FOURTH EDITION

managing ORGANIZATIONS FOR SPORT AND PHYSICAL ACTIVITY

a systems perspective

Packianathan Chelladurai

Distinguished Professor, Troy University

HHP

Holcomb Hathaway, Publishers

Scottsdale, Arizona

Library of Congress Cataloging-in-Publication Data

Chelladurai, P.
Managing organizations for sport and physical activity : a systems perspective / Packianathan Chelladurai. — Fourth edition.
pages cm
ISBN 978-1-62159-014-9 (print) — ISBN 978-1-62159-015-6 (ebook) 1. Sports administration. 2. Physical education and training—Administration. I. Title.
GV713.C52 2014
796.069—dc23
2014002816

Holcomb Hathaway, Publishers, Inc.
8700 E. Via de Ventura Blvd., Suite 265
Scottsdale, Arizona 85250
480-991-7881
www.hh-pub.com

10 9 8 7 6 5 4 3 2

Print book ISBN: 978-1-62159-014-9
Ebook ISBN: 978-1-62159-015-6

This book is dedicated to the women in my life:

my wife,
Ponnuthai,

my mother-in-law,
Kanagammal,

my mother,
Sornammal

contents

preface

Like its predecessors, the fourth edition of this book strives to facilitate a full understanding of management by applying relevant theories and concepts to the issues we face in managing organizations that deal with sport and physical activity. In essence, the book describes and discusses sport and physical activity organizations and their management from a systems perspective, as indicated in the title. Of course, most of the book's chapters are devoted to management and its functions, as outlined below.

My goal has been to incorporate new research and developments on the perspectives and models most relevant to managing sport and physical activity organizations. In the Introduction, I offer a brief historical view of the emergence of the field of sport management. In addition, I discuss the economic impact of the sport industry and its components. The immensity of the sport industry highlights the significance of managing the organizations that produce the sport product/services. Chapter 1 provides a comprehensive description of the sport management field in terms of the services produced and marketed. Chapter 2 is devoted to defining organizations and describing their attributes and forms. In Chapter 3, I discuss the concept of systems and systems thinking and present the perspective of organizations as open systems. It discusses the environmental influences on organizations, including those of the stakeholders, and institutional and resource-dependence theories as extensions of a systems-based view of organizations.

In Chapter 4, I describe management in terms of its functions, skills necessary for effective management, and the roles of managers. The chapter also includes a description of the executive core qualifications (ECQs) required of managers as outlined by the Office of Personnel Management (OPM) of the U.S. Government.

Chapter 5 outlines the process of planning in and presents the issues associated with organizational goals, the generation of information needed for effective planning, and the relationship between planning and budgeting. As almost every aspect of management is concerned with making decisions, Chapter 6 is devoted to managerial decision making and various models of decision making. I also discuss the social processes involved in making decisions and the appropriateness of varying degrees of member involvement in making decisions under diverse conditions.

Chapters 7 and 8 deal with the function of organizing. In Chapter 7, I briefly describe the classical principles of organizing, then delve into Weber's bureaucracy as a popular form of organizing—both its strengths and weaknesses. I also highlight the significant and complementary place of bureaucracy in a democracy. Chapter 8 outlines the systems perspectives on organizing and the need for differentiation and integration within organizations. It also highlights the importance of boundary-spanning units of an organization in its interactions with its environment. I have also included a discussion of contemporary organizational forms, including internal, external, and interorganizational networks. Chapter 9 covers staffing—the essentials of finding, recruiting, selecting, hiring, and training the right people for the job. Chapter 9 also outlines the processes of job analysis, job description, and job specification.

While the functions of planning and organizing, including staffing, are relatively more conceptual or cerebral in nature, the function of leading is relatively more interpersonal. Because the leading function is oriented toward influencing and motivating members, it is essential that we gain insight into individual motivation; thus, Chapter 10 addresses this topic. I describe the more significant and popular theories of motivation, focusing on content as well as process. I conclude the chapter with a description of an integrative theory of motivation. Chapter 11 discusses the critical interpersonal and behavioral process of leadership. I describe the classical theories of leadership that focus on the leader, the members, and the situational elements. In Chapter 12, I discuss the more contemporary approaches to leadership, including transformational and charismatic leadership and the leader–member exchange theory (LMX). I conclude the chapter with a description of my own multidimensional model of leadership as an integrative framework.

Chapter 13 discusses the emergent concerns with managing diversity. As the U.S. population becomes increasingly diverse, the clients/customers and employees of sport and physical activity organizations also become more diverse. Accordingly, I discuss issues associated with diversity and approaches to managing diversity.

The next three chapters expand on the managerial function of evaluation: program evaluation, service quality, and assessing organizational effectiveness, respectively. The other significant aspect of performance appraisal, the evaluation of individual performance, is covered in my companion book, *Human Resource Management in Sport and Recreation* (Human Kinetics, 2006). Chapter 14, on program evaluation, deals with purposes and processes of evaluating various programs of a sport or physical activity organization. Chapter 15, new to this edition, discusses quality targets and the standards to be applied in evaluating the quality of a given sport service, distinguishing between the standards for consumer services and those for human services. I note that because most of the products of the sport industry are services, sport managers must pay particular attention to enhancing and maintaining the quality of the services they provide. Chapter 16 emphasizes organizational effectiveness as the ultimate dependent variable of any organizational analysis or managerial action. I present the problems associated with defining and measuring the concept of organizational effectiveness as political and scientific issues. The political aspect refers to the question of whose views should prevail in the effectiveness judgments. In addition to the various perspectives advanced in this debate, I describe the "prime beneficiary" approach to resolving the issue of whose views should hold in the assessment of organizational effectiveness.

Each chapter contains useful pedagogy. In this edition, the new feature "An Expert's View" offers additional perspectives on relevant topics contributed by scholars who research and publish in that area. Other helpful tools include learning objectives, key terms, illustrative diagrams, boxed "In Brief" summaries of key concepts and sidebars on current topics relevant to the field of sport management and offering significant statements and excerpts from theorists or theories. At the end of each chapter, I provide a list of issues and questions under the heading "Developing Your Perspectives" and a comprehensive list of References.

Readers and instructors should find these learning aids useful. Further, instructors will be pleased to know that an Instructor's Manual, which includes case studies, and a PowerPoint presentation, including many of the book's exhibits, are available with adoption of the book.

Readers will recognize that this book does not provide details for "how to" carry out certain managerial activities. There are two reasons for this. First, as noted in Chapter 3, there is no "one best way" to carry out managerial activities. Second, a prescription of one way of doing things might lead readers to form habits. This would be fine with simpler and noncritical tasks. As Vroom (2003) pointed out, however, "habits typically reflect the learning environment at the time the habit was formed. As long as the environment is unchanging, this property is fine. But in a changing world, such as that which most managers currently experience, habits can be troublesome" (p. 977).

The most obvious audience for this book is students in sport management, broadly defined to include physical education, high school and collegiate athletics, campus recreation, community recreation, club management, aquatics management, and such other fields concerned with sport and physical activity. Further, because athletic coaching is a form of management, instructors of coaching courses may also find most of the content of the book relevant to their courses. Readers will find the content of the book straightforward. Instructors will have the flexibility to choose or emphasize specific chapters and introduce their own material to supplement the text.

The theories and models I have included may reflect my preferences, and the interpretations of them may be a function of my biases. This sets the stage for instructors and readers to debate contentious issues and to generate alternate views and solutions.

While acknowledging my debt to reviewers, colleagues, and co-investigators and to my students, who over the years have shaped my thoughts and perspective on sport management, I have this request for readers of the book: if you find conceptual or technical flaws in the text, please let me know. If you are pleased with the book, please tell others.

Reference

Vroom, V. H. (2003). Educating managers for decision making and leadership. *Management Decision, 41*(10), 968–978.

acknowledgments

I would first like to express my gratitude to my mentors and benefactors, Earle Zeigler and Garth Paton, who lured me into sport management, inspired me with their enthusiasm and love for the field, and groomed me to be a professional in the field. I also owe much to the following individuals, who have offered support in a multitude of ways over the years: Terry Haggerty, Bert Carron, Shoukry Saleh, Dorothy Zakrajsek, Mary Daniels, and Damon Andrew.

My special thanks to Makis Asimakopoulos, George Cunningham, Dimitris Gargalianos, Jon Iveson, Annelies Knoppers, Laura Misener, Kari Puronaho, Catherine Quatman-Yates, Claudio Rocha, and Jim Weese, who were kind enough to contribute their valuable "Expert Views" for this edition's new feature.

I must express my indebtedness to all of my doctoral and masters students at The Ohio State University who offered valuable insight and comments on this book in its earlier editions. I am also grateful to Lauren Graham and Mary Kaminsky, two of my final masters students at OSU, who generated many of the examples used in this fourth edition.

I wish to thank the following reviewers, who offered constructive suggestions for this and the previous edition: Brennan Berg, University of Texas at Austin; Douglas Callahan, Winona State University; Shirley Cleave, University of New Brunswick; Harry Davakos, The Citadel; Jaime DeLuca, Towson University; Courtney Flowers, University of West Georgia; Alan L. Geist, Cedarville University; Fred Green, Troy University; Laura Hatfield, University of Missouri; Dee Jacobsen, Louisiana State University; Floyd Jones, West Virginia University; Lisa Campanell Komara, The College of Wooster; Mary E. Kreis, California University of Pennsylvania; Keith W. Lambrecht, Loyola University Chicago; Milena Parent, University of Ottawa; Glen Schorr, Towson University; and Steven Waller, University of Tennessee.

I am indebted to Colette Kelly and Gay Pauley of Holcomb Hathaway, whose publishing insight and expertise have been valuable in fine-tuning the manuscripts over the years. While they deserve credit for shaping my manuscript into a publishable text, I am responsible for any remaining conceptual lapses and technical errors in the text. I also wish to thank Harold Riemer, Aubrey Kent, Keith Lambrecht, Dianna Gray, and David Hedlund for their contributions to the book's instructor's manual, case studies, and PowerPoint presentation.

Since I left India many years ago, my roots in North America have deepened, as has my association with the community of sport management scholars and students. Even more significantly, the emotional roots are represented by my grandchildren, Jason, Shane, Daniel, Andrew, and Michelle, and their parents, Ruban and Karen, and Chandran and Sally. These delightful families and the growth and development of the grandchildren into bright young adults keep my wife and me very happy and proud. They make me want to do more to be worthy of their affection and respect.

Of course, no words can express the depth of my gratitude to my wife, Ponnu, who is the most dominant influence in my life and who has over the years tolerated my foibles and helped me in all my efforts. Her love, patience, and support sustain me in all spheres of my life. She is my friend, philosopher, and guide.

about the author

Packianathan Chelladurai, or "Chella" as he is most widely and affectionately known, has clearly established himself as one of the preeminent scholars in sport management. Chella has left an indelible mark at two world-class universities, the University of Western Ontario and The Ohio State University. Currently, he is a distinguished professor at Troy University in Alabama. Throughout his career, he has directly influenced aspiring scholars and broadly influenced all of us within the field of sport management through his insightful writing, research, and counsel.

Chella's contributions have been recognized worldwide. Over the past three decades, Chella has become sport management's "international spokesperson." He has been invited to speak and consult on a worldwide basis, presenting at national and international conferences held in Belgium, Chile, Croatia, Cyprus, Denmark, England, Finland, France, Greece, Hungary, India, Italy, Japan, Malaysia, Mexico, Morocco, the Netherlands, Norway, Poland, Portugal, Republic of South Africa, Scotland, South Korea, Spain, Sri Lanka, Sweden, Taiwan, and Turkey.

Chella has also been long associated with the Olympic movement. He is among the few international scholars teaching and advising in the Olympic Solidarity's Executive Masters in Sport Organizations Management (MEMOS); he takes a leadership role in the human resource module of the MEMOS program. As a member of the Sport Commission and Scientific Board of the Olympic Council of Asia, Chella was involved in organizing the First Sport Congress in Kuwait City in March 2009.

Chella served on the NCAA-sponsored Board of Directors of the Forum for the Scholarly Study of Intercollegiate Athletics in Higher Education. He was also the Associate Editor for the *Journal of Intercollegiate Athletics,* which was sponsored by the NCAA.

Chella has established a prolific publishing record over the past 30 years. His articles have appeared in issues of the *Journal of Sport Management, Journal of Sport and Exercise Psychology, Research Quarterly for Exercise and Sport,* and others. Chella's first textbook, *Sport Management: Macro Perspectives,* published in 1985, represented a clear departure from the norm of earlier texts in the field; it was marked, and uniquely so at the time, by an integration of management theory with clear, practical applications for the field of sport management. He is also the author of *Human Resource Management in Sport and Recreation* (Human Kinetics, 2006).

Chella is the first recipient of the prestigious Earle F. Zeigler Award from the North American Society for Sport Management. The European Association for Sport Management honored him in 2005 with the Merit Award for Distinguished Service to Sport Management Education. In 2009, the Southern Sport Management

Conference of the United States bestowed on him the Sport Management Scholar Lifetime Achievement Award.

In 2012, the University of Western Ontario awarded Chella an honorary degree (LL.D.) for his contribution to the field of sport management. In 2014, the *International Journal of Sport Science* (Vol. 10, No. 5) recognized him as an Eminent Scholar with a tribute written by Dr. Donna Pastore of The Ohio State University.

The marriage of sound theory and excellent practice in the field of sport management has long been talked about but rarely achieved. Chella has dedicated his professional career to this goal, and this most recent book, *Managing Organizations for Sport and Physical Activity: A Systems Perspective,* Fourth Edition, represents a giant step toward its achievement.

Garth Paton

KINESIOLOGY, UNIVERSITY OF NEW BRUNSWICK, CANADA
NORTH AMERICAN SOCIETY FOR SPORT MANAGEMENT

INTRODUCTION

SPORT MANAGEMENT
ITS PAST, PRESENT, AND FUTURE

manage YOUR LEARNING

After completing this introduction you should be able to:

- **Understand the historical roots of sport management.**
- **Describe the current status of sport management.**
- **Explain the economic significance of sport.**
- **Know the career opportunities in sport management.**
- **Understand the prospects for sport management.**

strategic CONCEPTS

administration of physical education
career opportunities
gross domestic sports product (GDSP)
job types
organizational contexts
participant sport
professional associations
size of the sport industry
sport industry

MANAGEMENT THEN AND NOW

An indelible mark of civilization has been the pooling and management of human effort. Indeed, the progress of the human race has been based on various forms of management through which the efforts of people have been channeled in specific ways. Numerous examples can be drawn from early history to show the historical contributions of management. Hitt, Black, and Porter (2009) note that management was practiced even by the Mayans, Greeks, and Romans. More than 1,000 years ago, Chinese officials wrote about how to manage and control human activity. They note that "Chinese leaders discussed the value of specialized labor, hiring, promotions based on merit, and the need to clearly describe jobs. The modern field of strategic management owes its origin to an ancient Chinese warrior, Su Tsu, and his book, *The Art of War*" (p. 11).

Robbins (1976) cites an example from Exodus in the Bible. When Moses was overburdened with administrative and judicial duties, his father-in-law advised him that he should appoint able men as "rulers of thousands, and rulers of hundreds, rulers of fifties, and rulers of tens . . . and it shall be, that every great matter they shall bring unto thee, but every small matter they shall judge: so shall it be easier for thyself, and they shall bear the burden with thee" (Exodus 18:17–23). This is, in essence, the institution of a hierarchy and the delegation of authority—managerial processes that are much touted in modern literature.

Although the study and practice of management can be traced to earliest times, intense and thorough investigation, as well as propagation of the art and science of management, began in the early part of the twentieth century. Almost every university in North America now offers programs in Business Administration, Public Administration, Hospital Administration, and other such specializations.

EMERGENCE OF SPORT MANAGEMENT

One specialized field of management that has emerged is referred to as *sport management*. As sport and physical activity become dominant features of North American culture, and around the world, the number and types of organizations whose major domain of operation is sport and physical activity have multiplied dramatically over the past 50 years. In addition to the traditional concerns associated with the manufacture and retailing of sporting goods, various other organizations deal with sport and physical activity. A sampling of these organizations would include those that:

- offer the use of their facilities and equipment and provide training for sport and physical activity, as in health clubs,
- schedule and organize activities, as in youth sport leagues,
- offer instruction in specific activities, as in municipal recreation departments,
- organize competitions and promote excellence, as in university intercollegiate programs and professional sports, and
- regulate the affairs of the sport or activity within the state, province, or nation, as in national Olympic associations, or within the sport as in the NCAA and NFL.

These various kinds of organizations that deal with sport and physical activity need to be managed effectively, hence the importance and emergence of sport management.

THE PAST

The field of sport management as we know it had its beginnings in educational institutions. It was then called **administration of physical education**. Zeigler (1951) notes that a course in organization and administration of physical education and athletics was offered even as early as 1890. The subject matter of early courses was mostly concerned with maintenance of sport facilities in educational institutions, purchase and care of equipment, and organizing and conducting sport events.

A major impetus for sport becoming a dominant feature of American society was high school and collegiate sports. As we all know, no other country in the world places such emphasis on sports in educational institutions as the United States. The sport facilities in many high schools in America would be the envy of some of the larger universities around the world. As another example, the median total expenses of major intercollegiate athletic departments in 2010–2011 was over $50 million (Brown, 2012). That is more than many governments around the world spend on all of their sport and physical education programs.

With the increasing popularity of educational sports, including intramural sports and the associated financial outlay, came the emphasis on management. Several universities began offering programs on administration of high school athletics and intercollegiate sports. These professional preparation programs have been primarily confined to preparation of administrators or managers of sport in the educational institutions.

Landmark Thrusts

About 50 years ago, two significant moves came about to foster the emergence of sport management. First, James G. Mason at Ohio University began a program for

> **IN brief**
>
> The field of sport management grew out of the earlier fields of administration of physical education and athletics. Sport management is now broader in scope, and it includes the earlier fields.

training managers of professional sports. Although the program started in 1966, the idea was said to have been originally proposed to Dr. Mason in 1957 by Walter O'Malley, president of the Brooklyn Dodgers, a professional sport franchise (Stier, 1999). Many of the alumni of the program are now employed in various professional sport franchises. With that broad and deep network, the program is still going strong.

The other significant thrust was the move toward the academic study of sport management, spearheaded by Earle F. Zeigler in the 1960s (Paton, 1987). He and his students (including me) at the universities of Michigan, Illinois, and Western Ontario formed the vanguard of the academic study of sport management. They continue to be significant contributors to the field. In recognition of Zeigler's leadership and contribution, the North American Society for Sport Management (NASSM) instituted an award in his name to be presented to outstanding individuals in the field.

THE PRESENT

I describe the present status of sport management in two sections: the professional status of the occupation of sport management and the economic significance of the sport industry. We need to consider both of these aspects because the occupation of sport management is concerned with managing the sport industry.

Professional Status of Sport Management

The professional status of any occupation is defined by several factors. The following section outlines three significant factors elevating the status of sport management: degree programs, professional associations, and scholarly journals.

Sport management degree programs

The growth in the number of degree programs in the United States has been phenomenal. According to NASSM, as of 2013 there are 350 universities in the United States offering sport management degree programs at the bachelor's, master's, and doctorate levels (NASSM, 2013). It is among the fastest growing areas of study in U.S. universities. More and more students want to enroll in these programs, and universities are expanding their programs to accommodate this great demand. Many doctoral students have been able to find teaching jobs in universities either before or immediately after graduating. As another example of the growth of sport management, many universities and governments in Europe and the European Union have endorsed a program for a European master's degree in sport management.

Professional associations

The maturity of a profession is indicated by the existence of **professional associations** that bring together scholars and practitioners to exchange ideas and generate guidelines for self-regulation of the profession and its members. NASSM was formed in 1985. In July 2008, NASSM and the National Association for Sport and Physical Education (NASPE) jointly established the independent body known as the Commission on Sport Management Accreditation (COSMA) to provide accreditation and related services for sport management programs in colleges and universities. Another organization, the Sport Marketing Association (SMA), was founded in 2002 and held its first annual meeting in November 2003. In addition, the Sport and Recreation Law Association (SRLA), formed in 1986, addresses legal aspects of sport and recreation. Beyond North America are several other organizations. See Exhibit I.1 for a partial list of the professional associations and their websites.

Journals in sport management

Another hallmark of a profession's growth is the publication of scholarly and trade journals. The journals dedicated to sport management in North America are the *Journal of Sport Management,* first published in January 1987; *Sport Marketing Quarterly,* first published in 1992; and the *International Journal of Sport Management,* launched in 1999. Since then several other journals have come into existence, and they contribute greatly to expanding the knowledge pertinent to sport management. Exhibit I.2 is a partial list of sport management journals.

In addition to these dedicated journals, several other journals and trade publications publish sport management-related articles, including *Athletic Administration, Fitness Management, Interscholastic Athletic Administration, NCAA News, Facility Manager (IAAM), Journal of the National Intramural Recreation Sports Association (NIRSA), Athletic Business, Athletic Management,* and *Corporate Fitness and Recreation.* A more significant publication dedicated to the sport business is *Street & Smith's SportsBusiness Journal,* which began publication in 1998. This journal is an important source of current information on many matters related to sports as a business. These publications go a long way in sustaining and advancing the study and practice of sport management. They also indicate the growth of sport management as a profession.

IN brief

The professional status of sport management as an occupation is reinforced by the number and quality of degree programs offered by universities, its professional associations, and the number of journals published.

exhibit I.1 List of professional organizations with websites.

DATE FOUNDED	PROFESSIONAL ASSOCIATION	WEBSITE
1985	North American Society for Sport Management (NASSM)	www.nassm.org
1974	National Association of Sport and Physical Education (NASPE)	www.aahperd.org/naspe
2008	Commission on Sport Management Accreditation (COSMA)	www.cosmaweb.org
2002	Sport Marketing Association (SMA)	www.sportmarketingassociation.com
1986	Sport and Recreation Law Association (SRLA)	www.srlawebsite.com
	Japanese Society of Sport Industry (JSSI)	www.spo-sun.gr.jp/
1993	European Association for Sport Management (EASM)	www.easm.net
1995	Sport Management Association of Australia and New Zealand (SMAANZ)	www.smaanz.org
2003	Asian Association for Sport Management (AASM)	www.aasmasia.com/
2010	African Sport Management Association (ASMA)	www.asma-online.org/
2012	World Association of Sport Management (WASM)	www.worldsportmanagement.org/

exhibit I.2 A partial list of sport management journals.

NAME OF THE JOURNAL	STARTING YEAR
Journal of Sport Management	1986
Journal of Sports Economics	2000
International Journal of Sports Finance	2006
International Journal of Sports Marketing & Sponsorship	1999
International Journal of Sport Management and Marketing	2005
International Journal of Sport Management	2000
Journal of Intercollegiate Sports	2008
Sport Management Review	1998
Sport Marketing Quarterly	1992
Sport Management Education Journal	2007
European Sport Management Quarterly	2001
Journal of Quantitative Analysis in Sports	2005
Journal of Legal Aspects of Sport	1990
Journal of Sports Media	2007
Journal of Contemporary Athletics	2005
Journal for the Study of Sports and Athletics in Education	2007
Journal of Venue & Event Management	2007
International Journal of Sport Communication	2008
Journal of Sport Administration & Supervision	2009
The Sport Journal	1998

Economic Significance of the Sport Industry

The foregoing developments are also a reflection of the economic significance of sport. Several estimates on the **size of the sport industry** have been undertaken. They differ not only in the time frame for the estimate, but also in what they include as part of the **sport industry.** Despite these differences, they all show that the sport industry is vibrant and growing, ranking among the largest industries in the United States. For illustrative purposes, I summarize estimates in the following sections. Although more recent estimates would differ from these studies, the figures included here present a clear idea of the industry's size and significance and the differing methodologies used to derive the estimates.

Size of the sport industry

Broughton (2002) listed 15 categories of spending related to sport. See Exhibit I.3. He explains his method of estimating the size of the sport industry as follows:

> Start with the terminology—money spent related to sports. It is distinctly different than a measure of the size of the sport industry. Whereas an industry's size is typically connected with the amount of revenue generated, this endeavor at examining sports-related spending goes a step further. . . . Consider a company buying TV

exhibit 1.3 *SportsBusiness Journal's* estimate of dollars spent in sport (2001), in $ billions.

CATEGORY	SUB-CATEGORY	AMOUNT SPENT	TOTAL AND (PERCENTAGE) FOR CATEGORY
Advertising	Billboards, arena/stadium signage	16.39	27.430 (14.1%)
	National network TV	4.69	
	Radio	2.34	
	National cable TV	1.78	
	Sports magazines	1.45	
	Regional TV (network and cable)	0.57	
	National syndicated TV	0.21	
Endorsements	Endorsement of top 75 athletes, coaches, & personalities (estimated to be two thirds of all endorsements)	0.897	0.897 (0.5%)
Sporting Goods	Equipment used in competition	10.14	25.62 (13.2%)
	Sportswear used in competition	7.98	
	Footwear used in competition	7.50	
Facility Construction	U.S. stadiums/motor speedways	1.44	2.48 (1.3%)
	U.S. arenas	1.04	
Internet	Ad spending	0.230	0.239 (0.1%)
	Subscriber fees	0.009	
Licensed Goods	National Football League	2.50	10.50 (5.4%)
	All colleges	2.50	
	Major League Baseball	2.30	
	NASCAR	1.20	
	National Basketball Association	1.00	
	National Hockey League	0.90	
	Other	0.10	
Media Broadcast Rights	Big four leagues plus NASCAR	5.29	6.99 (3.6%)
	Colleges	1.06	
	Other	0.64	
Professional Services	Facility and event management	6.75	15.25 (7.8%)
	Financial, legal & insurance services	5.81	
	Marketing & consulting services	2.30	
	Athlete representation	0.385	

(continued)

Source: Broughton, D. (2002). Dollars in sport: Methodology. *Street & Smith's SportsBusiness Journal,* March 11, p. 25. Reprinted with permission.

exhibit I.3 Continued.

CATEGORY	SUB-CATEGORY	AMOUNT SPENT	TOTAL AND (PERCENTAGE) FOR CATEGORY
Spectator Spending	Ticket sales	11.74	26.17 (13.4%)
	Concessions, parking (on-site), merchandise	10.70	
	Premium seating	3.73	
Sponsorships	Sponsorship of leagues, teams, broadcasts, and events		6.40 (3.3%)
Medical Spending	Soccer	3.39	12.60 (6.5%)
	Baseball	2.16	
	Softball	1.28	
	Football	1.27	
	Track and Field	1.12	
	Gymnastics	1.08	
	Basketball	0.948	
	Wrestling	0.399	
	Volleyball	0.246	
	Ice hockey	0.183	
	Other	0.524	
Travel	Spectators	12.40	16.06 (8.3%)
	Colleges	1.11	
	Big four pro leagues	0.335	
	Minor leagues	0.113	
	Other	2.10	
Multimedia	Magazines (circulation revenue)	0.944	2.2 (1.1%)
	Computer and video	0.750	
	Videos and DVD	0.280	
	Books	0.146	
Gambling	Pari-mutuels (including horse/ greyhound racing)	14.69	18.90 (9.7%)
	Internet	2.17	
	Legal sports books	2.04	
Operating Expenses	Big four leagues payroll	6.10	22.98 (11.8%)
	Big four leagues other expenses	5.81	
	Colleges	6.04	
	Minor leagues	0.600	
	Other	4.44	
Total for All Categories			194.64

> time for a commercial during a game broadcast. Neither the teams participating in that game nor their league might get that money from the company; it could stay with the broadcast outlet. It is, however, money spent because of sports, just as the broadcaster likely spent money for the rights to broadcast the game. Looking at these and other different ways in which money changes hands provides a true sense of the mass of the sports-business industry. (Broughton, 2002, p. 25)

In the process of estimating the size of the sport industry, Broughton excludes certain kinds of expenditures. Focusing on what he calls organized sports, he excludes the expenditures on recreational activities (e.g., purchases, travel, and injuries related to recreational activities such as golf). Similarly, he includes travel expenses incurred in order to compete in an event or attend a sport event; but he excludes travel expenditures associated with sport-tourism spending such as "trips to resorts or camps, or cruises, where sports might have been part of the trip but not the trip's purpose" (p. 25). Note Broughton's emphases on (a) different ways money changes hands and (b) the sport business industry. The process of counting the number of times money changes hands with reference to a product is different from counting the final price consumers pay for a product. Counting the number of times money changes hands may result in some double counting. Consider, for example, the expenditures listed under advertising ($27.43 billion) and media broadcast rights ($6.99 billion). Some of the expenditures under advertising are channeled into the broadcast media. On a simpler level, assume that a broadcaster pays $10 million to broadcast a football game. The broadcaster then sells 30-second and 60-second spots to several corporations for a total of $12 million. Should we include both amounts (i.e., $22 million) in estimating the size of the industry? Or just the original $10 million paid by the broadcaster? Or just the $12 million paid by the advertisers?

The same question arises in buying a tennis racket (or a basketball shoe). I buy a racket for $100 from a retailer who paid $60 for it and incurred another $20 in expenses for transporting it and displaying it for customer convenience. If you are asked to estimate the size of the sport industry, which of these amounts would you include? Why?

The emphasis on the sport business industry also leads to the exclusion of expenditures associated with individuals and families participating in sports. These sport contexts may be highly organized, such as youth soccer leagues or adult bowling leagues. As this chapter will show, the expenditures on recreational or participant sport do constitute the larger percentage of the sport industry.

In another study, Plunkett Research placed the total value of the industry between $400 and $435 billion (Plunkett Research, 2012) although it is not clear how this estimate was derived. As noted above, one must consider double counting that can lead to exaggerated claims. In contrast to Broughton (2002) and Plunkett Research (2012), Meek (1997) applied the same rules and methodology used by the U.S. Department of Commerce in calculating the nation's gross domestic product (GDP) and reported that the size of the sport industry was $152 billion in 1995. He labeled this amount the **gross domestic sports product (GDSP)**, which represents the final consumption of sport products and services. Any intermediary transactions between production and final consumption are not included in this figure (Meek, 1997). For example, the $80 price for a tennis racket includes the price the retailer paid for the racket and all the expenses incurred in transporting, storing, and displaying the racket. Meek cautioned that including those expenses would amount to "double" counting. However, he also notes that such transactions do constitute economic activity.

In a third study, Milano and Chelladurai (2011) replicated Meek's (1997) work and presented three estimates for the GDSP of the United States of America in 2005. The reason for three estimates was because the government departments that collected the data had grouped the expenditures on some leisure- time activities and provided one estimate for all of them. For example, one item of expenditure included expenses on golf courses, country clubs, and other social organizations. Obviously, expenses on golf courses should be included in GDSP. But it is not clear how much of the expenses on country clubs or other social organizations should be included in estimating the size of the sport industry. Therefore, Milano and Chelladurai advanced three estimates: (1) a liberal estimate in which they included the entire amount; (2) a conservative estimate that excluded the amount entirely; and (3) a moderate estimate in which they included only one third of the government figures because there were three types of expenditures—golf courses, country clubs, and other social organizations. In the final analysis, the conservative estimate of the size of the sport industry in 2005 was $168.469 billion (excluding those items where expenditures on sport were combined with other leisure time activities), the liberal estimate was $207.503 billion (including those expenditures), and the moderate estimate was $189.338 billion (including only appropriate proportions of those expenditures). The items of expenditure and the amounts as per the moderate estimate are provided in Exhibit I.4.

Milano and Chelladurai made two important observations. First, the expenditures incurred by Americans for active participation in sport and physical activity were $107.9 billion. This figure represents about 57 percent of the total worth of the sport industry, which is less than the 60 percent spent for participation in Meek's (1997) estimate of the industry in 1995. Their second observation was that the sport industry—after correcting for inflation—had shrunk in size between 1995 and 2005. The authors opined that this decline could be due to the public consuming fewer of the goods and services of the sport industry or because the prices of sport-related goods and services decreased. Despite this decline in size, the sport industry ranked as the 17th largest industry in the United States, as shown in Exhibit I.5.

Other impressive figures that attest to the size of the sport industry include the following:

- Brown, Rascher, Nagel, and McEvoy (2010) report that the National Football League (NFL), the National Basketball Association (NBA), and Major League Baseball (MLB) receive annually from the media organizations $1.9 billion, $930 million, and $696 million, respectively.
- The National Collegiate Athletic Association (NCAA, 2012) expected that its revenue for the 2011–2012 year would be $777 million, of which $680 million would come from CBS Sports and Turner Broadcasting. The median budget of the NCAA institutions belonging to the Football Bowl Subdivision was about $50 million in 2010–2011 (Brown, 2012).
- Baade and Matheson (2011) noted that the construction costs alone for major league professional sports facilities exceeded $30 billion since 1990, with over half of the cost being paid by the public.
- The International Health, Racquet & Sports Club Association (IHRSA, 2012) reported that health club utilization reached an all-time high of 59 million consumers in 2011. These consumers paid an average monthly membership fee of $42.55, which adds up to $30.125 billion annually.

exhibit 1.4 Moderate estimate of the gross domestic sport product (2005), in $ billions.

SEGMENT	ESTIMATE	TOTAL
Entertainment & Recreation		
Season tickets to sporting events	3.237	
Golf courses, country clubs, & social organizations	4.011	
Health clubs, fitness centers, swimming pools, other recreational or sport organizations	7.743	
Fees for participating in sports (e.g., tennis, golf, etc.)	7.106	
Single admissions to spectator sports	2.719	
Recreational lessons or other instructions	6.720	
Sports expenses	0.252	
Renting of sports equipment	0.816	
Fees for participation in sport and fitness	1.982	
Entertainment and admission fees	3.645	
Sport expenses incurred for others	0.055	
Pari-mutuel net receipts	6.200	
Food and beverage	4.300	
Total for Entertainment and Recreation		48.786
Sports equipment	23.688	
Sports apparel	40.115	
Sports footwear	15.719	
Sport movies attendance	0.563	
Sport magazines	0.992	
Sport books	0.137	
Sport trading cards	0.325	
Sport video games	1.077	
Fantasy sport fees	1.395	
Sport medicine	15.150	
Sport licensing	6.514	
Total for Products and Services		105.675
Sponsorship	6.372	
Television and Internet advertising	7.510	
Magazines	0.902	
Total for Non–Sport-Related Advertising		14.784
Amusement, social, recreational buildings	9.283	
Indoor swimming pools	0.583	
Indoor ice rinks	0.024	
Outdoor swimming pools	7.344	
Outdoor recreational areas	5.732	
Total for Sport Investments		22.966
Sport-Related Government Expenditures		0.657
Sport Imports & Exports		–3.530
Gross Domestic Sports Product		**189.338**

Source: Adapted from Milano, M., & Chelladurai, P. (2011). Gross Domestic Sport Product: The Size of the Sport Industry in the United States. *Journal of Sport Management, 25(1)*, 24–35; *Consumer Expenditure Survey,* Washington, DC: Bureau of Labor Statistics.

exhibit I.5 Industry rankings by 2005 GDP, in $ billions.

RANK	INDUSTRY	VALUE
1	Real estate	1461.3
2	Retail trade	812.7
3	Wholesale trade	723.7
4	Construction	607.9
5	Miscellaneous professional, scientific, and technical services	542.5
6	Federal Reserve banks, credit intermediation and related activities	506.1
7	Ambulatory health care services	433.6
8	Hospital and nursing and residential care facilities	340.0
9	Administrative and support services	344.4
10	Broadcasting and telecommunications	324.2
11	Other services, except government	288.1
12	Insurance carriers and related activities	264.5
13	Utilities	249.5
14	Management of companies and enterprises	234.9
15	Food services and drinking places	225.8
	Sport (Liberal GDSP Estimate)	*207.5*
16	Manufacturing - Chemical products	199.8
	Sport (Moderate GDSP Estimate)	*189.3*
17	Securities, commodity contracts, and investments	183.8
18	Legal services	176.4
	Sport (Conservative GDSP Estimate)	*168.4*
19	Manufacturing - Food and beverage and tobacco products	163.7
20	Oil and gas extraction	149.6
21	Publishing industries (includes software)	142.2
22	Computer systems design and related services	133.0
23	Manufacturing - Computer and electronic products	132.7
24	Manufacturing - Fabricated metal products	123.3
25	Truck transportation	118.6

From: Milano and Chelladurai (2011). Used with permission from Human Kinetics.

Participant or recreational sport

These impressive figures include elite sport offered by organizations such as the professional sport leagues and the NCAA Division I schools. The expenses incurred for participation, however, are also impressive. As noted earlier, Milano and Chelladurai reported that $107.9 billion was spent for participation in sport and this figure amounts to about 57 percent of the total. Viewed from this perspective, **participant sport** is the core of the sport industry; it spawns the spectator sport, which in turn supports (and is supported by) other related industries (see Exhibit I.6).

exhibit I.6 Segmentation of the sport industry.

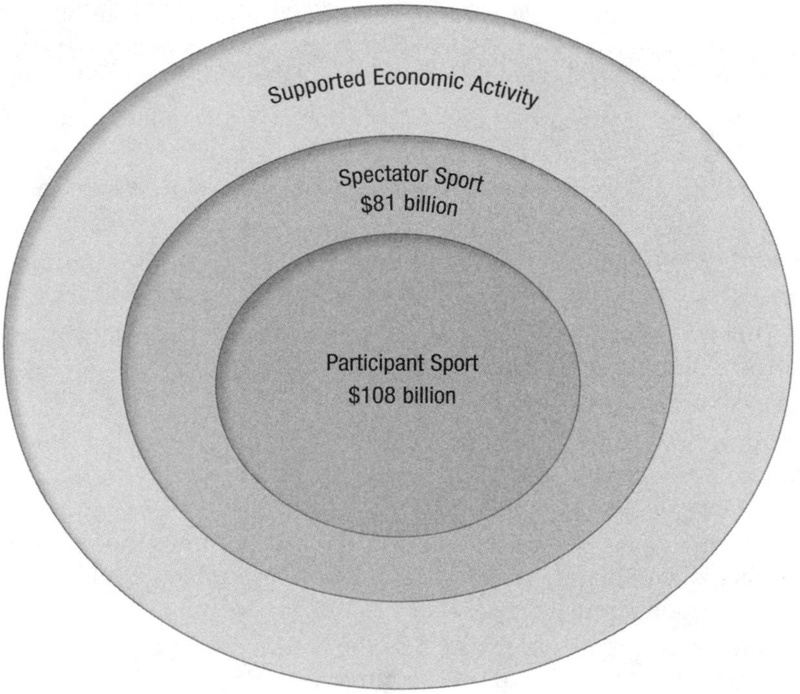

As one example, consider that more than 40 million U.S. youth participate in various sports outside of the programs organized by educational institutions (National Council of Youth Sports, 2008). We should remember to consider student participation in athletics at the elementary, middle, and high school levels, and the vast number of athletes in nonrevenue sports in collegiate athletics.

CAREER OPPORTUNITIES IN SPORT MANAGEMENT

The economic significance of the sport industry also underscores the wide variety of **career opportunities** available in the sport industry. Meek (1997), who estimated the GDSP to be $152 billion in 1995, also estimated that the sport industry employed nearly 2.32 million people who worked directly in generating the GDSP. This employment yielded a household income of $52 billion. In addition, another 2.33 million people were employed in the economic activities supported by the sport industry. This employment added $75 billion to household incomes. Overall, the sport industry facilitated the employment of 4.65 million people for a total household income of $127 billion. Despite these statistics, competition for entry-level positions is keen, and thus these positions can sometimes be difficult to secure.

Organizational Contexts

These employment opportunities are offered by different kinds of organizations pursuing different goals and employing different processes to achieve their goals within the sport domain. The following is a partial list of **organizational contexts** involved in sport:

- educational institutions, including elementary and high schools, colleges, and universities
- professional sport teams
- nonprofit organizations that offer sport, fitness, and wellness services, such as the YMCA and Boys and Girls Clubs of America
- profit-oriented firms dealing in sport, fitness, and wellness services
- corporate fitness and wellness units
- profit-oriented firms providing consulting, legal, agency, and marketing services
- government agencies such as city recreation departments and state parks and recreation departments
- the U.S. Armed Forces
- sport-governing bodies at the national and state levels (e.g., the United States Basketball Association, the United States Lawn Tennis Association, the Ohio State Volleyball Association)
- international sport-governing bodies such as the International Federation of Basketball Associations (FIBA) and International Federation of Football [Soccer] Associations (FIFA)
- umbrella sport organizations such as the National Collegiate Athletic Association and the U.S. Olympic Committee

Activity/Job Types

Careers in sport management also can be broadly classified on the basis of specific activities or **job types.** These activity/job areas include:

- event management
- facility management
- ticketing operations
- licensing operations
- concession operations
- legal issues
- scheduling of facility/equipment
- programming
- rental operations
- scheduling of games/activities
- tournament operations
- parking operations
- marketing operations
- public relations
- personnel management
- budgeting and accounting

Note that not all of the above classes of activities are relevant to all organizations. For example, ticketing operations are meaningful only where sport is offered as entertainment for a fee. Also, within any type of activity area, different levels of jobs may be arranged in a hierarchical order. For instance, in a large university athletic department, there may be a director of ticketing operations with one or more assistant directors who, in turn, may supervise several account executives. Similarly, the employees maintaining a city's ballparks usually are organized into two or more hierarchical levels. The aerobics instructors in a fitness club may be supervised by a higher-ranking person.

THE FUTURE OF SPORT MANAGEMENT

Pitts and Stotlar (1996) reported that the size of the sport industry was $47.3 billion in 1986, which jumped to $50.2 billion in 1987 and to $63.1 billion in 1988. They predicted that the industry would grow to be worth $139 billion, at an average growth rate of 6.8 percent. As noted, this figure was surpassed even by 1995 according to Meek (1997). The estimate by *Street & Smith's SportsBusiness Journal* (Broughton, 2002) showed the sport industry to be even larger—$194 billion in 2001. Despite the discrepancies in what items are included in the sport industry and how they are estimated, these figures do indicate substantial growth. We could also expect that at some point the sport industry might hit a plateau. In fact, as mentioned earlier, Milano and Chelladurai (2011) demonstrated that the total worth of the sport industry in 2005 was almost the same as it was in 1995 when corrected for inflation.

IN brief

The future of sport management looks bright because the prospects for the sport industry itself are promising. Increasing leisure time, the popularity of women's sports, and the globalization of sport are the bases for this optimism.

Now to a more optimistic forecast of the future of sport industry. In forecasting the patterns of economic growth in the next thousand years, Molitor (1996) proposed that economic growth will be powered by the "big five" engines: leisure time era, life sciences era, mega-materials era, new atomic age, and new space age. These eras are described in Exhibit I.7. What is most relevant to us is that Molitor predicts that the engine behind the economic growth as soon as the year 2015 will be the leisure time era. In his view, this sector will account for 50 percent of the U.S. gross national product (GNP). The sector would include, among several other activities, recreation, entertainment, gambling and wagering, travel, tourism, adventure-seeking, sports, exercising, and outdoor activities. These activities are similar to those included in the estimates of the size of the sport industry. Extrapolating from Molitor's perspective, we can say that the sport industry itself will be a driving force in the economic growth in the United States.

Molitor (1996) also notes that "leisure time, continuing to steadily increase, very soon will account for over 50 percent of lifetime activities in advanced-affluent nations" (p. 159). The increase in leisure time will be facilitated by shorter workdays and workweeks, increased number of holidays, longer vacations, increased leaves of absence, and early retirement. All of these scenarios augur well for the growth of the sport industry and sport management. We should also note two significant trends that affect sport management. The first is the globalization of sport. The second is the growing popularity of women's sports. Related to this increase in spectator appeal of women's sports will be growth in demand for sport services that promote more—and more intensive—participation by women and girls.

exhibit 1.7 Molitor's (1996) "big five" engines of economic growth in the next thousand years.

1. **LEISURE TIME ERA (BY 2015).** Hospitality, recreation, and entertainment. Leisure time pursuits have been a part of human activity from the very outset. The change about to be fully felt occurs when "free time" dominates total individual lifetime activity.
2. **LIFE SCIENCES ERA (2100).** Bio-tech, genetics, cloning, genetic engineering, transgenics, and "pharming," among others. Theoretical underpinnings trace back more than a century. The pace began to accelerate with the Human Genome Project, and it reached a dramatic turning point with the cloning of Dolly.
3. **MEGA-MATERIALS ERA (2200–2300).** Quantum mechanics, particle physics, nano-technologies, isotopes/allotropes/chirality, superconductors, and microscopic imaging systems constitute the major core technologies. This sector began to take off with the development of plastics, bulletproof Kevlar, ceramic engineering, high-strength alloys, composites, silicon, super-alloys, high-temperature superconductors, crystallography, cryogenics, semiconductors, time/temperature/pressure variable materials, designer materials.
4. **NEW ATOMIC AGE (2100–2500).** Thermonuclear fusion, hydrogen and helium isotopes, and lasers constitute the key technologies upon which almost every energy-dependent activity will depend. Paramountcy of these activities looms ever closer as finite fossil fuels—first petroleum, then natural gas, and finally coal—are depleted. This era reaches its apex a century or more into the future. Roots of coming change, however, trace far back in time. Commencing with theoretical foundations, this early phase came of age with "splitting the atom." Early experiments soon led to atomic fission, followed by development of thermonuclear explosives. Breakthroughs essential to harnessing fusion center on advances in magnetohydrodynamics, laser-induced implosion, and quantum physics.
5. **NEW SPACE AGE (2500–3000).** Astrophysics, cosmology, spacecraft development, exploration, travel, resource-gathering are pivotal activities propelling this stage of development. Beginnings for this sector trace back to gunpowder and rockets—developments over 2,000 years ago. World War II rockets and jet aircraft accelerated the pace. Sputnik, spy satellites, manned space missions, extra-planetary probes, and telescopic arrays that pierce the outermost limits of the universe are among the activities contributing to the conquest of space.

SUMMARY

The extent and significance of the sport industry are impressive. We must realize, however, that the sport industry did not just happen. Considerable entrepreneurial and managerial talents and efforts have fueled the phenomenal growth of the sport industry. Many organizations, both profit and nonprofit, have been and are responsible for the growth and sustenance of sport. These organizations produce and market sport-related products, and the extent of consumption of those products determines the size of the sport industry. The focus of this book is on managing those organizations and coordinating the processes of producing and marketing sport products. Accordingly, the ensuing chapters will provide a more detailed description of several processes of managing those organizations.

develop YOUR PERSPECTIVE

1. Consider Broughton's (2002) and Milano and Chelladurai's (2011) estimates of the size of the sport industry (see Exhibits I.3 and I.4). Compare and contrast the categories of industry segments employed in the two estimates. Identify the overlaps among them.
2. This introduction presents a list of organizational types that offer job opportunities in sport as well as a list of job or activity types in sport management. Would you add anything to those two lists? What kind of job would you like, and in what type of organization? Explain.

references

Baade, R. A., & Matheson, V. A. (2011). Financing Professional Sports Facilities. Working Paper Series, Paper No. 11-02. Department of Economics and Business, Lake Forest College. Retrieved from http://college.holycross.edu/RePEc/spe/MathesonBaade_FinancingSports.pdf.

Broughton, D. (2002, March 11). Dollars in sports: Methodology. *Street & Smith's SportsBusiness Journal*, p. 25.

Brown, G. (2012). NCAA report reveals consistent financial allocation among DI schools. Retrieved from http://www.ncaa.org/wps/wcm/connect/public/NCAA/Resources/Latest+News/2012/October/NCAA+report+reveals+consistent+financial+allocation+among+DI+schools.

Brown, M. T., Rascher, D. A., Nagel, M. S., & McEvoy, C. D. (2010). *Financial management in the sport industry*. Scottsdale, AZ: Holcomb Hathaway.

Higham, J., & Hinch, T. (2009). *Sport and tourism: Globalization, mobility, and identity*. Oxford, UK: Butterworth-Heinemann.

Hitt, M. A., Black, J. S., & Porter, L. W. (2009). *Management* (2nd ed). Upper Saddle River, NJ: Pearson-Prentice Hall.

IHRSA (2012). IHRSA releases annual Health Club Consumer Report: 2012 Health Club Activity, Usage, Trends & Analysis; Report explores consumer trends over economic recession and recovery. Retrieved from http://www.ihrsa.org/media-center/2012/9/6/ihrsa-releases-annual-health-club-consumer-report-2012-healt.html

Meek, A. (1997). An estimate of the size and supported economic activity of the sport industry in the United States. *Sport Marketing Quarterly, 6*(4), 15–21.

Milano, M., & Chelladurai, P. (2011). Gross domestic sport product: The size of the sport industry in the United States. *Journal of Sport Management, 25*(1), 24–35.

Molitor, G. T. T. (1996). The next thousand years: The "big five" engines of economic growth. In G. T. Kurian & G. T. T. Molitor (Eds.), *The 21st century*. New York: Simon & Schuster.

NCAA (2012). Revenue. Retrieved from http://www.ncaa.org/wps/wcm/connect/public/NCAA/Finances/Revenue.

NASSM. (2013). Sport management programs: United States. Retrieved from http://www.nassm.com/InfoAbout/SportMgmtPrograms/United_States.

National Council of Youth Sports. (2008). Market research report NCYS membership survey—2008 edition. Retrieved from http://www.ncys.org/pdfs/2008/2008-ncys-market-research-report.pdf.

Paton, G. (1987). Sport management research: What progress has been made? *Journal of Sport Management, 1*, 25–31.

Pitts, B. G., & Stotlar, D. K. (1996). *Fundamentals of sport marketing*. Morgantown, WV: Fitness Information Technology.

Plunkett Research (2012). Sport industry market research. Retrieved from http://www.plunkettresearch.com/sports-recreation-leisure-market-research/industry-and-business-data/statistics.

Robbins, S. P. (1976). *The administrative process: Integrating theory and practice*. Englewood Cliffs, NJ: Prentice Hall.

Stier, W. F. (1999). *Managing sport, fitness, and recreation programs: Concepts and practices*. Boston: Allyn & Bacon.

Zeigler, E. F. (1951). *A history of professional preparation for physical education in the United States, 1861–1948*. Unpublished doctoral dissertation, University of Oregon.

DEFINING THE FIELD OF SPORT MANAGEMENT

1

CHAPTER

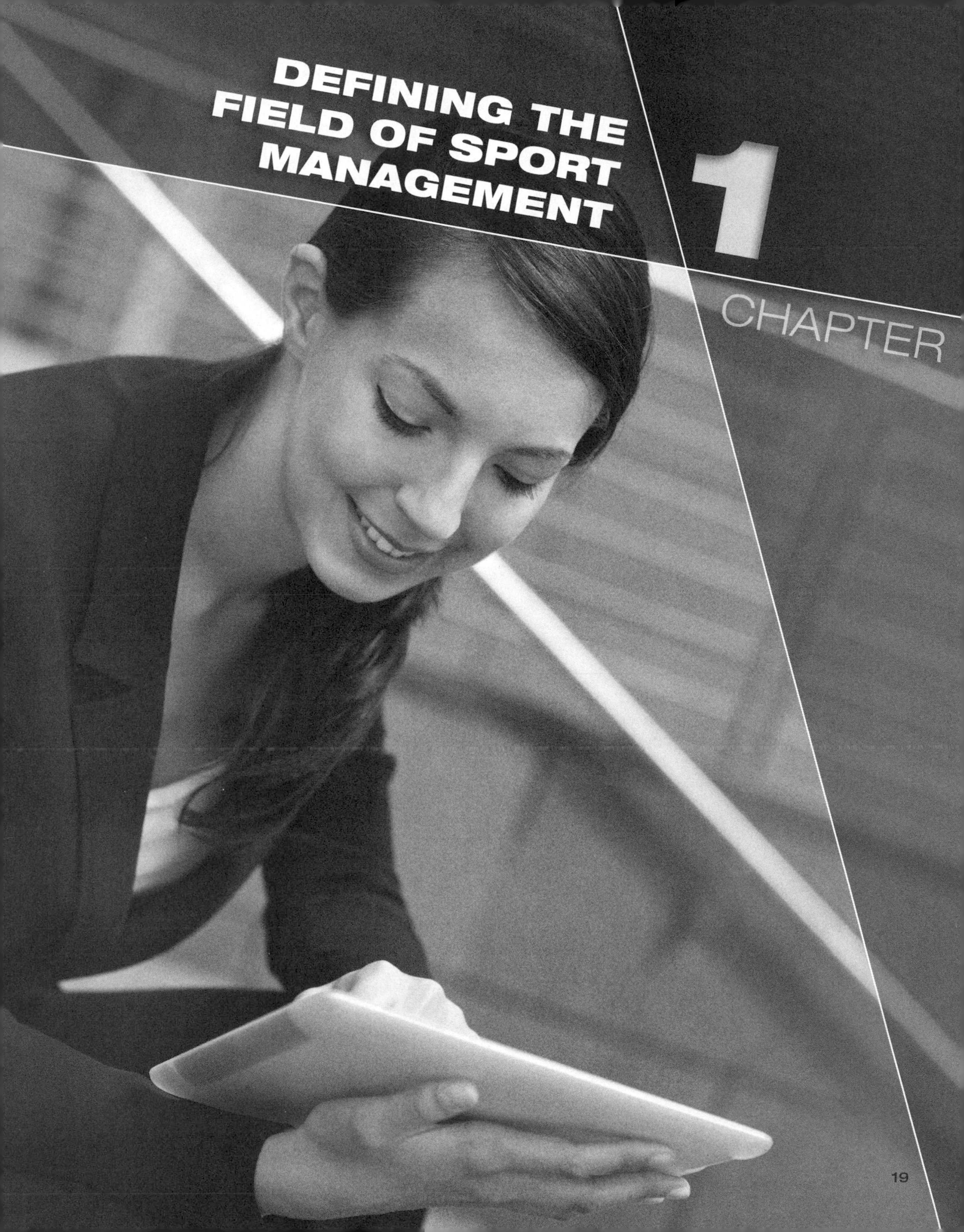

manage YOUR LEARNING

After completing this chapter you should be able to:

- Describe the differences between goods and services.
- Distinguish among consumer, professional, and human services.
- Discuss the motives for participation in sport and physical activity.
- Analyze the distinctions among participant, spectator, sponsorship, and donor services.
- Describe the primary purpose of sport management.

strategic CONCEPTS

consumer services
coordination
human resources
human services
management
marketing
participant services
production
professional services
service attributes
spectator services
sponsorship services
support units

THE FIELD DEFINED

I described the growth of sport management and its present scope in the Introduction. The figures that underscored the economic significance of the sport industry were quite impressive. Despite the enormous progress described in the Introduction, there is no comprehensive and coherent description of our field. Some of the existing definitions show a divergent or fragmented view of sport management. For example, Chelladurai (1985) defines sport management as

> management of those organizations whose major domain of operation is sport and physical activity. (p. 4)

Similarly, Slack and Parent (2006) define a sport organization as

> a social entity involved in the sport industry; it is goal directed with a consciously structured activity system and a relatively identifiable boundary. (p. 5)

Mullin (1980) defines a sport manager as

> a person whose job entails planning, organizing, staffing, directing, and controlling to be performed within the context of an organization whose primary or predominant product or service is sport and sport-related. (p. 3)

Note the emphasis on sport or sport-related products. Yet another definition was offered by the founders of the North American Society for Sport Management (NASSM, n.d.), including the venerable Dr. Earle F. Zeigler, considered by many to be the father of sport management. The constitution of NASSM (revised in 2013) states that

> the purpose of the Society shall be to promote, stimulate, and encourage study, research, scholarly writing, and professional development in the area of sport management (broadly interpreted).

It goes on to say that

> the members of this Society are concerned about the *theoretical* and *applied* aspects of management theory and practice specifically related to sport, exercise, dance, and play as these enterprises are pursued by all sectors of the population.

The inclusion of "exercise, dance, and play" in the above definition is noteworthy. In a similar vein, Pitts and Stotlar (2007) define sport management as

> The study and practices of all people, activities, businesses, and organizations involved in producing, facilitating, promoting, or organizing any product that is sport, fitness, and recreation related. (p. 4)

Note the reference to the term *industry* in the definition offered by Slack and Parent (2006). Many scholars and practitioners tend to use this term in its singular form. When we consider that an industry is a group of organizations that produce the same or similar products that are substitutable for each other (such as the paper industry and automobile industry) the question arises whether we are indeed a single industry. Are the products of a university recreation department substitutable for the products of a professional sport franchise? From this perspective, Mullin (1980) noted that "we have a collection of sport management occupations. The sports industry is fragmented. It is in fact a number of sports industries" (p. 8). If sport management is concerned with different industries, then it is useful to describe the field in terms of the products those industries produce. The remainder of this chapter is devoted to describing these products.

IN brief

The various definitions of sport management differentially emphasize sport organizations, careers in sport management, and the sport industry. In all these cases, the focus ultimately turns to sport products.

SPORT INDUSTRY PRODUCTS

Chelladurai (1993, 1994) defines the sport management field comprehensively by cataloging and classifying its products, alluded to by various scholars (e.g., Mullin, 1980; Mullin, Hardy, & Sutton, 2007; Pitts & Stotlar, 2007). The following pages offer the logic behind his definition and description of the field.

sidebar 1.1

MORE THAN A GAME

The definitions given in this chapter view sport management as a field concerned with several forms of participation in physical activity including recreational sport and fitness activities. The term *sport* in sport management is used in a generic sense to include all of these forms of participation. Unfortunately, a misconception exists that sport management in the United States is concerned only with elite sport such as intercollegiate athletics and professional and semiprofessional sports. This is not the case. Most practitioners and scholars would subscribe to the inclusive nature of sport management, and this text is based on the broader view of sport management. Readers will encounter references to recreational agencies, fitness clubs, sport clubs, and other such agencies and programs. Specialized fields such as recreation administration and fitness management, and most of what is taught and practiced in those fields, would parallel what is described in this text.

It has been argued that developing a classification of the observed phenomena is fundamental to any form of scientific inquiry. "To classify things is to bring parsimony and mental order to one's view of them" (Hambrick, 1984, p. 27). It is a fundamental characteristic of humans to gain a better understanding of the nature around them by classifying things.

The need to begin with the classification of the products of sport management rather than the organizations themselves comes from the growing interface between management and economics. The interest of management scholars in applying economic principles to the study of organizations, and of economists to look at their field from a managerial perspective, has resulted in a body of knowledge known as *organizational economics*. The major propositions of organizational economics are that (a) organizations are mechanisms that have evolved to facilitate the process of exchange of products, and (b) the organizational arrangements needed to support any particular exchange will depend on the inherent characteristics of the exchange (Hesterly, Liebeskind, & Zenger, 1990).

Consider the case of (a) a professional sport club, (b) a profit-oriented fitness club, and (c) a city recreation department. The professional sport club produces entertainment in the form of sport excellence and exchanges that product with the public for the price of admission to the game. The profit-oriented fitness club maintains the facility and equipment and rents them to its customers in exchange for a fee. It may also provide expert consultation, instruction, and leadership in fitness activities in exchange for a fee. The city recreation department maintains the playing fields and the arenas. What it offers is the use of those fields and arenas by the public at large. What the public offers in exchange is not so direct as in the previous two examples. Here, the exchange is in the form of taxes paid by members of the community, but the idea is the same—that is, somebody pays a price in exchange for the consumption of a sport product or service.

By the same token, these three organizations are structured and managed differently. For instance, the entertainment value of professional sport is a function of the competitiveness of the teams involved. To ensure competitiveness, professional leagues have rules for drafting and movement of players from team to team. The leagues also set salary caps for teams. League rules govern the individual clubs. The schedule of games is also largely left to the league. In contrast, a fitness club is autonomous from other fitness clubs. The owners can decide on the services to be offered and prices for those services based on market conditions. They can also set the schedule of activities. The city recreation department is a unit of the city government, which is controlled by elected representatives from various parts of the city. The department is normally structured to be responsive to the city council and its members. The variations in the structure and processes of these three different sport organizations reflect the products they exchange and the nature of that exchange.

From this perspective, the question of what is being exchanged becomes critical. What are the entities involved in the exchange that is being facilitated by sport organizations? If we can define, describe, and classify the products of exchange within the context of sport and recreation, then we should be able to capture the essential nature of the field and its boundaries.

Products as Goods and Services

The products of any organization may be goods or services or both. A good is a physical object that can be produced at one time and used later. In contrast, a service is a "time-perishable, intangible experience performed for a customer acting in the role of co-producer" (Fitzsimmons & Fitzsimmons, 2011, p. 4). In our context, the goods include all the equipment needed to engage in various kinds of sports and physical activity (e.g., golf clubs, tennis balls, soccer shoes, weight-training sets). In addition, promotional materials and merchandise (e.g., T-shirts, caps, banners) can also be included in the list of goods produced in the context of sport.

It should be pointed out that goods might be used in the production of services. For example, a fitness specialist may use highly sophisticated and expensive equipment to assess an individual's fitness status and then prescribe a suitable exercise program for that person. The equipment (i.e., goods) facilitates the service. In other words, the client has not bought the equipment, only the use of it by the specialist. A recreation department may use computers to assign participants randomly to various teams and draw up a schedule of competitions. The computer facilitates the service provided by the department. When a racquetball court is rented, the service involved is related to the renting of the court, an expensive good. A scoreboard (a piece of equipment) in an arena enhances the game experiences of the spectators (the service). These goods are properly called *facilitating goods and facilities* (Chelladurai, Scott, & Haywood-Farmer, 1987). Another example occurs when a baseball glove is purchased in a sport shop. The majority of the cost is for the glove (the good), but some of the cost is associated with the service rendered by the retailer, who purchased the good from the manufacturer and displayed it for the customer's convenience. The difference between the wholesale price and the retail price is the cost of the service to the customer.

IN brief

Every organization is a mechanism for exchange of one or more products with other elements in society. Thus, an understanding of the products of an organization is necessary to understand the organization itself.

According to the criterion of whether an organization is producing goods or services, almost all sports and recreation organizations can be classified as service organizations. Departments of sport management provide expert teaching in related subjects; athletic programs provide expert coaching for selected athletes; intramural programs provide opportunities for participation and competition among the general student population. Professional sport teams provide entertainment for the public. Government agencies, such as municipal recreation departments, may offer the use of facilities and opportunities to participate in organized competitions. Before we go on to describe and catalog the various services within sport and recreation, let us look in greater detail at the definition and description of services in general.

Services and Their Attributes

Service can be defined as an *intangible occurrence, process, or performance* that is produced and consumed simultaneously. The nature of a service is better understood by highlighting its pertinent attributes (characteristics). The **service attributes** most frequently discussed are *intangibility, perishability, heterogeneity,* and *simultaneity* (Grönroos, 1990; Lovelock, 1991; Sasser, Olsen, & Wyckoff, 1978; Schneider & Bowen, 1995).

A service is *intangible* in the sense that the client or customer cannot judge the quality of the product before actually obtaining it. The customer usually is guided by previous experience, the reputation of the organization, or the person(s) delivering the service. An athlete might base her choice of a university on the reputation of the coach or of the university itself or even on the recommendation of a friend. However, the athlete does not really know how good the service (i.e., the coaching and academic counseling) is until she experiences it. Similarly, clients have to experience the leadership of a fitness instructor or the lessons of a tennis pro before they can judge their quality. Intangibility stems from the sensual and psychological benefits that customers derive individually from a service. Feelings of comfort, status, and a sense of well-being are individualistic, so the services offered remain intangible.

Services are also *perishable;* a service cannot be produced and stored for future use. If no customer reports to a fitness consultant during a two-hour period, whatever services the consultant could have provided during that period have been lost. A high school coach may offer a free two-hour session of coaching for middle school players. If no players turned out for the session, the coaching service and its benefits would be gone. Similarly, if a racquetball court is not rented, the service (i.e., the use of the court during that period) has vanished. In contrast, a manufacturer can continue to produce goods and inventory them even though there may be no sales at any given moment.

Heterogeneity refers to the fact that whereas goods, such as a particular brand of tennis rackets, are usually of uniform quality (whether good or bad), services are relatively more variable in quality. A youth soccer league may have a good reputation, but the coaching experiences of players in the teams of that league may vary considerably. There are three reasons for this:

- First, individual differences among service providers in terms of personality, experience, and expertise result in different experiences for the clients. For instance, the leadership offered by various soccer coaches or fitness leaders or the lessons of different tennis pros may vary.
- Second, the same employee may not provide the same level of service from one time to another. For example, a soccer coach's lessons may vary in quality from day to day. This difference could be a function of the coach's level of motivation and fatigue (coaching following a busy day), stress (pressures affecting family life), and other such factors.
- Third, the quality of the experienced service can be affected by the consumer's psyche—a service may be judged good or bad depending upon the consumer's frame of mind. If motivation, fatigue, and stress can affect the service provider, the same factors could also affect the clients. For instance, not all the children on a soccer team will have similar experiences from the coaching offered by a single person. The member who is keenly interested in developing skills may not mind the coach pushing him or her to the limit, whereas a member who is there just for the fun of it may resent the coach's behavior. On the other hand, heterogeneity may not be as pronounced in the case of the rental of a tennis court, where the quality of the court will basically be the same day in and day out.

Simultaneity refers to the fact that a service has to be consumed as it is produced. When a coach is instructing, the athletes must be present. Because the production and consumption of a service are simultaneous, the interface between the employee (the producer of a service) and the client (the consumer of that service) becomes extremely important. In contrast, the production of tennis rackets happens at a place and time far removed from the customers. Thus, the interface between the producer and the consumer is much more important in the exchange of services than of goods. The term *inseparability* is also used to refer to this attribute, indicating that the production and consumption of a service cannot be separated.

Lovelock and Gummesson (2004) have argued that the attributes of intangibility, heterogeneity, simultaneity (inseparability of production and consumption), and perishability are not sufficient to distinguish a service from a good. In their view, the growth of telephone ordering and ecommerce means that the pre-purchase judgments about a good (e.g., a trampoline for the playground) cannot be made because the customer cannot touch it, feel it, or test it before the purchase. That is, the concept of intangibility extends to goods also. Moreover, some services can be verified before actual purchase, making the attribute of intangibility invalid in relation to that service. Suppose you plan on joining a fitness club to work out on your own. You may go to one or more fitness clubs to check the quality and layout of the equipment, parking facilities, locker room facilities, and similar items of concern to you. Based on these evaluations, you may join a particular club. The club's service to you is in fact the rental of its facility and equipment. Intangibility does not apply because you can test the equipment.

IN brief

A service is intangible because it cannot be scrutinized before purchase; it is perishable because it cannot be stored for future use; it is heterogeneous because it is variable from time to time; and its production and consumption occur simultaneously.

The concept of heterogeneity or variability loses its relevance in services where the process of service delivery is highly routinized and mechanized. Consider the case of club orientation in the fitness club. If the orientation is presented by several different employees, their mannerisms, attitudes, and behaviors may vary, thus making their services variable. Suppose the fitness club decides to educate new members using a video showing the facilities and equipment demonstrations. In such a case, there is little variability in the orientation process. As for inseparability, Lovelock and Gummesson (2004) point out that there are several *separable* services such as dry-cleaning your clothes and changing the oil in your car. In these cases, you do not get involved in the dry-cleaning process or the oil change, which are the core of these services. Stringing a tennis racket and sharpening skates would be examples of separable services in our context. As for perishability, Lovelock and Gummesson note that the concept is multidimensional in that it may refer to the actual *product* or service being perishable (e.g., tomatoes going bad or a professor giving a lecture that ends once class ends), or the *productive capacity* being perishable, as when a factory is shut down due to a power failure and its capacity to produce at that time perishes. In both of these perspectives, the concept of perishability applies to both goods and services. Some information-based services may not be perishable after all because they can be recorded and replayed later. For instance, if you take a video camera to your class and record the lectures of your professor (with permission of the instructor), his or her service in delivering the lecture is no longer perishable. Therefore, even perishability is not a good criterion to be used in distinguishing a service from a good.

Given the inadequacy of the four attributes to clearly delineate the boundaries of goods and services, Lovelock and Gummesson (2004) propose an alternative criterion to distinguish a service from a good—the *transfer of ownership*. Their essential argument is that in a service operation, there is no transfer of ownership of the service per se. They note that "marketing transactions that do not involve a transfer of ownership are distinctively different from those that do" (p. 34). Furthermore, they argue that "services involve a form of *rental* or *access* in which customers obtain benefits by gaining the right to use a physical object, to hire the labor and expertise of personnel, or to obtain access to facilities or networks" (p. 34). Within this nonownership framework they identify five broad categories of services:

1. *Rented goods services.* These services allow the customers the use of a physical good for a set time for a fee. For example, golf courses rent golfers the golf cart; bowling alleys rent shoes to their customers; and campus recreation centers rent out towels.
2. *Place and space rentals.* In this service, a customer uses a specified place or space for a fee. When I buy my season tickets for OSU Buckeye football games, I am allowed to occupy a particular seat number in a particular row in a particular section for the duration of the game. From this perspective, I am renting the space defined by that seat. Recreational and competitive leagues in several sports do not own their own facilities. Usually, they use the facilities of the city or the school district for a fee. This is similar to what happens when you park a car in a commercial parking lot—you rent the space and pay a certain amount for the period of time you occupy that space.
3. *Labor and expertise rentals.* In this form of service, the client simply rents the labor or expertise of another person or firm to carry out certain activities. The simplest example is when you or I hire somebody to mow our lawn. When someone pays for knee surgery, the payment includes the fee for the expertise of the surgeon and the surgical team. When a city recreation department hires a local marketing firm to survey the citizens on their sport and physical activity preferences, the department is renting the expertise residing in the marketing firm. As another example, The Ohio State University Athletic Department has outsourced the negotiation of sponsorship deals to International Marketing Group (IMG). In other words, the OSU Athletic Department has rented the expertise and labor of IMG.
4. *Physical facility access services.* When someone buys a ticket to the Hall of Fame in a given sport, the person receives access to the facility and the exhibits therein. Some famous sport venues sell tickets for access to their facilities; for example, Yankee Stadium in New York and Fenway Park in Boston. In contrast to buying a ticket for a game in which a seat is guaranteed, the client purchases general access to the facility.
5. *Network access and usage.* In this form of service, a client rents the right to participate in a network such as telecommunications, utilities, banking, insurance, or specialized information services. Some sports-related websites (e.g., NCAA, IEG) store enormous amounts of information and data. Although the information on some of the websites is free to access (e.g., NCAA), other commercial websites (e.g., IEG) charge a fee for access to their websites. An individual must also pay a fee (monthly, bi-annual, or annual) to access the "insider" portal on ESPN's website, which contains premium digital and print content as well as issues of *ESPN the Magazine* (http://insider.espn.go.com/insider/benefits).

Lovelock and Gummesson's (2004) introduction of the criterion of transfer of ownership (or absence of transfer of ownership, to be more correct) as the defining characteristic of a service represents a basic shift in assumptions. The former assumption that the four attributes of intangibility, heterogeneity, inseparability, and perishability distinguish services from goods is replaced by the assumption that what makes a service unique from a good is that there is no transfer of ownership in the case of a service but only the rental of or access to an object, labor and expertise, a facility, or a network.

Although Lovelock and Gummesson (2004) have made a logical argument for a more definitive distinguishing attribute of a service, they have not suggested the abandonment of the other four attributes as guiding managerial thought and actions but argue that they are not sufficient to define a service. If we accept their basic argument for transfer of ownership as the dividing line between a good and a service, we can also recognize that most services do differ from most goods on the four attributes. That is, most services are characterized by intangibility, heterogeneity, inseparability, and perishability. By the same token, we must understand that various services may differ among themselves in the degree of relevance of each of the four attributes. It would be very useful for us to conceive of four continuums representing the four attributes as shown in Exhibit 1.1.

CONSUMER, PROFESSIONAL, AND HUMAN SERVICES

Although the attributes given above are applicable to all services, we can also make distinctions among services based on their nature. The nature of the service provided is defined by what actually happens in the service provider–client interface. A significant aspect of the service provider–client interface is the amount and type of information exchanged between the client and provider in the production of the service (Grönroos, 1990; Mills & Margulies, 1980; Sasser et al., 1978; Schneider & Bowen, 1995). Sasser and colleagues (1978) used this construct to categorize services into consumer and professional services. In this section, both service categories will be discussed as well as human services, a subcategory of professional services.

exhibit 1.1 A framework for understanding the nature of services.

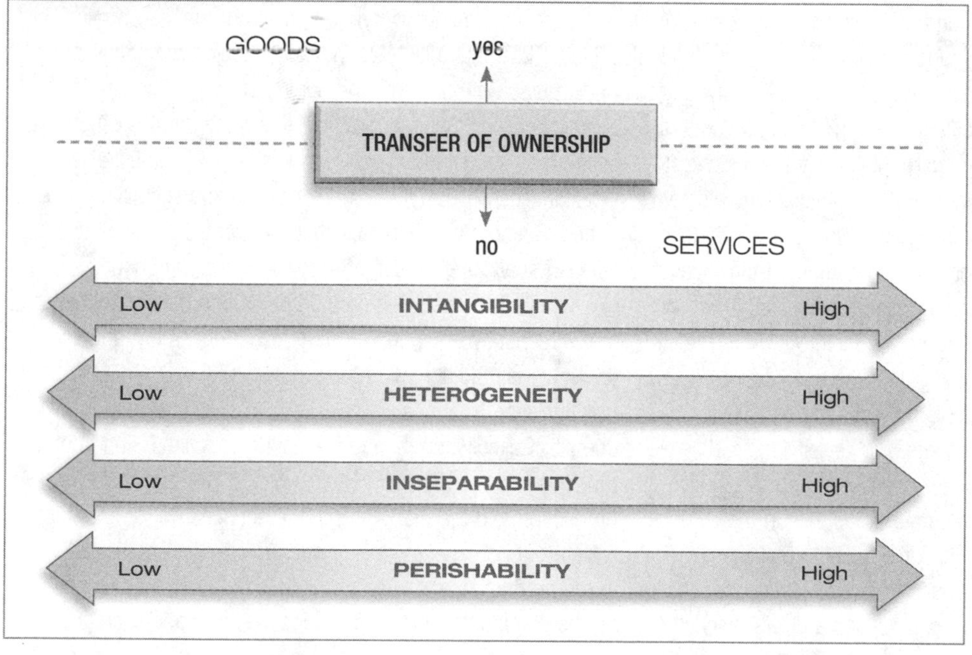

sidebar 1.2

SERVICE PARTICIPATION VERSUS SERVICE EXPERIENCE

While the classification offered by Lovelock and Gummesson (2004) is very useful when applied to a whole array of services produced in different industries, specific service industries (e.g., the fast-food industry, the entertainment industry, the transportation industry) may have their own defining characteristics that could require a different classification scheme. Based on this thinking, Chelladurai (2007) proposed a classification scheme for sport services. Earlier, a service was defined as a "time-perishable, intangible experience performed for a customer acting in the role of co-producer" (Fitzsimmons & Fitzsimmons, 2011, p. 4). Note the mention of the *customer* as a *co-producer.* That is, the customer is involved in the production of the service to some extent. Based on the idea of the client as a co-producer, Chelladurai (2007) advanced two criteria to classify sport services—(a) production participation and (b) service experience.

Production participation refers to the degree the client engages in the production of the service. With some sport services, customer involvement in the production of the service may be much more intensive and physical. Consider, for example, the services offered by a fitness club. The facility and the equipment are significant components of the service offered. However, the service is complete only when the clients engage physically in using it. Similarly, the city recreation department may build and maintain baseball fields, but the service is complete only when the citizens play on these fields. In other sport services, however, participation need not be as intensive or as physical. For example, most spectators at a sporting event do not engage physically in the contest. Although they are in the stadium, their physical involvement is minimal. Of course, some fans behave more physically than even the athletes themselves and do contribute to the spectacle of the event. Other fans, however, may enjoy the event with a few friends in their home or a restaurant. At any rate, the various services produced within the sport industry can be placed along the dimension of production participation.

Chelladurai's second criterion for classifying sport services, the dimension of service experience, refers to the extent to which such physical engagement of clients in the production of the service is hedonistic or agonistic. Keating (1964) distinguished between *sport* and *athletics. Sport* is derived from the French word *desporter,* meaning a diversionary activity to carry one away from work, and whose purpose is hedonistic, maximizing pleasure for all participants. Conversely, *athletics* is derived from the Greek words *athlos* (i.e., a contest), *athlon* (i.e., a prize), and *athlein* (i.e., to contend for a prize). Athletics is a *competitive* and *agonistic activity* to establish the superiority of one over others in seeking the coveted prize. It is characterized by a very high degree of devotion and commitment to the pursuit, extraordinary efforts over a prolonged period of training, and considerable personal sacrifice. In fact, the term *agon* refers to "the contest for a prize at public games," and *agony* refers to pain associated with athletic contests; more specifically, it refers to the painful preparation for athletic contests. But agony is not restricted to competitive sports. When individuals engage in jogging for the purpose of health, they are in an agonistic (i.e., painful) pursuit. In broader terms, anyone who engages in sport for some external benefits is involved in an agonistic activity. In sum, the experiences of an individual in a physical activity can be conceived of as hedonistic (i.e., oriented toward intrinsic rewards—pleasure of participation) or agonistic (i.e., oriented toward extrinsic rewards—victory in contests, fitness and health).

If these two dimensions are juxtaposed with experience (i.e., hedonistic versus agonistic) on the horizontal axis and production participation (i.e., high or low participation) on the vertical axis, we should derive four quadrants as shown in Exhibit 1.2. Quadrants 1, 2, and 3 are labeled spectator services, pursuit of pleasure, and pursuit of excellence and therapeutic services. Readers will note that quadrant 4 is empty because no sport and physical activity service is characterized simultaneously by low level of participation and agonistic experience. Readers will also note that quadrant 3 contains two types of services—pursuit of excellence and therapeutic services. In both cases, members participate in the production of the respective service, and their experiences are agonistic. However, the actual amount of activity (i.e., the intensity, duration, and frequency of activity) will be much greater in pursuit of excellence than in therapeutic services. The important point to note in this scheme is that the processes of production and the marketing of the services will be markedly different because of varying degrees of client participation in the production and varying degrees of client experiences on the continuum ranging from hedonistic to agonistic.

exhibit 1.2 Interplay of the extent of production participation and the type of experience.

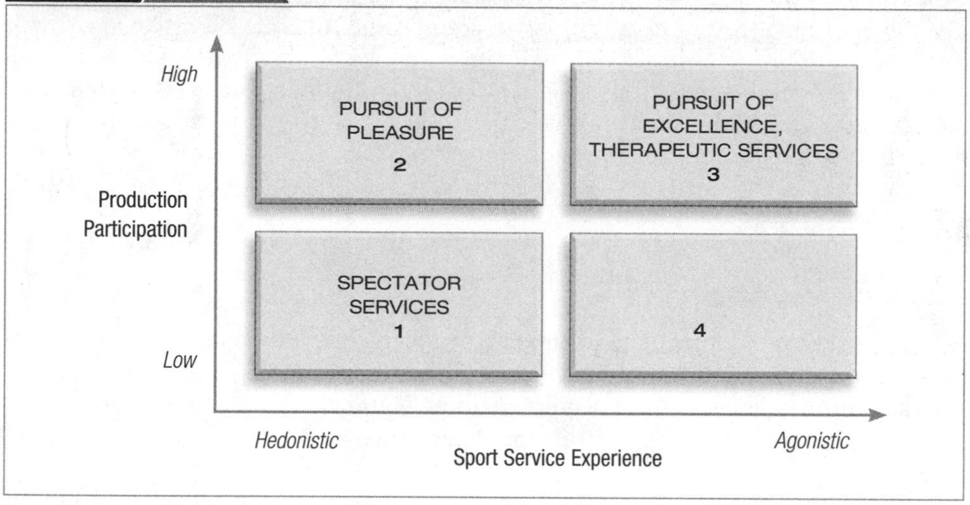

Consumer Services

Consumer services are largely based on low-skill and routine services including renting of facilities and retailing of goods. A reception clerk in a tennis club need only know the appropriate reservation procedures for the facilities or equipment, as well as guidelines for their use. Similarly, a locker room attendant need only know who is eligible for what equipment, and the procedures to sign out the equipment. As another example, a cashier at a sporting goods store need only to know how to scan the price of an item and how to receive payments.

Professional Services

Professional services are largely based on knowledge, expertise, and special competencies of the employee (the service provider). For example, an athletic trainer is trained to know the nature of sport injuries and what to do in the case of specific injuries, and a tennis pro's instructions are based on his or her respective expertise and knowledge. Similarly, a university provides a professional service when it offers expert coaching in various sports to selected students. In our context, the critical difference between a consumer service and a professional service is the direct and active leadership provided by the service worker in the assessment of clients' needs, the specification of appropriate activities, and the guidance and coaching provided during participation.

Most likely, an agency will offer both consumer and professional services to varying degrees, as in a university's intramural and intercollegiate athletic programs. A commercial fitness club may rent its facilities and equipment and, at the same time, offer professional services in the form of fitness testing, weight management, exercise prescription, and consultation.

Professional services themselves can be categorized into two major types: services involving something in which a client is interested and services involving

sidebar 1.3

FIX-IT SERVICES

Schneider and Bowen (1995), in contrasting a professional service with a fix-it service (i.e., to get a malfunctioning device working again), suggest that "a professional service is a high-falutin' synonym for a fix-it service provided by someone with a degree or license. Doctors, stockbrokers, architects, bankers, and professors deliver professional services. They also build things as well as fix things: stockbrokers build financial reserves, doctors build health, architects build buildings, and so forth" (p. 191).

the transformation of a client. For instance, lawyers, architects, accountants, and stockbrokers provide complex professional services to their clients or customers. By the same token, teachers, guidance counselors, and the clergy also provide professional services. But there is a distinction. The former type involves knowledge and guidelines regarding *something* in which the clients are interested (e.g., a legal issue, a building, or an investment). The latter type is engaged in transforming the *people* themselves (e.g., educating the child, guiding the students, and enhancing the spiritual life) (Hasenfeld, 1992; Hasenfeld & English, 1974). The latter services are human services.

Human Services

Human services "define or alter the person's behavior, attributes, and social status in order to maintain or enhance his well-being." Also, the "input of raw material are human beings with specific attributes, and their production output are persons processed or changed in a predetermined manner" (Hasenfeld & English, 1974, p. 1).

Thus, human services compared to the other professional services are unique because:

- the input (that is, the raw materials) is humans.
- the input/raw material is variable in terms of age, gender, health, fitness level, ability, and so on.
- the processes cannot be standardized because the input/raw material is variable.
- while client expectations are legitimate, only professional experts decide on the service to be provided (for instance, a coach decides on the strategies to be employed in a game; a fitness specialist decides on the exercise regimen).
- the clients who are the input get actively involved in the process of producing the relevant service (Chelladurai, 1996; Williamson, 1991).

The last factor is problematic in two different ways. First, a client's active involvement may hinder the employee's activities and judgment. For example, a client in an aerobics class who grunts too loudly while performing the routine, or one who shows off too much during the routine, may disrupt the activities of the instructor. The other problem is that the clients may not be compliant to expert directions (Hasenfeld, 1983, 1992). These two issues are accentuated in the sport context because the production of some of our services requires our clients to engage in quite *agonistic* (that is, painful) and *prolonged* activities. The provision of fitness- and health-oriented services, for example, is dependent on the extent to which the clients will adhere to the service provider's guidance and participate in vigorous activities. Similarly, pursuit of excellence in a sport requires the client to undergo strenuous practice sessions while forgoing other more pleasurable activities. These unique characteristics of human services in sport and recreation highlight the significance of ensuring that our service providers are professionally competent and, at the same time, skilled in social interactions.

Hasenfeld's (1983) three-level classification of (a) *people-processing,* (b) *people-sustaining,* and (c) *people-changing* functions of human services helps us to elaborate further on the nature of human services in sport and recreation organizations.

- **People-processing.** This function refers to testing or screening people and placing them in a particular class based on some specified criterion. Fitness-testing laboratories perform this function when they rate their customers on a scale of relative fitness. Classifying promising athletes after extensive assessment of their psychomotor abilities would be a people-processing service. Lifeguards may administer swim tests to decide which end of the swimming pool will be used by a client. Youth sport leagues may have schemes to assess the ability levels of the applicants before assigning them to specific teams. Similarly, testing athletes for drugs would also be designated as a people-processing service.

- **People-sustaining.** Another function of human service organizations may be to sustain people (that is, prevent or delay the decline in the welfare or status of the clients). This is the major function of social service, assisted living, and rehabilitation programs. In our context, cardiac rehabilitation programs and physical therapy and athletic injury clinics provide people-sustaining services. U.S. Masters Swimming programs, for example, aim to help participants develop and maintain a certain level of fitness.
- **People-changing.** People-changing services aim at some changes in the clients or customers in terms of one or more of the biophysical, psychological, or social attributes. For example, sport management degree programs change their clients into more knowledgeable persons in the field; fitness programs make people healthier; recreational programs make their clients more relaxed and energized; and coaching programs and sports camps make the clients better performers.

IN brief

Services can be broadly classified as consumer and professional services. Human services, a subcategory of professional services, may involve processing, sustaining, and/or changing people.

Hasenfeld's three-level classification of human services can be easily mapped onto sport and physical activity services in general. However, because our focus is on those services that involve the active participation of the clients, the people-processing services become less germane and the people-sustaining and people-changing services more pertinent.

CLIENT MOTIVES FOR PARTICIPATION

The description of the types of services is critical for developing managerial guidelines; however, it is equally important that we identify the motives of the clients who participate in our services. As noted before, participant services in sport require the active involvement of clients. Thus, the clients contribute as much as the service employees to the nature of the service.

Although the notion of consumer involvement is generic to the production of many services, it is of greater importance in our context because the production of a sport or recreation service often depends upon active *physical exertion* on the part of the consumer. As mentioned earlier, the efforts of an exercise leader will result in a service only if the clients physically participate in the exercise regimen. Hasenfeld (1983), referring to human services in general, noted that "Patients may refuse to comply with a physician's orders; students may ignore their teachers; and clients may resist discussing their interpersonal problems. . . . Consequently, the control of the client and the need to elicit conformity are critical issues in human service organizations and consume much of the efforts of their practitioners" (pp. 122–123). Getting the clients to participate in the sport and physical activity programs is critical for the service providers.

sidebar 1.4

EMPLOYEES DEFINE THE ORGANIZATION

Sasser et al. (1978) note with reference to professional services, "while employees may be replaceable, every replacement alters the nature of the organization . . . and the nature of the product" (p. 401). That is, the employees themselves define the organization, particularly a professional service organization. Thus, when a professor of sport management leaves a university, the course offerings in that field are altered, the research thrust also changes, and, in sum, the service product becomes different. This scenario is often repeated in the context of elite sport coaching. Every replacement of the head coach is followed by a different coaching philosophy and different strategies (that is, a different product).

The relative ease or difficulty of securing client motivation in sport and physical activity services varies from one context to another. The psychological dynamics of client motivation are best understood if we consider clients' motives for participation in physical activities. Several schemes have been proposed to classify participant motives and attitudes in (a) youth sports (Gill, Gross, & Huddleston, 1983); (b) school physical education (Jewett, 1987); (c) college physical activity classes (Mathes & Battista, 1985); (d) older adults (Heitmann, 1986); and (e) various life stages (Vuolle, 1987).

Ellis (1988) proposes a continuum of goals for activity and leisure in the community ranging from health care through health enhancement to enjoyment. These are further broken down into cure, rehabilitation, wellness promotion, self-expenditure on work/service, and self-actualization. Pelletier, Fortier, Vallerand, Tuson, and Briere (1995) developed the Sport Motivation Scale (SMS) to measure three forms of intrinsic motivation, three forms of extrinsic motivation, and amotivation (i.e., being neither intrinsically nor extrinsically motivated to participate). Roberts (1993) and Duda (1994, 1996) refer to two orthogonal goal orientations of participants in sport. *Task orientation* refers to success being judged on the basis of task mastery and personal improvement, and *ego orientation* refers to success being judged on the basis of one's performance relative to other performances.

For our purposes, we can group the motives, attitudes, and goals outlined by these scholars into (a) pursuit of pleasure, (b) pursuit of skill, (c) pursuit of excellence, and (d) pursuit of health/fitness.

Pursuit of Pleasure

People may participate in sport and physical activity because they enjoy the kinesthetic sensations or the competition provided by, say, a game of squash, pick-up basketball, or weekly bowling. The pleasures they seek can be enjoyed only during participation; that is, they are not seeking any other benefits outside of actual participation itself. It is easier to secure client motivation when such pleasure-seeking is the basis for participation; that is, the clients are intrinsically motivated. Thus, the elementary school teacher is not much concerned about motivating the children during recess. Similarly, fitness club employees need not focus on motivating those who participate in squash or tennis for pleasure.

Pursuit of Skill

The desire to acquire physical skills may compel people to participate in sport and physical activity. Individuals may focus on perfecting their skills through continued vigorous physical activity. Organized physical activity classes (such as wall climbing and judo, as well as sports camps and clinics) aim at imparting skills in various sports to members of the community. The popularity of such programs among people of all ages attests to the pervasiveness of the desire to learn skills.

Pursuit of Excellence

People may also participate in some form of sport or physical activity in pursuit of excellence in that activity. Pursuit of excellence is broadly defined as the effort to win in a contest against a standard. The standard may be your own previous performance, somebody else's performance, or simply winning against an opponent. Those individuals who pursue excellence prepare for the contests and are willing to comply with the instructions of the coach or teacher. The scenario of athletes going through painful exercises while chanting the motto "no pain, no gain" aptly illustrates the pursuit of excellence. Note that acquisition and mastery of skills are prerequisites for the pursuit of excellence.

The emphasis on achieving personal standards is best illustrated by most distance runners who strive to improve their personal best. As another example, NBA star Lebron James was doing very well with his former team, the Cleveland Cavaliers. The fans, the media, and the other players acknowledged that he was the best player on the team. But for him that was not good enough. He desired to win the ultimate prize in basketball—an NBA championship ring. So, he moved to the Miami Heat and won it.

IN brief

The reasons why people participate in sport and physical activity may be broadly classified as (a) pursuit of pleasure, (b) pursuit of skill, (c) pursuit of excellence, and (d) pursuit of health and fitness. Activities chosen to satisfy one motive may yield other outcomes as well.

Pursuit of Health/Fitness

Other participants in sport and physical activity strive mainly for those health-related benefits (such as fitness, stress reduction, and longevity) that result from such participation. In other words, the benefits of participating are extrinsic to the activity itself. They reside outside the actual physical activity and are derived after prolonged physical activity.

In this regard, Hasenfeld's (1983) distinction between those functioning adequately and those functioning below an adequate level has relevance for us. That is, many individuals who are sufficiently fit and healthy would like to maintain that level of fitness and health; therefore, they continue to participate in sport and physical activity. Such motives may be labeled *sustenance* motives. On the other hand, other people may participate in physical activity to improve fitness and health that has been judged inadequate. These motives may be labeled *curative.*

Although these motives are distinct from each other, the activities that people select to satisfy any one of them may result in other outcomes as well. For example, those who play squash in pursuit of pleasure may also gain in fitness and may also enhance their performance capabilities. Similarly, those who run for the sake of fitness may learn to enjoy the kinesthetic sensations as well as the sense of achievement in running farther or at a faster pace. However, it is critical from a managerial perspective that the primary purpose for participation in a program of sport or physical activity be established so that its development and implementation will be smooth and coordinated. For instance, the need for motivating clients before and during participation varies with the purposes of such participation. In pursuit of pleasure, the activity itself is the reward, and therefore it acts as the motivator for the participants. The service provider's role is then restricted to providing facilities and equipment, scheduling activities, and giving general supervision. On the other hand, in pursuit of excellence, skill, or fitness and health, the reward will not be immediate, and therefore the agency has a greater responsibility in motivating the participants.

CLASSIFYING SPORT SERVICES

Based on the distinctions among consumer, professional, and human services and on the motives of participants, the services (products) within the domain of sport management can be broadly classified into *participant services, spectator services, sponsorship services* (including licensing and merchandising), *donor services*, and *social ideas*. These are explained in the following sections. Some of these broad areas can be further broken down into specific services as shown in Exhibit 1.3. The manufacture and sale of sporting goods is a sport product that is relatively self-explanatory and will not be discussed here.

Participant Services

Participant services are those services offered in order for clients to engage physically in some form of sport or physical activity. A combination of the types of services (consumer and human) and client motives (pursuit of pleasure, health/fitness, skill, and excellence) yields six types of participant services: *consumer-pleasure, consumer-health/fitness, human-skill, human-excellence, human-sustenance,* and *human-curative* (Chelladurai, 1992). The descriptions of these participant services follow.

- *Consumer-pleasure* services refer to the scheduling or reserving of facilities or equipment as requested by clients who seek pleasure in physical activity. This class of service includes organizing and conducting different kinds of competitions for clients.

exhibit 1.3 Classification of sport services.

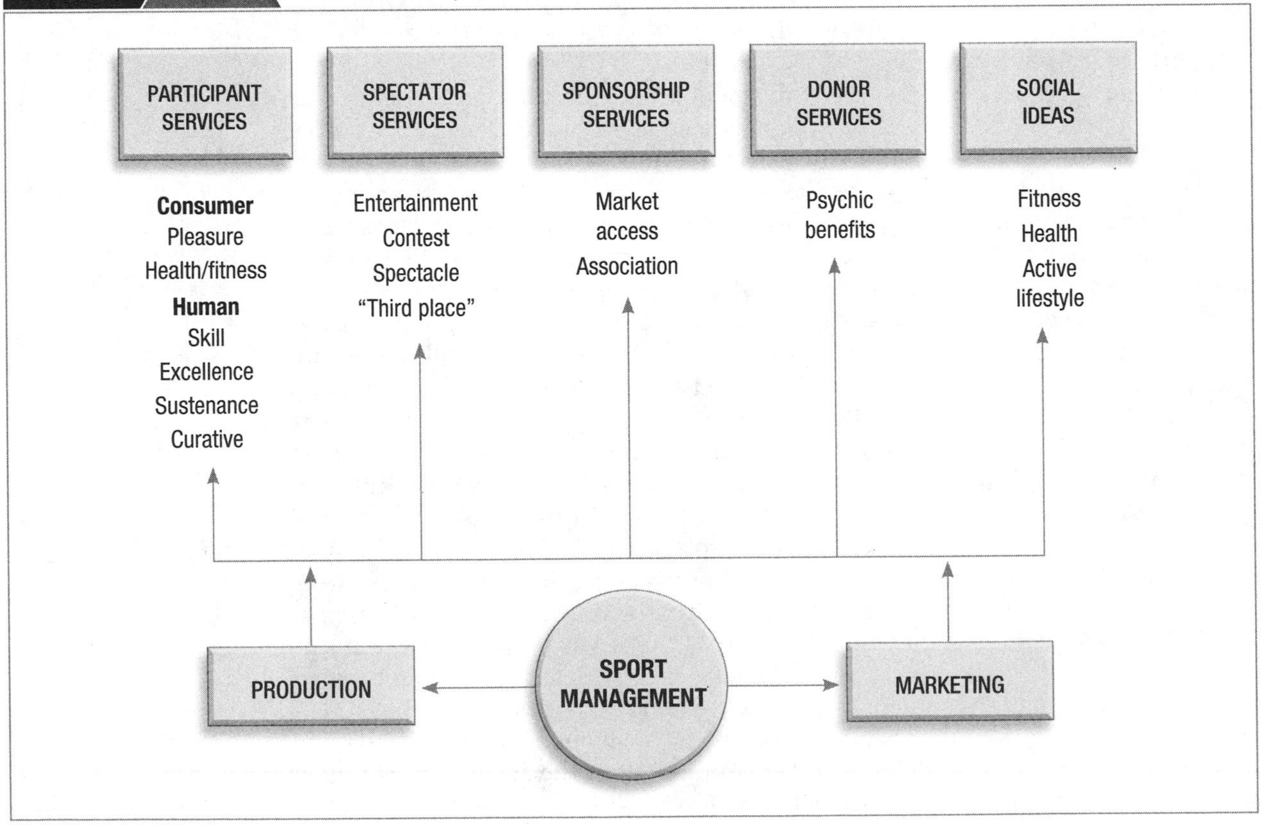

sidebar 1.5

AMERICAN FOOTBALL AROUND THE WORLD

Many Americans may not be aware of the International Federation of American Football (IFAF), made up of over 50 member countries, which holds a world championship every four years (see more at http://IFAF.org and http://www.usafootball.com). Furthermore, there are 68 professional or semi-professional American football leagues in Central and South America, Europe, Asia, and Oceania. It should also be noted that approximately 70 foreign-born players from 30 other countries play in the NFL (BusinessInsider, 2011). At one time only U.S.-born players were members of the teams in Major League Baseball and the National Basketball Association. Such U.S. dominance has diminished considerably with the influx of players from around the world in all major league sports. Given the worldwide television coverage of NFL games and the NFL's prestige and wealth, drafting foreign-born players will continue to become more commonplace for NFL teams.

- *Consumer-health/fitness* services involve scheduling or reserving facilities or equipment to satisfy clients' desire to maintain their fitness and health.

The next set of services includes human services that involve instruction, guidance, or coaching by experts.

- *Human-skill* services refer to the expert application of teaching technology and leadership in developing the skills (including techniques and strategies) of the clients in various forms of sport and physical activity.
- *Human-excellence* services provide expert guidance and coaching for clients in their pursuit of excellence in a chosen physical activity.
- *Human-sustenance* services are the organization and conduct of exercise and fitness programs on a regular basis under the guidance and supervision of an expert leader, as in the case of aerobics instructors leading a group of clients.
- *Human-curative* services involve designing and offering physical activity programs to rehabilitate those in need of improvement in fitness, health, or physical appearance in such areas as cardiac rehabilitation, relaxation and stress reduction, and weight management.

Spectator Services

Spectator services refer to the entertainment we provide to our clients. Not all sports have the same degree of entertainment value for all people. For instance, although soccer is the most popular sport in the world, it does not generate the same level of excitement in the United States as it does in many other countries. Similarly, cricket is quite popular in the British Commonwealth countries, whereas it remains virtually unknown in the United States. These differences are a function of culture and tradition. Even within one country or cultural context, individuals may be attracted to specific features of a sport. While the physical contact of football may be attractive to some, the quiet finesse of golf may appeal more to others. Our concern here is not with the entertainment value of a single sport but of sports in general.

The entertainment value of sport may be generated by two different ventures with different goals and processes. The primary purpose of professional sports is to make a profit through providing entertainment to the public. Therefore, pro leagues recruit excellence produced elsewhere and parade it before the paying pub-

sidebar 1.6

WINNING

In Broyles and Hay's (1979) view, "competitive athletic events are part of the entertainment business. Athletes are brought together to create a social event that is exciting and valuable to fans. These events are marketed to attract customers" (p. 3). And, "the primary objective of a successful business organization is to produce a quality product and/or service to satisfy the needs of the customers; similarly, the main goal of a successful athletic program is to produce a winning team to satisfy some of the entertainment needs of the fans. By winning more than half of its competitive events, an athletic program establishes itself as a winner. Winning is the name of the game for athletic administrators" (p. 27).

lic in the form of organized competitions. They ensure that the teams are of similar caliber so that the outcome of a competition is relatively unpredictable. In contrast, some organizations pursue the goal of excellence—for example, the traditional role of intercollegiate athletics in the United States. These athletic programs also organize competitions, though mainly to promote and prove excellence. In the process, they may also produce entertainment value for the public. Such entertainment may be viewed as a by-product of the pursuit of excellence. This is not to deny that the provision of entertainment and generation of revenue may indeed be the primary objectives for some universities. In fact, some authors maintain that intercollegiate athletics should be run as businesses that provide entertainment and generate revenue. For instance, as of 2009, the mission statement of The Ohio State University Athletic Department noted, "We will sustain a strong financial and community base of support by presenting outstanding intercollegiate athletic teams which provide quality entertainment and a positive public identity for the university."

The entertainment value of sport competitions stems largely from three different sources—*contest, spectacle,* and *third place experience.*

The contest

The entertainment value of a sport contest lies in (a) the excellence exhibited by the participants, (b) the unpredictability of the outcomes of a contest, and (c) the loyalty and attachment of people to certain sports, teams, and athletes. Thus, the higher the level of excellence, the higher the entertainment value. Contests of the Olympics, World Cup, and professional sports are more exciting to watch than high school contests. Next, the entertainment value of a contest increases if the outcome is not a foregone conclusion. Normally, the unpredictable nature of the contest stems from the equality of resources, such as skill, size, strength, and training, between the contestants, and from the element of luck (the bounce of the ball, or a referee's mistakes). Spectators are more interested in watching a game between two top-ranked teams than between a high-ranked team and a team in the cellar. The Dream Team (the U.S. men's basketball team for the Barcelona Olympics in 1992) was loaded with so much talent that every contest turned out to be a "no contest." However, in this case, it was not the competitions per se that were attractive but the ensemble of the most excellent talent in the sport. Another example is when the Miami Heat basketball team hired Lebron James and Chris Bosh to join Dwayne Wade in 2010. Many fans were excited about seeing the three stars play together.

The third element of the contest as a source of entertainment is the loyalty or attachment of individuals (the fans) to a particular sport, team, or athlete. There are those who like baseball and hate basketball; those who love the Los Angeles Dodgers and think less of the New York Yankees; and those who admire Serena Williams or Rafael Nadal and those who adore Maria Sharapova or Novak Djokovic. Thus, it is not surprising that considerable effort and money are spent in promoting (a) a sport (hence the NBA's commercial slogan, "Where Amazing Happens"); (b) a team (the promotion of the Dallas Cowboys as America's team); and (c) an athlete (the efforts to name a successor to Michael Jordan).

The spectacle

Although the contest forms the core of the event, spectacle is also a part of these contests. The opening and closing ceremonies of the Olympics, and the parades and half-time shows of football games in the United States, are added elements of the entertainment package (i.e., product extensions, in marketing terminology). The cheerleaders and the marching bands are also part of the spectacle. In fact, some of the more famous cheerleading squads (e.g., the Laker Girls of the Los Angeles Lakers basketball team) may be invited to perform during periods in a hockey game in a remote city. In 2004, the organizers of the Madrid Masters tennis tournament hired fashion models as ball girls for one televised match each day to add to the entertainment value (ESPN.com, 2004). Being skeptical about fashion models in skimpy outfits on the sidelines of a tennis court, Andre Agassi, a contestant in the tournament, noted, "I think it's important for our sport to understand its product clearly. And I'm not quite convinced it's part of our product" (Associated Press, 2004). However, for some of the paying public these elements are as important as the contest itself. Consider, for example, the public's focus on the tennis outfits of Venus and Serena Williams.

IN brief

The elements that characterize spectator sports are (a) the contest itself, (b) the spectacle, and (c) the stadium/arena serving as a "third place."

The "third place" experience

An equally important aspect of sport as entertainment is highlighted by Melnick (1993), who argues that the forces of urbanization, individualism, interpersonal competition, technology, and geographical mobility have made the primary social ties with family and friends tenuous. Individuals in these contexts seek to satisfy their social needs in less personal ways. The venues where such associations can take place are called "third places" (as distinct from the home and workplace). Third places offer opportunities for "casual encounters with strangers of a quasi-primary kind" (p. 49). Thus, "sports spectating has emerged as a major urban structure where spectators come together not only to be entertained [by the contest] but to enrich their social psychological lives through the sociable, quasi-intimate relationships available" (p. 44). Melnick goes on to argue that sport managers may benefit by emphasizing this particular service—the availability of a third place. The notion of a third place may extend beyond the stadium and arena into bars, restaurants, and even shopping malls where a group of individuals can watch a game on television.

The third place experience as defined above also serves as a forum for BIRGing—Basking In Reflected Glory (Cialdini et al., 1976; Wann & Branscombe, 1990)—and CORFing—Cutting Off Reflected Failure (Snyder, Lassegard, & Ford, 1986; Wann & Branscombe, 1990). BIRGing refers to the tendency for people to publicize their connection with others who have been successful (Cialdini et al., 1976). These authors note that college students tend to wear school-identifying apparel after their college football teams' victories and use the pronoun "we" when the team is victorious, thus strengthening their connection with the winning team. CORFing is the distancing of oneself from the failure of others (Snyder et al., 1986). People tend to increase distance between themselves and others who have been unsuccessful. It is argued here that the presence of quasi-intimate relationships in a third place permits both unmitigated expression of reflected glory and distancing from reflected failure.

Sponsorship Services

Corporate sponsorship is one of the fastest growing and richest areas within sport management. The IEG Sponsorship Report (2013) notes that worldwide corporate sponsorship in 2012 was $51.1 billion. This amount included $18.9 billion in the United States alone, of which $13.01 billion was devoted to sponsoring sports.

Why would corporations spend so much money on sponsoring sporting events and teams? What do they gain in return? The definition of sponsorship offered by Mullin et al. (2007) provides the answer to this question. They define sponsorship as "the acquisition of rights to affiliate or directly associate with a product or event for the purpose of deriving benefits related to that affiliation or association. The sponsor then uses this relationship to achieve its promotional objectives or to facilitate and support its broader marketing objectives" (p. 254). In a similar vein, both Shilbury, Quick, and Westerbeek (1998) and Milne and McDonald (1999) view sponsorship as a business reciprocal relationship in which the sponsor provides funds for a sports event or an organization in return for the rights of association, which can be used for commercial advantages. In Shank's (2005) view, sponsorship is "investing in a sports entity (athlete, league, team, or event) to support overall organizational objectives, marketing goals, and promotional strategies" (p. 330). Shank (2005) lists the following as the sponsorship objectives:

1. Creating awareness of the sponsor's products and services, and/or corporate name;
2. Competing with other companies;
3. Reaching new target markets composed of people with similar activities, interests, and opinions;
4. Establishing long-term relationships with clients;
5. Building up the image of the sponsor; and
6. Increasing sales.

Amis, Pant, and Slack (1997) list the following as additional objectives of sponsorship:

1. Linking with local businesses and political communities;
2. Entertaining corporate customers;
3. Improving employee relations; and
4. Testing of company products under "real-life" conditions.

The above definitions incorporate two significant elements: *market access* and *association.**

Provide market access

The major service offered to the sponsors is the access to communication with a specific market (the direct and indirect consumers of a sport). With such access, sponsors are able to pursue their promotional and marketing objectives. When a

*Some authors have identified hospitality services as a component of sponsorship (e.g., Howard & Crompton, 1995). While it is true that corporations use those services to entertain their significant customers and employees, such services are usually generated by the sponsors themselves; that is, the sport organization itself is not providing those services. Therefore, hospitality services are not emphasized in this section.

footwear company offers millions of dollars to promote a tournament, it gains in exchange the access to millions of spectators and TV viewers who watch the game. The significance of this market access for the corporate sector is reflected in the billions of dollars spent on sponsorships in the United States, in Europe, and throughout the world.

Although corporations spend huge amounts on sponsorship of elite sports (professional sports, intercollegiate athletics, and Olympic events), the idea and practice of sponsorship is spreading to other sporting contexts as well. For example, the American Youth Soccer Organization was sponsored in 2013 by eight corporations including FOX Soccer, Liberty Mutual Insurance, the National Guard, Kohl's, Sunkist, and Quaker Oats (U.S. Youth Soccer, 2013). At the high-school level, "the Hawaii High School Athletic Association (HHSAA) lists major corporations such as Chevron and Enterprise Rent-A-Car, as well as numerous Hawaii-based corporations such as Hawaiian Airlines and First Hawaiian Bank. The New Mexico Activities Association (NMAA) lists Farmers Insurance, Gatorade, and Sonic among its sponsors; the Iowa High School Athletic Association has the Iowa Farm Bureau; and the Nebraska State Athletic Association has US Bank and the U.S. Marines" (Hums & MacLean, 2013, p. 102). The basic reason why corporations are eager to sponsor these children and young adult sport enterprises is the access they gain to a market of millions of children and their households. It should also be recognized that many organizations sponsor some of the not-so-popular sports because of their sense of social responsibility.

sidebar 1.7

WHAT'S IN IT FOR ME?

According to Howard and Crompton (1995), "Voluntary exchange is the central concept underlying both sponsorship and donations. The concept requires something of value to be offered in exchange for something else of value. Before an investment or a donation is made, the contributor is likely to ask two questions, 'What is in it for me?' and 'How much will it cost me?' The trade-off is weighted between what will be gained and what will have to be given up. Both sponsorship and philanthropy offer sources of funds, resources, and in-kind services to sport organizations, but they differ in the nature of what they expect in exchange" (p. 226).

Create association

A related outcome of sponsorship is the *image building* or *image projection* by association for the sponsoring corporation. The image promoted may be related to the concept of social responsibility (as in corporations sponsoring specific teams for the Olympics) or to the idea of excellence (corporations identifying with winning teams or excellent athletes).

Donor Services

The products we propose to exchange when we seek a donation are merely the sources of *psychic benefits*. Such psychic benefits may be altruistic (the good feeling of having supported a worthy venture), or they may be egoistic (the personal gratification in seeing one's name on the list of donors). Two points are worth noting here: First, these psychic benefits are self-administered by the donors themselves. The sport organization simply provides a basis from which these benefits can be derived. Second, an act of donation may engender both altruistic and egoistic benefits simultaneously. Consider a donor giving thousands of dollars for the construction of a playing field named after her. The generous offer is borne out of both a real concern to fulfill a need in the community (altruistic benefit) and the desire to leave behind something bearing her name (egoistic benefit).

This is not to deny that some donors may have ulterior motives in giving donations. For example, donors who give to political parties may do so with a view to gain access to decision makers and the same may be true of donors to athletic departments. In fact, in January 2011 a donor to the University of Connecticut demanded the return of a $3 million contribution he had made to the athletic department when he felt he was not sufficiently consulted in the hiring of a new football coach (Associated Press, 2011). In a similar manner, a donor may give a sizable donation to a sport-governing body in the hope that the decision makers will be inclined to select the donor's son or daughter for the national team. Or, a person may give a large donation to the local Y's sports program with a view to influence the decision on a construction contract. You may also recall that the Salt Lake Olympic Committee members made donations to the projects of some of the members of the International Olympic Committee (IOC). Though such donations did help those projects and their intended clients, they were still questionable because they were made with a view to influence the IOC members to vote in favor of awarding the 2002 Olympic event to Salt Lake City. Illegitimate and corrupt efforts of influence should not be considered donations in the true sense.

Service to Social Ideas

Some sport organizations are also engaged in promoting social objectives such as fitness and health through physical activity. The Association for International Sport for All (TAFISA) and ParticipACTION (a term coined to indicate participation and action) in Canada are good examples of such organizations. The National Association for Sport and Physical Education (NASPE, 2000) in the United States promotes the idea of "quality sport and physical education" in the form of posters, brochures, press releases, and meetings. Although this campaign may be viewed as an effort to promote the profession itself, the underlying theme is participation in sport and physical activity. Similarly, Nike's advertising slogan "Just Do It" promotes the idea of participation in physical activity while at the same time promoting its own corporate image. All these efforts are aimed at exchanging with the public the social idea and practice of participation in physical activity and the benefits of such participation.

Production and Marketing of Sport Services

An important element in Exhibit 1.3 is the emphasis on both **production** and **marketing** of the various services. Consider, for example, some of the significant activities of a typical university athletic department. It is heavily engaged in recruiting high-quality coaches and athletes, facilitating their training by maintaining and scheduling facilities, allotting a budget to every team to cover its expenses, and organizing and conducting the contests. Through these processes the department produces excellence and entertainment. In addition, the department also engages in promotional and advertising campaigns to highlight its products—setting up an elaborate scheme to distribute the tickets for the contests and engaging in public relations efforts to justify the department, its processes, and its products. These are the marketing efforts of the department. In a similar manner, a city recreation department prepares and maintains the playing facilities, organizes youth leagues, schedules the games, and recruits volunteers as coaches and referees. These are the factors that go into the production of that particular service. The department may also publicize the existence of its sport programs through the media, billboards, social media sites, and mailings in order to attract more participation by community members. These

IN brief

Sport management is concerned with both the production and marketing of various sport services.

efforts are marketing oriented. Thus, sport management as a field is engaged in both the production and marketing of sport products.

RELATIONSHIPS AMONG SPORT PRODUCTS

Although the various sport products have been described separately, they are intricately related, as shown in Exhibit 1.4. For example, consider participant services. People who engage in a sport for the pleasure of it (consumer-pleasure service) may become highly skilled in that sport, which is the goal of human-skill service. Individuals who are pursuing skills in a sport may also become excellent in that sport (the goal of human-excellence service). Similarly, participants who engage in a sport in pursuit of pleasure, skill, or excellence may also enhance their fitness and health (the goal of consumer-health, human-sustenance, and human-curative services).

Next consider spectator services. The product that is being exchanged is entertainment, but entertainment is a function of contests among excellent teams or athletes. That is, the entertainment value of sport increases as excellence in the sport increases. Thus, spectator services are an offshoot of human-excellence services. Furthermore, spectator services imply that there are a host of fans of a sport (basketball), a team in a sport (Los Angeles Lakers), or an athlete (Kobe Bryant). These fans constitute a market—a market attractive to some corporations. These corporations, in turn, are willing to sponsor a competition, a team, or an athlete in return for access to the market. Thus, sponsorship services are born out of spectator services. Similarly, licensing services are also a function of spectator services. As noted earlier, sponsorship services are also applicable to participant services related to specific sports insofar as the participants themselves constitute a sizable market, as with Little League, the American Youth Soccer Organization, and Pop Warner Football.

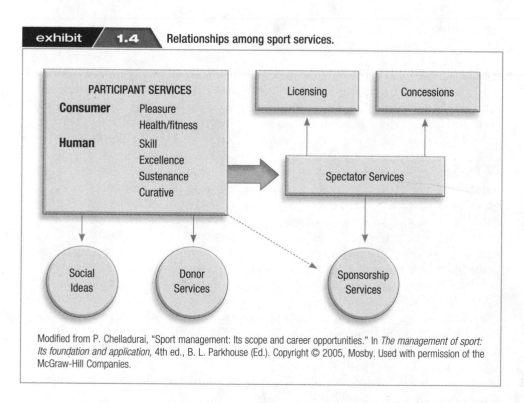

exhibit 1.4 Relationships among sport services.

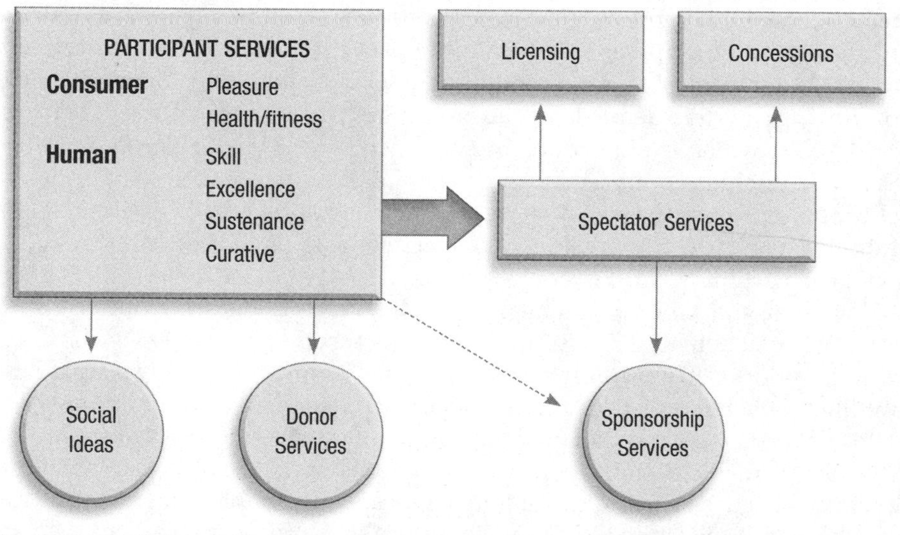

Modified from P. Chelladurai, "Sport management: Its scope and career opportunities." In *The management of sport: Its foundation and application,* 4th ed., B. L. Parkhouse (Ed.). Copyright © 2005, Mosby. Used with permission of the McGraw-Hill Companies.

MANIFESTATIONS OF SPORT

While the previous section shows how the various sport products are interrelated, it also masks the fundamental differences among the various products that, in turn, affect the ways in which those products are produced and exchanged. Chelladurai (2010, 2012) has suggested that sport managers should be attuned to three distinct *manifestations of sport,* which are based on the ways in which we engage in sport.

The label *egalitarian sport* refers to pursuit of pleasure in sport and *elite sport* refers to pursuit of excellence in sport. The term *egalitarian* refers to the inclusionary nature of the enterprise and equality among participants. In contrast, the term *elite* refers to an exclusive group of members considered to be the best in a particular context. In our case, these are the best performers in a given sport. It must be emphasized that elite sport involves an exclusionary process whereby those who do not meet the standards are excluded from the enterprise. When we say a coach selected his players, we also mean that he or she has excluded some others from becoming members of the team.

In addition to these two manifestations of sport, Chelladurai identified a third form of engagement in sport—*entertainment sport*—which is often referred to as spectator sport. The entertainment resides in the competition between two individuals or teams who compete arduously to be the victors in the contest and to win the prize associated with the competition. The entertainment value of such contests is also heightened by the rivalries cultivated among the contestants. For example, the contest between the Ohio State Buckeyes and the University of Michigan Wolverines football teams is the most anticipated and most entertaining game of the year for the teams' fans. While sports competitions between two rival entities are always entertaining (for example, between any two rival high school teams in any city), the entertainment value is greatly enhanced when the contestants are also excellent in a given sport. That is why competitions among NFL teams is generally held to be more entertaining than those among high school teams.

The three manifestations of sport as described above constitute the three segments of the sport industry. They may involve the same sport, but they are distinct enterprises with different purposes and processes. Egalitarian sport is fundamentally a gregarious activity engaged in for the pleasure derived from that activity. It is more closely related to the notion of play. Côté, Baker, and Abernethy (2007) and Huizinga (1955) defined play as a free activity outside of the strictures of everyday life, which is not serious but completely absorbs the participant. Egalitarian sport includes everyone irrespective of ability. In contrast, elite sport is an exclusionary process that restricts entry to persons of high ability with a determination to excel in the activity. It is characterized by high dedication, huge sacrifices, and extraordinary effort over a prolonged period of time. It has been estimated that ten thousand hours of training over a 10-year period are required to excel in one's chosen activity (Ericsson, Krampe, & Tesch-Römer, 1993). Thus, while egalitarian sport is playful, elite sport is a serious business requiring a great deal of planning, deliberate practice, and progressively challenging competitions.

In the case of entertainment sport, the popularity of the sport along with the excellence of the contestants contributes to the attractiveness of the competition. Popularity of a given sport varies among nations. For example, American football is most popular in the United States while it is unknown in many parts of the world, and cricket is popular in India, whose population is much greater than that of the United States. This explains why the NFL is a dominant player in the American sport scene while the Indian Premier League (IPL) in cricket is emerging as one of the strongest and wealthiest professional sport leagues in the world. The IPL's brand value was estimated to be US$3.98 billion in 2010, and it had the second highest budget for player salaries next to the NBA's. The major characteristic that distinguishes among the three manifestations is their differing purposes for engagement in sport. People engage in egalitarian sport for the pleasure of the game; participants in elite sports are striving for excellence; and those who engage in entertainment sport are of two kinds: (a) spectators who flock to see excellence in competition, and (b) the contestants who compete in the competition. We should note that in some cases people may not have to pay to watch excellence in action as, for example, in the case of television viewers. It should also be noted that somebody else is paying to facilitate the television viewing—the sponsors and the advertisers.

These three segments can also be distinguished by their environments, opportunities, and threats. The local community, government, social clubs, and the local educational institutions constitute the environment for egalitarian sport, while the environment of elite sport extends to regional and national governments and sport-governing bodies. For entertainment sport, while the paying public are mostly from the local community, the franchise (or a collegiate team) interacts with other teams located in far-off places as well as with sponsors, advertisers, and media agencies.

On a different note and following the lead by marketers (e.g., Highes & Sweeter, 2009), Chelladurai uses the term *farming* to refer to elite sport's long process of identifying, nurturing, and developing talent. The process is similar to a farmer engaging in the laborious acts of plowing, seeding, watering, and weeding a field in order to reap the harvest. In contrast, he uses the term *hunting* to refer to the major practice of professional franchises in entertainment sport drafting excellent athletes developed by other agencies and showcasing their excellence in organized competitions. This is similar to the hunters who are not involved in raising animals but only in hunting them. Finally, playing is simply enjoying the kinesthetic sensations of engaging in a sport; this is the major attribute of egalitarian sport. The three manifestations of the sport industry are illustrated in Exhibit 1.5.

exhibit 1.5 Manifestations of sport.

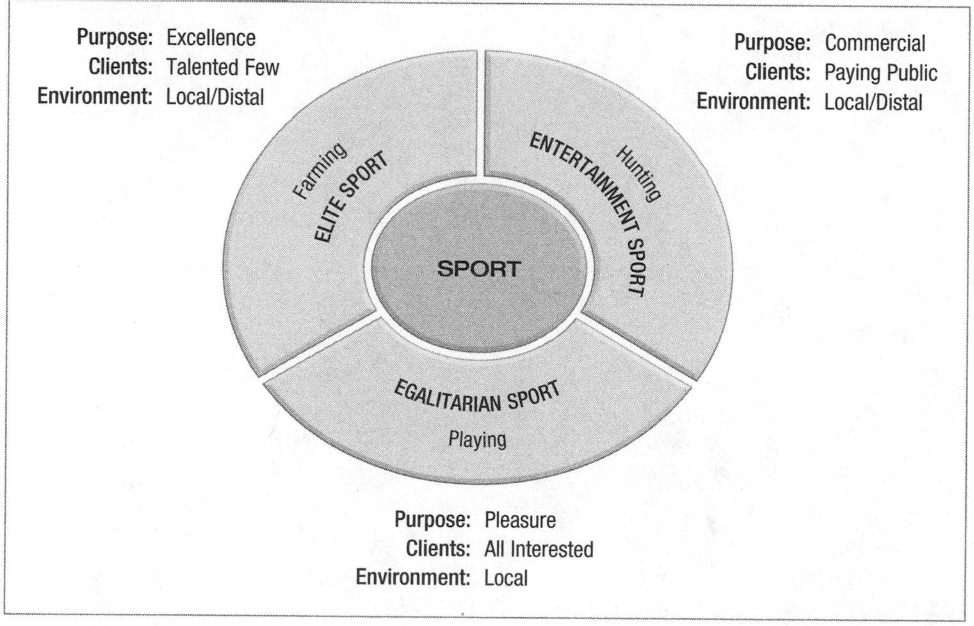

PRIMARY AND ANCILLARY (SATELLITE) SPORT PRODUCTS

The classification presented in this chapter (see Exhibits 1.3 and 1.4) lists the primary products of our field. There are, however, other significant products associated with sport. As noted in the Introduction, *Street & Smith's SportsBusiness Journal* includes the following as major segments of the sport industry: advertising, endorsements, equipment/apparel/shoes, facility construction, media broadcast rights, professional services, medical treatment, travel, publications/videos, and gambling (Broughton, Lee, & Nethery, 1999). The satellite operations associated with the primary products of participant and spectator sport are shown in Exhibit 1.6. These satellite services are noteworthy in that they are generated by the primary services while also facilitating the production and marketing of the primary services. Consider, for example, the player agency services. A player agent represents one or more athletes in bargaining with a professional team over the athlete's salary and contract. Player agents exist because professional teams produce spectator services and seek outstanding athletes. Player agents greatly facilitate the professional team's efforts to recruit and retain outstanding athletes. Similarly, several legal firms specializing in sport law provide critical services to sport organizations in terms of risk management and avoidance of legal liability. The broadcast media exist as a segment of the industry only because there are organizations such as the professional sport leagues and intercollegiate athletic leagues, which produce

exhibit 1.6 Examples of satellite services and primary products in sport industry.

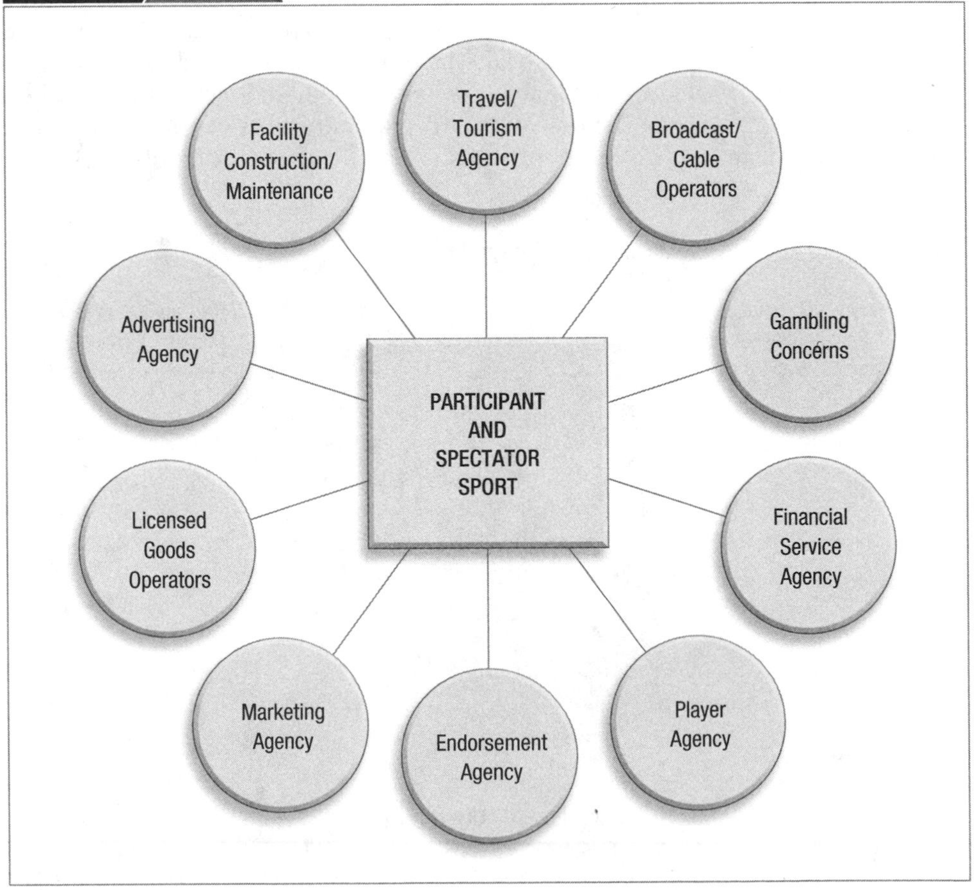

the excellence and entertainment in sport. In turn, the entertainment value and the prestige of the leagues are enhanced by the broadcast services.

In another example, a local university may hire the services of consultants in event management to run a weeklong program of basketball clinics for local youth (a human-skill service). The consultants bring their expertise in staging the event. They recruit renowned basketball players and instructors to run the clinics and volunteers to assist, and they recruit participants and assign them to various ability or age groups. The consultants also schedule the clinics and secure the use of facilities. In addition, they may also secure sponsorships to finance as well as publicize the clinics. These consultant services became necessary only because of the decision to provide the primary human service oriented toward skill development. Thus, as sport managers, we need to be able to identify the primary services offered in the field of sport management, as well as those ancillary services needed in the production and marketing of the primary services. Most of the ancillary or satellite sport services may be seen as springing from participant service associated with pursuit of excellence.

SPORT MANAGEMENT AS COORDINATION

Having listed and classified the products in our field, we will next describe management as it relates to both the production and marketing of those products. When we examine the various definitions and descriptions of management, we quickly see that the essence of **management is coordination** (Argote, 1982; Mintzberg, 1989; Thompson, 1967; Zalesny, Salas, & Prince, 1995). Mintzberg (1989) highlights the concept of coordination as follows:

> Every human activity—from making of pottery to the placing of a man on the moon—gives rise to two fundamental and opposing requirements: the division of labor into various tasks to be performed and the *coordination* [emphasis added] of those tasks to accomplish the activity. The structure of an organization can be defined simply as the total of the ways in which it is divided into distinct tasks and then its *coordination* [emphasis added] achieved among those tasks. (pp. 100–101)

Management as coordination is further elaborated in Chapter 4. For the moment, let us address the question, "What is being coordinated in sport management?" That is, what are the factors that need to be coordinated in the production and marketing of sport services? As shown in Exhibit 1.7, the more significant of these factors are *human resources, technologies,* and *support units,* which facilitate the production and marketing of sport services, and the *context* in which such production and marketing take place.

IN brief

Sport management is concerned with coordinating the activities of three sets of human resources: clients, paid workers, and volunteer workers.

Human Resources

The most significant factor that needs to be coordinated is the **human resources** —that is, the people involved in the production of the sport services. The people are the clients, the paid employees, and the volunteer workers.

Clients. The human resources of any venture offering sport and physical activity service will necessarily involve the clients of that service, because the service cannot be produced without their active participation (Chelladurai, 1992, 1999). Clients may vary in their orientation toward sport and physical activity and in

exhibit 1.7 Factors of coordination in sport management.

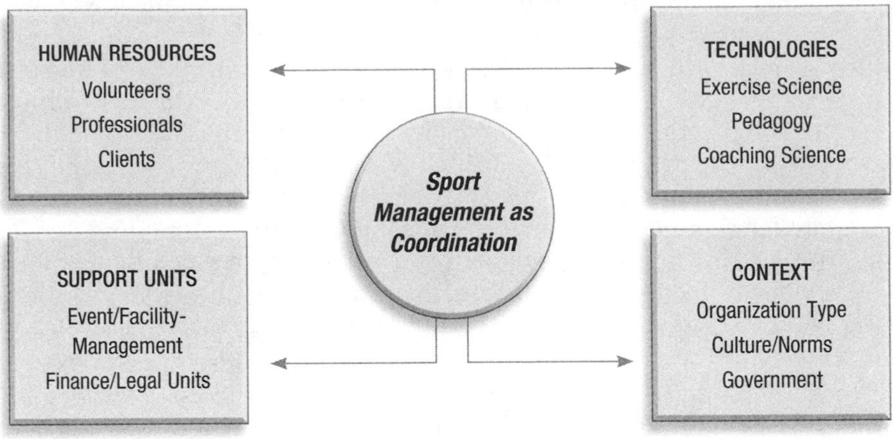

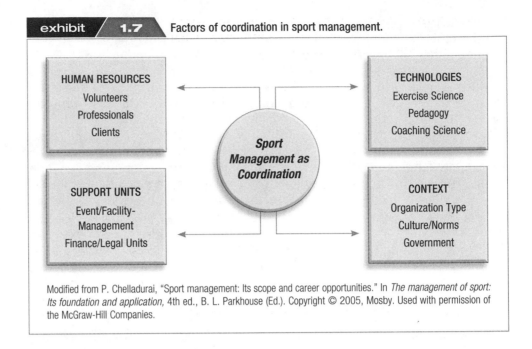

Modified from P. Chelladurai, "Sport management: Its scope and career opportunities." In *The management of sport: Its foundation and application,* 4th ed., B. L. Parkhouse (Ed.). Copyright © 2005, Mosby. Used with permission of the McGraw-Hill Companies.

their degree of commitment to such programs. Motivating the clients and gaining their compliance is a challenge to the service providers.

Employees. The next kind of human resources is the service employees. As noted earlier, employees may further be classified into consumer service or professional service employees. Consumer service employees engage in simple, routine activities requiring little training, whereas professional service employees provide complex, knowledge-based, and individualized service to their clients.

Volunteers. Heavy involvement of volunteers is also characteristic of sport organizations. These volunteers are the mainstay of such projects as the Special Olympics and youth sport organized by recreation departments in many cities. The conventional approaches to managing paid workers must be considerably modified in the case of volunteers. The coordination of the contributions of volunteers with those of paid employees is a critical area of sport management. In sum,

sidebar 1.8

STUDENT-ATHLETES OR VOLUNTEER EMPLOYEES?

The categorization of human resources of a sport organization into clients, employees, and volunteers is meaningful in most cases, but the athletes in American intercollegiate athletics do not fit neatly into one of these categories. University athletes are first and foremost clients of the university athletic department. Furthermore, their participation is voluntary. The scholarship assistance provided to athletes facilitates their academic pursuits and does not represent payment for athletic contributions. However, when thousands of spectators watch a game in which these athletes participate, they become service providers in creating the entertainment. From this perspective, the athletes become volunteer employees of the athletic department. The athletes in professional sport teams are, of course, professional employees of the franchise because they are paid for their contributions.

motivating these differing types of employees and coordinating their activities is a very significant component of sport management that offers both a challenge and an opportunity for sport managers.

Technologies

> "Technology is the combination of skills, knowledge, abilities, techniques, materials, machines, computers, tools, and other equipment that people use to convert or change raw materials, problems, and new ideas into valuable goods and services" (Jones, 2010, p. 240).

The technologies associated with the production of our services are generated by disciplinary fields such as exercise physiology, sport medicine, sport psychology, sport pedagogy, coaching education, health science, sport nutrition, and so on. The success of our endeavor depends on the proper use of the knowledge generated in those subdisciplines. Consider, for example, the services offered by a fitness club. The knowledge generated by exercise physiologists determines the appropriateness of a particular exercise regimen for a person or group. Similarly, the information generated by sport/exercise psychologists on factors that contribute to adherence (or nonadherence) to exercise programs has implications for sport managers. When sport sociology determines which groups of people tend to participate in what kinds of activities, this knowledge should affect marketing strategies and practices. Sport philosophy may guide us in ethical and moral issues concerning the management and delivery of our services. In addition to the sport-based subdisciplines, sport management may also draw on the knowledge generated in such fields as management science and consumer psychology.

The relative significance of these technologies clearly varies from service to service and also with regard to the quality levels expected of a service. For example, the importance of exercise physiology is higher in human-curative services than in consumer-pleasure services. Following this argument, we can expect a high school coach to be more highly trained than a volunteer youth coach. At high levels of performance, as in pursuit of excellence, we may even have specialists and experts such as a team doctor and team psychologist assisting the coach. Note that the concept of coordination of technologies implicitly refers to the coordination of the activities of those individuals or groups who actually use those technologies in producing the services. In other words, the sport manager does not have to be an expert in all the technologies associated with the production and marketing of the services offered by the organization. However, the manager must have a rudimentary knowledge of these technologies so that she can effectively coordinate the activities of the experts in their respective fields.

Support Units

Sport management is also concerned with the coordination of the **support units** that facilitate the production of a given service. These support units may deal with facility management, event management, personnel management, financial management, public relations, labor relations, sport law, and sport finance. The production and marketing of any product cannot be effectively achieved without the efficient and coordinated activities of the support units. The significance of these support units is reflected by the extent to which courses dealing with these support units are mandatory in almost all sport management degree programs. In fact, COSMA guidelines specify that a degree program will be certified only if it includes courses on these topics.

Context

An important aspect of sport management as coordination is the context in which production and marketing take place. In this phase, the sport manager is concerned with coordinating the production and marketing processes with the external forces represented by the interorganizational networks, market conditions, and government, culture, and community.

Interorganizational networks

Interorganizational networks such as the National Collegiate Athletic Association (NCAA) in the United States and Canadian Interuniversity Sport (CIS) link those organizations that produce the same services with similar goals and operate in comparable organizational contexts. For example, all universities that offer athletic programs do so with education and pursuit of excellence as the major goals. The NCAA supports this endeavor and provides the supervision and regulation necessary to ensure that the educational purposes are maintained by the entire membership. In a similar manner, such professional leagues as the NFL, NBA, and NHL also ensure that their members adhere to commonly agreed upon rules and regulations to govern their respective organizations. You may be familiar with similar bodies that govern high school sports at the state and national levels. One of the important responsibilities of the sport manager is to coordinate the activities of his own organization with the requirements of the appropriate interorganizational network.

Market conditions

The context also includes market conditions such as changes in the demand for services and in the organizations competing for the same clients/customers and resources. Thus, a professional sport franchise has to coordinate its own activities, tactics, and strategies to counteract those of its competitors, such as another sport franchise (which provides the same or similar service) or a theater (which provides a substitute service).

Government, community, and culture

Our operations should be consistent with government regulations, cultural norms, and societal expectations. The well-publicized difficulties often encountered by businesses trying to establish a branch in another country point to the challenge of coordinating organizational activities with the requirements of the situation. Even within a national context, changes in societal expectations may occur frequently. Social diversity, gender equity, and inclusion of individuals with disabilities have affected the practice of management in general and sport management in particular. The growing sport management literature on considerations of gender equity is a case in point, emphasizing the need for sport managers to alter their employment practices. For example, it is unlawful and bad managerial practice to inquire about the gender of an applicant for a job when gender does not have a bearing on the job. Similarly, gone are the days when management paid higher salaries for male aerobics instructors than for female instructors.

The need to coordinate the operations of a sport organization with the local community's interests and desires is illustrated by the influence exerted by alumni associations in intercollegiate athletics. Similarly, professional sport franchises depend on local governments for building or renting stadiums and arenas. Even smaller sport organizations look to the local community for concessions and tax exemptions.

DEFINITION OF SPORT MANAGEMENT

From what has been outlined so far, sport management can be defined as "a field concerned with the coordination of limited human and material resources, relevant technologies, and situational contingencies for the efficient production and exchange of sport services" (Chelladurai, 1994, p. 15). The essential elements of this definition are illustrated in Exhibit 1.8.

According to this definition, management encompasses both the production and the marketing (exchange) of sport services. Note also that the definition includes three distinct forms of endeavor: the *study,* the *teaching,* and the *practice* of sport management. Furthermore, according to the definition, sport management is not restricted to any organizational context. That is, different types of organizations may be involved to varying degrees in the production and marketing of one or more sport services.

Finally, the definition emphasizes the notion of coordination as the primary purpose of management. The coordination of various elements within and outside organizations, as described above, points to the enormity and complexity of the managerial job. The complexity may indeed lead to paradoxical situations where the manager is forced to carry out contradictory activities to satisfy various constituencies of the organization that have conflicting needs or expectations. Under these circumstances, the meaning of *managing* shifts from control and coordination to *coping,* where the manager attempts to overcome problems of contradictory demands and claims (Lewis, 2002).

The following chapters define and describe the managerial functions through which such coordination is achieved. The concept of organizations per se is explained in Chapters 2 and 3. An outline of the concept of management itself is provided in Chapter 4. Then follow descriptions of the functions of planning in Chapter 5, decision making in Chapter 6, organizing in Chapters 7 and 8, staffing in Chapter 9, leading in Chapters 10, 11, and 12, managing diversity in Chapter 13, program evaluation in Chapter 14, service quality in Chapter 15, and organizational effectiveness in Chapter 16. These managerial functions are in essence aimed at coordinating the factors of production and marketing toward the achievement of organizational goals with limited resources.

exhibit 1.8 **Sport management as coordination.**

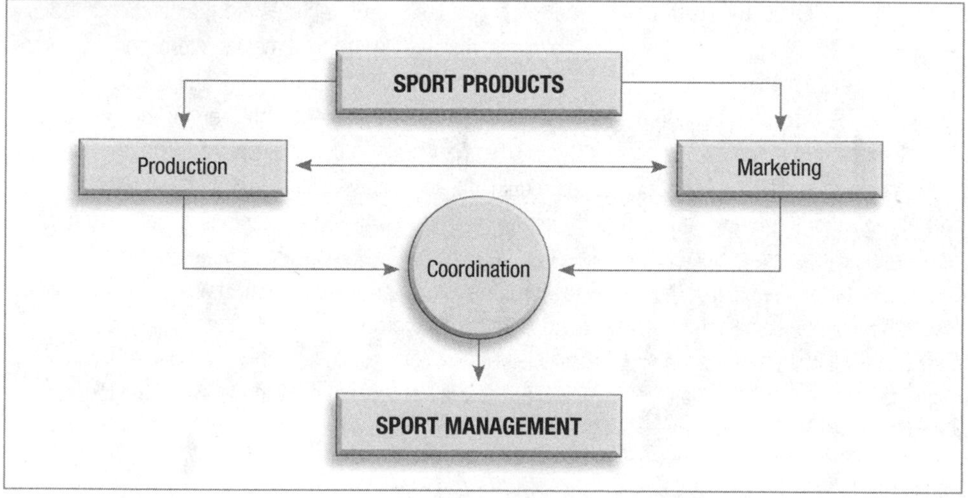

sidebar 1.9

SATELLITE ECONOMIC ACTIVITIES

Recall from the Introduction that in 1997 Meek estimated the worth of satellite economic activities of sport at about $260 billion. Our interest in these satellite activities is threefold. First, several aspects of these activities facilitate and promote our own services. When television networks broadcast certain sports programs, they do so to increase their share of television audience and thus their profitability. In the process, they promote that particular sport event, the athletes involved, and the organizations that stage the event. Consider the enormous publicity boost that the Wimbledon and U.S. Open tennis tournaments receive during their telecasts. The footwear produced by Nike, Reebok, Adidas, and other firms facilitates our participant sport services. In a similar manner, travel agencies, player agencies, and advertising agencies contribute to our efforts, albeit indirectly.

Second, satellite activities constitute a reservoir of financial resources that we may tap into. For instance, corporations such as General Motors, Coca-Cola, and Visa spend millions of dollars advertising their products. These organizations also like to promote themselves by associating with sport products and athletes, and they have huge budgets for sponsorship of sport events, sport organizations, and athletes. Thus, it is not surprising that sport advertising and sponsorship are hot topics of discussion within sport management.

Third, satellite activities offer more than 2 million jobs that graduates from academic programs can potentially occupy (Meek, 1997). Some critical areas of concern for sport management degree programs are (a) finding internship and practicum opportunities for the students, and (b) placing graduates in meaningful employment. The satellite operations provide such opportunities.

The relationships among sport organizations, sport industry, and satellite organizations can also be illustrated through Knoke's (2001, p. 39) three-level scheme of organizations. The first level, the *organizational society,* consists of all organizations in a nation. All sport organizations, manufacturing organizations, business concerns, political organizations, charitable organizations, governments, military units, and the endless list of other organizations in a country constitute the organizational society. At the second level is the *organization population,* which is "a homogeneous set consisting of all organizations of a specific type or form, such as restaurants, newspapers, or hospitals" (p. 39). An organizational population is the same as an industry, where the organizations within an industry produce the same or similar products (e.g., professional sport leagues). The third level, the *organizational field,* is represented by different organizations from different industries that carry out different activities that are functionally interconnected. Knoke gives the example of all corporations, interest groups, and government agencies that are involved with national defense. In our context, intercollegiate athletic departments, the NCAA, the local and national media, local businesses including hotels and tourism businesses, relevant government agencies (e.g., police controlling traffic for an event), other sport organizations in the community, interest groups, faculty, students, alumni, and such other vested interests constitute an organizational field. Exhibit 1.9 illustrates the relationships among organizational populations and organizational fields. Sport managers need to be attuned to the factors within an industry that affect their organizations, as well as the factors from their organizational field that impinge on their organizations.

Readers must note that the conceptual distinctions between Knoke's types of organizations and the products they produce become murky or blurry when organizations from one population (e.g., from media industry) get involved with another population (e.g., sport industry). Consider, for example, New York–based Cablevision's ownership of the NHL Rangers and the NBA Knicks featured on Madison Square Garden Network. It makes good business sense for a cable company to acquire the organizations that produce the content for cable television. For our purposes, the sport franchises are the sport organizations although they are owned by a media enterprise.

Another development is the emergence of cable networks associated with a specific college conference; for example, for the Big Ten Network, the universities in the Big Ten Conference produce the sports entertainment. Schools, conferences, and their representatives used to bargain and sign contracts with other networks for the broadcast rights. Now the Big Ten and other conferences produce the entertainment packages, show programs on their own networks, and may even seek to sell entertainment packages to the cable networks. Further, each of the Big 4 sports has its own network: NBA TV, the NFL Network, the NHL Network, and the MLB Network. These moves reverse the trend of media enterprises acquiring sport enterprises for their entertainment value.

Given the significance of these satellite economic activities, the study and analysis of this domain are meaningful and necessary (Slack & Parent, 2006). In Chapter 3, we will discuss organizations as open systems. In that view, an organization is engulfed by its environment, consisting of other organizations that have an impact on the focal organization, including television networks, footwear manufacturers, and travel and advertising agencies. From this perspective, it is imperative that we understand this part of our environment and cultivate our ability to communicate with it.

But at the same time, we should not let that interest determine how we define sport management. A case in point: The game of golf was not defined by the millions of dollars General Motors paid Tiger Woods to endorse Buick from 2004 to 2008. By the same token, General Motors and the automobile industry are not defined by the celebrities who endorse their products. Closer to home, Nike's or Reebok's sponsorship of our athletes, teams, or projects does not define our core products or our field. Thus, it is necessary to separate our field, defined by what we produce, from those enterprises that would buy and use our products or gain access to our markets for their own ends. We need to understand how these elements in the environment influence our operations, and how our products influence them, but we also need to understand that those elements do not define our field.

exhibit 1.9 **Relationships among organizational populations and organizational fields.**

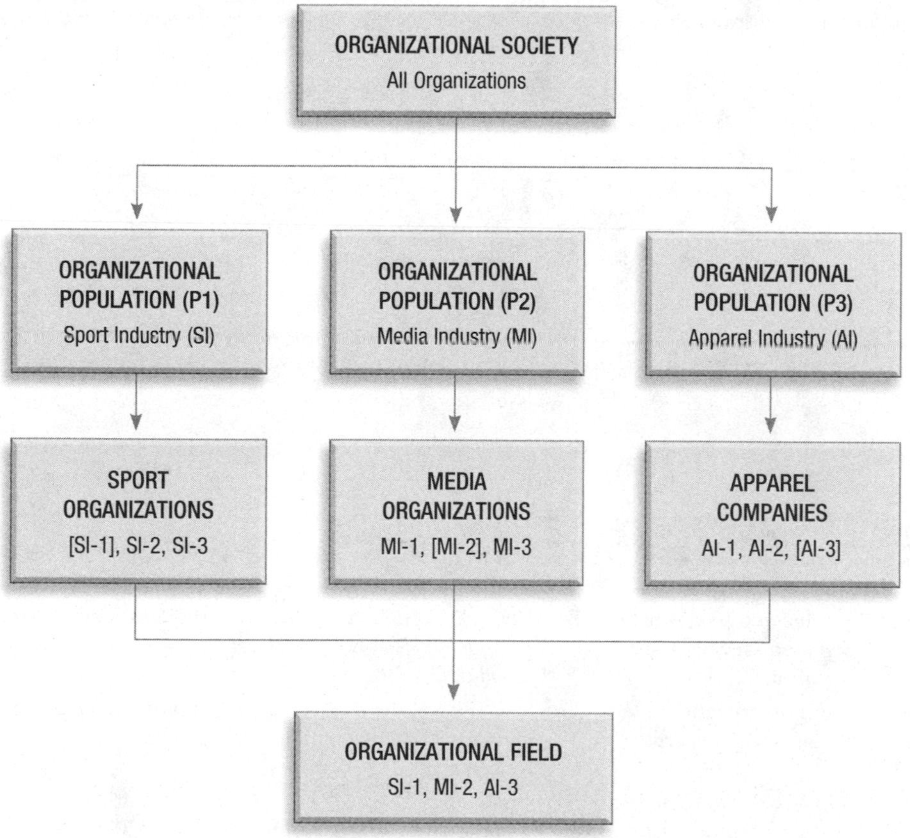

Modified from D. Knoke, *Changing organizations: Business networks in the new political economy.* Copyright © 2001 by Westview Press, a member of Perseus Books Group, Boulder, CO. Used with permission.

SUMMARY

This chapter has outlined the significant sport products within the purview of sport management: participant services, spectator services, sponsorship services, donor services, and social ideas. Participant services are in turn classified into six classes based on the distinctions between consumer and human services and participant motives. We noted that other significant products such as sport tourism, advertising, and endorsement flow from these primary products. As noted in the Introduction, these satellite segments contribute much to the sport industry. The chapter also described the factors that must be coordinated in the production and marketing of sport products. These factors include human resources, technologies, support units, and contextual factors. Finally, a definition of sport management was offered, emphasizing the production and marketing of sport products as well as the essential nature of management as coordination.

develop YOUR PERSPECTIVE

1. This chapter notes that the focus of sport management is not on sporting goods but on sport services. Discuss the relevance and role of sporting goods to a sport manager.
2. Describe the relative significance of technologies in the production and marketing of sport as entertainment.
3. Discuss the usefulness of the classification of sport products presented in Exhibits 1.3, 1.4, and 1.5.
4. This chapter identifies several factors that must be coordinated for effective production and marketing of sport products. In your view, which are the most critical? Are there any other factors that we should consider?
5. Is the definition of sport management as outlined in the chapter adequate? How would you modify it?

references

Amis, J., Pant, N., & Slack, T. (1997). Achieving a sustainable competitive advantage: A resource-based view of sport sponsorship. *Journal of Sport Management, 11*, 80–96.

Argote, L. (1982). Input uncertainty and organizational coordination in hospital emergency units. *Administrative Science Quarterly, 27*, 420–434.

Associated Press (2004, October 19). Models as ball retrievers draw notice. Retrieved from http://sports.espn.go.com/sports/tennis/news/story?id=1905266.

Associated Press (2011, January 26). Officials continue talks with donor. Retrieved from http://sports.espn.go.com/ncf/news/story?id=6062369.

Broughton, D., Lee, J., & Nethery, R. (1999, December 20–26). The answer: $213 billion. *Street & Smith's SportsBusiness Journal*, 2, 23–29.

Broyles, J. F., & Hay, R. D. (1979). *Administration of athletic programs: A managerial approach.* Englewood Cliffs, NJ: Prentice Hall.

BusinessInsider (2011, Nov. 17). Sports Chart of the Day: The international origins of NFL players. Retrieved from http://www.businessinsider.com/chart-international-origins-of-nfl-players-2011-11#ixzz2IRo22JJW.

Chelladurai, P. (1985). *Sport management: Macro perspectives.* London, Canada: Sports Dynamics.

Chelladurai, P. (1992). A classification of sport and physical activity services: Implications for sport management. *Journal of Sport Management, 6,* 38–51.

Chelladurai, P. (1993). *Sport management: Defining the field.* Invited inaugural address at the First European Congress on Sport Management of the European Association of Sport Management, University of Groningen, Netherlands, September 22–25.

Chelladurai, P. (1994). Sport management: Defining the field. *European Journal of Sport Management, 1,* 7–21.

Chelladurai, P. (1996). *The nature and dimensions of quality in sport services.* Invited keynote address at the Fourth European Congress on Sport Management. Montpelier, France. October 2–5.

Chelladurai, P. (1999). *Human resource management in sport and recreation.* Champaign, IL: Human Kinetics.

Chelladurai, P. (2007). *Marketing of sport services.* Keynote presentation at the First International Conference on Sport Marketing and Sport Business. Zakapone, Poland, June.

Chelladurai, P. (2010). *Human resource management in the sport industry.* Opening keynote paper at the 6th Congress of the Asian Association for Sport Management 13–16 October. Kuala Lumpur, Malaysia.

Chelladurai, P. (2012). Leadership and manifestations of sport. In S. Murphy (Ed.), *The handbook of sport and performance psychology* (pp. 328–342). New York: Oxford University Press.

Chelladurai, P., Scott, F. L., & Haywood-Farmer, J. (1987). Dimensions of fitness services: Development of a model. *Journal of Sport Management, 1,* 159–172.

Cialdini, R. B., Borden, R. J., Thorne, R. J., Walker, M. R., Freeman, S., & Sloan, L. R. (1976). Basking in reflected glory: Three (football) field studies. *Journal of Personality and Social Psychology, 34,* 366–375.

Côté, J., Baker, J., & Abernethy, B. (2007). Practice and play in the development of sport expertise. In G. Tenenbaum & R.C. Eklund (Eds.), *Handbook of sport psychology* (3rd ed., pp. 184–202). New York: John Wiley.

Duda, J. L. (1994). A goal perspective theory of meaning and motivation in sports. In S. Serpa (Ed.), *International perspectives on sport and exercise psychology* (pp. 127–148). Indianapolis, IN: Benchmark Press.

Duda, J. L. (1996). Maximizing motivation in sport and physical education among children and adolescents: The case of greater task involvement. *Quest, 48,* 290–302.

Ellis, M. J. (1988). *The business of physical education.* Champaign, IL: Human Kinetics.

Ericsson, K. A., Krampe, R. T., & Tesch-Römer, C. (1993). The role of deliberate practice in the acquisition of expert performance. *Psychological Review, 103,* 363–406.

ESPN.com (2004, October 18). Models replace ball kids in Madrid. Retrieved from http://sports.espn.go.com/sports/tennis/news/story?id=1904665.

Fitzsimmons, J., & Fitzsimmons, M. (2011). *Service management: Operations, strategy, and information technology* (7th ed.). Boston: McGraw-Hill.

Gill, D. L., Gross, J. B., & Huddleston, S. (1983). Participation motives in youth sports. *International Journal of Sport Psychology, 14,* 1–14.

Grönroos, C. (1990). *Service management and marketing: Managing the moment of truth in service competition.* Lexington, MA: Lexington Books.

Hambrick, D. C. (1984). Taxonomic approaches to studying strategy: Some conceptual and methodological issues. *Journal of Management, 10*(1), 27–41.

Hasenfeld, Y. (1983). *Human service operations.* Englewood Cliffs, NJ: Prentice Hall.

Hasenfeld, Y. (Ed.). (1992). *Human services as complex organizations.* Newbury Park, CA: Sage Publications.

Hasenfeld, Y., & English, R. A. (1974). Human service organizations: A conceptual overview. In Y. Hasenfeld & R. A. English (Eds.), *Human service organizations: A book of readings* (pp. 1–23). Ann Arbor, MI: University of Michigan Press.

Heitmann, H. M. (1986). Motives of older adults for participating in physical activity programs. In B. D. McPherson (Ed.), *Sport and aging* (pp. 199–204). Champaign, IL: Human Kinetics.

Hesterly, W. S., Liebeskind, J., & Zenger, T. R. (1990). Organizational economics: An impending revolution in organization theory? *Academy of Management Review, 15* (3), 402–420.

Highes, M., & Sweeter, A. (2009). *Successful e-mail marketing strategies: From hunting to farming.* Chicago: Racom Communications.

Howard, D. R., & Crompton, J. L. (1995). *Financing sport.* Morgantown, WV: Fitness Information Technology.

Huizinga, J. (1955). *Homo ludens; a study of the play-element in culture.* Boston: Beacon Press.

Hums, M. A., & MacLean, J. C. (2013). *Governance and policy in sport organizations* (3rd ed.). Scottsdale, AZ: Holcomb Hathaway.

IEG Sponsorship Report (2013). The latest on sports, arts, cause and entertainment marketing. Retrieved from http://www.sponsorship.com/IEGSR/2013/01/07/2013-Sponsorship-Outlook-Spending-Increase-Is-Dou.aspx

Jewett, A. E. (1987). Participant purposes for engaging in physical activity. In G. T. Barrette, R. S. Feingold, C. R. Rees, & M. Pieron (Eds.), *Myths, models, & methods in sport pedagogy* (pp. 87–100). Champaign, IL: Human Kinetics.

Jones, G. R. (2010). *Organizational theory, design, and change* (6th ed.). Upper Saddle River, NJ: Pearson.

Keating, J. W. (1964). Sportsmanship as a moral category. *Ethics, 75,* 25–35.

Knoke, D. (2001). *Changing organizations: Business networks in the new political economy.* Boulder, CO: Westview Press.

Lewis, M. (2002). Exploring paradox: Toward a more comprehensive guide. *Academy of Management Review, 25,* 760–776.

Lovelock, C. H. (1991). *Services marketing* (2nd ed.). Englewood Cliffs, NJ: Prentice Hall.

Lovelock, C., & Gummesson, E. (2004). Whither services marketing? In search of new paradigm and fresh perspectives. *Journal of Service Research, 7*(1), 20–41.

Mathes, S. A., & Battista, R. (1985). College men's and women's motives for participation in physical activity. *Perceptual and Motor Skills, 61,* 719–726.

Meek, A. (1997). An estimate of the size and supported economic activity of the sport industry in the United States. *Sport Marketing Quarterly, 6*(4), 15–21.

Melnick, M. J. (1993). Searching for sociability in the stands: A theory of sport spectating. *Journal of Sport Management, 7*(1), 44–60.

Mills, P. K., & Margulies, N. (1980). Toward a core typology of service organizations. *Academy of Management Review, 5,* 255–265.

Milne, G. R., & McDonald, M. A. (1999). *Sport marketing: Managing the exchange process.* Sudbury, MA: Jones & Bartlett Publishers.

Mintzberg, H. (1989). *Mintzberg on management: Inside our strange world of organizations.* New York: The Free Press.

Mullin, B. J. (1980). Sport management: The nature and utility of the concept. *Arena Review, 4*(3), 1–11.

Mullin, B. J., Hardy, S., & Sutton, W. A. (2007). *Sport marketing* (3rd ed.). Champaign, IL: Human Kinetics.

NASPE. (2000). *Sport management program standards and review protocol.* Reston, VA: NASPE.

NASSM. (n.d.). *Constitution* (revised June, 2013). Retrieved from http://www.nassm.com/files/NASSM%20Constitution%20June%202013.pdf.

Pelletier, L. G., Fortier, M. S., Vallerand, R. J., Tuson, K. M., & Briere, N. M. (1995). Toward a new measure of intrinsic motivation, extrinsic motivation, and amotivation in sports: The Sport Motivation Scale (SMS). *Journal of Sport and Exercise Psychology, 17,* 35–53.

Pitts, B. G., & Stotlar, D. K. (2007). *Fundamentals of sport marketing* (3rd ed.). Morgantown, WV: Fitness Information Technology.

Roberts, G. (1993). Motivation in sport: Understanding and enhancing the motivation and achievement of children. In R. N. Singer, M. Murphey, & L. K. Tennant (Eds.), *Handbook of research on sport psychology* (pp. 405–420). New York: Macmillan.

Sasser, W. E., Olsen, R. P., & Wyckoff, D. (1978). *Management of service operations.* Rockleigh, NJ: Allyn & Bacon.

Schneider, B., & Bowen, D. E. (1995). *Winning the service game.* Boston: Harvard Business School Press.

Shank, M. D. (2005). *Sports marketing: A strategic perspective* (3rd ed.). Upper Saddle River, NJ: Prentice Hall.

Shilbury, D., Quick, S., & Westerbeek, H. (1998). *Strategic sport marketing.* St. Leonards, NSW, Australia: Allen & Unwin.

Slack, T., & Parent, M. M. (2006). *Understanding of sport organizations: The application of organization theory* (2nd ed.). Champaign, IL: Human Kinetics.

Snyder, C. R., Lassegard, M. A., & Ford, C. E. (1986). Distancing after group success and failure: Basking in reflected glory and cutting off reflected failure. *Journal of Personality and Social Psychology, 51,* 382–388.

Thompson, J. D. (1967). *Organizations in action.* New York: McGraw-Hill.

U.S. Youth Soccer. (2013). Sponsors. Retrieved from http://www.usyouthsoccer.org/sponsors/.

Vuolle, P. (1987). Social motives as determinants of physical recreation at various life stages. In G. T. Barrette, R. S. Feingold, C. R. Rees, & M. Pieron (Eds.), *Myths, models, & methods in sport pedagogy* (pp. 169–179). Champaign, IL: Human Kinetics.

Wann, D. L., & Branscombe, N. R. (1990). Die-hard and fair-weather fans: Effects of identification on BIRGing and CORFing tendencies. *Journal of Sport and Social Issues, 14*(2), 103–117.

Williamson, J. (1991). Providing quality care. *Human Services Management, 87*(1), 18–27.

Zalesny, M. D., Salas, E., & Prince, C. (1995). Conceptual and measurement issues in coordination: Implications for team behavior and performance. *Research in Personnel and Human Resources Management, 13,* 81–115.

CHAPTER 2

CLASSICAL VIEW OF ORGANIZATIONS

manage YOUR LEARNING

After completing this chapter you should be able to:

- Define an organization.
- Identify and describe significant attributes of an organization.
- Describe the ways in which organizations can be classified and the significance of such classifications for management.

strategic CONCEPTS

attributes of an organization
boundaries
business concern
commonweal organization
division of labor
employee–customer interface
hierarchy of authority
identity
instrumentality
mutual benefit association
organization
permanency
prime beneficiary
profit orientation
service organization
source of funding
voluntary associations

IMPORTANCE OF ORGANIZATIONS

In Chapter 1, we defined and described the field of sport management from the perspective of the products (services) produced and marketed in the field. That approach was based on the notion that **organizations**, including sport organizations, are simply mechanisms for the exchange of products. If organizations are responsible for the production and marketing of sport products, then it is useful to gain an understanding of organizations and their properties. This chapter focuses on defining and describing organizations in general and sport organizations in particular.

Management, defined and described in Chapter 4, is relevant only in the context of organizations. Therefore, it is necessary to clarify the meaning of the term *organization,* its attributes, and its functions in the societal context. Moreover, since the methods and content of the four functions in the managerial process—that is, planning, organizing, leading, and evaluating—vary with differences between organizations, it is essential to analyze various organizations in terms of their similarities and dissimilarities. Then, these various organizations can be grouped according to some specific characteristics.

The chapter begins with a description of the critical elements included in various definitions of organizations. This is followed by an elaboration of the attributes that set an organization apart from other social entities.

DEFINING ORGANIZATIONS

The term *organization* has been defined by a number of authors. The following definitions are typical:

> An organization is a tool people use to coordinate their actions to obtain something that they desire or value—that is to achieve their goals. (Jones, 2010, p. 2)
>
> An *organization* is a deliberate arrangement of people to accomplish some specific purpose. (Robbins, Coulter, Leach, & Kilfoil, 2012, p. 10)
>
> An organization is a group of people working together in some type of concerted or coordinated effort to attain objectives. (Rue & Byars, 2009, p. 160)
>
> Organizations are interconnected sets of individuals and groups who attempt to accomplish common goals through differentiated functions and intended coordination. (Hitt, Black, Porter, & Hanson, 2007, p. 8)

In Simon's (1997) view:

> The term organization refers to the pattern of communications and relations among a group of human beings, including the processes for making and implementing decisions. This pattern provides to organization members much of the information and many of the assumptions, goals, and attitudes that enter into their decisions, and provides also a set of stable and comprehensive expectations as to what the other members of the group are doing and how they will react to what one says and does. The sociologist calls this pattern a "role system"; we are concerned with [the] form of role system known as an "organization." (pp. 18–19)

All of the definitions for an organization essentially incorporate four elements:

1. More than one person is needed.
2. The members' contributions are specialized.
3. These specialized functions are coordinated.
4. A common end/goal is being sought.

ATTRIBUTES OF ORGANIZATIONS

The foregoing definitions imply several **attributes of an organization**. A clearer understanding of an organization can be gained by probing further into these attributes: identity, instrumentality, program of activity, membership, clear boundaries, permanency, division of labor, hierarchy of authority, and formal rules and procedures.

Identity

The **identity** of the organization is separate from the identities of the members who make up that organization. That is, an organization has its own identity without reference to who the members and/or office-bearers are. For instance, although the mayor and council members may be in charge of the city recreation department, the identities of these individuals may change after every election. Similarly, the directors and assistant directors of the department may also leave for one reason or another. However, the department remains and is known as the recreation department based on its activities rather than on which individuals are in charge or are carrying out the activities. Similarly, a university athletic department has its own organizational identity independent of its directors, coaches, and athletes. As another example, the Y's mission of putting "Christian principles into practice through programs that build a healthy spirit, mind and body for all" is the same irrespective of a branch's location, its director, or members of the board (The Y, n.d.).

In legal parlance, this concept of separate identity is referred to as "corporate identity." "A corporation is a business formed under state or federal statutes that is authorized to act as a legal person. A corporation exists apart from its owners and can be taxed and sued like an individual. Corporate owners have limited liability; this means that they cannot lose their personal resources if the corporation fails. Only the corporation loses" (Rue & Byars, 2009, p. 104). To gain such a legal status, however, an organization must be registered according to the laws of the land. While the above statement refers to the situation in the United States, similar rules exist in most other countries.

Instrumentality

An organization exhibits **instrumentality** when it can achieve goals that are beyond the capacity of the individual members. This is the fundamental basis for an organization. If organizations were not the means to some end, there would not be any need for individuals to join an organization. For example, an individual joins a local sports club because it is instrumental in securing the necessary facilities, in providing expert training and coaching, and in bringing together people of similar interests and skills.

A Program of Activities

The notion that an organization is instrumental in achieving certain specific goals implies that the organization is involved in specific activities. For example, a fitness and tennis club is recognizable by the fact that it provides facilities for physical activities including tennis; it schedules those activities and competitions and it offers instructions in those activities. On the other hand, a firm retailing sporting goods is involved in the purchase, promotion, and sales of sporting goods. These programs of activities define, in part, the goals of the organization and the domain in which it operates.

Membership

Organizations tend to define who can have membership. They also establish procedures to replace members who leave for one reason or another. For example, to become a member of a university, one must either have a high academic degree (such as a Ph.D.) to be a faculty member, or have a high academic high school record to be a student. In a similar manner, membership in a university athletic department as either an administrator, a coach, or an athlete is contingent upon the individual possessing the requisite qualifications. Employees of a firm specializing in sport law are expected to have some training and education in law, specifically pertaining to sport law. Fitness clubs hire as fitness specialists those individuals who have had training in exercise physiology. This attribute ensures that the organization's members have the skills and expertise to carry out at least some of the activities undertaken by the organization.

In some sport organizations, the notion of membership may be restrictive in the sense that only members with certain assigned attributes (usually demographic characteristics) would be accepted as participants. For instance, the participants in Little League have to be within a certain age range. Several sport leagues offer competitions for different groups based on age and/or gender classification. These restrictions are attempts to ensure equality in maturity and development of the participants, but they also define who can be members of what teams or leagues.

Clear Boundaries

An organization's **boundaries** are defined by the attributes described above. That is, an organization's goals, its program of activity, and its roster of members clarify its boundaries in terms of its area of operation, its personnel, and its customers or clients. For example, a university's boundaries are defined by the activities that are carried out (teaching, research, service), its members (teachers and support staff), and its clients (the students). The boundaries defining a university athletic department or a department of recreational sports are their respective activities, personnel, and client groups. Similarly, a commercial fitness club's boundaries are defined by its fitness programs, its staff, and its clients. The distinction between a public golf course and a private nonprofit golf course is based on who can use the facilities and who the managers are.

Permanency

Generally speaking, an organization is relatively more permanent than the members who compose it. The Roman Catholic Church, government bureaucracies, large industrial and business corporations, universities, and voluntary organizations such as sport-governing bodies and Olympic associations are examples in which this attribute is clearly evident. Count Jacques Rogge, president of the International Olympic Committee (IOC), left office in 2013 but the IOC elected Thomas Bach to succeed him, and thus the IOC will continue to survive and thrive. Similarly, a golf club is likely to continue to exist despite turnovers in personnel such as managers, professionals, and groundskeepers. Or, consider a college athletic department. Over the years, its administrators, coaches, and athletes come and go, but the department itself continues to exist and carry on. There is **permanency** to these organizations, which outlasts the transfers, resignations, and deaths of individual members. It is conceivable, however, that smaller and not so well-established organizations could collapse with the departure of significant members.

Division of Labor

Division of labor and its consequence, specialization, makes the organization an efficient entity. As noted in the previous chapter, the managerial process of organizing should ensure that the division of labor is rational and consistent with the selected goals and programs of activities, which in turn promote efficiency. For example, the existence of special units in an athletic department to manage facilities, events, ticketing, and marketing indicates a division of labor in that department. A fitness club may divide its operations into specialized units for aerobics, weight training, swimming, tennis, and squash. A national sport-governing body may divide its total work into specific domains such as selection and training of national teams, training of coaches and officials, programs for mass participation, and marketing of its programs. Thus, every organization is characterized by division of labor.

Hierarchy of Authority

The coordination of individual members and their tasks requires a scheme in which one or more individuals specialize in coordinating the work of others. Moreover, persons in these positions of control and coordination must have the necessary authority to carry out these tasks. Thus, an organization is characterized by a

IN brief

Organizations are characterized by nine attributes: a separate identity, instrumentality, a program of activities, a roster of members, clear boundaries, permanency, a division of labor, a hierarchy of authority, and formal rules and procedures.

hierarchy of authority and an organizational chart that specifies who has authority over whom and for what purposes. This obviously results in unequal distribution of power, authority, influence, and status among organization members. In a department of sport management, the hierarchy of authority is represented by the positions of president and vice presidents of the university, the dean and assistant deans of the college, and the chair of the department. We can identify the positions arranged in a hierarchical manner in any athletic department, professional sport franchise, city recreation department, private golf club, or similar sport organization. Because the hierarchy of authority is necessary for the control and coordination of the activities of the members, it also carries with it the power to schedule the activities, allocate funds to the various programs, and monitor activities in general.

Formal Rules and Procedures

A dominant attribute in any organization is the presence of explicit rules and procedures to direct and control the behavior of members (employees as well as customers). For instance, the constitution and bylaws of a sport-governing body stipulate who can be office-bearers, and how and by whom they are selected. These rules also articulate the specific responsibilities of each office-bearer. Members of a tennis club are given a set of rules to follow in reserving a court and using the facilities. The NCAA is notorious for its voluminous set of rules relating to recruiting and eligibility. The purpose of rules is to ensure that the actions of individual members are consistent with the goals of the organization and coordinated toward the attainment of those goals. An equally important outcome of rules is that all clients of the organization are treated equally and fairly.

In summary, the above attributes are present to a greater or lesser extent in all organizations. Although various organizations—businesses and industries, hospitals, the military, athletic departments, volunteer organizations like the Red Cross, and educational institutions—possess these attributes, some are quite distinct from others in many respects. For example, the Red Cross and the military are dissimilar entities because they pursue different goals, carry out different activities, and adopt different internal processes. On the other hand, organizations such as universities and high schools can be very similar to each other because their main purposes and activities (i.e., educating individuals) are comparable.

ATHLETIC TEAMS AS ORGANIZATIONS

The above description of organizations is broad enough to include athletic teams as well as universities and industrial corporations. Ball (1975) pointed out that while athletic teams possess all the attributes of an organization, they are also unique in terms of (a) the constant roster size of members across teams in the same sport, (b) the codification of the activities of the team in rule books, and (c) the public and precise record of performances of the team. These attributes facilitate organizational analyses of teams, particularly in comparative and cross-cultural contexts.

In fact, many research efforts relating to athletic teams are based on the notion that they are similar to conventional organizations in many respects. This basic premise has led several authors to employ theoretical models from industry and business in the study of athletic teams and their effectiveness. For instance, Chelladurai's (1978, 1993) multidimensional model of leadership was developed to apply to athletic teams. This model, which will be discussed in detail in Chapter 12, was a synthesis and modification of leadership models in business and industry.

Riemer and Chelladurai (1998) developed a scale for measuring the satisfaction of athletes. This scale, known as the Athlete Satisfaction Questionnaire (ASQ), is based on the premise that athletic teams are organizations as already defined. The focus of their investigation was athletics in educational institutions. The ASQ relies on a conceptual framework derived from other satisfaction models in business and industry (Chelladurai & Riemer, 1997). According to the authors, there are two perspectives on athletes as members of the athletic team. In the first perspective, athletes are the clients or beneficiaries of the athletic team as the organization. Consistent with the emphasis in general management on client/customer satisfaction, measuring athlete satisfaction would be a measure of organizational effectiveness. The second perspective stems from the notion that athletic teams are providers of entertainment to the public. In this scenario, the athletes produce the entertainment through their excellent performance. Therefore, the athletes resemble the employees in business and industrial organizations. Thus, measuring athletic satisfaction would be akin to measuring job satisfaction of regular employees. In both perspectives, the athletic team is seen as an organization in itself.

Similarly, Chelladurai and Ogasawara (2003) investigated the satisfaction of coaches in intercollegiate athletics. Turner and Chelladurai (2005) also explored the extent to which intercollegiate athletic coaches were committed to their occupation and to their organization. These works were based on models of job satisfaction found in industrial and organizational psychology literature. The basic assumption in these investigations is that the coach is the manager of the athletic team—an organization in its own right.

Not only sport scientists view athletic teams as conventional organizations. Organization theorists also have noted how the various sport teams such as baseball, football, and basketball constitute ideal prototypes of organizations. For instance, Drucker (1995) compares work teams in organizations to three different types of sport teams. He notes that

> "Team-building" has become a buzzword in American business. The results are not overly impressive. . . . One reason—perhaps the major one—for these near failures is the all-but-universal belief among executives that there is just one kind of team. There actually are three—each different in structure, in the behavior it demands from its members, in its strengths, its vulnerabilities, its limitations, its requirements, but above all, in what it can do and should be used for. (pp. 97–98)

Drucker (1995) views an open-heart surgical team and an automobile assembly team as similar to baseball teams in that each member in these teams has a fixed position (e.g., second baseman and pitcher in baseball, and the anesthesiologist and the surgical nurse in the surgical team). Thus, "the players play on the team; they do not play as a team" (p. 98). Drucker compares the football team to the hospital unit that rallies around a patient who goes into shock, where the players play as a team despite their fixed positions. Finally, the tennis doubles team is compared to a musical band and to senior executives in a big company, where "players have a primary rather than a fixed position. They are supposed to 'cover'

IN brief

Athletic teams are organizations in their own right, possessing the same attributes as conventional organizations. Their uniqueness lies in their limited and specified membership roster and activities, as well as the publicity of their performance.

their teammates, adjusting to their teammates' strengths and weaknesses and to the changing demands of the 'game'" (p. 99). Drucker's essential point is that because the dynamics of each type of team are different, their success depends on how that type of team is composed and managed.

CLASSIFYING ORGANIZATIONS

It has been argued that "classifying things is perhaps the most fundamental and characteristic activity of the human mind, and underlies all forms of science" (Crowson, 1970, p. 1). In emphasizing the need for the development of an organizational typology (that is, a classification), Mills and Margulies (1980) stated that "Typologies play an important role in theory development because valid typologies provide a general set of principles for scientifically classifying things or events. What one attempts to do in such endeavors is to generate an analytical tool or instrument, not only as a way of reducing data, but more significantly to stimulate thinking" (p. 255). The significance of a typology for practicing managers was further highlighted by McKelvy (1975) as follows:

> Organization science, and especially the application of its findings to the problem of organizations and managers, is not likely to emerge with viable laws and principles until substantial progress is made toward an acceptable taxonomy and classification of organizations. The basic inductive–deductive process of science does not work without the phenomena under investigation being divided into sufficiently homogeneous classes. Managers cannot use the fruits of science unless they first can discover which of all the scientific findings apply to their situation. (p. 523)

Some of the criteria for classifying organizations that are more germane to sport/physical activity organizations are summarized in Exhibit 2.1 and described below.

Profit Orientation

Traditionally organizations are categorized on the basis of whether their purpose is to make a profit. An individual business providing fitness services is an example of a for-profit organization (even if it does not actually make a profit), whereas a university intramural department offering the same services is an example of a nonprofit organization (even if its receipts exceed expenses). Similarly, a professional sports club is a profit-oriented organization, while a national sport organization is not. All government agencies are nonprofit organizations. However, there is a debate over the use of the terms *profit* and *nonprofit*. Some individuals feel that it is more appropriate to use the terms *for-profit* and *not-for-profit* to indicate the **profit orientation** of the organization. In this view, if any profit-oriented organi-

exhibit 2.1 Criteria for classifying an organization relevant to sport management.

1. **Profit orientation:** Is the organization's purpose to make a profit?
2. **Source of funding:** What is the source of its funding?
3. **Prime beneficiary:** Who benefits from the organization?
4. **Employee–customer interface:** What type of interaction occurs between the customer and the employee?
5. **Volunteer participation:** Is it a voluntary association?

zation fails to make a profit, it would be labeled as nonprofit. However, the terms *profit* and *nonprofit* are most commonly used by scholars and practitioners.

A more serious issue is the similarity in structures and processes between profit and nonprofit organizations. One complaint relating to NCAA Division I athletics is that several of the athletic departments run their programs in such a way as to maximize their revenues. Although some of their methods may be unacceptable in a nonprofit and educational context, the idea of maximizing revenue should not be held against such institutions. A critical function of management is to ensure the survival of the organization. Such survival is based on securing resources not only for current operations but also for future operations. Thus, even managers of nonprofit sport organizations, including university athletic departments, are required to maximize their revenue to ensure the survival of their respective organizations and the continued provision of their respective services. Consider the case of Girls on the Run, an organization that engages girls from ages 8 to 13 in physical activity, life skills, and self-esteem (Girls on the Run, 2013). While it is a nonprofit organization, it does require participants to pay a registration fee and another fee to participate in the end-of-season 5K run. But the point is that these funds are reinvested into the organization's programs. If such maximization efforts result in an excess over expenses, such excess funds are rightly labeled *surplus* rather than *profit*. The surplus is, in fact, a reserve for a rainy day.

From a different perspective, many university athletic departments can generate revenue only on the strength of the popularity of certain sports, such as football and basketball. For instance, in 2010–2011, the football team of The Ohio State University generated nearly $52 million in revenue, about $39 million more than it costs to run the football program (Dosh, 2011). The excess funds were used to support teams in more than 36 other sports for both men and women at the university. If it were concerned with profit, OSU's athletic department would not support the other nonrevenue sports. This practice is consistent with Reynold's (2001) position that "the term *nonprofit organization* is used to refer to entities formed to provide social services rather than being formed to seek a profit. . . . The organizations do not have owners, and the ownership interest cannot be sold or traded. While the organization's revenues may exceed expenses, the excess must be used for the common good of society. It cannot directly benefit the members, and it cannot be referred to as profit" (pp. 432–433). Hopkins (2001) notes that from a legal perspective nonprofit organizations are distinguished from for-profit organizations by the doctrine of *private inurement*. This doctrine states that for a nonprofit to be tax exempt it "must be organized and operated so that no part of its net earnings inures to the benefit of any private shareholder or individual" (p. 900). Viewed from this perspective, it could be argued that revenue maximization is not only justified but also required.

IN brief

Organizations can be classified as profit or nonprofit based on their orientation to make profit. The excess of income over expenditures incurred by a nonprofit organization is considered a surplus that can be used only to further its goals.

Miller and Fielding (1995) provide another good example of a nonprofit organization engaging in revenue-generating activities. They document the history of the YMCA (now the Y) from its birth as a "noncommercial, protestant, religious organization endeavoring to spread the word of God through religious outreach, welfare, and relief-oriented activities" (p. 11). They describe the status of many branches of the Y that offer similar or identical services to those of profit organizations. For example, many Ys offer fitness programs that do not differ much from those found at privately owned profit-oriented fitness clubs. Referring to these Y branches as the "commercial YMCAs," Miller and Fielding point out that they not only offer the same programs as the profit-oriented organizations, but they also offer them to the same market segment, comprising of those who can pay for these services. Miller and Fielding also note that these Ys use the revenue generated by some of their activities to fund other non-revenue-producing activities in the service of the community. From this perspective, the excess revenues are considered surplus rather than profit.

The above references to revenue generation by university athletic departments and the Y may not be relevant to many other nonprofit organizations that depend primarily on donations for their income stream. In their mission to serve the public these nonprofits often may not be good models of financial management. As Howe (1997) points out, "In determining programs to undertake and in evaluating their effectiveness, [nonprofit organizations] depend inescapably on *subjective* judgments, on balancing imprecise benefits against precise costs" (p. 10).

The growth in the number and size of nonprofit organizations has been considerable in the past few decades. It is estimated that their operating expenses make up 6 percent of the U.S. gross national product (Pappas, 1996). Given the immensity of these operations, it has become commonplace to speak of the *nonprofit sector* in contrast to the *public* (or government) and *private* (restricted to profit-oriented businesses and industries) sectors (Pappas, 1996).

Source of Funding

The major **source of funding** has also been used to classify organizations broadly into private and public organizations. Those organizations that depend on private contributions or capital investments for their operation and survival are categorized as private organizations. Public organizations are those that are funded by tax monies at the national, state or provincial, or municipal level. Thus, all government agencies involved in the promotion of sport and physical activity are public sector organizations. All other sport organizations can be designated private sector organizations.

A number of authors such as Etzioni (1973) and McGill and Wooten (1976) have noted the emergence of a new class of organizations, which they call third sector organizations. The essential feature of a third sector organization is a partnership or collaboration between traditional private and public sector organizations. This partnership usually takes the form of financial support from the public sector, with the private sector being charged with the management of the organization toward well-defined purposes.

Third sector sport organizations may come about in two specific ways. First, the government or its agencies may create a new organization in the third sector. In Canada, for example, the federal government launched ParticipACTION Canada for the specific purpose of propagating fitness among the general public. The government provided a block grant of $500,000 and invited certain prominent members of the community, including business leaders, to carry out the functions outlined. Thereafter, the organization was left to its own devices to promote fitness. The government's contribution continued to be strictly monetary, but even that became

sidebar 2.1

FOTTLER'S CLASSES OF ORGANIZATIONS

Fottler (1981) identified four types of organizations based on a combination of profit motive and source of funding. These four classes are (1) private for-profit organizations, which are the businesses and corporations whose capital is provided by investors; (2) private nonprofit organizations, which are supported by donations, endowments, and government grants; (3) private quasi-public organizations, which are created and partly funded by government and authorized to provide particular goods or services; and (4) public organizations, whose primary form of financing is taxation.

negligible in comparison to the millions of dollars' worth of media advertisement generated by ParticipACTION Canada. Another example is the U.S. Department of Health and Human Services, which created *Healthy People 2020,* an organization with a set of health goals to be achieved by the year 2020. The department funds the activities carried out by several internal agencies and consortiums within the organization (Healthy People 2020, 2013).

The second way for a third sector organization to emerge is when the government begins to provide funds to private sector organizations in support of specific functions. For example, Sport Canada spent C$100 million in 2005 to support national sport organizations and their programs (Sport Canada, 2005), whereas the government's contribution was C$20 million in 1983. As contributions from governments increase, sport-governing bodies are more likely to become third sector organizations. As another example, the American Red Cross was developed as a private organization, but it receives U.S. federal funding in the form of grants for specific causes.

Thus, the distinction among public, private, and third sector organizations can be narrowed down to the extent to which funding for these organizations is supplied through legislation of a senior-ranking organization. If this criterion is used, a university athletic department, which is financed by student fees on a schedule set and approved by the university senate, is similar to a third sector organization. On a higher level, the university itself is a third sector organization if it is heavily funded by the government—even though it retains autonomy in its management.

IN brief

Organizations can be classified as public (funded by government taxation), private (funded by private capital), and third sector (subsidized by government finances).

The growing significance of third sector organizations was highlighted by Drucker (1989) decades ago. He noted that the United States' third sector institutions were rapidly becoming "creators of new bonds of community and a bridge across the widening gap of knowledge workers and the other half. . . . In well run third sector organizations, there are no more volunteers, there are only unpaid staff. . . . Unpaid staff are thoroughly trained, and given a specific assignment with performance goals" (p. 203).

Prime Beneficiary

Blau and Scott (1960) referred to four types of organizations based on the criterion of **prime beneficiary** of the organization. In their view, while several groups may benefit through an organization, one of those groups can be identified as the primary group for whose benefit the organization exists. For example, although the faculty, staff, and students benefit from a university, it is the students who are the prime beneficiaries of the university because they are the reason the university exists. In fact, the benefits that accrue to the faculty and staff may be viewed as costs a university incurs in order to serve the students. Based on this notion of prime beneficiary, Blau and Scott (1960) classified organizations as follows:

1. **Mutual benefit associations**, in which the members or rank-and-file participants are the prime beneficiaries, as in player unions and private nonprofit golf or tennis clubs.
2. **Business concerns**, in which the owners or managers of the organization are the prime beneficiaries, as in commercial fitness or golf clubs and professional sport franchises.

3. **Service organizations**, in which the clients or the "public-in-contact" (Blau and Scott's term) are the prime beneficiaries, as in athletic and recreational departments in educational institutions, city recreation departments, YMCA sports departments, and sport-governing bodies.
4. **Commonweal organizations**, in which the public-at-large is the prime beneficiary, as in prisons and police departments. Commonweal organizations are rare in society, and almost nonexistent in sport. Of course, some individuals may see a summer sports camp as one way of "keeping kids off the street" for the benefit of the other citizens. In this perspective, summer camps could be considered similar to commonweal organizations.

IN brief

Organizations can be classified as mutual benefit associations existing for the primary benefit of members, business concerns for the benefit of owners, service organizations for the benefit of their clients, and commonweal organizations for the benefit of the public.

As we will discuss later in the book, the criterion of prime beneficiary is the best basis for many organizational decisions where several groups are likely to be affected.

Employee–Customer Interface

In Chapter 1 we described several classes of sport services. One of the factors that differentiate among various forms of services is the type of interaction between the customer or client and the service employee. Based on what takes place in the **employee–customer interface** and the importance of the information component in that interface, Mills and Margulies (1980) classified service organizations as maintenance-interactive, task-interactive, and personal-interactive. In *maintenance-interactive* types of organizations, the information processed by the employee is rather limited, and the decisions he makes are simple. Consider, for example, the employee who handles the membership and reservations of a racquetball club or the person selling soda or popcorn at an MLB game. Each transaction with a customer involves little time, simple decisions, and minimal information processing. The services offered by this type of organization are usually consumer services, as discussed in Chapter 1.

In *task-interactive* service organizations, more time is involved, the decisions are more complex, and the employee has more information. As a consequence, the employee also has more power than the customer, who knows what she wants but not how to get it. For example, an entrepreneur, after deciding to build a new racquetball and fitness facility, must depend on an engineering and construction firm for a plan and the eventual construction of the facility. The entrepreneur—that is, the customer—depends on the construction firm employee's expertise and knowledge about the specific tasks to be completed. Similarly, the event manager in an athletic department may have to depend on the expertise of an outside security company for ensuring that no one is seriously injured during an event.

The services of this kind of organization are professional services, as discussed in Chapter 1. In *personal-interactive* service organizations, the clients or customers are "typically unaware or imprecise about *what* will best serve their interest and *how* to go about remedying a situation" (Mills & Margulies, 1980, p. 264). A fitness consulting firm or an athletic injuries clinic is an example from the field of sport/physical activity. Although the clients or customers may provide detailed information about their fitness level or the source and nature of their ailments, the employee processes this information and makes decisions. The customers may not be even aware if quality service is being provided. As another example, collegiate and professional sport teams have begun to hire sport psychologists to help athletes deal with challenges and problems. Athletes may recognize the problem but may rely on the psychologist to determine the cause and solution. Note that the services of this type of organization are human services, as described in Chapter 1.

Volunteer Participation

Most sport-governing bodies and their local units are **voluntary associations**—organizations run by volunteers. Sills (1972) defined a voluntary association as "an organized group of persons (1) that is formed in order to further some common interest of its members; (2) in which membership is voluntary in the sense that it is neither mandatory nor acquired through birth; and (3) that exists independently of the state" (p. 363).

Knoke (1990) described volunteer associations as "collective action organizations [that] (1) seek nonmarket solutions to particular individual or group problems; (2) maintain formal criteria for membership on a voluntary basis; (3) may employ persons under the authority of organizational leaders; and (4) provide formally democratic procedures to involve members in policy decisions" (p. 7). These associations are differentiated from primary groups (such as social circles, friendship cliques, and families) because the latter groups do not have clearly stated purposes and specific criteria for membership. Volunteer associations also differ from regular work organizations such as governments and business organizations, which are characterized by rigid hierarchical authority systems and a contract between labor and the organization in the form of financial compensation for full-time work (Knoke, 1990).

These definitions are broad enough to include not only sport-governing bodies and local sport clubs but also players' unions and referees' unions. However, the purpose of the unions is to protect the economic welfare of their members, whereas the former two—the truly voluntary associations—are not concerned with "making a living for the members," as Sills would put it. Furthermore, for an association to be legitimately called voluntary, the volunteers (as opposed to paid staff) must constitute the majority of the participants. For example, the board of governors of a university or a hospital consists of volunteer members. However, the proportion of other paid participants, such as professors, doctors, or staff, is much larger; therefore, these types of institutions lose the true flavor of voluntary associations. In contrast, in sport-governing bodies and their local units, almost all activities—top management as well as front-line activities—are run by volunteers. (A trend has emerged, however, to hire more and more paid staff to carry out the ever-increasing activities of sport organizations.) The presence of volunteers and their influence on organizational purposes and processes make the management of those organizations distinct from the management of other organizations. These differences in managerial processes are pointed out in subsequent chapters.

SUMMARY

In this chapter, we defined the organization as a social entity and described its characteristics. We discussed the significant attributes of an organization—identity, instrumentality, program of activities, membership, boundaries, permanency, division of labor, hierarchy of authority, and formal rules and procedures. We compared athletic teams to an organization as defined and described above. We noted that organizations can be classified on the basis of (a) profit orientation (profit and nonprofit organizations), (b) source of funding (public, private, and third sector organizations), (c) prime beneficiaries (mutual benefit, business, service, and commonweal organizations), (d) employee–customer interface (maintenance-interactive, task-interactive, and personal-interactive organizations), and (e) volunteer membership and governance (volunteer organizations). These classifications and the criteria on which they are based provide the sport manager with some insights regarding the context and people he is dealing with.

The various classifications of organizations are not mutually exclusive. The classification based on profit motive and that based on sources of funding are not independent of each other. For example, government (public) organizations are not profit oriented. Similarly, most third sector organizations are nonprofit in nature. Organizations could be placed in different classes of organizations proposed by Blau and Scott (1960) and Mills and Margulies (1980). For example, a university, which is a nonprofit, third sector organization, is also a service organization (Blau & Scott) providing personal-interactive services (Mills & Margulies). On the other hand, a sports arena run by a city is a public, nonprofit, service organization providing a maintenance-interactive service.

The above classification systems provide some insight into the types of products produced by different classes of organizations, and the nature of the exchange of those products with their respective client groups. They also highlight the specific constraints and exigencies faced by different kinds of organizations. Thus, an understanding of these classifications can help sport managers adapt to the specific organizational contexts they manage.

develop YOUR PERSPECTIVE

1. Consider the various definitions of an organization provided at the beginning of the chapter. Discuss the relative emphasis each one places on goals, people, specialization, and coordination.
2. This chapter describes several attributes of an organization. Select two sport organizations and describe them in terms of those attributes.
3. Considering the same two organizations, classify them according to the criteria provided in the chapter—profit orientation, sources of funding, prime beneficiary, and employee–customer interface.

references

Ball, D. W. (1975). A note on method in the sociological study of sport. In D. W. Ball & J. W. Loy (Eds.), *Sport and social order*. Reading, MA: Addison-Wesley.

Blau, P. M., & Scott, W. R. (1960). *Formal organizations: A comparative study*. San Francisco: Chandler.

Chelladurai, P. (1978). *A contingency model of leadership in athletics*. Unpublished doctoral dissertation, University of Waterloo, Waterloo, ON, Canada.

Chelladurai, P. (1993). Leadership. In R. N. Singer, M. Murphy, & K. Tennant (Eds.), *The handbook on research in sport psychology* (pp. 647–671). New York: Macmillan.

Chelladurai, P., & Ogasawara, E. (2003). Satisfaction and commitment of American and Japanese collegiate coaches. *Journal of Sport Management, 17*, 62–73.

Chelladurai, P., & Riemer, H. (1997). A classification of facets of athlete satisfaction. *Journal of Sport Management, 11*, 133, 159.

Crowson, R. A. (1970). *Classification and biology*. New York: Atherton Press.

Dosh, K. (2011, May 31). Ohio State's football budget. *The Business of College Sports*. Retrieved from http://businessofcollegesports.com/2011/05/31/ohio-states-football-budget/

Drucker, P. F. (1989). *The new realities*. New York: Harper & Row.

Drucker, P. F. (1995). *Managing in a time of great change*. New York: Truman Talley Books/Dutton.

Etzioni, A. (1973). The third sector and domestic missions. *Public Administration Review*, July–August, 314–327.

Fottler, M. D. (1981). Is management really generic? *Academy of Management Review, 6*, 1–12.

Girls on the Run. (2013). Nonprofit girls running program. Retrieved from http://www.girlsontherun.org.

Healthy People 2020. (2013). Consortium & partners. Retrieved from http://www.healthypeople.gov/2020/consortium/default.aspx.

Hitt, M. A., Black, J. S., Porter, L. W., & Hanson, D. (2007). *Management*. Frenchs Forest, NSW: Pearson Education Australia.

Hopkins, B. R. (2001). Law and taxation. In T. D. Connors (Ed.), *The nonprofit handbook: Management* (3rd ed., pp. 893–921). New York: John Wiley & Sons.

Howe, F. (1997). *The board member's guide to strategic planning*. San Francisco, CA: Jossey-Bass Publishers.

Jones, G. R. (2010). *Organizational theory, design, and change* (6th ed.). Upper Saddle River, NJ: Pearson.

Knoke, D. (1990). *Organizing for collective action: The political economies of associations*. New York: Aldine de Gruyter.

McGill, M. E., & Wooten, L. M. (1976). Management in the third sector. In J. L. Gibson, J. M. Ivancevich, & J. H. Donnelly (Eds.), *Readings in organizations: Behavior, structure, processes*. Dallas, TX: Business Publications.

McKelvy, B. (1975). Guidelines for the empirical classification of organizations. *Administrative Science Quarterly, 20*, 509–525.

Miller, L. K., & Fielding, L. W. (1995). The battle between the for-profit health club and the "commercial" YMCA. *Journal of Sport and Social Issues, 19*(1), 76–107.

Mills, P. K., & Margulies, N. (1980). Toward a core typology of service organizations. *Academy of Management Review, 5*, 255–265.

Pappas, A. T. (1996). *Reengineering your nonprofit organization: A guide to strategic transformation*. New York: John Wiley & Sons.

Reynolds, R. G. (2001). Nonprofit organizations as entrepreneurs. In T. D. Connors (Ed.), *The nonprofit handbook: Management* (3rd ed., pp. 432–442). New York: John Wiley & Sons.

Riemer, H. A., & Chelladurai, P. (1998). Development of the Athlete Satisfaction Questionnaire (ASQ). *Journal of Sport & Exercise Psychology, 20*, 127–156.

Robbins, S. P., Coulter, M., Leach, E., & Kilfoil, M. (2012). *Management* (10th ed.). Don Mills, Ontario: Pearson Canada.

Rue, L. W., & Byars, L. L. (2009). *Management: Skills and application* (13th ed). New York: McGraw-Hill Irwin.

Sills, D. L. (1972). Voluntary associations: Sociological aspects. In *International encyclopedia of the social sciences* (Vol. 16). New York: Crowell, Collier, and Macmillan.

Simon, H. A. (1997). *Administrative behavior: A study of decision-making behaviors in administrative organizations* (4th ed.). New York: The Free Press.

Sport Canada. (2005). Introduction. Retrieved from www.pch.gc.ca/progs/sc/pubs/tablesrondes-roundtables/synopsis/2_e.cfm.

Turner, B. A., & Chelladurai, P. (2005). Organizational and occupational commitment, intention to leave and perceived performance of intercollegiate coaches. *Journal of Sport Management, 19*, 193 211.

Y. (n.d.). About us. Retrieved from http://www.ymca.net/about-us/.

CHAPTER 3

SYSTEMS VIEW OF ORGANIZATIONS

manage YOUR LEARNING

After completing this chapter you should be able to:

- Explain the processes associated with an open system, and compare an organization to an open system.
- Describe the inputs, throughputs, and outputs of an organization from a systems perspective.
- Understand the significance of the environment for organizational survival and growth.
- Explain three theories of the environmental influences on organizations.

strategic CONCEPTS

coercive isomorphism
demand-side stakeholder
environment, external
environment, general (or distal)
environment, task (or operating or proximal)
equifinality
inputs–throughputs–outputs
institutional isomorphism
institutional theory
involuntary stakeholder
mimetic isomorphism
multifinality
negative entropy
normative isomorphism
open systems
primary stakeholders
progressive mechanization
progressive segregation
secondary stakeholders
self-regulation
supply-side stakeholder
system boundaries
systems thinking
voluntary stakeholder

ORGANIZATIONS AS OPEN SYSTEMS

In Chapter 2, we looked at a few definitions of organizations and described the significant attributes applicable to most organizations. We also discussed the different classifications of organizations, helping us to understand the differences among them. The foregoing descriptions provide a beginning understanding of organizations.

Take note of the word *systems* in the title of this chapter. The term *system* is descriptive of the complex interrelationships among elements within an organization. Studying sport delivery systems is consistent with the views of several authors who have suggested that an organization can be perceived as an *open system* (as in Bowman & Jarrett, 1996; Immegart & Pilecki, 1973; Katz & Kahn, 1966; Waring, 1996). Accordingly, this chapter outlines the concept of a system and its relevance to sport management. The advantages of viewing organizations as open systems (**systems thinking**) are also explained.

A system can be defined as "a set of interrelated and interdependent parts arranged in a manner that produces a unified whole" (Robbins, Coulter, Leach, & Kilfoil, 2012, p. 35). These interrelated and interdependent parts also tend to interact with each other in an orderly manner (Hitt, Black, & Porter, 2009). The notion of interactions is further explained by Morecroft, Sanchez, and Heene (2002) when they state that "the essential meaning of *interactions* between system elements, however, is that a change in one system element causes, induces, or otherwise leads to a change in one or more other system elements. . . .This *interdependence* of the elements is therefore a defining characteristic of a system" (pp. 7–8). In Ritchie-Dunham and Rabbino's (2001) view, "Systems thinking is about seeing, understanding, and working with 'the whole.' It focuses more on the relationships that link the parts of the whole than on the parts themselves" (p. 5).

The human body provides a good illustration of a system as defined above. It is composed of different parts (head, legs, eyes, heart, and so on) that are put together in such a way as to constitute a meaningful whole. Each of the parts has its own attributes or qualities, but what makes the human body a system is the interrelationships among the parts, and the specific qualities that result from these interrelationships. This is clearly illustrated when a short, mesomorphic body type is contrasted with a tall, ectomorphic body type. These two specific body types contribute to potential for excellence in specific activities. The contrast between the body types lies not only in the differences in the attributes (parts), but also in the qualities of the relationships among those parts.

A wooden table can also be viewed as a system. Four legs and a top, constructed in a particular way, make up the system of a table. The different configurations in which these parts can be put together make for different systems of tables. In similar ways, almost everything can be conceived of as a system.

There is, however, one fundamental difference between the human body and the table as systems. The human body shivers when exposed to cold, and it perspires in reaction to heat. The human body consumes oxygen from the air it breathes, and it disposes of carbon dioxide. These reactions to environmental conditions, and the exchange of energy with the environment, do not take place to the same extent in the case of a table. Thus, the human body can be thought of as an **open system** (relatively open to the influences of the environment in which it lives), whereas the table can be thought of as a closed system (relatively impervious to the environment).

The systems view of organizations draws out the basic elements common to all organizations, the relationships among these elements, and their interactions with the environment. Organizations are open systems in that they influence and are influenced by the social, cultural, and economic conditions of the community in which they operate. They depend on society for their resources, and, in

sidebar 3.1

OPENNESS VERSUS CLOSEDNESS

The designation of the human body as relatively open and the table as relatively closed is deliberate. The notions of "openness" and "closedness" should be viewed as two ends of a continuum, and the systems can be located at different points on that continuum. That is, some systems will be relatively more open (or closed) than others. In the preceding example, environmental influences will have an effect on the table, which, as a result, will decay over a period of time. However, when compared to the environmental influences on the human body, the table lies near the closed end of the continuum whereas the body is near the other extreme. Note also the possibility that the subsystems of a system may vary in the degree to which they are open or closed. Thus, the skeletal subsystem is relatively more closed than the circulatory system. Similar differences are likely to be found among the units of an organization.

exchange, they provide products or services for that society. For example, a professional sport franchise depends on the community for facilities, media coverage, corporate support, and attendance at its events. In return, the franchise provides entertainment for the public, generates a certain degree of economic activity, and brings prestige and publicity to the community.

PROPERTIES OF ORGANIZATIONS AS OPEN SYSTEMS

The view of organizations as open systems can be further clarified by examining some of the relevant system properties. The two that seem most pertinent here are boundaries and environments.

Subsystems and Boundaries

Every system (except the very smallest) has subsystems that can be conceived of as systems in themselves. For example, the circulatory system is a subsystem of the human body and is itself a complete system consisting of the heart, arteries, veins, capillaries in the muscles, alveoli in the lungs, and so on.

Similarly, a college athletic department consists of the administrators, the support staff, the various teams, the facilities, and the equipment. A team that is a subsystem in the athletic department is also a system in itself from another perspective. It is composed of the coach, the athletes, the team's facilities and equipment, and so on. Consider a large fitness club. Each of its programs such as fitness evaluation, aerobics, aquatics, and strength training is a subsystem. And each one of these programs consists of its own subsystems of specialized activities, equipment and facilities, and personnel. Yet another example is the Little League organization, which has a board and commissioners. The teams that make up the league are systems by themselves, having their own governing structure and operating rules.

Although the idea of a system and subsystems is quite straightforward, the notion of a system boundary is less so. The reason for this is that humans as analysts or managers must decide on what elements should be included in a system of interest. Moreover, humans are limited in their ability to analyze and manage. Thus, while in a sense everything is connected to everything else in this world, human analysis leads to the exclusion of a number of things and people only remotely related to the system in question. As Khandwalla (1977) stated, "It is because of our ability to fail to see many weak relationships that we are at all able to perceive 'systems'" (p. 224).

A good example of this problem lies in sport sciences. All the subsystems of the human body are integrally interrelated. However, an exercise physiologist tends to focus on the cardiovascular and muscular systems; a scholar in biomechanics emphasizes the skeletal and muscular systems and the mechanical laws that govern their actions; and a sport or exercise psychologist may be concerned with the personality and cognitive dynamics of individuals. Each of these scholars has set the boundaries of the system under investigation, but each also recognizes that the system is integrally linked to a suprasystem—the human.

In the case of organizations, the boundary of the system is also critical. For a city recreation department, the system would consist of all the arenas and playgrounds, the staff, and the participants. On the other hand, for an arena manager, the system would be delimited to such things as the building itself, the heating and refrigeration units, the electrical and plumbing arrangements, the employees, and the policies and procedures that regulate the management of the arena. **System boundaries**, then, are arbitrarily set to suit specific purposes, and anything and everything outside the selected boundaries is considered the focal system's environment.

External Environment

In any discussion of the properties of an organization as an open system, it is important to consider the external environment. The **external environment** "is the set of forces and conditions that operate beyond an organization's boundaries but affect its ability to acquire and use resources to create value" (Jones, 2010, p. 2). As shown in Exhibit 3.1, the environment is usually subdivided into two categories: (1) the *task* or *operating environment* (also called the *proximal environment*), and (2) the *general environment* (also called the *distal environment*).

Some of the elements in the environment are more clearly related to the system and influence it more directly. These elements make up what is referred to as the **task** (or proximal) **environment.** The other elements constitute the **general** (or distal) **environment.** Thus, for a profit-oriented tennis club, the task environment would include its competitors and the attitude of the community in which it operates. The general environment might include the television coverage of major tournaments that could positively influence the community's attitudes toward tennis. This, in turn, could increase the demand for the club's services. Note that the distinction between task and general environment refers to proximity not in geography but in tasks. For instance, the task environment for The Ohio State University football team would include the affairs of the University of Minnesota football team even though it is hundreds of miles away from Columbus, Ohio. However, the softball program of the Columbus City Recreation Department would not be within the task environment of the Buckeye football team.

exhibit 3.1 Distal and proximal environments of a system.

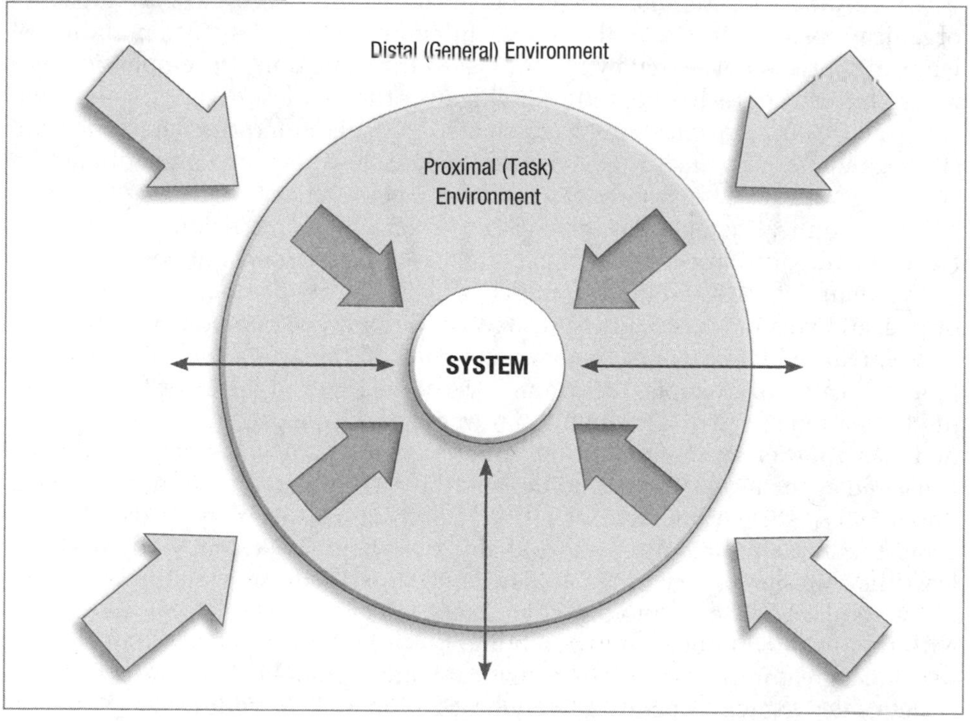

Key elements of the general environment

Elements in the general environment can be grouped in several ways (see Pierce & Dunham, 1990; Slack, 1997; Wehrich & Koontz, 1993). The following scheme is drawn from Certo and Certo (2009), who suggest that the environment consists of (a) the *economic component,* (b) the *social component,* (c) the *political component,* (d) the *legal component,* and (e) the *technology component.* The economic component for a fitness club would include the rates of wages paid to labor (fitness and aerobics instructors), availability of labor (trained instructors), the cost of the fitness equipment, and the market prices for the services offered by the club. Another critical issue in the economic component is the state of the economy itself. When the economy is expanding and incomes are rising, customers have more discretionary funds (funds over and above the minimum required for day-to-day expenses). Therefore, consumers are likely to spend more on leisure pursuits, including membership in fitness clubs. If, on the other hand, the economy is in decline, consumers are likely to cut back on such leisure expenses.

The social component of the general environment would include the demography, or characteristics, of the population. For instance, if the population is aging—as is happening in industrial nations—the fitness club's operations would have to be modified to attract and maintain its clients by adding programs and equipment suited to older adults. It is estimated that in the not-too-distant future, the majority of the American labor force will comprise nonwhites and females. This means that a large proportion of the national income will go to these diverse segments of the population. This trend in the population will affect how sport organizations could best serve their communities. For example, the National Football League could maintain its standing as the premier professional sports league in North America only if it could cater to the needs and preferences of these diversified income earners. In addition, the NFL would also be expected to court these market segments by directing its promotional campaigns toward them.

According to Certo and Certo (2009), social values also have an impact on organizations. For instance, the American emphasis on competition and excellence in sports is not shared by all nations. At the same time, the emphasis Americans place on sports has been intensifying over the past few decades. In line with this trend, sport organizations have changed. Media enterprises are tuned into sports, and other commercial enterprises look at sports, sports competitions, and sport organizations from more of a marketing perspective.

The political component includes the extent to which democracy and free trade are practiced in a country, the influence (or interference) of political parties in the affairs of industry and commerce, and the ability of labor unions to affect organizational practices. Closely related to the political component is the legal component, which refers to the laws and rules of the land. For a minor league baseball team, for example, the zoning laws of the city and the labor laws, including legislation specifying the minimum wage, would be part of the legal component. As another example, both the American and Canadian governments have legislated against sweatshop conditions in the workplace, as seen in the Occupational Safety and Health Act of 1970. Every sport organization needs to understand the legislated requirements and abide by them (for example, by paying at least the minimum wage and maintaining the specified range of temperature in the workplace). The technology component refers to the technology associated with the production of a firm's goods and services. The introduction of artificial turf had a great impact on how professional football franchises and intercollegiate athletics departments operated. Every fitness club and strength-training program would be affected if manufacturing firms were to come up with a series of new exercise equipment scientifically proven to be more effective. And of course firms in the sport management industry continue to be affected by and take advantage of online and social networking innovations, particularly in marketing and promoting teams and products. Another instance of technology impinging on sport organizations is the advances in manufacturing swimsuits that enhance the performances of competitive swimmers. Federation Internationale de Natation Amateur (FINA), the international governing body of swimming, once compared the use of these swimsuits to the use of performance-enhancing substances. Now it approves the swimsuits and they can be used by swimmers in FINA-approved competitions.

sidebar 3.2

GOVERNMENT AGENCIES AS OPEN SYSTEMS

There was a time when government agencies did not react to environmental pressures to the extent that private organizations did. However, this is no longer the case. Government agencies do adopt certain business practices as a result of economic, political, and social pressures, including building alliances and linkages with other organizations, both profit and nonprofit, in the private sector. Thibault, Frisby, and Kikulis (1999) examined this with three local government agencies in British Columbia providing leisure services, including fitness and sport services. They found that all three government agencies had built linkages with schools and nonprofit organizations. They have also begun to build such linkages with profit-oriented organizations. This illustrates that no organization should be impervious to its environment.

Key elements of the task environment

The task or operating environment includes those elements that have a more direct and immediate effect on the organization. The introduction of a scientifically improved exercise machine stems from the general or distal environment affecting all fitness clubs all over the country. In contrast, if a nearby fitness club buys these new machines, it has an immediate and direct effect on the focal club. Thus, the fitness club in the vicinity and its operation would be considered within the task or operating environment of the focal club. Similarly, the national economy is part of the general environment that could affect attendance at sporting events all over the country. By the same token, a specific professional sport franchise could be affected by the economy of the region and city where it is located. Thus, the regional economy is an element in the operating environment. Another example occurs when a university athletic department must cope with the competition posed when a new professional sport franchise is awarded to the city.

A major concern of management of a sport organization is to understand clearly the task or operating environment, the opportunities it offers, and the constraints it places on the organization. The success of the organization is a function of the extent to which it capitalizes on the opportunities and satisfies the demands placed on it. The operating environment can be broken down into the:

- *customer component* (those who buy the organization's goods and services, such as the spectators at a professional sporting event, players at a golf course, clients of an aerobics class, or students in a sport management program)
- *competition component* (all other individuals or organizations that produce the same type of services and goods and compete for the same customers or clients, such as other professional sport franchises, golf courses, and fitness clubs in the vicinity)
- *labor component* (availability of suitable employees, their demands, and their general attitude toward the professional sports club, golf course, or fitness club under consideration)
- *supplier component* (all the individuals and organizations that supply the equipment and other needed resources for the professional sports team, golf course, or fitness club)

Internal Environment

The concept of environment is also applicable to the internal operations of the organization. Consider, for example, two professional sport franchises in football. In one, the primary owner may take part extensively in the recruitment, training, and deployment of the players. In contrast, the primary owner in the other franchise may leave these affairs in the hands of the manager and coach. The two clubs may also differ in the extent and manner of planning that takes place, the arrangement of the relationships among the units and employees of the organization, the leadership provided, and the ways in which individuals or units are evaluated and rewarded. These topics will be covered in later chapters. At this point, just note that top managers create the internal environment through their specific policies and procedures. Employees' reactions (both positive and negative) and their adherence to these policies also contribute to the creation of the internal environment.

IN brief

An organization, like any other living system, is also characterized by subsystems—each interacting with its own tasks and general environments. However, it is up to the decision makers to define the system's boundaries to suit their specific purposes.

In Exhibit 3.1, the narrow two-sided arrows pointing outward from the system indicate the organization's efforts to influence its environment. For example, the NCAA sponsors youth and community programs such as youth sport skill clinics, the Ticket to Reading Rewards program, and forums on careers in sport (NCAA, 2011). These are in one sense attempts to inform the proximal environment of the NCAA's function as a nonprofit enterprise supporting athletics and education for youth. For that matter, all lobbying groups function essentially to influence the relevant environments of the organizations they represent.

PROCESSES IN OPEN SYSTEMS

The view of organizations as open systems can also be clarified by examining the processes of systems. The processes that are particularly pertinent in this regard are *negative entropy* (which is reflected in the processes of self-regulation, progressive segregation, and progressive mechanization) and *equifinality* and *multifinality*.

Negative Entropy

Entropy is the tendency of a system toward disorder and decay. However, open systems such as organizations can prolong the length of their life and enhance their quality by constantly evolving and adapting to environmental conditions. Such an attempt to reverse the entropic process is called **negative entropy**. As Immegart and Pilecki (1973) noted, "The open system has great control over its existence and destiny; it can choose whether or not to fight entropy or to maximize its existence. All living or open systems exist for a finite period in time/space. Few, indeed, have infinite lives. However, the duration and quality of life for the open system is, in large measure, in its own hands" (pp. 44–45).

The implication here is that the management of an organization must understand that unless it takes positive steps to adapt to the changing conditions, the entropic process cannot be arrested. In the case of a commercial golf course, the entropic process can be seen in the physical decay of the fairways and greens, the parking lots, the clubhouse, the restaurant, and the pro shop. The maintenance and upkeep of these facilities is, in fact, a process of arresting this decay of negative entropy. This concept applies to both physical facilities and managerial activities. The measures to arrest the decay (i.e., the entropy) can take several forms. The more significant measures are *self-regulation, progressive segregation,* and *progressive mechanization.*

Self-regulation

The notion that open systems/organizations tend to reverse the process of decay implies that these systems do, in fact, regulate their own activities. Just as the human body perspires to reduce the adverse effects of heat, organizations also react to fluctuations and disturbances in their environment. Such **self-regulation** may consist of changes in personnel, organizational structure, or internal processes. When a university athletic department fires a coach and hires a new one, it is regulating itself in order to arrest the presumed decline in its status. Every intercollegiate athletic program has a compliance department that is, in effect, a self-regulating mechanism. That is, its role is to ensure that the program complies with every rule of the NCAA athletic department. Attempts to modernize the reservation procedures at a golf course would also be a form of self-regulation. In addition, management may train the employees in the use of new computers and software. Similarly, a fitness club may send its fitness specialists to clinics in exercise physiology or fitness testing as a means of keeping up to date with emergent technology. These types of self-regulatory activities are aimed at stopping the decline and ensuring the growth of the organization.

In addition, these regulatory adaptations and adjustments maintain the system in a state of dynamic equilibrium. That is, the subsystems of an organization must be in harmony with each other, and the organization as a whole must be in tune with environmental influences and pressures. Thus, changes in our previous examples (reservation procedures in the golf club or exercise testing in a fitness club) must be consistent not only with the expertise of the members, but also with the requirements of the society. Subsequent changes in the environment necessitate suitable alterations in the system, which in turn result in a new state of equilibrium.

Progressive segregation

One of the regulatory processes of a system is its tendency to subdivide its subsystems into functional and specialized units and to order them in a hierarchy. Immegart and Pilecki (1973) comment on this process: "At a basic level, this is the tendency of an open system to determine what subsystems it will formally create, what subsystems it will use to process work, the nature and order of subsystem activity, and the priority of subsystem duties and obligations within the overall system perspective" (pp. 43–44).

The national sport organizations (NSOs) in several countries, in response to pressures to improve their operations and produce world-class athletes, have established special units to identify and develop athletic talent and to promote excellence in their respective sports. These units are differentiated from other units such as those that deal with promotion of the sport in the community and training of volunteer referees and coaches. This is an example of **progressive segregation.** As it grows in size and attendance, a golfing club may create and segregate the units that deal with (a) tournaments; (b) golfing for youth, adults, and seniors; (c) membership and reservations; and (d) ancillary services such as parking, child care, and the restaurant. This progressive segregation provides for greater specialization and regulation of work. Note that the process of creation and segregation of subsystems can take many forms. The question of which units need to be created or segregated in a golf or fitness club must be addressed only in the context of that club and its unique circumstances.

Progressive mechanization

As the system grows and the number of subsystems with specialized functions increases, the system faces the problem of coordinating all of its activities. Managers achieve such coordination by stipulating a set of procedures and regulations for each subsystem regarding what to do and when and how it should be done. These procedural and regulatory arrangements develop from the perspective of total system coordination. Girls on the Run, which promotes the sport of running among young women, has established procedures for starting each council, including the same training for all coaches, lesson plans, and activities for the participants. This form of mechanization allows the program to be standardized across the country (Girls on the Run, 2013).

On a larger scale, the NCAA offers another example of **progressive mechanization.** In order to coordinate and control intercollegiate athletics in the United States, the NCAA has instituted rules and regulations, such as recruiting and eligibility rules, and has created special units to monitor compliance to these rules (Departments of Legislative Services and of Enforcement and Appeals). To the extent that these rules and procedures are comprehensive, the tasks within the units tend to become more prescribed and routine.

Equifinality and Multifinality

Equifinality refers to the idea that two systems that initially start from different positions can end up at the same final position (Gresov & Drazin, 1997; Reeves, Duncan, & Ginter, 2003). It is "the idea that an objective—a final result or desired state—can be achieved in different ways by following different routes" (Roth, 2002, p. 14). That is, any two systems can be distinguished on the basis of the number and nature of their subsystems, and the particular internal processes within each system. However, either of the systems can be equally effective. For example, two football teams might differ on the basis of their coaches' authoritarian versus participative orientation. Both teams could be effective provided that in each team the types of players and their preferences were conducive to the coach's orientation. If players under an authoritarian coach preferred to be told what, when, and how they should do things, then that team would be internally consistent and, therefore, could be effective. Similarly, if the players under the participative coach were more autonomous and preferred to make their own decisions in the course of play, then they would be consistent with their coach's orientation and, thus, could be as effective as the first team. As this example suggests, the ability of differing organizations to achieve similar ends depends on the subsystems and their processes being consistent with each other and with the task environments.

As another example, China and the United States are both competitive in international sport competitions. Yet the two countries differ in many ways, including their process of identifying and grooming athletes. The two systems have different economic resources, adopt different processes, and yet arrive at the same point of international supremacy in athletics.

Similarly, two National Hockey League teams (or two Major League Soccer teams) may differ in the number and type of segregated subsystems and the

sidebar 3.3

DRESS CODES AND EQUIFINALITY

Consider school policies on dress code. Various groups of stakeholders may support a dress code based on their personal values and beliefs that may differ drastically from one another. A conservative group may prefer uniforms for school students because they value discipline and because they believe that such a code will help foster that discipline. In contrast, a more liberal group may prefer uniforms for students because they value equality and believe that a uniform evens out the playing field between the rich and the poor. Without it, some students may flaunt their wealth by wearing expensive clothes that other students cannot afford.

For a different reason, France passed a law in 2004 banning conspicuous religious symbols in its public primary and secondary schools. This ban was enacted to maintain secularity and the separation of state and religious activities. The law caused considerable furor at that time because many observers thought that the law was aimed at Muslim schoolgirls who wore a *khimar* or *hijab* (a head scarf) as part of their religious tradition. For yet another reason, the Whithall School Board in Ohio banned sleeveless shirts and baggy shirts and pants (DeMartini, 2008). The reason for the ban was the fear that a student could hide a gun in such an outfit. That is, the school systems in France and the United States began with different reasons (secularity and safety, respectively) but ended with the same decision to ban certain types of clothing.

All these examples show that different groups with different values, beliefs, and fears may come to the same conclusion on the need for a code of dress in schools. That is an illustration of *equifinality* in systems thinking.

extent and character of the rules they have instituted. Yet they may both be successful or unsuccessful.

Multifinality is "the idea that similar initial conditions can lead to different final states" (Roth, 2002, p. 14). For example, most universities structure their intercollegiate athletic departments in similar ways and institute similar processes to achieve their objectives. They are also governed by the rules and regulations of a common umbrella organization, the NCAA. Despite such similarities, not all athletic departments achieve their objectives. In fact, a particular university athletic department may not perform at the same level from year to year. This phenomenon of multifinality is found in other spheres of the sport industry such as recreation units, fitness clubs, professional franchises, and so forth.

In sum, the concepts of equifinality and multifinality simply mean that "managers must reject the 'one right way' concept because there are several ways in which an organization can succeed, just as there are several ways that lead to failure" (Reeves et al., 2003, p. 41). Each organization is unique; what is important is to ensure that the subsystems and their processes are consistent with each other and with the task requirements.

IN brief

Organizations tend to avoid decline by self-regulating their subsystems, creating specialized units, and instituting rules and regulations. Organizations with different resources and processes can achieve the same ends if the resources and processes are consistent with each other.

ORGANIZATIONS AS SYSTEMS OF INPUTS–THROUGHPUTS–OUTPUTS AND FEEDBACK

We noted earlier that an open system is in an exchange relationship with its environment. The system receives the necessary inputs (the resources) from the environment and processes these inputs into certain outputs (the finished products) for the benefit of the environment. These relationships were highlighted by Clegg, Kornberger, and Pitsis (2005) when they defined a system as involving "a stable set of relationships between inputs, transformation processes, and outputs. Outputs often have a feedback function on processes" (p. 504).

A conceptualization of a system consisting of **inputs**, **throughputs**, and **outputs** and two feedback loops is illustrated in Exhibit 3.2.

Inputs

The inputs or resources that flow into a system are many and varied. First, the organization needs material resources in the form of money, facilities, equipment, and supplies. Human resources in the form of professional and nonprofessional employees are also needed. The personal characteristics of those individuals coming into the organization define, to a large extent, the nature of an organization and set the tone for its operations. Although departments of sport management in neighboring universities may have identical goals and structures, the way they operate may vary because their professors and students (the inputs) may differ in many respects.

Although the organization actively secures the needed resources, the environment also imposes some demands and expectations on the organization. Societal values, norms, and expectations constrain the organization to operate in specific ways. For example, individual needs and desires are paramount in North American society, whereas group requirements override individual requirements in Japanese society. Accordingly, the structures of organizations and their managerial processes are different in the two cultures.

Throughputs

The throughputs in a system are all the processes instituted by the organization to convert or transform the inputs/resources into desirable outputs such as goods or services. The processes of planning, organizing, leading, and evaluating these processes (to be discussed in greater detail in later chapters) form part of the throughput. The specification of the means and ways of carrying out the organi-

exhibit 3.2 Input–throughput–output conceptualization of a system.

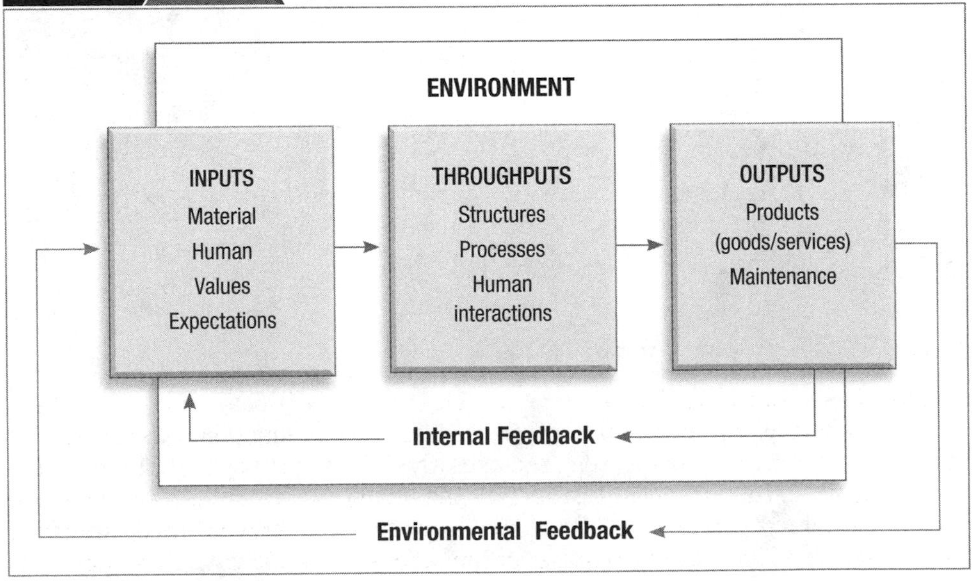

zation's production activities, the structure of authority and control, and the system of rewards within the organization are significant facets of throughput. The essence of good management is to make these throughput processes congruent with the attitudes, beliefs, skills, role orientations, and group affiliations of the employees in the organization. The processes employed by golf or fitness clubs would need to take into account the expertise of the employees, preferences of the clients, legal requirements, and societal expectations.

Outputs

The outputs of an organization can be neatly divided into product outputs and maintenance outputs. The products may be goods, as in sporting goods produced by a manufacturing firm, and/or services. (See Chapter 1 for a description of various types of sport services.) The outputs (products) of an organization should be acceptable to the environment. Milstein and Belasco (1973) emphasized this when they pointed out that "the system is as dependent upon environmental acceptance of its outputs or products as it is upon environmental resource inputs. In fact, the relationship between the two dependencies—resource needs and output acceptance—is direct, the one affecting the other, with systems thruput processes being the intervening variables" (p. 81).

Thus, a municipal recreation department can get the necessary resources (inputs) from the community only if its recreation services (outputs) are desired and consumed by the public. For example, the department will be able to get council approval for the construction of a new roller hockey rink only if there is a demand for it. As another example, an athletic department can get donations and public support only if it is run efficiently according to the educational goals of the university, and if it has a winning tradition in selected sports. To get the resources it needs it must satisfy the needs and expectations of the local community.

Apart from producing goods and services, the organization is also concerned with its own survival and growth. Therefore, the satisfaction of the employees and the ability of the organization and its members to cope with and adapt to external influences are critical to the maintenance of the organization, its growth, and its viability. When a fitness club institutes new technology and trains its employees in that technology, it is adapting to external influences.

Employee satisfaction is even more critical to sport organizations that concentrate on providing one sport service or another. Studies have shown that the extent of employee satisfaction is reflected in customer-perceived quality of services. If the aerobics instructors or the fitness leaders are dissatisfied with their work, their supervisors, or their club, such dissatisfaction will be reflected in how they deliver the service and how they treat the organization's clients. These aspects constitute what can be referred to as *maintenance* outputs. These maintenance outputs of an organization are as critical as the actual products of the organization.

Feedback

As Exhibit 3.2 illustrates, the system contains two feedback loops. One of these is internal to the organization; the other channel connects the organization to the environment. Organizational feedback provides an indication of the degree to which the organization has achieved or is achieving its objectives. Any shortfall in the attainment of objectives, as well as deviations from the originally specified patterns of operation, would require modifications in the inputs or throughputs.

One of the concerns of the director of a city recreation department is the efficient operation of the areas under his jurisdiction. Periodic inspections and reports provide the feedback that becomes the basis for corrective action.

The second feedback loop helps keep the organizational products (the outputs) in tune with the environmental needs. The acceptability of organizational products is contingent upon both the quality of the product and the needs of the environment. As the needs of the environment change, so must the organizational outputs. For example, at one time, institutions offering degree programs in physical education emphasized teacher training because of the great demand for physical education teachers. Environmental needs changed, however. Thus, the content and structure of many of these institutions also changed. Now, these institutions have diversified their programs under different names that include exercise physiology, sport and exercise psychology, sport sociology, sport management, and other specializations. The growth of educational programs in sport management shows one way that universities adapt to environmental needs.

Another important feature of this environmental feedback loop is that it also provides information on the sources for needed inputs and the means to those sources. If an organization is not actively seeking information about its boundary conditions and adapting to changes in its environment, it may not be able to dispense its products and, in turn, will fail to secure resources. Thus, the boundary-spanning activity becomes critical to the organization. For example, the success of the city recreation department lies in its ability to recruit volunteer and part-time help to oversee its various programs. Success also depends upon the department's continued search for information relating to the likes and dislikes of the public with respect to the programs offered. Thus, the director of the recreation department and specified individuals within it must be in constant touch with the community.

IN brief

From a systems perspective, organizations receive resources from society (input) and convert those resources (throughput) into products for the society (output).

THE SYSTEMS APPROACH IN OVERVIEW

A systems view of organizations is extremely useful for portraying the social, cultural, and economic forces that impinge upon the organization; the people and the interplay of their personal characteristics; the internal processes of authority, control, and task activities; and the dynamic interactions among all these variables. On the other hand, a systems view is also exceedingly complex. Because there are a number of variables in a system and their interactions are diverse, a systems approach does not permit detailed specifications for the optimal relationships among these variables. Neither does it suggest a managerial approach to a given configuration of system variables.

> In systems theory, or systems thinking, a system is merely a way of thinking about, or understanding, any dynamic process, whether the dynamic process is riding a bicycle, or a process, or an organization, or a job, or a machine, or any other entity we care to think of which involves a dynamic process. (Cusins, 1994, p. 19)

The systems approach *does* provide a framework for the analysis of an organization or a subsystem within it. The manager must first define the boundaries of the system of interest by including the relevant elements and identifying the forces in the task environment. The throughput processes within the system also must be clearly spelled out. Next, any inconsistencies must be identified with a view to correcting the problem or improving the performance of the unit. When any action is taken, the effect of such action on other subsystems and on the whole system must be examined. Bowman and Jarrett (1996) note that "[the systems view] of what is an organization is comprehensive, sufficiently inclusive and robust as a test of reality. It covers the rational, emotional and political aspects of organizational life yet provides a baseline to explore organizational relationships in a systematic and organized manner, without losing some of the complexity" (p. 7).

Thus, a systems approach emphasizes the gestalt, or total, view of the organization while at the same time providing opportunities to focus on well-defined subsystems for the purposes of analysis and action. Accordingly, we will refer to the systems approach in discussing the managerial processes in subsequent chapters.

ENVIRONMENTAL INFLUENCES ON ORGANIZATIONS

In discussing the systems theory, we placed a great emphasis on the notion of the environment in which an organization is embedded. We noted that the environment consists of both internal and external segments. The internal environment includes the goals, structures, and processes of the organization; the employees; and the leaders and supervisors. The external environment consists of suppliers, clients or customers, other organizations competing for the resources or to sell their products, government agencies, political groups, social activists, and so forth. The importance and impact of the organizational environment has led to the articulation of three different theoretical frameworks for understanding environmental dynamics. They are (1) stakeholder theory, (2) institutional theory, and (3) resource dependence theory.

Stakeholder Theory

Several factors, such as economic and technological components, have been described as part of an organization's environment. These factors are largely inanimate in the sense that they refer to organizations and political, social, or legal systems. Bearing in mind that these systems are created and directed by people, we can look at an organization's environment in such a way as to include various groups of stakeholders. The term *stakeholder* is derived from the word *stake*. Stakes are used to mark off a field or territory to be claimed, and hence the usage of the phrase "to stake a claim." In the context of organizations and their management, *stakeholders* are the "persons or groups that have or claim ownership, rights, or interests in a corporation and its activities, past, present, or future" (Clarkson, 1995, p. 106). Freeman (1984) defines a stakeholder as "any group or individual who can affect or is affected by the achievement of the organization's objectives" (p. 46).

Clarkson (1995) notes that stakeholder rights and interests stem from stakeholders' interactions with the focal organization. For instance, the police who are involved in directing the traffic for a professional sport competition have a stake in how and when the franchise schedules its competitions. Those groups affected by the organization's actions can also be considered stakeholders.

Classifications of stakeholders

Stakeholders can be individuals or groups of people who share similar interests, claims, or rights. Such groups might be composed of the athletes, the coaches, the spectators, the media, the alumni, or the employees of the athletic department. We

sidebar 3.4

EXPANDING VIEW OF STAKEHOLDER MANAGEMENT

In the past, the discussion regarding stakeholders has focused on how managers of an organization should manage the relationships between the organization and its stakeholders. In that line of thinking, an organization's activities would demark the organization's stakeholders. Typically, the stakeholder groups would include the workers, the buyers of organization's products (customers/clients), the suppliers of finished or raw materials that facilitate the organization's activities, other organizations in a locality or in the industry, and so on. In sum, the organization is at the center of the network of stakeholder groups, and its activities define its stakeholders. That is, those who could affect the activities of the organization and/or who could be affected by organizational activities would be legitimate stakeholders.

However, a new line of thinking has emerged that views the organization as being caught up in issues unrelated to organizational activities yet compelled to act or react to solve those issues (Roloff, 2008). In this view, the organization is part of a larger network of organizations and the stakeholders are seen as those associated with all of those organizations. For example, the NCAA's activities would clearly show that all the intercollegiate athletic departments would be the organization's primary stakeholders. In addition, the activities associated with organizing tournaments (e.g., the March Madness basketball championships) would bring in the media companies, the sponsors, the donors, and the fans as stakeholders. Rarely would the NCAA be interacting with the governor of a state. But an issue could arise in which both the NCAA and a state government could become stakeholders of each other. A case in point is the NCAA sanctions against Penn State University in the aftermath of the Jerry Sandusky scandal. The sanctions included a fine of $60 million, a four-year post-season ban, a reduction in the number of scholarship players, and a probation period of five years (Yanda, 2012). Most readers will remember that these penalties were imposed on Penn State not because of any violations by the Penn State athletic department, its coaches, or its players, but because a former employee of the athletic department had sexually abused young boys on the premises of the athletic department. The authorities of Penn State, including the legendary football coach Joe Paterno, knew of Sandusky's behavior but tried to sweep it under the rug. The public outcry over the affair was such that the NCAA felt compelled to impose strict penalties. In January 2013, the governor of Pennsylvania filed a lawsuit against the NCAA saying that the sanctions were hurting the people and the state of Pennsylvania (Tully, 2013). In suing the NCAA, Governor Tom Corbett of Pennsylvania noted that Sandusky's case involved criminal activity and should be settled in court. Thus, the state's government and its citizens became stakeholders of the NCAA, although in an adversarial capacity. As commentators take differing positions on the NCAA actions, they also become stakeholders.

Another example is Hank Williams, Jr., who in 2011 made disparaging remarks on Fox News about U.S. government leaders. ESPN is not affiliated with either Fox News or the U.S. government, yet it became a critical stakeholder in the issue because at that time Williams sang the theme song for ESPN's *Monday Night Football*. In reaction to Williams's comments, ESPN rescinded its contract with the singer (ESPN, 2011). A third example is the case of People for the Ethical Treatment of Animals (PETA) and the NFL Atlanta Falcons. These two organizations had nothing in common, yet in late July 2007 PETA suddenly became a significant stakeholder of the Falcons when nearly 50 PETA members protested in front of the team's headquarters. The protest was triggered by the charges brought against Falcons quarterback Michael Vick for dog fighting. This incident is an example of how unrelated activities (dog fighting and football) and unrelated organizations (PETA and the Atlanta Falcons) can be brought together in a protest situation. The Atlanta Falcons organization was forced to respond to the protest, even though it was sparked by an activity unrelated to football that was undertaken by a team member on his own time. It is unclear if the protest and response would have been comparable if the player in question was not the star quarterback.

Clarkson (1995) notes that the interests of some stakeholders may be strictly moral. In the cases of Hank Williams, Jr. and Michael Vick, many divergent groups expressed a revulsion with their behavior based on moral grounds. Another example of stakeholders reacting on moral grounds is the groups who have expressed concerns about sweatshop conditions under which some sports products are made. The foregoing examples show clearly that sport organizations must be prepared to satisfy the preferences and alleviate the concerns of stakeholders that may emerge during unforeseen events that are not part of routine operations.

can identify similar groups of stakeholders in any sport organization—for example, the shareholders and player agents in the case of a professional sport franchise, or community organizations and taxpayer groups in the case of a city recreation department. These various stakeholders can be classified as voluntary and involuntary, primary and secondary, and demand-side and supply-side stakeholders.

Voluntary and involuntary stakeholders. The previous example of the Atlanta Falcons and PETA, whose various stakeholders reacted to an action by an organization, illustrates the distinction between *voluntary* and *involuntary* stakeholders. The players, the media personnel, the coaches, and the team themselves are in close proximity, and they have a direct stake in the operation of the organization. In contrast, the politicians and social activists who reacted to Vick's case do not have any close association with the Atlanta Falcons. Thus, the former set are **voluntary stakeholders** who create and distribute the products of the Atlanta Falcons. The latter groups are **involuntary stakeholders** who are indirectly and unwittingly involved with the organization's results (Clarkson, 1995).

The distinction between voluntary and involuntary stakeholder is best illustrated by the case of a professional sport franchise moving to a new city. The players and other employees would have to go through the troubles of moving to a new location. But because they are voluntary members of the franchise, they are voluntary stakeholders. On the other hand, consider the residents living where the new stadium is to be built. Some people will likely be displaced from their homes; even those who are not displaced will be inconvenienced in terms of increased traffic, noise, and other nuisances. These people, then, become involuntary stakeholders. As another example, consider a riot breaking out after a home team loses that causes significant damage to university property. The fans also may suffer loss of property or bodily injuries, and students and faculty may also suffer from the university's tarnished reputation. But these groups are voluntary stakeholders in the sense that they wanted to be part of the organization and its proceedings. In addition, they stand to gain from the athletic department and the performance of its teams. In contrast, the homeowners outside the university grounds who suffer damage or injury may not be fans of the team or students or faculty of the university. Such groups are labeled involuntary stakeholders because they tend to be affected by whatever happens in the organizational context despite not having chosen the association.

Primary and secondary stakeholder groups. According to Clarkson (1995), stakeholders can also be classified as primary and secondary stakeholders based on the contributions they make to the survival and growth of the organization. A **primary stakeholder** is one "without whose continuing participation the corporation cannot survive as a going concern" (Clarkson, 1995, p. 106). For instance, the players of a professional sport league are a primary stakeholder group because the league cannot exist without their participation. By the same token, the employees and coaches of a university athletic department are one of its primary stakeholder groups because the department cannot offer its programs without them. Even spectators at university football games become a significant stakeholder group if they disrupt the event with unruly behavior. The significance of spectators as a stakeholder group is very much understood by soccer leagues in Europe and South America, where violence among the crowds has disrupted many games. Similarly, the lawmakers and people of communities that provide the stadiums and arenas are primary stakeholder groups for professional sport franchises. In sum, a sport organization is very dependent on the cooperation and participation of its primary stakeholders.

Secondary stakeholder groups are those that do not directly interact with the focal organization but that can affect or be affected by it (Clarkson, 1995). We already noted that stakeholder groups had an impact on ESPN because of the comments Hank Williams, Jr. made. Several of the groups did not have any direct transactions with ESPN, yet they were able to mobilize public opinion against the network and thereby influence its decisions. Similarly, citizen groups that complain about student behavior on their streets after a football game are not directly involved with the athletic department. From this perspective they are not primary stakeholders, and yet their influence is great enough for the department and the university to take actions to address their concerns. Thus, they constitute a secondary stakeholder group. From a different perspective, Donaldson and Preston (1995) note that "stakeholders are identified by their interest in the corporation and not necessarily by whether the corporation has any corresponding functional interest in the stakeholders." These authors also note that an organization must be concerned with and learn to manage all stakeholder groups because the interests of these groups have merit.

IN brief

Persons and groups that have an interest or a right in an organization are labeled its stakeholders. Primary stakeholders are those whose participation is necessary for the growth and survival of the organization. Secondary stakeholders do not directly interact with the organization but do have an influence on it.

Demand-side and supply-side stakeholders. Ben-Ner and Gui (1993) provided yet another classification of stakeholders. Referring to nonprofit organizations, they made a distinction between demand-side stakeholders and supply-side stakeholders. **Demand-side stakeholders** include all those who consume the products of an organization. The payment for these products may be from the consumers themselves, as in the case of members of a local YMCA paying for the use of the weight room or the services of a yoga instructor. The payment could also be made by a sponsor, as in the case of a local business sponsoring a youth sports camp.

The **supply-side stakeholders** are all those individuals, groups, or organizations that facilitate the production and distribution of the focal organization's products. The volunteer coaches and officials of a youth sport league are supply-side stakeholders. The municipal council financing the recreation department and the school district subsidizing athletic programs would also be supply-side stakeholders. In the case of USA Diving, the national governing body for the sport of diving, the divers would be the demand-side stakeholders, and the supply-side stakeholders would be the coaches, trainers, scientists, and the pool staff who provide the necessary service for the divers.

Managing stakeholders

The concept of an organization with multiple constituencies has been in vogue for several decades. However, the emphasis on management of stakeholders is newer. An important component of effective stakeholder management is to gain a clear understanding of stakeholder perceptions and preferences.

In intercollegiate athletics, the values and preferences of specific stakeholder groups, such as students, student-athletes, alumni, faculty and athletic program employees, media, the community, and local businesses, have been the focus of several investigations (see Putler & Wolfe, 1999; Trail & Chelladurai, 2000; Wolfe & Putler, 2002). Putler and Wolfe investigated the perceptions of six different stakeholders of intercollegiate athletics: students, prospective students, student-athletes, alumni, faculty, and athletic program employees. They found that members of these stakeholder groups fell into four distinct groups with unique priorities: athletic program revenue, winning, education, and ethics. Interestingly, the degree to which the respondents endorsed these priorities did not parallel their membership in the stakeholder groups. This means that members within a single stakeholder group may differ widely in the priorities they place on organizational goals and processes.

Trail and Chelladurai (2000) investigated the extent to which two stakeholder groups of intercollegiate athletics (faculty and students) differed in the importance they attached to 10 selected goals and their approval of 11 selected processes within intercollegiate athletics. The researchers found that the subgroups as defined by faculty—student status and gender—differed significantly in the relative importance they placed on various intercollegiate athletic goals, as well as in their approval of the different processes of intercollegiate athletics. (These goals and processes are further explained in Chapter 5, in which we examine the concept of organizational goals.) All subgroups were congruent in rating development goals (that is, those focused on development of athletes) as more important than performance goals (those focused on winning and generating revenue). Similarly, the groups endorsed developmental processes at a higher level than performance processes. Notably, the females of the study were more concerned with the process of creating gender equality and the goal of a diverse culture.

Salience of stakeholders

It is one thing to identify stakeholders and categorize them as voluntary or involuntary, primary or secondary, and demand-side or supply-side. But it is different and more difficult to rank them in terms of their salience or criticalness to the organization. For instance, a fitness club depends on the managers who maintain the facility and equipment as well as the personal trainers and group activity leaders who provide the services for the clients. Both groups are easily categorized as either primary or voluntary stakeholders. But which one of the two groups is more critical to the club than the other? That is, how does an organization with several stakeholder groups with varying interests, demands, and expectations decide whose interests or demands are critical to the organization? In other words, how does one decide on the relative *salience* of the various stakeholders? Mitchell, Agle, and Wood (1997) noted that the stakeholders can be distinguished on the basis of three significant attributes—power, legitimacy, and urgency.

Power. Stakeholders may differ in the power they hold over the focal organization, which reflects their capacity to influence the organization. For example, contributors of large donations may have greater influence over an athletic department than those who contribute smaller amounts. Because media controls the avenues of publicity (both positive and negative) for the institution, the media personnel possess greater power over the athletic department than does an alumni or fan club in a neighboring small town.

Legitimacy. The legitimacy of a stakeholder is based on contractual or legal obligations, as well as moral interests in the harms and benefits that an organization creates (Mitchell et al., 1997). Thus, every entity that has a business contract with the athletic department (e.g., the contract to sell one brand of beverage in the stadium) has legitimacy of the claims that the contract permits. As another example, the claims of student-athletes for academic support from the athletic department will be far more legitimate than such claims from the general student body. Recall the concept of prime beneficiary. That is, every organization exists primarily for the benefit of a particular group. In the present case, the athletes are the prime beneficiaries; therefore, their claims on the athletic department are more legitimate than are those of other students. Similarly, the concern of a parent of a youth soccer player about the safety of her child is a legitimate concern and thus is more salient than a parent's expectation that the child play all the time.

Apart from legal titles and rights and contractual obligations, legitimacy may also stem from moral grounds and value-based beliefs. For example, every university athletic department takes extraordinary measures to control crowd behavior within and outside of the university boundaries. The concern with what happens outside its own boundaries is based more on moral grounds than on any legal or contractual obligations. By the same token, the university's neighboring residents do have a legitimate claim that the university safeguard their persons and property.

Urgency. Urgency refers to the speed with which a claim by a stakeholder group should be attended to. Consider the athletes involved in a competition and the spectators watching the contest. Consider also the athletic trainers and the medical staff on the sidelines. The athletes' claims on the services of these medical staff are far more legitimate than those of any of the spectators. Yet, if a spectator shows symptoms of a heart attack, the medical staff would certainly jump into action and drop their work on an athlete's minor injury to help the spectator. That is the notion of urgency: it implies that the claims of some stakeholders may be more pressing than those of others, irrespective of their power or legitimacy.

Another simple example concerns an event manager approached by Coach A and Coach B with demands on how their events should be managed. Coach A's event is two months away and Coach B's event is two weeks away, so urgency dictates that the event manager will attend to Coach B's demand before resolving Coach A's concerns. Or, a minor league baseball team has planned pre-game activities for a Saturday game. But a prominent member of the community and a supporter of the club dies of cancer two days beforehand. The club may drop its original plans and replace them with an activity to honor the departed and promote cancer awareness. The death of a prominent citizen and stakeholder in this case is an urgency that necessitates changes in other stakeholders' plans.

Mitchell and colleagues (1997) hold that power and legitimacy are the core attributes that can be used to identify a stakeholder group. They also note that stakeholder power to influence the organization may or may not be legitimate and that the impact of power or legitimacy is a function of the urgency of the claims of a stakeholder group.

An important point Mitchell and colleagues (1997) make is that power, legitimacy, and urgency are not mutually exclusive. Instead, they interact with each other. A powerful stakeholder may have an urgent and at the same time legitimate claim. For instance, let us assume that a television network has a legal contract with a university athletic department to televise its football games, with a stipulation that the network has the final say in the starting time of the game on a given day. Let us also assume that the network approaches the athletic department just a week before a game with a request to change the starting time of the game because of its own scheduling problems. The television network is a powerful stakeholder because it helps the athletic department generate revenue. The claim is also legitimate, because it is within the limits of the contract. In addition, the claim has urgency, because the network has to know the response immediately so that it can proceed with other arrangements.

Institutional Theory

Institutional theory may be seen as another extension of systems theory. The basic premise of institutional theory is that just as individuals try to respond to significant others and behave in ways that are consistent with the orientations and expectations of significant others, organizations also seek legitimacy or approval from their respective environments. That is, institutional theory postulates that every organization is influenced by the institution of similar organizations and by its social system (Scott & Meyer, 1994). An organization gains the legitimacy it seeks by strong association with similar other organizations and by adopting structures and processes similar to those of other organizations. For example, the legitimacy of a fitness club is enhanced when it becomes a member of the International Health, Racquet & Sports Club Association (IHRSA); accepts the mission of the association; and abides by the association's code of conduct. Frequent interactions with other fitness clubs and other agencies promoting fitness (e.g., an exercise physiology lab in a university setting) would further the legitimacy of the fitness club.

Institutional isomorphism

A significant corollary of institutional theory is that an organization tends to imitate other organizations in the same institutional sphere. For example, a university athletic department is likely to be very similar to other athletic departments in the same conference in terms of the mission and values it espouses, the structures and processes it adopts, the kinds of services it offers, and its interactions with external agents. The process of organizations becoming similar to each other is called **institutional isomorphism** (DiMaggio & Powell, 1983, 1991; Scott, 2001). DiMaggio and Powell (1983) suggested that three different forces may lead to institutional isomorphism—coercive, mimetic, and normative isomorphism.

Coercive isomorphism. **Coercive isomorphism** occurs when external political and social influences direct organizations to behave in similar ways. For instance, the governments in many countries provide a large portion of the budgets of their respective national sport-governing bodies. In conjunction with the financial support, the governments stipulate that the sport-governing bodies adopt specific structures and processes. When these organizations do this, they become isomorphic (alike). This is the effect of the coercion of the government through its funding procedures (see, e.g., Silk & Amis, 2000; Slack & Hinings, 1994). In the American context, the NCAA as the apex body of the intercollegiate athletic network imposes certain demands and constraints on all member institutions. Consider all the rules and regulations concerning critical operations in athletics such as recruitment, number of practices and games, number of scholarships, and academic requirements. These rules cause member athletic departments to become similar in orientation as well as operations.

Mimetic isomorphism. A second force that may be operative is **mimetic isomorphism.** As noted, organizations may imitate other organizations in their quest for legitimacy and support from their environments. Sport teams are famous for copying the strategies and tactics of other, successful teams. Intercollegiate ath-

sidebar 3.5

GOVERNMENT AND SPORT

A major player in the general environment of any organization is the government itself either at the federal level or at the state level or at both levels. Just like any other organization, a sport organization is recognized by the government and is expected to abide by government rules and regulations. Further, sport has become one of the most globalized entities in the world, and sport competitions at the international level are seen as the platforms for nations to showcase the superiority of their respective athletes, their systems of governance of sport, and their processes of grooming athletic talent. Consequently, national governments have taken an ever increasing interest in the promotion of sport and the governance of sporting operations.

Any organization from any industry in any country exists as a social mechanism recognized by the government of the country, which requires every organization to be registered and to follow existing laws, rules, and regulations. Beyond this basic and necessary condition, governments may support certain organizations or industries because their products (goods or services) are critical to the welfare of the society as a whole. For example, several governments including the U.S. government and the European Union provide agricultural subsidies to ensure that certain crops are readily available to the people in the country.

Along similar lines of thinking, governments do support sport organizations in order to promote participation in sport and physical activity and to produce excellent athletes who can compete in international competitions. Extensive sport participation is expected to contribute to the health of the participants while excellent athletes bring glory to the country and a sense of pride among people.

Involvement of various governments in sport can be charted along four dimensions: (1) regulation of the sport governing organizations, (2) financial support to sport organizations, (3) engagement in the governance of sport, and (4) identification and development of talent.

Regulation of Sport Governing Organizations

While, as noted, every organization has to be approved and registered by the government, sport-governing organizations present a special case because (a) they perform state-like functions such as representing the country in international forums, (b) they use the name of the country in their own names (e.g., USA Volleyball; Skate Canada), and (c) they select and field the teams in the name of the country. Hence, one can argue that the government has a vital interest in ensuring these national sport organizations are run properly.

In the United States, the United States Olympic Committee (USOC) is chartered by the Ted Stevens Olympic and Amateur Sports Act under Title 36 of the United States Code. The federal government has also specified the goals and purposes for USOC and its rights and powers. More specifically, the USOC is granted exclusive jurisdiction over the representation of the nation in the Olympic Games and the use of the words *Olympic* and *Olympiad* and the motto *Citius Altius Fortius* and any other combination or simulation of these protected words. In addition, the President's Council on Fitness, Sports & Nutrition promotes programs and initiatives that motivate people of all ages, backgrounds, and abilities to lead active, healthy lives. In 2009, President Obama established the White House Office of Olympic, Paralympic and Youth Sport to promote the Olympic Movement and its principles and to encourage increased youth participation in athletics. Also noteworthy is the unit named SportsUnited under the Bureau of Educational and Cultural Affairs within the United States Department of State. It engages in sport diplomacy to bring together people of diverse cultures building on the universal passion for sport. Apart from these general oversight influences, the U.S. government refrains from interfering in the affairs of USOC or any other sport organization.

In contrast, the Chinese government at all levels controls China's sport organizations and their operations (Ko, Xie, & Kimura, 2012). Currently, the State General Administration of Sports (SGAS) is the government unit that oversees sports in the country. This government unit is closely linked with the Chinese Olympic Committee and the All-China Sports Federation. More germane to the present discussion, the SGAS is heavily involved in the management of national sport events and international sport events held in China, promoting participation in sport and physical activity, implementing government regulations related to sport industry and sport businesses, and other matters of national importance. Most other countries fall within the two extremes of the United States and China.

Government involvement among Western countries in promoting and governing sport is highest in France (Camy, 2004).

According to Camy, France holds the view that star athletes are the representatives of the nation and, therefore, they need the support of the nation and its government. In line with this perspective, the French government has enacted a law to bring sport within its purview and has enacted several other laws to promote and regulate sport within its borders. Furthermore, the Ministry of Sports employs 6,000 civil servants, of whom 1,600 are assigned to work for the governing bodies of various sports. As another example, Venezuela's government provides support, leadership, and direction for national sport. The governments of Canada, the United Kingdom, and Australia do get involved in sport but not to the same extent as the government of France. They limit their involvement to providing funds to sport-governing bodies for specific projects and refrain from managing the organizations or embedding government employees in them, as is done in France.

Financial Support to Sport-Governing Organizations

Most governments, with the notable exception of the U.S. government, spend considerable tax dollars to support national sport governing organizations and other sport and fitness organizations that operate nationally. For instance, Sport Canada, a unit of the Canadian government concerned with sport, allocated nearly C$199 million during the budget year 2011–2012 to 106 organizations, which included provincial government units that deal with sport in their respective provinces. Much poorer nations may not be able to match in dollar terms the support by Sport Canada; however, countries like Australia, France, Germany, and Great Britain have been promulgating policies to support the promotion of sport and have also funded their sport organizations as heavily as Canada.

Identification and Development of Talent

Another way governments get involved in sport is to engage directly in the identification and development of sporting talent. In the United States, the task of identifying and developing talent is largely in the hands of educational institutions. No country in the world comes even close to the extent and intensity of scholastic and collegiate competitions found in the United States. In addition, private enterprises handle the development of talent in some individual sports like tennis. The government, however, refrains from engaging in any activities associated with talent development.

In contrast, China is well known for its government-run sports schools. Its estimated 3,000 sports schools train about 400,000 youth in various sports. The system of sports schools was originally instituted in the former Union of Soviet Socialist Republics (USSR). Several other countries attempt to emulate the system of sports schools but have not been as successful as the Chinese in producing medal-winning athletes. Other governments, such as Canada and Great Britain, support and finance the establishment of sports centers where high-level athletes practice for international competitions. At the moment, Canada has seven Canadian Sport Centers spread throughout the country. These were created by Sport Canada in partnership with Canadian Olympic Committee, the Coaching Association of Canada (a government sponsored unit), and the provincial governments. The Canadian amateur sport system gets the largest investment from Sport Canada through its programs, including the Hosting Program, the Sport Support Program, and the Athlete Assistance Program (Canadian Heritage, 2013). Many other nations follow the patterns of Australia, Canada, and Great Britain.

letic departments adopt the managerial and marketing practices of other athletic departments in order to legitimize their own operations and gain support from their own stakeholders. Also, when an organization is not certain about its actions and its future, it is likely to imitate others to reduce the uncertainty. Consider, for example, the colors of automobiles produced by different companies. If five colors are available in a given year for a given make, it is likely that you will find different shades of the same five colors in other makes, too. Because every manufacturer is not sure which colors will gain popularity among consumers, they all avoid the risk due to uncertainty by picking shades of the same colors.

Normative isomorphism. The third force is **normative isomorphism**, in the sense that all organizations behave similarly because of the value and belief systems of decision makers. It is likely that the decision makers or managers have been trained and educated in institutions advocating similar business strategies and tactics. For example, the MBA programs of most universities teach very similar curricula and the students are exposed to similar textbooks. Despite the disparity in reputation of universities, graduating MBAs across the nation (indeed around the world) are likely to have cultivated very similar value and belief systems regarding what and how things should be done. This similarity in values and beliefs will be reflected in the structures and processes the graduates institute in their respective organizations. This is also the case with sport management graduates, who tend to be exposed to similar curricula and literature. External agencies, such as the professional associations, may advocate similar professional practices, which are likely to be adopted across many organizations. Furthermore, managers tend to be transferred from one organization to another, and they are likely to carry their previous practices, experience, and knowledge with them to their new institutions.

In the context of sport organizations, Danylchuk and Chelladurai (1999) found that the intercollegiate athletic departments in Canada tended to become similar in structural and procedural properties. They attributed this tendency to institutional forces as outlined above. Silk and Amis (2000) have shown that telecasts of sporting events in different countries (e.g., Indonesia) are subjected to institutional pressure to conform to production practices elsewhere. In contrast, Cunningham and Ashley (2001) found considerable variation in the structural properties of the NCAA athletic programs. They concluded that environmental pressures may not be as dominant as suggested by institutional theory. In other words, their results support the notion of equifinality discussed earlier.

The third theoretical framework for articulating environmental influences on organizations is resource dependence theory.

Resource Dependence Theory

Recall that the systems view of organizations holds that the organization is in an exchange relationship with its environment. In other words, the system imports its resources from the environment and exports its outputs to the environment. The notion that an organization is dependent on other entities in its environment for its resources is the basis of *resource dependence theory*. The basic thrust of the theory is that because the organization depends on other entities in the environment for its resources (e.g., land, labor, capital, information), those entities gain power over the focal organization (Knoke, 2001). For example, the broadcast media is a major source for publicity for a university athletic department and is a conduit for information from the department to the public. Hence, the broadcast media has some power over the athletic department. Or, consider the collective bargaining agreement negotiations that occurred with both the NFL and NBA in 2011. Because the two leagues depend on the players as the major component of their business, the players have power over the league such that they are able to effectively negotiate more favorable contracts. A city recreation department is beholden to the elected politicians because those politicians influence the budget allocations to the department.

sidebar 3.6

RESOURCE IMBALANCE

"A fundamental exchange principle is that actor A becomes dependent on actor B to the extent B controls a resource or behavior highly valued by A, which A can neither do without nor obtain elsewhere. Hence to acquire that vital resource, A must comply with the exchange conditions that B imposes, particularly by paying whatever price B demands. In any exchange relationship, A's dependence is inverse to B's power: the more A depends on B for an essential resource, the greater is B's power to control A's actions. These basic resource imbalance principles apply to social exchanges across many levels of analysis, ranging from small work groups to giant international corporations to national governments" (Knoke, 2001, pp. 54–55).

The power differential between two organizations is conditioned by (a) the importance of a resource to an organization, (b) control by another party (i.e., other organization or group) over the resource, and (c) a lack of other alternatives for securing that resource (Knoke, 2001). Given the above, it follows that the dependence relationship between any two organizations is fluid and can change with alterations in one or more of the conditions listed above. For instance, the dependence of professional sport organizations on traditional media for publicity has changed with the advent of social media. Teams as well as individual players can promote themselves through social networking sites, microblogs, blogs, content-sharing sites, and so forth. In a similar manner, a sports club can depend on local businesses and its municipality for its resources (i.e., finances and facilities), but this can change if a wealthy person bequeaths a large sum of money to the club.

The significance of stakeholder influence and management of stakeholders will be illustrated at various points in the following chapters.

SUMMARY

In this chapter, we described an organization as an open system—that is, a set of interrelated parts making up an integrated whole. After defining the concept of a system, we looked at the concepts of subsystems and their boundaries, and we related the concepts to an organization. We described in detail the types and significant elements of the environment of a system or an organization. We discussed the applicability of the processes of a system (negative entropy, self-regulation, progressive segregation, progressive mechanization, and equifinality and multifinality) in relation to an organization. This chapter also presented the input–throughput–output conceptualization of a system, and how the same perspective applies to organizations. We saw how the systems approach provides a framework for the analysis of an organization or its units and gives us a handy way of thinking about the organization, its units, and its processes. The final segment of the chapter dealt with environmental influences on organizations and three theories regarding an organization's relationship with its environment.

develop YOUR PERSPECTIVE

1. Choose an organization you are familiar with and identify its subsystems. Discuss the bases on which the subsystems of that organization can be defined.
2. Bearing in mind the same organization, describe it in terms of its inputs, throughputs, and outputs.
3. How would you describe the organization's environment? What elements would you include in the environment, and how would you classify those elements?
4. Explain who would be the stakeholders of the organization you have chosen, and why.
5. Identify the organizations on which a focal organization depends for its resources.
6. Explain your organization's similarities to other organizations delivering the same kind of services.

Ben-Ner, A., & Gui, B. (1993). Nonprofit organizations in the mixed economy: A demand and supply analysis. In A. Ben-Ner & B. Gui (Eds.), *The nonprofit sector in the mixed economy* (pp. 27–58). Ann Arbor: The University of Michigan Press.

Bowman, C., & Jarrett, M. G. (1996). *Management in practice: A framework for managing organizational change* (3rd ed.). Oxford, UK: Butterworth-Heinemann.

Camy, J. (2004). *Configurations of national sports systems in the E.U. countries: Their impact on training in the sports sector.* Paper presented at the 12th Congress of the European Association of Sport Management, Ghent, Belgium. September 22–25.

Canadian Heritage. (2013). Sport Canada. Retrieved from http://www.pch.gc.ca/eng/1268160670172/1268160761399.

Certo, S. C., & Certo, S. T. (2009). *Modern management: Concepts and skills* (11th ed.). Upper Saddle River, NJ: Prentice Hall.

Clarkson, M. B. E. (1995). A stakeholder framework for analyzing and evaluating corporate social performance. *Academy of Management Review, 20,* 92–117.

Clegg, S., Kornberger, M., & Pitsis, T. (2005). *Managing organizations: An introduction to theory and practice.* London: Sage.

Cunningham, G. B., & Ashley, F. B. (2001). Isomorphic tendencies in NCAA athletic departments: The use of competing theories and advancement of theory. *Sport Management Review, 4,* 47–63.

Cusins, P. (1994). Understanding quality through systems thinking. *The TQM Magazine, 6,* 19–27.

Danylchuk, K. E., & Chelladurai, P. (1999). The nature of managerial work in Canadian intercollegiate athletics. *Journal of Sport Management, 13,* 148–166.

DeMartini, A. (2008, January 11). Whitehall restricts student attire. *Columbus Dispatch,* p. 03B.

DiMaggio, P., & Powell, W. (1983). The iron cage revisited: Institutional isomorphism and collective rationality in organizational fields. *American Sociological Review, 48,* 147–160.

DiMaggio, P., & Powell, W. (1991). Introduction. In W. Powell & P. DiMaggio (Eds.), *The new institutionalism* (pp. 1–38). Chicago: University of Chicago Press.

Donaldson, T., & Preston, L. E. (1995). The stakeholder theory of the corporation: Concepts, evidence, and implications. *Academy of Management Review, 20,* 65–91.

ESPN (2011). ESPN, Hank Williams Jr. part ways. Retrieved from http://espn.go.com/nfl/story/_/id/7066449/espn-hank-williams-jr-theme-song-return-monday-night-football.

Freeman, E. R. (1984). *Strategic management: A stakeholder approach.* Marshfield, MA: Pitman.

Girls on the Run (2013). Start a council. Retrieved from http://www.girlsontherun.org/Get-Involved/Start-a-Council.

Gresov, C., & Drazin, R. (1997). Equifinality: Functional equivalence in organizational design. *Academy of Management Review, 22,* 403–428.

Hitt, M. A., Black, J. S., & Porter, L. W. (2009). *Management* (2nd ed.). Upper Saddle River, NJ: Pearson.

Immegart, G. L., & Pilecki, F. J. (1973). *An introduction to systems for the educational administrator.* Reading, MA: Addison-Wesley.

Jones, G. R. (2010). *Organizational theory, design, and change* (6th ed.). Upper Saddle River, NJ: Prentice Hall.

Katz, D., & Kahn, R. L. (1966). *The social psychology of organizations.* New York: John Wiley.

Khandwalla, P. N. (1977). *The design of organizations.* New York: Harcourt Brace Jovanovich.

Knoke, D. (2001). *Changing organizations: Business networks in the new political economy.* Boulder, CO: Westview Press.

Ko, Y. J., Xie, D., & Kimura, K. (2012). Sport in Northeast Asia. In M. Li, E. W. Macintosh, & G. A. Bravo (Eds.), *International sport management* (pp. 199–217). Champaign, IL: Human Kinetics.

Milstein, M. M., & Belasco, J. A. (1973). *Educational administration and the behavioral sciences: A systems perspective.* Boston: Allyn & Bacon.

Mitchell, R., Agle, B., & Wood, D. (1997). Toward a theory of stakeholder identification and salience: Defining the principle of who and what really counts. *Academy of Management Review,* 22(4), 853–886.

Morecroft, J., Sanchez, R., & Heene, A. (2002). Integrating systems thinking and competence concepts in a new view of resources, capabilities, and management processes. In J. Morecroft, R. Sanchez, & A. Heene (Eds.), *Systems perspectives on resources, capabilities, and management processes* (pp. 3–16). Amsterdam: Pergamon.

NCAA. (2011). Community & youth initiatives. Retrieved from www.ncaa.com/news/basketball-men/2011-01-25/ncaa-community-youth-initiatives.

Pierce, J. L., & Dunham, R. B. (1990). *Managing.* Glenview, IL: Scott Foresman/Little, Brown Higher Education.

Putler, D. S., & Wolfe, R. A. (1999). Perceptions of intercollegiate athletic programs: Priorities and tradeoffs. *Sociology of Sport Journal, 16,* 301–325.

Reeves, T. C., Duncan, W. J., & Ginter, P. M. (2003). Strategic configurations in health services organizations. *Journal of Business Research, 56*(1), 31–43.

Ritchie-Dunham, J. L., & Rabbino, H. T. (2001). *Managing from clarity: Identifying, aligning, and leveraging strategic resources.* Chichester, NY: John Wiley & Sons.

Robbins, S. P., Coulter, M., Leach, E., & Kilfoil, M. (2012). *Management* (10th ed.). Don Mills, Ontario: Pearson Canada.

Roloff, J. (2008). Learning from multi-stakeholder networks: Issue-focused stakeholder management. *Journal of Business Ethics, 82,* 233–250.

Roth, W. (2002). Business ethics: Grounded in systems thinking. *Journal of Organizational Excellence, 21*(3), 3–16.

Scott, R., & Meyer, J. (1994). *Institutional environments and organizations: Structural complexity and individualism.* Thousand Oaks, CA: Sage.

Scott, W. R. (2001). *Institutions and organizations.* Thousand Oaks, CA: Sage.

Silk, M. L., & Amis, J. (2000). Institutional pressures and the production of televised sport. *Journal of Sport Management, 14,* 267–292.

Slack, T. (1997). *Understanding sport organizations: The application of organization theory.* Champaign, IL: Human Kinetics.

Slack, T., & Hinings, C. R. (1994). Institutional pressures and isomorphic change: An empirical test. *Organization Studies, 15,* 803–827.

Thibault, L., Frisby, W., & Kikulis, L. M. (1999). Interorganizational linkages in the delivery of local leisure services in Canada: Responding to economic, political and social pressures. *Managing Leisure, 4,* 125–141.

Trail, G., & Chelladurai, P. (2000). Perceptions of goals and processes of intercollegiate athletics: A case study. *Journal of Sport Management, 14,* 154–178.

Tully, J. (2013). Pennsylvania suing NCAA over Sandusky penalties. *USA Today Sports.* Retrieved from http://www.usatoday.com/story/sports/ncaaf/bigten/2013/01/02/penn-state-jerry-sandusky-child-abuse-law-suit-governor/1804119/.

Waring, A. (1996). *Practical systems thinking.* London: International Thomson Business Press.

Wehrich, H., & Koontz, H. (1993). *Management: A global perspective.* New York: McGraw-Hill.

Wolfe, R. A., & Putler, D. S. (2002). How tight are the ties that bind stakeholder groups? *Organization Science, 13,* 64–80.

Yanda, S. (2012, July 23). Penn State football punished by NCAA over Jerry Sandusky scandal. *Washington Post.* Retrieved from http://www.washingtonpost.com/sports/penn-state-football-punished-by-ncaa-over-sandusky-scandal/2012/07/23/gJQAGNeM4W_story.html.

CHAPTER 4

MEANING OF MANAGEMENT

manage YOUR LEARNING

After completing this chapter you should be able to:

- Understand the general meaning of management.
- Explain the functions of management, including planning, organizing, leading, and evaluating.
- Discuss the distinctions among technical, human, and conceptual skills.
- Explain the 10 roles of a manager and the relationships among them.
- Explain what is meant by the "universal nature of management."

strategic CONCEPTS

decisional roles
evaluation
informational roles
interpersonal roles
leading
management
managerial roles
organizing
planning
skills—technical, human, and conceptual

ROOTS OF MANAGEMENT

Let us begin this chapter on the roots of management as outlined by the great management guru Peter F. Drucker:

> Management as a *practice* is very old. The most successful executive in all history was surely that Egyptian who, 4,700 years or more ago, first conceived the pyramid—without any precedent—designed it, built it, and did so in record time. Unlike any other work of man built at that time, that first pyramid still stands. But as a *discipline,* management is barely fifty years old. It was first dimly perceived around the time of World War I. It did not emerge until World War II, and then primarily in the United States. Since then, it has been the fastest-growing new function, and its study the fastest-growing new discipline. No function in history has emerged as fast as management and managers have in the last fifty to sixty years, and surely none has had such worldwide sweep in such a short period. (Drucker, 2009, p. 210)

As in the case of general management that was practiced 2500 years before the common era, sport management has also been practiced for millennia. Consider the ancient Olympic Games, which began in 776 B.C. It was a sporting competition among city states of ancient Greece conducted in a specially constructed facility. But the discipline of sport management and the specialty of event management or facility management are very recent. As noted in the Introduction, the academic study of managing sport began less than 50 years ago and has rapidly grown to cover all continents of the globe.

MANAGEMENT DEFINED

All of us have a general idea of what the term *management* means. Some of us may think of the field of study called management. Others may think of a group of people at the top of an organization who guide the affairs of that organization, and still others may think of the actual processes of managing the organization. Although all three meanings are commonly employed, this chapter focuses on the third meaning—that is, describing management as the act of managing, by which we are referring to the functions and activities of managers. Let us begin with some of the numerous definitions of **management:**

> Management is the process of reaching organizational goals by working with and through other people and other organizational resources. (Certo & Certo, 2009, p. 8)
>
> Management is the process of working with people and resources to accomplish organizational goals. (Bateman & Snell, 2007, p. 16)
>
> Management is co-ordinating work activities so that they are completed efficiently and effectively with and through other people. (Robbins, Coulter, Leach, & Kilfoil, 2012, p. 5)
>
> Management is a form of work that involves deciding the best way to use an organization's resources to produce goods or provide services. (Rue & Byars, 2009, p. 3)

The above definitions highlight three common elements with which management is concerned: (1) goals and objectives, (2) limited resources, and (3) people. Management's fundamental task is to coordinate these three elements so that the goals will be achieved. Note that the description of management as a process parallels the definition of sport management as a field provided in Chapter 1. Sport management was defined as "a field concerned with the coordination of limited human and material resources, relevant technologies, and situational contingencies for the efficient production and exchange of sport services."

Robbins and colleagues (2012) draw two other implications from their definition of management. The first one is that management is concerned with effectiveness in achieving the goals. The second, equally critical implication is that management is concerned with efficiency. Efficiency refers to maximizing the benefits for a given cost (limited resources). Insofar as resources are limited, it is important that managers attempt to get the most out of those resources—that is, minimize the inputs and maximize the outputs. We will deal with these two concepts—effectiveness and efficiency—in greater detail in later chapters.

IN brief

Management is the process of achieving organizational goals with and through other people within the constraints of limited resources.

An emphasis on the importance of goals and people dominated the earliest scholarly work in the area of management. For example, in 1911, Taylor proposed that all work could be analyzed scientifically, and that one best way could be determined for its execution. He also suggested that incentive pay schemes—that is, basing salary on how much is produced—could be used to ensure that employees followed this one best way. Such an analysis of work entails time and motion studies and the design of appropriate workstations and equipment. This classical approach to the design of work, known as scientific management, still pervades business and industry in all developed nations. In the domain of sport and physical activity, teachers and coaches speak of the best way to execute a skill or implement a strategy. There is a constant endeavor to design new tools and equipment (fiberglass poles for vaulting, new rackets made of different materials for tennis and badminton).

In contrast to Taylor's exclusive focus on work, in 1933 Mayo emphasized the human element in the organization. His research led him to suggest that people are not cogs in a machine, and that the satisfaction of personal needs and desires is a prerequisite to productivity. This swing toward the human aspects of management, referred to as the human relations movement, has contributed greatly to the development of managerial thought. However, like the scientific management approach, the human relations movement has been the object of criticism because it also focuses exclusively on only one main element in the management process. Not surprisingly, as modern definitions of management would suggest, approaches to management now emphasize both the work and the people. In these approaches, it is still important, as Taylor noted, to design the work for efficiency (how best to store the equipment in a locker room, set up the reservation system, or organize the fitness testing of several clients). At the same time, however, managers should consider the issue of individual differences in ability, attitudes, and preferences in designing jobs and assigning them to employees. Who is best suited to manage the locker room? What are the preferences of the reservation clerks? How will the clients react? In addition, the structure and processes that coordinate the various jobs and the people performing them should also be consistent with the human dimensions. Thus, this approach, referred to as the behavioral movement, is concerned with the work, the people, and the processes that bring them together.

THE FUNCTIONS OF MANAGEMENT

We can gain a clearer grasp of the concept of management by exploring what functions are necessary for managers to perform. These functions were described by Fayol in 1916 in his book *General and Industrial Management* (Fayol, 1949). Fayol saw management as composed of planning, organizing, commanding, coordinating, and controlling. Considerable discussion has ensued around the functions of management since Fayol presented his list. As a result, the number and types of functions have undergone changes. From the perspective of modern sport management, four functions are worth emphasizing: planning, organizing, leading, and evaluating.

Planning

Planning involves setting the goals for the organization and its members, and specifying the activities, or programs, through which to achieve those goals. Robbins and colleagues (2012) note that "planning is often called the primary management function because it establishes the basis for all the other functions that managers perform. Without planning, managers wouldn't know what to organize, lead, or control. In fact, without plans, there wouldn't be anything to organize, lead, or control" (p. 160).

In the process of planning, the manager needs to identify the constraints within which the organization must operate. For instance, the goals set for the organization and the means selected to achieve them should be within the financial capabilities of the organization, and at the same time they should be acceptable to the society in which the organization operates. Planning also entails forecasting the future. In setting up a private fitness club, the manager or owner must be concerned not only with the current market but also with the future potential of the market, as well as probable trends in the activity preferences of the population (e.g., Pilates versus spinning). Similarly, when a professional sport league wants to expand and sanction new franchises in specific cities, it has to consider the financial strength of the backers of the franchise, the support from the city and the surrounding community, and the potential for growth in the market.

An organization generally announces its area(s) of business, its general aims to serve the customers/clients, and its social responsibility in a mission statement. Mission statements are general in nature and reflect the long-term orientation of the organization. The mission statement indicates to clients what is to be expected of the organization and its members. Once the specific goals for the immediate future and the means of achieving them have been identified, these must be formally stated in the form of policies, procedures, methods, standards, and rules. The purpose of such formal statements is to outline clearly to the members of the organization what is to be done and how.

Consider the example of a head coach of a university football team. He sets the goals for his team in terms of a championship or a certain number of wins. In doing so, he takes into account constraints such as the finances, the quality of players, and the opposition. Furthermore, the means adopted to achieve the goals must be within the rules of the sport, the governing organization, and the university, and they must be consistent with societal expectations. The coach then states these goals and the means to the goals in the form of strategies and tactics to be adopted. The plan may encompass the whole season or even beyond (a long-range plan), or it may pertain only to the first few games (a short-range plan).

The total planning process is often subdivided and a specific distinctive label then attached to the various components—policy setting, strategy formulation, and so on. In this text, we will use the general term *planning* to cover all of the different components.

sidebar 4.1

POSDCORB VERSUS POLE

A comprehensive list of managerial functions would include planning, organizing, staffing, directing, coordinating, reporting, and budgeting (POSDCORB). Some of these functions can be considered aspects of the four functions emphasized: planning, organizing, leading, and evaluating (POLE). For instance, budgeting is one aspect of planning, and staffing can be considered a part of the organizing function. Similarly, coordinating is ensured through the organizing and leading functions. For this reason, and because the concern in this book is with macro issues in sport management, this text deals only with the four main functions.

IN brief

Planning includes setting goals within constraints, selecting activities to achieve the goals, and establishing policies and procedures to carry out those activities.

Organizing

The second function of management, **organizing**, involves breaking down the total work specified in the planning process into specific jobs, and then establishing a formal relationship among these jobs and among the individuals assigned to carry them out. Whereas the planning process specifies *what* should be done and how, the organizing process elaborates on *who* should do it.

Organizing involves the management of not only each individual employee, but of the employees in a group. In every large organization, managers formally create and designate groups as separate departments or units. This grouping, or departmentation, as it is also called, is a critical component of the organizing process.

After the creation of jobs and units, the task of assigning the right people to do the right job becomes important. All the efforts that have gone into the earlier steps are to no avail if the staffing procedures are inefficient or ineffective. In fact, a number of theorists place such great importance on this step that they treat it as a separate function.

IN brief

Organizing involves creating jobs, grouping them, establishing relationships among them, and establishing a formal authority structure.

Another essential element in the organizing process is specifying the methods for coordinating the activities of the many individuals involved. We achieve this by establishing a formal hierarchy of authority specifying the chain of command within the organization. Every organization except the very smallest prepares an organizational chart showing the relationships among individuals and departments within the organization.

For example, a football coach must assign the available players to the offensive, defensive, and special squads. Within each squad, the appropriate individual must fill each position, and each individual must be told what is expected in every situation. The playbook is a planning document and serves as a coordinative mechanism. Another mode of coordination is the development of a hierarchy of authority consisting of the head coach, assistant coaches, specialty coaches, offensive and defensive captains, and quarterback. Similarly, in a national sport-governing body, the marketing and sponsorship activities designed to increase revenue will be assigned to a specialized unit with the necessary expertise, and the activities associated with increasing the number of members will be assigned to another unit. In addition, each unit may have its own manager who, in turn, would be answerable to a higher position supervising both of these units.

Leading

The third function of management, **leading**, has been defined as the management function that energizes people to contribute their best individually and in cooperation with other people (Gomez-Mejia, Balkin, & Cardy, 2005, p. 11). Whereas the planning and organizing functions set the stage for the work activities to be carried out, the leading function deals with influencing or motivating individual members to carry out their specific assignments efficiently.

IN brief

Leading is the process of influencing members to achieve organizational goals. It is an interpersonal process in which the manager and member(s) interact directly.

In order to be an effective leader, the manager must have a working knowledge of the motivational processes of individuals—their needs and dispositions as well as the situational elements that help or hinder motivation. Because leading focuses on the interactions and reciprocal influence among the manager, the subordinates, and the situation, and because differences among individuals are numerous and complex, some researchers have suggested that this is the most difficult and critical of the managerial functions. For example, Likert (1967) states that "managing the human component is the central and most important task because all else depends on how well it is done" (p. 1).

Referring back to the example of a football team, when the coach and his assistants encourage the players individually or in groups toward greater effort, or when they compliment them for a good performance, they are engaged in the leading function—that is, motivation. The pre-game speeches and various motivational posters in a locker room are examples of techniques used by coaches as leaders or motivators.

Evaluating

Finally, a manager must be concerned with assessing the degree to which the organization as a whole, as well as the various units and individuals comprising

sidebar 4.2

MANAGERIAL CONTROL

Many authors (e.g., Bateman & Snell, 2007; Robbins et al., 2012) would list *control* as a major function of management. Control is "the process of monitoring activities to ensure that they are being accomplished as planned, and correcting any significant deviations" (Bateman & Snell, 2007, p. 440). The control process involves first comparing the current performance to the standards set in the planning stage. If the set standards are not met, managers then scrutinize the people–work interface created in the organizing function to determine if any mismatch therein could be the cause of failing to meet the standards. In addition, they will examine if the leadership/guidance provided by the managers and supervisors fails to inspire the workers to better performance. Note that the above description of the function of control parallels the evaluating function outlined in the text. In fact, many researchers hold that managerial control is the fourth major function of management.

it, have accomplished what they set out to do. This is the **evaluation** function. Evaluation provides the manager with the feedback necessary to take corrective action when organizational performance does not match expectations.

The evaluation process involves measuring performance and comparing that performance to standards set in the planning process. If performance does not meet established standards, the manager may lower the organizational expectations if they are judged to be unrealistic. On the other hand, changes in the organizational structure, communication patterns, the type of leadership, or the reward systems may bring about the desired level of performance. In order to determine the proper course of action, evaluation is essential. Also note that evaluation must be carried out at strategic points from the initiation of a program of activities to the conclusion of those activities.

When the football coach views a game film or scrutinizes the statistics of a game, he is carrying out the evaluating function. The feedback he gains from his own personal observation and from the recorded details provides a basis for refining or redesigning the strategies and tactics to be used in future games.

The above discussion of the four managerial functions may imply that they are necessarily carried out in the sequence in which they have been described. This, however, is far from the case. Although such sequencing of the managerial functions is possible when setting up a new organization or starting an independent project, it is more realistic to view these as ongoing processes occurring simultaneously sometimes and sequentially other times. Note also that these functions are not independent of each other. For example, the feedback from the evaluation function can affect goal setting (the planning function), the distribution of particular activities to specific individuals (the organizing function), and leadership behavior (the leading function).

IN brief

Evaluation is measuring performance of individuals, units, and the total organization and comparing it to the standards set in the planning process.

The reference to coaching may seem out of place. However, as noted in Chapter 2, if sport teams are organizations in their own right, then the teams' coaches can be compared to managers and leaders. In fact, the leader of a baseball team is called a manager. That many outstanding coaches are invited to speak to groups of managers or to conduct motivational seminars is proof that coaching is closely related to management. Robbins (1997) has this to say about coaching and management:

> Today's manager is increasingly more like a coach than a boss. Coaches don't play the game. They create a climate in which their players can excel. They define the overall objectives, set expectations, define the boundaries of each player's role, ensure that players are properly trained and have the resources they need to perform their roles, attempt to enlarge each player's capabilities, offer inspiration and motivation, and evaluate results. Contemporary managers look much more like coaches than bosses as they guide, listen to, encourage, and motivate their employees. (pp. 42–43)

Macguire (2013) cites Mike Carson, author of *The Manager: Inside the Minds of Football Leaders:* "Football [i.e., soccer] management is not unlike being a senior executive, where you have to balance the needs of multiple parties: investors, shareholders, committees, customers, clients, consumers and stakeholders in general," and "Whether you're leading a football club and all the infrastructure behind that . . . or whether you're leading an executive company, the human skills are quite similar" (unpaged).

THE SKILLS OF MANAGEMENT

The concept of management can be understood not only by looking at the four managerial functions of planning, organizing, leading, and evaluating, but also by determining the skills necessary to carry out these functions effectively. Katz (1974) takes this approach. He proposed that three main types of skills—*technical, human,* and *conceptual*—are necessary for management. Katz also placed each of these skills within a three-tier hierarchy, with technical skills being the most fundamental, followed by human skills and then by conceptual skills.

Katz developed his three classes of managerial skills as a counter to the traditional view that managers are born, not made. Although he originally maintained that all these skills could be developed independently of inborn traits, he later modified his position and noted that conceptual skill cannot be easily developed after adolescence.

Technical Skills

According to Katz (1974) **technical skills** involve "an understanding of and proficiency in a specific kind of activity, particularly one involving methods, procedures or techniques" (p. 91). Katz sees technical skill as specific to that area of specialization in which the organization is engaged. For example, the technical skills associated with manufacturing tennis rackets may not be relevant to running a fitness club. However, some technical skills are transferable across organizations. Because every organization must manage its finances efficiently, budgeting and accounting skills are necessary in all types of organizations.

The technical skills required of a manager of a fitness club include a working knowledge of and experience in the use of the equipment (such as various weight-training machines and bicycle ergometers); an understanding of the physiological effects of exercise and the interrelationships of exercise, diet, and body composition; expertise in exercise testing and exercise prescription; and so on. The manager also needs to be proficient in accounting, legal liability, and other concerns related to operating a fitness club. Similarly, a facility manager in a large university athletic department should be familiar with the technologies associated with the ice rink, the maintenance of playing fields, and such other technical aspects of the facilities she manages.

Human Skills

As the term would suggest, the human skills of managers center on their interactions with people. Katz (1974) emphasized this point when he defined **human skill** as the

> executive's ability to work effectively as a group member and to build a cooperative effort within the team he [/she] leads. As *technical* skill is primarily concerned with working with "things" (processes or physical objects), so *human* skill is primarily concerned with working with people. The skill is demonstrated in the way the individual perceives (and recognizes the perceptions of) his [/her] superiors, equals, and subordinates, and in the way he [/she] behaves subsequently. (p. 91)

The human skills of a fitness club manager are demonstrated in the effectiveness of his interactions with the customers and the other employees of the organization (instructors, personal trainers, marketing/membership specialists, and front desk staff). As another example, the director of a university intramural recreation department needs good human skills to interact effectively with the participating students and staff, the employees of the department, the heads of other departments, and the university administrators. Clearly, because there is much more variety and variability among human beings than among processes or physical objects, human skill is of a higher order than technical skill.

Conceptual Skills

The highest, most complex type of skill in the hierarchy is **conceptual skill.** Katz (1974) defined it as the "ability to see the enterprise as a whole; it includes recognizing how the various functions of the organization depend on one another, and how changes in any one part affect all the other; and it extends to visualizing the relationship of the individual business to the industry, the community, and the political, social, and economic forces of the nation as a whole" (p. 93).

For the manager of a fitness club, this definition of conceptual skills implies that she must be capable of perceiving the organization as a gestalt, or whole, and be cognizant of the effects of every managerial decision on the total organization and its various parts. The manager should be aware that a decision to buy more costly equipment might reduce the funds available for part-time help, which in turn may affect the morale of the full-time employees. It also implies that the manager must be concerned with the relative emphasis placed on the various goals of the club (such as whether to increase the number of customers or enhance the quality of the service).

IN brief

To be an effective manager, one needs to possess technical skills (an understanding of the methods, procedures, and techniques), human skills (interpersonal skills), and conceptual skills (the ability to see the organization as a whole).

Finally, Zeigler (1979) proposes that two more skill categories should be added to the three proposed by Katz (1974)—conjoined skills and personal skills. Conjoined skills are a mixture of Katz's technical, human, and conceptual skills. Zeigler's inclusion of this as a combined category is meaningful because an effective manager needs to be proficient in all three skills. Personal skills refer to the ability to manage personal time efficiently, organize and articulate personal thoughts, and keep abreast of current events and innovations, along with other attributes that make a good manager.

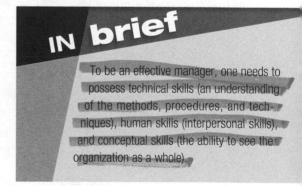

Along similar lines, Klemp and McClelland (1986) suggest that successful managers are characterized by three sets of competencies—intellectual competencies, influence, and self-confidence. Intellectual competencies consist

sidebar 4.3

THE SKILLS REQUIRED AT THE EXECUTIVE LEVEL

Following are two lists of skills of executives in the context of sport and government. Note that despite the vast differences between managing sports and managing government units, the two lists are very similar to each other.

Quarterman (1998) collated from the literature the following skills necessary for transformational leadership as perceived by commissioners of intercollegiate athletic conferences:

- Empowerment skills—sharing power, promoting others' development, and realizing that visions are achieved by teams
- Visioning skills—using persuasion and inducing individuals and groups to achieve visions
- Self-understanding skills—being aware of one's strengths, weaknesses, wants, and needs
- Value congruence skills—understanding and teaching the organization's guiding beliefs and values
- Anticipatory skills—developing and utilizing foresight and strategies consistent with the changing environment
- Intuitive skills—utilizing "gut feelings" and "hunches" in decision making and problem solving

The concept and features of transformational leadership are discussed in Chapter 12.

The U.S. government's Office of Personnel Management (2008) outlined the following five Executive Core Qualifications (ECQs) required for entry into Senior Executive Service:

1. Leading change—This involves an individual's ability to bring about strategic change, both within and outside the organization, to meet organizational goals. Inherent to this ECQ is the aptitude to establish an organizational vision and to implement it in a continuously changing environment. The competencies associated with this core qualification include *creativity and innovation, external awareness, flexibility, resilience, strategic thinking,* and *vision.*
2. Leading people—This core qualification involves the ability to lead people toward meeting the organization's vision, mission, and goals. Inherent to this ECQ is the skill to provide an inclusive workplace that fosters the development of others, facilitates cooperation and teamwork, and supports constructive resolution of conflicts. Effective leading of people would require the abilities of *conflict management, leveraging diversity, developing others,* and *team building.*
3. Results driven—A results-driven individual demonstrates the ability to meet organizational goals and customer expectations. Inherent to this ECQ is the capability to make decisions that produce high-quality results by applying technical knowledge, analyzing problems, and calculating risks. A results-driven qualification would involve the competencies related to *accountability, customer service, decisiveness, entrepreneurship, problem solving,* and *technical credibility.*
4. Business acumen—This can be defined as the knack for managing human, financial, and information resources strategically. This qualification will be exemplified in *financial management, human capital management,* and *technology management.*
5. Building coalitions—A person who demonstrates this core qualification is able to build coalitions internally and with other federal agencies, state and local governments, nonprofit and private sector organizations, foreign governments, or international organizations to achieve common goals. This qualification will be enhanced by *partnering, political savvy,* and *influencing/negotiating.*

of seeing implications and consequences, analyzing causal relationships, seeking information from multiple sources, and making plans and strategies to achieve goals. They also include understanding how parts fit together and identifying and interpreting patterns of events. The next set, influence competencies, includes desiring to persuade people, directing them to do things in specific ways, effectively interacting with groups to influence outcomes, letting key members be part of decisions, setting a personal example, and using symbols for group identity. The final competency is self-confidence, which is seeing oneself as the prime mover and the most capable person to get the job done.

THE ROLES OF A MANAGER

The discussion of both managerial functions and managerial skills contributes to a picture of the manager as a person who is concerned with and has ample time, scope, and ability to carry out these functions. It also implies that the manager is not likely to be involved in routine and mundane activities. This is far from the case, as a number of researchers have clearly shown.

Mintzberg (1975), whose research is considered the most definitive of its kind, concluded that the classical descriptions of managerial jobs are myths. He found that instead of being reflective and systematic planners, managers "work at an unrelenting pace . . . their activities are characterized by brevity, and discontinuity, and . . . they are strongly oriented to action and dislike reflective activities" (p. 50). Furthermore, Mintzberg found that contrary to general impressions, "managerial work involves performing a number of regular duties including ritual and ceremony, negotiations, and processing of soft information that links the organization with its environment" (p. 51). Instead of relying on formal information systems, according to Mintzberg, "Managers strongly favor the verbal media—namely, telephone calls and meetings" (p. 51). We may add that modern-day managers are likely to rely on emails and such other electronic communications.

> "Before we made the study, I always thought of a chief executive as the conductor of an orchestra, standing aloof on his platform. Now I am in some respects inclined to see him as the puppet in a puppet-show with hundreds of people pulling the strings and forcing him to act in one way or another."
>
> **CARLSON,** *1979, p. 52*

Rather than adopting the classical descriptions of management, Mintzberg suggests that management can best be described in terms of the roles managers play in their day-to-day activities. Ten **managerial roles** were identified within three broad categories: interpersonal roles, informational roles, and decisional roles. These are illustrated in Exhibit 4.1.

exhibit 4.1 Mintzberg's 10 managerial roles in three categories.

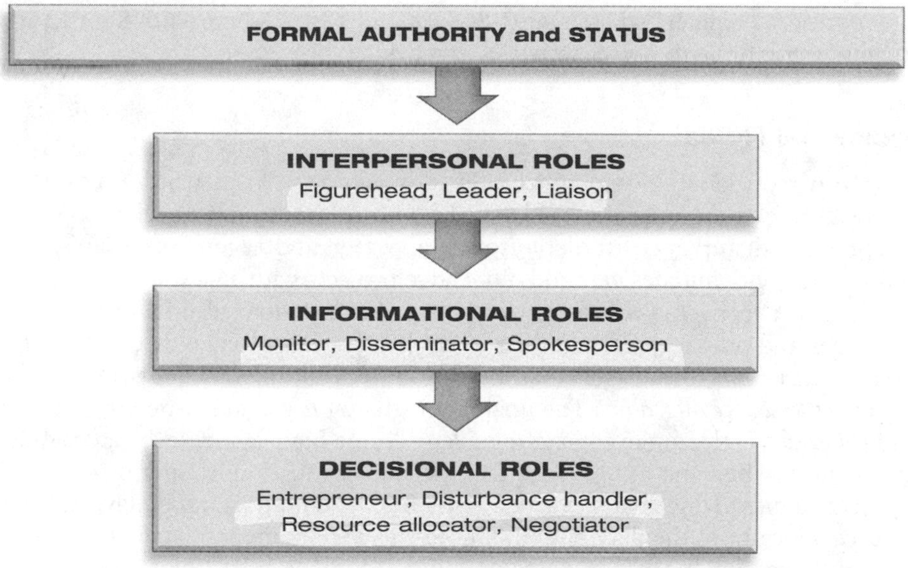

Adapted and reprinted by permission of *Harvard Business Review*. From "The Manager's Job: Folklore and Fact," by H. Mintzberg, July–August, 1975, p. 55. Copyright © 1975 by the Harvard Business School Publishing Corporation; all rights reserved.

Interpersonal Roles

The formal position of manager involves three separate **interpersonal roles:** figurehead, leader, and liaison. The *figurehead* role involves ceremonial duties in which the manager represents the organization in public functions. This role is particularly important in larger organizations. In the *leader* role, of course, the manager supervises and motivates subordinates, whereas the *liaison* role involves the establishment and maintenance of contacts outside the department, unit, or group. Examples of the interpersonal roles in operation are when the director of an athletic department addresses a meeting to honor sport persons in the community (figurehead); talks to her assistants individually or collectively about the importance of generating more donations (leader); or meets with other departmental heads, the president of the university, or other administrators (liaison). A head football coach is the ceremonial *figurehead* of the team when receiving the trophy on behalf of the team; he is also the *leader* of both the players and assistant coaches in motivating them; and he is also the *liaison* in linking the team and the public.

Informational Roles

The contacts emerging from the three interpersonal roles enable managers to become the nerve-centers of their groups because of the amount of information that flows through them. This informational base leads the manager to become a monitor, disseminator, and spokesperson. In the *monitor* role, the manager consciously seeks information from within the unit as well as from outside it. The concern here is to obtain any and all kinds of information that will have a bearing on the organization. At this point, the manager assumes a *disseminator* role as he passes relevant information on to his subordinates. The third **informational role** is that of *spokesperson.* In this role, a manager is mainly involved in lobbying for and justifying what goes on within the unit or the organization. In all contacts with external as well as internal agents, the director of athletics consciously seeks out information that will affect the department (monitor), conveys the pieces of information to concerned assistants and unit heads (disseminator), and carries out public relations in any external interactions (spokesperson).

Decisional Roles

The interpersonal and informational roles, along with the formal authority vested in the position, cast the manager in four **decisional roles.** Mintzberg refers to these as entrepreneur, disturbance handler, resource allocator, and negotiator. As an *entrepreneur,* the manager initiates new and innovative projects with a view to enhancing the viability and effectiveness of the organization. Managers may also be forced to react to changes and pressures beyond their control. Thus, the manager becomes a *disturbance handler.* When managers distribute resources to different units or members, they act as *resource allocators.* The final role is that of *negotiator,* whereby a manager resolves issues with employees and outsiders. At the high school level, a coach is an entrepreneur when she comes up with creative ideas for fundraising or team training; she is a disturbance handler when resolving the conflict among players; she is a resource allocator in the distribution of uniforms and equipment; and she is a negotiator in canvassing the athletic director and boosters for more funds.

Mintzberg (1975) has stated that these roles are inseparable and that every manager needs to be effective in all 10. He acknowledges, however, that "to say that the ten roles form a gestalt is not to say that all managers give equal attention to each role" (p. 59). Furthermore, Mintzberg describes the inaccuracy of traditional descriptions of managerial work—a view he illustrates by contrasting the folklore about management with the facts (see Exhibit 4.2).

Countering Mintzberg's claims, Carroll and Gillen (1987) argue that observing a manager in action does not provide a clear grasp of the total work she does because (a) managerial work is largely mental and therefore cannot be observed; (b) mental time is different from physical time; and (c) the activity of the brain during the mental time, including the thought trials, can be enormous and efficient. The researchers go on to say that in any interaction with subordinates, peers, and superiors, the manager gets not only basic information but also attitudinal and emotional clues that are critical for decision making. Finally, Carroll and Gillen suggest that managers have their own mental agenda, and they use all the pieces of information they get to revise and implement that agenda. We may add that the supposedly soft information the manager gets through verbal communications may be based on hard data. The manager's subordinates may have worked long on a large set of data before passing on this information to the boss in a distilled and simple format. For the observer, it is soft information, but in truth it is based on hard data.

IN brief

Management also consists of behaviors associated with interpersonal roles (figurehead, leader, liaison), informational roles (monitor, disseminator, spokesperson), and decisional roles (entrepreneur, disturbance handler, resource allocator, negotiator).

exhibit 4.2 Mintzberg's management folklore and facts.

FOLKLORE	FACT
The manager is a reflective, systematic planner.	Study after study has shown that managers work at an unrelenting pace, that their activities are characterized by brevity, variety, and discontinuity, and that they are strongly oriented to action and dislike reflective activities.
The effective manager has no regular duties to perform.	In addition to handling exceptions, managerial work involves performing a number of regular duties, including ritual and ceremony, negotiations, and processing of soft information that links the organization with its environment.
The senior manager needs aggregated information, which a formal management information system best provides.	Managers strongly favor the verbal media—namely, telephone calls and meetings. [Today we would add email as a preferred contact method.]
Management is, or at least is quickly becoming, a science and profession.	The managers' programs—to schedule time, process information, make decisions, and so on—remain locked deep inside their brains.

Managerial Roles and Managerial Levels

Although identifying and describing the various managerial roles is essential, determining which roles are critical to which level of management is also important. Note that Mintzberg's work was based on his observation of the chief executive officers (CEOs) of five large corporations, and therefore, his classification may not be relevant to lower levels of management. In their study of managerial jobs, Kraut, Pedigo, McKenna, and Dunnette (1989) identified seven critical managerial roles that are differentially important to three levels of management—first-line supervisors, middle managers, and executives. Their findings show that the managers in their study rated certain roles as more critical for each of the three levels of management (see Exhibit 4.3).

Managerial Roles in Athletic Contexts

Mintzberg's (1975) scheme of managerial roles has been the basis for the investigation of a manager's job in some athletic contexts. Quarterman (1994) used Mintzberg's model of managerial roles to examine the different managerial roles played by athletic conference commissioners in carrying out their job-related responsibilities. Quarterman saw collegiate athletic conference commissioners as the highest ranked managers in the conference setting. They belong to the cadre of top-level managers because they are responsible for the organization and conduct of athletic competitions in their conference. In addition, the commissioners monitor and supervise the activities of other units dealing with compliance, game officials, public relations, and other vital activities of the conference.

Quarterman's (1994) respondents, 63 intercollegiate athletic conference commissioners from all three divisions of the NCAA, rated the importance of the 10 roles. The results show that these commissioners considered the roles of disseminator, liaison, disturbance handler, and monitor as the four most important, in that order. According to Quarterman's findings, the following define the major functions of a commissioner:

1. communicating relevant information to member institutions and subordinate managers within the conference office (the disseminator role);
2. interacting with presidents and athletic directors of member institutions and the NCAA (the liaison role);

exhibit 4.3 Managerial levels and importance of managerial tasks.

MANAGEMENT LEVEL	MAJOR THRUST	MANAGERIAL TASKS
First-Line Supervisor (e.g., Stadium Manager)	Supervising individuals	1. Managing individual performance 2. Instructing subordinates
Middle Manager (e.g., Assistant Athletic Director)	Linking groups	1. Planning and resource allocation 2. Coordinating interdependent groups 3. Managing group performance
Executive (e.g., Athletic Director)	Monitoring the business environment	1. Monitoring the environment 2. Linking the organization with the environment

3. resolving conflicts among member institutions (the disturbance handler role);
4. monitoring the environment for useful information (the monitor role).

These results make sense when we take into account that a commissioner's major responsibility is to organize and conduct the competitions within the conference. The actual preparation of the teams for the competitions, and the costs of such preparation, are left to the individual institutions. Thus, the roles of leader, entrepreneur, spokesperson, figurehead, negotiator, and resource allocator were not rated as high as the former four roles. In fact, resource allocator was rated the least important.

Danylchuk and Chelladurai (1999) examined the total managerial work (including the managerial activities of assistant athletic directors and staff) in a university athletic department in Canada. Expanding on Mintzberg's conceptual scheme, they proposed 19 managerial activities associated with an intercollegiate athletic department. For each activity they sought to assess (a) its importance, (b) the time devoted to it, and (c) the manager's percentage of responsibility for it. Athletic directors of 37 Canadian universities perceived financial management, leadership, policy making, disturbance handling, revenue generation, and concern for athletes as the most important and most time-consuming activities. In essence, these athletic directors considered the roles of resource allocator (financial management and revenue generation), leader and entrepreneur (policy making), and disturbance handler to be the most important. Given the financial constraints faced by Canadian university athletic departments, not surprisingly the directors emphasized resource management (both securing and distributing the resources) as most important. This contrasts with Quarterman's finding that the commissioners of athletic conferences in the United States rated this the least important of the 10 roles. If we were to ask the U.S. athletic directors the same questions, they would probably rate resource allocation among the most important roles. These findings collectively suggest that the relative significance of Mintzberg's managerial roles varies from one context to another.

The athletic directors in Danylchuk and Chelladurai's (1999) study reported that they were largely responsible for the more important tasks, with average responsibility of 55 percent. The average responsibility assigned to assistant directors was 29.5 percent, and this limited responsibility was significantly but inversely related to the importance of the tasks. This finding substantiates Mintzberg's claim that managerial work involves a number of regular duties.

IN brief

Management consists of planning, organizing, leading, and evaluating, which require conceptual, human, and technical skills. In performing these functions, the manager fills interpersonal, informational, and decisional roles.

THE MANAGEMENT PROCESS IN OVERVIEW

The descriptions of management as a set of functions, skills, and roles are simply different perspectives on the same phenomenon. As such, these functions, skills, and roles are highly interrelated (Rue & Byars, 2009). An examination of the 10 roles of management and the three skills of management reveals considerable overlap among these and the four functions of management (see Exhibit 4.4). For example, Katz's three managerial skills can easily be synthesized with the four managerial functions: the planning and organizing functions entail a great amount of conceptual skill, whereas the leading function presup-

exhibit 4.4 Correspondence among managerial functions, skills, and roles.

MANAGEMENT FUNCTIONS	MANAGERIAL SKILLS	MANAGERIAL ROLES
Planning	Conceptual	Monitor Disseminator Entrepreneur
Organizing	Conceptual	Disturbance handler Resource allocator Negotiator
Leading	Human	Leader
Evaluating	Technical	Spokesperson Liaison Figurehead

poses higher levels of human skill. Finally, technical skill is more closely associated with the evaluation phase of management.

In a similar vein, there is also considerable overlap among Mintzberg's 10 roles and the four managerial functions. For example, a manager's decisions in the roles of entrepreneur and resource allocator are based on the information gained in the role of monitor, and these are, in fact, the essential elements of the planning function. The manager sets the priority of objectives and selects the appropriate means only after securing all the relevant information. Resources are then distributed on the basis of the priority of objectives. As Rue and Byars (2009) noted, "All three approaches to examine the management process look at the process from a different perspective. All have their merits. But in the final

sidebar 4.4

MANAGEMENT AS A PROFESSION

Despite the enormous growth in the study of management, the field cannot be considered a profession in the same sense medicine and law are. In Barker's (2010) words, "Neither the boundaries of the discipline of management nor a consensus on the requisite body of knowledge exists. No professional body is granted control, no formal entry or certification is required, no ethical standards are enforced, and no mechanism can exclude someone from practice" (p. 56).

Because the elements in the above quote are prerequisites for an occupation to be considered a profession, Barker concludes that management is not a profession and it can never be a profession. This extends to sport management, but it does not suggest that sport managers should be anything but professionals. And becoming a professional entails advanced education and training, formal testing of competence, application of skills based on technical knowledge, existence of professional associations, existence of a code of conduct or ethics, and a commitment to the occupation (Morrow & Goetz, 1988, p. 94).

analysis, a successful manager must (1) understand the work that is to be performed (the managerial functions); (2) understand the organized set of behaviors to be performed (the managerial roles); and (3) master the skills involved in performing the job (managerial skills)" (p. 10).

THE UNIVERSAL NATURE OF THE MANAGEMENT PROCESS

Anyone who has any experience with various organizations as an employee, customer, or client is aware that organizations differ dramatically from one another in size, complexity, products, objectives, and so on. Thus, common sense dictates that they cannot all be managed in the same way. Nevertheless, Robbins et al. (2012) speak of the *universality of management*. In their words, "We can say with absolute certainty that management is needed in all types and sizes of organizations, at all organizational levels, in all organizational work areas, and in all organizations, no matter what country they're located in" (p. 19). This assertion means that all organizations, without reference to their shape, size, goals, purposes, or cultural context, need to be managed. Simply stated, management in any organization consists of planning, organizing, leading, and evaluating. This does not mean, however, that the methods and consequences of these four functions will be the same from one organization to another. By the same token, the significance of each of these functions and the extent to which a manager emphasizes one function over another depend on the hierarchical level at which the manager operates. For instance, the commissioner of a professional sport league will spend more time on strategic planning for the entire enterprise than will the supervisor of interns in the marketing department. The supervisor, on the other hand, is likely to be more engaged in the leading function than the commissioner. With reference to Mintzberg's managerial roles, a high school coach concerned with shaping young athletes into adults will be more engaged in interpersonal roles, while the coach of a professional team will be more engaged in the informational and decisional roles because he or she is largely responsible for the success of the team.

To see how organizations may differ, consider the organizing function. It involves breaking down the total work into specific jobs and then grouping those jobs into meaningful units or departments. Closer to home, all collegiate athletic departments promote excellence in sports. Furthermore, they all follow the rules set by the NCAA. Yet, they are structured differently in different universities. Some are independent units within their respective universities, and others are part of a larger unit that may house other units such as campus recreation. Some are heavily funded by their universities, and others are left to fend for themselves.

The previous example illustrates that although the consequences of the organizing process may be different, the process of organizing itself is universal across all organizations. In short, all four of the managerial functions—planning, organizing, leading, and evaluating—must be carried out if an organization is to be effective. Only the decisions made under each process are unique to and contingent upon the specific circumstances of the organization and the manager's orientation. In later chapters, we will explore similarities and differences among sport organizations and how they facilitate or constrain the managerial processes.

sidebar 4.5

MANAGEMENT VERSUS MARKETING

It is not uncommon for people to distinguish between management and marketing based on the idea that management is concerned with production whereas marketing is concerned with the exchange of products. This is far from the truth. As you will understand from reading this chapter, the concept of management refers to coordination of people, their activities, and limited resources to achieve goals and objectives. A goal of a sport enterprise could be to produce an excellent team and stage exciting sport competitions. Similarly, another goal of the same enterprise could be to sell all the seats in the stadium and secure sponsorships for its programs. The enterprise may set up two units to achieve these objectives. Each unit may consist of several positions hierarchically organized, and these positions would carry out different activities and be allotted a certain budget. If the units are to achieve their respective objectives, their resources, activities, and people need to be coordinated properly. And that is management. So it is more meaningful to consider management as a process applicable to both production and marketing.

A related debate is whether production or marketing is more important to an organization. Obviously, production and marketing are highly interrelated, and both are critical to an organization. You cannot market anything if it is not produced, and there is no point in producing anything if it cannot be marketed. Despite this, marketing is considered more critical in many types of organizations, and rightly so. Why? We can identify several differences between the two functions that make marketing more critical for an organization.

First, the production function is internal to the organization, whereas marketing is externally oriented. The production of an excellent team in our example is carried out within the organization. The coaches and the facility and event managers are employees of the organization. The athletes are employees, students, or members of the organization, depending on whether it is a professional franchise, scholastic institution, or sports club. In contrast, marketing is externally oriented in the sense that the spectators and the sponsors are external to the organization. This distinction leads to the difference in the relative control the organization has in the production versus the marketing of its products. The people, processes, and resources involved in production are under the control of the organization, whereas the spectators or sponsors are independent of the organization. Thus, it is easier to manage the production function than it is to manage the marketing function. We can also argue that the technology associated with the production of an excellent team is, relatively speaking, better known and better mastered (e.g., coaching, event management, and facility management) than the technology associated with marketing (e.g., consumer psychology/behavior).

A final distinction is that the production function involves the expenditure of resources, whereas the marketing function involves the acquisition of such resources. In many types of organization, the units that deal with elements in the external environment or secure the necessary resources are likely to have greater power and influence. Accordingly, marketing is likely to be given greater status than production in most sport organizations. However, those units that produce exceptional products and that are most sought after by the public, such as the football and basketball programs in Division I universities, are likely to have clout equal to if not greater than that of marketing.

SUMMARY

This chapter describes the concept of management—the process of achieving organizational goals with and through other people, given limited resources. Management was described from three different perspectives: functions, skills, and roles. Managerial functions include planning, organizing, leading, and evaluating. To carry out these functions, managers need to have three kinds of skills: conceptual, human, and technical. Management was also described as consisting of interpersonal roles (figurehead, leader, and liaison), informational roles (monitor, disseminator, and spokesperson), and decisional roles (entrepreneur, disturbance handler, resource allocator, and negotiator). These three perspectives complement each other in describing management in detail. We also discussed the idea that management is a universal process.

In Chapter 1, we defined sport management as the coordination of limited human and material resources, relevant technologies, and situational contingencies for the efficient production and exchange of sport services (refer back to Exhibit 1.6). The four functions of management as outlined above, in fact, are aimed at coordination of the activities of organizational units and their members (see Exhibit 4.5). The goals set and the activities chosen to achieve those goals in the planning process, the creation of organizational units and hiring of the right people to run those units, the guidance and coaching provided in the leading function, and the evaluations of individual-, unit-, and organizational-level performances all aim at coordination. Accordingly, we will elaborate further on these four functions in the next chapters.

exhibit 4.5 Managerial functions as means of coordination.

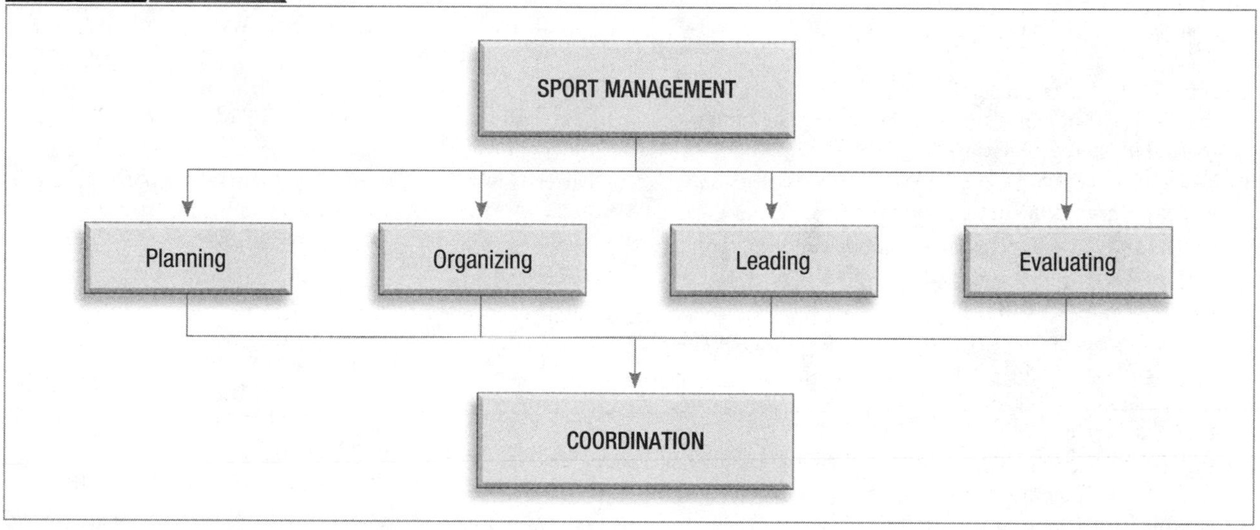

develop YOUR PERSPECTIVE

1. Compare any two sport organizations in terms of the relative importance of the four managerial functions of planning, organizing, leading, and evaluating.
2. Select a large sport organization (for example, a Division I athletic department) and discuss how, and to what degree, the various levels of managers are involved in the four managerial functions.
3. In the organization you choose, which of the technical, human, and conceptual skills are most important at each level of management?
4. What does the head of your unit or department actually do in a typical day? How is his or her time apportioned among the 10 managerial roles described by Mintzberg?
5. Compare the daily activities of the coach of an athletic team to those of the athletic director. Discuss the differences in their roles and in the time they spend in each of the roles.

Barker, R. (2010). No. Management is not a profession. *Harvard Business Review, 88* (7/8), 52–60.

Bateman, T. S., & Snell, S. A. (2007). *Management: Leading & collaborating in a competitive world* (7th ed.). Boston: McGraw-Hill Irwin.

Carlson, S. (1979). *Executive behavior: A study of the workload and the working methods of managing directors.* New York: Arno Press. (Original work published in 1951.)

Carroll, S. J., & Gillen, D. J. (1987). Are the classical management functions useful in describing managerial work? *Academy of Management Review, 12,* 38–51.

Certo, S. C., & Certo, S. T. (2009). *Modern management: Concepts and skills* (11th ed.). Upper Saddle River, NJ: Prentice Hall.

Danylchuk, K. E., & Chelladurai, P. (1999). The nature of managerial work in Canadian intercollegiate athletics. *Journal of Sport Management, 13,* 148–166.

Drucker, P. F. (2009). *Managing in a time of great change.* Boston: Harvard Business Press.

Fayol, H. (1949). *General and industrial management.* London: Pitman. (First published in French in 1916.)

Gomez-Mejia, L. R., Balkin, D. B., & Cardy, R. L. (2005). *Management: People, performance, and change* (2nd ed.). Boston: McGraw-Hill Irwin.

Katz, R. L. (1974). Skills of an effective administrator. *Harvard Business Review, 52,* 90–102.

Klemp, G. O., Jr., & McClelland, D. C. (1986). What characterizes intelligent functioning among senior managers? In R. J. Sternberg & R. K. Wagner (Eds.), *Practical intelligence: Nature and origins of competence in the everyday world* (pp. 31–50). New York: Cambridge University Press.

Kraut, A. I., Pedigo, P. R., McKenna, D. D., & Dunnette, M. D. (1989). The role of the manager: What's really important in different management jobs. *Academy of Management Executive, 3,* 286–293.

Likert, R. (1967). *The human organization, its management and value.* New York: McGraw-Hill.

Macguire, E. (2013, October 1). What football managers can teach you about leadership. CNN. Retrieved from http://www.cnn.com/2013/10/01/business/can-football-managers-coach-leadership/

Mayo, E. (1933). *The human problems of an industrial civilization.* Cambridge, MA: Harvard University Press.

Mintzberg, H. (1975). The manager's job: Folklore and fact. *Harvard Business Review, 53,* 49–61.

Morrow, P. C., & Goetz, J. F. (1988). Professionalism as a form of work commitment. *Journal of Vocational Behavior, 32,* 92–111.

Office of Personnel Management (2008). Executive core qualifications. Retrieved from www.opm.gov/ses/recruitment/ecq.asp.

Quarterman, J. (1994). Managerial role profiles of intercollegiate athletic conference commissioners. *Journal of Sport Management, 8,* 129–139.

Quarterman, J. (1998). An assessment of the perception of management and leadership skills by intercollegiate athletics conference commissioners. *Journal of Sport Management, 12,* 146–164.

Robbins, S. P. (1997). *Managing today!* Upper Saddle River, NJ: Prentice Hall.

Robbins, S. P., Coulter, M., Leach, E., & Kilfoil, M. (2012). *Management,* (10th ed.). Don Mills, Ontario: Pearson Canada.

Rue, L. W., & Byars, L. L. (2009). *Management: Skills and application* (13th ed.). Boston: McGraw-Hill/Irwin.

Taylor, F. W. (1911). *The principles of scientific management.* New York: Harper & Bros.

Zeigler, E. F. (1979). *Elements of a competency based approach to management development: A preliminary analysis.* Paper read at the Convention of the Canadian Association for Health, Physical Education and Recreation. Winnipeg, Manitoba.

CHAPTER 5
PLANNING

manage YOUR LEARNING

After completing this chapter you should be able to:

- Understand the steps in the planning process.
- Explain the significance of the various steps in the planning process.
- Define and describe strategic management.
- Understand the significance of mission statements.
- Explain tactical/operational plans.
- See the relationship between planning and budgeting.
- Explain how goals can be constraints.
- Explain the significance of information in planning and discuss the methods used to gather information.
- Understand knowledge management.
- Understand the need for planning without goals or directional planning.

strategic CONCEPTS

alternative
brainstorming
budgeting
constraint
Delphi technique
directional planning
forecasting
goal
knowledge management
means and ends
mission statement
nominal group technique
planning
real/operative goal
stated/official goal
strategic planning
tactical/operational planning

THE PLANNING FUNCTION

In the first four chapters, we described the field of sport management (Chapter 1), the concept of organizations (Chapter 2), organizations as open systems (Chapter 3), and the act of management (Chapter 4).

The previous chapters set the stage for an in-depth discussion of management itself. As we noted in Chapter 4, management can be described from several different perspectives. The approach of this book is to describe and discuss management as a set of functions: planning, organizing, leading, and evaluating. This chapter is devoted to the function of planning. We begin with a definition of planning and go on to describe the steps in the planning process. Then, we explore the distinctions between strategic planning and operational planning. Following this is a description of the elements of a good mission statement—an integral part of strategic management. Then, after contrasting long-range planning with short-term planning, we look at the issues surrounding organizational goals. The chapter concludes with a discussion of directional planning as a viable option for managers and organizations.

DEFINITION OF PLANNING

Although all of the four managerial functions referred to in Chapter 4—planning, organizing, leading, and evaluating—are integrally linked, the planning function must precede the others. Let us therefore look at how some authors define **planning**:

> *Planning* . . . is essentially a decision making process that focuses on the future of the organization and how it will get where it wants to go. (Hitt, Black, Porter, & Hanson, 2007, p. 268)

> Planning involves defining goals, establishing an overall strategy for achieving those goals, and developing a comprehensive set of plans to integrate and coordinate the work needed to achieve the goals. (Robbins, Coulter, Leach, & Kilfoil, 2012, p. 185)

> *Planning* is the conscious, systematic process of making decisions about goals and activities that an individual, group, work unit, or organization will pursue in the future. (Bateman & Snell, 2007, p. 118)

> Planning encompasses defining an organization's goals, establishing an overall strategy for achieving those goals, and developing a hierarchy of plans to integrate and coordinate activities. It is concerned, then, with *ends* (what is to be done) as well as with *means* (how it is to be done). (Robbins, 1997, p. 130)

key definitions

In the previous chapters, we defined sport management as the coordination of resources (human and material), relevant technologies, and situational contingencies for the efficient production and exchange of sport services. We defined an organization as consisting of people whose specialized activities are coordinated to achieve specified goals. Management is the specialized activity of coordinating the activities of others, and limited resources, toward efficiently achieving the goals.

TO recap

These definitions suggest that planning is concerned with establishing goals for the organization and identifying the activities and programs to achieve those goals. There is also the underlying notion that planning precedes other managerial activities. This process of deciding on what is to be achieved and how it should be done involves several steps, which we will now examine.

STEPS IN THE PLANNING PROCESS

We can use the framework illustrated in Exhibit 5.1 to help define and discuss the total planning process. In the model, planning is composed of the stages of specifying goals, identifying opportunities, identifying constraints, generating alternatives, establishing performance criteria, evaluating alternatives, selecting an alternative, and presenting the plan document. First of all, note that the specification of organizational goals takes place along with identification of opportunities and constraints, even though they are discussed sequentially.

Specifying Goals

As we noted earlier, the first step in the planning process is to set out the **goals** for the organization. An organization may have more than one goal, and these may relate to profitability, growth, market share, productivity/efficiency, leadership, client satisfaction, or social awareness (Pettinger, 1997; Robbins, 1997; Rosen, 1995; Rue & Byars, 2009). We will now describe these various goals.

Profitability refers to the fact that a profit-oriented sport organization may aim to secure a specified number of dollars as its profits. Alternatively, it may seek a certain percentage of its capital outlay as profits. Thus, a fitness firm may aim for a profit of $50,000 or a 15 percent return on its capital outlay. Most professional sport organizations are likely to have profitability as the primary goal, and they

exhibit 5.1 Steps in the planning process.

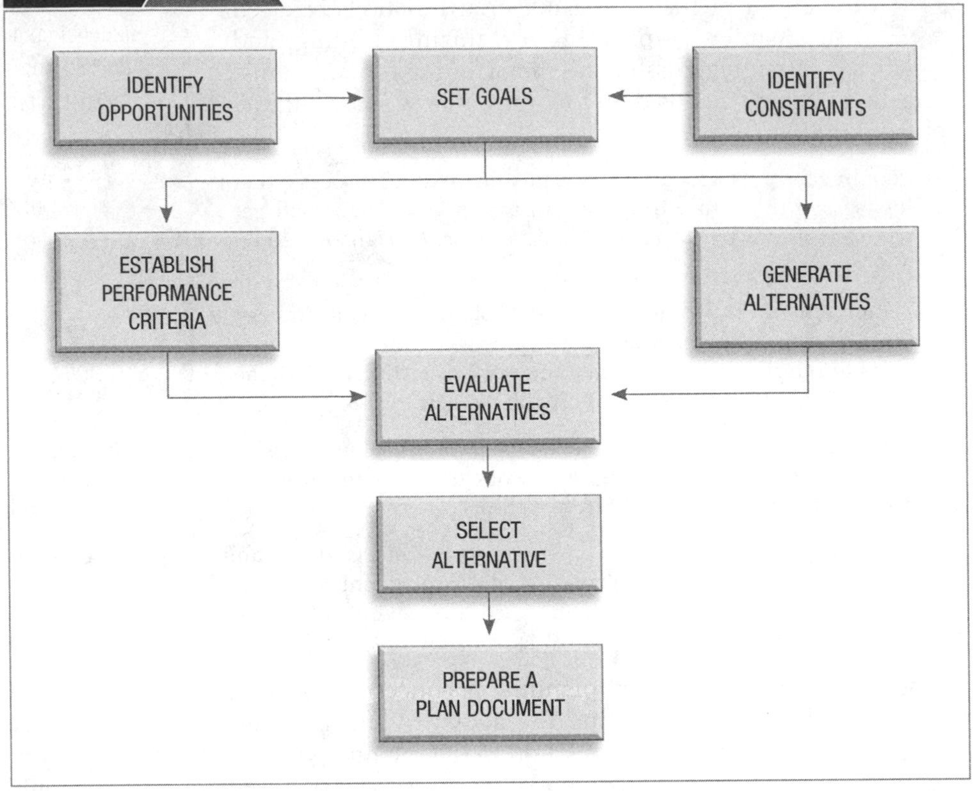

run their business with that motive firmly in mind. However, this is not to deny that some professional sport franchises may tolerate monetary losses in favor of other benefits such as winning, creating a tax shelter, and gaining prestige.

Another goal might be related to the *growth* of the organization—growth in terms of profits, total revenue, market share, number of employees, or the number of products or activities. The growth concept is equally relevant to both profit and nonprofit organizations. For instance, a department of sport management may seek to increase its number of faculty members and the number of courses it offers. One growth objective of an organization such as the North American Sports Group's "Hoop-It-Up" is to stage its three-on-three basketball tournaments in a growing number of cities. Profit-oriented fitness clubs may view the increase in number of members as a sign of growth. By the same token, they may also seek to grow by opening new clubs in different locations in the same city or in a different city. Because size is often equated with status, it is not uncommon for nonprofit organizations to emphasize growth as their primary objective. For the Y, growth may be measured by enrollments in its various physical activities programs.

Market share refers to the fact that some organizations may have the securing of a certain share of the market as their goal. In fact, relative market share has been used as a measure of effectiveness in many comparative studies of organizations. Even universities tend to have as an objective the recruitment of a certain percentage of the total student population. Businesses providing fitness and sports services also compete for a larger percentage of the market in their geographical area. Sporting goods manufacturers such as Under Armour and Nike are also sure to work toward gaining a larger share of the market. Consider a professional sport franchise that has to compete for a significant share of the entertainment dollar (i.e., the total amount of dollars the local citizens are willing to shell out for entertainment) with not only other professional sport franchises in the locality but also with other entertainment ventures like movie theaters. Similarly, as the leading cable channel for sports broadcasting, ESPN is striving to increase its market share (or at the least maintain its current share of the market) by going mobile and using social media. The concept of *productivity/efficiency* refers to the maximization of the output relative to a given input. Though all organizations are concerned with efficiency, it becomes a singular concern in times of crisis. For example, educational institutions have been forced to consider efficiency in their operations as a result of dwindling financial resources. The practices of downsizing and restructuring are often a part of efforts to enhance productivity by paring down the labor force and eliminating inefficient operations. When a professional sport franchise attempts to trade a high-salaried athlete, it could be for the purpose of reducing expenses and thereby becoming more efficient. Of course, it is assumed that the franchise will perform as well without the star player. Similarly, a fitness club may drop a program for a special group, such as seniors, because the program is not profitable—that is, the program costs more to run than it generates in revenue. In a similar manner, a profit-oriented golf club may reduce the number of employees in order to become more efficient. In these examples, the organization may already be successful in other respects (such as making a profit), but not necessarily efficient.

Organizations may also aspire to *leadership in the market* in terms of the products they produce or the methods of production. For example, many computer companies compete to produce new and innovative products, both hardware and software. Universities and departments of sport management also take pride in offering new and more relevant courses or programs and in being known as leaders in the educational domain. University athletic departments also strive to be leaders in terms of number of sports supported, extent and quality of facilities, athlete assistance programs, and so on. Fitness club chains seek to be the leaders of the industry by offering new activity classes and new equipment, which are then copied by other chains and independent clubs.

Client satisfaction also may be an important objective sought by an organization. Such satisfaction is, of course, primarily contingent upon whether the products (goods or services) are of sufficiently high quality. Rigorous quality control measures, procurement of high-quality raw materials, and improvement of production processes are indicative of the importance that sporting goods manufacturers place on this objective. Golf courses make every effort to satisfy their patrons, including making sure that tee times are scheduled efficiently. Major sporting event organizers offer entertainment during game breaks, concessions, and other activities both before and after the game with a view to satisfying their fans.

Many organizations may also set goals in terms of *social awareness*—being socially responsible and responsive. The problem of childhood obesity is behind the NFL's Play60 campaign, the goal of which is to increase physical activity among children to fight obesity by encouraging children to be active for 60 minutes a day. An example from intercollegiate athletics is The Ohio State Athletic Department declaring its Ohio Stadium as a "zero waste" facility in 2011, meaning that 90 percent of all the waste generated at the stadium is to be recycled or composted. In addition, all items sold within the stadium are either recyclable or compostable. The actions of municipal recreation departments to improve safety features in playgrounds or the actions of a professional sport franchise in controlling the crowd could be a function of social awareness as well as the desire to avoid legal liability. In fact, you could say that risk management must be primarily a social responsibility.

Most nonprofit organizations are guided by their awareness of societal needs. The Red Cross and the Salvation Army are two examples in which social awareness is the main guide for action. Schools and universities are also sensitive to the fact that their contributions are to society as a whole and not just to their current students. One of the purposes of any intercollegiate athletic department is to ensure that athletes obtain a quality education so that they can become useful citizens.

It is neither necessary nor practical for an organization to limit its goals to any one of the above areas. In fact, most organizations have multiple goals. (The concept of multiple goals and their effect on rational planning are discussed in a later section of this chapter.) However, specification of one or more goals should be undertaken only after thoroughly considering the opportunities available to, and the constraints faced by, the organization.

Identifying Opportunities

The choice of organizational goals depends on the opportunities available in the organization's environment. For instance, a fitness club may find that many senior citizens have moved into its locality. This presents an opportunity for the club to start a fitness program for seniors. A charitable organization may find that it cannot maintain and run its recreational facility for lack of funds. This may provide an opportunity for a commercial sport enterprise or the city recreation department to take over the facility. The NCAA's expectation that all university athletic departments should attempt to achieve gender equity may prove to be an opportunity for a university to start new programs for women. Generally, the opportunities are a function of economic, social, cultural, demographic, environmental, political, legal, technological, and competitive trends (David, 1997).

Opportunities may also arise out of conditions internal to the organization. For example, a fitness club may be building a reserve fund for use in case of emergencies. Over the years, the fund may have exceeded the planned-for level of emergency. In such a case, the club has the opportunity to invest the excess money in additional facilities, equipment, or programs. Similarly, the employees of the fitness club may have gained additional certifications that will enable the club to offer more programs that require such certification.

Identifying Constraints

The third stage in the planning process involves identifying **constraints** (refer back to Exhibit 5.1). Although an organization may desire to achieve a number of goals, some of them may not be attainable owing to specific constraints. These constraints may be in the form of limited resources—finances, time, or personnel. Thus, a fitness club may wish to expand its program of offerings but be unable to do so because of limited capital or staff. Additional constraints may also be placed on an organization by virtue of societal norms, government regulations, or competition from other organizations. A firm specializing in representing athletes, for example, is constrained by legal requirements in several states.

We noted earlier that the NCAA's expectation regarding gender equity could be an opportunity for some university athletic departments. By the same token, it could be a constraint on a university considering adding one more men's sport. As is the case with opportunities, constraints may stem from environmental influences such as regulations by the government or interorganizational networks. A university athletic department must consider the financial rules of the Internal Revenue Service and the regulations of the NCAA regarding amateur status in its recruiting efforts. (Unlike a pro sport franchise, it cannot simply outbid other schools competing for a talented player.) Another example of environmental con-

sidebar 5.1

THE SMART WAY TO SET GOALS

We noted that setting goals for the organization is the first step in the planning process, and that these goals may relate to different areas such as profitability, growth, and efficiency. While our discussion has been general, organizations must specify each and every goal in concrete terms so that those who are charged with carrying out the goals know exactly what is to be accomplished and when. For example, a sport organization may say that its goal is to increase its membership. Compare this general statement to one in which an organization says that it wants to increase membership by 20 percent by the end of the year. The goal statement has become specific in terms of percentage increase in membership and the time period within which it should be accomplished. In business literature, this line of thinking has been described in the form of the acronym **SMART,** which indicates goals that are **S**pecific, **M**easurable, **A**chievable, **R**elevant, and **T**ime-bound (e.g., Platt, 2002), as illustrated in Exhibit 5.2.

Based on the acronym SMART, for example, the United States Track and Field (USATF) organization set nine goals for itself at the beginning of 2013 (USATF, 2013). They are:

1. Increase membership by 20 percent without reduction in net income through a membership drive and creating new membership categories.
2. Secure $1 million each year through sponsorship, membership, TV and media contracts, merchandizing, and rights fees.
3. Create financial savings of 1 to 3 percent by making the existing operations more efficient.
4. Find partners to promote USATF events so as to create a surplus from them.
5. Increase the popularity of USATF by increasing attendance at our events, TV ratings by 20 percent, and exposure through social media by 50 percent.
6. Develop strategy for events to include all segments of participants (e.g., youth, masters).
7. Create an operating reserve to cover nine months of expenses within five years.
8. *and* 9. Collaborate with USATF Foundation to raise $20 million in the next five years to set up an endowment to support USATF operations.

Let us look at the acronym in greater detail with reference to a college athletic department's goal of increasing attendance at women's basketball games.

Specific: Instead of setting a global goal to increase attendance next season, a specific goal is set to increase next season's attendance by 20% over this season. The marketing department is designated as the agency that will work to achieve this targeted increase in attendance.

Measurable: The goal of achieving a 20% increase can easily be measured by comparing next season's attendance with this season's attendance.

Achievable: Assuming that the athletic department in question had not done much in terms or promoting women's basketball, expecting a 20% increase in attendance is realistic and achievable.

Relevant: The goal is consistent with the functions of the marketing department and is aligned with the athletic department's mission of promoting both men's and women's teams.

Time-bound: The goal is time-bound as the 20% increase in attendance is expected to be achieved by the end of next season (a 12-month time span).

exhibit 5.2 SMART acronym for goal setting.

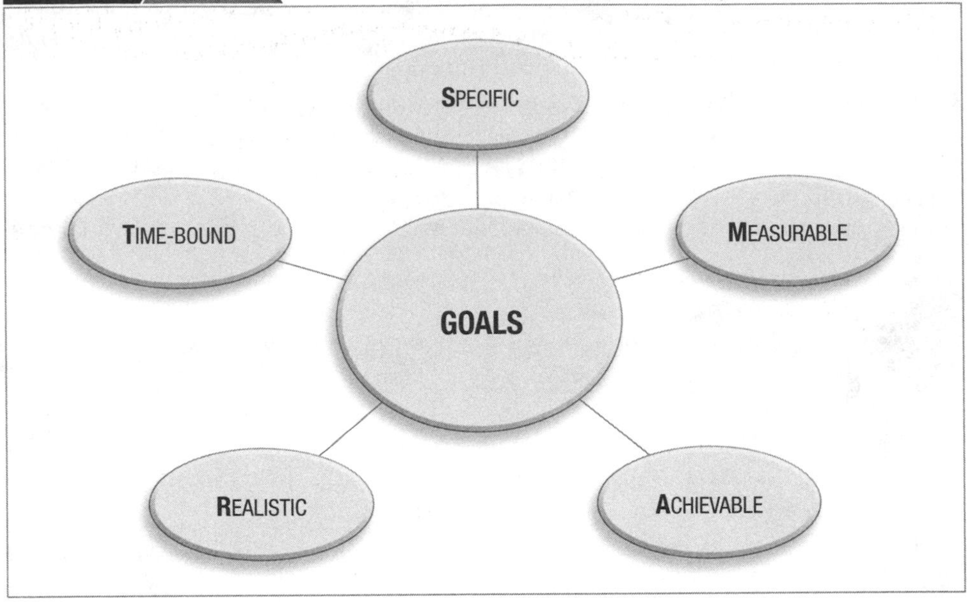

straints is the existence of competition in the market. For example, a fitness club may not be able to extend its operations to another locality if another fitness enterprise is already there. Geography, climate, and physical resources can impede the implementation of a plan. A plan for the development of ice hockey could not be easily implemented in a tropical country because of the climate conditions.

Constraints may be internally generated as well. Although many university athletic departments are quite willing to make gender equity a goal, they may be constrained in implementing it due to a scarcity of funds. As another example, a fitness firm may not be able to offer fitness appraisal as one of its services because the available expertise and equipment may not meet the technological standards, and the firm does not have the capital to acquire the needed equipment. A sport marketing firm wishing to expand its operations to include social media marketing may not be able to do so because its employees do not have the necessary training or experience, and hiring people with such expertise may be too expensive.

In the foregoing analysis of opportunities and constraints, we noted that these can be a function of both internal and external (or environmental) conditions. The emphasis on environmental conditions takes us back to the notion of organizations as open systems, as discussed in Chapter 3. That is, any plan to be successful needs to be formulated so that it is aligned with the organization's environment. Stated another way, planners must hold a systems view of the organization, taking into consideration the external environment as well as the internal conditions in setting goals for the organization. A review of all the opportunities and constraints in the environment would show which of the desired goals are within reach and which are not feasible.

Generating Alternative Courses of Action

After specifying the goals, two sets of activities must be carried out independently: generation of **alternative** courses of action for achieving the specified goals, and

sidebar 5.2

SWOT AND THE TENNIS CLUB

The three stages of identifying opportunities, identifying constraints, and setting goals as outlined in the text involve environmental analyses and internal evaluations. Our discussion implies that such analyses would show the strengths and weaknesses of the organization in question. These analyses are popularly known by the acronym SWOT: Strengths, Weaknesses, Opportunities, and Threats (Pettinger, 1997; Robbins, 1997; Rosen, 1995). Consider, for example, Dan Jackson, a former member of a local university tennis team in a mid-size city who wants to start his own tennis club. As shown in Exhibit 5.3, his strengths include his tennis expertise. (He was an outstanding player trained by expert coaches.) Jackson is very knowledgeable in tennis instruction and coaching and could prove to be an outstanding pro. Furthermore, former teammates have agreed to help out with the tennis club. Both Jackson and the teammates are well known in and around the city, having won several tournaments and championships as members of the local university team. Jackson has continued to play competitive tennis with some success.

His weaknesses include a lack of experience in running a business. Jackson majored in social work, and none of the teammates has any background in business. Furthermore, he lacks the initial capital necessary to start up a business. Jackson would have to rely on well-wishers and banks to provide such capital. However, there is some indication that such capital might be forthcoming.

His opportunities include the fact that the city is one of the fastest growing in the region. It boasts an above-average median family income. In addition, the citizens are highly involved in sport and physical activity. These factors indicate that there are likely to be enough people willing to pay to join a tennis club. If the facility could be located near the university, it may be successful in targeting students for membership. Furthermore, the city itself is promoting new businesses by offering sizable incentives.

As for threats, the city's two existing fitness clubs are both planning to expand into tennis operations. There may not be enough customers in the city to sustain all three tennis enterprises.

With careful consideration of this situation's strengths, weaknesses, opportunities, and threats, Jackson will be able to make a decision regarding whether to start the business. This process is illustrated in Exhibit 5.3.

exhibit 5.3 The SWOT approach to organizational planning.

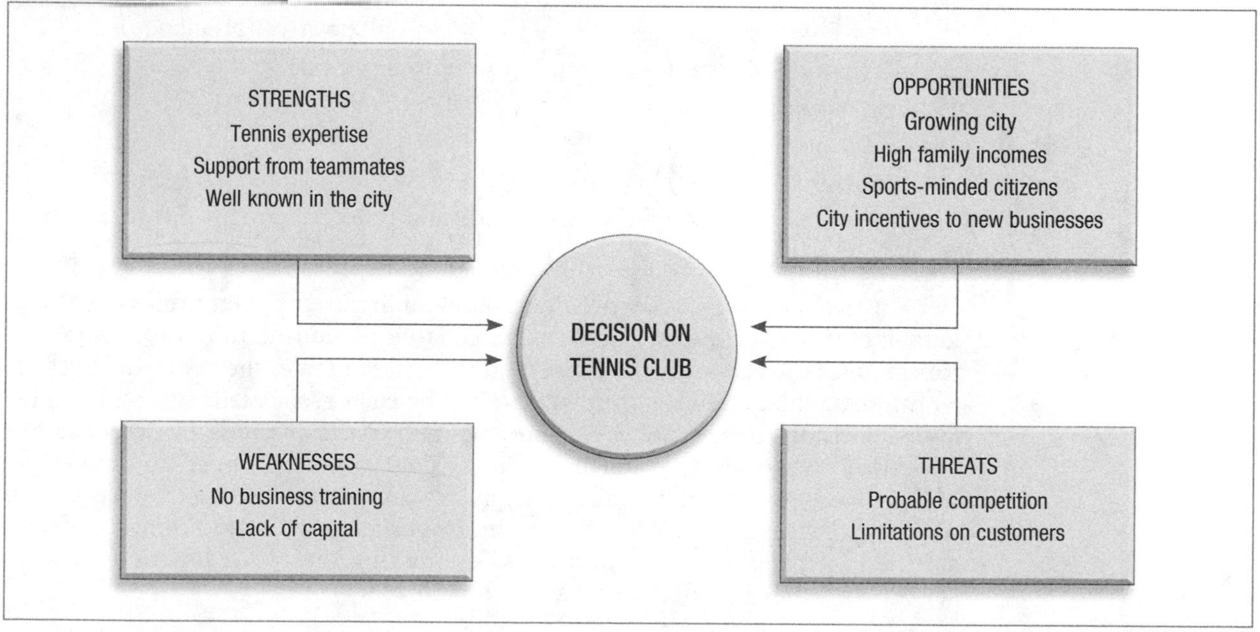

sidebar 5.3

BENCHMARKING AS A PLANNING TOOL

To generate alternative courses of action, managers can adopt *benchmarking.* "Benchmarking is the investigation of the best results among competitors and the practices that lead to those results" (Hitt et al., 2007, p. 274). The emphasis here is on the practices or activities of the other organizations that lead to their successes. To the extent the focal organization has not engaged in those activities in the past, they can be considered a feasible set of alternate courses of action.

the establishment of criteria to evaluate these alternatives with a view to selecting the best ones (see Exhibit 5.1).

The term *generation* implies that planners are involved in an attempt to develop new and untried alternatives and are not satisfied with simply considering the existing and tried alternatives. Filley, House, and Kerr (1976) have pointed out that perhaps the greatest danger to effective decision making is "the tendency to ignore the practical difficulty of developing alternatives and to place greater emphasis on goal definition and the process of weighting alternatives" (p. 431). In order to ensure that a variety of alternatives are generated, planners must foster open communication among relevant members of the organization. Creativity and ingenuity in developing new ways of doing things must be encouraged. For instance, some universities, faced with the necessity of accommodating increasing numbers of spectators in their football stadiums, have come up with the innovative idea of digging up the ground and lowering the football field. In addition, if the track around the football field is removed, there will be room for many more spectators. Such an idea may eliminate the need for an expensive brand-new stadium. To bring in more revenue, many intercollegiate athletic programs offer tours of their athletic facilities. In addition, they also offer special ticketing packages such as family packages, theme nights, and discount concessions nights.

Establishing Performance Criteria to Evaluate Alternatives

After alternatives have been generated, the best one is selected. Doing so requires that guidelines or performance criteria have been established (see Exhibit 5.1). These criteria must be established independently from the process by which the alternatives were generated. Otherwise, there is a tendency to fit the evaluative performance criteria to a preferred alternative, and the resulting choice might not be optimal. The following criteria may be useful in evaluating the alternatives:

1. relative cost and associated benefits of each alternative (efficiency)
2. alternative's potential contribution to more than one goal
3. ease of implementation
4. ease of measurement
5. conformity to societal norms and government sanctions
6. availability of personnel with requisite ability to implement the alternative
7. other similar factors

For instance, a city may decide to build an arena to attract professional basketball and hockey teams. The decision is based on consideration of several factors such as the economic activity the arena will generate, the pride and prestige a professional team would bring to the city, the costs associated with building the arena, and the reaction (positive and negative) of the citizens. The city has two options on where to build the arena: in the core of downtown or on the periphery of downtown where two major highways intersect. The downtown option is more expensive primarily because of the real estate cost. In addition, it will create traffic problems. On the positive side, building the arena downtown is consistent with the city's determination to revitalize its core.

The other option—building the arena out of the downtown area—is attractive because of the reduced costs for the real estate. In addition, it will not create any significant traffic congestion in the vicinity of the arena. However, the arena in that location will not contribute much to the downtown revitalization project. The costs, the traffic congestion, and the contribution to more than one goal (the revitalization project) are just a few examples of criteria the decision makers can use in evaluating the two options. Once again, the idea of a systems view comes into play. The analyses of internal and external environments and the organization's strengths and weaknesses will indicate which of the alternatives is more feasible as well as more acceptable to the environment.

Evaluating Alternatives

The evaluation of alternatives follows the establishment of performance criteria and the generation of alternative courses of action (see Exhibit 5.1). This process involves the comparison of alternatives to the performance criteria. It might be solely computational in nature if the established performance criteria are all quantitative in nature. Under these circumstances, there is no need for the planners to make any judgment decisions. For example, in planning the transportation of a football team for a bowl game, the athletic department may have several alternatives. Because each alternative will have clear quantifiable data on the expenses, time lost, and other criteria, it is easy to evaluate these alternatives and choose the best one according to the set performance criteria. For a more critical decision, consider again the case of the city considering building its arena either in the downtown area or outside it. We said that the real estate cost would be much lower outside the downtown area, so if the only criterion were the cost, then the decision would be clear: build outside the downtown area. These are examples of quantitative criteria applied to planning.

IN brief

The critical steps in the planning process are specifying goals after identifying the constraints, generating alternatives to achieve those goals, and evaluating these alternatives on previously stated criteria.

However, in most instances the performance and measurement criteria are qualitative in nature. When this is the case, greater care must be taken to be as objective as possible in evaluating each alternative on the selected performance criteria. Any variability in such assessment could falsely indicate one alternative's superiority over the others. A case in point is the hiring of a football coach. Many of the selection criteria, such as years of experience and past performance records of the candidates, are quantifiable; therefore, it is easy to evaluate and compare the candidates. On the other hand, other selection criteria, such as disposition, interpersonal skills, values, and ethics, are qualitative in nature. A candidate's capacity to interact effectively with the players, administrators, other coaches, and the media is a function of personality and interpersonal skills. Similarly, whether a candidate shares the values of the organization in promoting the welfare of the athletes, and whether the candidate will refrain from violating the letter and spirit of the NCAA rules, are based on her own values and ethical standards. These are not as easily measured as years of experience or a win/loss record. Therefore, the evaluation of the pool of candidates on these criteria becomes problematic, and the selectors have to use their best judgment. In the case of the city building an arena, consider that two different designs for the exterior of the arena have been presented. Though cost may be one criterion in the selection of one design over the other, there is also the criterion of aesthetics. Does one design present a more tasteful, elegant, and pleasing appearance? Because this criterion is qualitative in nature, decisions made in this regard will be more subjective than objective.

Selecting an Alternative

Selection of an alternative as outlined in Exhibit 5.1 is technical and routine in nature. That is, the alternative with the highest rating on the evaluative criteria is selected automatically as the means to a given goal. If two or more alternatives are given the same highest rating, the choice can be made simply by tossing a coin! The simplicity of this step emphasizes the fact that serious thought, careful deliberations, and necessary computations need to have gone into the previous steps of the planning process. A common fallacy is to equate this final step with the entire planning process. When a high school athlete signs with a university on the National Signing Day, everybody would say that the athlete has made a decision. Such a simple statement overlooks the fact that the athlete had carefully gone through a long process of looking at all the alternatives and evaluating them over several months. Similarly, when the city officials announce the chosen site or design for a new arena, their decision usually is the result of many discussions and debates, media scrutiny, polls, and political struggles that are all part of the decision-making process.

Presenting the Plan Document

As the final step in the planning process, the administrators must draw up a document for the benefit of all members of the organization (see Exhibit 5.1). This document should specify (a) the goals being sought, (b) the activities to be carried out to achieve those goals, (c) the initiatives of the management in this regard, (d) the corresponding responsibilities of the members or units, (e) the standards to be maintained, (f) the methods and measures of performance, and (g) the controls to be exercised at various levels to ensure conformance to the plan.

STRATEGIC PLANNING

So far we have discussed the dynamics of the planning process and several guidelines to make it more effective. Note that the scope of planning, the time frame for it, and the rigor with which it is formulated will all vary with the type of problem addressed and the organizational level at which the planning occurs. The planning that occurs at the top level of management is called strategic planning (David, 1997; Rosen, 1995). Interestingly, "the term *strategy* is derived from the Greek word *strategos*, which means 'a general.' In ancient times, it meant the art and science of managing military forces to victory" (Megginson, Mosley, & Pietri, 1992, p. 197). The idea is that planning at the highest levels is strategic because it affects the whole organization and its future. Such strategic planning encompasses all the units within the organization and their operations. **Strategic planning** is defined as "the process of formulating, implementing, and evaluating organizational changes in ways that enable an organization to achieve its objectives" (Greenberg, 2005, p. 462).

The first step in strategic planning is to determine the *strategic intent*, which "captures the general identity, direction and level of aspirations of the organization" (Hitt et al., 2007, p. 192). For example, the NFL can have the intent of being the most popular league around the world and of having several competi-

Dr. Laura Misener is a rising star among sport management scholars and has contributed the following discussion of the Critical Path Method, a popular tool in mainstream management.

PLANNING TOOL: CRITICAL PATH METHOD

Laura Misener, Western University

Managers in sport and physical activity have an assortment of tools to help them with the planning processes in organizations. Technological advances have made it possible to access these tools easily, and managers should employ them to achieve desired outcomes.

The Critical Path Method (CPM) is a longstanding approach to planning that breaks down complex plans into manageable, achievable tasks with associated guidelines for coordination and timing. CPM is a project management technique developed in the late 1950s by Morgan R. Walker of DuPont, a U.S.-based chemical company, and James E. Kelley, Jr. of Remington Rand, a business machine manufacturer. The term *critical path* was developed as a response to the Program Evaluation and Review Technique (PERT), which was developed and used by the U.S. Navy. The precursors of what came to be known as Critical Path were developed during the Manhattan Project and put into practice by DuPont in the early 1940s. CPM is commonly used with all forms of projects, including construction, aerospace and defense, software development, research projects, product development, engineering, and plant maintenance, among others. It is a useful tool for any project with interdependent activities. For the most part, the original concept of the CPM mathematical program and approach is no longer used, but the term is generally still applied to any approach used to analyze a project network logic diagram. Thus, it is a worthwhile tool for sport managers in project management.

The Critical Path Method is an effective and powerful method of assessing:

- Specific tasks that must be carried out
- Where parallel activities and tasks can be performed
- The shortest time in which a project can be completed
- The necessary resources to execute individual tasks and the overall project
- The sequence of tasks and activities
- The priorities of each task
- The timing of the tasks and related activities
- The most efficient way of shortening time on urgent projects

An effective analysis of the critical path can make the difference between success and failure on complex projects. It can be very useful for assessing the importance of problems faced during the implementation of the plan. There are essentially four steps necessary to implement CPM:

Step One: Determine Tasks

In order to develop the list of a project's particular tasks and activities, it is necessary to determine the discrete tasks needed to accomplish the project. In examining the overall task to be accomplished, write down each individual task necessary to complete the overall goal. For example, if the project at hand is running a charity road race the tasks might include plotting and mapping the course, obtaining necessary permits for the course, meeting with city personnel regarding road closures, coordinating with police regarding road closures, securing volunteers for race stations, developing sponsorship packages, etc. In this way, each of the tasks for that particular race project has been identified, thus ensuring the necessary steps are taken to produce this event.

Step Two: Estimate Times for Each Task

Once the tasks for the project have been identified, it is then necessary to estimate the earliest start date for each task and the estimated length of time each task will take. In addition, it is important to determine if a task is a parallel task (i.e., can occur simultaneous to other tasks) or sequential to other tasks (i.e., dependent upon completion of previous task). If tasks are sequential, it is also vital to show which stage they depend on in order to properly plot the CPM task chart. In Table 1, an example from the charity road race event demonstrates task breakdown, begin date, estimated time, and sequencing. Note that often the timing of a task will require specific knowledge of the task. In this example, the race event managers need to know that the city has up to three weeks from the date of application to process the course permits.

Step Three: Plot Tasks as "Activity-on-Arc" Diagram

Critical Path analyses are presented using circle and arrow diagrams showing events within the project, and the relationship between the tasks. An "activity-on-arc" (AOA) diagram has numbered "nodes" that represent stages of project completion. The diagram is constructed to represent particular stages in task completion. The nodes are connected with arrows or arcs that represent the activities that are listed in the previously created task table. The letter corresponds to a particular task and the number in brackets corresponds to the start time for the particular task. An arrow between two event nodes shows the activity needed to

TABLE 1 Sample partial task list: charity road race.

TASK	EARLIEST START	LENGTH	TYPE	DEPENDENT ON . . .
A. Drive tentative routes	Week 0	5 days	Sequential	
B. Obtain city for road permits	Week 1	3 weeks	Parallel	A
C. Meet with City Clerk regarding road closures	Week 2	2 weeks	Parallel	B
D. Contact emergency services	Week 4	4 days	Sequential	A
E. Draw detailed map with checkpoints and road descriptions	Week 6	1 week	Sequential	A, B, C, D
F. Secure insurance certificates	Week 3	3 weeks	Parallel	B
G. Create list of locations associated with emergency services	Week 5	1 week	Sequential	D
H. Print copy of map and route descriptions for participants	Week 5	5 days	Sequential	F, D

complete that task. A description of the task can be written underneath the arrow. The length of the task is shown beside the task, and sometimes the start times can also be included. An example of a very simple diagram is shown in Figure 1. The simple diagram shows important information about the task: the sequential nature of the task and time in days for the task to be completed.

FIGURE 1 Simple CPM diagram.

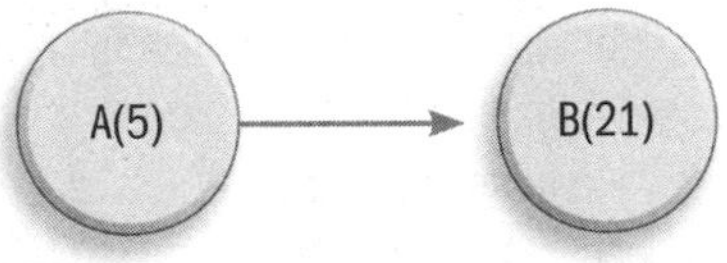

In drawing the CPM diagram, it is necessary to consider the tasks that are to be completed sequentially and those that can be completed in parallel. See Figure 2 for a more complex diagram, which demonstrates how some activities can take place at the same time as others. The consideration for this logic is based on a number of factors, including human resources, capacity, and financing available to undertake these tasks.

FIGURE 2 Increasingly complex CPM diagram.

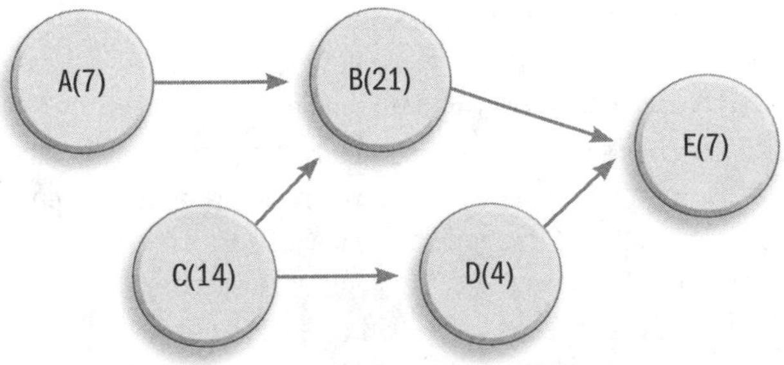

Step Four: Determine Critical Path

Having determined the tasks necessary to complete the project and their time estimations, it is necessary to determine the critical path. The critical path consists of the activities that have to be completed on time; if they are not, the whole project is put in jeopardy. When designing the CPM diagram it is a good idea to highlight the vital sections of the plan to show that they are of utmost importance to the successful completion of the project. In the charity race example, applying for the course permits on time is an example of a critical task. It may occur that a project needs to be completed earlier than determined possible in the Critical Path analysis, for example, if the event managers find out that the city needs more than three weeks to process the permits. In this case it would then be necessary to re-plan the project. This would necessitate re-assessing the impact of this on the project's cost, quality, and time required to completion. For example, additional resources may need to be secured for each activity to lessen the time spent on each task.

Drawing nodes, tables, and arcs can be tricky, particularly when it comes to connecting nodes with arrows and giving direction to the arrows. A number of software programs available online employ mathematical modeling and creative drawing features that can assist in this process. These programs provide an intuitive interface and network templates to assist in each of the steps in the CPM. A free online Critical Path Calculator is available from Sporkforge.com.

The Critical Path Method is one tool to aid sport managers in helping to certify that extra time and resources are not wasted on noncritical parts of a project and to ensure that programmed projects are completed efficiently and on time.

tive divisions in various countries, all culminating in a final world championship, as with the World Cup of soccer. With this strategic intent in mind, the NFL may begin to operate in different continents. Hitt et al. (2007) suggest that strategic intent is the heart of strategic planning or management. Thus, strategic planning includes "those activities that involve defining the organization's mission, setting its objectives, and developing strategies to enable it to operate successfully in its environment" (Megginson et al., 1992, p. 197).

The emphases in the above definitions are twofold. First, strategic planning (or strategic management) involves the entire organization and its units. Second, strategic planning is concerned with matching the organization with the external environment. In other words, those who are involved with strategic planning must take into account the opportunities available in the larger environment and the obstacles and constraints (including competition) posed by the environment. Strategic planning addresses the challenge of exploiting the opportunities while at the same time overcoming the obstacles.

Once a strategic decision is made, other planning activities follow. For example, the strategic decision to build an arena is followed by planning by the architects, builders, facility managers, marketing units, concert managers, and others.

Strategic planning differs from other forms of planning because it

1. involves decisions by top management
2. requires allocation of large amounts of resources
3. has significant long-term effects
4. focuses on the organization's interactions with the external environment

Of course, such planning should take into account the internal strengths and weaknesses of the organization itself. In other words, although strategic planning focuses primarily on environmental contingencies, it cannot be effective if it does not consider the resources available within the organization.

On occasion, the effects of strategic planning/management may be quite drastic. For instance, consider the efforts by many corporate managers to downsize their enterprises, whereas some other executives take the path of acquisitions and diversification. These differing strategic processes are undertaken only after careful analysis of the opportunities and obstacles posed by the external environment and an audit of internal dynamics and the resources, strengths, and weaknesses of the organization.

When an entrepreneur holding a franchise in one sport in one city bids for a franchise in a new league in another sport in another city, such a move is said to be strategic. Such moves involve an extensive analysis of several factors, including the growth in the popularity of the sport, the sporting tradition of the city and the community surrounding it, and even the viability of the new league.

In another example, a university athletic department has to decide whether to renovate an existing arena or build a new one. This strategic decision involves many factors—the cost of each alternative, inputs from various contributors, and the long-term viability of the old arena. If a new arena is built, there is the opportunity to name it after a person or an organization and thereby secure a large donation for it. On the other hand, it is possible that the pub-

sidebar 5.4

STRATEGIC PLANNING ON A SMALLER SCALE

Strategic planning does not necessarily involve huge sums of money. When students choose one university over another, they have engaged in strategic planning. When two or more entrepreneurs decide to form a company to get into the golf business instead of real estate, they have performed strategic planning. If they decide to construct a new golf course instead of buying an existing one, they have made a strategic decision. Similarly, when a fitness club extends its operations to provide tennis facilities, the decision is born of strategic planning.

lic and funding agencies such as the state government may question having two arenas at one university. The decision makers may also consider renting the new facility for additional entertainment purposes such as concerts to offset maintenance costs. But then others may question the notion of the university getting into the entertainment business. These are just two examples of opposing forces operating in the environment. Decision makers have the formidable task of weighing all these factors and making the most appropriate strategic decision—one that will have a long-lasting effect on the department and the university.

IN brief

Strategic planning focuses on the direction that the total organization and its units will take over the long run. Such planning takes place at the organization's top levels and covers a long time frame. More importantly, it links the organization with its environment.

A professional sport club moving from one city to another, a city replacing its old arena with a new one, and the NBA launching the Women's NBA (WNBA) are other examples of strategic planning. These are impressive decisions, chiefly because of the millions (if not billions) of dollars involved. Brown, Rascher, Nagel, and McEvoy (2010) report that in the years between 2000 and 2010, $14.26 billion (in 2013 dollars) was spent on sport facilities.

Deciding to build a new arena, whether a university or professional facility, is not a random act. These kinds of expenses reflect strategic planning, and "Strategy is the art and science of combining the many resources available to achieve the best match between an organization and its environment" (Pierce & Dunham, 1990, p. 170). In the case of university arenas, the decision follows from the global approach and strategic direction proposed by the athletic department and the university administrators. That direction may include becoming a leader in university athletics, being known for the department's athletic and academic achievements, and being acknowledged for its facilities. From this perspective, building a new arena is one step toward attaining national prominence. Thus, we see that setting and articulating the mission for the organization is critical to strategic management.

Readers will recognize similarities between what modern-day advocates such as Iveson advance, and McCaskey's (1974) directional planning described in this chapter. The major difference between the two conceptualizations is that while McCaskey laid out his *directional planning* as an option for management, Iveson and other modern management experts imply that managers do not have any other choice but to think in terms of *strategic advancement*.

Mission and Mission Statement

According to Pearce and David (1987), a **mission statement** (a) sets a business apart; (b) reveals an organization's product or service, markets, customers, and philosophy; (c) provides the foundation for priorities, strategies, plans, and work assignments including managerial jobs and structures; and (d) specifies the fundamental reason why an organization exists.

According to Pearce and David (1987), a mission statement should include the following eight elements:

1. Specification of key elements in the company philosophy
2. Identification of the company's self-concept
3. Identification of the company's desired public image
4. Specification of target customers and markets

an expert's view / ON STRATEGIC PLANNING

Dr. Jon Iveson is the founder and head coach of *LEARNING to Be a Champion.* Echoing thoughts of experts on strategic planning, Iveson notes that the strategic planning process itself has evolved to fit the changing times and the changing nature of our work. In his view, it is more appropriate to think in terms of strategic advancement rather than strategic planning. Here is his argument.

STRATEGIC ADVANCEMENT VERSUS STRATEGIC PLANNING

Jon Iveson

Advancement is the act of advancing, progressing, and improving. Thus, *strategic advancement* is the process of strategically progressing. It goes well beyond tactical improvements but does not include controlled, conservative, planned, organized, sequential, and detailed plans.

Strategic advancement contains many elements of the classical strategic planning process but it is more fluid and dynamic, encompassing the number one strategic asset, the human brain. Given the vast changes occurring in organizational environments due to technology and globalization, managers need to focus on capitalizing the collective wisdom of all their employees in tackling the exigencies and emergencies that arise. It is also necessary for organizations to recruit and retain the best brains to gain a competitive advantage over rival organizations. Accordingly, whoever taps the collective intelligence for the given situation wins. It's about creating and sustaining an "ultra-brain" for the organization.

While strategic advancement concerns the configuration of the "brainy workforce," the process of strategic planning has also changed. Following the example of General Electric, every organization should simply have a long-term goal with a central strategic idea and a 90-day plan. In this perspective, the traditional processes of articulating a vision and core ideologies, conducting a market analysis of the classic strengths, weaknesses, opportunities, and threats (SWOT), using brand positioning, and setting annual goals and objectives are still appropriate and necessary. However, the notion of detailed intermediate plans is obsolete. Strategic advancement is based on the idea that you do need a plan to start but the advancement can occur only when there is flexibility. Flexibility allows people to align with emerging circumstances and act fluidly and dynamically to suit the circumstances at hand. That is, an organization does need a strong plan to start but must realize that the plan will need to evolve to get you to where you want to go. There is no perfect plan, and you can and should attempt to improve the plan you started with and align it with current environmental conditions. That is, choose progress, not perfection when it comes to strategic planning. In the final analysis, while the old saying that "If you fail to plan, you can plan to fail" is still true, don't attach yourself to detailed long-term strategic planning. Embrace and play at strategic advancement and you will most certainly make many winning moves and perhaps win a few "championships."

5. Identification of principal products/services
6. Specification of geographic domain
7. Identification of core technologies
8. Expression of commitment to survival/growth/profitability

The mission statements of The Ohio State University's Department of Athletics and Department of Recreational Sports are shown in Exhibit 5.4. Exhibit 5.5 shows the mission statement of the organizing committee of the 2007 Special Olympics World Games. A perusal of these mission statements shows that they follow the relevant guidelines proposed by Pearce and David (1987).

Note that they are general but at the same time specific about the direction in which the enterprises want to move, the target populations they want to serve, and the products they will deliver. Because it is free from details, "[the] mission statement has breadth of scope; it provides for the generation and consideration of a range of alternative objectives and strategies because it does not unduly stifle management" (p. 109). In sum, a mission statement and a strategic plan make the organization more systematic, direct its efforts to specific objectives, and reduce guesswork for the managers.

exhibit 5.4 Mission statements of the athletic and recreation departments of The Ohio State University.

THE OHIO STATE UNIVERSITY

DEPARTMENT OF ATHLETICS

Mission Statement

The OSUDA supports the University mission by providing student athletes with exceptional educational and athletic opportunities. We commit to national leadership, excellence and the highest ethical standards in intercollegiate athletics. We will sustain a strong financial and community base of support by presenting outstanding intercollegiate athletic teams which provide quality entertainment and a positive public identity for the university. We will embrace our community through public service and as a source of pride by representing the state of Ohio with nationally successful athletic programs.

DEPARTMENT OF RECREATIONAL SPORTS

Mission Statement

We are committed to providing the finest programs, services, facilities, and equipment to enrich the University learning experience. We also want to foster a lifetime appreciation of wellness and recreational sports and activities among our students, faculty, and staff.

Used with permission of the Department of Athletics and the Department of Recreational Sports, The Ohio State University.

exhibit 5.5 Mission statement of the 2007 Special Olympics World Games Organizing Committee.

The mission statement of the Special Olympics is to provide year-round sports training and athletic competition in a variety of Olympic-type sports for children and adults with intellectual disabilities, giving them continuing opportunities to develop physical fitness, demonstrate courage, experience joy and participate in a sharing of gifts, skills and friendship with their families, other Special Olympics athletes and the community.

Source: 2007 Special Olympics World Games.

TACTICAL/OPERATIONAL PLANNING

The description of strategic planning highlights its significant attributes: (a) a long-term plan, (b) devised by top level managers, (c) involving considerable outlay of resources, and (d) affecting the entire organization. This description implies that other forms of planning need to follow the strategic plan. These other plans are called **tactical** or **operational plans**.

In general, the implementation of the grand strategy outlined in the strategic plan is the responsibility of several units of the organization. Thus, each unit will develop its own plan, which includes the goals for the unit and the activities

sidebar 5.5

KEY WORDS IN A MISSION STATEMENT

Management consultant Scott Simmerman offers a simple toolkit that uses the following and other key words and activities designed to quickly and interactively generate an organization's mission statement:

best, most, dedicated, consistently, outstanding, helpful, customer service, image, service, returns, relationships, price, dependable, guarantee, dedication, largest, commitment, competition, treatment, adaptable, security, trust, people, personal, growth, company growth, responsiveness, profit, customer care, strategic, fashion, training, support, principles, beliefs, competent, sincerity, self-confident, sincere, interest at heart, relationships, efficient, adaptable, insure, ensure, career path, opportunity, honesty/honest, thru training, productivity, performance, ability, professionalism, competence, longevity, skills, retain, develop, number one, hassle-free, reasonable, energetic, loyal, family, low-key, no hype, sincere, friendly, cohesive, consistent, visible, positive, priceless, trustworthy, low pressure, genuine, real, excellent, sensitive, astute, knowledgeable, synergy, maximum value, minimum, professionalism, professionals, technicians, reliable, stand behind our work, people, complete satisfaction, long-term relationships, seen by our customers as high standards of service, our customers and our associates, our customers and our people, our family of employees, our family of services, long-term view of the business, relationships for the long term, do what's right, referrals and customer goodwill, high expectations of performance and reliability.

See Dr. Simmerman's materials at www.performancemanagementcompany.com.

that unit will engage in to achieve its goals. In essence, the strategic goal is broken down into smaller goals and restricted sets of activities specific to each unit. If a unit contains subunits, then the subunits will have their own goals and plans. This phenomenon of every set of goals acting as a means to the achievement of goals at a higher level is referred to as a chain of **means and ends.**

Suppose the strategic goal of a certain professional sport franchise is to increase rate of return on investment, achieve 5 percent growth in gross revenue, and provide excellent entertainment to customers. The attainment of this overall goal is possible only if the various units in the organization improve their operations (units dealing with player personnel, ticketing operations, marketing, event management, public relations, finance, administration, and so on). That is, each unit will set its own goals to be consistent with the overall strategic goal and will identify a set of activities to achieve its specific goals. For example, the administrator of player personnel could set the goal of forming an outstanding team with charismatic performers in the pursuit of winning championships and providing quality entertainment. At the same time, the administrator will also be concerned about containing costs because the strategic goal aims to increase the rate of return. One way of doing this is to become more efficient by reducing operating costs. Similarly, the marketing unit may set its goal to raise more money through securing more corporate advertisements and selling luxury boxes and seat licenses while curtailing its own operating costs. The event managers could set their goal to make their operations more efficient, smooth, and user-friendly to customers. In a similar manner, every unit within the organization would set its goals with a view to reaching the strategic goal.

But these goals of the individual units are only means to the goals of the larger organization, that is, the professional franchise. Thus, a goal for a lower level is a means to achieve the goals at a higher level. Fink, Jenks, and Willits

exhibit 5.6 Tactical/operational goals and plans as a chain of means and ends.

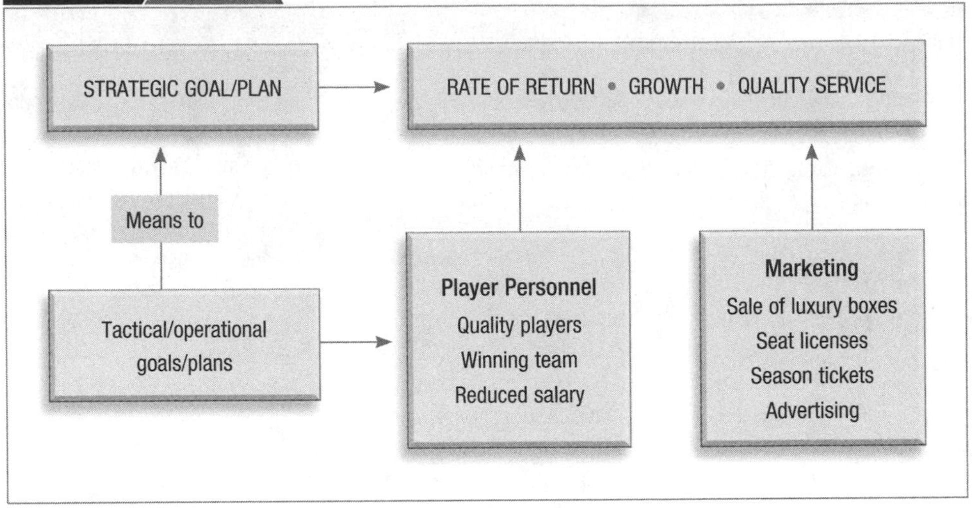

(1983) clarify this notion of a means–ends chain as follows: "Two characteristics of such means to a final goal are noteworthy. The means themselves constitute ends (goals). . . . Thus, each major goal of an organization is the beginning of a chain of goals and sub-goals, in which each sub-goal is a means to a larger goal. Second, each sub-goal tends to be more concrete and tangible than the related goal" (p. 22).

This view of goals and subgoals as a chain of means and ends is illustrated in Exhibit 5.6. Each unit prepares its own tactical and operational plans to achieve its goals. Traditionally, tactical goals and plans refer to those at middle levels of management, and operational goals and plans to the subunits within each unit. In other words, the strategic plan is devised at the top management level, the tactical goals at the middle management level, and the operational goals at the supervisory level. However, as most sport organizations are not characterized by three levels of management, the tactical and operational plans are likely to be combined into one, as shown in Exhibit 5.6.

PLANNING AND BUDGETING

Although it is customary to discuss budgeting as a managerial process separate from planning, the two functions are integrally linked. When an objective is identified and suitable alternatives are selected based on some evaluative criteria, those alternatives must be funded so that they can be carried out. As Robbins et al. (2012) state, "A budget is a numerical plan for allocating resources to specific activities" (p. 242). Insofar as these activities have been specified in the planning process, **budgeting** is actually a reflection of the plan in monetary terms. Therefore, the allocation of funds to specific activities becomes a simple technical/clerical detail because the cost of a chosen alternative will have been worked out before it was chosen. That is, all of the preliminary steps associated with budgeting have been carried out in the planning process.

Haggerty and Paton (1984) distinguished between two forms of budgeting: the incremental approach and the rational–comprehensive approach. In

sidebar 5.6

STANDING PLANS AND SINGLE-USE PLANS

Consider the case of the professional sport franchise referred to earlier. It needs to organize and conduct a certain number of home games in a year. In the initial year of operation, the organization and event managers will have gone through elaborate planning. Then, after a few games, the activities and processes of event management will have become routine—the plan that was originally prepared and revised during the first few games will be good enough for the next set of games. In fact, with some minor adjustments, it may be sufficient for the next few seasons. Thus, the plan becomes a *standing plan.*

In contrast, sport organizations may undertake a one-time project that is not likely to repeat in the near future. A good example is a U.S. city hosting the Olympics (summer or winter). Of course, the Organizing Committee will have begun its planning at least 10 years in advance of the Olympics. Such planning will involve the International Olympic Committee (IOC), the U.S. Olympic Committee (USOC), federal and state governments, the media, and other stakeholders. This elaborate plan, involving so much effort and resources, will be put to use only once in the foreseeable future. Such plans are called *single-use plans.* Single-use plans are not restricted to large undertakings such as the Olympics. A small city recreation department may undertake to stage the state championships in some sporting events. A fitness club may embark on a unique promotional campaign without the intention of repeating it in the future.

its most basic form, *incremental budgeting* exists when decision makers look at the total amount of money available and distribute it to various activities, programs, or departments based on precedent. This could take the form of a fixed percentage of increase or decrease for every unit based on previous budget(s). Haggerty and Paton (1984) point out that "The incremental approach does not require much information concerning what programs are actually doing, nor the manner in which budget units spend dollars. Rather, the focus is on percentage (or dollar) increments or decrements from the previous year or historical base" (p. 6).

An implication of the incremental approach is that the decision makers are satisfied with the status quo in terms of the objectives sought, the programs instituted to achieve those objectives, and the degree to which those objectives were reached in the previous budget year. It is also conceivable that the decision makers may adopt the incremental budgeting approach in order to avoid conflicts with the units. Thus, the incremental approach to budgeting resembles the planning process, even though serious thought and discussion have not been invested in the identification of objectives and the generation and evaluation of alternatives.

The *rational–comprehensive budgeting* approach forms a marked contrast to the incremental approach. One rational–comprehensive budgeting technique is known as the Planning–Programming–Budgeting System (PPBS). As the name suggests, this is actually a planning process in a different guise. The steps involved in PPBS highlight this fact.

> "Budgeting is nothing more than planning translated into sums of money. Money is the only common denominator into which all activities in the organization can be translated. This is because planning must always have a financial aspect: budgeting is a logical consequence of planning. Just like planning, budgeting has an active character."
>
> **KEUNING,** *1998, p. 486*

"Planning," in PPBS, involves defining the objectives to be accomplished; "programming" entails designing various alternative programs to accomplish these objectives; and "budgeting" involves funding some of these programs and eliminating others based on the evaluative information on the various programs (Gannon, 1977). Briefly, a program is a collection of activities aimed at achieving specified goals; a detailed description of a program is provided in Chapter 13. Thus, the steps in PPBS are exactly the same as the steps in the planning process outlined earlier. In sum, PPBS and other similar budgetary systems are, in fact, planning techniques. However, some authors find it convenient to deal with budgeting as a separate topic because other related financial issues (like accounting) can also be considered along with budgeting.

In summary, from an organizational point of view, sport managers must always attempt to be rational in their planning and other critical decisions. That is, they must try to generate as many alternatives as are feasible, evaluate them on previously specified criteria, and select the best alternative(s) to achieve the desired ends. In short, they must strive to be rational in their approach. This, however, is not always the case. Two factors limiting rationality in the planning process are problems that arise in the determination of organizational goals and problems that arise from a lack of information. These are examined in the sections that follow.

RATIONAL PLANNING AND ORGANIZATIONAL GOALS

An episode from Lewis Carroll's *Alice's Adventures in Wonderland* (1969, p. 160) is quoted in several management science textbooks to illustrate the significance of goals for an organization:

> Alice: "Would you tell me, please, which way I ought to go from here?"
>
> Cat: "That depends a great deal on where you want to get to."
>
> Alice: "I don't much care where—"
>
> Cat: "Then it doesn't matter which way you go."

Goals provide the direction and the source of motivation for the behavior of the organization's members. Goals also determine the standards for performance and evaluation. From the earlier description of the planning process, it would appear that planning cannot proceed without goal specification. "Thus, goals and objectives permeate the whole management process, providing an underpinning for planning efforts, direction, motivation, and control" (Richards, 1978, pp. 8–9). Given the importance of goals in organizational activities, examining some of the issues raised about goals/objectives in management literature is beneficial.

Perrow (1961) has made a distinction between the official goals and the operative goals of an organization. Some authors have labeled this distinction as stated (official) goals and real (operative) goals (see Robbins, 1997). Because this distinction is so critical in the operation of any organization, it is elaborated in the following sections.

Stated Goals

Perrow (1961) states that "Official goals are the general purposes of the organization as put forth in the charter, annual reports, public statements by key executives and other authoritative pronouncements" (p. 855). To Robbins (1997), **stated** or **official goals** "are official announcements of what an organization says—and what it wants various constituencies to believe—are its objectives. However, they are often conflicting and excessively influenced by what society believes organizations *should* do" (p. 149). For example, the type of statement likely to be found in the official pronouncement of a university is that "the purpose of intercollegiate athletics is to provide an opportunity for the pursuit of excellence in physical activity." But, as Perrow (1961) points out: "Official goals are purposely vague and general and do not indicate two major factors which influence organizational behavior: the host of decisions that must be made among alternative ways of achieving official goals, and the priority of multiple goals and the many unofficial goals pursued by groups within the organization" (p. 855).

For example, the global statement of "pursuit of excellence" as the purpose of intercollegiate athletics does not provide any clue as to whether a large number of sports will be fostered or excellence in a few sports will be emphasized.

Genesis of stated goals

If goals are to provide the direction and motivation for the behavior of the organization and its members, they must be concise, clear, and specific. Furthermore, if there are several goals, they should be consistent with each other in order to provide a unified thrust for the organization. However, in many organizations, the formal goals are stated in vague and global terms. Such global statements are necessary to accommodate the desires and preferences of those associated with the organization, both internally and externally.

From a systems perspective (as noted in Chapter 3), the organization is in an exchange relationship with the environment. The organization is dependent upon various subgroups in the environment for its inputs and for the disposition of its outputs. In order for such a relationship to continue to exist, the organization must meet the goals that those subgroups hold for the organization. In the case of an intercollegiate athletic program, for example, the alumni, the faculty, the students, other universities, and other sport organizations are some of the stakeholders that would expect the organization to pursue specific goals. The administrators, the coaches, and the athletes are some of the internal groups with different expectations for the athletic program. If all of these goals are taken together, some may conflict with others. For instance, promotion of all sports versus pursuit of excellence in specific sports is an example of conflicting goals sought by two different groups. Insofar as an organization cannot afford to alienate any of the groups with conflicting orientations and preferences, it tends to proclaim its goals in general and vague terms. As noted before, most athletic programs state their goal as "the provision of opportunities for students to pursue excellence in sports." No subgroup can take exception to such a broad and all-encompassing goal statement. Thus, general goal statements are abstractions distilled from the

stakeholders

In Chapter 3, stakeholders were defined as individuals or groups that have a stake (some rights or interests) in the organization. A group of stakeholders, such as the athletes, coaches, spectators, media people, alumni, or employees of the athletic department, may share similar interests, claims, or rights. These stakeholder groups can be classified as *primary* stakeholder groups, whose participation in the organization and its affairs is necessary for organizational survival. In contrast, the *secondary* stakeholder groups are not necessary for the organization, although they could influence the affairs of the organization.

TO recap

> "Formal goal statements are "a fiction produced by an organization to account for, explain, or rationalize its existence to particular audiences rather than . . . valid and reliable indicators of purpose."
>
> **WARRINER,** *1965, p. 141*

demands of the external and internal environments (Hall, 1996). Perrow (1961) also suggests that stated goals serve the purpose of legitimizing the organization in the societal context and, thus, of securing the necessary resources.

Real Goals

Although the stated goals are an attempt to justify the existence of the organization and the support extended to it, they do not provide the focus and direction the organization needs to function effectively. However, stating broad goals allows the key administrators the opportunity to emphasize specific subdomains within these broad goals. Most university athletic departments state their official goal is "developing student athletes." But this could mean development in terms of athletic potential, their academic potential, or both. For another example, under the rubric of pursuit of excellence, one intercollegiate athletic program may support the popular sports while another may support some of the less popular international sports. These contrasting orientations and thrusts are the **real** or **operative goals** pursued by the organizations. Perrow (1961) describes them as "Operative goals [that] designate the ends sought through the actual operating policies of the organization; they tell us what the organization is actually trying to do, regardless of what the official goals say are the aims" (p. 855).

We have already referred to two contrasting real goals in intercollegiate athletics—support of locally popular sports versus support of international sports. If various intercollegiate athletic programs are analyzed, it is possible to identify a number of real goals. Chelladurai et al. (1984) identified nine real goals of university athletic programs in the Canadian context. Then, Trail and Chelladurai (2000) investigated the importance attached to 10 goals of intercollegiate athletics by faculty and students of one Midwestern university. They further divided the 10 goals into those focusing on the development of the athletes (developmental goals) and those focusing on the performance of the teams that provide entertainment, generate revenue, and bring prestige and visibility to the university (performance goals). As shown in Exhibit 5.7, both schemes are quite similar, although the labeling of the goals differs.

Note the features of the real goals shown in Exhibit 5.7. First, all of them are contained in the official goal of pursuit of excellence in physical activity. That is,

sidebar 5.7

DEVELOPMENTAL GOALS VERSUS PERFORMANCE GOALS IN THE NCAA

In a study of NCAA Division IA, IAA, IAAA, and III university presidents' perspectives on athletic department goals, McGuire and Trail (2002) found that all Division I presidents placed greater importance on the goals of entertainment, financial security, visibility and prestige, and winning than Division III presidents did. These differences do reflect the policies and practices of the Division I athletic departments, which emphasize recruiting outstanding athletes, paying high salaries to coaches of major sports, building bigger and better facilities, and organizing major events. They also found that presidents of all divisions included in the study were less satisfied (relative to the importance they attached) with the extent to which the athletic departments achieved the developmental goals of academic achievement, social moral development, culture of diversity, careers, and health/fitness. These latter results are encouraging in that the presidents are aware that these developmental goals are not achieved to the same extent as the performance goals. Such awareness should move them to take actions to rectify the deficiencies.

exhibit 5.7 Two lists of goals of intercollegiate athletics.

LIST OF GOALS CHELLADURAI ET AL. (1984)	**LIST OF GOALS** TRAIL & CHELLADURAI (2000)
DEVELOPMENTAL GOALS	
Athletes' Personal Growth: Promotion of athletes' personal growth and health (physical, mental, and emotional)	Academic Achievement: Academic progress and achievement of athletes
Career Opportunities: Provision of those athletic experiences that will increase career opportunities for the athletes	Health/Fitness: Health and physical well-being of athletes
	Social/Moral Citizenship: Development of athletes into social, moral, and ethical citizens
	Careers: Career development and growth of athletes
	Culture of Diversity: Racial, ethnic, and gender equality, and respect for diversity
PERFORMANCE GOALS	
Achieved Excellence: To support those athletes performing at a high level of excellence	Winning: Conference and national championships, winning record, and victories over traditional rivals
Entertainment: To provide a source of entertainment for the student body, faculty/staff, alumni, and community	Entertainment: Entertainment for university, local, regional, and national communities
Financial: To generate revenue for the university	Visibility and Prestige: Positive public identity, national image, and prestige for the university
Public Relations: To enhance university–community relations	Financial Security: Revenue generation, financial self-sufficiency, and financial surplus
Prestige: To enhance the prestige of the university	National Sport Development: Excellent performances of athletes in Olympic and international sports/competitions
National Sport Development: To contribute to national sport development and performance in the international context	
Transmission of Culture: To transmit the culture and tradition of the university and community	

each of the real goals does not in any way violate the general thrust of the stated goal. Exhibit 5.8 illustrates this relationship between the stated (official) goal and the real (operative) goals within it.

Although some of the real goals are complementary to each other, others are in conflict. In general, the goals classified as performance-oriented are complementary to each other. For example, insofar as providing entertainment, enhancing prestige, and creating good public relations are all a function of winning teams, they are complementary to each other—an emphasis on any one of the objectives would result in the enhancement of the other two objectives. On the other hand, transmission of culture and national sport development may be in conflict with each other. To be more explicit, if transmission of culture implies support of locally popular sports such as football, and if national sport development suggests support for internationally played sports, then these are obviously in conflict. That is, a greater emphasis on one objective could mean

exhibit 5.8 Official and operative goals in intercollegiate athletics.

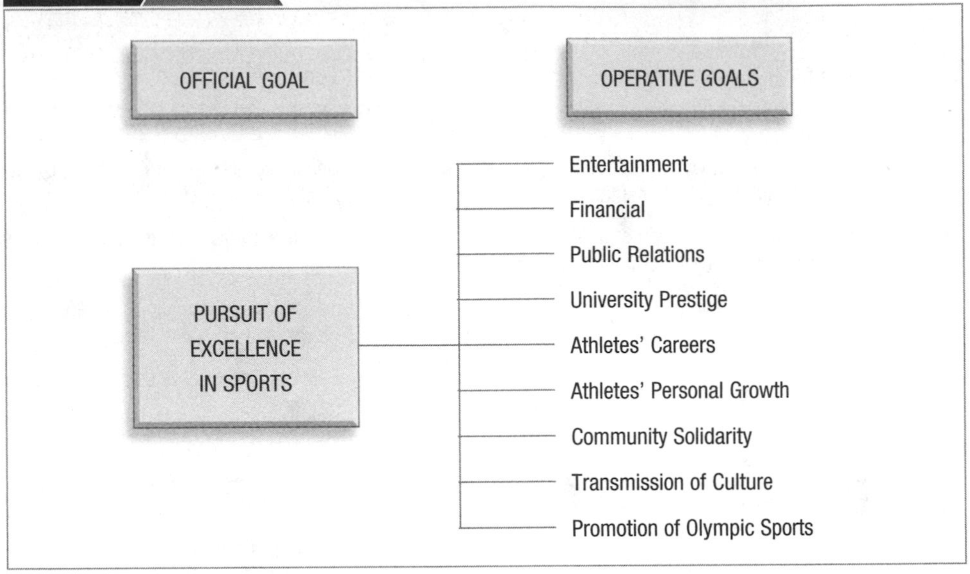

a reduction in the other (given that resources are limited). The nature of complementary and conflicting goals is illustrated in Exhibit 5.9.

The third feature of real goals is that decisions on the competing values represented by the goals "influence the nature of the organization, and distinguish it from another with an identical official goal" (Perrow, 1961, p. 856). This was brought out in a study of the operative goals of intercollegiate athletics in Canadian universities (Chelladurai & Danylchuk, 1984). Using the list of operative goals developed by Chelladurai et al. (1984), the authors found that those athletic administrators in Canadian universities who emphasized public relations, prestige, entertainment, national sport development, and/or financial objectives tended to favor athletic scholarships and unrestrained

exhibit 5.9 Complementary and conflicting goals.

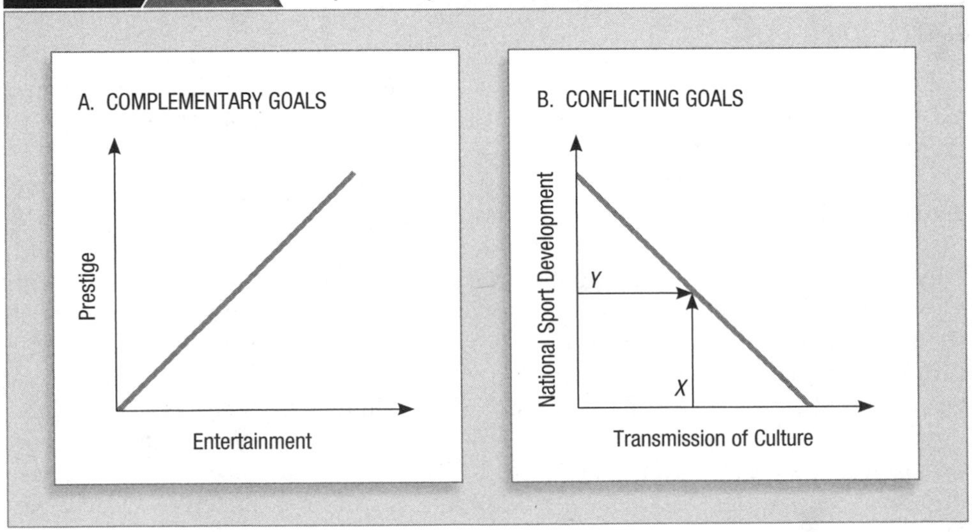

sidebar 5.8

INTERCOLLEGIATE ATHLETICS IN THE UNITED STATES AND OLYMPIC SPORTS

Despite the relatively lower support for Olympic sports compared to the support for locally popular sports such as football, basketball, and baseball, current and former athletes from the NCAA won 47 medals including 22 gold, 11 silver, and 14 bronze in the 2012 London Olympics (NCAA, 2012). Nevertheless, both the U.S. Olympic Committee and the NCAA have been concerned with the decline of Olympic sports on the collegiate scene. For example, only 61 Division I and 17 Division I universities support women's and men's gymnastics respectively. Furthermore, men's sports such as fencing (supported by only 21 universities), rifle (27 universities), volleyball (23 universities), water polo (21 universities), and wrestling (85 universities) are considered at risk of being dropped. The USOC and the NCAA set up a 15-member task force in May 2004 to study and recommend ways to raise money, manage, and market these sports.

recruitment of athletes.* "To elaborate, the objectives of enhancing the image of the university, generating revenue, and satisfying the entertainment needs of the fans can all be achieved through a winning team. One way of producing the winning team is to recruit the best available talent by offering athletic scholarships and other perks as inducements" (Chelladurai & Danylchuk, 1984, p. 40).

Exhibit 5.10 shows the processes that could be adopted by two universities differentially emphasizing two contrasting real objectives—educational and athletic objectives. It should be apparent from Exhibit 5.10 that the real goals of the two universities set them apart, although the official goals of both are the same.

exhibit 5.10 Contrasts in real goals and processes.

STATED OBJECTIVE FOR UNIVERSITIES A AND B
"Provide Educational and Athletic Opportunities for Student-Athletes"

	UNIVERSITY A	UNIVERSITY B
Real Objectives	Student development/growth	Entertainment/University prestige
Processes	Less focus on winning	More focus on winning
	Developing students	Recruiting athletes/athletic scholarships as incentives
	Treating athletes as students	Special treatment of athletes
	Teaching the spirit of rules	Flouting the spirit of rules (e.g., teaching good fouls, employing time-wasting tactics)

*Intercollegiate athletics in Canada and the United States differ on two counts: Most Canadian universities do not offer athletic scholarships. When offered, the scholarships are very few in number, and the dollar value is much less than in the United States. Also, recruiting of athletes is rather restricted when compared to in the United States. Many Canadian coaches prefer the American model, as shown by the above research. .

Another feature of real goals is that whereas the official goals are found in the charter, annual reports, and pronouncements of the top officials of the organization, the real goals can be inferred only through a scrutiny of the decisions made in key areas such as budgeting and personnel. For example, the objectives of entertainment, publicity, and so on were not stated explicitly by universities in the past. On the contrary, many scholars have proscribed such objectives in the educational context. For example, Mathews (1974) emphasized that the success of an intercollegiate athletic program should not be gauged by the prestige it brings to the university, the revenue it generates, or the entertainment it provides. If, however, the actual decisions relating to budget allocations and staffing procedures were analyzed, it would quickly become evident that many universities are pursuing the objectives of entertainment, prestige, and public relations.

As early as 1979, Broyles and Hay provided an alternate view of the objectives of intercollegiate athletics. They were quite explicit in stating that the prime objective of intercollegiate athletic programs is to satisfy the entertainment needs of fans. Starting with this premise, the authors proceeded to outline logically the processes that create entertainment value. These processes include recruitment of athletes, athletic scholarships, high-quality coaching, and emphasis on those sports with entertainment value.

Along similar lines, Chelladurai and Danylchuk (1984) argued that entertainment and prestige are legitimate objectives for a university athletic program because they benefit the institution and the student body, respectively. If universities and their units publicize their various academic and non-academic programs (employment rate of students, research grants secured, facilities) with a view to enhancing prestige, then they can also use intercollegiate athletics as a vehicle for prestige. Similarly, if universities arrange plays, music festivals, and other entertainment events, then it could be argued that intercollegiate athletics, recognized as an integral part of the total educational process, can also be used for the same purposes.

IN brief

Stated goals are broader statements, whereas real goals are the actual goals sought by the organization. Stated goals are general in order to accommodate the preferences of several constituents of the organization. They also tend to encompass all real goals, even if some of the real goals conflict with each other.

Many universities in the United States now emphasize entertainment, prestige, and publicity as legitimate goals of intercollegiate athletics. However, they state these as secondary to the goals oriented toward the development of student-athletes. Once again, a scrutiny of the decisions made by administrators and coaches might lead us to question the primacy of student-athlete development. This has been the focus of criticism by several authors who suggest that educational or developmental goals are not promoted to the same extent as performance goals (see Andre & James, 1991; Bailey & Littleton, 1991; Sperber, 2000). In Telander's (1989) view, coaches are primarily interested in winning, athletic administrators in revenue generation, and university presidents in prestige for the university. Thus, the stated goals of athletic departments may not reflect what the departments are in fact pursuing.

Genesis of real goals

It has been stated that organizations do not have goals; only the individuals in the organization have goals. This is particularly true in the case of the real goals that are set by the top administrators of the organization. Although external agents such as resource providers, clients, and governments largely influence the choice of the real goals, internal groups and administrators also exercise their influence in the choice of these goals. The conflict over these real goals leads to the formation of coalitions among groups and individuals (Cyert & March, 1963; Rosen, 1995). According to Hasenfeld (1983),

> Typically, these negotiations are marked by the emergence of various coalitions whose members can agree on a common set of goals for the organization, and thus can pool their resources to influence the organizational decision making in their direction. The relative power of each coalition is determined by the total amount of resources needed by the organization that it can control and mobilize. The most powerful among them will be the dominant coalition. The negotiations and compromises among the members of the dominant coalition will determine the nature of the organizational [real] goals. (p. 96)

A coalition exists when the alumni of a university or college and the businesses in the local community band together to influence the goals and processes of the intercollegiate athletic program. Their dominance over the program is mainly due to the control they exercise over the resources needed by the program or the university.

This does not mean, however, that the administrators will entirely disregard the preferences of others. Administrators, and members as well, respect precedents. Insofar as the conflicting orientations have been supported in the past, administrators will likely continue to cater to those orientations. It is also possible to satisfy sequentially the conflicting preferences. (However, in those instances where the organization is blessed with abundant resources, the conflicting goals can be simultaneously satisfied.) These factors permit the administrators to pursue their operative goals in a steady manner.

Goals and Constraints

The fact that two conflicting goals cannot be maximally pursued with limited resources led Eilon (1971) to suggest that goals may also be perceived as constraints. In Exhibit 5.9, for example, it is apparent that if one goal, such as transmission of culture, is to be secured to a minimum level (as indicated by point *X* on the horizontal axis), it acts as a constraint on the other goal (national sport development). That is, national sport development cannot be pursued beyond point *Y* on the vertical axis. This notion of one goal acting as a constraint on another is valid only under the condition of limited resources—but, of course, the fact of limited resources is one of the main reasons for setting up an organization and emphasizing its management in the first place.

Eilon (1971) pointed out that, from a different perspective, the constraints "may be regarded as an expression of management's desire to have minimum attainments or levels of performance with respect to various criteria [goals]. *All constraints are, therefore, expressions of goals*" (p. 295).

Thus, when the athletic department declares its support for a minimum number of women's sports, it imposes on itself a constraint as well as a goal. The emphasis on gender equity in U.S. intercollegiate athletics is perceived as a constraint by some and a goal by others, although in fact it is both.

In summary, two goal-related factors reduce the rationality of the planning process. First, ambiguity in the statement of official goals (and the inherent instability of the operative goals) does not permit rational planning over a period of time. Second, conflicts among the goals of an organization can make one goal a constraint on another.

RATIONAL PLANNING AND INFORMATION GATHERING

Another factor that limits the rationality and effectiveness of the planning process is paucity of information. Although information (or the lack of it) bears directly on any decision, its impact is more pronounced in (a) **forecasting** the future and (b) generating or developing alternative solutions, both of which are essential steps in the planning process. These two sub-processes of planning require a special type of skill and knowledge base.

Forecasting

Planning, by definition, deals with the future. That is, specific programs or activities are instituted in the expectation that they will lead to some desired outcomes at a future point in time. In addition, the plan itself, or parts of it, will be implemented in the future. Morden (1993) noted that

> An enterprise cannot plan ahead without making forecasts, and it cannot make forecasts without having some kind of plan to act as a framework for the forecasting process. The process of forecasting attempts to produce a picture of the kind of *future environment* in which enterprise plans and activities are likely to be implemented. It makes assumptions about the future conditions that are likely to determine the success of these plans. And it attempts to predict the outcome from the implementation of these plans. (p. 54)

These expectations are based on some assumptions regarding the state of affairs in the future. Although the future cannot be perfectly predicted, individuals (whether they are administrators or not) do make some assumptions about the future in almost every activity in which they engage. For instance, if children make plans to play soccer tomorrow afternoon, they assume that it will not rain during then. Such a forecast may be based on the weather reports, intuition, or even a belief in luck. Since children's soccer is not a significant spectator event, the presence or absence of rain is relatively unimportant. However, if the event being planned is a World Cup championship several years in the future, the accuracy of the forecast is critical. In this case, the planners must look into the forecasts, records of rainfall in previous years, the texture and drainage of the playing fields, and their durability in rainy conditions. The forecasts should also include details about economic, political, and social conditions that might prevail at the time of the world championships. All of these factors could affect the successful conduct of the World Cup. Thus, planners must make every effort to gather all available information and tap all possible sources. This, in effect, is forecasting.

One focus of forecasting may be to determine the demand for the products of the organization. In this focus, the purposes of forecasting are to "predict future *demand* for the organization's goods or services; future *trends* in demand; future *changes* in these trends; and the *magnitude* of change in the trends" (Gannon, 1977, p. 119). An entrepreneur who plans to start a commercial golf course needs to forecast the number of people who will play golf on the course, whether the customer base will increase or decrease over time, and whether the changes in demand will be substantial. Similarly, prior to constructing a new facility, a city recreation department must forecast the demand for the facility.

Forecasting may also be concerned with (a) predicting the outcome of a future event and (b) the timing of a future event (Rue & Byars, 2009). When the decision is being made to build a new arena, the senior athletic administrators will be concerned about the final cost of the arena. That is, given that the arena will be built (a definite event), the outcome (the final cost) needs to be forecast.

> "A trend is a trend. The question is when will it bend? Will it climb higher and higher, or eventually expire, and come to an untimely end?"
>
> **CHAIRNCROSS,**
> *quoted in Dessler, 1979, p. 57*

Similarly, the administrators will be interested in when the construction of the arena will be completed and ready for events (event timing forecast).

The importance as well as the difficulty of forecasting increases with the planning time frame. That is, forecasting tomorrow's weather is much easier than forecasting the weather two years in advance. Using past trends and present situations to predict tomorrow's conditions is an uncertain enterprise, as seen in the plight of educational institutions. In all long-range plans, enrollment figures must be forecast. These figures depend on population trends, the job market, and the orientation of new generations toward higher education. History abounds with instances in which the forecasts of educational institutions were far from the real occurrences.

Planners can profitably use many of the reports published by government agencies and other private research organizations. There are numerous statistical reports relating to the gross national product (GNP), other leading indicators of economic growth, population trends, and so on. Planners may also gather information by polling relevant individuals. For instance, the director of a city recreation department can poll the residents of the city concerning their preferences for activities or programs for the future. The director can also ask the city administrators about future trends in the budgetary allocations for recreation.

Planners can profitably employ spreadsheet programs to facilitate their forecasting efforts. For instance, a fitness club can use a spreadsheet to project membership three years hence by using (a) the historical average of membership patterns and (b) the capacity of the club to serve the clients. Similarly, a golf course can use spreadsheets to project its revenues by using the data on (a) membership patterns, (b) membership fees, (c) rates of participation by members and nonmembers, and (d) greens fees for members and nonmembers.

Forecasting by experts

Planners may also consult with experts in the field to help them in the formulation of forecasts. Two specific techniques used to capitalize on the skills of experts are the nominal group technique and the Delphi technique (see Exhibit 5.11).

Nominal group technique. In the **nominal group technique**, approximately eight to ten experts are brought together in a structured format. After learning about the problem, the group members think about it for a short period of time. Then each expert presents his or her ideas. After all the experts have presented their ideas, limited interaction is permitted. Following this, each expert ranks the ideas on the basis of the probability of their occurrence. The average of these rankings is then accepted as the forecast for that particular question. In the nominal group technique, it is important that all of the ideas are given equal importance. Therefore, a secretary or moderator must be present not only to record the proceedings but also to ensure that every idea is given equal time and attention.

Delphi technique. The general concept underlying the **Delphi technique** is the same as in the nominal group technique. In the Delphi technique, however,

exhibit 5.11 Nominal group technique versus Delphi technique.

NOMINAL GROUP TECHNIQUE

Involves a meeting of experts

Experts think about an issue or questions, present ideas to the group, and then interact with each other

Experts rank the ideas on the basis of probability of their occurrence

Average of the rankings is accepted as the forecast

All ideas are given equal time and attention

Requires the presence of a secretary or moderator

DELPHI TECHNIQUE

Experts do not meet; they remain anonymous

Experts are presented with an issue or a question and respond in writing

Summary of opinions is prepared and sent back to experts

Experts revise their opinions based on the summary

Process is repeated as often as needed

Final report summarizing the opinions is submitted to top management

experts arrive at a consensus without ever meeting together to discuss the issue in question—that is, the opinions of experts are sought individually. The anonymity of the participants is crucial for the process. Typically, a problem such as "Will men's soccer or women's basketball enjoy greater success as a professional sport in North America?" is mailed to experts, who respond in writing with their opinions. A summary of these opinions is prepared and sent back to each expert, and the experts are then allowed to revise their estimates based on this feedback. This entire process may be repeated a number of times. Those experts whose estimates deviate from the average are asked to justify their position. A final report summarizing the opinions of the group is then submitted to top management. One problem associated with this technique lies in accurately describing the problem to the experts (Byars, 1987). Another problem is to interpret the opinions of the experts and to summarize them accurately.

IN brief

Information is important in all decision making, particularly about future trends and available alternatives. The nominal group and Delphi techniques are useful in forecasting future trends, whereas brainstorming is most useful in generating alternatives.

Gannon (1977) has suggested that organizations should update their forecast when new information about the future becomes available. An organization might draw up a five-year plan only to find that after a year, new evidence reveals that the earlier forecasts were not accurate. Therefore, a new set of forecasts is required. Also, of course, the five-year plan will have to be redrawn to agree with the new forecast. This is not an unusual scenario. Many organizations draw up a three-year or five-year plan, *but they do it every year*. During the periodic planning phases, the original forecasts, budget estimates, and other vital parameters of planning are revised on the basis of new information available to the planners.

sidebar 5.9

FORECASTING AND SPORT MANAGEMENT

The nominal group, Delphi, and brainstorming methods discussed in this section have been used to generate information on varied matters. The following are a few examples from our field.

- Ball, Simpson, Ardovino, and Skemp-Arit (2008) employed the Delphi method to identify the leadership competencies necessary to be successful in a collegiate recreational setting. The three rounds of Delphi method involving 10 university recreation directors resulted in the selection of five leadership competencies—communication, management of the budget, personal management, adaptability to change, and commitment and integrity.
- Lam, Zhang, and Jensen (2005) employed the Delphi method in developing their Service Quality Assessment Scale (SQAS), which measures six dimensions of service quality in health-fitness clubs—staff, program, locker room, physical facility, workout facility, and child care.
- In her study of the future of sport management, Costa (2005) engaged a panel of 17 leading sport management scholars from around the world. Three iterations of a Delphi questionnaire showed that these experts felt that more research, including cross-disciplinary research, efforts to link theory and practice, and improved doctoral training, would facilitate the growth of sport management. They disagreed, however, on the appropriate academic home for sport management, the ingredients of quality research, the significance of qualitative and quantitative research, and the relative value of basic and applied research.
- Hurd (2005) employed the Delphi technique with 16 employees to determine the competencies needed by entry-level employees in public parks and recreation agencies. The resultant Entry-Level Competency Framework (ELCF) includes five general competency categories, 15 primary competency areas, and 53 specific competencies. She also found that (a) the ability to communicate clearly with customers, (b) the ability to listen to staff and customers, (c) the ability to deal with the public, (d) the ability to communicate clearly with staff, (e) knowing how to act professionally, and (f) the ability to manage multiple tasks were rated as most important.
- The 25 jurors in Austin, Lee, and Getz's (2008) Delphi study reported a promising future for special and inclusive recreation, and it is becoming more widely embraced. Moreover, programs and services are increasingly focused on inclusive recreation.

Generation of Alternatives

Forecasting requires expert knowledge about past historical data, trends, and the future, whereas alternative generation requires innovative ability and creativity. Alternative generation is perhaps the most critical step in planning, and therefore, management must attempt to harness the creative abilities of relevant members during this stage of the planning process.

Brainstorming

One technique that has been used successfully to encourage and marshal the creativity and ingenuity of members is **brainstorming.** Osborn (1953), who developed this technique, suggested that the brain is used to "storm" a creative problem in the same fashion that commandos might audaciously attack a fortress. The brainstorming process calls for relevant members to come together and think of solutions or alternatives for a particular problem. Members present their ideas one at a time. A significant guideline of this process is that no one is permitted to evaluate the ideas as they are presented (Byars, 1987). This restriction enables individuals to come up with a variety of ideas without fear of being ridiculed or criticized. A basic premise in brainstorming is that it is important to encourage a large number of different ideas even if they seem improbable, preposterous, or foolish. In Osborn's view, it is much more difficult to come up with new ideas than it is to evaluate them.

Another crucial aspect of the brainstorming process is that members are allowed to "hitchhike" on the ideas of others. That is, after hearing one member's idea, others may be able to improve on it or combine two or more ideas to make a better idea. Some members may be better hitchhikers than originators of ideas, and planners must capitalize on both types of talent.

KNOWLEDGE MANAGEMENT

It is commonly noted that organizations need to learn to adapt to the changing environment owing to advances in information technology and knowledge explosion. Some researchers argue that managers must understand the value of knowledge as a resource just as they value the material and monetary resources. Given this need, it is not surprising that a new discipline called *knowledge management* is gaining popularity. Some universities now offer courses in **knowledge management**; several books have been written on the topic; and several consultant services focus exclusively on it. But what is it? "Knowledge management is the developing body of methods, tools, techniques and values through which organisations can acquire, develop, measure, distribute and provide a return on their intellectual capital assets" (du Plessis, 2008, p. 285). It is a planned and structured managerial function to identify, create, and share the knowledge to further the organization's capacity to compete effectively with other organizations. With an internal focus, knowledge management is aimed at discovering and harnessing the intellects of the employees of the organization. "Knowledge management is about finding, unlocking, sharing, and altogether capitalizing on the most precious resources of an organization: people's expertise, skills, wisdom, and relationships" (Bateman & Snell, 2007, p. 9).

Traditionally, employees are hired on the basis of whether the person has the requisite skills to carry out the specific job. The point is that one or more persons in a specific job may have more skills and abilities than what the job requires. For instance, several immigrants new to this country may possess some expertise (e.g., in engineering, medicine, computer science, psychology, coaching). But because they are not fluent in English or lack a degree from a local university, they may not find a job in their specialty. Thus, they may settle for jobs as janitors or taxi drivers. Consider a sport management student with a minor in computer science or accounting who joins a fitness club as an intern. The fitness club assigns the student to work in the locker room. But the student's expertise in computer technology or accounting is ignored. If the fitness club had a knowledge management system in place, it would have recognized and recorded the expertise of all its employees, including interns, and would have implemented that knowledge whenever such expertise was needed. Simply stated, knowledge management is cataloguing "who knows what?" (Greenberg, 2005, p. 105).

DIRECTIONAL PLANNING

In the conventional view of planning, the first step in the process involves setting specific, concise, and clear goals. Given the clarity and specificity of the goals, the plan itself will be quite clear and specific in its details. However, "formal planning efforts can lock an organization into specific goals to be achieved within specific timetables" (Robbins et al., 2012, p. 197). Moreover, formal plans cannot adequately deal with the constantly changing environment. Given these issues, plans should be flexible. In a similar vein, McCaskey (1974) proposed another mode of planning whereby "the planner or planners identify a domain and direction. *Domain* is the area in which the organization or individual will work. The *direction* is the actor's tendencies, the favored styles of perceiving and doing. Instead of specifying concrete, measurable goals, the planners work more from who they are and what they like to do" (p. 283).

McCaskey suggested that in those cases where the organization cannot spell out specific goals, it should set the domain for its activities and let the organization members move ahead in that domain according to their preferred ways of acting. It is quite conceivable that as the organization moves it will discover goals. For example, a private profit-oriented firm might decide that its domain is fitness. The proprietor would then lease some exercise equipment and set up a fitness center. This initial business activity could be based on the proprietor's personal expertise and experience in fitness activities. After a period of time, the proprietor may note that customers are bored with the monotonous and tedious workouts. Based on this observation, the proprietor may open up a few racquetball courts with a view to providing variety for the customers. Over time, the firm might expand to include a tennis court, badminton court, sauna, pool, and possibly even an area for food and liquor (products not directly related to fitness). In the end, the firm might turn out to be in the recreation business rather than the fitness business.

Another example is that of a Swiss watch company that started out manufacturing watches for the general public but ended up producing high-priced watches for the wealthy. The chairman of the company is reported to have denied that his company was in the watch business. He insisted that it was in the "luxury" business. Some university athletic departments in the United States are capitalizing on the entertainment opportunities offered by their teams as well as their facilities. The preceding examples illustrate McCaskey's suggestion that new goals can be discovered and highlighted after the organization begins operating in a particular domain.

McCaskey emphasized the flexibility that **directional planning** offers. The specific goals sought are determined only after interaction with environmental forces—an approach that is consistent with the systems view of organizations (see Chapter 3). Planning in this manner permits planners to capitalize on unexpected opportunities and adapt to new constraints that may arise after the organization has entered a domain.

Although McCaskey (1974) has advocated a general directional approach to planning (whereby a domain and direction are initially identified), he has also acknowledged that planning with specific goals is appropriate under certain conditions. According to McCaskey, planning with goals is more suitable when

1. planners want to narrow the focus so that the efforts of members will converge
2. the environment of the organization is stable and predictable
3. there are severe time and resource limitations that call for programming of activities
4. members prefer well-defined conditions for their work

Similarly, planning without goals (directional planning) is appropriate when

1. the organization has just come into existence
2. the environment is unpredictable
3. members cannot build enough trust or agreement to decide on a common goal

Directional Planning and Stated Goals

Note that the distinction between planning with goals and directional planning (planning without goals) is conceptually similar to Perrow's (1961) notion of dichotomizing goals into stated versus real goals. Stated goals are couched in very broad, general terms, and thus they serve to outline a general domain for organizational activity.

On the other hand, the choice of real goals is a reflection of the specific thrust of the organization at a given point in time. Thus, real goals may shift with changes in administrators, personnel, or environmental conditions. This is directly comparable to the flexibility afforded by directional planning. The overlapping of these two conceptual schemes is illustrated in Exhibit 5.12. In this example, the real goals are within the domain agreed upon for intercollegiate athletics. Also, although the shifts in focus are drastic, the organizational efforts remain within the general domain.

Directional Planning and Information

One of the main reasons for directional planning is that planners seldom have all the necessary information to permit them to be specific about their goals. In directional planning, it is possible to work around the scarcity of information and to proceed in the general domain or direction. In the course of time, as new information becomes available, planners can become more specific in their goal setting.

SUMMARY

In this chapter, we defined the planning process as the specification of goals to be achieved and the activities to be carried out to achieve those goals. We described the steps in the planning process—identifying constraints, generating alternatives, and evaluating those alternatives. We distinguished between strategic plans and tactical plans and looked at budgeting as it relates to planning, and at the types of budgeting processes. We explored the differences between,

exhibit 5.12 Shifts in operative goals within directional planning.

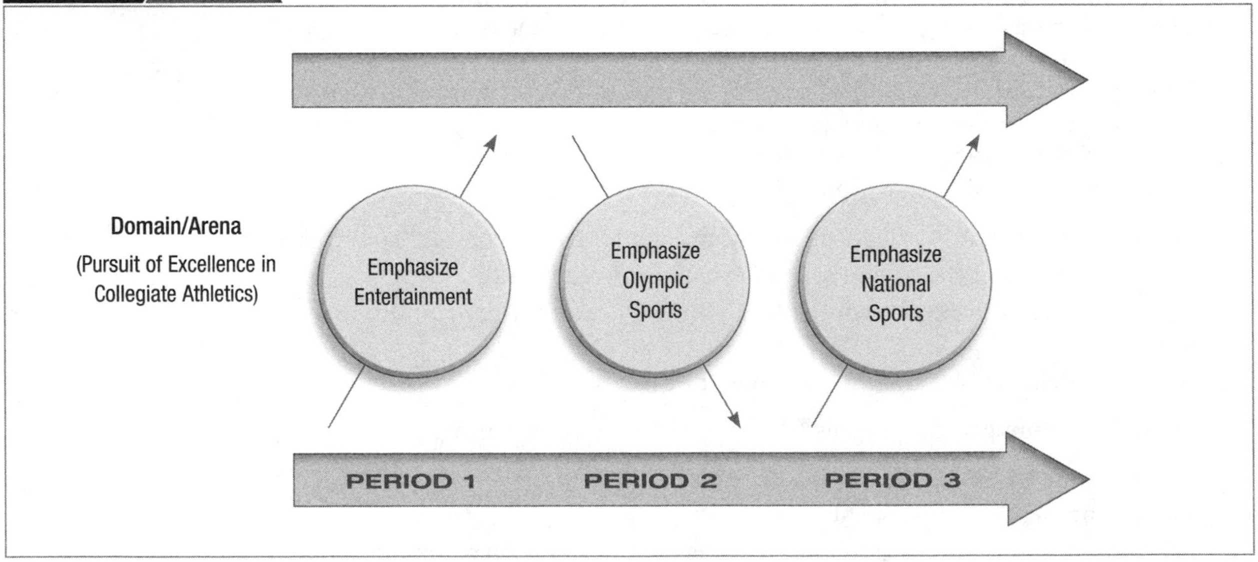

and genesis of, stated goals and real goals. Having noted the crucial importance of information and forecasting to decision making, we explored several methods of seeking information: nominal group technique, Delphi technique, and brainstorming. Finally, the need for directional planning—planning without specific goals—as an alternate mode of planning was explained.

develop YOUR PERSPECTIVE

1. What real (operative) goals are emphasized in your intercollegiate athletic program or school? Explain the basis of your opinion.
2. Discuss the environmental factors, including stakeholder groups, that influence the goals of your intercollegiate athletic program. Is there a dominant coalition among these stakeholder groups? How does this coalition achieve dominance over others?
3. Consider the mission statement provided in Exhibit 5.5. Discuss the extent to which this mission statement reflects what this organization is actually doing.
4. Consider all the programs, processes, and decisions of the athletic department in your university, and identify those that reflect each of the eight components of a mission statement. Are there any programs, processes, or decisions that do not fit into the mission statement? Are all the programs, processes, and decisions consistent with each other?
5. Using the key words provided in Sidebar 5.5, write a mission statement for the organization of your choice.
6. Discuss the relevance of (a) planning with specific goals and (b) planning without specific goals to any two or three sport organizations you are familiar with.
7. Give examples of problem situations in which the nominal group technique, Delphi method, and brainstorming could be used.

references

Andre, J., & James, D. N. (Eds.). (1991). *Rethinking college athletics*. Philadelphia: Temple University Press.

Austin, D. R., Lee, Y., & Getz, D. A. (2008). A Delphi study of trends in special and inclusive recreation. *Leisure/Loisir,* 32(1), 163–182.

Bailey, W. S., & Littleton, T. D. (1991). *Athletics and academe*. New York: Macmillan.

Ball, J., Simpson, S., Ardovino, P., & Skemp-Arit, K. (2008). Leadership competencies of university recreational directors in Wisconsin. *Recreational Sports Journal, 32,* 3–10.

Bateman, T. S., & Snell, S. A. (2007). *Management: Leading & collaborating in a competitive world* (7th ed.). Boston: McGraw-Hill Irwin.

Brown, M., Rascher, D., Nagel, M., & McEvoy, C. D. (2010). *Financial management in the sport industry*. Scottsdale, AZ: Holcomb Hathaway.

Broyles, J. F., & Hay, R. D. (1979). *Administration of athletic programs: A managerial approach*. Englewood Cliffs, NJ: Prentice Hall.

Byars, L. L. (1987). *Strategic management: Planning and implementation*. New York: Harper & Row.

Carroll, L. (1969 [1865]). *Alice's adventures in wonderland*. Quoted in D. Rackin (Ed.), *Alice's adventures in wonderland: A critical handbook*. Belmont, CA: Wadsworth.

Chairncross, A. (1975). Quoted in Thomas E. Milne, *Business for forecasting: A managerial approach*. London: Longman.

Chelladurai, P., & Danylchuk, K. E. (1984). Operative goals of intercollegiate athletics: Perceptions of athletic administrators. *Canadian Journal of Applied Sport Sciences, 9,* 33–41.

Chelladurai, P., Inglis, S. E., & Danylchuk, K. E. (1984). Priorities in intercollegiate athletics: Development of a scale. *Research Quarterly for Exercise and Sport, 55,* 74–79.

Costa, C. A. (2005). The status and future of sport management: A Delphi study. *Journal of Sport Management, 19,* 117–142.

Cyert, R. M., & March, J. G. (1963). *The behavioral theory of the firm.* Englewood Cliffs, NJ: Prentice Hall.

David, F. R. (1997). *Concepts of strategic management.* Upper Saddle River, NJ: Prentice Hall.

Dessler, G. (1979). *Management fundamentals: A framework.* Reston, VA: Reston Publishing.

du Plessis, M. (2008). What bars organisations from managing knowledge successfully? *International Journal of Information Management, 28*(4), 285–292.

Eilon, S. (1971). Goals and constraints. *Journal of Management Studies, 8,* 292–303.

Filley, A. C., House, R. J., & Kerr, S. (1976). *Managerial process and organizational behavior.* Glenview, IL: Scott Foresman.

Fink, L. F., Jenks, R. S., & Willits, R. D. (1983). *Designing and managing organizations.* Homewood, IL: Richard D. Irwin.

Gannon, M. J. (1977). *Management: An organizational perspective.* Boston: Little, Brown.

Greenberg, J. (2005). *Managing behavior in organizations.* Upper Saddle River, NJ: Pearson-Prentice Hall.

Haggerty, T. R., & Paton, G. A. (1984). *Financial management of sport-related organizations.* Champaign, IL: Stipes.

Hall, R. H. (1996). *Organizations: Structure, processes, and outcomes* (6th ed.). Englewood Cliffs, NJ: Prentice Hall.

Hasenfeld, Y. (1983). *Human service organizations.* Englewood Cliffs, NJ: Prentice Hall.

Hitt, M. A., Black, J. S., Porter, L. W., & Hanson, D. (2007). *Management.* Frenchs Forest, NSW: Pearson Education Australia.

Hurd, A. R. (2005). Competency development for entry level public parks and recreation professionals. *Journal of Park and Recreation Administration, 23*(3), 45–62.

Keuning, D. (1998). *Management: A contemporary approach.* London: Pitman.

Lam, E. T. C., Zhang, J. J., & Jensen, B. E. (2005). Service Quality Assessment Scale (SQAS): An instrument for evaluating service quality of health–fitness clubs. *Measurement in Physical Education and Exercise Science, 9*(2), 79–111.

Mathews, A. W. (1974). *Athletics in Canadian universities: The report of the AUCC/CIAU study of athletic programs in Canadian universities.* Ottawa: Association of Universities and Colleges of Canada.

McCaskey, M. B. (1974). A contingency approach to planning: Planning with goals and planning without goals. *Academy of Management Journal, 17,* 281–291.

McGuire, R., & Trail, G. (2002). Satisfaction and importance of athletic department goals: The views of university presidents. *International Journal of Sport Management, 3,* 53–73.

Megginson, L. C., Mosley, D. C., & Pietri, P. H., Jr. (1992). *Management: Concepts and applications* (4th ed.). New York: HarperCollins.

Morden, A. R. (1993). *Business strategy and planning.* London: McGraw-Hill.

NCAA (2012, August 13). Student-athletes shine at Olympics. *Latest News.* Retrieved from http://www.ncaa.org/wps/wcm/connect/public/NCAA/Resources/Latest+News/2012/August/Student+athletes+shine+at+Olympics.

Osborn, A. F. (1953). *Applied imagination.* New York: Charles Scribner's Sons.

Pearce, J. A., II, & David, F. (1987). Corporate mission statement: The bottom line. *Academy of Management Executive, 1*(2), 109–116.

Perrow, C. (1961). The analysis of goals in complex organizations. *American Sociological Review, 26,* 854–865.

Pettinger, R. (1997). *Introduction to management* (2nd ed.). London: Macmillan Business.

Pierce, J. L., & Dunham, R. B. (1990). *Managing.* Glenview, IL: Scott Foresman/Little, Brown.

Platt, G. (2002, August). SMART objectives: What they mean and how to set them. *Training Journal,* 23–26.

Richards, M. D. (1978). *Organizational goal structures.* St. Paul, MN: West.

Robbins, S. P. (1997). *Managing today!* Upper Saddle River, NJ: Prentice Hall.

Robbins. S. P., Coulter, M., Leach, E., & Kilfoil, M. (2012). *Management* (10th ed.). Don Mills, Ontario: Pearson Canada.

Rosen, R. (1995). *Strategic management: An introduction.* London: Pitman.

Rue, L. W., & Byars, L. L. (2009). *Management: Skills and application* (13th ed.). Homewood, IL: Irwin.

Sperber, M. (2000). *Beer and circus: How big-time college sports is crippling undergraduate education.* New York: Henry Holt.

SquareWheels (2008). Mission statement and consensus exercise. Retrieved from www.squarewheels.com/scottswriting/mission.html.

Telander, R. (1989). *The hundred yard lie: The corruption of college football and what we can do to stop it.* New York: Simon & Schuster.

Trail, G., & Chelladurai, P. (2000). Perceptions of goals and processes of intercollegiate athletics: A case study. *Journal of Sport Management, 14,* 154–178.

USATF (2013, February). USATF stages annual meeting. *Track and Field News,* 60.

Warriner, C. K. (1965). The problem of organizational purpose. *Sociological Quarterly, 6,* 139–146.

CHAPTER 6 MANAGERIAL DECISION MAKING

manage YOUR LEARNING

After completing this chapter you should be able to:

- Understand the significance of decision making in management.
- Define the steps in decision making.
- Explain the programmability and significance of decisions.
- Explain the rationality of decisions as related to the means and goals.
- Discuss the differences among the economic person, administrative person, and implicit favorite models of decision making.
- Explain the advantages and disadvantages of member participation in decision making.
- Understand decision styles.
- Know the critical attributes of a problem situation that determine the appropriate level of participation by members.

strategic CONCEPTS

administrative person model
alternative
bounded rationality
economic person model
framing the problem
implicit favorite model
nonprogrammed decision
opportunity
participative decision making
problem
programmed decision
significance of a decision

THE SIGNIFICANCE OF DECISION MAKING

The last chapter was devoted to the managerial function of planning. A look at the different steps in the planning process shows us that planners make decisions at every step of the process. For instance, in the first step of goal setting, the planners might have several choices, but they select one or more of them as the goals and then set priorities among these selected goals. Even constraints require decisions, and the planners must decide which of the constraints are more critical than the others. Similarly, the environment may offer several opportunities, which the planners must narrow down to just a few. In all these ways decision making is critical to planning.

Decision making, defined as "the process of choosing the best alternative for reaching objectives" (Certo & Certo, 2009, p. 181), underlies all managerial activities—not just planning. In fact, Nobel laureate H. A. Simon (1977) equates decision making with management. As he points out, "The task of 'deciding' pervades the entire administrative organization quite as much as does the task of 'doing'—indeed, it is integrally tied up with the latter. A general theory of administration [management] must include principles of organization that will insure correct decision-making, just as it must include principles that will insure effective action" (p. 1).

The city council has to make a decision on constructing a $100 million arena. The player personnel management unit in a professional franchise needs to decide which players to draft and which ones to trade. The management committee of the Y has to decide whether to extend the building to make way for more exercise and dance rooms. A fitness club manager has to decide who and how many personal trainers to hire and which classes to offer. The marketing director of a university athletic department has to choose a printing firm to print promotional materials. The assistant to the director of a city recreation department has to decide how to reorganize the office. The locker room attendant has to decide if a particular client should be given a towel. The receptionist in a tennis club has to decide if he can reserve a court for a member at a particular time and date. These are all examples of decisions made in sport organizations. In one sense, every action by every member and unit in an organization is based on a decision some person or group has made. From this perspective, we can say that an organization is a forum for making decisions. In the same vein, we can also say that managers are there *only to make decisions*.

managerial roles

Recall that we discussed Mintzberg's 10 managerial roles in Chapter 4. In each of these roles, the manager must make decisions. The significance of those decisions is much more pronounced in the last four roles. As entrepreneur, the manager has to choose new projects for implementation to ensure the viability and growth of the organization. That is, the manager conceives of effective ways to capitalize on the opportunities offered by the environment. In the role of disturbance handler, the manager decides how to respond to changes in the environment. As resource allocator, she also makes critical decisions regarding which individual or unit will get what resources. Finally, as negotiator, the manager has to make decisions to resolve the problems and conflicts that arise within the organization. In both the disturbance handler and negotiator roles, the manager is solving problems that abound in organizations. In fact, there would not be much need for managers if there were no problems.

TO recap

OPPORTUNITIES AND PROBLEMS

Opportunities and problems perceived by the manager present the occasions for making decisions. An **opportunity** is a situation that, when acted upon, could benefit the organization in such areas as profitability, productivity, and growth. For instance, assume that the aerobics instructor in a fitness club has obtained nutritionist credentials. The manager can see this opportunity for nutrition counseling as a new service to club clients. When a professional sports team wants to move to a city, authorities can use that opportunity to revitalize the area and improve the transportation system. In fact, a large part of the rationale for holding large-scale events (e.g., the Olympics) or offering incentives to a professional franchise to move to a city is because it will foster improvement to the infrastructure, create jobs, and improve the welfare of the citizens.

A **problem** is a situation that reduces or could reduce the effectiveness of the organization or disrupt operations. For instance, two aerobics instructors argue constantly in front of clients. This does not project a good image of the club and reduces the quality of the club's services. Or, consider the aerobics instructor who has just been certified as a nutrition counselor. We noted that this could be an opportunity for the club to introduce nutrition counseling, but it could also be a problem if the instructor decides to leave the club for a better-paying job. A different kind of problem occurs when the building's heat pump breaks down, disrupting operations. All of these situations call for decision making, either to seize the opportunities or to solve the problems.

Because of the central place of decision making in management, sport managers need a comprehensive understanding of the process of managerial decision making and the difficulties associated with it. Accordingly, we explore the process of decision making in the following sections. Then, we examine the distinction between two broad classes of decisions—programmed decisions and nonprogrammed decisions. Following this, we discuss the issue of rationality in decision making and learn to distinguish between the *ethical* and *factual* content of a decision. Finally, we look at different models of decision making that reflect varying degrees of rationality.

STEPS IN DECISION MAKING

Exhibit 6.1 shows the steps in decision making. Note the resemblance between this exhibit and Exhibit 5.1. This similarity exists because planning is a special aspect of decision making.

Problem Statement/Framing the Problem

As shown in Exhibit 6.1, the first step in decision making is to define the goal to be achieved or the problem to be solved. Managers must be clear about the problem they are trying to solve. If the problem is not clearly defined and clarified, the subsequent steps will be futile. Great managers look into the nature of the problem, its frequency and causes, and the elements involved (people, place, or things). Based on this analysis, they then state the problem in unambiguous terms.

This first step is also called **framing the problem**. Variations in defining the same problem could lead to different and often meaningless solutions. For example, suppose you are the major partner in a tennis club in a mid-size city. Your business is not doing as well as expected, because another tennis club close to your facility has poached many of your members. In fact, your club has become a losing proposition. You are at the point of letting go some of your employees in an attempt to reduce costs. Just as you are getting ready to downsize, you learn that your competitor is going out of business and would like to sell his club to you. You want to capitalize on this opportunity, but you need the approval of your partners. You can frame the situation in two different ways:

exhibit 6.1 Steps in the classical model of decision making.

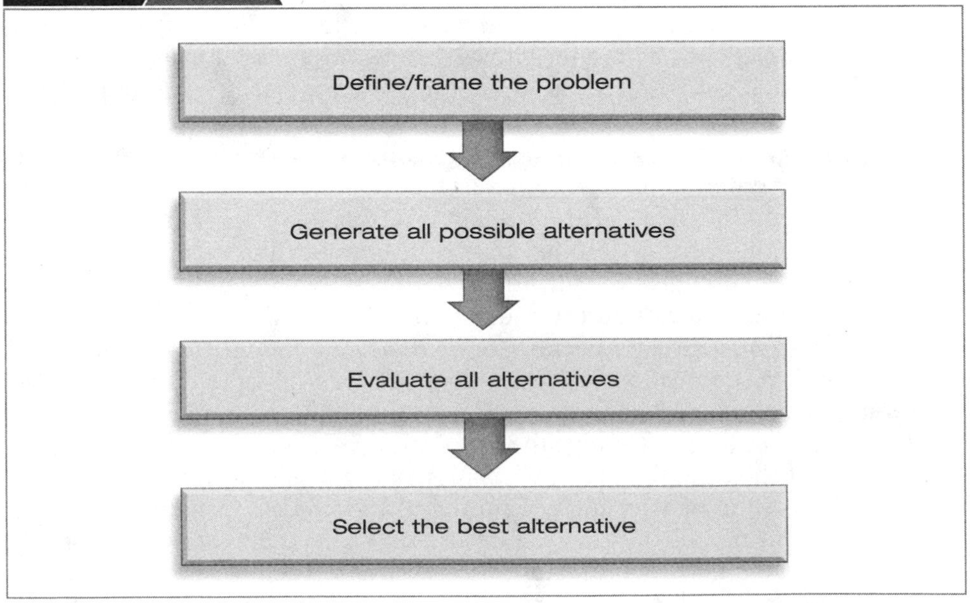
Define/frame the problem
Generate all possible alternatives
Evaluate all alternatives
Select the best alternative

Frame 1. If you buy the other club, there is a 100 percent chance that you can retain 10 of your 15 employees, and there is a 75 percent chance that you will make a profit.

Frame 2. If you buy the other club, there is a 100 percent chance that you will have to let go five of your 15 employees, and there is a 25 percent chance of losing money.

Although both frames contain the same information, the partners may be more inclined toward the acquisition of the other tennis club in the first frame but less likely in the second frame, because the second frame is negative in its tone. A more comprehensive frame would combine both frames and present a holistic picture. For example, it would emphasize the positive outlook for making a profit (75 percent chance) while also pointing out the negative impact of letting go five of 15 employees.

Black and Porter (2000) offer a good example of the effects of framing a problem that relates to the space shuttle *Challenger*, which exploded 73 seconds after its launch on January 18, 1986. The explosion was caused by a leaky O-ring seal that failed due to the cold weather. On previous launches, NASA had asked engineers to confirm that a launch was 100 percent ready and that the circumstances presented no risk. But because this launch had already been delayed once, NASA was intent on going ahead. Thus, in this case the engineers were asked to "prove absolutely that the shuttle would fail. . . . The engineers could not provide definitive quantitative evidence of a failure that had not yet occurred" (Black & Porter, 2000, p. 313) and thus the launch proceeded.

Generating Alternatives

The second step involves the generation and evaluation of possible **alternative** courses of action or solutions to the problem. In the earlier example, the alternatives for the tennis club owners could be to (a) downsize, (b) acquire the neigh-

sidebar 6.1

PERCEIVED LOSS VS. PERCEIVED GAIN

Here is another case where two different ways of framing a problem lead to different decisions. Chou and Murnighan (2013) investigated the effects of two types of appeal for blood donations. In the first appeal, prospective donors were asked to donate blood in order *to save the lives* of many. In the second appeal, people were asked to donate blood in order *to prevent the deaths* of many. Their research showed that college students who received the appeal to prevent deaths donated significantly more blood than those who got the appeal to save lives. That is, students were more willing to avoid losses (i.e., deaths of recipients) than they were to secure gains (i.e., lives of recipients). The point is that saving lives and preventing deaths are one and the same. Yet saving a life is seen as a gain (for the recipients of blood) and death is seen as a loss. Perceived loss has a greater impact on individual decision making than perceived gain.

But the above point that "perceived loss has a greater impact on individual decision making than perceived gain" did not hold in the Michigan–Ohio State football game played in November, 2013. The game was exciting, with 14 touchdowns scored (7 for each team). With 32 seconds left in the game, Michigan scored its seventh touchdown to make the score 42–41 in favor of Ohio State. The coach and players of the Michigan team knew very well that trying a two-point conversion would result in either a successful attempt and a win for the Wolverines or an unsuccessful attempt and a loss for them. In making the decision to go for it, the possible perceived gain outweighed the prospect of perceived loss. After losing the game, Michigan coach Hoke said, "We played the game to win."

boring club, (c) expand the current operations to include a restaurant and a swimming pool, or (d) get out of the business altogether. If the problem is arguing and fighting aerobics instructors, the solutions could be to (a) have a face-to-face discussion with both instructors, (b) schedule their hours so they do not overlap, (c) fire instructor A, (d) fire instructor B, or (e) fire both instructors. If the fitness club has more than one branch, then transferring one of the instructors to another branch is an alternative. The point is that all possible alternatives must be explored.

Evaluating Alternatives

The third step in decision making is to evaluate all the alternatives generated in the second step. Such evaluation must be based on meaningful criteria. In the case of the tennis club, the cost, the risk, and the expected payoff of each option are some of the criteria that could be employed in this step. The concern for retaining the employees versus making profits could also come into play at this step. Another example involves hiring a new head coach for an intercollegiate athletic team. The decision makers may consider such criteria as cost of the contract with each prospective candidate, the candidates' past successes in elevating their teams' performances in both athletics and academics, and projected acceptance of the candidate by the existing staff of the department. The fourth and final step in decision making is to select and implement the alternative that is rated the best based on the selected criteria.

PROGRAMMABILITY AND SIGNIFICANCE OF DECISIONS

The above description of the decision process is applicable to all kinds of decisions faced by managers. However, the extent to which a manager would spend effort and time over a decision is based on two issues: (a) the programmability of the decision and (b) the significance of the decision. Earlier in the chapter, we listed several decision situations in sport management. Let us take three of those examples to illustrate these two issues.

Programmed and Nonprogrammed Decisions

The first case is a locker room attendant giving out towels to clients. This is a repetitive action in that the attendant gives out hundreds of towels every day. Because of the task's repetitive nature, the decision becomes routine. Furthermore, the decision criteria are simple and straightforward. The attendant has to check if the client is a member of the club and if he or she has paid for the towel service. Because clubs usually have a card or token to indicate these criteria, the attendant's decision process is even more simplified. This kind of decision is called a programmed decision. A **programmed decision** is one made by applying decision rules in response to recurring situations or problems.

On the other hand, take the case of the player personnel unit of a professional club deciding whom to draft and whom to trade. This is much more complex than handing out towels. The decision makers must consider the current status of the team in terms of team performance, team composition, salary total for the team, and attributes of individual players (performance capabilities, physical and psychological profiles); the dollar amount management is willing to invest in players; and what is offered in return for a trade. Because the players in the pool change every year and because the order of pick changes every year, the decision makers cannot set specific decision criteria that can be applied from year to year. That is, these decisions cannot be programmed in advance, as can towel service. Instead, the decision makers need decision rules specific to that year of draft. These are nonprogrammed decisions. A **nonprogrammed decision** is one made in a situation that is unique and poorly defined.

Typically, a manager is faced with a series of both programmed decisions and nonprogrammed decisions. Because of time pressures and because it is easier to attend to programmed decisions than to nonprogrammed decisions, managers usually focus more on clearing the programmed decisions and let the more complex and important decisions take a backseat (Black & Porter, 2000). An effective manager would set aside the necessary time to focus exclusively on the complex decisions without being sidetracked by programmed decisions.

Significance of Decisions

The extent to which a manager focuses on a particular decision is also a function of the significance of the problem and the consequences of making a specific decision. In the above example, the programmed decision of the locker room attendant is not as significant as the nonprogrammed decision of drafting players. Errors made in the locker room will not gravely impact the club; a few towels lost or ineligible clients' use of the service is not going to affect the club's bottom line to any extent. On the other hand, the nonprogrammed decision of drafting a player is significant and has great consequences for the club in that it takes away the resources available for drafting or signing other players or carrying out other franchise needs. This issue becomes even more pronounced when the franchise approaches the salary cap imposed by the league. The decision to draft or sign a high-ranking player also has long-term consequences. For instance, the decision

sidebar 6.2

ESCALATING COMMITMENT AND THE NBA

The drafting of an NBA player has long-term consequences in terms of structuring the operations around that player. This tendency, known as *escalating commitment,* means that the managers commit themselves more and more to the earlier decision even though it may not yield the desired results. It is "the tendency for decision makers to persist with failing courses of action" (Brockner, 1992, p. 39). That is, "The fact that resources have already been committed to such a player leads to a situation where escalation might arise: rather than decrease the player's court time based on poor performance, a team may over-use a player relative to his value if a large previous commitment has been made" (Camerer & Weber, 1999, p. 61). This tendency to be committed to decisions could be based on self-justification, meaning an unwillingness to admit past incorrect decisions (Arkers & Blumer, 1985; Brockner, 1992). In order to avoid admitting a faulty decision, managers may allocate more resources to that course of action. The escalating commitment to the drafting of the player could also be based on the expectancy that additional resource allocations (in terms of playing time, drafting of other players to complement the talents of the drafted player, and so on) will lead to better results (Brockner, 1992, p. 40). Matsuoka and Chelladurai (2000) use this perspective to explain sports fans' continued commitment to a team. Unwilling to admit that their attachment to an unsuccessful team is futile and incorrect, fans may devote more resources in terms of money, effort, and time to the team, and thus become more attached to it. Also, fans of that team may expect that it will do better in the future, and based on that expectation, they continue to support the team.

by the Lakers to re-sign Kobe Bryant in November, 2013, at a cost of $48.5 million for two years (Amick, 2013) will impact future decisions the Lakers make concerning the make-up of the team, its promotion, and so on.

Although the relationship between programmability and the **significance of a decision** is true in many cases, it does not extend to all situations. Consider event management at a large university. Most of the decisions (traffic routes, traffic signals, and so on) are programmed to a great extent. These decisions are critically important despite the fact that they are programmed. Another example is a football coach who emphasizes set plays. He has programmed specific plays for specific circumstances, and he has given specific responsibilities to every player and drilled them in their specific responsibilities—programmed them to act in specific ways. These decisions are as significant as those made by any other coach who works without programming plays.

RATIONALITY IN DECISION MAKING

The rationality of decisions is an issue that has been debated at length. What is rationality? How rational are the decisions made by individuals and organizations? Can someone be fully rational in all decisions? We will discuss these and other questions in the following sections.

A decision is said to be rational when the best means are selected to achieve a given end. Note that rationality refers to the *selection of the best means* to achieve a goal and not to the *selection of the goal itself*. Thus, if an individual wishes to own a car primarily as a means of transportation, then the purchase of an inexpensive, efficient model would represent a rational decision. On the other hand, if that same individual purchases a Rolls Royce, the decision would not be rational. A second individual might wish to achieve status and prestige through car ownership. Thus, if this individual purchased a Rolls Royce, the decision would be rational. In short, the purchase is a means to an end, and consequently, purchase of the Rolls Royce may or may not be rational depending on the goal.

Simon (1976, 1977) made a distinction between the ethical content and the factual content of a decision. The ethical content refers to the decision maker's beliefs of "what ought to be," and thus it reflects the goal that an administrator may pursue. However, the choice of that goal cannot be proved to be true or false. Simon points out that the concept of rationality strictly applies only to the factual elements of a decision and not to its ethical components. For example, if the athletic department's goal is to achieve national standing in one sport but then it decides to hire a specific coach because he is available at a lower salary, the decision would not be considered rational. On the other hand, if minimizing expenses in order to balance the budget is the main objective, then the decision to hire a less expensive coach would be rational. Note that the choice of the goal (attaining national status versus balancing the budget) cannot be subjected to the test of rationality because it is based on beliefs and values. On the other hand, the choice of a coach can be judged rational or not based on the extent to which it relates to the specified objective. For another example, consider a youth sports program with the goal of providing access to a program for all youth within its community. A decision to charge high registration and participation fees for entry into the program would not be rational because these fees would bar several youth from poor families from entering

IN brief

Rationality in planning refers to generating many alternatives and choosing the best one to achieve a goal. It does not refer to the goal itself.

the program. However, reducing these fees for poor families would be consistent with the original goal and thus would be a rational decision. Again, note that the goal of providing access to sports for all youth in a community cannot be subjected to the test of rationality because it is based on beliefs and values.

The idea that rationality refers to the choice of the *best* means to achieve a goal implies that several alternative means would be considered and evaluated against specified criteria. This comprehensive and rigorous process of comparing several alternatives and selecting the best is labeled the *economic person model* of decision making.

Economic Person Model

In the **economic person model**, or classical model, the decision maker wishes to maximize the benefits and minimize the costs (Simon, 1977). To do this, the decision maker will rigorously follow the steps outlined in Exhibit 6.1. This is the ideal model of rationality. It is *prescriptive* in the sense that it details what ought to be done. The economic person model is based on certain fundamental assumptions. Naylor (1999, p. 349) notes these:

1. Objectives are clear and agreed.
2. Problems are clearly defined.
3. The manager seeks and gains full information on all possible alternatives before making any choice.
4. The criteria for evaluation can be unambiguously drawn from the objectives and problem definition.
5. Decision makers will make logical decisions to satisfy objectives as well as possible.

Although the economic person model has an inherent appeal, problems arise because human capacity is rather limited (Schermerhorn, Hunt, & Osborn, 1997). Recognizing these human limitations, Simon (1957) introduced the key notion of bounded rationality.

Bounded rationality

As we noted earlier, rationality implies that managers gather all the necessary information, identify all possible alternatives, evaluate each one carefully, and select the best one. In Simon's view, this is simply impossible. First, organizational problems are so complex that it is not possible to collect all the information needed. In fact, the manager may not know all the factors that contribute to the problem and therefore cannot collect the relevant information. Moreover, not all the possible choices will be known and/or evaluated. In addition, because human capacity is limited, managers may not be able to process the available information. Thus, despite the manager's best intentions, she can exercise only **bounded rationality**. That is, the rationality of the decision is bounded by the complexity of the problem, the lack of information, and the limits on human capacity.

Administrative Person Model

Based on his notion of bounded rationality, Simon (1945, 1977) proposed an alternate model of decision making that is based on assumptions contrary to those of the economic person model. His **administrative person model** is *descrip-*

tive in that it describes how managers actually make decisions. As we have noted, decision makers are inherently limited in terms of their knowledge and capacity to evaluate all possible alternatives. Given such limitations, it is not possible to maximize a decision as the economic person model would suggest. Therefore, the decision maker is prepared to "satisfice" rather than maximize. The term *satisfice* was coined by Simon from the two words *satisfy* and *suffice*. It means that the decision maker is willing to accept an alternative that is minimally sufficient in meeting the goal. In the model of the administrative person, a decision maker specifies evaluative criteria that are minimally acceptable. Then a few alternatives are evaluated against these criteria, and the first alternative that meets the criteria is selected. Thus, a decision is made with the least cost of search. The next alternative to come along might have been far superior to the one selected, but the decision maker is not concerned with this possibility. The manager is satisfied with the choice that has been made because it is sufficient for the purpose. Exhibit 6.2 illustrates this process of decision making.

The critical distinction between the economic and administrative models of decision making is that the economic person lists and evaluates all possible alternatives before selecting the best one, whereas the administrative person evaluates the alternatives one at a time and selects the first alternative that is satisfactory/sufficient. According to Simon (1976), the decisions of the administrative person are characterized by "bounded rationality," which he describes as follows: "The individual can be rational in terms of the organization's goals only to the extent that he is *able* to pursue a course of action, he has a correct conception of the *goal* of the action, and he is correctly *informed* about the conditions surrounding his action. Within the boundaries laid down by these factors his choices are rational-goal oriented" (p. 241).

exhibit 6.2 **Steps in the administrative person model of decision making.**

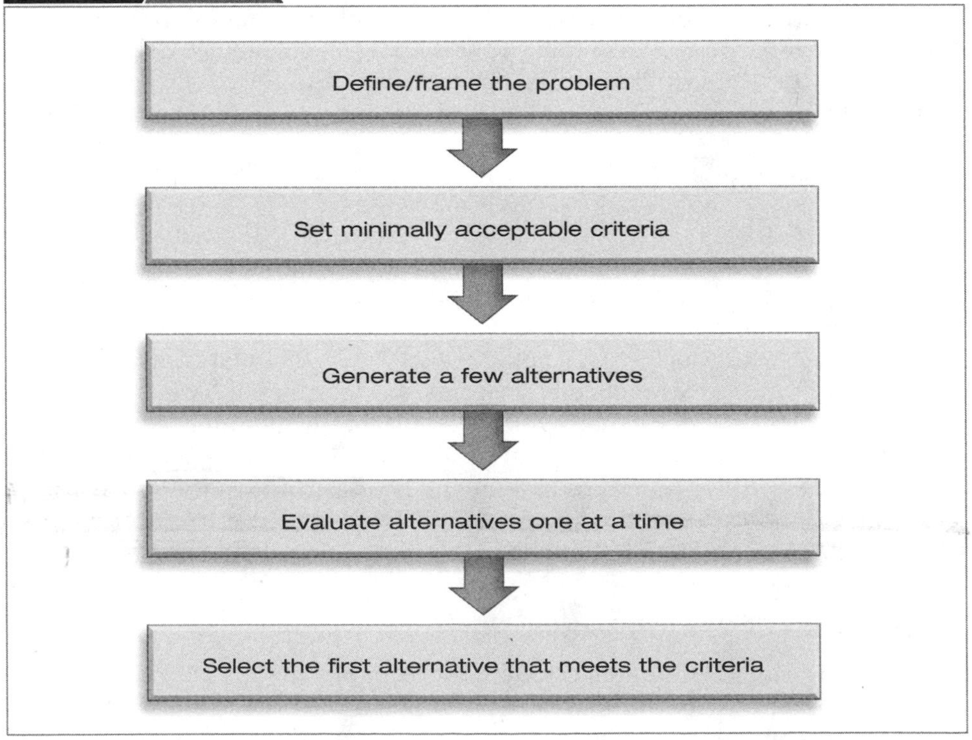
Define/frame the problem
Set minimally acceptable criteria
Generate a few alternatives
Evaluate alternatives one at a time
Select the first alternative that meets the criteria

Simon also used the term *subjective rationality* (as opposed to *objective rationality*) to refer to decisions made with little information about the alternatives and their consequences. Insofar as a decision maker has made the best choice with the available information, he is said to be rational—but only subjectively. The objectively rational decision—the decision made with all the necessary information available—could prove to be an entirely different one. Thus, in Simon's (1976) view, "The need for an administrative theory resides in the fact that there *are* practical limits to human rationality, and that these limits are not static, but depend upon the organizational environment in which the individual's decision takes place. The task of administration is to design this environment so that the individual will approach as close as practicable to rationality (judged in terms of the organization's goals) in his decisions" (pp. 240–241).

IN brief

In critical issues, managers may have to maximize in making decisions by evaluating a large number of feasible alternatives. They may "satisfice" in less critical issues by selecting the first alternative that meets the minimal criteria.

Both models of decision making are relevant to management. In situations critical to an organization's growth or survival (as in the planning process), managers must try to use the model of the economic person. In less critical situations, such as buying a water cooler for the office, the model of the administrative person is adequate. In decisions regarding the transportation for the football team or the hiring of a coach, the managers may lean toward "satisficing" (the administrative person model) in the transportation issue and toward "maximizing" (the economic person model) in hiring a coach.

Note that even satisficing—making a decision that is merely sufficient and satisfactory—can be rational, if the decision maker's objective is to minimize the cost of the search and the decision situation is not highly critical to the organization's functioning. The critical thrust of the administrative person model is the notion of satisficing based on the concept of bounded rationality. That is, managers tend to satisfice because they do not have the information or capacity to maximize the benefits. On the other hand, managers could be rational in deliberately choosing to satisfice rather than maximize. For example, the marketing manager who is seeking a printing firm may choose the first firm that meets his minimal criteria (a certain cost, a certain quality of output, and commitment to deadlines). The manager may satisfice in this case because the decision is not that critical and the additional benefits one may get through maximizing may not be worth the time and effort of the manager and the department. Viewed from this perspective (minimizing cost in less critical decisions), satisficing may indeed be a maximizing strategy.

Implicit Favorite Model

Another model of decision making, the **implicit favorite model**, was proposed by Soelberg (1967). In this model, while searching for a number of alternatives, the decision maker develops a preference for one alternative early in the search. Soelberg refers to this alternative as the implicit favorite. The subsequent search for alternatives and their evaluation is aimed at confirming the suitability of the implicit favorite. As Filley, House, and Kerr (1976) noted:

> The final decision process is one of *decision confirmation*. The decision maker will not enter into this period until one of the alternatives discovered thus far can be identified as an *implicit favorite*. In other words, decision making during the confirmation stage is an exercise in prejudice—in rationalization rather than in ratio-

nality. The decision maker ensures during the confirmation phase that the implicit favorite will indeed turn out to be the "right" choice. (p. 122)

Confirmation of the implicit favorite is achieved by selecting evaluative criteria that when applied to the other alternatives automatically result in their elimination.

Athletes choosing from among a number of universities that have similar scholarship offers, programs, facilities, and opportunities often adopt an implicit favorite approach. They make a choice early and then examine alternative universities as a means of confirming their initial selection. Similarly, when an organization has a preference for a particular individual and then places an advertisement for the position with job specifications that only the preferred candidate can meet, it is following the implicit favorite model. Exhibit 6.3 illustrates this process.

The implicit favorite model may be employed by individuals in making personal decisions like buying a car or going to a particular college or university, but managers need to exercise caution in using the model in an organizational context. The implicit favorite model may prove functional in decisions relating to buying equipment, supplies, and other decisions not involving humans. For instance, a manager and her assistants may decide to buy one brand of lawn mowers because the manager has always favored that brand. However, the model should not be used in any decisions involving humans, such as hiring, training, and promotions. Although buying a lawn mower may be influenced by the implicit favorite model, hiring those individuals who would use the lawn mower cannot be based on that model. First, there are laws and government regulations that prohibit such practices. Second, it would be unwise and unethical to shut out other candidates merely because the manager favors one individual based on characteristics irrelevant to the job in question. The risk of falling into the traps of the implicit favorite model can be avoided if, and only if, the setting of the evaluation criteria is established independently of and concurrently with the generation and search for alternatives.

We can draw one important guideline from the implicit favorite model. Once the decision maker has identified the implicit favorite, the subsequent

exhibit 6.3 **Steps in the implicit favorite model of decision making.**

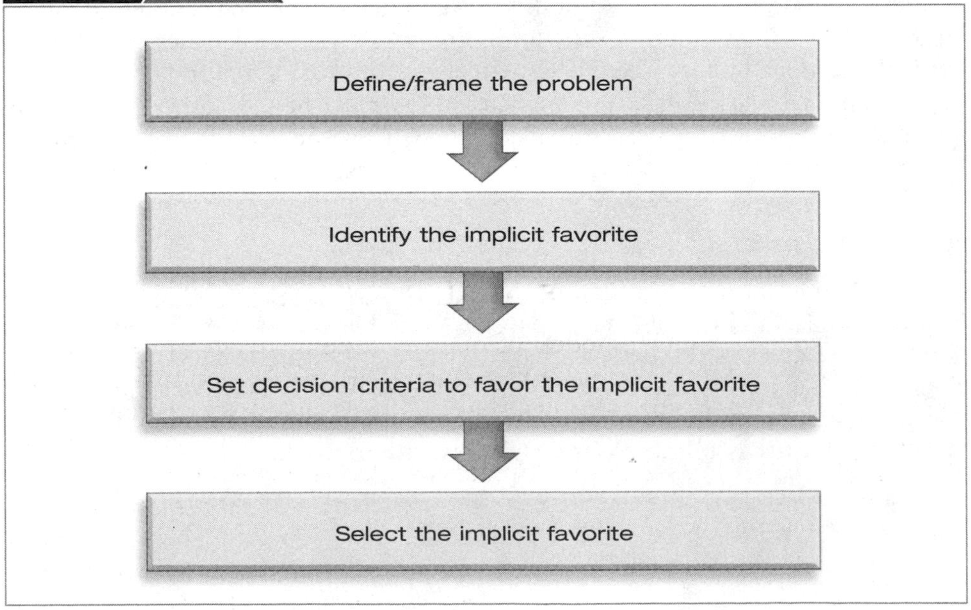
Define/frame the problem
Identify the implicit favorite
Set decision criteria to favor the implicit favorite
Select the implicit favorite

sidebar 6.3

BIASES IN THE DECISION-MAKING PROCESS

The models of decision making, whether prescriptive or descriptive, alert us to the biases that often creep into the decision-making process and thus reduce the decision's effectiveness. Vecchio (2003) refers to six kinds of biases that might influence a decision. First is the *availability bias,* which refers to the availability of relevant information through one's memory or perception. Such information could be limited and misleading, thus resulting in a faulty decision. Consider, for example, a ticket sales manager of a minor league baseball club who neglects to target the Mexican American population based on his memory of years ago when that segment of the population was rather small. Statistics suggest that Mexican Americans now constitute a large segment of fans and warrant the attention of marketers. In short, a manager's readily available knowledge may be limited and dated.

The second bias, *representativeness bias,* stems from the tendency of decision makers to rely on their sense that one person (or object or event) resembles another and lump them together in making judgments. Suppose, for example, a high school coach encounters a tall, athletic-looking African American student and immediately considers him for the basketball team. The coach (just like you and me) is likely to see the features of the potential player as similar to those of excellent athletes and would tend to judge him as ~~qualified~~ based on assuming he is an athlete. It could turn out, however, that the student was never an athlete but instead a scholar and musician.

The *implicit favorite bias* is the tendency of a decision maker to justify the choice of an alternative without realizing that it was his preference in the first place. Another bias is the *loss-aversion bias,* where the decision maker tends to avoid alternatives that run the risk of a loss. That is, such a person would go with the "sure bets." The *selective perception bias* is the tendency for a decision maker to interpret the available information selectively. For instance, a manager of a golf course, having recruited a groundskeeper, might have positive impressions of that person. That positive expectation could be reflected in the subsequent performance evaluation of the groundskeeper.

Finally, the *personal experience bias* is the influence of one's personal experiences to cloud judgment. For instance, if an event manager of a local professional franchise has a negative encounter with a group of high school students, he may think that all high school students engage in unruly behavior.

processes *confirm* the favorite choice. Good managers can use the same processes to *disconfirm* the favorite choice. That is, even though the favorite is chosen based on meaningful criteria, such criteria tend to show the choice in a good light. The problem here is that the process tends to overlook other equally qualified candidates or alternatives. In order to guard against making a mistake, the decision maker may purposely attempt to evaluate the favorite on other criteria that might show weaknesses. If in this process the candidate or alternative is not discredited or disconfirmed, then the decision maker can be more confident of the choice.

DECISION MAKING AS A SOCIAL PROCESS

The above-mentioned models of decision making are cognitive processes. But there is another equally important aspect of decision making—social processes. The social process of decision making refers to the degree to which members of a group are allowed to participate in decision making and can actually influence decisions. The social process of decision making may vary from autocratic decision making by the manager to varying degrees of participation by members (consultation with one or a few members, consultation with all members, group decision making, or delegation). These variations have been called the *decision styles* of the manager (Chelladurai & Haggerty, 1978).

Because member involvement in decision making is a major concern in management, let us look at the social processes of decision making in greater detail. We all know some leaders and managers who are autocratic and others who are democratic. For example, coaches of sport teams in general are said to be autocratic (Ogilvie & Tutko, 1966). Some researchers suggest that one's personality predisposes that person to be autocratic (Hendry, 1968). A different perspective holds that instead of viewing individuals as autocratic or democratic, we must view the situation as calling for autocratic or democratic decisions (Vroom & Yetton, 1973). In this view, being autocratic is in itself neither good nor bad. For instance, when a parent decides autocratically that a preschooler should go to bed, the parent is concerned about the child's welfare and is making an optimal, albeit autocratic, decision. On the other hand, a parent would be expected to allow a teenager to participate in the decision regarding his or her choice of a college. The difference between the preschooler's and the teenager's capacity to participate meaningfully in decisions calls for different social processes of decision making. From the human resource management perspective, it is critical that a manager be aware of the benefits and drawbacks of **participative decision making** and the appropriate degrees of participation under varying circumstances.

IN brief

Decision making as a cognitive process involves an analysis of the problem, generation of alternative solutions, and choice of the optimal solution. Decision making as a social process uses member participation to solve various problems.

Advantages of Participative Decision Making

The benefits of allowing members to participate in decision making can be summarized as (a) higher rationality of the decisions, (b) better understanding of the decisions, (c) broader ownership of the decisions, and (d) better execution of the decisions. The rationality of a decision depends on the amount of available information relevant to the problem at hand. Recall from Chapter 5 that the nominal group and Delphi techniques involve experts to forecast the future. Similarly, brainstorming is a process in which members engage in generating alternatives. The basic principle behind those methods is that a group harbors more information and insight than an individual. This wider and deeper base of information and expertise allows the manager to clarify the problem and identify and evaluate alternative solutions. Consider, for example, a marketing unit in a large fitness and recreation club or a university athletic department. The employees will look at a problem from different perspectives and with different insights stemming from their varied backgrounds and experiences. By the same token, they will also have different pieces of information about the problem. Thus, the unit as a collective has more information than any individual. Let us assume that a Y would like to market its programs to various segments of the local population, including the elderly and women. The seniors and women in the marketing unit are likely to have some pertinent information on how to reach these groups. This information, combined with the marketing expertise of the entire group, is likely to result in a comprehensive marketing plan. The idea that people of diverse backgrounds have different contributions to make is explored further in Chapter 13, on management of diversity.

An equally important benefit of participative decisions is that they enable members to comprehend more clearly the problem and its solution. Because employees of the marketing unit in the above example participated in decisions concerning the marketing strategies, they gained a better understanding of the rationale behind those decisions. They are therefore better equipped to implement the strategies. In addition, when members participate in decision making, they feel a sense of ownership in the decision. This sense of ownership motivates them to execute the strategies more efficiently and effectively. All of these advantages contribute to the success of the decisions. This view is supported by Nutt's (2002) finding that although more than half of the decisions made by organizations failed, 80 percent of the decisions involving significant participation of members succeeded.

An additional advantage of participation in decision making relates to development of individual employees. Participation in decision making makes the members more knowledgeable and capable of analyzing problems and evaluating options. These experiences are critical to individuals' personal growth and development, which in turn enhances the human resources of the organization.

The idea that several members with different backgrounds can contribute to good decision making is not restricted to just employees. For example, consider a community youth recreation program governed by a board of directors. The board probably includes influential members of the community, parents, coaches, and recreation leaders with varied backgrounds. They are likely to bring a variety of opinions and insights to the table and thus enable the board to make informed and better decisions.

Disadvantages of Participative Decision Making

Of course, participative decisions have their drawbacks. One obvious problem is that participative decisions take time. Have you ever seen a basketball coach engage in participative decisions during timeouts? There simply is not enough time. Also, it is possible that the leader may have more information than the group as a whole. In our previous example of the marketing unit of a local Y, we made an implicit assumption that the employees offered different sets of knowledge and experience. This is not necessarily true in all circumstances. Consider the case where the department hires an experienced marketing manager and five or six graduates. If the new graduates do not possess the relevant knowledge and experience, participative decision making would simply be "pooling of ignorance" (Chelladurai, 1985), and may not lead to higher-quality decisions.

Another significant factor influencing the effectiveness of participative decisions is the extent to which the group is integrated. If a group is poorly integrated and is marked by conflicts and cliques, the leader should be very careful in engaging that group in participative decisions. In our example of the marketing unit, it is possible that its members could have formed cliques (e.g., along age or gender lines), and the cliques could have developed animosity toward each other. In such a case, the leader of the marketing unit should be wary of engaging these members in participative decision making.

IN brief

Participative decision making capitalizes on the abilities and knowledge of the members, which typically results in better decisions. In addition, a participative process creates a better understanding of the problem and the solution, and ensures the acceptance of a decision. Disadvantages of group decision making include the cost of the time it takes to make decisions, possible "pooling of ignorance," and the possibility of group conflicts arising out of differences in preferred solutions to a problem.

Decision Styles

We noted earlier that the social process of decision making refers to the *degree* to which members participate in decision making. The degree of participation leads to the suggestion that participation in decision making may take several forms. A few decades ago, Vroom and his associates (Vroom & Jago, 1978, 1988; Vroom & Yetton, 1973) embarked on a concerted effort to study the social processes of making decisions. The cumulative results of this extensive and intensive research were summarized by Vroom (2000, 2003). Basically, Vroom's model includes five social processes involved in making a decision. They are described in Exhibit 6.4. Chelladurai and his associates (Chelladurai, 1993; Chelladurai & Arnott, 1985; Chelladurai & Haggerty, 1978; Chelladurai, Haggerty, & Baxter, 1989; Chelladurai & Quek, 1995) labeled these varying degrees of participation as *decision styles*.

Note that in Exhibit 6.4, the last two procedures (facilitate and delegate) are participative decisions, whereas in the other three procedures (decide, consult individually, and consult group) the leader is the sole decision maker. However, the influence of members in the decision progressively increases from "decide" to "delegate." In fact, Vroom (2000) provides a rating of member influence on each of the decision styles on a 10-point scale by 40 specialists. These ratings are shown in the far right column of Exhibit 6.4.

Problem Attributes

The issue now centers on the extent to which group members are allowed to influence the decisions and in what situations. In other words, which of the decision styles will be appropriate under which conditions? Vroom (2000, 2003) suggested that every situation could be described in terms of seven attributes:

1. *Decision significance:* the extent to which the decision in question is important to the project or the organization. In our example of a marketing unit,

exhibit 6.4 Decision styles and their descriptions.

DECISION STYLE	DESCRIPTION	MEMBERS' INFLUENCE (10-point scale)
1. Decide	The leader makes the decision based on available information, and announces it.	0
2. Consult individually	The leader explains the problem to members individually, gets their feedback, and then makes the decision.	3
3. Consult group	The leader explains the problem to the group as a whole, gets their feedback, and then makes the decision.	5
4. Facilitate	The leader explains the problem to the group, sets the limits to the decision, and attempts to get the members to concur on a decision. Leader's influence is minimal.	7
5. Delegate	The leader permits the group to make a decision within certain limits. The group defines the problem and its characteristics, generates alternative solutions, and decides on one or more of the alternatives.	10

the choice of a marketing strategy is a more significant decision, because it impacts a company's sales and growth, than the purchase of a table for the conference room. This distinction is analogous to the distinction between maximizing and satisficing processes discussed earlier. The greater the significance of the decision, the greater the need for member participation that brings in more information and insights.

2. *Importance of commitment:* members' commitment to the decision. If members will be called upon to implement the decision diligently (e.g., the selected marketing strategy), their commitment to the chosen strategy becomes critical. As noted earlier, such commitment can be secured by having the members participate in making the decision, thus giving them a sense of ownership. In other cases, a manager or her immediate assistants may execute the decision without the involvement of the members (for example, deciding to interact with the media). The higher the requirement of member commitment, the higher the need for member participation.
3. *Leader's expertise:* the amount and quality of information, knowledge, and expertise the leader has in relation to the problem at hand. When the leader does not have all the information, it is prudent for him to get members involved in decision making. On the other hand, group decision making may not be worth the time and effort involved when the leader has all the information.
4. *Likelihood of commitment:* the degree to which members will be committed to a decision even when the leader makes the decision by herself. Earlier we suggested that members' commitment can be secured by engaging them in making the decision. If the leader is well respected and liked, it is possible that members may be committed to a decision made by the leader. In such a case, participation in decision making may not be necessary.
5. *Group support for objectives:* the extent to which members of the group accept and support the goals and objectives of the group and organization. If they all share the group goals, they can be expected to participate diligently in making an optimal decision. If, however, some members have divergent perceptions of what the group goals should be, their participation may not be wholehearted. In such a case, participative decision making would likely be futile. In the example of the marketing unit, some members may believe that the organization or the unit should concentrate on satisfying the exist-

sidebar 6.4

DECISION STYLES AND WINDOW DRESSING

Chelladurai (1993) cautioned against confusing a person's decision style with his personality. For instance, consider a football coach who presents his playbook for the season to the quarterback with the apparently menacing command: "This is your bible. You'd better master it." In contrast, another coach may present his playbook with a smile and the comment: "Here is the playbook I drew up during the summer. You may get a kick out of reading it." The difference in their mannerisms should not be allowed to mask the fact that both coaches autocratically decided on the plays.

Chelladurai (1993) also suggests that we should not be misguided by "window dressing." That is, a person may project herself as very democratic by letting members make decisions in trivial matters. For instance, a basketball coach may allow his players to choose the starting five for a game. How does that make the coach more democratic when he substitutes those players at the first whistle? The coach has just created a façade of democratic leadership.

ing customer base instead of attempting to expand its market. If so, their participation in the choice of strategies for expansion may not be worthwhile. The lower the goal congruence among members, the lower the need for group decisions.

6. *Group expertise:* the amount and quality of information and expertise the members have relative to the problem at hand. A basic premise for participative decision making is that there is more information in the group. However, as noted above, in certain circumstances the members may lack the necessary information or experience to contribute to group decision making. Therefore, engaging them in group decisions would not be fruitful.
7. *Team competence:* the ability of the members to work together on the problem and come up with a solution. It is expected that the members get along as a group and have learned to interact with each other and participate effectively in decision making. If, in contrast, the group is characterized by internal cliques and conflicts, members' self-interest is likely to interfere with effective decision making.

Vroom and his associates also took into account the leader's concern with the time it takes to make decisions on the one hand and, on the other hand, her desire to develop the subordinates' cognitive abilities to analyze problems and evaluate alternatives. There may be occasions when the leader does not have much time to engage the members in decision making, as in the case of a timeout during a basketball game. Even when there are no such constraints, the leader needs to balance the labor costs associated with the time it takes to make participative decisions with the developmental benefits of participation. Thus, the leader may engage less in participative decision styles if there are time concerns and more in participative styles if the developmental benefits outweigh the time concerns.

The above attributes can be categorized on the basis of whether they relate to the problem per se, to the leader, or to the members in juxtaposition with the problem. Thus, the attribute of decision significance refers to the problem itself. Leader's expertise refers to the leader's information relevant to the problem. The remaining attributes pertain to the group members, their interrelationships, and their relationship to the leader and the problem.

As Vroom and Yetton (1973) pointed out, "The quality of the decision is dependent not only on the information and expertise of those participating in it, but also on their disposition to use their information in the service of the goal stated in the problem" (p. 29). In reading the above attributes, you will recognize that some of the attributes refer to members' information and expertise whereas others relate to their willingness to participate meaningfully in making decisions. The effects of problem attributes on the choice of decision styles are summarized in Exhibit 6.5.

A consistent finding from the 25-year research on the model proposed by Vroom and his associates is that the influence of situational attributes on a manager's decision style dwarfs the influence of individual difference (i.e., personal) factors (Vroom, 2000). A similar trend appears in an athletic context. Chelladurai and his associates (Chelladurai & Arnott, 1985; Chelladurai et al., 1989; Chelladurai & Quek, 1995) investigated basketball players' preferences for a particular decision style under various problems that were defined by selected problem attributes—quality requirement, coaches' information, players' information, problem structure, and team integration. High and low levels of these attributes were built into differing scenarios or problem situations. Basketball players at the

exhibit 6.5 Relationships between problem attributes and subordinate participation in decision making.

WHEN THIS PROBLEM ATTRIBUTE IS HIGH . . .	MEMBER PARTICIPATION IS
Decision significance	High
Importance of commitment	High
Leader expertise	Low
Likelihood of commitment	Low
Group support	High
Group expertise	High
Team competence	High

Adapted from P. Chelladurai, *Human Resource Management in Sport and Recreation,* 2nd ed., p. 209. © 2006 by Packianathan Chelladurai. Champaign, IL: Human Kinetics. Data from Vroom, 2003.

university and high school levels were asked to indicate which decision style they would prefer their coach to employ. Results indicated that the majority of the players agreed that their coaches should make the decision even without consultation with the players. Furthermore, the results showed that the problem attributes built into the scenarios had three to four times more influence on decision style preferences than individual differences did. That is, the players' preferences for specific decision styles varied with the type of situation.

Thus, an analysis of the specific attributes of a problem should assist the leader in deciding on a specific decision style. It is important that the leader take into consideration the attributes in totality instead of focusing on just one or two of them. Along with viewing the problem attributes comprehensively, managers must also consider four possible outcomes of a given decision style—(a) the quality of the decision that is consistent with organizational goals, (b) the extent to which subordinates understand and accept the decision, (c) the cost in terms of time, and (d) the development of group members (Vroom, 2003).

From this perspective, deciding on the social process to be employed in decision making itself is a cognitive process. The ideas presented here represent a logical and rational framework with which managers may analyze problem situations and select an appropriate decision style. Also, this framework minimizes the importance of a manager's personal characteristics, including personality, as determinants of decision style choices.

Vroom (2000) noted that over his 25-year research period, managers' decision styles shifted to relatively more participative processes. He speculated that this shift reflects (a) the higher rates of change in and increased complexity of the environment, (b) a move toward flatter organizational structures, (c) improved information technology, and (d) a more

IN brief

Though a leader would be better off allowing his members to participate in decision making, the extent to which such participation should occur is a function of the attributes of the problem and the characteristics of individual members and the group. A leader should evaluate these attributes and choose the most appropriate decision style in a given problem situation.

sidebar 6.5

POLITICAL DEMOCRACY VERSUS ORGANIZATIONAL DEMOCRACY

There has always been a strong push to *democratize* the organization. Increasing participation by workers in making decisions on organizational policies and processes has been advocated on the grounds either that it is the moral or right thing to do or that such an approach would lead to a more committed workforce and thus to better organizational performance. Yet the practice of democracy in organizations has never kept pace with the rhetoric for it. Kerr (2004) points to the fallacy of two assumptions behind the push for democracy. First is the assumption that the *political* democracy as we know it in the United States and other Western countries can be translated into *organizational* democracy. The second assumption is that such organizational democracy would be the best method of governance and decision making in all organizational settings.

Kerr (2004) notes that (a) organizations are not the same as societies where democracy is practiced; (b) managers are not elected, as are representatives to legislative bodies; and (c) the roles and responsibilities of employees are not the same as those of citizens. The critical democratic characteristics of accountability to the governed, equal rights of participation, free exchange of information, and representation of the governed are not relevant to or even existent in organizations. That is, while the elected in a political democracy are accountable to the governed (i.e., the electorate), managers are accountable to the owners and not the employees. In a political democracy, equal participation is guaranteed by law, whereas in an organization such participation is controlled by management. As for free exchange of information, the electorate in a democracy has unconstrained access to almost all information, whereas such access and exchange is controlled by management in an organization. Finally, representation of the people in a democracy is guaranteed through the electoral process; such representation is incidental in an organization. It must also be noted that the legitimacy of those who govern in a society is derived from the democratic process, whereas such legitimacy in an organization stems from the legal ownership of the organization. For all these reasons, democracy has not taken root in organizations:

> The "problem" with organizational democracy is that it is not a trivial or superficial adjustment. . . . It requires a fundamental redistribution of responsibility, authority, power, and resources that affects every member of the organization and the relationships between them. It is also not an easy system to live with once established. In place of straightforward commands and controls, every interaction is a potential negotiation, every decision a potential political moment. (Kerr, 2004, p. 93)

Kerr (2004) also suggests that the democratic process in an organization can be successful only if (a) the process will enhance the work of the organization, (b) the workforce has the talent and attitude to engage in the process, (c) the cost and risk of changing to a democratic process would be minimal, and (d) the upper management is prepared for and committed to democratic values and practices.

highly educated and sophisticated labor force. He also noted that women managers tended to be more participative than men. Finally, he noted that managers at higher levels of the organization tended to be more participative than those at lower levels.

SUMMARY

The emphasis in this chapter was on decision making as a significant component of management. The importance of clearly stating and framing the problem or opportunity was highlighted. We noted that the way a problem is framed can influence subsequent decisions related to it. As in the planning process, we recognized the need to generate alternative solutions and evaluate them. We identified the differences between a programmed decision and a nonprogrammed decision, and the relationship between a decision's programmability and its significance. We examined how the classical model of decision making is aimed at being rational; however, managers' rationality is bound by their lack of information and their own inability to digest all the information. We discussed Simon's concept of bounded rationality and the three models of decision making—economic person, administrative person, and implicit favorite. We discussed the concepts of maximizing and "satisficing" and the appropriateness of each to different problems. Finally, we looked at decision making as a social process, the advantages and disadvantages of participative decision making, and problem attributes.

develop YOUR PERSPECTIVE

1. Explain the steps in decision making and its significance to a sport manager.
2. Consider a sport organization you are familiar with. Give examples of the opportunities and problems that the manager may have to decide on.
3. Which of the examples you gave would involve programmed decisions and which nonprogrammed decisions? Explain.
4. Describe what you think would be the short-term and long-term consequences of the decisions you listed in number 2.
5. What is meant by rationality of a decision? Describe a decision made by a sport manager that, in your opinion, was not rational. Explain.
6. Explain the concepts maximizing and satisficing. Give examples in which a manager should maximize or satisfice.
7. Recall a situation where you were involved in participative decision making. Describe the situation in terms of the problem attributes explained in the chapter. Was the group effective in making a decision? What were the strengths and weaknesses of the group in making the decision?

references

Amick, S. (2013, November 25). Kobe Bryant, Lakers sign two-year contract extension. *USA TODAY Sports*.

Arkers, H. R., & Blumer, C. (1985). The psychology of sunk cost. *Organizational Behavior and Human Decision Processes, 35,* 124–140.

Black, J. S., & Porter, L. W. (2000). *Management: Meeting new challenges*. Upper Saddle River, NJ: Prentice Hall.

Brockner, J. (1992). The escalation of commitment to a failing course of action: Toward theoretical progress. *Academy of Management Review, 17*(1), 39–61.

Camerer, C. F., & Weber, R. A. (1999). The econometrics and behavioral economics of escalation of commitment: A re-examination of Staw and Hoang's NBA data. *Journal of Economic Behavior and Organization, 39,* 59–82.

Certo, S. C., & Certo, S. T. (2009). *Modern management: Concepts and skills* (11th ed.). Upper Saddle River, NJ: Prentice Hall.

Chelladurai, P. (1985). *Sport management: Macro perspectives*. London, Canada: Sports Dynamics.

Chelladurai, P. (1993). Styles of decision making in coaching. In J. M. Williams (Ed.), *Applied sport psychology: Personal growth to peak performance* (2nd ed., pp. 99–109). Palo Alto, CA: Mayfield.

Chelladurai, P., & Arnott, M. (1985). Decision styles in coaching: Preferences of basketball players. *Research Quarterly for Exercise and Sport, 56*(1), 15–24.

Chelladurai, P., & Haggerty, T. R. (1978). A normative model of decision styles in coaching. *Athletic Administrator, 13,* 6–9.

Chelladurai, P., Haggerty, T. R., & Baxter, P. R. (1989). Decision style choices of university basketball coaches and players. *Journal of Sport and Exercise Psychology, 11,* 201–215.

Chelladurai, P., & Quek, C. B. (1995). Situational and personality effects on the decision style choices of high school basketball coaches. *Journal of Sport Behavior, 18*(2), 91–108.

Chou, E. Y., & Murnighan, J. K. (2013). Life or death decisions: Framing the call for help. *PLoS ONE, 8*(3). Retrieved from http://www.plosone.org/article/info%3Adoi%2F10.1371%2Fjournal.pone.0057351.

Filley, A. C., House, R. J., & Kerr, S. (1976). *Managerial process and organizational behavior*. Glenview, IL: Scott, Foresman.

Hendry, L. B. (1968). A personality study of highly successful and "ideal" swimming coaches. *Research Quarterly, 40*, 299–305.

Kerr, J. L. (2004). The limits of organizational democracy. *Academy of Management Executive, 18*(3), 81–95.

Matsuoka, H., & Chelladurai, P. (2000). *Components of psychological attachment to sport teams*. Unpublished manuscript, The Ohio State University.

Naylor, J. (1999). *Management*. London: Financial Times Management.

Nutt, P. C. (2002). *Why decisions fail: Avoiding the blunders and traps that lead to debacles*. Williston, VT: Berrett-Koehler.

Ogilvie, B. C., & Tutko, T. A. (1966). *Problem athletes and how to control them*. London: Pelham Books.

Schermerhorn, J. R., Hunt, J. G., & Osborn, R. N. (1997). *Organizational behavior* (6th ed.). New York: John Wiley.

Simon, H. A. (1945). *Administrative behavior*. New York: Macmillan.

Simon, H. A. (1957). *Models of man*. New York: John Wiley.

Simon, H. A. (1976). *Administrative behavior: A study of decision-making processes in administrative organizations*. New York: Free Press.

Simon, H. A. (1977). *The new science of managerial decision making*. Englewood Cliffs, NJ: Prentice Hall.

Soelberg, P. (1967). Unprogrammed decision making. *Industrial Management Review, 8*, 19–29.

Staw, B. M., & Hoang, H. (1995). Sunk costs in the NBA: Why draft order affects playing time and survival in professional basketball. *Administrative Science Quarterly, 40*, 474–494.

Vecchio, R. P. (2003). *Organizational behavior: Core concepts*. Mason, OH: Thompson/South-Western.

Vroom, V. H. (1959). Some personality determinants of the effects of participation. *Journal of Abnormal and Social Psychology, 59*, 322–327.

Vroom, V. H. (2000). Leadership and the decision-making process. *Organizational Dynamics, 28*(4), 82–94.

Vroom, V. H. (2003). Educating managers for decision making and leadership. *Management Decision, 41*(10), 968–978.

Vroom, V. H., & Jago, A. G. (1978). On the validity of the Vroom–Yetton model. *Journal of Applied Psychology, 63*, 151–162.

Vroom, V. H., & Jago, A. G. (1988). *The new leadership: Managing participation in organizations*. Upper Saddle River, NJ: Prentice Hall.

Vroom, V. H., & Yetton, R. N. (1973). *Leadership and decision-making*. Pittsburgh: University of Pittsburgh Press.

PRINCIPLES OF ORGANIZING

CHAPTER 7

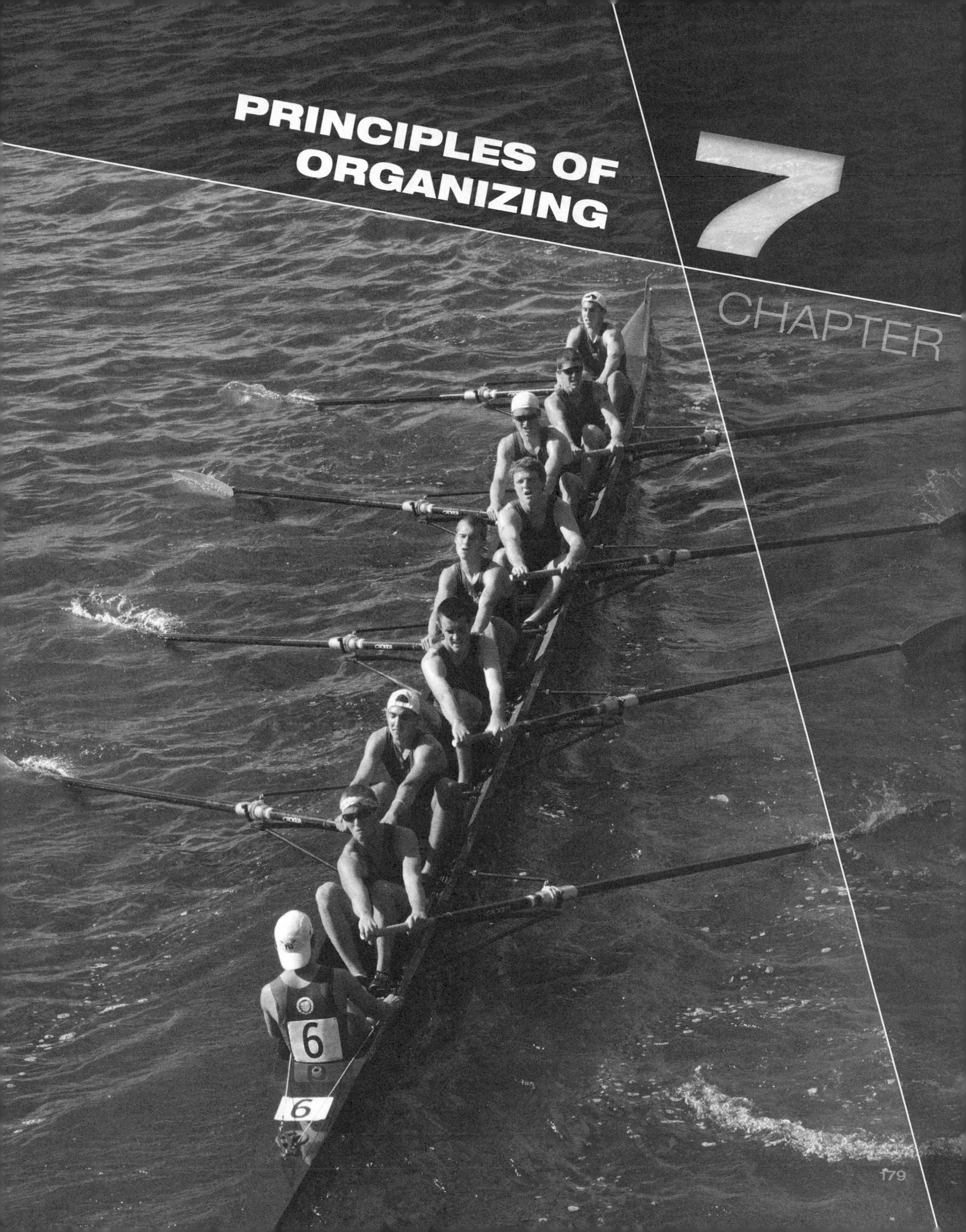

manage YOUR LEARNING

After completing this chapter you should be able to:

- Describe the classical principles of organizing.
- List the tenets of a bureaucracy.
- Discuss the relevance of bureaucracy and its tenets to sport organizations.
- Describe the dysfunctional aspects of bureaucracy.
- Explain the place of bureaucracy in a democracy, and how the two complement each other.

strategic CONCEPTS

abstract rules
bureaucracy
democracy
departmentalization
division of labor
hierarchical authority structure
impersonality
span of control
specialization
stability
technical competence
unity of command

ORGANIZING DEFINED

In Chapter 5, we described the planning function of organizations. The fundamental tasks of that function are identifying and clarifying goals and specifying the activities and programs needed to achieve those goals. In essence, the sum of these activities and programs constitutes the total work to be accomplished. For instance, a commercial fitness club may set as its goal a 5 percent increase in the number of its clients. This simple goal stated in a straightforward manner belies the numerous activities employees must engage themselves in. First, they must increase the quality of services offered, which will involve all employees—instructors in weight training, aerobics, swimming, and tennis; receptionists; locker room attendants; and day care supervisors. Second, they must become more efficient in scheduling the activities and instructors. This may also entail rearranging the equipment and activity spaces. Then they must market the improved services. These are just a few examples of how a simple goal generates a host of activities.

Once the goals have been specified and the courses of action have been selected (that is, after the planning process has been completed), the work must be divided into specific jobs, those jobs must be assigned to individuals, and all activities must be coordinated toward achieving the organizational goals. This is the process of organizing:

> Organizing is assembling and coordinating the human, financial, physical, informational, and other resources needed to achieve goals. Organizing activities include attracting people to the organization, specifying job responsibilities, grouping jobs into work units, marshalling and allocating resources, and creating conditions so

that people and things work together to achieve maximum success. (Bateman & Snell, 2007, p. 17)

> The process of organizing is the grouping of activities necessary to attain common objectives and the assignment of each grouping to a manager who has the authority required to supervise the people performing the activities. (Rue & Byars, 2009, p. 160)

> Organizing is a management function that involves determining what tasks are to be done, who is to do them, how the tasks are to be grouped, who reports to whom, and where decisions are to be made. (Robbins, Coulter, Leach, & Kilfoil, 2012, p. 7)

In essence, then, the organizing process results in an organizational structure that specifies the relationships among tasks and among the people who perform them. These definitions imply that

- there is division of labor in the sense that different people are asked to carry out different activities (ticketing personnel, marketing personnel, and event management personnel in a professional sport franchise), and
- there is a hierarchy in the sense that some are placed in supervisory roles over other persons (e.g., ticketing manager, marketing manager, event manager, and the general manager, who supervises the other managerial positions in a professional sport franchise).

Such a structure is expected to maximize the use of all available resources within the organization. As Hall (1996) noted, the organizational structure facilitates (a) the production of organizational outputs, (b) regulation of individual variations from organizational requirements, and (c) definition of power hierarchy (i.e., which positions exercise power over other positions). Hall also noted that organizational structure defines the flow of information needed for effective decision making. Thus, "structure becomes one of the most important issues because it is structure that holds the whole organization together, keeps it afloat, and separates the inside from the outside" (Clegg, Kornberger, & Pitsis, 2005, p. 120).

The fundamental purpose of organizing (and the resultant organizational structure) is to establish a means of coordination. You will recall that sport management is defined as the coordination of the activities in the production and marketing of sport services. You also saw that the managerial functions of planning, organizing, leading, and evaluating are the means of such coordination. The focus here is on organizational structure as a coordinating mechanism. The structure enables coordination through systematically allocating diverse tasks, creating specified means of cooperation among people and units, establishing channels of communication among people and units, and allocating decision-making powers to those people or positions most qualified to make the decisions (Robbins et al., 2012). In the following sections, the various principles of organizing are outlined. Because these principles have been in vogue for several decades, they are called

> "Every organized human activity—from the making of pottery to the placing of a man on the moon—gives rise to two fundamental and opposing requirements: the division of labor into various tasks to be performed and the coordination of those tasks to accomplish the activity. The structure of an organization can be defined simply as the total of the ways in which its labor is divided into distinct tasks and then its coordination achieved among tasks."
>
> **MINTZBERG,**
> *1989, pp. 100–101*

the *classical principles*. The fact that management scholars and many management textbooks adhere to these principles attests to their veracity and utility.

CLASSICAL PRINCIPLES

The classical principles that have been the cornerstones of organizing include specialization, span of control, departmentalization, unity of command, and responsibility and authority.

Specialization

Specialization refers to the notion that individuals in an organization perform tasks that are narrow in scope. Specialization calls for each person to perform one function if it is feasible. An extreme example is an assembly line in a factory, where one individual's task may be reduced to placing a bolt on a product. The idea is germane to all kinds of organizations. For example, a fitness club may employ specialists in weight training, aerobics, swimming, tennis, exercise physiology, nutrition, accounting, marketing, and so on. Similarly, a professional sport franchise may have specialists in media relations, marketing, sport law, accounting, and so on. Sport management degree programs in many universities have professors specializing in sport marketing, sport finance, sport law, organization theory, human resource management, and facility and event management.

Specialization may be necessary because one person does not have the time, energy, or knowledge to carry out a number of tasks associated with an organization. An added advantage of specialization is that it allows for those with the knowledge and ability to perform skilled tasks, and those without the competency to perform the unskilled tasks.

Specialization contributes to efficiency in the following specific ways:

1. Specialization in a limited number of tasks increases the skill or ability to perform those functions.
2. Specialization eliminates the time spent putting away tools and equipment from one step and preparing for the next.
3. Specialization facilitates the training of workers. It is easier and more effective to train individuals in a restricted number of specific and routine tasks than an array of different tasks.

Span of Control

Span of control refers to the number of people, units, and operations that a manager can control effectively and efficiently in a given time period. Research generally supports the suggestion that the span of control should be narrow at the top level of management (a ratio of approximately four subordinates to one manager) and wide at the lower levels (a ratio of approximately eight or more subordinates to one manager). Research also suggests that seven is the optimum number of subordinates a manager should supervise. However, Fink, Jenks, and Willits (1983) outlined the following series of factors that will affect the actual span of control in an organization or a unit.

Type of work done. If the employees are engaged in similar and routine tasks, then it is possible for one manager to supervise a large number of personnel. For example, in a professional sport franchise, an individual may be able to supervise effectively a number of ticket takers for a game because they are all involved in similar tasks (checking the tickets and directing the spectators to their location). If, however, the tasks of the employees are complex and changing, then a narrower span of control is necessary. Returning to the professional franchise marketing example, the personnel would be performing relatively more complex tasks than the ticket takers. In addition, if they were involved in tackling different segments of the market, they would be dealing with different sets of customer information and differing opportunities and barriers. One supervisor cannot effectively deal with this complexity. Therefore, such a situation would call for a narrow span of control.

Competence/expertise of the person doing the job. If employees are well trained and dedicated to their respective jobs, then close supervision is not necessary. Therefore, the span of control can be wider. For instance, if the subordinates of a marketing director in a university athletic department have good training in marketing, have experience in sport marketing, and are committed to their tasks, the director will not need to spend much time and energy supervising them. Thus, she can supervise more employees. On the other hand, if the employees are new to the organization, and to sport marketing in particular, the director will have to spend more time giving them guidance and direction. Therefore, the manager can effectively supervise fewer employees. Similarly, greater supervision and therefore a narrower span of control are required where workers are indifferent to their task.

Competence/expertise of the supervisor. A more competent and technically qualified supervisor is able to supervise a greater number of subordinates than a less qualified and less skilled supervisor.

Relationship between the supervisor and employees. In situations where there is respect for the supervisor and his role and supervisor and employees enjoy a warm interpersonal relationship, a wider span of control is feasible. As we will note in a later chapter on leadership, respect for and approval of the manager can motivate employees to carry out their responsibilities in order not to let the manager down.

IN brief

Span of control refers to the number of people, units, and operations under the control of a manager. The width of the span is influenced by the type of work, the competence of the employees and the supervisor, the relationship between them, and the pressure for production.

Pressure for production. If there is pressure on the organization to produce more or higher-quality goods or services, then the organization must impose greater control and supervision over its employees, which in turn leads to a narrower span of control. Note that a narrower span of control implies greater control and more supervision, whereas a wider span entails less supervision and less control. Therefore, whenever it is deemed necessary to exert greater control over the subordinates and their tasks, the number of subordinates under a manager is reduced.

When an organization institutes a narrow span of control in its mode of operation, the result is a greater number of levels in the hierarchy. On the other hand, if an organization adopts a wider span of control, there will be fewer levels in the hierarchy. The former situation results in a "tall" structure and the latter a "flat" structure. Suppose 12 employees are working under one marketing director. That means only two levels of hierarchy exist in the marketing unit—the director level and the employee level—resulting in a flat structure. Now suppose that for some reason, the organization finds it necessary to supervise these 12 employees more closely to improve the efficiency and quality of the marketing operations. Accordingly, the decision is made to promote two of the senior employees to the rank of assistant directors of marketing. This arrangement results in a narrow span of control in the unit. The reorganization has created one more level of hierarchy in the unit, as shown in Exhibit 7.1, making the structure taller than before.

Departmentalization

The principle of span of control leads to the concept of departmentalization. That is, as organizational activities increase in number and complexity, they need to be grouped into homogeneous sets: the organization needs to be departmentalized (Bateman & Snell, 2007). This process of forming homogeneous groupings is called **departmentalization.** There are two broad types of departmentalization.

Process-oriented or functional departmentalization. This grouping is based on the concept of specialization. That is, individuals performing the same functions, or in positions involving similar skills, expertise, and resources, are grouped into a department. A ticketing department in a professional sport franchise, an accounting department in a large fitness club, and a sport management department in a university are examples of departmentalization according to specialized functions. In a university's athletic department, specialized units often are related to compliance, event management, ticketing, and marketing.

IN brief

Departmentalization is forming homogeneous groupings of tasks based on either the functions they perform (functional departmentalization) or the products they produce (product departmentalization).

Product- or goal-oriented departmentalization. This way of grouping is basically a division of the organization according to different products, different geographical areas, different customer types, or different projects. In this type of departmentalization, each unit consists of members with different specialized skills performing different functions. Consider a profit-oriented

exhibit 7.1 Flat and tall structures.

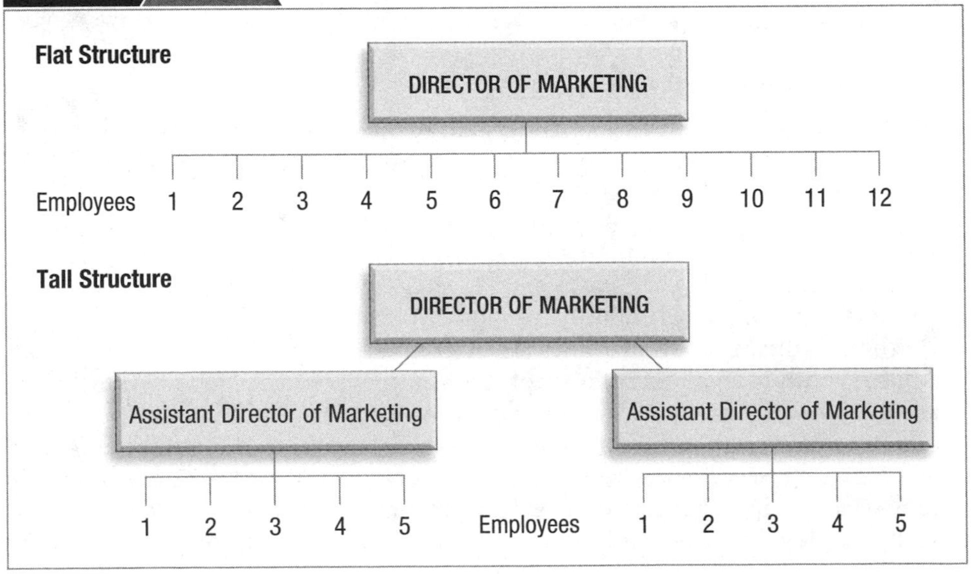

fitness club that has expanded its business to different geographical areas. Each geographical unit must hire people with various skills to perform the necessary functions. Similarly, when a university athletic department assigns athletic trainers and public relations personnel to specific teams and expects them to work under the supervision of the coaches or managers of the respective teams, it is following goal-oriented departmentalization.

A number of advantages and disadvantages are associated with the two forms of departmentalization. Functional departmentalization provides for the development of subspecialties (a division of labor within a specialty); advancement in the specialty; supervision by a specialist; professional contagion (the opportunity to learn from professional colleagues and to be motivated by them); efficient and maximum use of resources (that is, the use of existing personnel or equipment to the maximum extent before additions are made); and satisfaction with work (members of functional departments are more satisfied with their work than members of goal-oriented departments).

On the negative side, functional departmentalization leads to difficulties in coordinating and scheduling the activities of different units. Also, functional structures lead to conflict and competition between departments owing to differences in professional orientations of the personnel. That is, the professional goals of the members, for example, in the marketing department, the event management unit, and other functionally specialized units in an organization may be in conflict with each other for two reasons: First, they compete with each other for resources as well as for the status and prestige accorded to each unit within the organization. Second, the conflicts (or at least lack of harmony) may be a function of their differing ways of looking at problems and arriving at solutions.

In a goal- or product-oriented department, the glue that binds the members together is the goal of the project and its customers. Therefore, each of the units and its members are focused on their respective customers and the requirements of the project or goal. Also, in such departmentalization, personnel of different specialized skills function under one manager, resulting in greater coordination and less conflict among members. However, goal-oriented departmentalization is less efficient in the sense that skills and equipment are duplicated and are not fully utilized. Furthermore, since most members are not supervised by a specialist, they may feel isolated—particularly if there are no others in the same specialty within the department. That is, the opportunities for learning and professional growth are reduced.

sidebar 7.1

TURF WARS

R. J. Herbold (2004), former Chief Operating Officer of Microsoft, had this to say on interdepartmental rivalries and turf wars:

> Over the course of my thirty-six years in business, I have come to realize there is a set of behaviors that people exhibit that remind me very much of the feudal fiefdoms of the Middle Ages. Individuals and groups tend to isolate themselves from the larger organization, and worry more about defending their turf and protecting the status quo than in moving the organization forward. I call such behavior the Fiefdom syndrome. (p. 1)

Herbold found this syndrome in organizations in every sector (private, profit, nonprofit, public, educational, etc.). Noting that the behaviors associated with fiefdom go against common sense and innovation and lead to destructive turf wars, he also said that "it's not that people who exhibit fiefdom tendencies are mischievous or unethical. These behaviors are simply natural human tendencies that emerge as people try to exercise control over their workplace environment, protect their domain, and avoid change that might upset the present order" (p. 1).

Matrix. Matrix structure is another form of departmentalization that attempts to meld the advantages of both functional and goal-oriented departmentalization. A matrix organization is simply the imposition of one structure over the other. In Exhibit 7.2, members of an athletic department of a university belonging to a particular functional specialization are grouped together as a functional unit. At the same time, each individual member belongs to a goal-oriented unit—that is, a team. This grouping allows for greater and more efficient coordination in a team's activities while at the same time providing a "home base" for each member. In a similar manner, a fitness club with two or more locations within a city may decide to adopt the matrix structure. In this scheme, functional units such as aerobics, weight training, swimming, and so on are supervised by a functional specialist. At the same time, members of the functional units are assigned to different branches supervised by the club manager. The matrix structure has one serious drawback: each member is supervised by two different managers—a violation of the principle of *unity of command,* which is discussed below.

IN brief

The matrix structure is a combination of process- and product-oriented departmentalization in which an individual reports to a functional unit as well as a product unit.

Unity of Command

Unity of command is similar to the biblical principle "No one can serve two masters." The principle of **unity of command** means that each member of the organization should follow the orders of only one supervisor and be accountable only to that supervisor. This principle serves to protect against the possibility that conflicting commands will be given by different superiors. Although this concept is useful in highly structured organizations such as a government bureaucracy, it

exhibit 7.2 Matrix structure for a department of athletics and for a fitness center.

DEPARTMENT OF ATHLETICS	Project Grouping (Programs)			
Functional Grouping	Football	Basketball	Hockey	Gymnastics
Athletic Training				
Marketing				
Public Relations				
Academic Counseling				

FITNESS CENTER	Location Grouping		
Functional Grouping	Location A	Location B	Location C
Aerobics			
Weight Training			
Swimming			

is likely to be disregarded in more modern, complex forms of organizational structures such as the matrix organization. In such structures, an employee may be expected to follow the advice and suggestions of more than one person rather than to comply strictly with the directives of one supervisor. The athletic trainer in a university athletic department, for example, may be asked to serve under both of the supervisors of the athletic training units catering to the football and basketball teams. Similarly, a marketing specialist may serve under the supervisor of marketing for the athletic teams as well as the supervisor of marketing for the large arena.

IN brief

Unity of command states that a worker should report to a single supervisor. Another principle states that those individuals who have a responsibility must have the authority to carry out the responsibility.

Responsibility and Authority

The classical principle of responsibility with equal authority states that an employee must be given the necessary authority to carry out an assigned responsibility. It is readily apparent that individuals cannot carry out their duties if they do not have the authority to make decisions relating to their tasks. Thus, a manager put in charge of a sports event must have the authority to decide on the traffic and security measures necessary to carry out the responsibility effectively and efficiently. This notion of authority equaling responsibility becomes critical in the case of those managers who have to monitor and control the activities of subordinates. A manager should have the authority to assign different people to different tasks, ask them to perform certain duties, correct them when they are not doing things accurately, and reward (or punish) them for their performance. In the absence of such authority, the manager cannot be held responsible if the subordinates do not carry out their duties effectively. A good example of this principle in practice is when the head coach of a university team is given the autonomy and authority to decide on team members, tactics and strategies, practice sessions, and the game plan for every competition.

BUREAUCRACY

Bureaucrats have been likened to cockroaches. The reasoning is that like cockroaches, they are everywhere; like cockroaches, they do not seem to serve any useful purpose and they seem to defy all attempts at their extinction. (Watch Donald Brittain's documentary *Paperland: The Bureaucrat Observed*—the source of this comparison—for a savagely funny criticism of bureaucrats.)

This description sums up the negative attitude of anybody who has come up against a bureaucracy. Nevertheless, despite all criticisms, bureaucratic organizations are prevalent in all nations, whether democratic or totalitarian, rich or poor, large or small. Professional sport clubs, commercial fitness clubs, city recreation departments, national sport-governing bodies, and international sport federations are all patterned as bureaucracies. Even the departments of intercollegiate athletics and recreational sports in American universities are organized as bureaucracies.

Tenets of a Bureaucracy

Although bureaucracy has been practiced in some form or another since ancient times, the analysis and discussion of the phenomenon has gained momentum only since the beginning of the 20th century. Classical theorists such as Frederick

Winslow Taylor and Henri Fayol emphasized some of the characteristics of a bureaucratic organization, but it was left to Max Weber, a German sociologist, to coin the term **bureaucracy** and write extensively on the concept in the early part of the 20th century. In his writings, Weber (1947) emphasized that an organization, if it is to operate rationally and efficiently, must be structured to include certain fundamental characteristics. His bureaucratic tenets, or principles, are described below. Note that some of these tenets are the same as or similar to the classical principles of organizations detailed earlier.

- **Division of labor.** In any organization, the total work must be broken down into simple, well-defined tasks, and these tasks must be distributed to members as official duties.
- **Hierarchical authority structure.** The positions in an organization are arranged in a hierarchical authority structure, meaning that progressively increasing authority is vested at each successively higher level.
- **A system of abstract rules.** This principle refers to the fact that an organization will specify a set of rules to regulate what is to be done, by whom, for whom, and under what conditions.
- **Impersonality.** Bureaucracies also exhibit impersonality, the notion that employees of an organization must deal with clients/customers, subordinates, and superiors on the same categorical basis without any personal, emotional, or social considerations.
- **Technical competence.** In a bureaucracy, employees should be hired and promoted on the basis of their technical competence relevant to a particular office or position in the organization.

The concepts of division of labor and hierarchy of authority are usually represented in an organizational chart. Exhibit 7.3 shows a typical organizational chart for a professional baseball team. The horizontal row of five boxes represents the division of labor into player personnel, scouting, public relations, ticket operations, and finance and administration. The vertical arrangement of the boxes shows the hierarchy of authority within the organization, beginning with the chief executive officer (CEO) and extending down to the directors of marketing and operations, the controller, and the information systems manager. Note that there may be other employees below the lowest level shown in Exhibit 7.3.

Weber (1947) was convinced that bureaucracy is "superior to any other form in precision, in stability, in the stringency of its discipline and its reliability. It thus makes possible a high degree of calculability of results for the heads of organization and for those acting in relation to it" (p. 334). In his view, bureaucracy was like a mechanistic means of production while other forms of organizations were non-mechanistic means of production.

Criticisms of Bureaucracy

It is worth noting that Weber was describing an ideal construct. As is most often the case, the ideal is never reached. This conundrum has resulted in serious criticisms being leveled against bureaucracy and its prescriptions.

The major criticism against the creation of a *division of labor* is that each individual's job is reduced to a monotonous and degrading routine. This, in turn, leads to decreased initiative, creativity, and motivation. The resulting boredom and frustration have been known to reduce worker productivity. Thus, a division of labor that produces expertise and, through it, efficiency, can also lead to boredom and ineffi-

exhibit 7.3 An organizational chart for a typical professional baseball franchise.

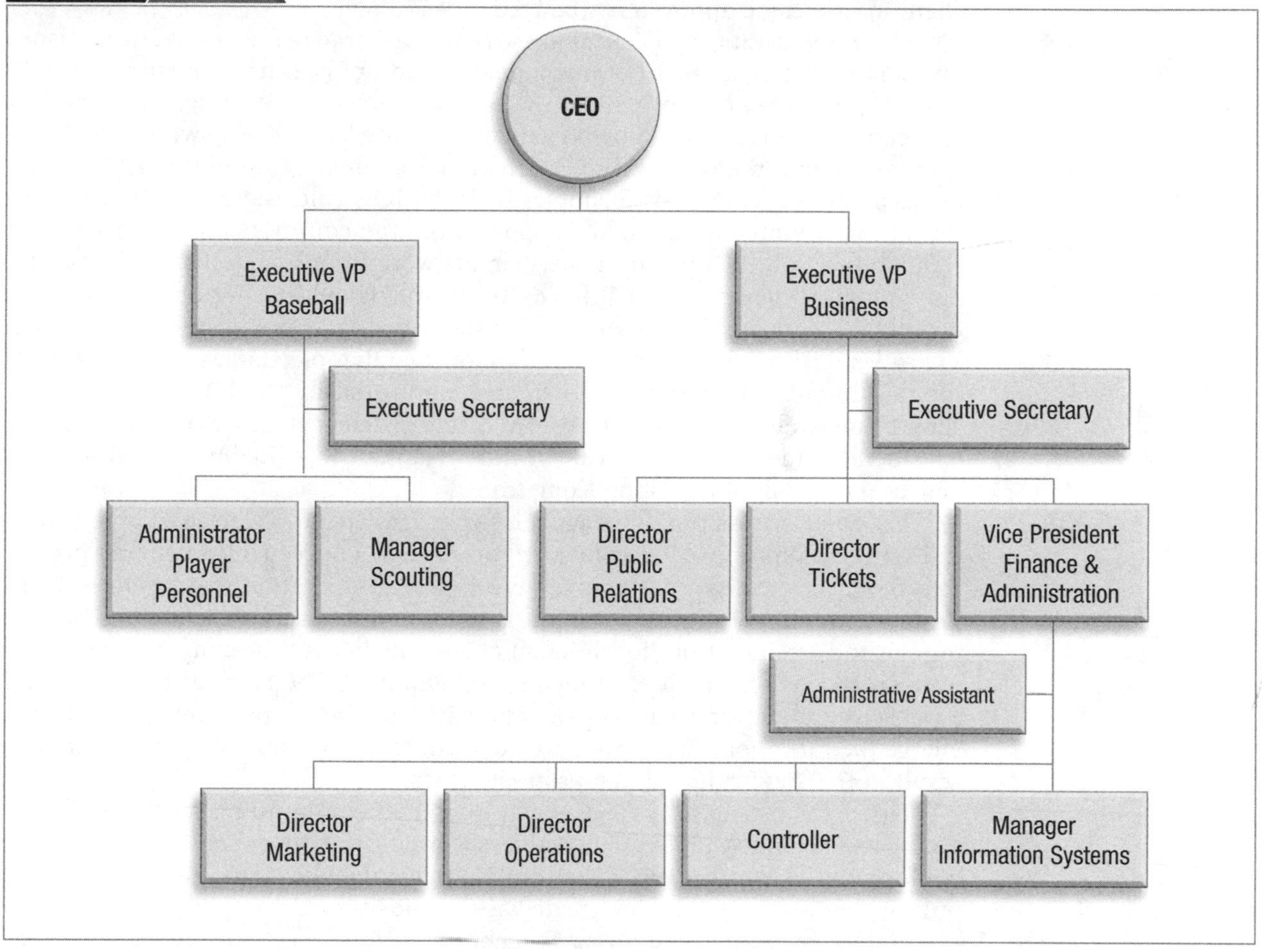

ciency. For example, the work in a ticketing operation could be divided into attending the phone, recording written requests, keeping track of tickets issued, and so on. If such division of work were done carefully, it would no doubt increase the efficiency of the operations. On the other hand, those persons who carry out these divided pieces of work are likely to be bored and frustrated with the routine.

Another tenet of bureaucracy to come under fire is *departmentalization*—the division of labor at the unit level. This division creates interdepartmental rivalry, which in turn leads to the displacement of organizational goals. That is, each department sets and pursues its own goals without reference to the wider organizational goals.

A serious drawback to *hierarchy of authority* is that the communication flow ultimately becomes inconsistent with the workflow. As an example, consider the case of a client who is eligible for specific seats in the football stadium because she has made a donation or paid for an advertisement in the stadium. The ticketing clerk is not aware of the client's status, but the employee in the marketing department knows the details. The most prudent and efficient treatment is for the two employees to confer and issue the ticket to the client. However, if the bureaucratic principle of hierarchy of authority is strictly and blindly followed, then the two employees cannot consult with each other but must go through their respective bosses. In such a case, the operation becomes inefficient and the client may become annoyed by the "red tape."

The bureaucratic tenet of *abstract rules* has drawn the severest criticisms. First, quite often the rules become outdated and out of tune with current conditions. Consider the case of Hannah Wilson, who was born in Hong Kong and had participated in the Asian Games as a member of the Hong Kong swim team. However, she was forbidden by the International Olympic Committee (IOC) from participating in the Athens Olympics in 2004. IOC rules state that the competitors at the Olympics must hold passports from the countries they represent, but Hannah held a British passport. Her parents were from England and she was not old enough to renounce her British citizenship. To add to her distress, she was not allowed to represent Britain because she had already represented Hong Kong. The rules of the Asian Games and those of the Olympic Games were contradictory although both were sanctioned and monitored by the IOC. This example shows how well-intentioned rules can actually defeat their own purpose. After considerable media and political pressure, Hannah was finally allowed to compete as a member of the Hong Kong team.

A second criticism of abstract rules concerns the application of appropriate rules. In handling a particular incident or subject, a bureaucrat must first place it into the proper category. Moreover, errors in categorization may result in inappropriate treatment in some cases. It is not uncommon for fitness clubs to have unique and separate rules for different classes of clients. The simplest example is differential rates for seniors, students, and children. The employee dealing with a particular client first has to place the client in the proper category and then charge the rate applicable to that category. An error in categorizing the client can result in the application of inappropriate rules.

Third, the existence of rules effectively sets the minimum acceptable level of performance for employees. This reduces workers' initiative, because they tend to conform strictly to the rules. The result is that rules that were intended to serve only as a means to an end are treated as the ends themselves.

Finally, strict reliance on rules makes employees rigid in their interactions with clients. This rigidity produces tension between employees and clients, which in turn leads the employees to adhere even more closely to the rules. This phenomenon is reflected in the phrase "throwing the book at you." For instance, consider a locker room attendant who refuses a towel or some equipment to a regular client who has left her identity card at home. The attendant is adhering to the rules in refusing the request. However, his reliance on the rule only, instead of the fact that the person is a regular client with a valid excuse, makes him too rigid. Such rigidity is likely to lead to resentment and friction in future interactions on the part of the client.

The bureaucratic notion of *impersonality* ignores human nature inside and outside the organization. Critics of the impersonality of a bureaucracy have argued that it is not realistic to expect employees to suppress all their feelings and attitudes.

Technical competence is generally accepted as a requisite for organizational efficiency and effectiveness. However, bureaucracies tend to promote individuals to higher positions on the basis of seniority, not competence. Although seniority often reflects experience and accrued knowledge at various lower-level positions, promotion on the basis of seniority alone denies the best and brightest the opportunity to move up the hierarchy. Moreover, it could be argued that in some bureaucracies "20 years' experience is one year's experience 20 times over."

sidebar 7.2

BUREAUCRATIZATION VERSUS MCDONALDIZATION

The term *bureaucratization* refers to the processes of division of labor, specialization, routinization of jobs controlled by rules, and hierarchy of authority. Ritzer (1997) discussed the *McDonaldization* of the workplace. The term, derived from the fast-food giant McDonald's, refers to the application of the production principles and processes of the fast-food industry to other workplaces. The process is based on:

- *Efficiency,* which is assured when the best means is chosen to achieve a particular goal.
- *Calculability,* which is attained by quantifying everything the worker does (e.g., time and motions involved in a task).
- *Predictability,* by making sure that the products and services are the same every time they are produced.
- *Control,* whereby the behaviors of both workers and customers are guided by the technology of the production process.
- *Irrationality of rationality,* where the above rational processes lead to an irrational outcome, particularly the dehumanization of the people involved.

Ritzer (1997) noted that the process is an offshoot of earlier approaches such as bureaucracy and scientific management. He contended that the process of McDonaldization creates "McJobs," which

- involve simple tasks designed for efficiency
- are simplified
- are predictable (e.g., in terms of work done and interactions with customers)
- are controlled by nonhuman technologies
- are dehumanizing

Ritzer (1997) noted that McJobs are tightly scripted. In his words, "McDonaldized jobs tend to be characterized by *both* routinized actions (for example, McDonald's hamburgers are to be put down on the grill moving from left to right, six rows of six patties, and the burgers are to be flipped beginning with the third row, with the first two rows to be flipped last) and scripted interactions (examples include, 'May I help you?'; 'Would you like a dessert to go with your meal?'; 'Have a nice day!')" (unpaged). Readers should recognize that both bureaucratization and McDonaldization are designed to increase efficiency and consistency in the operations. Both also involve impersonal interactions with customers. Although McDonald's employees are trained to be courteous to the customer, they are also trained to be consistent in how they deal with individual customers.

Despite these criticisms, many organizational theorists support Weber's ideas and endorse the view that the bureaucracy should be the dominant mode of structuring large and complex organizations. Perrow (1972) has gone even further, suggesting that "the sins generally attributed to bureaucracy are either not sins at all or are consequences of the failure to bureaucratize sufficiently" (p. 6). On the other hand, Perrow also acknowledges that the "ideal" form of a bureaucracy is never realized. One of the reasons for this is that members of the organization "track all kinds of mud from the rest of their lives with them into the organization, and they have all kinds of interests that are independent of the organization" (p. 5). Another reason is that people "are only indifferently intelligent, prescient, all-knowing, and energetic. All organizations must be designed for the 'average' person one is likely to find in each position, not the superman" (p. 5).

Perrow also pointed out that a bureaucracy is structured to be stable in order to be efficient. In the case of governments, the **stability** requirement may be the most critical criterion. One paradox, however, is that if stability is achieved, the bureaucracy becomes impervious to change. In turn, this results in the development of so-called red tape and inefficiency. Government bureaucracies are often strongly criticized for the red tape and inefficiencies that result from their stability. However, it is important to remember that the stability of a bureaucracy is the very thing that provides some form of consistency during periods of rapid and dramatic change (democratic or revolutionary) in the government. Stability may also be needed in nongovernmental organizations. Consider a new CEO of a university athletic department or a professional franchise. She may be considering drastic changes to transform the organization into a better and more efficient organization. However, she needs time to study the situation and identify the best areas to implement changes in structure and processes. The existing bureaucracy (division of labor, hierarchy of authority, rules and procedures, and so on) provides stability until the CEO initiates organizational changes.

Bureaucracy in a Democracy

Some believe that the emphasis on a hierarchy and the discipline and obedience to superiors that are necessary in a bureaucracy are antithetical to the democratic notions of equality, freedom of choice, and dissent. If this is the case, how can a bureaucracy be tolerated and allowed to grow in a democracy?

Blau (1956) resolved this issue by outlining the contrasting purposes and processes of a democracy and a bureaucracy. The purpose of a **democracy** is to identify commonly agreed-upon social objectives. The process of identifying these goals occurs through freedom of expression and dissent. Based on these differing expressions, the electorate and lawmakers can make informed decisions.

In contrast, the purpose of a bureaucracy is to achieve specified goals. Its concern is with the implementation of efficient ways of achieving those goals. Efficiency requires rules and procedures and an authority structure that ensures adherence to those rules. Also, members must exhibit disciplined compliance to the rules and obedience to authority. Thus, as Blau (1956) pointed out:

> Bureaucratic and democratic structures can be distinguished, then, on the basis of the dominant organizing principle: efficiency or freedom of dissent. Each of these principles is suited for one purpose and not the other. When people set themselves the task of determining the social objectives that represent the interests of most of them, the crucial problem is to provide an opportunity for all conflicting viewpoints to be heard. In contrast, when the task is the achievement of given social objectives the essential problem to be solved is to discover the efficient, not the popular, means for doing so. Democratic values require not only that social goals be determined by majority decision, but also that they be implemented through the most effective methods available, that is, by establishing organizations that are bureaucratically rather than democratically governed. The existence, therefore, of such bureaucracies does not violate democratic values. (p. 107)

The contrasting objectives and processes of a democracy and a bureaucracy are illustrated in Exhibit 7.4 (p. 194).

Although theorists like Perrow and Blau have supported the concept of bureaucracy, they have also pointed out the threat posed by large bureaucracies. Because of their control over vast amounts of resources (people and money), large bureaucracies have the power to influence democratic processes. In fact, their tendency to perpetuate themselves and to increase their power leads them to interfere in democratic affairs. For instance, the lobbying efforts of large corporations and special interest groups, such as cigarette manufacturers or gun ownership organizations, to influence the decision-making processes of democratically elected bodies are just

IN brief

Democracy's purpose is identifying majority goals, whereas bureaucracy's purpose is achieving those goals. In order to identify majority goals, democracy permits debates and dissension. In contrast, bureaucracy emphasizes obedience and compliance in order to efficiently achieve democracy's goals.

an expert's view / ON BUREAUCRACY IN ACTION

A good example of bureaucracy in action is in the organization and conduct of Olympic Games. Dr. Makis Asimakopoulos was the General Manager of Sports for the Athens 2004 Olympic Games Organizing Committee (OGOC). Dr. Dimitris Gargalianos is a professor at Democritos University of Thrace, Komotini, Greece.

COMPLEXITY AND SIMPLICITY OF ORGANIZING OLYMPIC GAMES

Makis Asimakopoulos,
Dimitris Gargalianos

The complexity of organizing and conducting the Olympic Games is illustrated by the following:

- the number of people to be hosted (10,500 athletes, 5,500 team officials, 45,000 volunteers, 21,500 media representatives, 5.3 million ticketed spectators);
- number of sports and events (35 sport disciplines, 6,000 sessions of competitions, 301 medal ceremonies, 35 competition venues and 60 fields of play, and 72 training facilities in five cities);
- the functions (accreditation, ceremonies, communication, education, environment, finance, food services, image & identity, international relations, language services, logistics, marketing, medical services including doping control, merchandising, media services, risk management, security, site management, spectators services, staffing, technology, ticketing, transportation, venue operations); and
- organizations to interact with (28 international federations, 28 national federations, 202 National Olympic Committees, the Greek government and its 20 ministries, the city of Athens and four other cities, sponsors, broadcasters and media, owners of venues) (Asimakopoulos, 2006).

Later, Gargalianos, Asimakopoulos, and Chelladurai (2012) noted that despite this level of complexity, the ticketed spectators and billions of TV viewers did not recognize any of this complexity. All they saw was events proceeding like clockwork. The authors argued that all the complexity was reduced to the simplicity that spectators saw through the application of Weber's (1947) tenets of bureaucracy—division of labor, hierarchy of authority, system of abstract rules, impersonality, and technical competence.

The OGOC created divisions of labor that fell into the following units: (a) *Sport* concerned with implementing the technical requirements of all sports; (b) *Athens Olympic Broadcasting* for the production of the television and radio coverage of the games; (c) *NOC Relations and Services* to facilitate the participation of the National Olympic Committees and their teams; (d) *IOC Relations & Protocol,* including language services and translation services; (e) *Security;* (f) *Technology;* (g) *Information and Press Operations;* (h) *Spectator Services;* (i) *Communications;* (j) *Marketing,* including sponsorship, licensing, ticketing; (k) *Games Services,* including accommodation, accreditation, transportation, food services, medical services and doping control; (l) *Administration/Finance,* including office and building administration, legal services, brand protection, financial services, procurement, logistics, rate card and risk management; (m) *Human Resources;* (n) *Volunteers;* (o) *Venue Operations;* and (p) *Programs.* Note that each of these units had several subunits to handle more specific responsibilities and issues.

The system of abstract rules was defined by the Olympic Charter, the host city contract, the IOC contracts, national laws, the OCOG's extensive operations policies and procedures, memoranda of understanding, and the rules and regulations of each of the international sports federations. The authority structure was reflected in the hierarchy of the 17-member board of directors, the five-member steering committee, the president, the group general managers, the general managers, the department managers, the competition managers, the venue managers, the project managers, the coordinators of various tasks, and the supervisors of activities. The tenet of impersonality was emphasized by Fundamental Principle No. 6 of the Olympic Charter, which states that "Any form of discrimination with regard to a country or a person on grounds of race, religion, politics, gender or otherwise is incompatible with belonging to the Olympic Movement." The personnel's technical competence was ensured by following conventional hiring processes, which included documenting the necessity for recruitment, accurate descriptions of the positions, qualifications of the applicants, and hiring only the qualified candidates. As noted in the chapter, bureaucracy properly applied facilitates the efficiency and effectiveness of operations as evidenced by the success of the Athens Olympics.

exhibit 7.4 Purposes and processes of a democracy and a bureaucracy.

	DEMOCRACY	BUREAUCRACY
PURPOSE	Identify majority goals ▼	Achieve majority goals ▼
CONCERN	Informed opinion ▼	Efficiency ▼
PROCESS	Freedom of expression Discussion Dissent	Disciplined obedience Compliance to procedures and authority

two examples. Perrow (1972) cautioned that "it is also crucial to understand not only how [bureaucracy] mobilizes social resources for desirable ends, but also how it inevitably concentrates those forces in the hands of a few who are prone to use them for ends we do not approve of, for ends we are generally not aware of, and more frightening still, for ends we are led to accept because we are not in a position to conceive alternative ones" (p. 7).

In conclusion, it seems reasonable to suggest that a bureaucracy in a democracy is "value neutral"—that is, its positive and negative consequences are produced by humans and not a function of the bureaucracy itself.

Relevance of Bureaucracy Today

Many researchers have questioned the utility of bureaucracy in the current era of information technology and globalization. These individuals say bureaucracy is irrelevant to *market-oriented or entrepreneurial* organizational forms in which every unit within an organization should react to and compete with other relevant organizations or the *network* organizations where cooperation with other organizations is sought. But others suggest that the bureaucratic form of organizing is still relevant and needed. For instance, Olsen (2005), focusing on public administration, notes:

> Bureaucratic organization and the success criteria in which it is embedded are still with us. . . . The juridification [i.e., the proliferation of regulations, standards and codes of practice] of many spheres of society, human rights developments,

sidebar 7.3

REVERSAL OF ROLES

In our discussion of the role of bureaucracies in a democracy, we have made the implicit assumption that the bureaucracies (including the military) exist to serve the democratically elected government and that the democratic government has control over the bureaucracies in its service. This is true in the United States and other Western nations. But other parts of the world have suffered military coups in which the military deposes the elected government and rules the country by itself or sets up a government of its choice. One example from 2013 was Egypt, where the military dismissed the elected government and appointed a president and other ministers to run the country. While such occurrences are repugnant to those who subscribe to and adhere to democratic ideals, such military coups are sometimes tolerated by democratic nations around the world, as is the case with the coup in Egypt. Unfortunately, such tolerance can lend legitimacy to the coup.

increased diversity, lack of common overriding goals, and renewed demands for public accountability may furthermore contribute to a rising interest in the legal bureaucratic aspects of administration and governing. (p. 18)

Similarly, Walton (2005) has shown that

the very model of bureaucratic control, abhorred by many, facilitates opportunities for developing new organizational forms . . . including flatter hierarchies, temporary structures, flexible work systems and networked activities. . . . The model of bureaucratic control accommodates such new forms precisely because reducing divisions of labour and reorganizing workflows do not alter overall control of activities significantly. . . . The findings demonstrate the general validity of the model of bureaucratic control. (p. 589)

Bureaucracy in Sport Organizations

We have discussed the concept of bureaucracy at length for two main reasons. First, modern society is controlled to a greater and greater extent by bureaucracies (the government, large corporations, universities, hospitals, unions, political parties, etc.). Thus, all individuals need to understand and appreciate the principles underlying bureaucratic structures. Second, although the concept of bureaucracy appears to be more relevant to large organizations, the elements that make a bureaucracy rational and efficient can also be profitably applied to smaller organizations. For example, football teams are clearly characterized by a division of labor (offensive and defensive units, and the specializations within each); a hierarchy (the chief coach, assistant coach, coaches for specialized units, captain, quarterback); impersonality in selection, utilization, and rewarding of athletes; and technical competence on the part of the coaches and players. Furthermore, rules are numerous in football—from the rules of the sport to league rules to team rules that even control the athlete's life away from the field. What is most significant is that these rules are closely followed by the players. There is perhaps no better example of members' willing compliance and obedience to the rules and authority of a bureaucracy.

Frisby (1983) noted that a number of authors have "bemoaned the loss of personal autonomy on the part of the participants and volunteers, the intrusion of the law and government into the arena of sport, and the usurpation of expressive values by instrumental values as sport has become more bureaucratic in nature" (p. 80). These concerns that the fundamental elements of sport are lost with bureaucratization are somewhat analogous to the concerns expressed about bureaucracy as it relates to a democracy.

In the latter context, Blau (1956) argued that the contrasting purposes of a democracy and a bureaucracy necessitate as well as justify different processes—freedom of expression and dissent in a democracy versus compliance and obedience in a bureaucracy. Similarly, an examination of the purposes of competitive and recreational sports reveals that they are radically different, and, consequently, the process within each differs. In this regard, Keating (1964) has distinguished between *athletics,* the purpose of which is pursuit of excellence, and *sport,* the purpose of which is pleasure for contestants: "In essence, sport is a kind of diversion which has for its immediate and direct end fun, pleasure and delight and which is dominated by a spirit of moderation and generosity. Athletics, on the other hand, is essentially competitive activity which has for its end victory in the contest and which is characterized by a spirit of dedication, sacrifice, and intensity" (p. 28). If the differences between recreational sport (which is concerned with the pursuit of pleasure) and athletics or competitive sport (which is concerned

an expert's view / ON MOCK BUREAUCRACY

I am grateful to Claudio Rocha of the University of São Paulo in Brazil, a former student of mine, for providing this discussion. He did his doctoral research on the patterns of bureaucracy in intercollegiate athletic departments.

MOCK BUREAUCRACY IN SPORT ORGANIZATIONS

Claudio Rocha

Organizations are usually expected to follow institutional rules. Nevertheless, on some occasions, these rules conflict with the technical imperatives of daily internal activities of an organization. For example, the central office of a chain of fitness centers might impose the rule that each piece of equipment in a center needs to be cleaned every hour. While all the employees and managers in the franchises follow the rule implicitly most of the time, there may be occasions when this procedure may impede the flow of work. When a large number of clients are waiting to use the equipment, the employees may delay cleaning till there is a lull in its use. The manager, being aware of this exigency, may tacitly approve postponing the cleaning. Gouldner (1954) called this the *mock bureaucracy,* where both the managers and the employees agree on adapting the rule to meet the task imperatives. Mock bureaucracy is a way organizations have found to remain legitimate and, consequently, survive.

The issue of the need to adapt the rules to meet the task imperatives is more acute when an organization pursues differing goals, and a set of rules applicable to one goal interferes with the activities associated with another goal. That is the case with intercollegiate athletic departments, which pursue both academic and athletic goals. Athletic departments have been criticized on the grounds that student-athletes are encouraged and/or made to spend more time on athletics than academics, thereby jeopardizing their chances of achieving academic success. Rocha and Chelladurai (2013) found that mock bureaucracy has been a strategy to deal with conflicts between institutional rules and technical needs of athletic departments. Results of this research showed that different patterns of bureaucracy arise as a consequence of the emphasis athletic departments place on either performance or developmental goals. Emphasis on performance goals (e.g., winning) leads to a pattern of loose coupling between rules and actual activities, that is, mock bureaucracy. Emphasis on developmental goals (e.g., academic achievement) leads to a pattern of tight coupling between rules and actual activities, implying either representative or punishment-centered bureaucracy. *Representative bureaucracy* implies full compliance of the rules by agreement between managers and employees; while *punishment-centered bureaucracy* implies full compliance of the rules by enforcement. In summary, both patterns of loose and tight coupling arise depending on the goals emphasized by athletic department managers. That is, different patterns of bureaucracy are used as an effective strategy to respond to different goals of athletic departments.

It is noteworthy that respondents in that research (i.e., college coaches) reported minimal levels of mock bureaucracy in their universities. But this should not mask the fact that it could be extensively practiced in a few institutions. On the other hand, the respondents perceived a very high degree of representative bureaucracy in their departments. The view advanced by some (Benford, 2007; Sperber, 2000; Zimbalist, 1999) that the coaches are ready to bend or break the rules is negated by the results of this research. The coaches in the study appear to recognize the significance of athletics in the educational sphere and accept the need for them to abide by the letter and spirit of the rules from the NCAA and their own respective universities.

with the pursuit of excellence) are taken into account, then it is only logical to expect that the two endeavors will be structured differently. Recreational sport should be loosely structured; competitive sport, bureaucratically structured.

The relevance of bureaucratic concepts to national sport organizations is illustrated by Frisby's (1983) study of those organizations in Canada. She found that those national sport organizations that were more bureaucratic were also more effective in terms of both goal attainment and resource acquisition. Consider the International Olympic Committee and the National Collegiate Athletic Association. These two large sport organizations with different goals, areas of operation, membership, and stakeholders are both effective in achieving their respective goals. The common element that facilitates their effectiveness is that both of them follow the bureaucratic tenets in their operations.

ORGANIZATIONAL DESIGN

As noted, the process of organizing results in an organizational structure, which is usually simplified and depicted as an organizational chart, as seen in Exhibit 7.3. An organizational chart usually shows the hierarchical arrangement of organizational positions from top to bottom. This arrangement would be the *vertical structure* of the organization. Looking at the chart from left to right, we notice the different departments and the sections within each department are shown in a horizontal arrangement—the *horizontal structure* of the organization. The term *organizational design* refers to the process of creating or changing the organizational structure. In designing or redesigning an organization, senior managers will consider several key elements discussed earlier, such as specialization, division of labor, span of control, departmentalization, and unity of command.

When Gene Smith became the Athletic Director at The Ohio State University in 2005, one significant change he made was to design a new organizational structure for the department. Prior to his arrival, there were five major departments with the five chiefs of those departments reporting directly to the Athletic Director. Smith redesigned this structure to have only three major departments with the three chiefs reporting to the Athletic Director. In fact, the three chiefs were promoted to the rank of Senior Associate Athletic Director. According to Smith (2006), the changes were meant to "improve the department's planning, structural accountability, communication and overall cohesiveness." In essence, this redesign resulted in a narrower span of control (from five to three people reporting to Smith) and a taller structure (one more position added at the top). Also, while three of the former senior positions were elevated to the rank of Senior Associate Athletic Director, the two other positions were relegated to the third tier in the hierarchy.

SUMMARY

This chapter outlined the classical principles of specialization, span of control, departmentalization (both functional and product), unity of command, and responsibility and authority. We discussed the organizational form known as bureaucracy, including its tenets of division of labor, hierarchy of authority, system of abstract rules, impersonality, and technical competence, and we looked at various criticisms of these tenets. Despite some criticisms, bureaucracy is the best form for managing organizations. We explained the role of bureaucracy in achieving the goals determined by a democracy and noted the contradictory processes of dialogue, debate, and dissension in a democracy on the one hand and obedience to authority and compliance to rules in a bureaucracy on the other. We saw how the differing processes are consistent with the respective purposes of democracy (identifying majority goals) and bureaucracy (achieving those goals efficiently). Finally, we discussed the relevance of bureaucracy for sport organizations.

develop YOUR PERSPECTIVE

1. Recall a job you have had. Describe the extent to which it was specialized. Did that specialized work contribute to efficiency of the organization? Did it allow you to become an expert in the task? Did it contribute to your personal growth?

2. Describe a significant experience you have had with a bureaucracy in terms of both the positive and negative aspects of that experience.
3. What is a mock bureaucracy? Cite an example of such a bureaucracy from your experience as a student or in a job.
4. To what degree are the programs (graduate, undergraduate, athletic, intramural) in your university or college bureaucratized? What changes, if any, would you make in the administrative structure of these programs? Why?
5. Which of the bureaucratic tenets do you favor and which ones do you dislike? Why?
6. Consider two or three sport management jobs you are familiar with. Describe the extent to which each of them has been or could be McDonaldized.

references

Asimakopoulos, M. (2006, September 8). The role of the sport manager in the organization of the Olympic Games. Proceedings of the European Association for Sport Management Congress, Nicosia, Cyprus.

Bateman, T. S., & Snell, S. A. (2007). *Management: Leading & collaborating in a competitive world* (7th ed.). Boston: McGraw-Hill Irwin.

Benford, R. D. (2007). The college sports reform movement: Reframing the "edutainment" industry. *Sociological Quarterly, 48*,1–28.

Blau, P. M. (1956). *Bureaucracy in modern society*. New York: Random House.

Child, J. (2005). *Organization: Contemporary principles and practice*. Malden, MA: Blackwell.

Clegg, S., Kornberger, M., & Pitsis, T. (2005). *Managing and organizations: An introduction to theory and practice*. London: Sage Publications.

Fink, S. L., Jenks, R. S., & Willits, R. D. (1983). *Designing and managing organizations*. Homewood, IL: Richard D. Irwin.

Frisby, W. M. (1983). *The organizational structure and effectiveness of Canadian national sport governing bodies*. Unpublished doctoral dissertation, University of Waterloo, Waterloo, Canada.

Gargalianos, D., Asimakopoulos, M., & Chelladurai, P. (2012, August 7). Complexity and simplicity of organizing Olympic Games: The role of bureaucracy. Proceedings of the 5th International Sport Business Symposium, London.

Gouldner, A. (1954). *Patterns of industrial bureaucracy*. New York: Free Press.

Hall, R. H. (1996). *Organizations: Structures, processes, and outcomes* (6th ed.). Englewood Cliffs, NJ: Prentice Hall.

Herbold, R. J. (2004). *The fiefdom syndrome*. New York: Currency/Doubleday.

Keating, J. W. (1964). Sportsmanship as a moral category. *Ethics, 75*, 25–35.

Mintzberg, H. (1989). *Mintzberg on management: Inside our strange world of organization*. New York: Free Press.

Olsen, J. P. (2005). Maybe it is time to rediscover bureaucracy. *Journal of Public Administration Research and Theory, 16*, 1–24.

Perrow, C. (1972). *Complex organizations: A critical essay*. Glenview, IL: Scott, Foresman.

Ritzer, G. (1997). McJobs. Retrieved from http://icdl.uncg.edu/ft/051199-05.html.

Robbins, S. P., Coulter, M., Leach, E., & Kilfoil, M. (2012). *Management* (10th ed.). Don Mills, Ontario: Pearson Canada.

Rocha, C. M., & Chelladurai, P. (2013). Patterns of bureaucracy in intercollegiate athletic departments. *Journal of Sport Management, 27*, 114–129.

Rue, L. W., & Byars, L. L. (2009). *Management: Skills and application* (13th ed.). New York: McGraw-Hill Irwin.

Smith, G. (2006). Department of athletics announces reorganization. Retrieved from www.ohiostatebuckeyes.com/ViewArticle.dbml?&DB_OEM_ID=17300&ATCLID=1024018&SPID=10402&SPSID=87726.

Sperber, M. A. (2000). *Beer and circus: How big-time college sports is crippling undergraduate education*. New York: Henry Holt.

Walton, E. J. (2005). The persistence of bureaucracy: A meta analysis of Weber's model of bureaucratic control. *Organization Studies, 26*(4), 569–600.

Weber, M. (1947). *The theory of social and economic organization* (Translated by A. M. Henderson & T. Parsons). New York: Oxford University Press.

Zimbalist, A. S. (1999). *Unpaid professionals: Commercialism and conflict in big-time college sports*. Princeton, NJ: Princeton University Press.

CHAPTER 8 SYSTEMS-BASED ORGANIZING

manage YOUR LEARNING

After completing this chapter you should be able to:

- Explain the need to view organizations from a systems perspective and design them to be responsive to environmental conditions.
- Understand the concepts of differentiation and integration of organizational units, and explain why organizations need to undertake both simultaneously.
- Discuss the methods of integrating differentiated units.
- Explain the applicability to sport organizations of Thompson's idea of insulating the technical core.
- Understand the significance of boundary-spanning units.
- Discuss Parsons' notions of vertical differentiation of the institutional, managerial, and technical subsystems.
- Explain the role of the technical core in service organizations in boundary-spanning activities.
- Describe the types of network organizations and identify their purposes.

strategic CONCEPTS

authority	flexiform model	managerial subsystem
authority structure	functional power	network organization
boundary-spanning unit	institutional subsystem	operational unit
differentiation	integration	soft bureaucracy
environmental influences	internal network	systems perspective
external network	interorganizational network	technical core

ORGANIZING: OPEN SYSTEMS PERSPECTIVES

In the previous chapter, after describing the classical principles of organizing, we investigated bureaucracy as an organizational form. Although bureaucracy has its strengths, we also noted several criticisms of it. One of the strengths, as well as a weakness, is the fact that it is slow to change. Although that slowness may be a virtue in terms of the stability it offers, it also underscores its closed nature as an organizational system. In a bureaucracy, organizational goals are assumed to be clear and fixed, and the organization and its processes are designed to be efficient in all internal operations. However, in its drive for efficiency, a bureaucracy tends to ignore **environmental influences.**

Organizations do not operate in a vacuum. In Chapter 3, we began exploring the **systems perspective**, viewing an organization as a system interacting with its environment. We also discussed the types and significant elements of the environment with which an organization interacts. This chapter discusses the application of those systems-based concepts in designing an organization and its units.

Fundamentally, an organization is an instrument of society, and, consequently, it has a primary responsibility to society and its needs. For instance, a high school athletic department promotes the pursuit of excellence among its students and provides entertainment for the school population and the community. Therefore, it needs to be aware of the needs and preferences of the student-athletes, the students at large, the teachers and administrators, and the community. In addition, it has to compete with the athletic departments of other area high schools in order to create good community entertainment and bring prestige to the school. Thus, it needs to monitor what is happening in other high schools, its state high school athletic and activity association, and the National Federation of State High School Associations (NFHS), and be open to changing its own operations. In addition, the athletic department must be responsive to stakeholder groups and their demands.

open systems

In Chapter 3, organizations were described as open systems. A system is a set of interrelated parts organized in such a way as to make a recognizable whole (Robbins, Coulter, & Langton, 2006; Waring, 1996). The attribute that makes an organization an open system is its need to interact and be consistent with its environment. Note that an organization is dependent upon the environment for its resources as well as the disposal of its outputs; therefore, it is imperative that an organization be attuned to the vagaries of the environment.

TO recap

From a different perspective, organizations are self-serving in that they pursue their own goals. For instance, a profit-oriented sport organization such as a professional sport franchise exists to make a profit for the owners. Insofar as the fans and corporate sponsors are the source of such profits, the franchise must be attuned to the needs and preferences of those customers. Also, the franchise can make a profit only if it competes effectively with other franchises providing the same products or services (another team in the same league or geographical market). Thus, a professional sport franchise must recruit outstanding athletes in order to present a winning team and quality entertainment to the public. If its products are not acceptable to the public, the franchise will eventually go out of business. In addition, the professional franchise must also ensure that the athletes do not violate the moral and ethical standards of society (for example, by illegal drug use). The professional sport franchise needs to change its managerial practices if and when the ethical and moral standards of society change. Otherwise, it could eventually be forced out of business.

The sponsors and the advertisers are also a source of income, and therefore the franchise must deal with them effectively. Because media coverage is essential for the franchise, the media's demands and requirements must be addressed. Finally, the franchise must also be aware of and follow government regulations and guidelines. Considering that all sources of profit and constraints to profits are part of the organization's environment, the franchise must adapt and change with the environment in order to survive. Similar arguments can be advanced in the case of other profit-oriented sport enterprises such as a commercial fitness club, a golf course, a sport law consulting firm, a player agency, or a footwear and apparel company.

The idea of environment and the need to monitor and adapt to changes within it are implied in some of the topics covered so far. For instance, in Chapter 4, we found that the conceptual skills needed for effective management must include an awareness of the relationship of the organization to the industry, the community, and the political, social, and economic forces of the nation as a whole (Katz, 1974). Similarly, three of the 10 managerial roles described by Mintzberg (1975) in Chapter 4 deal specifically with environmental conditions, including the opportunities and restraints they provide. Likewise, the planning function discussed in Chapter 5 rests heavily on identifying opportunities and constraints in setting goals for the organization. This sensitivity to environmental demands forms the basis for the approach taken by many theorists in designing organizations. In the following sections, we will look at the approaches taken by some of these theorists—Lawrence and Lorsch (1967), Thompson (1967), and Parsons (1960).

The Lawrence and Lorsch Model

Lawrence and Lorsch (1967) compiled data on manufacturing organizations. Their basic premise was that a manufacturing organization is divided into three major subsystems: sales, production, and research and development. Each of these subsystems must deal with different segments of the environment—market, technical–economic, and scientific subenvironments, respectively.

The three subsystems differ with respect to three elements: (1) the rate at which their respective subenvironments change, (2) the relative amounts of information they have about their environments, and (3) the feedback they receive from the environment. These three elements constitute what Lawrence and Lorsch called the "certainty of the environment." According to these authors, the relative certainty of the environment faced by the subsystems creates two specific problems for the organization—differentiation and integration.

Differentiation

Differentiation occurs when an organization is divided into units according to environmental exigencies, and those units are then staffed with people of the appropriate aptitude and skills. Note that the concept of differentiation is not identical to the concept of departmentalization. According to the classical and bureaucratic approaches, departmentalization occurs when an organization is divided into units that are concerned with specific functions or purposes. The internal structure within the various units is similar and is characterized by hierarchy of authority and rules and regulations.

Differentiation, on the other hand, according to Lawrence and Lorsch, is the division of labor based on differing environmental conditions. Because each unit is required to interact with different segments of the environment (and these segments differ in terms of certainty, feedback, and rate of change), each organizational unit must be organized differently to enable it to cope with the particular subenvironment and its requirements. A further condition necessary for differentiation is that the members of a unit possess those specific talents and aptitudes that match the demands of the environment. For instance, a sales agent for a manufacturing company needs to interact with reluctant customers and convince them of the benefits of buying the company's products. On the other hand, the purchasing agent for the company often has to resist attempts by sales agents of other companies who want to sell their products to the focal company. Thus, the sales agent and the purchasing agent need different persuasive and analytical skills in responding to their respective environments.

IN brief

Differentiation refers to structuring organizational units in specific ways to meet the environmental requirements of each, and to staffing the units with personnel who possess the necessary skills and aptitudes. Integration refers to the ways in which the differentiated units are brought together to cooperate with each other in the pursuit of organizational goals.

Integration

Lawrence and Lorsch pointed out that although differentiation is relatively easy to implement, integrating the subunits into a meaningful and effective whole is a problem. Because differentiated units have differing structures and follow different operating procedures (and, more importantly, the members of these units have different training and orientations), the task of **integration** is more difficult than the task of differentiation. It is possible for organizations to achieve the difficult task of integration by creating liaison or integrator roles, by making interactions across groupings mandatory, by promoting joint responsibilities for common goals, by developing task forces or committees with joint memberships, and by holding meetings to foster understanding among various groups. As for integration, a fundamental tenet to be followed is that the individuality and independence of the differentiated units will not be violated through the efforts to integrate.

Although the Lawrence and Lorsch model was developed for business firms and industries, the concepts of differentiation and integration are also useful in the context of sport organizations. This is certainly the case in the organization of programs of intercollegiate athletics, as evident in Sidebar 8.1.

Implications for sport managers

The concepts of differentiation and integration are critical to management of any sport organization. As we noted in Chapter 1, sport management is concerned with the production and marketing of sport services. Accordingly, the subunits concerned with the production of these services will be differentiated in terms of both structure and personnel from those subunits marketing the same services. For instance, the unit producing excellence and the associated entertainment (the team and the coaching staff) in a professional sport franchise will be structured differently than the marketing unit or the ticketing unit. In a similar man-

sidebar 8.1

DIFFERENTIATION AND INTEGRATION WITHIN AN ATHLETIC DEPARTMENT

The following is a case of differing perspectives on how to structure an intercollegiate athletic department and its departments. At The Ohio State University, the units that (a) provide academic support to student-athletes (named Student-Athlete Support Services at OSU), (b) investigate rule violations (i.e., the Compliance Office at OSU), and (c) interact with boosters and alumni were all housed in the same administrative department under the supervision of the athletic director. This organization makes sense if the focus of analysis is the athletic department. That is, coordination and integration of units within intercollegiate athletics is improved by this arrangement. However, when the university faced problems with rule violations and academic integrity, the president and the athletic director decided to restructure the department to place the academic support services under the supervision of the Office of the Provost and the Compliance unit in the Office of Legal Affairs. Although the interaction with boosters and alumni remained under the athletic director's supervision, it was mandated that all correspondence to these groups and other donors was to emphasize the rules governing their activities, and there was to be greater vigilance of those activities. This reorganization makes sense from the perspective of the university as the focus of analysis. That is, the units that ensure academics are emphasized and the rules followed in intercollegiate athletics are assigned to university units specializing in those two areas. At the least, this restructuring should eliminate the perceptions that rule violators and rule enforcers are colluding with each other.

ner, event and facility management may entail other differentiated structures and processes. Exhibit 8.1 illustrates this view of differentiated units in a professional sport franchise.

Note that the production of various services will also entail differentiated structures. A good example is the differentiation between structures and personnel in the athletic department and the recreation department in a university. Because the athletic department is concerned with producing excellence and entertainment, whereas the recreation department's focus is on participant services, the expectations of their respective stakeholders are different. For instance, the public and the media will be extremely critical of the athletic department if the athletic teams are not performing well. Because such a situation is likely to reflect on the image of the university, the university authorities will also be concerned. In contrast, such negative consequences are not likely when specific units within the recreation department are not performing well. Accordingly, the structures, processes, and personnel of the two departments will differ from each other.

The Thompson Model

Thompson (1967) endorsed the Lawrence and Lorsch view that an organization should be subdivided into units on the basis of the segments of the environment with which they interact. Thompson, along the lines of Parsons (1960) (discussed later in the chapter), endorsed the view that organizations must attempt to seal off one of the units—the *technical core*—from environmental uncertainties. Those units that have direct contact with the external environment are called the *boundary-spanning units*.

exhibit 8.1 Differentiation and integration of units within a professional franchise.

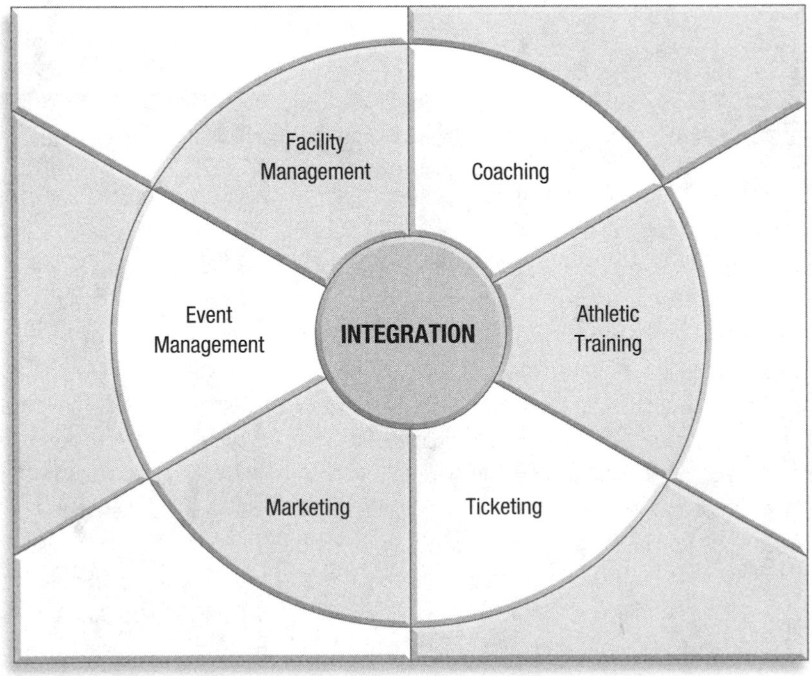

Technical core

Technical core refers to the unit that is most directly concerned with the production of goods or services. The assembly line in an automobile factory, the classrooms in a high school, and an athletic team in an intercollegiate athletic program are examples of the technical core in their respective organizations. Consider a fitness club. The aerobics instructor, the clients, the music, and the room where the class is conducted constitute one part of the technical core of the fitness club—the part associated with the production of the aerobics service. The weight training instructor, the clients, and the equipment in the weight room would be another part of the technical core.

Thompson argued that if the technical core is to be efficient, it must be able to work in a stable environment in terms of a steady flow of resources (inputs), prompt disposal of its products (outputs), and minimal interference from other units and organizations. That is, the technical core must be able to focus on its fundamental task of producing goods or services without being distracted by environmental concerns such as securing resources and disposing of products. Note that the notion of disposing of products is more germane to manufacturing organizations where the production and consumption (buying) of the product are separated. We noted in Chapter 1 that a service is produced and consumed simultaneously. In the previous example of the fitness club, the production and consumption of the aerobics service (the participant service) are simultaneous. Despite this difference between producing a good and producing a service, the idea of a stable environment for the production is equally applicable to both goods and services. The efficiency and quality of the aerobics class cannot be ensured if the instructor is distracted by the malfunctioning public-address system or worried about how to sell memberships to the general public.

Boundary-spanning units

Environmental stability is provided by what Thompson (1967) calls the **boundary-spanning units**, in which "organizations subject to rationality norms seek to isolate their technical cores from environmental influences by establishing boundary-spanning units to buffer or level environmental fluctuations. These responsibilities help determine the structure of input and output units" (p. 67).

In business and industry, units dealing with marketing, purchasing, legal affairs, and public relations interact with their respective environments in specific ways, and in so doing secure the resources needed for the technical core, dispose of its outputs, and thereby create a relatively stable environment for the technical core.

Implications for sport managers

The relevance of the Thompson model to sport organizations can be highlighted through one or two examples. The operation of a university athletic team illustrates the notion of insulating the technical core from environmental disturbances. As shown in Exhibit 8.2, the athletic team (including the athletes and coaches) is the technical core. The boundary-spanning units are the athletic department, university administration, the physical plant, and the university board of governors. Because the athletic team must strive for excellence in the sport and attempt to win as many games as possible, its major focus must be on training and preparation. All factors and influences that might detract from this exclusive focus must be blocked out. Athletic departments do this, in part, by providing athletic scholarships in order to relieve athletes of concerns for

exhibit 8.2 Application of Thompson's model to an athletic department.

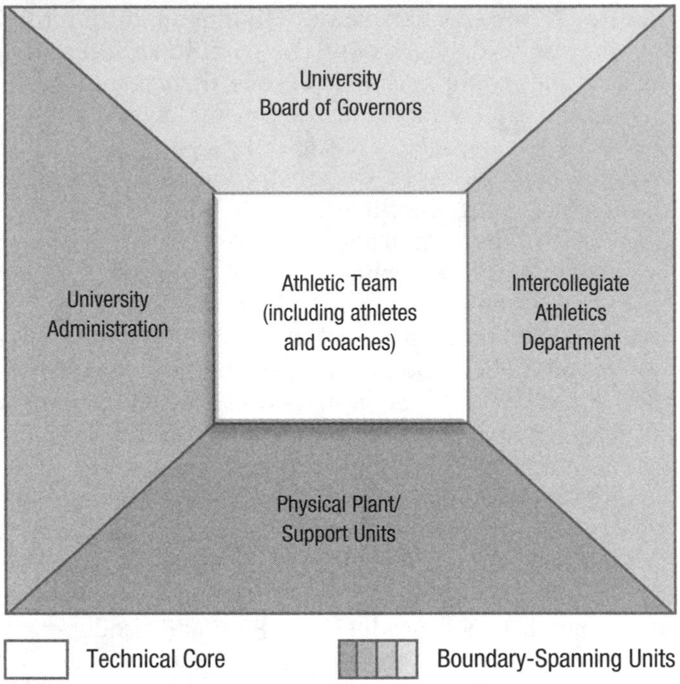

their upkeep. Some universities used to have separate dormitories for athletes in order to filter out the "distracting influences" of other students. In some universities, special classes or instructors are provided so that practices and games are not affected by regularly scheduled classes. Although many educators question such practices in a university setting, it cannot be denied that those institutions that adopt these strategies—providing a buffer between the technical core and the outer environment—are able to nurture, develop, and produce the best athletic talent.

IN brief

The units involved in the production of organizational outputs must be insulated by boundary-spanning units from environmental disturbances.

In addition, the athletic department, through its various subunits such as academic counseling, facility management, event management, marketing, and ticketing, acts as a boundary-spanning unit and insulates the athletic teams from environmental influences. By being the buffers between the athletic teams and the environment, these units facilitate the smooth functioning of the university teams.

This concept of insulating the athletes from environmental influences was also evident in the manner in which the former Soviet Union used to prepare its athletes. Good athletes were recruited and employed by a factory or a government agency such as the army. Typically, the coaches were also employees of the organization. Salaries for the athletes were equivalent to the athletic scholarships provided by a North American university. Instead of reporting for regular work, the athletes reported for athletic practices. The work requirements were rescheduled to fit the athletic schedule, just as is the case in some North American universities. Thus, both cases illustrate Thompson's idea of insulating the technical core.

The Parsonian Model

Parsons' (1960) model is particularly relevant to those sport organizations that have both an elected and an appointed body of administrators—that is, both volunteer administrators and paid professional administrators. This is presently the case in most sport-governing bodies in North America (as in Basketball Canada and USA Cycling).

In Parsons' view, an organization consists of distinct hierarchical suborganizations—the technical, the managerial, and the institutional subsystems. These subsystems are illustrated in Exhibit 8.3.

Technical subsystem

The technical subsystem is concerned with those activities that are directly associated with the major tasks of the organization. The nature of the technical task and the processes involved define its fundamental requirements. This is identical to Thompson's concept of technical core discussed earlier.

Managerial subsystem

The **managerial subsystem** is a higher-order system that both administers and serves the technical system. Parsons (1960) attributed two major areas of responsibility to the managerial subsystem: "The primary one is to mediate between the technical organization and those who use its 'products'—the 'customers,' pupils,

exhibit 8.3 **Parsons' hierarchical differentiation of subsystems, as applied to a sport-governing body.**

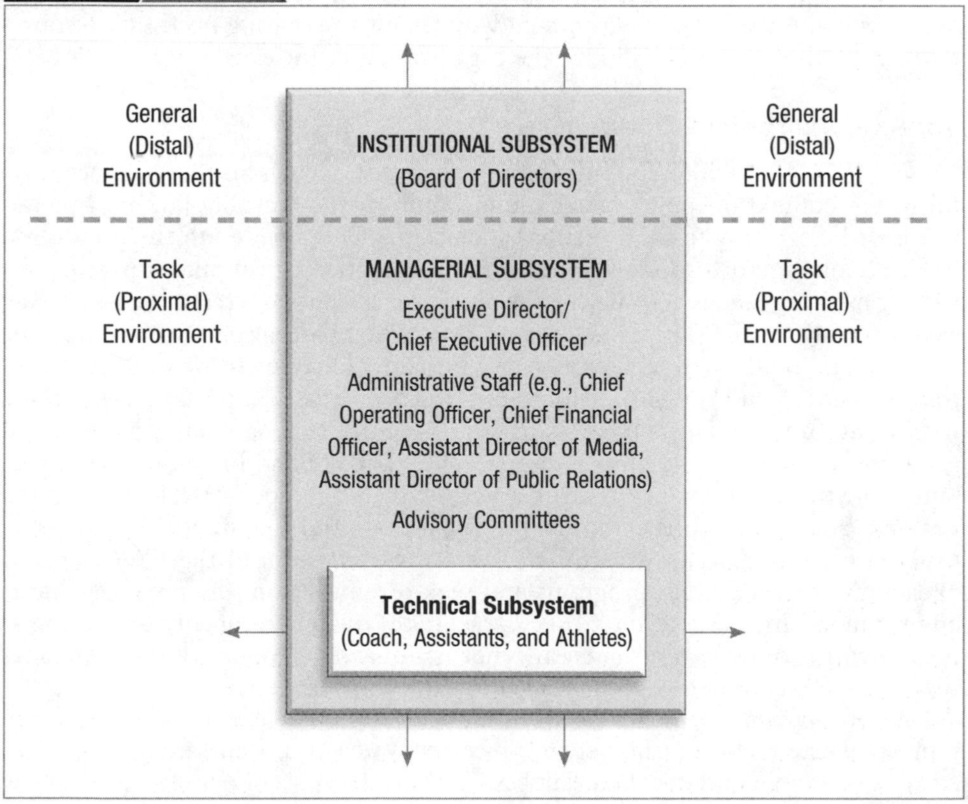

or whoever. The second is to procure the resources necessary for carrying out the technical functions (i.e., financial resources, personnel and physical facilities)" (p. 62). Thus, the managerial subsystem carries out part of the boundary-spanning functions included in Thompson's model. In the case of a professional sport franchise, the general manager and the managers and personnel of player operations, marketing, and facility and event management would constitute the managerial subsystem. This subsystem is the buffer insulating the team and its coaches from environmental disturbances.

Institutional subsystem

The function of the **institutional subsystem** is to interact with the wider environment with which the organization must deal. As Parsons (1960) noted, "The organization which consists of both technical and managerial suborganizations never operates subject only to the exigencies of disposal to and procurement from other agencies (which stand on an approximately equal level) as customers or as sources of supply. There is always some 'organized superior' agency with which the organization articulates" (p. 63). This interaction with the wider social system serves to legitimize the existence of the focal organization and justify the societal support extended to it. From this perspective, the institutional subsystem also serves the boundary-spanning function as outlined by Thompson.

From Parsons' perspective, the institutional subsystem in a typical organization consists of the board of governors or directors. Their functions are mainly to set the objectives and policies of the organization, to recruit the top managers, and, more importantly, to direct the institutional subsystem's efforts toward the management of that segment of the environment for which it is responsible. Thus, after charting the major course for the organization, the institutional subsystem must deal with the larger environment with a view to securing necessary resources. It must also work to legitimize the organization in the eyes of the public.

Implications for sport managers

Parsons' concept of differentiation along hierarchical levels also is very meaningful in the context of sport organizations. With sport-governing bodies, generally a board of governors (or directors) is elected and charged with the promotion and development of a sport. The board represents the institutional subsystem for the organization and is responsible for hiring the executive director (ED) or chief executive officer (CEO) for the organization. The board also approves projects, such as sending the national team to an international competition or setting up a training center, and budgets for those projects. An equally important, if not more important, function of the board is to interact with the general environment and generate resources for the organization. The ED/CEO and his immediate assistants constitute the managerial subsystem, which is responsible for hiring the national coaches (with the approval of the board) and for supervising the day-to-day operations of his subordinates. A critical function of the ED/CEO is to market the organization's programs and seek revenues from the proximal (task) environment. In addition, the ED/CEO facilitates the technical core by serving as liaison with external agents such as other national sport organizations, agencies that control facilities, government agencies, and travel agencies.

A national team, which consists of the athletes, the coach, and the assistants, represents the technical subsystem. Since the coach has been hired or appointed (put in charge of the technical subsystem) on the basis of expertise, the entire operation of the team should be left to her discretion. If Parsons' prescriptions are followed, the technical subsystem (the coach, assistants, and athletes) will be allowed to carry out its activities without undue influence from the managerial subsystem or the institutional subsystem. The coach should be allowed to select the athletes for the national team and decide on the training regimen and the competitive schedule. She should also be free to take disciplinary actions in the case of any rule violations.

This ideal of Parsons is followed mostly in university athletics in the United States and Canada. Unfortunately, the principles are often flouted among sport-governing bodies. For example, individuals who are elected to the board of directors are often former athletes or club representatives. Thus, all their skills, capacities, and orientations may be most strongly related to the internal operations of the organization, such as the selection and operation of the national team. That means they may not have the capacity, inclination, or experience to deal with external groups. When this is the case, it is not surprising to see considerable confusion and conflict in the management of the team. Even in the case of professional teams, owners are known to interfere with the affairs of the technical core (the team and the coaches).

task and general environments

We noted in Chapter 3 that an organization as an open system interacts with elements that lie outside its boundaries. Those elements that affect the organization more directly, and with which the organization interacts constantly, belong to the *task* (or *proximal*) environment. The other elements that impact the organization indirectly are labeled the *general* (or *distal*) environment. The organization does not interact with the elements in the general environment as often as it does with the elements in the task environment.

TO recap

Comparison of the Thompson and Parsonian Models

Numerous similarities exist between Thompson's model and Parsons' model. This is not surprising, because Thompson's model is partly derived from Parsons'. Both models acknowledge the need to seal off the technical core from environmental influences and to create boundary-spanning units. However, there is a difference in how the two models distribute the boundary-spanning activities to the various subsystems. In Thompson's model, various departments are expected to deal with various segments of the environment. In the case of a fitness club, the marketing unit will deal largely with the media and advertising people in marketing the services offered by the club. The unit in charge of facilities will interact with suppliers and technicians associated with such needs as plumbing, air conditioning, and so on. In contrast, in Parsons' model, the total environment is subdivided into proximal (or task) and distal (general) environments (see Chapter 3). Parsons proposed that the responsibilities for these two segments of the environment be split by hierarchical levels. That is, while the managerial subsystem must deal with the immediate task environment (including customers and suppliers), the institutional subsystem must interact with the larger segment of the environment (the society at large). The board of governors of a university, after approving a new stadium, embarks on securing resources from the general environment. The athletic department itself also engages in securing funds, but only by marketing luxury seating and seat licenses to the fans and spectators and advertising space to commercial interests, and by engaging in other activities involving elements in the task environment.

Parsons further argues that although the hierarchy places the institutional subsystem above the managerial system (which is, in turn, above the technical subsystem), there must be a clear break in the simple continuity of the **authority structure.** The two interfaces (that between the institutional and manageri-

sidebar 8.2

COMPLEXITY, FORMALIZATION, AND CENTRALIZATION

The previous two chapters focused on how organizations are structured in terms of roles, responsibilities, and coordination and control. In Chapter 7, we discussed some of the classical principles of structuring an organization and one of the dominant forms of organizational structure: bureaucracy and its tenets. In this chapter, we have looked at organizational structure from a systems perspective and emphasized the notions of differentiation and integration.

Readers should be aware of other concepts associated with organizational structure. For instance, Slack and his associates (e.g., Amis, Slack, & Berrett, 1995; Kikulis, Slack, & Hinings, 1995; Slack & Parent, 2006; Thibault, Slack, & Hinings, 1991) employed the notions of *complexity, formalization,* and *centralization* in their studies of sport organizations. *Complexity* refers to the various ways in which the units within an organization are differentiated (Slack & Parent, 2006). It includes horizontal, vertical, and spatial (that is, geographical) differentiation. Horizontal and vertical differentiation are similar to the concepts of differentiation discussed in this chapter. Spatial differentiation refers to different units being located in different geographical locations. The higher the various types of differentiation, the higher the complexity of that organization, and the higher the difficulty of managing it (Slack & Parent, 2006).

Formalization refers to the extent to which "mechanisms such as rules and regulations, job descriptions, and policies and procedures govern the operation of a sport organization" (Slack & Parent, 2006, p. 67). *Centralization* refers to whether authority to make critical decisions resides in the top-level positions (centralized decision making) or is distributed to lower-level positions in the organization (decentralized decision making). A bureaucracy, as discussed in the previous chapter, tends to be high on both formalization and centralization.

al subsystems, and that between the managerial and technical subsystems) must be designed in such a way that one subsystem does not interfere with the functioning of the other two subsystems. That is, "the institutionalization of these relations must typically take a form where the relative independence of each is protected" (Parsons, 1960, p. 69).

Technical Core in Service Organizations

Both Thompson and Parsons argue that the technical core of an organization must be insulated from environmental disturbances, but their models overlook one significant factor relating to service organizations—the interface between the customer and the employee. Chapter 1 emphasized that the customer–employee interface differentiates service organizations from organizations that produce goods. Whereas the notion of insulating the technical core is most meaningful and practical in organizations producing goods, it may not be appropriate or practical in the case of service organizations. This is certainly the case in those organizations that depend on their employees to seek and recruit more customers from among a larger population. In many service organizations, employees who belong to the technical core (which, according to theory, should be insulated) are expected to interact with the public in providing their services and recruiting more customers. Consider, for example, the intramural department in a university. Its major purpose is to provide recreational opportunities for all the students on the campus. Consequently, it organizes various competitions and instructional classes in as many activities as possible. The task of managing these various programs is left to paid or volunteer leaders. These are, in essence, the employees who provide the services. However, their effectiveness is related not only to their ability to provide quality service but also to their ability to interact with and recruit from the student population. That is, the boundary-spanning activities relating to both current and prospective customers are left to the technical core employees. Thus, the notion of insulating the technical core appears to be irrelevant in the context of the intramural department and other similar service organizations. From another perspective, though, it is apparent that the departmental chairpersons and their assistants do in fact shield the technical core from some environmental segments. For example, in matters relating to other academic departments, the board of governors, the physical plant, and so on, the managerial system acts as a buffer. This partial insulation from some segments of the environment and openness to relevant publics in the immediate task environment is illustrated in Exhibit 8.4.

AUTHORITY STRUCTURE IN DIFFERENTIATED ORGANIZATIONS

It follows from what has been discussed about differentiation among organizational units that such differentiated units cannot be subjected to a bureaucratic form of governance. Nor can all units be managed the same way. To the extent that different units operate in and react to differing environmental conditions, they must be given the freedom and authority to make decisions regarding the types of services that should be offered, how these should be produced, and how those services should be delivered. It follows that the conventional bureaucratic notions of a hierarchy of authority and a set of abstract rules

exhibit 8.4 Partial openness of technical core in service organizations.

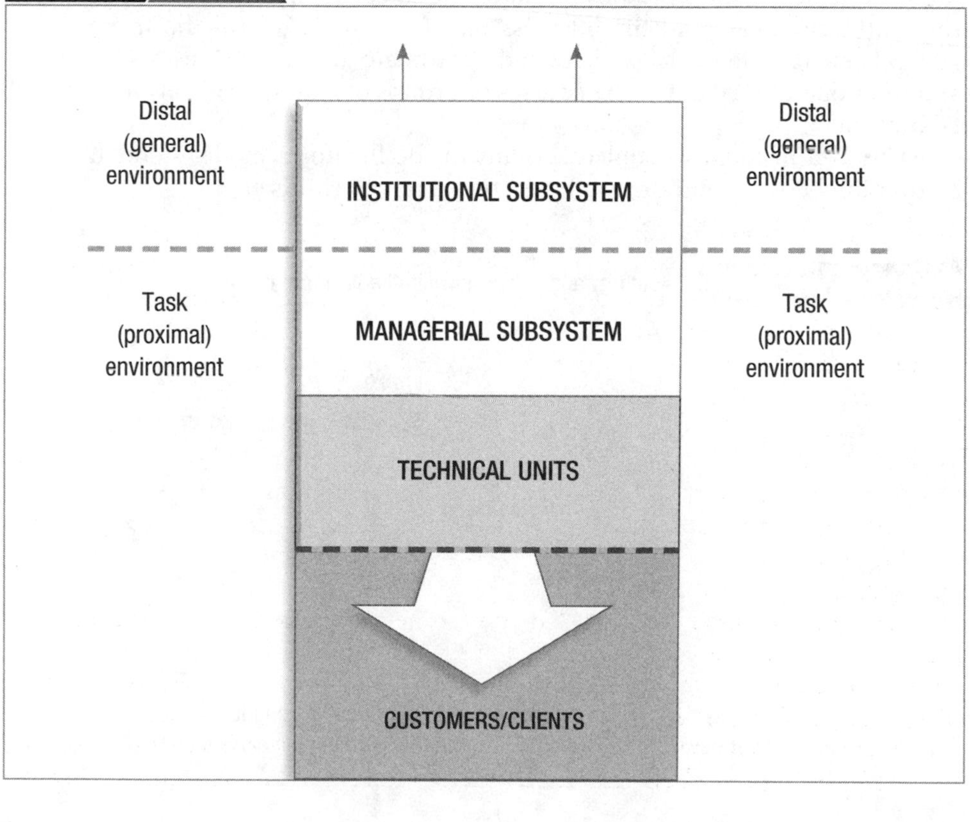

for all units may not be meaningful in the context of differentiated organizations. Two schemes of authority structure—**flexiform** and **soft bureaucracy**—provide some insights on how the differentiated units should be managed.

Flexiform Model

Noting the unique properties of professional and human service organizations, Mills, Hall, Leidecker, and Margulies (1983) proposed a structural model for these organizations—the **flexiform** (see Exhibit 8.5). The essence of the flexiform model is that the **operational units** (which are conceptually similar to the technical subsystem discussed earlier) and the administrative core (the managerial subsystem) are loosely coupled to each other.

The operational units are those involving the professionals and their customers. Each unit may consist of one professional or a team of professionals interacting with their customers. For example, the personal trainer and his clients in a fitness club, and the team and its coach in an athletic department, are examples of operational units in their respective organizations.

According to Mills and colleagues (1983), these operational units "need to be basically self-contained, relatively autonomous units and essentially to operate as mini-companies; the service is being produced and delivered concurrently" (p. 125). Thus, coaches of athletic teams are given autonomy and authority to select the athletes and train them in the strategies and tactics they (the coaches) selected.

Mills and colleagues (1983) point out that the functions of the administrative core include setting broad policies, controlling the boundary conditions, linking and coordinating the activities of the operational units, and systematizing routine activities. In the example of the department of sport management, the chair, the dean, and the business managers, if any, form the management team. Their function is to mediate and coordinate among the various professors and their operational units (the courses or groups of courses and various research laboratories).

The idea of loosely coupled systems in the flexiform model stems from the distinction between authority and functional power (Mills et al., 1983). The con-

exhibit 8.5 Authority and power flows in the flexiform model.

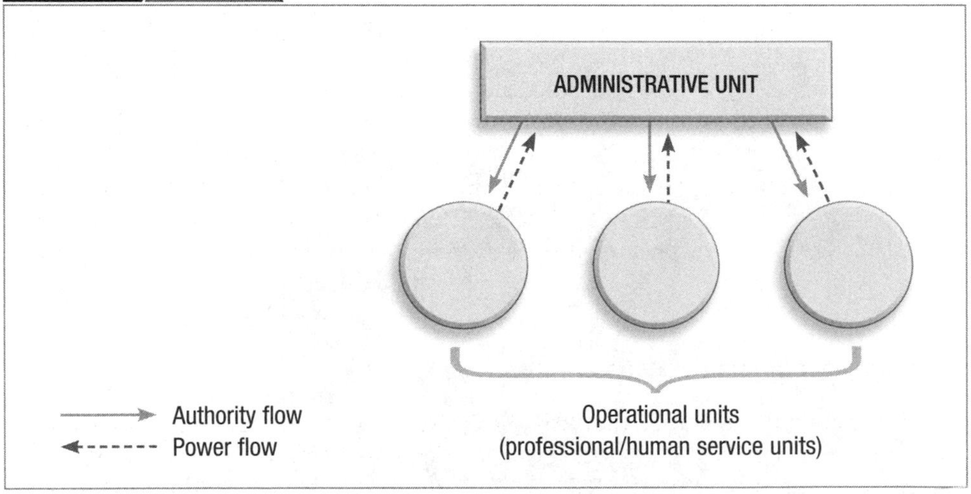

cept of authority, as perceived by Mills and colleagues, is similar to the concept of bureaucratic authority as perceived by Weber (1947). It refers to the right of superiors to make decisions that affect all subordinates of the organization. In the case of a sport-governing body, the CEO and other administrators have the authority to decide on the budget allocations for various programs. In contrast, functional power emerges from the expertise of the coaches, and the exigencies of the situations they face. Thus, as we noted before, each of the coaches has the functional power to select the athletes and decide on their training.

Simply stated, **authority** relates to decisions that affect all units (or most of them), and it resides in the administrative core. **Functional power** relates to what happens within individual units, and it stems from the expertise residing in the units. In the flexiform model (see Exhibit 8.5), functional power is greatest at the operational unit level. It decreases as it moves toward the administrative core at the center. Conversely, authority resides in the administrative core and flows toward the outer operational units. For example, the professors in sport management in a university have the functional power to make decisions over the processes in their operational unit, whereas the chairpersons and the dean have the authority to make decisions affecting all of the units in the school or college. As another example, consider the case of a professional sport franchise—the marketing, the public relations, the event management, and the coaching units would have functional power in their specific operations, whereas the general manager would have administrative authority over all those units.

Soft Bureaucracy

Ideas similar to those expressed by Mills et al. (1983) in their *flexiform* model have been advanced with the newer label of *soft bureaucracy* (Robertson & Swan, 2004; Vaast, 2007). In discussing the governance of knowledge-based firms that are involved in innovations, such as a sport marketing firm using technologies to develop social network marketing programs for their clients, the operational units are operating in novel fields where there is not much prior experience or convention to guide them.

Therefore, bureaucratic rules of what should be done, who should do it, and how it should be done would not be meaningful. And that is why such organizations would likely eschew any such rules governing the activities of the units and their members. However, there is still the need for coordination and control, particularly when several organizational units are engaged in knowledge and innovation. Thus, there would be a requirement for periodic reports on the progress of individual units in their respective ventures, the disposition of the budgets allotted to individual units, and future forecasts for achievements. In essence then, these operational units are free to take actions they deem fit, but they are answerable to the larger unit for those actions. Hence, the term *soft bureaucracy* is applied to this form of organization. Readers will recognize the similarities among the concepts of functional power and authority, loosely coupled systems, and soft bureaucracy.

NETWORK ORGANIZATIONS

Readers will recognize that the organizational forms suggested by Lawrence and Lorsch (1967), Thompson (1967), and Parsons (1960) are based on open systems thinking, particularly the notion of an organization interacting with and adapting its structures to the contingencies posed by its environment. Theoretical and practical approaches to structuring an organization also emphasize the turbulence posed by technological advances in production and communication, as well as the impact of globalization. In order to interact effectively with these ever-changing environments, some more innovative organizations have tended to adopt forms of structuring that are loosely labeled **network organizations.** As the label implies, a certain number of elements or units internal or external to the organization are linked in a network fashion such that the interactions among them are fast and effective.

As we noted, the bureaucratic form of organization emphasizes the hierarchy of authority and strict rules and procedures. We also noted that such rules and procedures are established to meet the situations that the organization or its employees face. That is appropriate if those situations are finite and known—that is, if the environment is stable. However, if the environment changes in fast and unpredictable ways, one cannot set rules and regulations for every contingency. Hence, the idea of networking those units that will be affected. In a network, members are allowed to interact with each other to make decisions as they see fit to meet the environmental challenges or opportunities they face.

Several authors (e.g., Birkinshaw, 2000; Hall, 1996; Kanter & Myers, 1991; Knoke, 2001; Miles & Snow, 1996) have discussed the emergence of various forms of networked organizations. This discussion follows Birkinshaw (2000) in classifying network forms of organization into *internal* and *external* networks. An **internal network** involves individuals within the organization interacting with each other to solve problems or to innovate new methods and techniques. Such interactions may be in response to internal issues or external events. An **external network** involves one or more internal units interacting with units external to the organization. Such interactions may be to facilitate the work processes within the organization or to outsource processes. Internal and external networks are described below, followed by a discussion of a third form of network—interorganizational—which is particularly relevant in sport management.

Internal Networks

As noted, internal networks may be formed to address the work processes within the organization or to respond to events occurring outside the organization.

Internal networks for work processes

In a traditional organization, specialized work units are hierarchically organized, and the communications among them are channeled through the hierarchical ranks. We noted that such arrangements can lead to delays and distortions in communication and that the communication flow can be inconsistent with the workflow. Another problem with centralized decision making is that the decision makers at the top may not be aware of or understand the demands of the work carried out at the front line (see criticisms of bureaucracy in Chapter 7). To alleviate these problems, many organizations have adopted the network form of organization as shown in Exhibit 8.6.

The first notable feature of this form is the absence of a strict formal hierarchy like that of traditional organizations. In other words, the communication channels are more lateral instead of vertical; every unit or employee interacts with any other unit or person as the situation warrants. Consider the case of an arena used by several teams. It is conventional for someone in authority to schedule the practices and

exhibit 8.6 Example of an internal network for work processes.

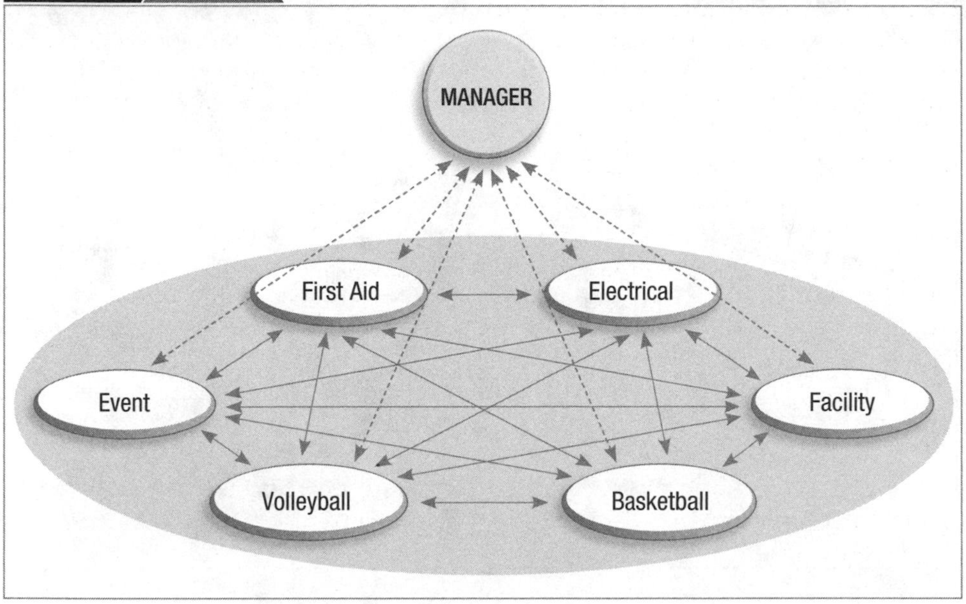

games for the teams using the arena. It is also conventional to have a unit in charge of managing the facility and another unit to manage the events (i.e., the competitions). It is also not uncommon to have other units take care of the electrical, heating, ventilation, and similar systems. In a traditional organization, a clear hierarchy and communication channels would be established to coordinate the activities. In a network organization, the units or persons would be permitted and encouraged to communicate among themselves to solve any problems they may face. For instance, suppose the volleyball coach wants to switch the practice time with the basketball coach for the next day. In a conventional organization, the volleyball coach would have to submit the request to a superior (e.g., the associate athletic director in charge of volleyball), who would, in turn, communicate formally with the associate director in charge of basketball and others in charge of facility management and first-aid services. In a networked organization, the volleyball coach would directly request the basketball coach for a change in the practice time. If the basketball coach accedes to the request, the volleyball coach would then inform the event and facility managers and those who provide first-aid services. In this example, the network arrangement facilitates smooth and speedy internal workflow.

Internal networks for external events

Another form of internal network organization permits the units to interact with each other to react collectively to an external and unexpected event. Exhibit 8.7 illustrates this arrangement: here, Units 1, 5, and 6 jointly react to external Event 1, and Units 2, 3, and 4 interact to counter Event 2. Which units will interact will depend on the nature of the event. Examples from athletic contests abound. The special teams in football (i.e., the offense, defense, punt-return) are made up of athletes with specialized skills to tackle specific problems. Basketball, hockey, and volleyball coaches shuffle their line-ups to counter the strategies of their opponents.

Consider a riot that breaks out on the campus after a football game. The units within the university in charge of security, traffic, physical plant, and fire preven-

exhibit 8.7 Example of internal networks dealing with external events.

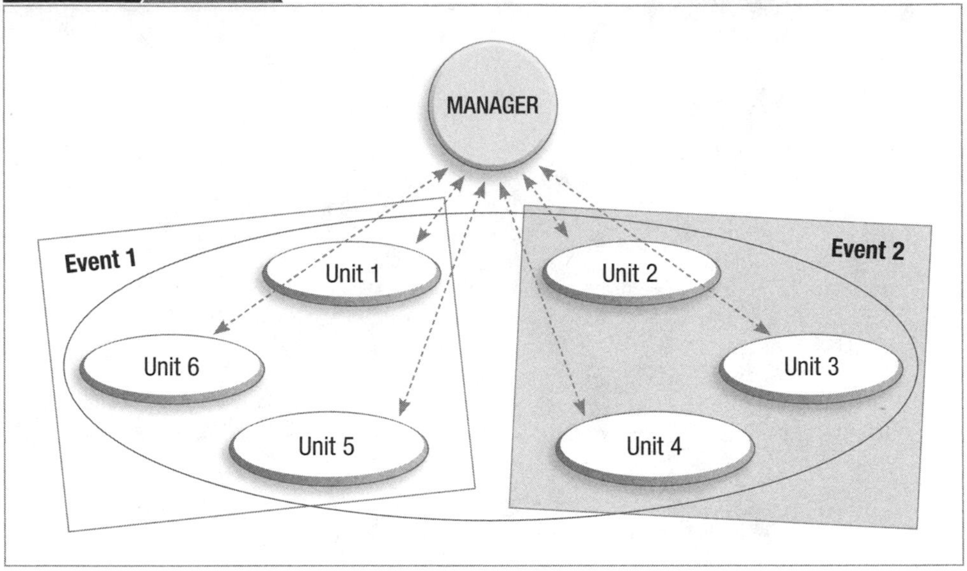

tion, as well as other emergency units, would interact with each other to control the riot. If necessary, these units would also be empowered to interact with external agencies, such as the city police and fire departments. The idea here is that these units interact with each other directly instead of going through the president or the board of governors.

External Networks

External networks may be formed to facilitate processes within the organization, or they may be formed to outsource these processes.

External networks facilitating internal processes

It is becoming increasingly necessary for the units within a given sport organization to interact with other organizations in the environment to facilitate internal processes (see Exhibit 8.8). Earlier in the chapter, we referred to units such as the marketing and development departments as boundary-spanning units (i.e., the boundary between the organization and its environment). If the marketing department wants to send a mass email promotion to fans, it can directly contact and negotiate a contract with an organization specializing in the design and implementation of mass email campaigns. Similarly, the event management unit would be permitted to contact the local police department and make traffic and security arrangements for a playoff game. The units within a city recreation department promoting sport and recreation programs would be at liberty to contact local high schools, associations of retirees, and other agencies to publicize their programs.

External networks for outsourcing

Another type of external network is formed when an organization decides to let another organization take on production or marketing functions. For example, the focal organization may buy its supplies from other organizations, may con-

exhibit 8.8 Example of external network facilitating internal processes.

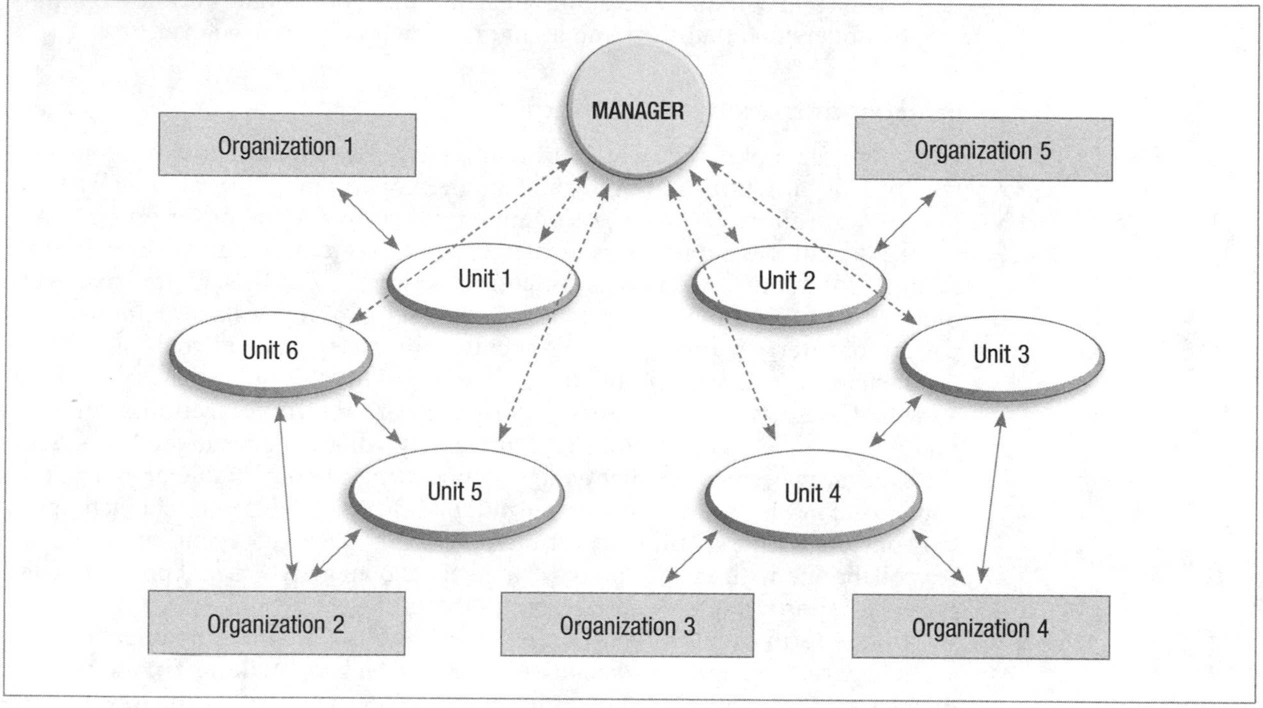

tract out the manufacturing function (i.e., the conversion of the supplies into its products) to other organizations, and may enlist the services of retailers to sell the products. This idea is catching on in the case of facility and event management. For example, SMG (2004) is an external agency managing arenas, facilities, and events for other organizations, including NFL teams, MLB, and NCAA sporting events. Another firm, BKB Limited (2010), specializes in organizing and conducting road races, triathlons, and Nordic events. Its services include

- full event management from initial concept to event day staff and equipment
- e-newsletters for client event publicity
- tailored vendor and supplier selection, bidding, and referral
- course creation and procurement of certification
- event announcing and consulting

External networking also occurred in March 2009, when The Ohio State University (OSU) athletic department announced a contract unprecedented among university athletic departments. With this deal, OSU awarded its marketing and media rights to IMG College, a division of IMG Worldwide Inc., and RadiOhio Inc. for $110 million over 10 years while also assuming $18 million in production, payroll, tickets, and other expenses (Matuszewski, 2009). Eugene Smith, Associate Vice President and Director of Athletics of The Ohio State University, noted that this arrangement would ensure long-term financial stability for Ohio State Athletics by continuing to fund its 36-sport program. Previously, the university was making $6.3 million a year through its own in-house marketing efforts (Price, 2009).

Readers should note that in the networked organizational forms described above, the top management still has hierarchical authority over all operations of the organization. It is just that the lower-level units are given the flexibility and authority to manage day-to-day operations and coordinate horizontal workflows. It must also be understood that these modes of organizing have evolved over time.

Interorganizational Networks

One other form of network organization is very relevant to sport management—the **interorganizational network.** This network is made up of "legally independent, autonomous, interdependent organizations with converging, but also diverging, interests and characteristics, which are connected with each other through interactive, reciprocal exchange relations" (Van Gils, 1998, p. 92). The member organizations engage in a common set of activities and demonstrate a pattern of interrelationships to attain collective and individual goals and resolve problems that arise among them (Hall, 1996). The NCAA in the United States and the Canadian Interuniversity Sport (CIS) are interorganizational networks that link member organizations (i.e., university athletic departments) producing the same services with similar goals and operating in comparable organizational contexts. That is, the member organizations (a) possess different characteristics, (b) compete with each other in various sports (i.e., have divergent interests), and (c) collaborate with each other to regulate their own activities and promote intercollegiate sport (i.e., have convergent interests).

In one form of interorganizational networks, the member organizations create an external agency to (a) facilitate collective decision making, (b) monitor the members' behaviors, and (c) coordinate and direct members' efforts toward common goals. The central agency is given the power to make decisions that bind the member organizations and to impose sanctions when a member organization violates its rules (Park, 1996). This form of interorganizational network is illustrated in Exhibit 8.9, with the NCAA as the apex organization of the network.

exhibit 8.9 The NCAA as an interorganizational network.

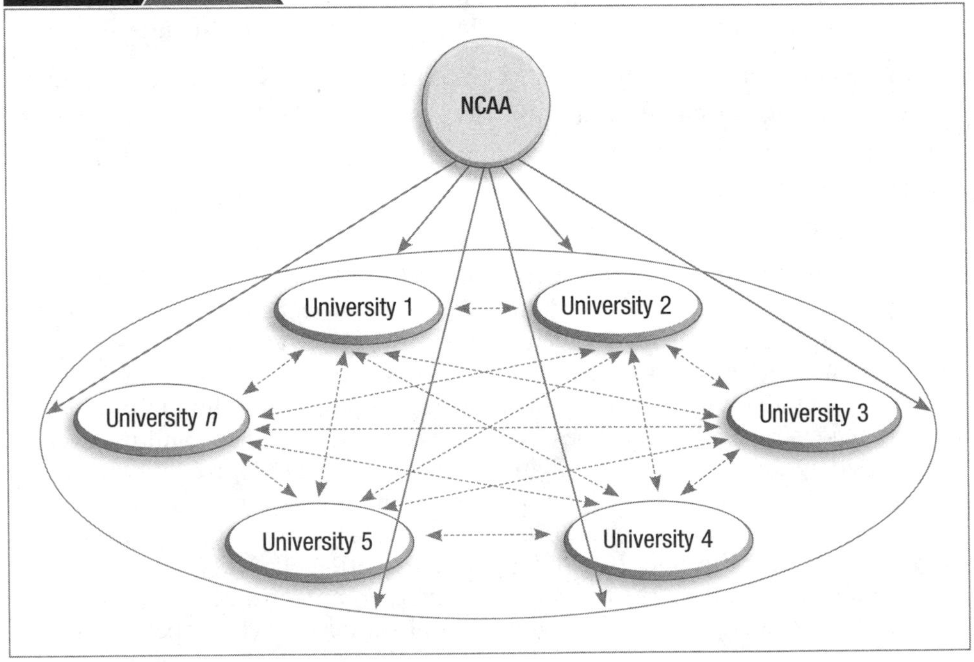

sidebar 8.3

OUTSOURCING ATHLETIC COACHING

Ponder the following scenario (illustrated in Exhibit 8.10). Let us assume that a wealthy individual buys an expansion franchise in the National Football League. She decides to outsource almost every activity fundamental to the operation of the franchise. The owner may decide to sign a contract with a university (e.g., Oklahoma State University) for the use of its stadium for all the team's home games. The university athletic department may maintain the facility as well as manage every game for the new franchise. Such an arrangement would be tantamount to outsourcing the functions of facility and event management. It is also possible to outsource the functions of promotions, marketing, ticketing, security, and other essential functions to the university itself or to agencies like SMG. Then there are the most important functions: forming the team and coaching the team during practices and games. The owner is contemplating outsourcing even those functions to an external enterprise.

Can we conceive of an outstanding coach forming a business enterprise consisting of himself plus assistant coaches, trainers, recruiting staff, and other essential personnel associated with coaching? Many business consulting firms and detective agencies operate this way with specialists under their employ. If there were such an athletic coaching enterprise, the new franchise owner could outsource the coaching function to that enterprise. With all these functions outsourced, the owner needs to have just a few professional assistants to help with the overall supervision of the franchise. Discuss the feasibility of this scenario.

Although there are firms that specialize in managing stadiums and organizing competitions, currently no firm specializes in forming and coaching teams. But the concept is not far off. Consider the coaches of NCAA Division I football and basketball teams. Their services are contracted for huge salaries for a certain number of years. They are permitted to hire their own assistant coaches and support staff. They are in full charge of which players they will recruit and which players will play in a given game. If the team performs well over the period of the contract, the contract may be extended. If not, the contract may not be renewed. The coach may even be fired before the end of the contract, if the team is not faring well. When a new coach is hired, he brings in his own lawyers and accountants to make sure that the contract and its provisions are in order and to safeguard his interests. From this perspective, the coaches of NCAA Division I football and basketball teams are in fact private enterprises without being formally and legally incorporated as businesses. And the process of hiring and firing a coach resembles outsourcing in many respects.

exhibit 8.10 **Example of an external network for outsourcing.**

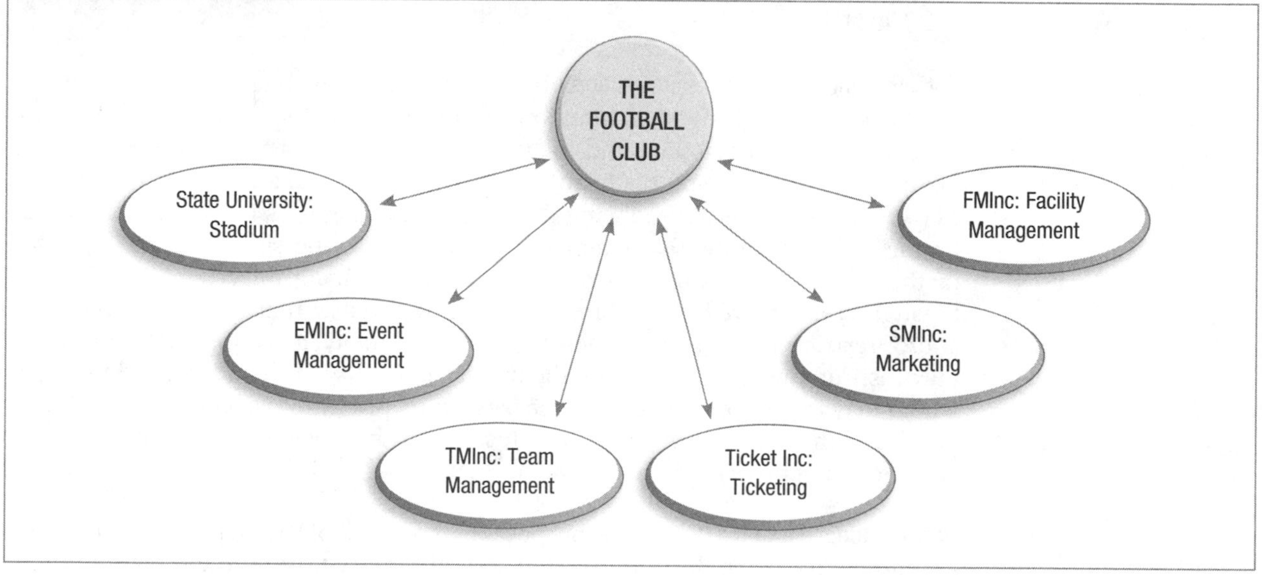

In the case of the NCAA, the member institutions granted the NCAA regulatory authority in 1952 that gave the NCAA "the right to control the athletic programs through rule-making and sanctions" (Stern, 1979, p. 247). It serves as the private regulatory network and coordinates the intercollegiate activities through surveillance and sanctioning (Stern, 1981). In fact, the NCAA has become a powerful control agent capable of punishing member schools for violating its rules (particularly recruiting rules) and providing a growing number of valued resources and services, including financial rewards and legitimacy (Knoke, 2001).

The National Basketball Association (NBA) and other professional sport organizations (e.g., National Football League, National Hockey League) are also interorganizational networks. The International Olympic Committee and international sport federations such as FIFA (football) and FIBA (basketball) are interorganizational networks at the global level. At the national level, the national Olympic committees and national sport federations such as USA Cycling fall under this category. Units of these organizations at the regional and state levels would also fall under the category of interorganizational networks. Similarly, state high school athletic associations and their national counterpart, the National Federation of State High School Associations, as well as various national youth sport organizations such as the American Youth Soccer Organization, are interorganizational networks.

Network functions

Interorganizational networks create greater access to resources for member organizations and help to increase the financial performance of members (Human & Provan, 1997). Furthermore, an interorganizational network is expected to

1. facilitate innovation and share knowledge and learning among member institutions (Goes & Park, 1997; Kraatz, 1998)
2. reduce variety and uncertainty in transactions (Park, 1996)
3. economize the costs of information gathering and dissemination (Kraatz, 1998; Park, 1996)
4. coordinate the interdependent activities among member institutions (Provan, 1983)

Network functions in professional sport. In the context of professional sport, Gerrard (2003) identifies three basic functions of a professional sport league: (1) administrative, (2) sport viability, and (3) financial. The administrative function entails planning and conducting a schedule of sport contests and a tournament structure, as well as instituting and policing the rules of the game. As for sport viability, the league's responsibility is to maintain the interests of the spectators and sponsors in the league. This is often accomplished by "ensuring uncertainty of outcome through competitive balance brought about by revenue redistribution, salary caps and/or restrictions on player mobility" (p. 219). Finally, a professional sport league may institute measures to ensure the financial viability of the league and its teams, which may involve restrictions on the bargaining power of players in the labor market and "limiting the number of franchises such that the demand from big-market cities for franchises exceeds the available supply" (p. 219).

Network functions in the NCAA. The purposes and services of the NCAA (2004a, 2004b) are shown in Exhibit 8.11. Readers will note that these purposes and services reflect

exhibit 8.11 The purposes and services of the National Collegiate Athletic Association.

The National Collegiate Athletic Association's purposes are:

- To initiate, stimulate and improve intercollegiate athletics programs for student-athletes and to promote and develop educational leadership, physical fitness, athletics excellence and athletics participation as a recreational pursuit.
- To uphold the principle of institutional control of, and responsibility for, all intercollegiate sports in conformity with the constitution and bylaws of the Association.
- To encourage its members to adopt eligibility rules to comply with satisfactory standards of scholarship, sportsmanship and amateurism.
- To formulate, copyright and publish rules of play governing intercollegiate athletics.
- To preserve intercollegiate athletics records.
- To supervise the conduct of, and to establish eligibility standards for, regional and national athletics events under the auspices of the Association.
- To legislate, through bylaws or by resolutions of a Convention, upon any subject of general concern to the members related to the administration of intercollegiate athletics.
- To study in general all phases of competitive intercollegiate athletics and establish standards whereby the colleges and universities of the United States can maintain their athletics programs on a high level.

The NCAA serves as a governance and administrative structure through which its members:

- Enact legislation to deal with athletics problems when the problems spread across regional lines and when member institutions conclude that national action is needed.
- Interpret legislation adopted by the membership.
- Provide financial assistance and other help to groups that are interested in promoting and advancing intercollegiate athletics.
- Combine to represent intercollegiate athletics in legislative and regulatory matters on the state and Federal levels. This involvement includes such areas as Federal taxes affecting college athletics, antibribery and gambling laws, television, international competition, and Federal aid to education affecting sports and physical education.
- Promote their championship events and all intercollegiate athletics through planned activities of the NCAA national office. In addition to general public relations activities, the Association publishes *The NCAA News* and dozens of other publications on behalf of its members.
- Compile and distribute football, basketball, baseball, ice hockey, men's and women's lacrosse, and women's softball and volleyball statistics. Regular-season records are maintained in women's volleyball, football and basketball; championships records are maintained in all sports in which the members sponsor NCAA championship competition.
- Maintain committees to write and interpret playing rules in 13 sports.
- Conduct research as a way to find solutions to athletics problems. These efforts include surveys about academics, television, postseason events, athletics and recreational facilities, sports injuries and safety, recruiting, financial aid, playing seasons, the cost of intercollegiate athletics, and the effects of participation on the student-athlete.

(continued)

exhibit 8.11 Continued.

- Annually produce, in conjunction with NCAA Productions, special programs for television along with television coverage of NCAA championships not carried by a national network. This operation includes a library of films and videotapes of more than 100 titles available for purchase and rental, plus the NCAA Television News Service, which supplies information to television and cable networks.
- Maintain a compliance services program that assists members in conducting institutional self-studies through a central resource clearinghouse and counseling agency to answer questions about intercollegiate athletics and athletics administration.
- Administer insurance programs, including a lifetime catastrophic injury insurance program, to ensure that member institutions can provide protection for student-athletes during competition, practice and travel. The Association also arranges disability insurance protection for elite student-athletes.
- Promote and participate in international sports planning and competition through membership in the U.S. Olympic Committee, USA Basketball, the United States Collegiate Sports Council, The Athletics Congress (track and field), the U.S. Volleyball Association, and the U.S. Baseball, Gymnastics and Wrestling Federations.
- Sanction postseason competition and certify certain noncollegiate contests to protect their institutional interests and those of their student-athletes.
- Support several community service programs, including NYSP (National Youth Sports Program), and offer Youth Education through Sports (YES) Clinics at numerous NCAA championship locations.
- Administer national and international marketing and licensing programs to enhance intercollegiate athletics and to expand youth development programs.

Sources: NCAA (2004a, 2004b).

the network functions described above. Establishing and monitoring eligibility rules, publishing rules of play governing intercollegiate athletics, and organizing and conducting regional and national athletics events are examples of critical network functions of the NCAA that bind its members and coordinate their activities.

SUMMARY

This chapter began with a critique of Weber's (1947) bureaucracy as a closed system. We saw that organizations need to be open to the influences of the greater environment. Accordingly, the chapter presented three different models of organizing based on the systems perspective. We explored the concepts of differentiation and integration proposed in the Lawrence and Lorsch (1967) model. Following this we described the Thompson (1967) model, which focused on the concept of insulating the technical core of an organization via its boundary-spanning units. The third model we covered in the chapter was that of Parsons (1960), with its three hierarchically arranged subsystems—technical subsystem, managerial subsystem, and institutional subsystem. We then looked at the relevance of these models to different kinds of sport organizations and also examined the distinction between the authority flowing from the administrative unit and the power flowing from the professional (operational) units. Finally, we discussed the various network structures that are becoming popular.

an expert's view / ON SOCIAL NETWORK THEORY

Our discussion so far has been on internal and external networks of organizations. But the idea of networks is not confined to organizations only. Readers are familiar with the importance of establishing and maintaining a strong network of people for either social or career purposes. But the concept of network is relevant in many other contexts. Catherine Quatman-Yates has introduced to the field of sport management an approach to the study of relationships among individuals and/or units in an organization (Quatman & Chelladurai, 2008a, 2008b). In reading this discussion, keep in mind that the principles and perspectives of social network theory are consistent with the systems view of organizations as discussed in Chapter 3.

SOCIAL NETWORK THEORY AND ANALYSIS

Catherine Quatman-Yates

Regardless of the type of formal structure an organization implements, managers should be conscious of the fact that the patterns of interaction (both formal and informal) among organizational members can influence the outcomes of organizational activities in powerful ways. Ultimately, managers face a great challenge in this regard. The abstract and inconsistent nature of both formal and informal interactions between members of an organization can hinder and perhaps even damage decision-making and administrative processes. However, from a different perspective, managers are presented with a great opportunity to capitalize on an inexpensive and readily accessible resource: the organization's underlying social network infrastructure. Often, an organization's informal infrastructure can be used to facilitate the endeavors and processes of the formal infrastructure. But, how can a manager strategically utilize an organizational variable that seems so unpredictable, intangible, and subjective?

One promising approach has emerged in the literature and in managerial practices that precisely addresses this question. Commonly referred to as *social network theory and analysis,* this approach has been identified by scholars and practitioners alike as being both scientifically and pragmatically worthwhile. *Social network theory* is more of a lens for viewing the world than a "theory" per se. The focus of this lens is a robust emphasis on considering and understanding the structural patterns of relationships between entities that exist within a system. *Social network analysis* is a measurement and analytical tool that draws upon visual representations and quantified measurements to assess the patterns of relationships that exist within a system.

The essence and utility of social network theory and analysis is perhaps best explained through the use of a contextual example and a few basic illustrations. While viewing Exhibit 8.12, imagine the points that are labeled "a"–"f" to represent the leading offensive players of an opposing team scheduled for an upcoming soccer match. Suppose you want to identify which player is most likely to receive and give a majority of the passes from and to her teammates. You watch a 10-minute segment of one of their previous matches and draw the diagrams shown in Exhibit 8.12 in an attempt to systematically identify passing patterns between players. Take a few minutes now to think about what you might conclude from these three diagrams.

One conclusion you may draw based upon diagram (1) is that player d tends to pass to players a, b, c, e, and f but does not receive many passes back from other players. Likewise, diagram (2) might lead you to the conclusion that player d receives

exhibit 8.12 Samples of passing patterns among five players of the opposing team.

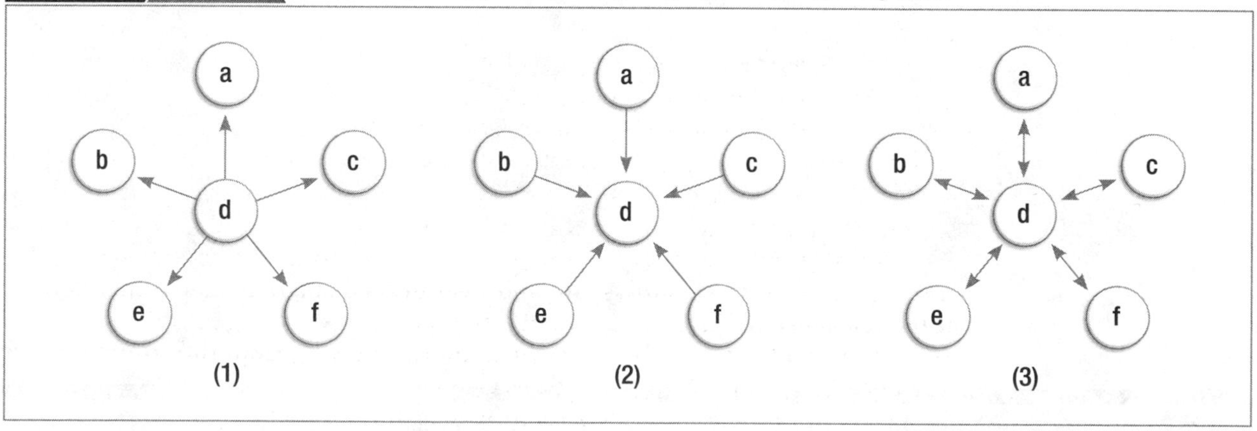

a lot of passes from several players whereas in diagram (3) player d both receives passes from and sends passes to the other players. Given this information, can you think of some defensive strategies you might employ? For example, for diagram (3), which player on the opposing team might you have your best defensive player mark during the game? (Answer: Player d appears to send to and receive from many other players. Thus, it might be prudent to put one of your strongest defensive players on this person.) This example is a very basic representation of what social network theory and analysis entails.

Intuitively, it is easy to see how studying such patterns of interaction might be useful for managers in a variety of contexts. However, one of the most novel and perhaps most useful aspects of social network theory and analysis is the emphasis that is placed on considering how the relationship between any two entities is embedded within the larger infrastructure of the system as a whole. In other words, consider Exhibit 8.13 using the example from earlier. Imagine that this example represents the passing patterns between all players on the opposing team over the course of an entire match.

What strategies might you devise based on Exhibit 8.13? For example, this diagram clearly identifies player d as being more active in the team's passing patterns than player a. Hence, a useful strategy might be to put one of your stronger defensive players on player d and one of your weaker defensive players on player a. Can you see why it is valuable to consider the patterns of interaction between entities in a system as being embedded within the entire system?

Together, social network theory and analysis can be useful for studying how the patterns of relationships within a system influence and affect the behavior of individual entities within the system and the system as a whole. Make note of the vague use of the terms "entities" and "system" as units of analysis. The use of these indistinct terms is intentional because social network theory and analysis is designed to be a flexible approach that can be used to investigate the interconnectedness of any type of things, beings, or events. For example, social network theory and analysis can be equally useful to study such trends as exchange of information patterns among employees in a department, friendships between employees in an organization, or the exchange of resources between organizations in an industry. Although social network theory and analysis can become complex depending upon the questions you are interested in addressing and the context you are studying, in many ways the basics of the approach are quite intuitive.

The purpose of the diagrams and examples in this discussion was to introduce you to social network theory and analysis as a tool for viewing and strategically managing systems. Of course, this serves as only a rudimentary overview of some of the concepts and applications of social network theory and analysis. Many sources are available in the form of textbooks, journal articles, and software packages, which provide a more comprehensive and in-depth description of the tools and strategies that may be of use for those individuals who wish to explore these techniques further.

Resources:

Quatman, C. C., & Chelladurai, P. (2008). Social network theory and analysis: A complementary lens for inquiry. *Journal of Sport Management, 22*(3), 338–360.

Love, A., & Andrew, D. P. S. (2012). The intersection of sport management and sociology of sport research: A social network perspective. *Sport Management Review, 15*(20), 244–256.

exhibit 8.13 **Passing patterns of all players on the opposing team during the entire game.**

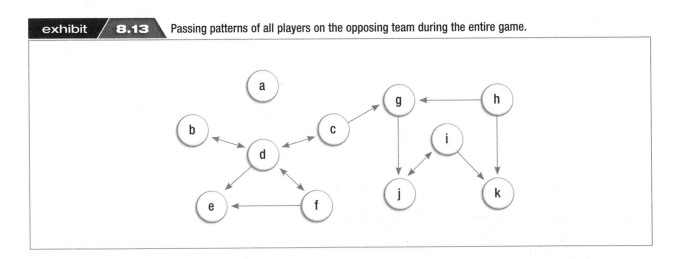

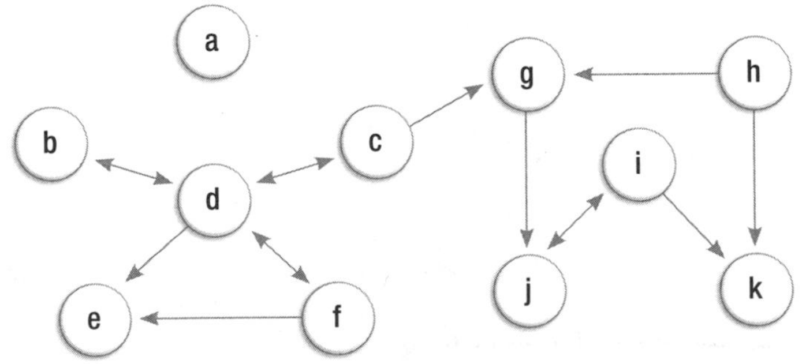

develop YOUR PERSPECTIVE

1. Select one sport organization of your choice (other than a university athletic team), and define and describe its environment. Explain the influences of different elements in the environment.
2. Describe the extent to which your organization's units are differentiated. Explain how integration among the differentiated units is achieved.
3. Considering the same organization, describe its "technical core." To what extent is that technical core protected from the external environment? How is this insulation achieved?
4. Identify an organization characterized by Parsons' three levels of subsystems—technical subsystem, managerial subsystem, and institutional subsystem. Explain the extent to which Parsons' perspectives are reflected in that organization.
5. Explain the concepts of authority flow and power flow. How relevant are these concepts to the various types of sport organizations?

references

Amis, J., Slack, T., & Berrett, T. (1995). The structural antecedents of conflict in national sport organizations. *Leisure Studies, 14,* 1–16.

Birkinshaw, J. (2000). Network relationships inside and outside the firm, and the development of capabilities. In J. Birkinshaw & P. Hagstrom (Eds.), *The flexible firm: Capability management in network organizations* (pp. 4–17). Oxford, UK: Oxford University Press.

BKB Limited (2010). Retrieved from www.bkbltd.com.

Gerrard, B. (2003). Editorial introduction: Efficiency in professional sports leagues. *European Sport Management Quarterly, 3,* 219–220.

Goes, J. B., & Park, S. H. (1997). Interorganizational links and innovation: The case of hospital services. *Academy of Management Journal, 40,* 673–696.

Hall, R. H. (1996). *Organizations: Structures, processes, and outcomes* (6th ed.). Englewood Cliffs, NJ: Prentice Hall.

Human, S. E., & Provan, K. G. (1997). An emergent theory of structure and outcomes in small-firm strategic manufacturing networks. *Academy of Management Journal, 40,* 368–403.

Kanter, R. S., & Myers, P. S. (1991). Interorganizational bonds and intraorganizational behavior: How alliances and partnerships change the organizations forming them. In A. Etzioni & P. R. Lawrence (Eds.), *Socioeconomics: Toward a new synthesis* (pp. 329–344). Armonk, NY: M. E. Sharpe.

Katz, R. L. (1974). Skills of an effective administrator. *Harvard Business Review, 52,* 90–102.

Kikulis, L., Slack, T., & Hinings, C. R. (1995). Does decision making make a difference?: Patterns of change within Canadian national sport organizations. *Journal of Sport Management, 9,* 273–299.

Knoke, D. (2001). *Changing organizations: Business networks in the new political economy.* Boulder, CO: Westview Press.

Kraatz, M. (1998). Learning by association? Interorganizational networks and adaptation to environmental change. *Academy of Management Journal, 41,* 621–643.

Lawrence, P. R., & Lorsch, J. W. (1967). Differentiation and integration in complex organizations. *Administrative Science Quarterly, 12,* 1–47.

Matuszewski, E. (2009, March 30). *Ohio State, IMG, RadiOhio agree to $128 million deal.* Bloomberg Press. Retrieved from http://www.bloomberg.com/apps/news?pid=20601079&sid=aelJHEQSZYPw&refer=home.

Miles, R. E., & Snow, C. C. (1996). Twenty-first century careers. In M. B. Arthur & D. M. Rousseau (Eds.), *The boundaryless career: A new employment principle for a new organizational era* (pp. 97–115). New York: Oxford University Press.

Mills, P. K., Hall, J. L., Leidecker, J. K., & Margulies, N. (1983). Flexiform: A model for professional service organizations. *Academy of Management Review, 8,* 118–131.

Mintzberg, H. (1975). The manager's job: Folklore and fact. *Harvard Business Review, 53,* 49–61.

NCAA (2004a). NCAA purposes. Retrieved from www.ncaa.org/about/purposes.html.

NCAA (2004b). NCAA services. Retrieved from www.ncaa.org/about/services.html.

Park, S. H. (1996). Managing an interorganizational network: A framework of the institutional mechanism for network control. *Organization Studies, 17,* 795–824.

Parsons, T. (1960). *Structure and process in modern societies.* New York: The Free Press of Glencoe.

Price, R. (2009, March 30). OSU getting richest multimedia contract. *Columbus Dispatch,* pp. A1, A4.

Provan, K. G. (1983). The federation as an interorganizational linkage network. *Academy of Management Review, 8,* 79–89.

Quatman, C. C., & Chelladurai, P. (2008a). Social network theory and analysis: A complimentary lens for inquiry. *Journal of Sport Management, 22*(3), 338–360.

Quatman, C. C., & Chelladurai, P. (2008b). The social construction of knowledge in the field of sport management: A social network perspective. *Journal of Sport Management, 22*(6), 651–676.

Robbins, S. P., Coulter, M., & Langton, N. (2006). *Management* (8th Canadian ed.). Toronto: Pearson Prentice Hall.

Robertson, M., & Swan, J. (2004). Going public: The emergence and effects of soft bureaucracy within a knowledge-intensive firm. *Organization, 11*(1), 123–148.

Slack, T., & Parent, M. M. (2006). *Understanding sport organizations: The application of organization theory* (2nd ed.). Champaign, IL: Human Kinetics.

SMG (2004). Retrieved from www.smgworld.com.

Stern, R. N. (1979). The development of an interorganizational network: The case of intercollegiate athletics. *Administrative Science Quarterly, 24,* 242–266.

Stern, R. N. (1981). Competitive influences on the interorganizational regulation of college athletics. *Administrative Science Quarterly, 26,* 15–31.

Thibault, L., Slack, T., & Hinings, C. R. (1991). Professionalism, structures and systems: The impact of professional staff on voluntary sport organizations. *International Review for the Sociology of Sport, 26,* 83–99.

Thompson, J. D. (1967). *Organizations in action.* New York: McGraw-Hill.

Vaast, E. (2007). What goes online comes offline: Knowledge management system use in a soft bureaucracy. *Organization Studies, 28*(3), 283–306.

Van Gils, M. R. (1998). Interorganizational networks. In P. J. D. Drenth, H. Thierry, & C. J. de Wolff (Eds.), *Organizational psychology. Volume 4 of Handbook of organizational psychology* (2nd ed.). Hove, East Sussex: Psychology Press.

Waring, A. (1996). *Practical systems thinking.* London: International Thomson Business Press.

Weber, M. (1947). *The theory of social and economic organization.* (Translated by A. M. Henderson & T. Parsons). New York: Oxford University Press.

CHAPTER 9
STAFFING

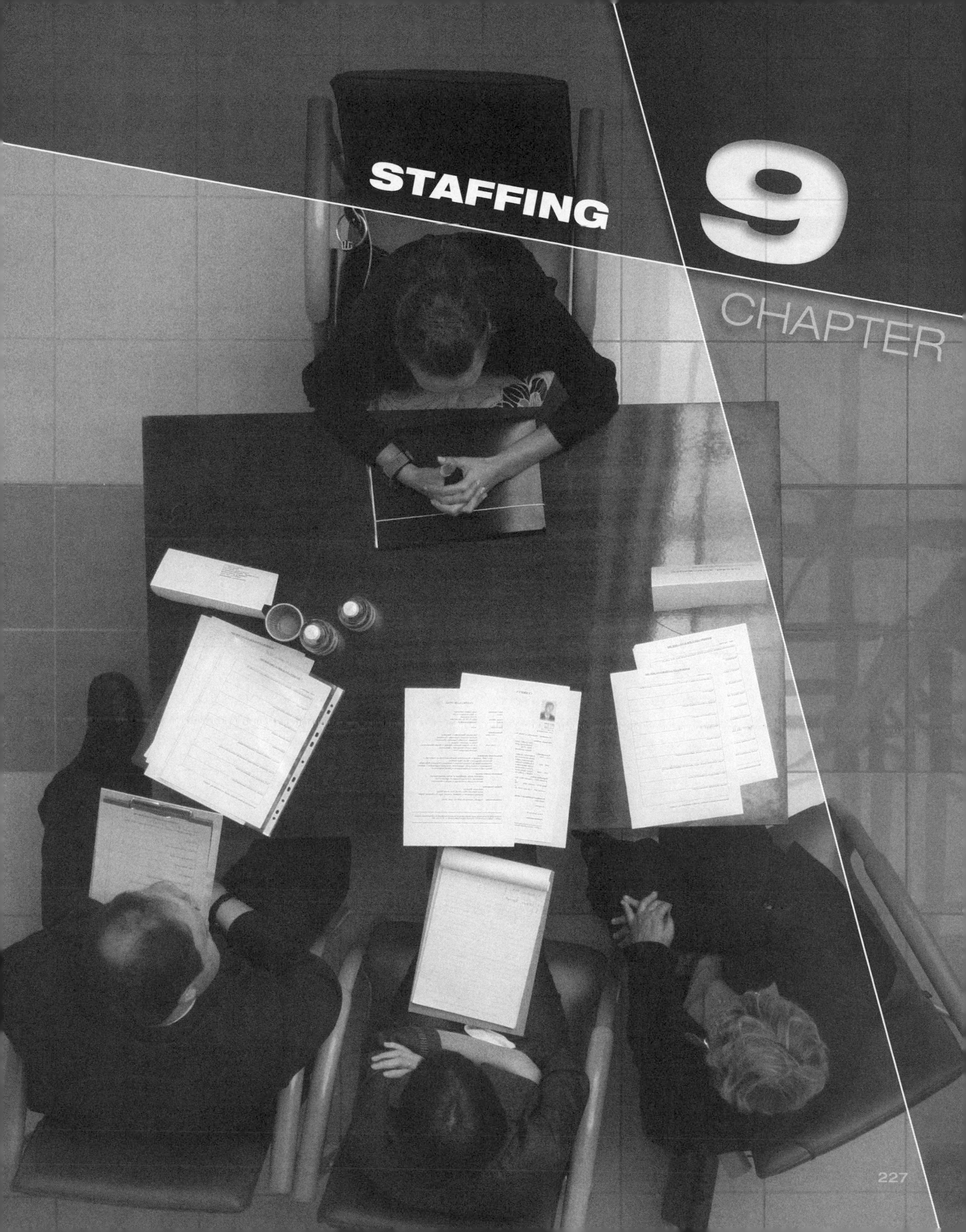

manage YOUR LEARNING

After completing this chapter you should be able to:

- Understand the purpose and focus of staffing as a managerial function.
- Know the processes of job analysis, job description, and job specification.
- Explain the process of matching people with jobs through recruiting and hiring.
- Understand the concepts of person–job fit and person–organization fit.

strategic CONCEPTS

assessment of staffing needs
coaching
development
employee referral
hiring
job analysis
job description
job rotation
job specification
mentoring
person–organization fit
person–task fit
recruiting
selection
staffing
training

INTRODUCTION

Chapters 7 and 8 indicated that a significant element of the organizing function is to allocate well-defined jobs to appropriately qualified individuals. For instance, a major tenet of bureaucracy is *technical competence,* which implies that the person who occupies a given position in a bureaucracy will be competent enough to carry it out. In systems-based organizing, *differentiation* refers to the distinctiveness of the structure and processes of units within the organization. This distinctiveness arises from the need for a unit to be consistent with the environmental conditions that it faces. The individuals in such differentiated units must possess the knowledge, skills, and attitudes suited for the tasks within the unit.

We must also recognize that no matter how sophisticated the management system is, it is the workers who make it work. All the elegant plans and the efficient organizing procedures would be useless if the members of the organization do not understand the systems, accept them, and execute them efficiently. Hence it is important that the most appropriate people are brought into the organization and assigned to appropriate positions. As Sullivan (1997) noted, "Building good staff is like making homemade soup. The people you hire are the ingredients you mix in. High-quality ingredients guarantee a first-rate meal. . . . It is not magical. It takes patience and effort to make it work. The sweat equity invested will reap high dividends" (p. 2).

Given the importance of the employees in an organization, several specialized fields of study and practice have emerged over the decades, such as personnel administration, personnel psychology, organizational behavior, and human resource management. Many large organizations have a specialized unit to manage the human resource issues within their respective organizations. Though the field of human resource management deals with several topics (e.g., employee relations, performance appraisal, personnel management, reward systems, work schedules) this chapter is confined to finding the right people for the organization (i.e., *recruiting*), and *hiring* and *training* them.

THE IMPORTANCE OF STAFFING

The importance of **staffing** is best understood from the perspective of a sport team like football, basketball, and soccer. Coaches and managers of these teams have a clear understanding of the task requirements of various positions in their respective sport. They know the role of each position and what kinds of skills and personal attributes are needed to be effective in a specific position. So, the first problem they address is to identify the best players and then recruit them for these positions. We all know how the professional sport franchises scramble for the best available players. Recruiting is also a major function of collegiate sport coaching programs. In fact, the recruiting costs for an intercollegiate athletic program can run up to $2 million a year (Jessop, 2012). As the demand for these talented players increases and as the players themselves

sidebar 9.1

SIGNIFICANCE OF HUMAN RESOURCES

Chelladurai (2006) argued that the people are the most important resource of an organization. As a resource, they impact other resources (money and materials). That is, it is the people (i.e., managers, employees, and clients or customers) who influence the decisions and goals of the organization and the distribution of available resources in pursuing those goals. Those same people also make the money and materials meaningful as resources and turn them into wealth. For instance, any technological innovation (e.g., cloud computing or smartphones) becomes an organizational resource only when the employees have the skill and inclination to use it effectively for business purposes. In essence, a material resource is a resource only when individuals with the "know-how" use it to serve the needs of other people. All innovations in technologies and processes rely basically on people who implement the policies and procedures of the organization. Any attention to human resource management, beginning with employee hiring and training, is likely to yield greater returns through greater productivity of the workers and their commitment to the organization. Therefore, managers should be concerned with managing the human resources at their disposal more effectively.

Chelladurai (2006) also noted that apart from the financial imperatives posed by people, there are two other significant reasons to focus on human resource management. The first reason is that the increasing sophistication of both employees and consumers (i.e., making them more educated and better informed) leads to their better understanding of what constitutes good human resource management practices, and their higher expectations in that regard. The cumulative effects of modern worker–client awareness, alertness, influence, and altered values have refocused management attention toward human resources. The second reason arises from the place of organizations in society: they serve as agencies of society at large, are sustained by society, and almost all adults within a society are workers of one organization or another. Organizations, therefore, have a societal duty to consider the well-being of their workers and strive to enhance the quality of their lives. Thus, management of human resources merits extreme care not only from the economic, efficiency, and quality perspectives, but also from the social responsibility perspective.

have their own preferences regarding where and for whom they want to play, the coaches (and their organizations) have to make their offer extremely attractive for the players under consideration. Of course, most work organizations are not competing for such a limited pool of talent to the extent professional sport teams are. Nonetheless, a work organization's effectiveness and productivity (or profitability) is highly dependent on the workforce in its fold. Hence, the significance of the function of staffing in an organization.

PURPOSES OF STAFFING

The goals of staffing can be viewed from two perspectives—**person–task fit** (P–T fit) and **person–organization fit** (P–O fit). The concern with person–task fit is to ensure that a person in a job has the right skills to perform that job effectively. Accordingly, the emphasis is on hiring the people with the right technical skills and providing more training in those skills. In the person–organization fit, the concern shifts to whether or not the person shares the values, norms, goals, and objectives of the organization. Another concern is with whether the person to be hired fits into the social milieu of the organization.

Taken together, the two perspectives (i.e., P–T fit and P–O fit) underscore the need to consider the requirements of the job as well as those of the organization. That is, organizations must attempt to attract people with the requisite personality and ability to participate in and promote its organizational values and goals and, at the same time, with the skills needed to perform the tasks of the job effectively. In other words, the person must fit both the content and the context of the job. That is, "applicants are hired based upon who they *are,* not just what they can *do*" (Schneider & Bowen 1992, p. 11). In summary, staffing is concerned with creating a fit between the individual's skills and the job requirements, and matching the individual orientations with organizational goals, values, and culture. First, let us focus on the person–task fit.

Person–Task Fit: Focus on Job Content

As we noted in earlier chapters, organizational work is broken down into specific jobs. These individual jobs cumulatively contribute to organizational outputs. To the extent any of the jobs are not carried out as expected, the total effort will also be affected adversely. That is why it is important that managers assign jobs to the right individuals. In the staffing function, the manager must address the issues discussed in the next sections.

Staffing needs assessment

Obviously, the manager must first determine how many and what types of jobs need to be filled. This **assessment of staffing needs** should consider the immediate as well as future needs. For instance, the manager of a large fitness club has to determine how many fitness instructors, personal trainers, childcare providers, reception desk personnel, and marketing people are needed to run the club efficiently and effectively. Such an assessment must consider the number and type of current employees, the possibility of some employees leaving (e.g., retiring or moving to other locations or jobs), and any future plans for expanding the club. Having determined the number and types of jobs to be filled, the manager then analyzes each of the jobs.

Job analysis

Job analysis involves studying a job and the activities associated with that job. For example, a coaching job in a high school may involve coaching one or more sports for both boys and girls of specific age groups. In some schools, the coaches may also be asked to teach physical education or other classes. Once all the tasks associated with a job are listed, the manager should collect information on the operations and responsibilities of the job. The manager may rely on his or her own insights to list duties and responsibilities of a job. In addition, the manager may observe others working on similar jobs and list the operations. Another useful approach would be to interview the employees who carry out similar jobs in order to identify the critical operations and responsibilities. The purpose of job analysis is to gather the information about the job, the duties and responsibilities involved in that job, the working conditions, the human characteristics (physical and mental attributes) required in that job, and such other details. Exhibit 9.1 lists and describes the critical elements of job analysis.

With the information gathered in the job analysis, the manager prepares a job description and job specification.

exhibit 9.1 Critical elements in a job analysis.

ELEMENT	DESCRIPTION
Job identification	Including job title, its department or division, and titles of supervisors
Job summary	Brief description of the job including its purpose and activities
Duties	Primary duties classified as technical, clerical, or professional; major duties and the proportions of time involved; and other duties and their time involvement
Responsibility	Extent of responsibility over use and care of equipment and tools, personal safety and safety of others, and the performance of others
Human characteristics	Extent to which certain human characteristics are required, including physical attributes such as vision, eye–hand coordination, strength, height, initiative, ingenuity, judgment, writing, education, experience, and training
Working conditions	Description of the physical conditions (usual or unusual) under which the job is to be carried out and any unusual psychological demands
Health and safety features	Description of health or safety hazards including special training or equipment needed
Performance standards	Description of how performance on the job is measured and the identifiable factors that contribute to successful performance

Used with permission from P. Chelladurai, *Human resource management in sport and recreation* (2nd ed.), Table 10.1. ©2006 by Packianathan Chelladurai. Champaign, IL: Human Kinetics.

Job description

A **job description** is a "written statement of what a jobholder does, how it is done, and why it is done. It typically describes job content, environment, and conditions of employment" (Robbins, Coulter, Leach, & Kilfoil, 2012, p. 328). When developing a job description, a good manager ensures that it is concise and clear. The job description must define broadly the scope of the job in terms of the nature of the work and its relationships with other jobs. At the same time, it also should be specific to indicate the complexity of the job, the skill required to manage it, and the worker's responsibility for each aspect. A job description would also include the job title, the immediate supervisor of the job, the number and type of jobs that the incumbent supervises, and specific activities of the job. Exhibit 9.2 provides an example of a job description for a sports director for a fitness center. The applicant is given information on the organization as well as a complete description of what the jobholder has to do to be effective in that job.

exhibit 9.2 A sample job description.

The **Sports Director** manages all athletic facilities and personnel at our year-round fitness center. This position reports to the General Manager.

In this role, the Sports Director

- Selects, trains, supervises, schedules, and evaluates all athletic staff
- Develops all monthly and annual programming (pool, fitness, tennis, aerobics)
- Oversees all athletic activities
- Coordinates the purchase of departmental supplies
- Accounts for member charges, payroll information, maintenance and engineering work
- Oversees facilities and equipment to ensure safety, cleanliness, and maintenance
- Oversees pool maintenance and ensures compliance with all regulations
- Oversees tennis court maintenance on a daily basis
- Ensures that all applicable daily reports are completed in a timely and accurate manner
- Conducts fitness testing and health screening of members and guests
- Inspects locker areas
- Contributes articles for the club's newsletter
- Initiates community-wide presentations on fitness, wellness, and health
- Assists departmental management staff in implementing club policies, goals, operating procedures, and standards
- Attends management meetings and conducts staff meetings
- Prepares and monitors operating and capital budgets
- Completes various other tasks as assigned by the General Manager

Qualifications: The Sports Director must be self motivated with a willingness to do whatever is necessary to ensure a positive experience is had by all. Strong organization skills, superior people skills, and knowledge of fitness equipment/specifications are required.

sidebar 9.2

PART-TIME WORKERS

Many organizations have adopted the practice of hiring contract employees and/or part-time workers on a short-term basis for specific tasks. Many sport organizations such as intercollegiate athletic departments and professional sport franchises hire people for short-term employment during the season. Golf courses in areas with long and severe winters are likely to hire groundskeepers on a part-time basis for the summer months only, because their services are not required during the winter months. The prevalence of part-time employment is said to arise from three reasons (Chang & Chelladurai, 2003):

1. The shift from a manufacturing economy to a service economy, where part-time employment has always been common.
2. The preference for part-time work because it allows people the flexibility to balance their family and work obligations.
3. The fact that part-time employees reduce costs. The savings stem from paying part-time workers less than full-time workers, not paying benefits to the part-time workers, and that part-time workers are generally not in line for promotion to higher-level positions.

This shift toward part-time employment has spawned many private employment services and employee leasing firms that facilitate part-time employment. In sport, many organizations rely on part-time employees. A good example are part-time or full-time workers who are employed during a specific season, such as a football season. During the football season, many people are needed to carry out various tasks associated with managing the home games. Although many volunteers offer to help with such events, the athletic department is likely to pay a few people to carry out specific tasks whose services will not be required after the season. That is, these employees are hired on a seasonal basis. This practice is also prevalent among professional sport franchises. As another example, a large fitness club may hire part-time employees during the peak hours of its operation (e.g., 4:30 to 9:30 P.M., when a large percentage of members show up to work out).

Sport managers must realize that although there are financial benefits of hiring part-time workers, there are also some deficits. Some evidence suggests that part-time employees are not as committed or as productive as full-time workers, and that although they may prefer to work part-time, many of these individuals may be less satisfied with their careers than full-time workers.

Job specification

As noted, job analysis determines the abilities and skills needed for a job. Based on that information, the manager then prepares the **job specification**, which is a statement of the minimum qualifications that a person must possess to perform a given job effectively. In some cases, the job may involve physical requirements as in the case of an aerobics instructor or a groundskeeper. In such cases, the physical characteristics of the jobholder should also be specified. Whereas the job description is a profile of the job, the job specification is a profile of the person who would carry out that job.

IN brief

Whereas job analysis identifies the activities, tasks, skills, and predispositions involved in a specific job, a job description lists the duties and responsibilities of a job, its relationships with others in the organization, and the working conditions. Job specification outlines personal characteristics such as education, experience, and abilities that are needed to carry out the job successfully.

Person–Organization Fit: Focus on Job Context

Although it is important that the employee has the necessary skills, abilities, and other personal and physical traits required to perform the task (i.e., the person–task fit), compatibility is also needed between people and the organization (Kristof, 1996); this is known as person–organization fit. Several aspects of an organization and several attributes of individuals may contribute to the notion of P–O fit, but researchers have typically focused on

1. whether the person shares the goals of the organization,
2. whether the individual's needs and preferences are met by the organization's systems and structures, and
3. whether the values of the person and the organization are compatible.

Of these three factors, the most dominant determinant of person–organization fit has been the compatibility between the values of the person and the organization (Chatman, 1989; Kim, Chelladurai, & Trail, 2007; O'Reilly, Chatman, & Caldwell, 1991). Accordingly, P–O fit is defined as "the congruence between the norms and values of the organizations and the values of persons" (Chatman, p. 339). In Rokeach's (1973) view, a value represents an enduring personal belief about and preferences for specific modes of conduct and end states. From this perspective, "an individual's beliefs of what ought to be attained and how it should be attained should be consistent with the goals and processes of the organization and its expectations for the behaviors of its members" (Kim et al., 2007, p. 155).

When one's personal values are in conflict with those of the organization, the person is not likely to perform the assigned tasks well and, more drastically, may refrain from performing the task entirely. A case in point is Muhammad Ali, who declared himself a conscientious objector and refused to be drafted into the U.S. Army in 1964 during the Vietnam War, because he believed that war was wrong according to his religion (Islam). However, such discomfort with organizational values and processes need not be confined to high-profile individuals or jobs. A well-qualified sport management student placed in a good job in an intercollegiate athletic department may find after a while that the exclusive focus on excellence and winning is not compatible with his or her personal values. Accordingly, the person may leave that job for another one in the city recreation department, which may focus more on participation for fitness and fun. In this scenario, both the person and the organization have lost something. The person has endured an incompatible situation for some time, whereas the organization has lost an experienced employee and now has to expend resources to recruit and train another candidate. Hence, it is important that the organization consider both the person–task fit and person–organization fit when interviewing candidates. By the same token, job seekers should consider whether the values and goals of the organization are consistent with their own personal values and goals.

THE HIRING PROCESS

The next step is identifying and attracting the people who could carry out the jobs effectively. In this step, the manager engages in three interrelated activities—recruiting, selecting, and hiring.

Recruiting

Recruiting is the process of "increase[ing] the pool of candidates that might be selected for a job" (Bateman & Snell, 2007, p. 324). It involves identifying and attracting qualified individuals. As Chelladurai (2006) noted, "This step is similar to how one goes about buying a car, a suit, or a computer. Take the case of buying a car. After deciding on the type of car he or she wants, an individual visits more than one car dealer to ensure that he or she has a selection of that particular type of car from which to choose. In a similar manner, an organization in search of employees also must reach out to many different types of sources of future employees" (p. 169).

Typical methods of recruiting involve advertising the position on multiple online sites, whether specific to the industry or general employment sites, and/or in several newspapers, journals, and trade publications, whether print or online. Many organizations also take advantage of the opportunities offered by universities and colleges to recruit future employees on campus. In fact, if an organization is seeking entry-level professionals, campus recruiting may prove to be the best method because universities and colleges are a good source of young professionals. At a campus job fair, for example, the recruiter has the advantage of interviewing several candidates in one spot and then contacting the more desirable candidates for subsequent interactions.

Another option open to the manager is to ask current employees to pass on the information on job openings to their acquaintances and relatives and ask the employees to suggest names of those who would be suitable. This process is known as **employee referral.** The advantage of this process is that the current employee knows the organization and its workings along with the nature of the job under consideration. Therefore, the employee is in a good position to determine which friend or relative might be the right person for the job. Unfortunately, current employees may recommend people similar to themselves, which could restrict diversity in terms of sex, race, ethnicity, and other demographic characteristics.

A final and practical option is considering current employees who may qualify for the advertised positions. This approach is cost effective since the candidates are already under observation and their performance capabilities are on record; that is, there is no further need to assess some of their aspects, such as their dependability or willingness to learn. An added advantage is that if the organization does recruit internal candidates often enough, it will serve as motivation for the employees to do well in their current jobs. By the same token, ignoring the current employees who are qualified may be a loss to the organization and unfair to the employees.

IN brief

Recruiting focuses on attracting a number of prospective employees from whom the manager can select and hire the best. Recruiting can employ advertising online or in the media, campus recruiting, employee referrals, and internal recruiting in attracting qualified candidates.

Managers also can request their counterparts in other organizations to ask qualified candidates to apply for the position. The essential point is that the organization must make every effort to reach out to qualified prospects for a job.

Selecting

Selection is the "process of screening job applicants to ensure that the most appropriate candidates are hired" (Robbins et al., 2012, p. 330). Once the manager has analyzed and described the jobs in question, specified the appropriate human factors needed, and designed the application to encompass all these elements, selecting and hiring a person would appear to be an easy step. But this is not so. Be aware that job analysis, job description, and job specification only match the right person with the right job (i.e., create the person–job fit). An equally important consideration is the fit between the organization and the person to be hired. As stated previously, such a person–organization fit is based on the personal needs, attitudes, and values of the individual, and the values and culture of the organization. Therefore, organizations and their managers commonly resort to other procedures to select an individual who fits the organizational context. These procedures include checking biographical background, considering reference letters, conducting interviews, and using personal judgment.

Unfortunately, the selection process may allow biases—consciously or unconsciously—to creep into the hiring process, thus resulting in discrimination against some applicants. Managers must carefully avoid this pitfall in the selection process. On the one hand, the sport manager wants to be fair to all the candidates. On the other hand, the manager should follow proper procedures and avoid making a decision that could lead to litigation. The federal and state governments have passed several laws to ensure that the recruiting and hiring processes are fair and nondiscriminatory. Exhibit 9.3 lists the significant government regulations that impact the staffing function of management. The sport manager must, of course, abide by the legal requirements. More importantly, sport managers must scrutinize their own thoughts and actions to ensure that they are free of any personal biases, particularly if they are not related to the job in question. Even asking apparently harmless questions may be reflective of one's own biases and/or may lead to subsequent biases. Exhibit 9.4 lists some of the lawful and unlawful questions or requirements asked of candidates for a job as articulated by the Ohio Civil Rights Commission.

IN brief

Selection is the process of screening the applicants and selecting a person to fit the job as well as the organization. Managers must employ only those criteria that relate to job performance and must disregard irrelevant factors. The manager must also conform to government regulations that pertain to the employment process.

Hiring

The final step is the **hiring** of the selected candidate (or candidates, if there is more than one position to be filled). In this step, the candidate is offered the job and is typically presented with some form of an employment agreement or contract. A letter of offer from an appropriate supervisor will state the salary and benefits for the position and establish the job relationships (i.e., to whom the candidate will report and whom the candidate will supervise and/or interact with), and any other special benefits and/or commitments that the organization and the candidate have agreed upon. The employment agreement normally includes the start date, provisions for termination of employment by the organization or the employee, the period of notice for such termination, and the compensation arrangements in the event of termination. When the candidate accepts the offer and signs the contract, the candidate is hired and he or she becomes an employee of the organization.

TRAINING AND DEVELOPMENT

According to Bateman and Snell (2007), **training** usually refers to teaching lower-level employees to do their specific jobs, whereas **development** is focused on enhancing the skills of an employee to do higher-level jobs in general. For instance, a sport management graduate may be hired by a ticketing department in an intercollegiate athletic department. The first job may be selling tickets to students, faculty, alumni, and other fans. The student must be trained in that specific job, which would entail answering the phone in a courteous manner, taking down details of the buyer of tickets, and entering them correctly in the

exhibit 9.3 Significant government regulations on staffing procedures.

LAWS AND EXECUTIVE ORDERS	PURPOSE OR INTENT
Equal Pay Act (1963)	Forbids sex-based discrimination in rates of pay for men and women working in the same or similar jobs.
Age Discrimination in Employment Act (1967)	Forbids discrimination against individuals between 40 and 70 years of age.
Title VII, Civil Rights Act, as amended by the Equal Opportunity Act (1964, 1972)	Forbids discrimination based on race, sex, color, religion, or national origin.
Rehabilitation Act, as amended (1973)	Forbids discrimination against persons with disabilities and requires affirmative action to provide employment opportunity for persons with disabilities.
Vietnam-Era Veterans Readjustment Assistance Act (1974)	Forbids discrimination in hiring disabled veterans with a 30% or more disability rating, veterans discharged or released for a service-connected disability, and veterans on active duty between August 5, 1964, and May 7, 1975.
Equal Employment Opportunity Commission Guidelines (1978)	Created by the 1964 Civil Rights Act, this commission investigates and eliminates employment discrimination against certain groups of individuals (e.g., women and African, Asian, Hispanic, and Native Americans).
Pregnancy Discrimination Act (1978)	Requires pregnancy to be treated as any other medical condition with regard to fringe benefits and leave policies.
Immigration Reform and Control Act (1986)	Prohibits hiring of illegal aliens.
Americans with Disabilities Act (1990)	Provides for increased access to services and jobs for persons with disabilities.
Older Workers Benefit Protection Act	Provides protection for employees who are more than 40 years of age (1990) regarding fringe benefits and gives employees time to consider an early retirement offer.
Civil Rights Act (1978)	Allows women, persons with disabilities, and persons of religious minorities to have a jury trial and to sue for punitive damages if they can prove intentional hiring and workplace discrimination.

Used with permission from P. Chelladurai, *Human resource management in sport and recreation* (2nd ed.), Table 10.3. © 2006 by Packianathan Chelladurai. Champaign, IL: Human Kinetics.

exhibit 9.4 Sample of lawful and unlawful questions asked of candidates.

INQUIRIES BEFORE HIRING	LAWFUL	UNLAWFUL*
Name	Name	Inquiry about any title that indicates race, color, religion, sex, national origin, disability, age, or ancestry
Address	Inquiry about place of residence and length at current address	Inquiry about any foreign addresses that would indicate national origin
Age	Inquiry limited to confirming that the applicant meets a minimum age requirement that may be established by law	Requiring a birth certificate or baptismal record before hiring; any inquiry that would reveal the date of high school graduation; any inquiry that would reveal whether the applicant is at least 40 years of age
Birthplace, national origin, or ancestry		Any inquiry about place of birth; any inquiry about place of birth of parents, grandparents, or spouse; any other inquiry about national origin or ancestry
Race or color		Any inquiry that would reveal race or color
Sex		Any inquiry that would reveal sex; any inquiry made of members of one sex but not of the other
Height and weight	Inquiry about the ability to perform	Considering height or weight as an actual job requirement without showing that no employee with the ineligible height or weight can do the work
Religion or creed		Any inquiry that would indicate or identify religious denomination or custom; telling the applicant the employer's religious identity or preference; requesting the pastor's recommendation or reference
Disability	Any inquiry necessary to determine the applicant's ability to substantially perform a specific job without significant hazard	Any inquiry about past or current medical conditions not related to the position for which the person has applied; any inquiry about workmen's compensation or similar claims
Citizenship	Inquiry about whether the applicant is a U.S. citizen; inquiry about whether a noncitizen applicant intends to become a U.S. citizen; inquiry about whether U.S. residence is legal; inquiry about whether the applicant's spouse is a U.S. citizen; requiring proof of citizenship after hiring; any other requirements mandated by the Immigration Reform and Control Act of 1986, as amended	Inquiry about whether the applicant is a native-born or naturalized U.S. citizen; requiring proof of citizenship before hiring; inquiry about whether the applicant's spouse or parents are native-born or naturalized U.S. citizens

exhibit 9.4 Continued.

INQUIRIES BEFORE HIRING	LAWFUL	UNLAWFUL*
Photograph	Requiring photograph after hiring	Requiring photograph before hiring for identification
Arrests and convictions	Inquiry about conviction of specific crimes related to qualifications for the job for which the person has applied	
Education	Inquiry about the nature and extent of academic, professional, or vocational training; inquiry about language skills, such as reading and writing of foreign languages, if job related	Any inquiry that would reveal the nationality or religious affiliation of a school; inquiry about what the applicant's mother tongue is or how foreign language ability was acquired
Relatives	Inquiry about name, relationship, and address of person to be notified in case of emergency	Any inquiry about a relative that would be unlawful if made about the applicant
Organizations	Inquiry about membership in professional organizations and offices held, excluding any organization that has a name or character indicating the race, color, religion, sex, national origin, disability, age, or ancestry of its members	Inquiry about every club and organization where membership is held
Military service	Inquiry about service in U.S. armed forces when such service is a qualification for the job; requiring military discharge certificate after hiring	Inquiry about military service in armed service of any country except the United States; requesting military service records; inquiry about type of discharge
Work schedule	Inquiry about willingness or ability to work required work schedule	Inquiry about willingness or ability to work any particular religious holidays
References	General personal and work references that do not reveal the race, color, religion, sex, national origin, disability, age, or ancestry of the applicant	Requesting references specifically from clergy or any other persons who might reflect race, color, religion, sex, national origin, disability, age, or ancestry of applicant

I. Employers acting under bona fide affirmative action programs or acting under orders of equal employment law enforcement agencies of federal, state, or local governments may make some of the prohibited inquiries listed to the extent that these inquiries are required by such programs or orders.

II. Employers having federal defense contracts are exempt to the extent that otherwise prohibited inquiries are required by federal law for security purposes.

III. Although not specifically listed above, any inquiry is prohibited that elicits information as to, or that is not job related and may be used to discriminate on the basis of race, color, religion, sex, national origin, disability, age, or ancestry in violation of the law.

*Unless bona fide occupation qualification is certified in advance by the Ohio Civil Rights Commission.

Used with permission from P. Chelladurai, *Human resource management in sport and recreation* (2nd ed.), Table 10.4. © 2006 by Packianathan Chelladurai. Champaign, IL: Human Kinetics.

sidebar 9.3

RECRUITING AND RETAINING VOLUNTEERS IN SPORT ORGANIZATIONS

According to VolunteeringInAmerica.gov (2012), 64.5 million Americans gave 7.9 billion hours of volunteer service worth $171 billion in 2011. Estimated value per hour of volunteer time was $22.14. It is not clear how much of that total figure can be assigned to volunteering in sport and recreation in America. We have an estimate from Canada showing that nearly 28 percent of all Canadian volunteers work with sport and recreation (True Sport, 2013). If we assume that a similar rate applies to the United States, we can assign nearly 25 percent of the $171 billion of all volunteering to sport and recreation, giving us approximately $43 billion. This impressive sum equals nearly 25 percent of the moderate estimate of the entire sport industry's worth as reported in the Introduction.

Many sport organizations cannot flourish or even survive without volunteer involvement. Volunteer involvement may be at the top levels of administration as in international, national, and regional sport-governing bodies. Volunteers at that level are called *policy volunteers* because they set the policy for their respective organizations. Just as important are the volunteers at the grassroots level who help provide the services of the organization to its clients. These volunteers are the *service volunteers* and can be seen running the youth sports programs all over the country (administering, coaching, and officiating); ushering the spectators in all major sport events, including professional sport events; and running the mega sport events. International mega sport events such as the Olympics and the World Cup cannot be successful without the help of the volunteers. For instance, the success of the 2012 London Olympics was due largely to the contributions of the 70,000 volunteers. The *Independent* (2012) noted that these unpaid heroes contributed eight million hours of voluntary work behind the scenes. According to this report, more than 240,000 people applied to volunteer, of whom 86,000 were interviewed before the final selection. The final set of volunteers were involved in selling 8.8 million tickets and providing services to the 10,490 athletes competing in 26 sports supervised by 5,770 team officials.

The importance of the work volunteers perform in a sport organization should not be minimized because they are not paid. On the contrary, sport managers must be eager and effective in recruiting and retaining volunteers because it is perhaps the most cost-saving effort a manager can undertake. A point to note here is that the processes of recruiting and retaining volunteers are very similar to those used in the case of paid workers. However, because by definition volunteers do not work for pay, pay cannot be used to attract and/or motivate the volunteers. What motivates volunteers to join a specific sport organization includes the goals of an organization, the context (i.e., people and processes) in which they work, and the tasks that they perform. Some of the difficulties in recruiting and retaining volunteers are:

- The skills the volunteer wants to use may not be the same as what the organization needs.
- The level of responsibility that the volunteer wants may not be consistent with what the organization can assign.
- The volunteer may want to work with certain people, but the organization needs the volunteer to work with other people.

Positive negotiations on these issues between management and volunteers should focus on creating as good a fit as possible between the person (i.e., the volunteer) and the job, and between the person and the organization.

Based on their own research and that of others relating to volunteers in different sport settings, Kim and Bang (2012) offer the following guidelines for sport managers:

1. Remember that volunteers form a crucial labor force.
2. Understand motivations of potential volunteer groups.
3. Match the knowledge and skills of volunteers and their job requirements.
4. Provide proper orientation and training.
5. Express personal interest in volunteers and their performance.
6. Constantly express appreciation for volunteer services.
7. Try to satisfy volunteers' motivational needs.
8. Evaluate the performance of volunteers.
9. Try to retain quality volunteers.

computer. In addition, the new employee must learn the rules and regulations regarding the distribution of tickets. That is, a university may specify who is eligible for which type of tickets, the prices of tickets for students, staff, and faculty, and so on. So the student must become familiar with those rules and regulations. These skills are called technical skills, which we discussed in Chapter 4.

Development is more concerned with enhancing the human (interpersonal) and conceptual skills of the new employee. In our context, the new employee may be given opportunities to interact with other employees and supervisors that will help him develop his human skills. The employee may also be exposed to the structure and processes of decision making at higher levels and the environmental conditions that influence such decision making. These exposures may include communication of the organization's goals and future strategies, opportunities for more interesting and challenging jobs, financial assistance, and time off to undergo training elsewhere. These experiences are likely to cultivate the conceptual and human skills of the employee. In addition, the training program should facilitate the assimilation of cultural values and norms of the organization. In essence, employee training and development programs are designed to promote the person–task fit as well as person–organization fit.

Domains of Training

Training programs may encompass one or more of the following domains (Robbins et al., 2006).

Interpersonal skills

A priority domain is interpersonal skills, where the employees learn the skills necessary for effective leadership, communication, conflict resolution, and team building. In addition, the trainees are taught the interpersonal skills in dealing with customers and diversity issues (see Chapter 13).

Technical skills

As noted in Chapter 4, some of the technical skills are specific to a given job and some others are transferable across different jobs. For instance, employees in a fitness club may be assigned to the specialized areas of aerobic training, weight training, and yoga. The skills associated with these specialized classes will be unique. However, the instructors in these areas deal with such common issues as customer relations, information, and computer technology. Accordingly, the training programs should focus on improving both kinds of skills.

Business skills

Employees can also be trained in the areas of finances, marketing, planning, and service quality. These skills are essential to employee productivity and advancement in both for-profit and nonprofit organizations.

Mandatory skills

These skills refer to areas with legal requirements; for example, safety of workers and clients, working conditions, and sexual harassment. Although these legal requirements are imposed by government regulations, they can also be established by organizations such as the International Olympic Committee, the International Basketball Federation (i.e., Fédération Internationale de Basketball, or FIBA), and the International Federation of Association Football (i.e., Fédération Internationale de Football Association, or FIFA). Closer to home, the NCAA has rules governing the activities of university athletic departments, coaches, and athletes. The NCAA also has rules governing the interactions of department employees with outside entities such as the booster clubs and player agents. Employees in university athletic departments should be trained to be familiar with and adhere to these rules.

Performance management

An obvious area for the sport organization is the performance of employees. Thus, it is natural that organizations offer training programs aimed at improving the performance of individual employees.

Personal skills

Training programs can also help employees develop skills that will benefit them personally. The focus here is on helping individual employees plan their careers, manage their time and finances, and improve their health. Note that although these skills are oriented toward the personal welfare of the employees, they have an impact on organizational effectiveness, too. After all, a person can perform better when he or she is healthy (physically and psychologically) than when unhealthy.

Methods of Training

Robbins et al. (2012) classify training methods into traditional and technology-based methods.

Traditional methods

Traditional training methods include on-the-job training in which the employee learns how to perform tasks by doing them with a little introductory help. **Job rotation** is another form of training in which the employee is periodically shifted to another job in the organization. Over time, the employee becomes proficient in many of the jobs within the organization. **Mentoring** and **coaching** constitute another method of training wherein an experienced employee teaches the novice the nuances and workings of the organization as a whole. Sidebar 9.4 explicates this process further. Employees may also be trained through experiential exercises in which they participate in role playing and other forms of face-to-face interactions. Workbooks, manuals, and classroom lectures may also facilitate the learning process.

IN brief

Training is the process of helping new employees learn the technical skills associated with the job, develop the interpersonal skills needed to interact with the customers, and understand the culture of the organization.

Technology-based methods

As an alternative or supplement to classroom training, many organizations use DVDs and web-based tools to educate and train their employees. In addition, organizations may also use videoconferencing or teleconferencing, whereby employees listen to or participate in conferences that take place at remote locations. Finally, employees may be asked to learn through podcasts, videos, and webinars using sites provided by the sport manager.

sidebar 9.4

MENTORING AND EMPLOYEE DEVELOPMENT

Although training is an effective way of teaching technical skills, the process of mentoring may be used to develop the members of an organization for advancement in their careers. Mentoring is defined as "a process in which a more experienced person serves as a role model, and provides guidance and support to a developing novice, and sponsors that novice in his/her career progress" (Weaver & Chelladurai, 1999, p. 1). This general description applies to our parents, our teachers, and our coaches who have helped us in our progress through life. Though their influences are immense, the present discussion will be confined to the mentoring process within organizations.

Kram (1983) noted that mentoring in organizations consists of two major sets of functions—career and psychosocial functions. In the career functions, the mentor first tries to increase the skills and abilities of the junior employee by exposing the protégé to challenging tasks. As the protégé improves his or her skills, the mentor assigns even more challenging tasks. This progressively increasing difficulty of assigned tasks facilitates the protégé becoming as good as can be. As the protégé becomes progressively more efficient and effective, the mentor exposes the protégé to the other senior decision makers in the organization and lets them know how good the protégé is. Such access to senior managers is one pathway to promotions and advancement in the organization.

The second set of functions focuses on building up the protégé's sense of competence, self-esteem, and self-identity. This significant influence ultimately allows the protégé to strive for higher positions and prove that he or she is worthy of such gains. The effort and initiative has to come from the protégé before the mentor can promote the protégé to the others. The personal characteristics of determination and initiative come from one's sense of worth and self-esteem. The mentor cultivates these traits in the protégé by being a good role model. In addition, the mentor accepts the protégé as he or she is and expresses confidence in the protégé's talents and abilities. Equally important is that the mentor shows friendship and counsels the protégé on important aspects of the protégé's career.

Although the protégé is the major beneficiary of the mentoring process, the mentor also gains. The mentor enjoys intrinsic satisfaction for having helped someone by increasing the person's sense of competence and confidence in his or her own abilities. In addition, the mentor enjoys the extrinsic rewards of status and esteem from peers and superiors and the network of protégés who now support her. The organization benefits as well from the mentoring process in terms of identifying and grooming worthy candidates for promotion to higher-level positions and by developing more satisfied and committed protégés. All of this is done at no cost to the organization.

As described above, the mentor is most often an older person with a higher-level position within the organization. But the actual mentoring does not have to be confined to high-level positions. Consider the case of a student. A freshman in your university or college may have learned a lot from the seniors about the ins and outs of university life, including whom to contact for what and what courses and professors are interesting. Those interactions and exchanges are one form of mentoring. In a similar manner, an employee with some experience at lower levels can help a novice learn the ropes. For instance, a five-year employee of a city recreation department can help the new employee learn the structure and processes of the work context, the specific duties associated with the jobs, and the general workings of their department. By the same token, the veteran can provide support by being a role model, accepting the newcomer for who he is, providing counseling, and offering friendship. These are psychosocial functions. Thus, being a mentor is not restricted to senior executives. Even lower-level workers who have gained expertise through experience, and who have the inclination to help novices, can be effective mentors. Being aware of this opportunity, sport managers should encourage such mentoring relationships among workers.

Domains of training and training methods

Exhibit 9.5 shows the domains of training and the methods of training. The domains and methods of training grid can also be applied to university sport management programs. Many courses (e.g., sport marketing, sport finance, sport law, event management, facility management) are, in fact, the domains of training. The methods of training are those followed by sport management faculty. For instance,

exhibit 9.5 Domains and methods of training.

		METHODS					
		On-the-job	Job Rotation	Mentoring	Workbooks/ Manuals	Lectures	Technology-based Methods
DOMAINS	Interpersonal Skills						
	Technical Skills						
	Business Skills						
	Mandatory						
	Personal Skills						

practicum and internship requirements parallel the on-the-job training referred to earlier. Of course, the classroom lectures, either live, online, or a hybrid of the two, are the basic and more common form of training in the university programs. Students have become adept in using the Internet to secure most of the information they need to write their class assignments.

SUMMARY

This chapter presented the purposes of staffing and the steps involved in that process. The steps include assessing the type and number of jobs needed to be filled, analyzing the job, describing the job in terms of requirements and responsibilities, and specifying the attributes required to perform the job well. After these steps have been completed, managers must embark on recruiting a large number of candidates for a position, then identify and hire the best candidate for a job. In addition, the chapter described the training and mentoring of newly hired individuals.

develop YOUR PERSPECTIVE

1. Consider a job you have had as a paid employee, a volunteer, or an intern. Prepare a job description and a job specification for that job.
2. Focusing on the above job, describe the extent to which you felt there was person–job fit. Which of your skills and abilities were suited for that job? What skills did you lack for good performance in the job?

3. As you look toward your future career, describe the organization you would like to work for. What aspects of the organization would be appealing to you? What other features of the organization would be unattractive to you? In other words, what aspects of the organization would create (or detract from) the person–organization fit?
4. Did you experience any mentoring in the workplace? Describe that experience in terms of the persons involved and the work setting in which the mentoring took place.

references

Bateman, T. S., & Snell, S. A. (2007). *Management: Leading & collaborating in a competitive world* (7th ed.). Boston: McGraw-Hill Irwin.

Chang, K., & Chelladurai, P. (2003). Comparison of part-time workers and full-time workers: Commitment and citizenship behaviors in Korean sport organizations. *Journal of Sport Management, 17,* 394–416.

Chatman, J. (1989). Improving interactional organizational research: A model of person organization fit. *Academy of Management Review, 14,* 333–349.

Chelladurai, P. (2006). *Management of human resources in sport and recreation* (2nd ed.). Champaign, IL: Human Kinetics.

Chronicle of Higher Education (2008, July 28). Hey, big spender.

Independent (2012, August 10). London 2012: Olympics success down to 70,000 volunteers. Retrieved from http://www.independent.co.uk/sport/olympics/news/london-2012-olympics-success-down-to-70000-volunteers-8030867.html.

Institute for Volunteering Research (2004). 1997 National Survey of Volunteering in the UK. Retrieved from www.ivr .org.uk/nationalsurvey.htm.

Jessop, A. (2012). Notre Dame recruiting expenses. *Business of College Sports.* Retrieved from http://businessofcollege sports.com/category/recruiting/.

Kim, M., & Bang, H. (2012). Volunteer management in sport. In L. Robinson, P. Chelladurai, G. Bodet., & P. Downward (Eds.), *Routledge handbook of sport management* (pp. 159–177). New York: Routledge.

Kim, M., Chelladurai, P., & Trail, G. T. (2007). A model of volunteer retention in youth sport. *Journal of Sport Management, 21,* 151–171.

Kram, K. E. (1983). Phases of the mentor relationship. *Academy of Management Journal, 26,* 608–625.

Kristof, A. L. (1996). Person–organization fit: An integrated review of its conceptualizations, measurement, and implications. *Personnel Psychology, 49*(1), 1–49.

O'Reilly, C. J., Chatman, J., & Caldwell, D. F. (1991). People and organizational culture: A profile comparison approach to assessing person–organizational fit. *Academy of Management Journal, 34,* 487–516.

Robbins, S. P., Coulter, M., Leach, E., & Kilfoil, M. (2012). *Management* (10th ed.). Don Mills, Ontario: Pearson Canada.

Rokeach, M. (1973). *The nature of human values.* New York: Free Press.

Schneider, B., & Bowen, D. E. (1992). Personnel/human resource management in the service sector. *Research in Personnel and Human Resource Management, 10,* 1–30.

Sullivan, W. (1997). *Entrepreneur Magazine: Human resources for small businesses.* New York: Wiley.

True Sport (2013). What sport can do: The True Sport Report. Retrieved from http://www.truesportpur.ca/en/tools-29-true-sport-report.

VolunteeringInAmerica.gov (2012). Volunteering and civic engagement in the United States. Retrieved from http://www.volunteeringinamerica.gov/national.

Weaver, M. A., & Chelladurai, P. (1999). A mentoring model for management in sport and physical education. *Quest, 51,* 24–38.

CHAPTER 10
MOTIVATIONAL BASIS OF LEADING

manage YOUR LEARNING

After completing this chapter you should be able to:

- Explain the importance of individual motivation in managing sport delivery systems.
- Distinguish between need-based and process-based theories of motivation.
- Explain the hierarchy of needs proposed by Maslow (1943).
- Understand the two-factor theory of Herzberg (1968) and explain the effects of motivators and hygiene factors.
- Explain how individuals' preferences for specific rewards and perceptions of the probability of receiving the rewards result in motivated behavior.
- Describe the concept of inequity of rewards as judged by individuals.
- Explain the concepts of justice and fairness in the workplace.
- Develop a comprehensive framework to incorporate the various perspectives on motivation.

strategic CONCEPTS

abilities and traits	hygiene	motivator
content and context of work	individual motivation	needs
critical incident method	inequity	outcomes
effort–performance relationship	inputs	physiological needs
effort–reward probability	instrumentality	role perception
esteem needs	intrinsic and extrinsic rewards	safety and security needs
expectancy	job enrichment	self-actualization
hierarchy of needs	love needs	valence

LEADING AND MOTIVATING

After defining the goals for the organization and specifying the ways of achieving those goals (planning), then clarifying who should do what (organizing), managers must motivate their subordinates to carry out their assignments so that the goals can be achieved (leading). Whereas the planning and organizing functions require more of the technical and conceptual skills, the leading function is based on the human skills (see Chapter 4). Furthermore, though the planning and organizing functions can be carried out without a great deal of interpersonal interaction with members, the leading function entails considerable face-to-face interactions—either collectively or individually. Effective managers need a clear understanding of how individuals are motivated and what factors influence motivation. Even though insights into member motivation are gained through personal experience, it is useful to consider the theories of motivation applied to an organizational context. This chapter presents some of the more relevant theories of work motivation.

Because human behavior is highly variable and individual differences in terms of needs and personality are numerous, none of the theories discussed in this chapter can be applied in all circumstances. However, understanding these theories does provide the manager with a gestalt view of the intricacies and complexities of human motivation, as well as insight into the appropriateness of the theories to specific situations. Moreover, although the various theories have a more direct bearing on the leading function, their relevance to the planning, organizing, and evaluating functions is also important.

MOTIVATION DEFINED

What is motivation in the context of leading? According to Greenberg (2005), motivation is "the process of arousing, directing, and maintaining behavior toward a goal" (p. 188). For Luthans (2011), motivation is "a process that starts with physiological or psychological deficiency or need that activates a behavior or a drive that is aimed at a goal or incentive" (p. 157). In Hitt, Black, and Porter's (2009) view, "motivation can be thought of as the set of forces that energise, direct and sustain behavior. These forces can come from the person, the so-called 'push' of internal forces, or they can come from the environment that surrounds the person, the so-called 'pull' of external forces" (p. 277).

These definitions point to five critical elements of **individual motivation**: (1) *forces* within the individual, (2) the *energy* for actions/behaviors, (3) *direction* of such behaviors, (4) *intensity* of those behaviors, and (5) *persistence* of the behaviors. The forces refer to the needs, drives, and motives to be satisfied. The energy is the activation of the individual to pursue satisfaction, whereas direction implies the specific goals an individual is seeking. Intensity refers to the magnitude of determination to achieve the goal, and persistence refers to an individual's continued effort to achieve the goal.

IN brief

Motivation is reflected in the level and direction of the effort an individual expends and the extent to which he or she persists with that effort.

As with many concepts in organizational psychology, several theories of motivation are useful in the workplace. These theories generally fall into two broad classes—content theories and process theories (see Exhibit 10.1). Some theories focus on the **needs** within individuals that provide the motivational energy. When needs are unsatisfied, the individual experiences a tension and is motivated to engage in some activity to satisfy them. That is, these theories address the issue of what motivates individuals. Thus, they are called *content* theories. In the following sections, we will explore the following content-based theories: Maslow's (1943) need hierarchy theory and Herzberg's (1968) motivation–hygiene theory.

Although the issue of what motivates an individual is critical, it is also important to understand *how* and *why* individuals choose one form of behavior over another in their efforts to satisfy their needs or desires. The process that individuals go through in selecting one course of action over another is the focus of the second set of theories of motivation. Accordingly, they are called *process* theories of motivation. The process theories considered in this text are Vroom's (1964) expectancy theory, Adams's (1963) inequity theory, and justice and fairness theories. The final theory discussed in the text is Porter and Lawler's (1968) model of motivation, a framework that integrates both the need-based and process theories.

exhibit 10.1 Classes of motivational theories.

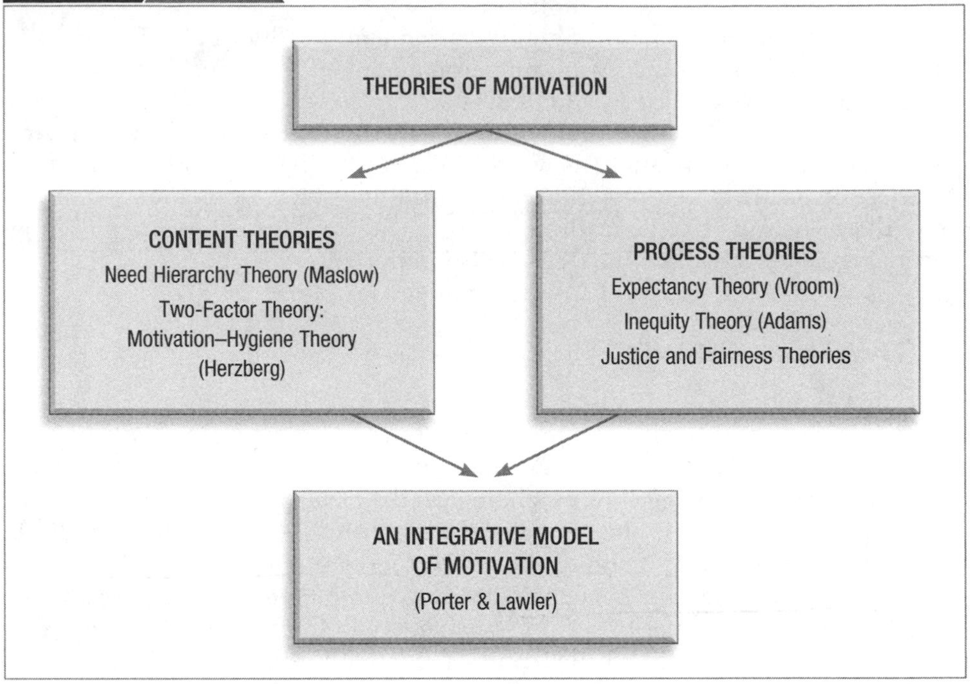

NEED-BASED (OR CONTENT) THEORIES

The general paradigm for motivational theories based on needs is that when an individual is deprived of a need, he or she is driven to satisfy that need. The need-based theories are also called content theories because they indicate what (content) motivates individuals to engage in specific behaviors.

We can assume that needs underlie every action; however, there is some question about which of the numerous needs is most important in the determination of behavior. Does one need take precedence over another when two needs are withheld? Does one class of needs predominate in influencing behavior? These are the types of questions addressed by the various content theories of motivation.

sidebar 10.1

MOTIVATION, BEHAVIORS, AND PERFORMANCE

Commenting on the relationships among motivation, behavior, and performance, Kanfer (1992) noted that "the constructs of motivation subsume the determinants and processes underlying the development of intentions, choice behaviors, and volitional activities. The products of these motivational processes are the individual's overt and/or covert behaviors. In contrast, performance in organizational psychology typically refers to an evaluation of the individual's behaviors. For example, a salesperson motivated to perform his or her job well may make many customer contacts and still perform poorly according to a criterion based only on sales volume. Performance theory differs from motivation theory in that prediction of performance requires consideration of additional factors, including individual differences in variables such as abilities and task comprehension, and environmental factors such as situational constraints and task demands" (p. 80).

The Need Hierarchy Theory

The essence of Maslow's (1943) need hierarchy theory lies in its specification of five classes of needs that are ordered in a hierarchy of prepotency (i.e., power or force). After stating that only unsatisfied needs are the basis of behavior and that satisfied needs lose their potency to instigate behavior, Maslow argued that people focus on meeting their basic needs and then move up the scale of the **hierarchy of needs** when the lower-order (prepotent) needs are satisfied. Maslow proposed five categories of needs in order of importance to the individual: physiological, safety and security, love and belonging, esteem, and self-actualization.

- **Physiological needs** relate to the more fundamental and biological requirements of a human being, such as food and shelter and the need to avoid pain. From an organizational perspective, then, the employee must be provided with sufficient financial rewards (such as salary and bonus) to ensure that the physiological needs are satisfied.
- **Safety and security needs** refer to an individual's preference for "a safe, orderly, predictable, organized world, which he can count on, and in which unexpected, unmanageable or other dangerous things do not happen" (Maslow, 1943, p. 378). In an organizational context, job security, health coverage, and retirement schemes are related to security needs, while safe working conditions, precautions against accidents, and other such organizational efforts are aimed at satisfying the safety needs of employees.
- **Love needs** represent the desires of people for friendship and warm interpersonal interaction with others—to be associated with and accepted by others. The satisfaction of the social needs in an organization depends on the employee's coworkers, work groups, and supervisors, and the intensity of their social needs.
- **Esteem needs** are considered to be higher-order needs that relate to a person's desire to be recognized by others and to have status among them. According to Maslow, the esteem needs include a desire for strength, achievement, adequacy, confidence (self-esteem), recognition, and respect (esteem) from others. The title and status accorded to individuals in an organization, and the respect with which they are treated by peers, are the kinds of factors that cater to esteem needs.
- **Self-actualization** lies at the highest level in Maslow's hierarchy. Individuals operating at this level endeavor to be what they can be. According to Maslow, people who have satisfied their self-actualization need will provide the fullest and healthiest creativity. He also acknowledged that such people are the exceptions rather than the rule—that is, most people do not progress up the ladder to the level of self-actualization.

sidebar 10.2

NEEDS

"Needs and the drive to fulfill them are two of the cornerstones of motivation. Although some common needs can be identified, the intensity of these needs, their priority, and therefore the impact they have on behavior can be different between people of different cultures and even between individuals within a culture. Understanding your own needs can be an important step in selecting appropriate jobs or careers; understanding the needs of others can be critical in your attempts to motivate and influence them" (Steers & Black, 1994, p. 156).

The need for self-actualization is not as clear as the other needs for two reasons. First, individuals reach that stage, if at all, very late in their life. Second, individuals at that stage transcend the realities of organizational life and are likely to be impervious to managerial actions. However, the idea of a self-actualizing person is attractive in itself. Advertisers sometimes exploit this idea in creating slogans for their clients; for example, the classic U.S. Army recruiting slogan, "Be all you can be," connotes self-actualization.

One important component of Maslow's theory is often overlooked. Conventionally, the deprivation of a need is seen as the driving force, and scant attention is given to the effects of gratification of that need. In Maslow's theory, gratification of a need is as important as deprivation, because gratification releases the organism from one set of needs and activates another set. The process of the deprivation of a need dominating the individual and its gratification activating the next higher-level need is illustrated in Exhibit 10.2.

IN brief

In Maslow's view, human needs can be hierarchically organized into physiological, safety and security, love, esteem, and self-actualization needs. The hierarchy is based on their relative prepotency (or power) to motivate the individual.

The notion of the hierarchy of the prepotency of needs is illustrated in the following example. A recent sport management graduate is offered a position in a distant location. In order of priority (prepotency), the graduate will be concerned with (a) salary and availability of housing (physiological needs); (b) job security and safety of the prospective residential area and the working conditions, including equipment (safety and security needs); and (c) type of coworkers and neighbors, including their personalities and their interpersonal orientation (social needs). After visits and interviews, the graduate might be reasonably confident that these needs will be satisfied, and consequently, she will accept the job and work hard at it. After a time, her superiors might recognize her effective performance and reward her with a promotion and an increase in salary (esteem needs). The graduate will be highly satisfied and will continue to work diligently and obtain the rewards and recognition associated with good performance. After a number of years, however, a sense of restlessness might develop. The graduate might feel that she requires a different and more challenging task, one involving innovation and creativity (self-actualizing needs). Therefore, she might leave the job and seek a different position. She might undertake further education in the same or some other field to be qualified for a more challenging job. It is also possible that she may start her own business in fitness, sponsorship, player agency, or consulting in marketing.

IN brief

Individual differences in personality and experience might affect the hierarchy. Some people may be fixated at one level, whereas others may renounce a higher level of needs. It is also not necessary for one level of needs to be completely satisfied before the next level is activated.

Self-esteem and self-actualization are commonly designated as *higher-order needs* or *growth needs*, and physiological, safety/security, and love needs as *lower-order needs* or *deficiency needs* (see Steers & Black, 1994).

Maslow viewed the classification of the needs as general in nature. However, he was the first to acknowledge that individual differences in personality and experience might make the hierarchy of needs irrelevant in some cases. For instance, individuals who have been deprived of a lower-order need for any length of time might either "fixate" at that level even after gratification of that need, or they might "renounce" that need and focus on a higher need. It is also possible that for some individuals, self-esteem might become prepotent even before the satisfaction of the love and social needs. In innately creative people, creativity could supersede all other needs, whereas in some others, "the level of aspiration may be permanently deadened or lowered. That is to say, the less prepotent goals may be lost, and may disappear forever, so that the person who has experienced life at a very low level, i.e., chronic unemployment, may continue to be satisfied for the rest of his life if only he can get enough food" (Maslow, 1943, p. 386).

exhibit 10.2 Maslow's need hierarchy theory applied to a sport management graduate's future employment.

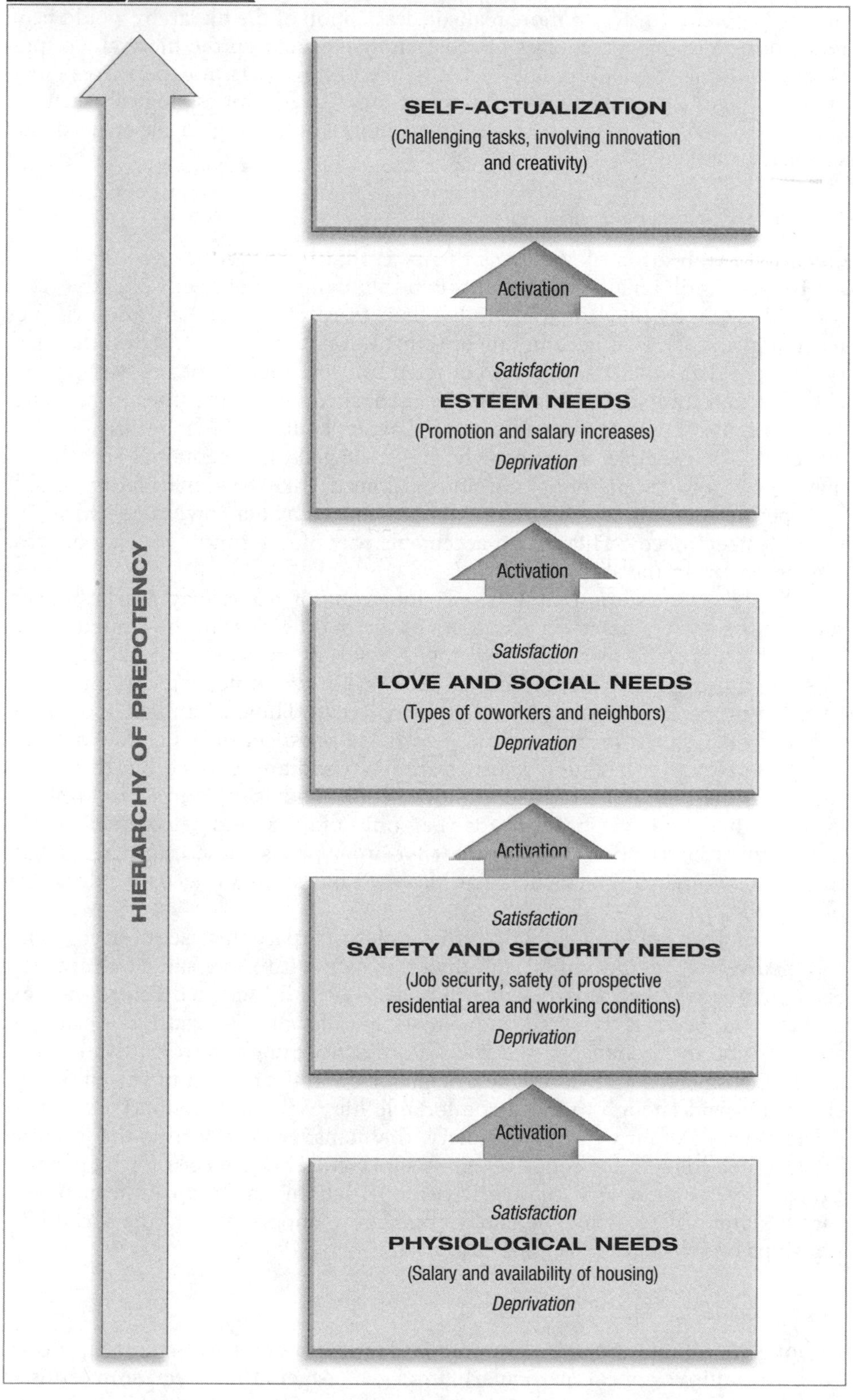

Maslow also emphasized that the notion of a hierarchy of needs does not imply that one set of needs has to be fulfilled completely before another set becomes potent. In fact, "a more realistic description of the hierarchy would be in terms of decreasing percentages of satisfaction as we go up the hierarchy of prepotency" (Maslow, 1943, p. 388). That is, the average person experiences greater percentages of satisfaction of the lower-order needs (physiological, security, and love needs) while much smaller percentages of the higher-order needs are satisfied.

Limitations of need hierarchy theory

One major limitation of Maslow's theory is that it cannot be adequately tested. Because individuals progress through the hierarchy of needs one at a time, it could take a lifetime for some individuals to reach self-actualization (if they reach it at all). Thus, it becomes inconvenient, if not impossible, to test the theory, because data would have to be collected over the lifetime of subjects.

A second limitation of the theory is associated with difficulties in measurement. It is also possible that one set of behaviors could satisfy more than one set of needs. For example, a person who has managed an exceptional sport event may receive a financial bonus (physiological need), may be seen as indispensable by superiors (security need), and may be recognized by her coworkers and supervisors (esteem need). There is no acceptable way of determining which of these was prepotent in the above case.

Another criticism is that Maslow's hierarchy of needs may not be universal. The theory was based on the values of the middle class in the United States. Thus, the hierarchy of needs may not be relevant in other cultural contexts. In some cultures such as the Indian culture, for example, esteem needs may be more prepotent than safety and security needs. Thus, an Indian sport journalist is likely to be more concerned with the prospect of his or her writings being in print and that such writings are liked and appreciated by the readers than with the salary for, and security of, the job. This is in contrast to Maslow's position that the lower-order needs (i.e., physiological and safety and security needs) must be satisfied before the higher-order needs come into play. In fact, there is no convincing evidence that Maslow's hierarchy of needs is relevant in other cultures.

Yet another criticism is that the thresholds of a particular set of needs being satisfied vary from individual to individual even within the same culture. The issue here is whether a particular need has to be fully satisfied before the next higher set of needs is triggered. Individuals do differ in this regard. For example, a facility and event manager in a Division III school might have cultivated good social relationships with colleagues, neighbors, and the community even though she is not paid enough to live a comfortable life. When a Division II university offers her a position with higher salary, the manager may decline the job offer because her concern for social relations supersedes her concern for higher pay. Conversely, a colleague at another Division III school may jump at the chance to earn a higher salary, which he may view as more important than the social relationships established in his current job.

Implications for sport managers

Although Maslow's theory is not readily subject to empirical research, it does have an intuitive appeal, particularly from a managerial perspective in terms of the emphasis placed on needs. The theory's simple and useful classes of a wide range of needs provide a basis for instituting reward systems and for judging their effectiveness. For example, a sport organization aims its salary increases at satisfying physiological needs. When a sport organization provides for medical or life insurance or pays into the employees' pension fund, it is catering to its employees' safety and security needs. The picnics and celebrations organized by a sport organization address the love and social needs of its employees. The titles bestowed on employees (Assistant to the Associate Athletic Director, Coordinator of Aerobics, Manager of Facilities) and the privileges offered to specific employees (larger offices, offices with windows or carpeting, keys to the executive washroom) satisfy some of the esteem needs. The attraction the theory holds for managers is that, to a large extent, they are in control of the monetary and material resources that they can manipulate to satisfy all of the classes of needs in the hierarchy except the self-actualization need.

The Two-Factor Theory: Motivation–Hygiene Theory

Whereas Maslow felt that even the lower-order needs could serve as motivators when they were deprived, Herzberg and associates (Herzberg, 1968; Herzberg, Mausner, & Snyderman, 1959) contended that the two sets of needs (higher-order and lower-order needs) are associated with satisfaction and dissatisfaction differentially. In contrast to the common view that satisfaction and dissatisfaction are two extremes on one continuum, Herzberg considered them to be on two separate continua. Herzberg (1968) explained:

> The factors involved in producing job satisfaction (and motivation) are separate and distinct from the factors that lead to job dissatisfaction. Since separate factors need to be considered, depending on whether job satisfaction or job dissatisfaction is being examined, it follows that these two feelings are not opposites of each other. The opposite of job satisfaction is not job dissatisfaction, rather *no* job satisfaction; and, similarly, the opposite of job dissatisfaction is not job satisfaction, but *no* job dissatisfaction. (p. 56)

The fundamental postulate of the theory is that only higher-order needs affect satisfaction, and the lower-order needs are associated with dissatisfaction. As a consequence, Herzberg's theory is called a two-factor (or dual factor) theory. To understand the theory better, it is useful to examine how it evolved.

In their analysis of previous research results, Herzberg and his colleagues found no consistent results relating needs to motivation. The authors felt that the available research supported the conclusion that different classes of needs are differentially associated with satisfaction or motivation. To test this proposition, they interviewed and administered a semi-structured questionnaire to approximately 200 engineers and accountants. The questionnaire required the respondents to think back to one incident in their work that made them feel extremely happy and satisfied, and to another incident that left them feeling extremely unhappy and dissatisfied. The subjects indicated what effects these feelings of happiness and unhappiness had had on their subsequent work, and how long these feelings lasted. The authors then analyzed the content of the responses and identified 16 factors as the causes of satisfaction or dissatisfaction. The data analysis showed that one set of factors, called the satisfiers or **motiva-**

IN brief

One set of job factors, called motivators, relate to the content of the job, whereas the second set, called hygienes, relate to the context of the job. Motivators influence satisfaction, whereas hygienes influence dissatisfaction.

tors, showed up more often in reference to satisfaction than to dissatisfaction. Another set, called the dissatisfiers or **hygienes**, showed up more often in incidents of dissatisfaction than of satisfaction. As mentioned previously, all of the satisfiers or motivators were related to higher-order needs, and the dissatisfiers were associated with lower-order needs. Exhibit 10.3 presents the composite of the results of this and 12 subsequent research studies.

The most important product of Herzberg's work was the finding that the motivators (or growth factors) were all related to the **content** of the work itself, while the hygiene factors were all related to the **context** in which the work was carried out. The content factors are achievement, recognition for achievement, the work itself, responsibility, and growth or advancement. The contextual factors are company policy and administration, supervision, interpersonal relationships, working conditions, salary, status, and security.

On the basis of his research findings, Herzberg concluded that management must be concerned with eliminating dissatisfaction by improving the hygiene factors. He also pointed out that these hygiene factors alone do not result in motivated or satisfied workers. Management must also change jobs in order to provide for the psychological growth of employees.

exhibit 10.3 Herzberg's motivation–hygiene theory.

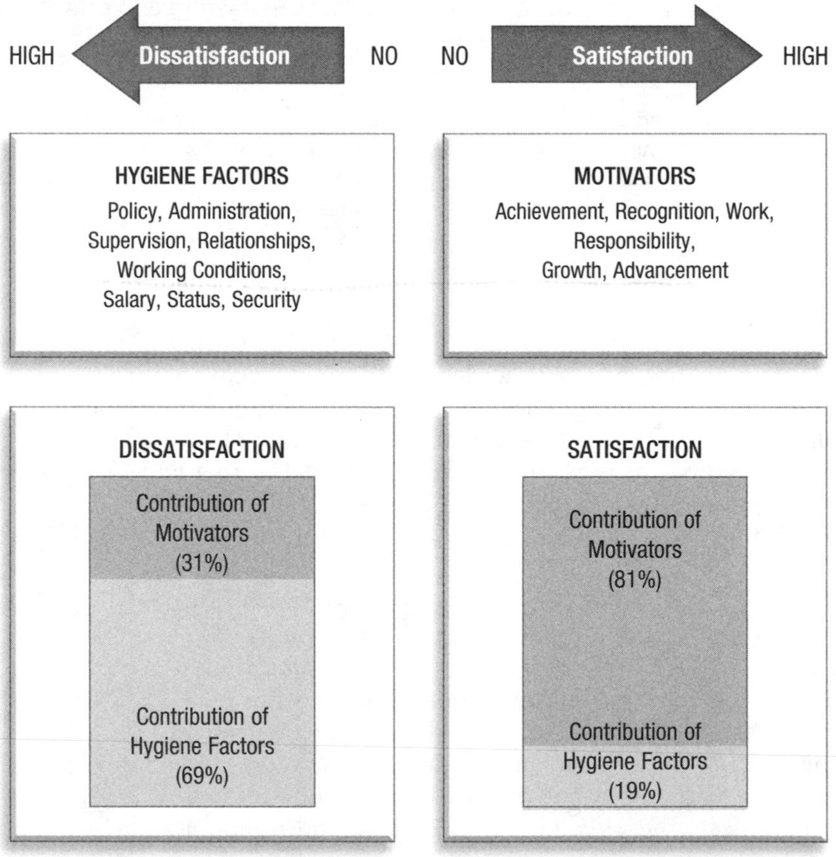

Source: Adapted and reprinted by permission of *Harvard Business Review*. From "One more time: How do you motivate people?" by F. Herzberg, Jan.–Feb., 1968.

Implications for sport managers

The two-factor theory has relevance for sport management contexts also. For instance, a manager of a commercial golf course needs to ensure that her employees are well paid in relation to the labor market. In addition, the manager should make the working conditions (lighting, ventilation, office furniture, and so on) adequate. Equally important, the manager's supervision of the employees should be fair, and the interactions among the employees need to be warm and pleasant. Deficiencies in one or more of these hygiene factors will cause dissatisfaction among the employees. Cumulatively, these deficiencies can cause great dissatisfaction and lowered morale. Therefore, the manager should make every effort to ensure these hygiene factors are maintained at acceptable levels. However, when the manager succeeds in ensuring adequate levels of these factors, only the dissatisfaction among employees disappears—greater motivation and higher performance do not miraculously result. According to Herzberg's two-factor theory, only the job and its content can provide the motivational force. That is, only when the job offers responsibility, a sense of achievement, and opportunities for growth and advancement will the employees be motivated. Accordingly, the manager should progressively increase the challenge and responsibility for the employees in their respective jobs.

The process of job enrichment is the practical application of Herzberg's theory. **Job enrichment**, or vertical job loading, involves redesigning jobs to satisfy higher-order needs. Some of the ways in which this can be accomplished are to assign whole units of work to employees (rather than having different employees responsible for different segments), to remove or reduce control and supervision, to grant additional authority, and to increase the difficulty of the tasks assigned (Herzberg, 1968). In the case of a golf club, the manager could assign more responsibilities to the front desk attendant (such as supervision of the locker rooms) and let him make decisions on how and when things will be done. The manager could also assign more challenging tasks, such as involving the front desk attendant in a promotional campaign. Such increases in the job content will increase his motivation, resulting in personal growth (a benefit to the employee) and higher performance (a benefit to the organization).

Limitations of two-factor theory

The two-factor theory is, perhaps, the most controversial theory of work motivation. Two serious criticisms detract from the usefulness of this theory. First, although two distinct sets of factors are assumed to influence satisfaction and dissatisfaction, Herzberg's data do not completely support this assumption. In some individuals, many of the same conditions contribute to both satisfaction and dissatisfaction. For example, although it has been suggested that hygiene factors alone influence job dissatisfaction, in Herzberg's research, 31 percent of all the factors contributing to job dissatisfaction were motivators (see Exhibit 10.3). Similarly, although it was suggested that the motivators alone influence job satisfaction, 19 percent of all the factors contributing to job satisfaction were found to be hygiene factors. In short, individual differences impact the manner and extent to which hygiene and motivator factors affect different people. However, Herzberg's emphasis on the generality of the impact of each factor overlooked or minimized such individual differences.

In our example of the golf club, one of the front desk attendants may be attracted to and motivated by the enriched job. Thus, her experience would fall under the 81 percent of motivators on the right side of Exhibit 10.3. In contrast, another front desk attendant may be more interested in and motivated by an increase in salary and less appreciative of the enriched job. In fact, the second attendant could be dissatisfied with the enriched job because it is beyond his abilities. Thus, he would fall under both the 19 percent of hygiene factors on the right-hand side and the 31 percent of the motivators on the left side of Exhibit 10.3. The implication for the manager is that while the theory offers some guidelines on enriching the jobs she supervises, the use of those guidelines should be consistent with individual differences and preferences. Accordingly, the golf club manager would attempt to enrich the job for the first front desk attendant and refrain from doing so in the case of the second.

The second criticism relates to the methodology used by Herzberg and his associates. The respondents were asked to recall incidents in which they felt satisfied or dissatisfied—an approach known as the **critical incident method.** However, when individuals are asked to recall incidents and express their reactions to them, they tend to attribute all the positive or happy events to their own efforts and achievements. Conversely, all negative outcomes are assigned to some external agent like company policy, supervision, and so on. This is a defense mechanism individuals use to protect their image and self-esteem. As Vroom (1964) stated, "Persons may be more likely to attribute the causes of satisfaction to their own achievements and accomplishments on the job. On the other hand, they may be more likely to attribute their dissatisfaction not to personal inadequacies or deficiencies, but to factors in the work environment, i.e., obstacles presented by company policies or supervision" (p. 129).

Studies that attempted to use other methods found that Herzberg's theory was not supported by the results (see Dunnette, Campbell, & Hakel, 1967; Hulin & Smith, 1967). Consequently, it has been suggested that the two-factor theory is limited by the method used to develop it. It must however be noted that although his motivation–hygiene theory was much criticized when it was advanced more than 50 years ago, its predictions and thus its utility have been supported in more recent times (e.g., Bassett-Jones & Lloyd, 2005).

The motivators in the two-factor theory are similar to Maslow's higher-order needs. However, this is where the similarity ends. As we noted previously, although Maslow contended that even lower-order needs can motivate workers, Herzberg stated that only factors intrinsic to the job can serve as motivators.

Implication of Need-Based Theories for Sport Managers

Despite the differences, the need-based theories have one general implication for management—that management should be concerned with making work meaningful for the workers. This viewpoint contrasts with the classical and bureaucratic approaches, which emphasized the fractionation of work (resulting in narrow routine and monotonous jobs) to ensure efficiency and productivity (see Chapter 7 for a discussion of classical principles). Also, earlier approaches that emphasized uniformity and consistency of operations tended to impose restrictive rules and procedures that governed the activities of the workers. These two aspects of the classical approach to management are not conducive to the pursuit or fulfillment of higher-order needs. Thus, the need-based theories of motivation discussed above—particularly the job enrichment recommended by Herzberg—are in sharp contrast to the classical approach to job design.

The upshot of the need theories for sport managers is that they must balance the concern for efficiency on one hand with providing growth opportunities for employees on the other. The efficiency concern can lead to simplifying jobs and making them routine, whereas concern for employee growth and motivation can lead to job enrichment. These are the golf club manager's choices when she decides whether to keep the job of the front desk attendant simple as it is now or improve it by adding more responsibility and autonomy.

The difficulty in designing jobs to meet the needs of individuals while maintaining efficiency is real. The happy fact is, however, that not all individuals are motivated by higher-order needs and higher skills. Those who do not seek fulfillment of higher-order needs and those who do not have the skills necessary for enriched jobs can be assigned relatively more simple and routine tasks. Accordingly, the manager of the golf club in the previous example may assign the simpler task of front desk attendant to an employee who prefers to be involved in such simple tasks. By the same token, she may assign the relatively more enriched jobs to those who seek such jobs and have the ability to do them well. In fact, this rationale should be the basis of promotions and job upgrades.

PROCESS THEORIES

As noted earlier, the content theories are concerned with the factors that motivate the worker—personal factors like individual needs and organizational factors like task assignment and rewards. However, they do not explain how individuals choose one behavior from the several available to them. The process theories of motivation deal with the individual's evaluation and choice of certain courses of action, and how other factors influence the results of such courses of action. The following sections describe three process models of motivation—Vroom's expectancy theory, Adams' theory of inequity, and organizational justice theory. The final section presents Porter and Lawler's model of motivation, which integrates the main thrusts of the three prior theories. These models are considered to be most relevant to organizations.

Vroom's Expectancy Theory

The main postulate of expectancy theory is that individuals evaluate the various courses of action that are available to them and choose the one that they expect to lead to the outcomes they prefer. Vroom's expectancy theory incorporates four major variables (or concepts)—valence, outcomes (or results), expectancy, and instrumentality.

Valence

An individual's preferences for particular outcomes is referred to as **valence.** If a particular result is very strongly preferred (for example, a trade from one team to another in professional baseball), then the valence for the result will approach the value of +1. If, on the other hand, an outcome is strongly detested (as in, say, a transfer to a distant locality), then the valence will approach –1. According to the theory, the actual valence for the trade is based on the relative weighting of the positive and negative aspects of that result. Thus, if a trade is a valued outcome, but it entails a transfer to another place that is negatively valued, the degree to which the trade is preferred is indicated by the average value of the two outcomes (the trade and the transfer). When an individual is indifferent to a particular outcome, the valence is considered to be zero. Other terms that can be used to refer to the concept of valence are *incentives, rewards,* and *utility*.

Outcomes

Outcomes or results refer to the consequences of a given act. For instance, an employee's promotion is an outcome. But this promotion is only a consequence of the employee's having achieved certain performance standards set by the organization. Thus, there are two sets of outcomes or results that stem from the efforts of the employee. Vroom calls these the first-level and second-level outcomes. The first-level outcome refers to the performance standards achieved by the employee; the second-level outcome refers to the rewards for that performance. Note that the first-level outcome is what the organization expects (productivity), whereas the second-level outcomes are what the employee desires (promotion, a pay increase).

Expectancy

Expectancy is the probability estimate that effort will lead to the first-level outcome or result—the performance standards set by the organization. If, in the above example, the employee believed that his efforts would result in superior performance, then the expectancy would approach the value of +1. If, however, the employee felt that his capacities were not sufficient to reach that level of performance, then the expectancy would approach the value of zero. Note that expectancy refers to the individual's *perception* of the probability that effort will lead to a standard of performance.

Instrumentality

The individual's estimate of the relationship between first-level results and second-level results is called **instrumentality**. If the employee in the above example believed that performing at a high level would automatically result in promotion, then instrumentality would approach the value of +1. If, however, he believed that promotion was based only on seniority and not on performance, then instrumentality would drop to zero. In contrast to expectancy (perceived probability), instrumentality reflects the individual's perception that there is a strong relationship between first-level and second-level outcomes. Expectancy connects individual effort to first-level outcomes, whereas instrumentality links the first- and second-level results. A coach might have a strong belief that if she recruits heavily her team will be successful (expectancy). She might also hold the strong belief that if her team is successful, she will receive a pay increase (instrumentality).

Interplay of concepts

The relationships among the preceding variables or concepts are illustrated in Exhibit 10.4. Vroom's expectancy theory assumes that the force (equated here with motivation) with which an individual engages in an activity depends on the valence or attraction for the outcomes (rewards or incentives the organization has to offer), the expectancy that the effort will result in a certain level of performance, and the instrumentality of performance in the attainment of those rewards.

exhibit 10.4 Vroom's expectancy model of motivation.

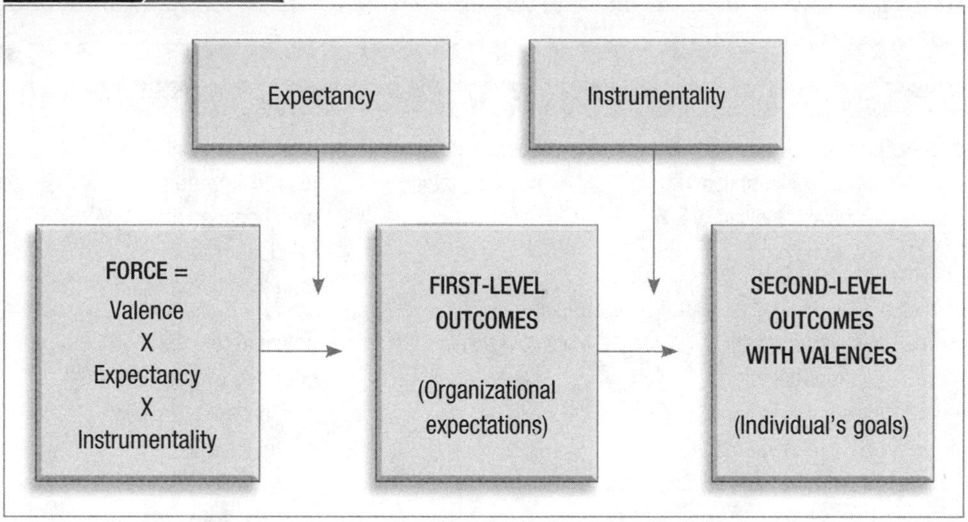

This interplay among the factors of Vroom's theory can be expressed as follows:

Force = Valence x Expectancy x Instrumentality

In this equation, the values for all of the variables on the right-hand side must be positive (and not equal to zero) if the force is to be positive (that is, if the individual is to be motivated). In simpler terms, if an individual dislikes an outcome (the promotion), the valence will be negative and there will be no motivation toward that outcome. If anything, behavior aimed at *avoiding* that outcome will be motivated. Similarly, both expectancy and instrumentality must be greater than zero. That is, the individual must believe that effort will ultimately result in the preferred rewards.

Consider a student contemplating a future career (see Exhibit 10.5). The career could be in any of several professional areas such as engineering, law, medicine, education, or sport management. The student is likely to choose one of these areas based on the rewards and satisfactions (the positive outcomes in Vroom's model) that each professional area is expected to offer. A career in medicine is likely to yield more income and a higher social status. On the other hand, a career in sport management is likely to offer the satisfaction of being involved with youth and excellence in sport, whereas medicine often deals with disease and decay. A student is likely to evaluate both the positive outcomes (higher salary and status in medicine, and exposure to youth and excellence in sport management) and negative outcomes (exposure to disease and decay in medicine, and, perhaps, lower status or salary in sport management). Based on these evaluations, the student finds one career choice more attractive than another (one career has greater valence than another). Thus, the student is motivated toward that career.

However, the student must also evaluate the likelihood of achieving that career. For instance, he may believe that he does not have the orientation and potential to succeed in a professional career. If so, he is likely to shun that career even though it is attractive from several other perspectives. This assessment corresponds to the expectancy estimates in Vroom's model.

A final evaluation the student may make is the extent to which her performance in professional preparation will actually lead to getting a good job in that

exhibit 10.5 Vroom's expectancy model applied to career choice.

	FORCE	= VALENCE *(expected outcome)*	X EXPECTANCY	X INSTRUMENTALITY
Medicine:		+ higher income + higher social status – exposure to disease and decay	– doing well in courses, taking exams	– limited potential for jobs in immediate area because more medical graduates than jobs in the area
Sport Management:		+ involvement with youth/athletes + excellence in sport – possible lower status/salary	+ doing well in courses, taking exams	+ potential for jobs high because of number of sport organizations in the area

career. For instance, a student may like the prospects of working with youth and excellence in intercollegiate athletics or professional sports (high valence) and may be convinced that she can do very well in preparing for a career in those areas (high expectancy). However, she may believe that getting a good job in one of those areas will be difficult owing to the limited number of jobs or discriminatory practices in hiring (low instrumentality). In such a case, the student may not choose to enter that career. This process of computing or estimating valence, expectancy, and instrumentality is the essential thrust of Vroom's expectancy model of motivation.

IN brief

The three significant concepts in Vroom's model are (1) valence (one's preferences for specific outcomes), (2) expectancy (one's estimate that effort will lead to achievement of organizational expectations), and (3) instrumentality (one's estimate that performance of what the organization expects will lead to personal rewards). The interplay of these three elements determines motivation.

We used the example of a student's choice of a career because many readers of this text are likely to be in the process of making such choices. However, the model is relevant to any job context in any sport organization. For instance, the degree of effort an employee puts into a job could be based on such calculations. In the discussion of bureaucracy (see Chapter 7), we saw that the extensive rules and regulations of a bureaucracy may actually set the minimum standards for performance. Furthermore, bureaucracies also tend to promote employees based on seniority rather than performance. If these are the convictions of an employee in a bureaucracy, that person is not motivated to put in extra effort. On the other hand, an employee in a private profit-oriented sport enterprise may perceive the organization as rewarding employees only on performance and firing those who do not perform adequately. With such perceptions, the employee is likely to put a lot of effort into his job.

Implications for sport managers

The practical implication of Vroom's model is that a sport organization and its managers can intervene in the process of individual motivation. For instance, an individual may believe that she does not have the ability to carry out a particular task or project (say, a promotional campaign for a fitness club), and, therefore, she may not be willing to take on the task or project (that is, she may have low expectancy). On the other hand, the manager knows the requirements of the task better and also knows that the employee can perform well in it. The manager's duty is to convince the employee of this fact, provide background or training the employee may feel she is lacking, and motivate the employee to undertake the job. That is, the manager needs to help the employee revise her expectancy estimate.

Similarly, the employee may not be convinced that successful performance in the task is likely to lead to any additional rewards. Once again, the manager can clarify the relationship between level of performance in the project and the associated rewards and outcomes. Thus, the manager corrects the employee's misperceptions of instrumentality. From this perspective, Vroom's model is very useful in managing employees' motivational processes. In fact, a very popular theory of leadership—the path–goal theory of leadership—is based on the concepts of Vroom's model. That theory will be explained in the next chapter.

In overview, Vroom's model outlines relevant variables associated with motivated behavior and their interrelationships. More importantly, through the introduction of concepts such as valence, expectancy, and instrumentality, Vroom's model helps to account for individual differences in motivated behavior. However, an assumption implicit in the model is that individuals always behave in a rational manner. This is simply not the case. As was already noted in Chapter 6, individuals often do not have the capacity or time to go through all the complicated calculations.

Adams' Theory of Inequity

Although the content theories of Maslow and Herzberg emphasize the concept of satisfaction, they are simplistic in their assumption that when a need is fulfilled, satisfaction automatically follows. From an organizational perspective, this is not necessarily true. For instance, when an individual gets a raise in pay, does it automatically lead to satisfaction? Or does the person compare the raise to some standard and then experience satisfaction or dissatisfaction? For instance, a raise of $1,000 in salary may not provide happiness for an assistant director of marketing in a professional sport franchise if he is aware that the other assistant director received $1,100. The important point in this example is that the absolute amount does not have a bearing on the estimation of inequity; it is the relative amount that is critical.

Input/outcome balance

According to Adams (1963, 1977) the individual's internalized standard could be simply a comparison between personal effort (**inputs**) and the rewards of that effort (outcomes). For example, if someone makes great sacrifices in an effort to lose weight but loses only two pounds in six months, he may have a feeling of inequity. The assistant director of marketing in the preceding example may be dissatisfied because his salary increase is not commensurate with all the time and effort he has put into the job. A feeling of inequity results from a simple comparison of personal cost versus personal benefit. In an organizational context, however, the cost–benefit comparison extends to referent others in the organization. That is, the assistant director compares the personal cost–benefit ratio to the cost–benefit ratio of others in the work group, as indicated below:

Personal Benefits (Outcomes)	Other's Benefits (Outcomes)
$1,000	$1,100
Compared to	
Personal Costs (Inputs)	**Other's Costs (Inputs)**
45-hour work week	40-hour work week
Extensive travel/time away from family	Minimal local travel

Adams' theory is anchored on this comparison to a referent other(s). As he noted: "Inequity exists for *Person* [italics added] whenever he perceives that the ratio of his outcomes to inputs and the ratio of *Other's* [italics added] outcomes to Other's inputs are unequal" (Adams, 1977, p. 113). The *other* in Adams' theory could be a subordinate, a supervisor, a coworker, or an employee in another comparable organization or occupation. It is also possible for an individual to compare the input/outcome balance of a current situation to that experienced in a previous one.

IN brief

According to Adams (1977), individuals tend to compare their outcomes and their inputs to the outcomes and inputs of comparable others. If the comparison is equal, there is equity. If not, the individual experiences inequity and tension.

The concept of *inputs* in Adams' theory refers to the personal contributions for which the individual expects to receive a reward. Some of the factors that a person may consider as inputs include intelligence, education and training, experience and seniority, personal appearance or attractiveness, health, and effort on the job. *Outcomes* in an organizational context include pay, seniority, and other fringe benefits; working conditions (including status and perquisites); and the psychological or intrinsic rewards of the job. Outcomes may also be negative, as in the case of poor working conditions. Thus, the theory of **inequity** is based on an individual's perception of the balance between personal outcomes (benefits) and inputs (costs) relative to the outcomes and inputs of others.

Implications for sport managers

There are three possible results of such comparisons—equity, inequity unfavorable to the individual (a referent other's cost–benefit ratio is greater), and inequity favorable to the individual (the individual's cost–benefit ratio is greater). A person who perceives inequity and feels the tension and discomfort associated with such inequity may attempt to restore equity (or reduce the inequity) in a number of ways. Obviously, the person may attempt to alter the values of any of the four elements of the inequity formula—personal outcomes, personal inputs, others' outcomes, and others' inputs. The most frequently used strategy is to attempt to increase personal outcomes. Thus, an individual is most likely to approach the employer and ask for more pay, greater benefits, and so on. If that approach fails, the individual may attempt to increase personal outcomes by putting in a greater number of hours or producing better-quality work. It is also possible, of course, to minimize the feeling of inequity by reducing personal inputs through decreased productivity or increased absenteeism. Inequity could also be minimized by reducing others' outcomes or inputs. However, the individual may be constrained from adopting this strategy. Others' outcomes, such as pay and promotion, are most likely to be determined by superiors, and others' inputs are most strongly influenced by the other individuals themselves. More importantly, a strategy that focuses on others' inputs or outcomes may not be psychologically acceptable to the person. Very few employees go to a supervisor and ask that the pay of another employee be reduced. Also, very few employees would sabotage or destroy a colleague's work.

Although the possibility exists that inequity in favor of the individual may occur (for example, someone receives a higher pay raise than is deserved), that individual may not express a feeling of inequity as often (or as strongly) as when perceiving inequity of the opposite type. However, feelings of discomfort and guilt could arise. If this is the case, the individual is likely to put in greater efforts in an attempt to justify the rewards received.

Apart from manipulating personal outcomes and inputs, there are other ways of reducing inequity. Adams suggested that individuals might alter their perceptions of personal and others' outcomes and inputs in such a manner that equity is perceptually restored. Alternatively, a person may change the referent other of comparison. Thus, a sport marketer might believe that she had a productive year and, therefore, deserves a high merit increase. However, this perception could change if she were to know the actual accomplishments of others. Another possibility is that the sport marketer could leave the current organization and join another organization.

It is clear from this discussion that a sport manager can intervene in restoring equity perceptions among his employees. First, because equity perceptions are based on relative performances of individuals, managers must ensure that their evaluation of employee performance is fair and accurate. Any errors in this area will naturally lead to inequity in the distribution of rewards. Thus, performance evaluation is a significant area of human resource management. Second, distribution of rewards or resources must also be equitable—that is, equal rewards for equal performance or contributions. Managers must take care to avoid any personal biases or preferences in such decisions. Third, because feelings of inequity in most cases are based on inadequate information or misperceptions, managers should publicize all the bases and rules of distribution of rewards. Being secretive about performance evaluations and distribution of rewards is a sure means of creating misperceptions and subsequent feelings of inequity. This issue is further discussed below under "Justice and Fairness Theories."

Although Adams considered his theory relevant to any situation of social exchange (husband and wife, partners in tennis, and so on), he used the organizational context as the backdrop for its development, and most of the examples listed in his writings relate to organizations and their members. The significance of the Adams theory lies in the fact that organizational reward systems are considered meaningful and effective only insofar as they create a sense of equity among the members of the organization. This notion is further elaborated in the Porter and Lawler model of motivation discussed later in this chapter.

Note here that the emphasis so far has been on the outcomes for individual members, such as pay and promotions. The concept of fairness and equity, however, extends as well to distribution of resources among groups and units within the organization. For instance, allocation of additional resources to specific teams is frequently a point of perceived unfairness by other teams. Similarly, improved office space for units such as marketing and event management may become the focus of perceived unfairness.

Justice and Fairness Theories

Our discussion of Adams' theory of inequity focused on an individual's reactions to the perceived fairness of outcomes for that individual alone. An extension of this view holds that members of an organization value and seek fairness in all employee–employer exchanges (Kanfer, 1992). For example, an employee in a sport organization may perceive that some of his colleagues are not dealt with fairly in pay raises or promotions. If these perceptions are strong and they lead to negative feelings, the focal employee may become disenchanted with the organization and its practices as much as when he himself is affected by such unfairness. These feelings may lead to lowered motivation.

Distributive justice versus procedural justice

In our discussions so far the emphasis has been on the outcomes to individuals or units—that is, the concern is with the distribution of available resources to individuals or groups. This aspect of justice and fairness is known as *distributive* justice or fairness. Another aspect of justice deals with the procedures that determine how resources are distributed. Although a person may be concerned primarily with her personal outcomes, she may also be concerned with the rules and procedures that determine the distribution of outcomes to members of the group or units of the organization. This aspect of justice is called *procedural* justice and refers to the degree to which those affected by allocations of resources or rewards perceive them to have been made according to fair methods and guidelines (Niehoff & Moorman, 1993).

Procedural justice refers to *how* various ends, or content or consequences (distributive justice), are attained (Folger & Greenberg, 1985). Thus, procedural justice is an intermediary stage that is instrumental in the attainment of distributive justice. However, procedures may have equal if not more weight than the actual outcomes in perceptions of justice (Folger & Greenberg, 1985). For example, employees of a sport marketing firm may perceive organizational justice when the criteria for evaluating their performance and the processes of such evaluation are clear and just, even though the actual salary increases they received were less than expected.

In their attempts to ensure procedural justice, sport managers should strive to formulate procedures that adhere to the following rules outlined by Leventhal (1980):

- *Consistency* specifies that allocation procedures should be consistent across persons and over time. For instance, managers cannot use performance as the basis of allocation for one or more employees and seniority for another set of employees.
- *Bias suppression* implies that decision makers should not let self-interest or biases affect the allocation process. Recall the implicit favorite model of decision making (see Chapter 6). A manager in a city recreation department would be succumbing to this process if he gives a higher salary increase to an employee because the manager likes the employee's athletic prowess. That would not be bias suppression! For another example, take the case of a person who networks and gets to know people within an organization so he can get a job in that organization. If a sport manager hires this individual just because he knows him, the manager is violating the principle of bias suppression.
- *Accuracy* means that all allocation decisions must be based on accurate information.
- *Representativeness* refers to making the allocation process representative of the concerns of all recipients. It is conceivable that a sport manager might decide on the allocation procedures based on input from her favorite subordinates, whereas the rest of the employees may prefer some other allocation rules. In such a case, the allocation process chosen by the manager would not be representative.

- *Ethicality* requires that allocations adhere to prevailing ethical and moral standards of the community.
- *Correctibility* acknowledges that decision makers may unintentionally violate one or more of the foregoing rules and err in making allocations. According to this rule, it should be possible for allocation decisions to be modified and the errors corrected. One tactic a sport manager may adopt is to set aside a certain amount of rewards or resources in order to correct any errors. If the manager distributes all the rewards at the outset, he will find it difficult to correct any errors down the road.

Interactional justice

Yet another aspect of justice, known as *interactional justice,* refers to the manner in which the distribution of outcomes is explained to recipients and to the procedures employed in such distribution (Bies & Moag, 1986; Bies & Shapiro, 1987; Greenberg, 1990; Tyler & Bies, 1990). The focus here is on communication about the outcomes and procedures. Any insufficient or erroneous communication is seen as unjust. By the same token, a lack of respect, concern, pleasantness, and warmth in such communications will also be seen as unjust. For instance, when an athletic director tells a subordinate abruptly that "that's the way it's done here," he is violating both aspects of interactional justice. First, he provided no explanation. Second, he conveyed his point coarsely, without conveying any respect or concern for the employee. Greenberg (1993) views these two components of interactional justice as *interpersonal justice* (in which individuals are treated with dignity and respect) and *informational justice* (in which adequate and correct information regarding procedures and outcomes is provided).

Implications for sport managers

Organizational justice (including distributive, procedural, and interactional aspects of justice) has two important implications for sport managers. First, any violation of organizational justice may lead to legal ramifications. That is, the affected employees may seek legal redress through litigation or other means. It is not uncommon for organizations to set up a procedure for the employee to appeal the decision made by a manager. Equally important is the idea that the affected employees, and even those who are not affected, are likely to see the organization and its managers as unjust. These feelings may influence the employees to change their attitudes and behaviors toward the organization. In other words, such perceived injustice may reduce employees' motivation to work hard and achieve organizational goals. Thus, sport managers must understand that the concepts of equity and justice are pervasive in their organizations. Almost every decision they make is subject to standards of equity and fairness.

AN INTEGRATIVE FRAMEWORK: THE PORTER AND LAWLER MODEL OF MOTIVATION

Each of the theories of motivation discussed thus far deals with significant but limited aspects of human motivation. Each theory provides some insights for the sport manager that will facilitate appropriate organizational practices. However, reliance on one single theory may not be a prudent approach for a manager. Instead, managers should attempt to develop a mental model of how motivation works and how it can be enhanced in an organizational context. With this in view, we now describe a motivational model that represents an attempt to synthesize the significant elements of other theories.

The model of motivation proposed by Porter and Lawler (1968) is an extension and elaboration of Vroom's expectancy theory, as well as a synthesis of the content and process theories discussed previously. The model is schematically represented in Exhibit 10.6. To facilitate discussion of the model, numbers have been placed in the boxes in Exhibit 10.6.

Effort (Box 3), which is equivalent to the force concept in Vroom's model, refers to the motivation behind an individual's effort. That is, the degree of effort expended is a reflection of an individual's motivational state. This motivation is a function of the value that the individual attaches to the possible rewards (Box 1) and the individual's perception of the probability that effort will result in reward (Box 2). It should be apparent that "value of rewards" and "perceived effort–reward probability" are equivalent to Vroom's concepts of "valence" and "expectancy," respectively. The effort expended results in a certain level of performance (Box 6). Performance in this context refers to what is expected of the employ-

exhibit 10.6 Porter and Lawler model of motivation.

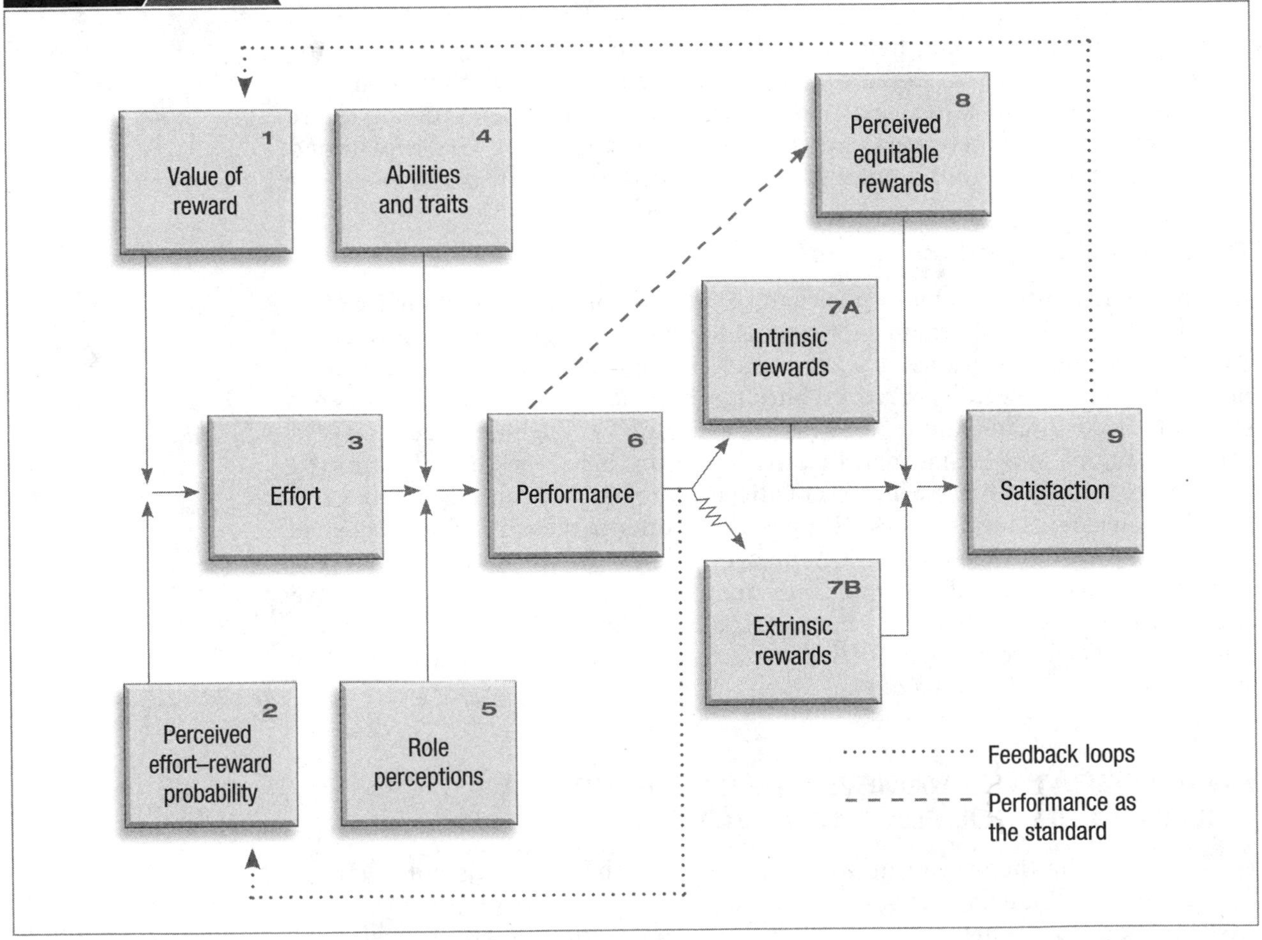

Used by permission from L. W. Porter and E. E. Lawler, 1968, *Managerial attitudes and performance.* (Homewood, IL: Richard D. Irwin. Library of Congress Catalog Card No. 67-29148.)

ee by the organization. That is, individuals may have their own standards of performance, but in an organization performance is measured in terms of organizational standards, rules, expectations, and so on. Thus, an employee of a city recreation department assigned the task of organizing competitions would be expected to do an adequate job in soliciting participants, forming teams, drawing up a schedule of competitions, reserving facilities, and supervising the conduct of the tournament. The individual could do an outstanding job of coaching various community volleyball clubs, but this would be irrelevant to the assigned job and of minimal value to the city recreation department.

IN brief

With sufficient effort an individual can perform adequately in the assigned job, but only if that individual has the necessary abilities and a clear understanding of the role. Without a correct perception of the role, the individual may be wasting time and energy in unrelated activities.

Effort–Performance Relationship

One of the significant contributions of the Porter and Lawler model is to highlight the complexity of the **effort–performance relationship.** Effort does not always lead directly to good performance. For effective performance to occur, an individual must have the necessary **abilities and traits** (Box 4). From a managerial perspective, an employee can perform adequately in a job only if she has the abilities and traits necessary for the job. For example, the employee of the city recreation department could organize competitions effectively if she is adept at forming teams and drawing up schedules, and if she possesses the interpersonal and communicative skills for recruiting participants and volunteers. Similarly, a fitness instructor can be successful only if he has the necessary physical abilities (e.g., muscular endurance, cardiovascular stamina, and flexibility). The instructor would also be expected to possess a positive attitude toward the clients, as well as patience and concern for them. Note that whereas abilities are transient and trainable qualities, traits are enduring and stable characteristics.

Another factor that affects the effort–performance relationship is the accuracy of the individual's **role perception** (Box 5). Each employee must have a complete understanding of what activities are necessary and how these activities should be carried out. Thus, the marketing director in an athletic department spends time and effort identifying potential sponsors, contacting them, and persuading them to sponsor events organized by the department. As another example, a coach or fitness trainer does not train marathon runners the same way as he trains weight lifters.

Performance–Reward Relationship

If the individual has the necessary abilities and traits and perceives her role correctly, it is reasonable to expect that she will achieve an acceptable level of performance (acceptable in terms of organizational expectations). Such a performance will result in certain rewards. Intrinsic rewards (Box 7A) relate to the higher-order needs of the individual. These rewards are personally derived from the accomplishments. That is, the individual receives a sense of achievement and experiences growth on the successful completion of a challenging task. In contrast to the intrinsic rewards that are personally derived, the extrinsic rewards (Box 7B) are administered by external agents (such as the supervisors). These rewards are the equivalent of Herzberg's hygiene factors and Maslow's lower-order needs. They are usually manifested in such things as salary increases and promotions. The fact that the intrinsic rewards relate directly to personal performance is indicated by the solid connecting line in Exhibit 10.6. The criteria on which extrinsic rewards are distributed may not be related to performance. Thus, in Exhibit 10.6 a wavy line connects performance with extrinsic rewards. As an example, promotion could be based on seniority, not on performance. Likewise, salary increases could be fixed for every employee; relative performance may not be taken into account.

Reward–Satisfaction Relationship

Receiving rewards should lead to satisfaction (Box 9 in Exhibit 10.6). However, the relationship between receiving the rewards and deriving satisfaction from them depends on whether or not the individual perceives the rewards as equitable (Box 8). Thus, the Porter and Lawler theory incorporates constructs from Adams' theory of inequity.

The relative performances of a person and his coworkers have a significant effect on how equity is perceived. Individuals who believe that they have performed well tend to emphasize performance as a standard for equity of rewards rather than the cost–benefit comparisons suggested by Adams' theory. An NBA player is not as concerned about the effort he put in to get to the NBA (or the effort put in during the season) as he is about receiving a salary comparable to that of other players whose performance contributions are similar. Thus, the importance of performance in one's determination of equity of rewards is illustrated by the dashed line going straight between performance (Box 6) and perceived equitable rewards (Box 8). Also note that the perceived equity of rewards does not affect the relationship between intrinsic rewards and satisfaction, because this relationship is internally experienced.

Feedback Loops

Finally, Exhibit 10.6 shows two feedback loops—one leading from satisfaction back to value of reward, and the other leading from the relationship between performance and rewards back to perceived **effort–reward probability.** The first feedback loop reflects the fact that the receipt of rewards affects the values attached to those rewards. In the case of **extrinsic rewards** such as pay, the value employees attach to these rewards is likely to be lowered as more and more of them are received. Thus, an athlete who receives a high salary is less likely to emphasize salary increases as much as an athlete on the low end of the pay scale. This view is consistent with both the Maslow and Herzberg theories. They suggest that the lower-order needs, once satisfied, cease to be motivators. However, Porter and Lawler acknowledged that the satisfaction derived from the **intrinsic rewards** is likely to lead the individual to value these rewards more.

IN brief

The value that a person attaches to intrinsic rewards increases as more of them are received, whereas the value a person places on extrinsic rewards decreases as more of them are received. In addition, a person's belief that effort will lead to rewards is affected by organizational practices.

The second loop relates to the employee's perception of the probability that his efforts will result in the rewards sought. If a baseball organization habitually promotes its managers on the basis of seniority, the perceived relationships of effort–performance–promotion will be weakened. That is, an individual desiring promotion might not be motivated to work hard, owing to her perception that the best way to get a promotion is to get old. Thus, as Porter and Lawler point out, organizational practices have a great influence in determining the perceived connection between performance and rewards.

In overview, the Porter and Lawler model of work motivation is comprehensive enough to include the concepts of Maslow's need hierarchy theory, Herzberg's two-factor theory, Vroom's expectancy theory, and Adams' theory of inequity. Accordingly, the implications of the model are cumulative with respect to each of the other theories included in the model.

MOTIVATION IN SPORT ORGANIZATIONS

The practical implication of the need theories, particularly Herzberg's motivation–hygiene theory, is that a job must be designed in such a way that it triggers as well as satisfies the higher-order needs of the worker. As stated previously, however, the principles behind job enrichment run counter to bureaucratic prescriptions. For instance, on the one hand, the principle of job enrichment suggests that a person must be given "a complete natural unit of work." On the other hand, the bureaucratic concept of division of labor suggests that the job should be broken down into smaller units. Similarly, removing controls over employees and giving them additional authority (techniques of enriching a job) are contrary to the bureaucratic principles of division of labor and hierarchy of authority, respectively.

We noted in Chapter 7 that concerns for rationality and efficiency, and for uniformity and consistency in organizational activities, are the basis for the bureaucratic way of structuring jobs. On the other hand, individual needs are the basis for the practice of promoting job enrichment. These two apparently contradictory approaches to the design of jobs can be reconciled if individual differences in needs, and their relative strengths, are taken into account. As noted before, individuals with a strong desire for achievement, responsibility, and recognition can be given enriched jobs, whereas those persons who are low on those needs can be assigned to fractionated and routine jobs.

In addition, organizations differ in their purposes and processes, as well as in their environmental conditions. Such differences can also facilitate the matching of jobs, individuals, and organizational characteristics.

Professional Service Versus Consumer Service Organizations

The categorization of sport organizations into professional service organizations and consumer service organizations (see Chapter 1) provides a basis for recommendations relating to the matchup of jobs, individuals, and organizational characteristics. We saw that professional service and consumer service organizations differ in the types of services they provide. Professional services are nonstandardized in the sense that they are individualized to suit the needs of customers and their unique problems. Thus, a professional employee is required to use personal expertise and knowledge to solve the problem. If help from professional colleagues or associations is needed, it is still the employee's prerogative to seek that help. That is, the professional employee has almost complete autonomy and control. In addition, a job in a professional service organization has greater task significance attached to it than a job in a consumer service organization. Furthermore, it possesses greater variety and variability and involves whole units of work. From this perspective, jobs in professional service organizations are "enriched." Mills, Hall, Leidecker, and Margulies (1983) emphasized this notion when they proposed the flexiform model for the organization of a professional service organization (see Chapter 8). Examples of these types of organizations include a sport marketing firm with different experts dealing with different groups of clients; a sport law firm with lawyers specializing in different fields of law; and a university athletic department, in which the coaches are the professionals.

The services in a consumer service organization are usually standardized in the sense that they involve minimal information processing by employees, and they are governed by rules and procedures to a much greater extent than is the case in professional service organizations (see Chapters 1 and 2). Thus, the employees in consumer service organizations do not experience autonomy and responsibility to the same extent as employees of professional service organizations. Furthermore, their jobs are also lower on task significance, variety, and variability, and they tend to be more specialized and routine in nature.

This discussion leads us to conclude that there is great potential for enriching the jobs in consumer service organizations, but is this feasible or practical? This question must be answered from two perspectives—the perspective of the employee and the perspective of the organization.

If the perspective of the employee is considered, it is obvious that an attempt must be made to match the person and the job. That is, job enrichment is meaningful only to the extent that the strength of the employee's growth need warrants such enrichment, and to the extent that the employee is capable of handling an enriched job. In the absence of either or both of these conditions, job enrichment will not have the desired effect of motivating the individual. In fact, it could be damaging to the individual's self-esteem if he fails to deal effectively with the enriched job because of a lack of expertise and ability.

If the organizational perspective is considered, job enrichment is feasible in a consumer service organization, provided that the organization is relatively small with few employees. In the initial stages of growth, it would be possible, and indeed desirable, to permit employees autonomy and freedom to be individualistic in providing services to customers. As the organization grows and expands, however, there is an increase in services to a large number of customers. The need for standardization then increases, and with it the need for more rules and procedures for employee guidance. Given a choice between cost effectiveness and job enrichment, a profit-oriented consumer service organization will choose cost effectiveness. An organization responsible for the management of a professional sport arena must have a standard protocol for its ticket sellers. That protocol may be monotonous and boring, but it will also be cost effective.

The resolution of the dilemma concerning whether to emphasize uniformity and consistency or a job enrichment protocol lies in the staffing procedures. Managers of consumer service organizations must determine the extent to which they can afford job enrichment, and thereby recruit individuals whose needs and abilities match the characteristics of the target jobs that they offer.

Even in situations where it is feasible and practical to redesign a job for enrichment purposes, a manager may not have the authority to do so. A middle line manager in a large organization, for example, may not be permitted to alter a job description that was drawn up by superiors. This problem is more acute in those organizations that are bureaucratically organized. A supervisor of ticket sellers, to use the previous example, may not have the liberty to alter the protocol set by the director of operations. This does not, however, preclude the manager from exercising a leadership function by intervening in the motivational process. This issue is discussed in the next chapter.

Volunteer Organizations

The notion of matching individual needs to the job is more pertinent to volunteers in organizations. That is, those who join an organization as employees might be prepared to accept a job and its requirements for economic reasons; the satisfaction of other needs may be relatively less important. Volunteers, by definition, do not seek economic benefits through their membership in an organization. A volunteer might join an organization for several reasons—learning and growing, helping others, cultivating friendships, using present skills and learning new skills, gaining work experience, repaying a debt to society, and using leisure time more effectively.

Although it is true that the volunteer organization and the services it provides may be innately attractive to volunteers, their continued membership and commitment to the organization largely depend on the type of work assignment they receive as well as the satisfaction they derive from it. For example, when a community association requests assistance to organize a basketball league, handle registration and organize a schedule, and coach the teams, several members of the community might volunteer. The total organizational effort must be broken down into specific units of work. In turn, this work must be assigned to the volunteers. Some of the work units, such as coaching a team, are high on autonomy, responsibility, significance, and variety. Others, such as answering the telephone during registration, are simple and routine. It is likely that the coaches will find their work more rewarding than the registration agents.

From a different perspective, some volunteers are high on the need for growth and power. They desire more complex and challenging tasks, like coaching a team. Others prefer to handle the simpler and more routine tasks. The proper matching of these individuals with the right type of work is the manager's job. When there is a good fit between the task demands and the personal needs of the volunteers, the volunteers feel satisfied and are likely to continue to participate. When there is a mismatch, however, the experience is frustrating for the volunteer. Individuals who have a high need for growth find the simple tasks meaningless and unfulfilling. Conversely, individuals who are low on the growth need find the more complex jobs frustrating and stressful. To decrease the likelihood of a mismatch, managers of volunteer organizations should draw up job descriptions for all the activities to be carried out. Then, the volunteers can better choose the activity they prefer.

SUMMARY

Our discussion of theories of motivation emphasized the motivational basis of the leading function. The "content" theories of motivation include Maslow's need hierarchy theory and Herzberg's two-factor theory. We discussed Maslow's conception of prepotency (the force in effect) for his hierarchical ordering of human needs, and then clarified the various classes of needs. Then we looked at Herzberg's two-factor theory and distinguished between hygiene factors and motivators and their effects on individual motivation.

We noted that whereas the content theories discuss external factors that motivate individuals, the process theories deal with the internal processes that motivate individuals. The "process" theories covered in the chapter are Vroom's expectancy theory; Adams' theory of inequity, justice, and fairness theories; and Porter and Lawler's model of motivation. We explained Vroom's concepts of valence, expectancy, and instrumentality and then discussed the concept of inequity (or equity) as espoused by Adams and the motivational impact of perceived inequity. Porter and Lawler's model of motivation provided an integrating framework for the relationships between motivation and performance, between performance and reward, and between reward and satisfaction. Finally, we discussed the implications of these theories for sport managers.

develop YOUR PERSPECTIVE

1. Consider a few people you know well. With respect to Maslow's need hierarchy theory, can you identify the level at which one of them is operating? Explain how you make those assessments.
2. From your experience as a student or an athlete, recall a situation in which you felt the happiest (or most satisfied). Narrate the sequence of events that led to this high feeling. How long did this feeling last? How did it affect your subsequent work, interpersonal relations, and your well-being? Similarly, recall an incident when you felt most unhappy (or most dissatisfied), and describe it along the same lines. Does your experience support Herzberg's two-factor theory? Explain.
3. You have your own career aspirations, and you are striving hard to reach them. Discuss your motivation from the perspective of Vroom's expectancy theory.
4. In your experience as either a paid or volunteer worker, did you ever feel that inequity was affecting you or your coworkers? If so, narrate the incident and explain how equity could have been restored.
5. Porter and Lawler's model suggests that motivation or effort is a function of the value one attaches to the rewards attainable through such efforts. Considering your own career aspirations, what are the rewards you expect in that career?

references

Adams, J. S. (1963). Toward an understanding of inequity. *Journal of Abnormal Social Psychology, 67*, 422–436.

Adams, J. S. (1977). Inequity in social exchange. In B. M. Staw (Ed.), *Psychological foundations of organizational behavior*. Santa Monica, CA: Goodyear.

Bassett-Jones, N., & Lloyd, G. C. (2005). Does Herzberg's motivation theory have staying power? *Journal of Management Development, 21*(10), 929–913.

Bies, R. J., & Moag, J. S. (1986). Interactional justice: Communication criteria of fairness. In R. J. Lewicki, B. H. Sheppard, & M. H. Bazerman (Eds.), *Research on negotiations in organizations* (Vol. 1, pp. 43–55). Greenwich, CT: JAI Press.

Bies, R. J., & Shapiro, D. L. (1987). Interactional fairness judgments: The influence of causal accounts. *Social Justice Research, 1*, 199–218.

Dunnette, M. D., Campbell, J. P., & Hakel, M. D. (1967). Factors contributing to job satisfaction and job dissatisfaction in six occupational groups. *Organizational Behavior and Human Performance, 2*, 143–174.

Folger, R., & Greenberg, J. (1985). Procedural justice: An interpretive analysis of personnel systems. In K. M. Rowland & G. R. Ferris (Eds.), *Research in personnel and human resource management* (Vol. 3, pp. 141–183). Greenwich, CT: JAI Press.

Greenberg, J. (1990). Organizational justice: Yesterday, today, and tomorrow. *Journal of Management, 16,* 399–432.

Greenberg, J. (1993). The social side of fairness: Interpersonal and informational classes of organizational justice. In R. Cropanzano (Ed.), *Justice in the workplace: Approaching fairness in human resource management* (pp. 79–103). Hillsdale, NJ: Erlbaum.

Greenberg, J. (2005). *Managing behavior in organizations* (4th ed.). Upper Saddle River, NJ: Pearson-Prentice Hall.

Herzberg, F. (1968). One more time: How do you motivate people? *Harvard Business Review,* Jan.–Feb., 53–62.

Herzberg, F., Mausner, B., & Snyderman, B. B. (1959). *The motivation to work.* New York: John Wiley & Sons.

Hitt, M. A., Black, J. S., & Porter, L. W. (2009). *Management* (2nd ed.). Upper Saddle River, NJ: Pearson Prentice Hall.

Hulin, C. L., & Smith, P. A. (1967). An empirical investigation of two implications of the two-factor theory of job satisfaction. *Journal of Applied Psychology, 51,* 396–402.

Kanfer, R. (1992). Motivation theory and industrial and organizational psychology. In M. D. Dunnette & L. M. Hough (Eds.), *Handbook of industrial and organizational psychology* (2nd ed., pp. 75–170). Palo Alto, CA: Consulting Psychologist's Press.

Leventhal, G. S. (1980). What should be done with equity theory? New approaches to the study of fairness in social relationships. In K. J. Gergen, M. S. Greenberg, & R. H. Willis (Eds.), *Social exchange: Advances in theory and research* (pp. 27–55). New York: Plenum.

Luthans, F. (2011). *Organizational behavior* (12th ed.). New York; McGraw-Hill Irwin.

Maslow, A. H. (1943). A theory of human motivation. *Psychological Review, 50,* 370–396.

Mills, P. K., Hall, J. L., Leidecker, J. K., & Margulies, N. (1983). Flexiform: A model for professional service organizations. *Academy of Management Review, 8,* 118–131.

Niehoff, B. P., & Moorman, R. H. (1993). Justice as a mediator of the relationship between methods of monitoring and organizational citizenship behavior. *Academy of Management Journal, 36,* 527–556.

Porter, L. W., & Lawler, E. E. (1968). *Managerial attitudes and performance.* Homewood, IL: Richard D. Irwin.

Steers, R. M., & Black, J. S. (1994). *Organizational behavior* (5th ed.). New York: HarperCollins College Publishers.

Tyler, T. R., & Bies, R. J. (1990). Beyond formal procedures: The interpersonal context of procedural justice. In J. S. Carroll (Ed.), *Applied social psychology and organizational settings* (pp. 77–88). Hillsdale, NJ: Erlbaum.

Vroom, V. H. (1964). *Work and motivation.* New York: John Wiley & Sons.

BEHAVIORAL PROCESS OF LEADING

CHAPTER 11

manage YOUR LEARNING

After completing this chapter you should be able to:

- **Define leadership.**
- **Describe the behavioral and situational approaches to leadership.**
- **Discuss the focuses of the contingency model and the path-goal theory of leadership effectiveness.**
- **Describe the five categories based on the sources of social power.**

strategic CONCEPTS

achievement-oriented behavior
adaptive behavior
behavioral approach
coercive power
consideration
contingency model
employee orientation
environmental factors
expert power
influence
initiating structure
instrumental behavior
leader–member relations
leadership
leadership style
least preferred coworker
legitimate power
managerial motivation
member factors
need for achievement
need for affiliation
need for power
organizational set
participative behavior
path–goal theory
personal power
position power
production orientation
reactive behavior
referent power
reward power
situational approach
situational favorableness
supportive behavior
task structure
trait approach

THE LEADING FUNCTION

The concept of leadership can be viewed from two perspectives. In the etymological sense, a leader is a person who actually goes ahead of the group to show the way. Thus, in early military history, a captain would lead the charge or attack for the brigade that followed. In other contexts, individuals such as Winston Churchill, Mohandas Gandhi, Martin Luther King Jr., and Nelson Mandela all initiated actions based on personal convictions. Others followed in their footsteps, both because they were convinced of these leaders' causes and because they were inspired by them. In this type of leadership, leaders not only initiate a movement but also spearhead it.

From an organizational perspective, however, leadership is just one of the functions of a manager who is placed in charge of a group and its activities and is, in turn, guided by superiors and organizational factors. Leadership in this context does not require the leader to be out in front or working alongside the members, or even to be chosen by the members. Rather, the organization has named the leader on behalf of its members. This form of organizational leadership is the focus in the sections that follow.

Planning and organizing involves specifying goals, identifying the actions to achieve those goals, assigning individuals to carry out those actions, and appointing managers to coordinate those actions. It is the manager's responsibility to ensure that individuals carry out their assigned duties. This function is leadership.

LEADERSHIP DEFINED

Consider the following definitions of organizational leadership:

> A leader is one who influences others to attain goals. (Bateman & Snell, 2007, p. 394)
>
> Leadership is imagining, willing and driving, and thereby making something happen which was not going to happen otherwise. (Fineman, Gabriel, & Sims, 2010, p. 99)
>
> Leadership is a process whereby an individual influences a group of individuals to achieve a common goal. (Northouse, 2010, p. 3)
>
> Organizational leadership [is] an interpersonal process that involves attempts to influence other people to attain goals. (Hitt, Black, & Porter, 2009, p. 244)
>
> Leadership [is] the process of influencing others to facilitate the attainment of organizationally relevant goals. (Ivancevich, Konopaske, & Matteson, 2011, p. 440)

All of these definitions of **leadership** embody three significant elements: (1) leadership is a behavioral process; (2) it is interpersonal in nature; and (3) it is aimed at influencing and motivating members toward group or organizational goals. That is, the notion of influencing others is a significant component of leadership. In fact, Hollander and Julian (1969) have suggested that the terms *leadership* and *influence* are synonymous. Furthermore, the process of **influence** is, in its very essence, interpersonal in nature. This is what distinguishes leading from the other functions of a manager. In other words, whereas the planning, organizing, and evaluating can be largely carried out without significant interaction, leading requires interpersonal contact between a manager and the organization's members.

IN brief

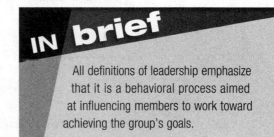

All definitions of leadership emphasize that it is a behavioral process aimed at influencing members to work toward achieving the group's goals.

The definitions presented above also specify that leadership is a behavioral process that emphasizes what the leader *does* rather than what the leader *is*. Although there is general consensus on this issue, the dialogue continues as to whether what the leader does is a function of what the leader *is*, or whether *doing* and *being* are independent factors. This dialogue is reflected in the various theories of leadership, which fall into three main categories: (1) those that deal with the traits of leaders (the **trait approach**); (2) those that deal with the behaviors of leaders (the **behavioral approach**); and (3) those that deal with the leaders' traits or behaviors in a specific situational context, taking into account the characteristics of both the members and the organization (the **situational approach**).

THE TRAIT APPROACH

Early leadership researchers attempted to identify a finite set of personal characteristics that distinguish good leaders. The characteristics studied included physical traits such as height, weight, age, and appearance; mental

sidebar 11.1

GENES AND TECHNOLOGY OF LEADERSHIP

Advances in research on genes and neurotechnology provide insights into the question of whether leaders are born or made. De Neve and colleagues (2013) studied 4,000 individuals from two large data sets and found that a specific genotype was associated with individuals who occupied supervisory positions in the workplace. The researchers equate occupying the supervisory role with leadership. While they acknowledge that leadership is a trainable skill, they also suggest that "about a quarter of the variation in leadership role occupancy is heritable" (p. 55). Thus, this research lends some support to the view that leaders are born.

In contrast, Hill (2013) reports on neuroleadership, an emerging area of study that suggests that a leader can be trained when wired to a computer. This high-tech process is also direct and simple in that the technology identifies the weaknesses in brain activity of the leader (e.g., in handling anger). Once such weaknesses are identified, the next step is to train the manager in addressing those weaknesses. If this line of research is repeated in several cases, the technology would uphold the idea that leaders are made (or trained).

traits such as intelligence; personality traits such as aggressiveness, dominance, extroversion, self-esteem, achievement motive, and task orientation; social background characteristics such as education and socioeconomic status; and social or interpersonal skills. However, these research efforts did not yield any consistent findings—no universal set of traits characterized effective leaders. Understandably, the general trait approach to the study of leadership fell into disfavor. Furthermore, as Szilagyi and Wallace (1980) point out, this general trait approach was concerned with the *emergence* of leaders and not their *effectiveness*.

THE BEHAVIORAL APPROACH

The futility of the trait approach led researchers to focus on what a leader actually does to contribute to group performance and satisfaction. The most notable among these efforts were the major research programs conducted at The Ohio State University and the University of Michigan. The contributions of these scholars are discussed below.

Ohio State Studies

A major thrust in the Ohio State studies was to identify and describe leadership behaviors relevant to the organizational context. To this end, researchers identified a large number of leader activities and classified them into nine categories (Hemphill & Coons, 1957). Subsequent research, however, concluded that it would be difficult to use nine dimensions of leader behavior effectively, because some were highly intercorrelated. Thus, the nine dimensions were combined into four (Halpin & Winer, 1957). Further research indicated that even these four behaviors could be condensed into two broad categories—consideration and initiating structure (Halpin & Winer, 1957).

Consideration is defined as leader behavior that reflects a leader's concern for members' well-being and concern for warm and friendly relations within the group. **Initiating structure** is defined as leader behavior that reflects a leader's concern for clarifying the roles for both the leader and the members and a concern for effective performance of the group's tasks. According to the Ohio State scholars, it is possible for a leader to be described as high on both dimensions, low on both, or high on one and low on the other. Thus, a leader's style can be located in one of the quadrants in Exhibit 11.1. In a study of NCAA Division I athletic directors, Branch (1990) found that successful athletic directors were perceived to be high on initiating structure and low on consideration. Thus, they would fall into quadrant 4 in Exhibit 11.1.

Although there was a general expectation that leaders falling in quadrant 2—those who exhibit high levels of both consideration and initiating structure—would be most effective, research results did not support this position. This was mainly attributed to the fact that the Ohio scholars did not consider the situational elements that can interact with the behaviors of a leader to influence effectiveness.

Michigan Studies

Scholars at the University of Michigan were also concerned with the description of leader behaviors (Katz, Maccoby, Gurin, & Floor, 1951; Katz, Maccoby, & Morse, 1950). In a manner identical to the Ohio State researchers, the Michigan group also identified two styles of leader behavior—an employee orientation or employee-centered leadership style, and a production orientation or job-centered leadership style. The **employee orientation** dimension reflects the degree to which a leader is concerned with the human relations aspect of the job. The **production orientation** dimension reflects the degree to which the leader is concerned with the technical aspects of the job and productivity.

The Michigan team found that emphasis on either one of the dimensions resulted in increased productivity to almost the same extent. However, they also observed that a production orientation caused a greater degree of employee resentment, dissatisfaction, turnover, and absenteeism (Morse & Reimer, 1956). The positive and detrimental effects of production orientation are shown in Exhibit 11.2. Note that the Michigan studies, which were carried out concurrently with

exhibit 11.1 The Ohio State leadership styles.

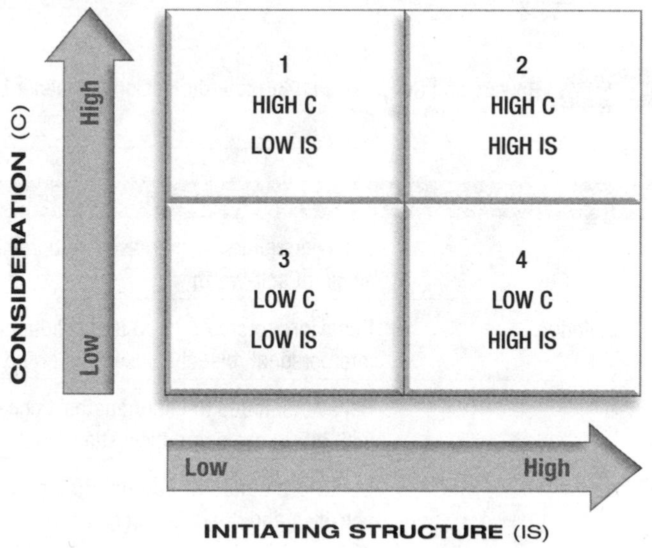

exhibit 11.2 Positive and negative effects of production orientation in leadership as found in the Michigan studies.

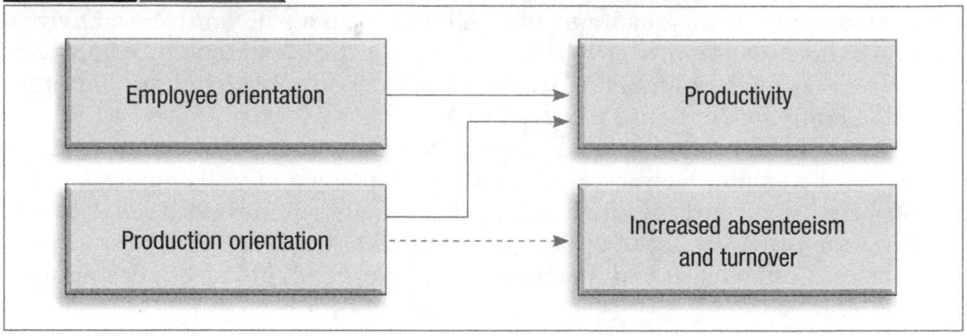

but independently of the Ohio State studies, yielded conceptually similar dimensions of leader behavior.

In 1966, Bowers and Seashore of the University of Michigan, in an effort to synthesize the results of earlier research involving both the Michigan and Ohio State descriptions of leader behavior, proposed a four-dimensional description of leader behavior. As shown in Exhibit 11.3, their four dimensions included support, interaction facilitation, goal emphasis, and work facilitation. The scales to measure these four dimensions of leader behavior are found in *Survey of Organizations* (Taylor & Bowers, 1972).

Limitations of Ohio State and Michigan Studies

In overview, these earlier research efforts were successful in identifying and describing relevant categories of leader behavior. However, they have been criticized for a number of reasons, including the fact that the complexity of leadership cannot be adequately described by two dimensions of leader behavior (House & Dessler, 1974; Stogdill, 1974; Yukl, 2006). In fact, in Stogdill's (1974) extended version of the Leader Behavior Description Questionnaire (LBDQ), there are 12 dimensions of leader behavior.

exhibit 11.3 Bowers and Seashore's (1966) four dimensions of leader behavior.

DIMENSION OF LEADER BEHAVIOR	DESCRIPTION
Support	Behaviors aimed at increasing subordinates' sense of self-worth
Interaction Facilitation	Behaviors to create good and productive interpersonal relationships in the group
Goal Emphasis	Behaviors aimed at subordinates' concern with group goals and their attainment
Work Facilitation	Behaviors aimed at coordinating group activities and providing technical guidance

Yukl and his associates (Yukl, 2006; Yukl, Gordon, & Taber, 2002) also proposed 12 leadership behaviors and then grouped them into three meta categories—*task-, relations-*, and *change-oriented behavior*—as shown in Exhibit 11.4. Task-oriented behaviors focus on improving the internal efficiency and coordination of the work unit. Relations-oriented behaviors aid in enhancing members' commitment to work objectives, in improving the trust and cooperation among members, and in cultivating member identification with the work unit. Change-oriented behaviors are focused on adapting to the external environment by modifying the objectives, strategies, and work processes. Readers should note that the task- and relations-oriented behaviors are similar to the Ohio State dimensions of initiating structure and consideration. The third of Yukl's categories aims at transforming the team or organization in significant ways. This is the central thrust of what is called transformational leadership, which is discussed in the next chapter.

However, questions relating to the appropriate number of leader behaviors are not as critical as the issue of the relationship between leader behavior and group performance. That is, it is immaterial how many dimensions are required to describe leader behavior if these dimensions do not show any relationship to the desired outcomes of group performance and member satisfaction. When viewed from this perspective, the earlier leadership studies have not been successful.

exhibit 11.4 Yukl's specific and mega categories of leadership behaviors.

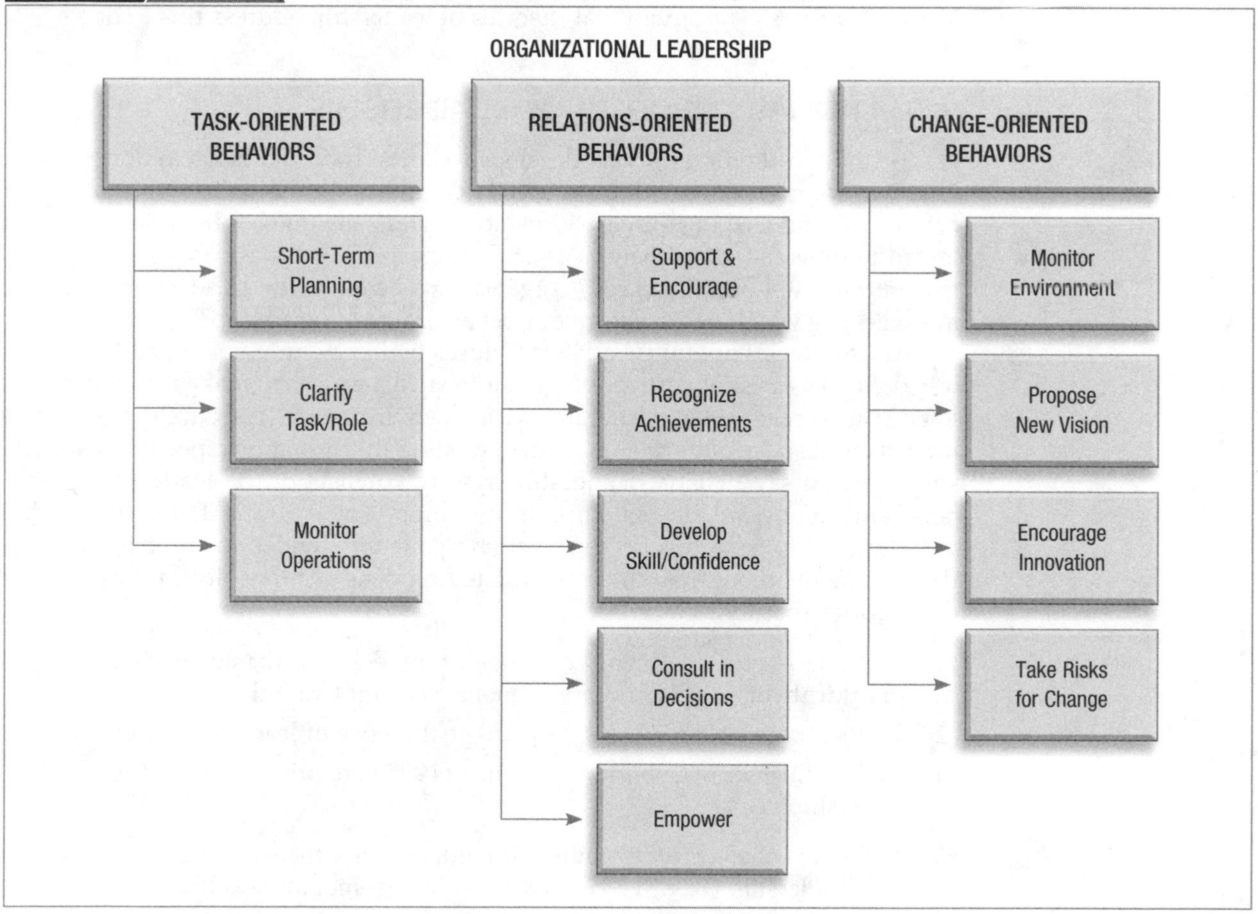

These research efforts were also criticized because they confounded the *style* of making a decision with the *substance* of the decision. For instance, in the LBDQ, the subscale that assesses initiating structure contains items that reflect the degree to which a leader uses an autocratic manner to make decisions. Similarly, the consideration subscale includes items that reflect the degree to which the leader possesses a participative orientation. Several authors (Chelladurai, 1993; House & Dessler, 1974; House & Mitchell, 1974; Sheridan, Downey, & Slocum, 1975; Yukl, 1971, 1981) have argued that the decision-making aspects of leadership (autocratic, participative, delegative, and so on) should be viewed in isolation from other aspects (task-oriented versus person-oriented). In this regard, House and Mitchell (1974) distinguished among participative behavior (behavior that allows members to participate in decision making), instrumental behavior (behavior that serves to control and coordinate activities), achievement-oriented behavior (behavior that sets challenging goals and serves to express confidence in subordinates), and supportive behavior (behavior concerned with the welfare of the members and the creation of a pleasant work environment). Similarly, in Yukl's (1981) scale, *decision participation* measures "the extent to which a leader consults with subordinates and otherwise allows them to influence his or her decisions" (p. 122).

Finally, a third general criticism of the Ohio State and Michigan studies is that they do not assess the specific dimensions of leader behavior appropriate to specific contexts (House & Dessler, 1974; Sheridan et al., 1975; Yukl, 1971). That is, certain leader behaviors might be effective in certain situations and ineffective in others. The situational theories of leadership address this issue.

SITUATIONAL THEORIES OF LEADERSHIP

Although the descriptions developed via the trait and behavioral approaches were good, they did not specify circumstances in which a given trait or behavior would lead to group performance. That is, the traits or behaviors were not linked to differences in situations. The theories described in the following sections take into account the differences in organizational contexts and leadership situations in suggesting which particular trait or behavior would be appropriate in each.

In Chapter 3, organizations were described as open systems, and a system was defined as a set of parts put together in such a way as to make up a whole. An open system reacts to and interacts with its environment to secure the resources it needs to dispose of its products. In extending the system perspective to leadership, we can say that the leadership system consists of the leader, the members, and the organizational context in which they operate. The theories that view leadership from this perspective have generally tended to emphasize one of these elements more than the others. The following sections deal, in order, with the theories that focus on:

1. the leader—Fiedler's (1967) contingency model of leadership and McClelland and Burnham's (1976) theory of managerial motivation;
2. the members—House's (1971) path–goal theory of leadership; and
3. the organization—Osborn and Hunt's (1975) adaptive–reactive theory of leadership.

In the next chapter, we examine the contemporary theories relating to transformational leadership (Bass, 1985, 1990) and leader–member exchange. Finally, the multidimensional model of leadership (Chelladurai, 1978, 1993), a synthesis of the above theories, is presented in the next chapter as an integrative framework.

The Contingency Model of Leadership Effectiveness

The impetus toward situational approaches to leadership was first provided by Fiedler (1954, 1967, 1973). His **contingency model** of leadership effectiveness proposes that (a) a leader's style (task orientation versus employee or interpersonal orientation) is a relatively stable personality characteristic; (b) the situation in which the leader operates may be more or less favorable to the leader (that is, favorable in the leader's exercise of influence over the subordinates); and (c) leadership effectiveness is contingent upon the fit between the leader's style and the situational favorableness.

Leadership style

Leadership style refers to the tendency of an individual to emphasize task accomplishment (task orientation) or interpersonal relations (employee orientation) in a given situation. For instance, a fitness club manager may be concerned with efficiency, productivity, and profitability in operating the club. She would express this concern (task orientation) by closely monitoring the activities of the employees and directing them on what should be done and how it should be done. On the other hand, the manager of another fitness club may be more concerned with the employees and their welfare. This manager would express his employee orientation by making the working conditions better for the employees, by being flexible in scheduling their assignments, and by being more supportive of the employees in general.

Fiedler (1967) introduced a unique method for assessing leadership style. The respondent is asked to recall a **least preferred coworker** (LPC); that is, a person the respondent has had the greatest amount of difficulty working with in the past. The respondent is then asked to evaluate that least preferred coworker on a scale that consists of 16 to 20 items (depending on the form used) that are bipolar adjectives. The following are three sample items from the scale:

Pleasant . . 8 7 6 5 4 3 2 1 . . . Unpleasant

Tense . . . . 1 2 3 4 5 6 7 8 . . . Relaxed

Efficient . . . 8 7 6 5 4 3 2 1 . . . Inefficient

An individual's score on this LPC scale is considered to reflect the individual's leadership style. In Fiedler's (1967) view, "We visualize the high-LPC individual (who perceives his least preferred coworker in a relatively favorable manner) as a person who derives his major satisfaction from successful interpersonal relationships, while the low-LPC person (who describes his LPC in very unfavorable terms) derives his major satisfaction from task performance" (p. 45). Thus, the basic motivation of the leader who gives a high-LPC rating is primarily toward the development of warm and friendly interpersonal relations with subordinates, whereas the basic motivation of a leader who gives a low-LPC rating is primarily toward task accomplishment. In a later revision of the theory, Fiedler (1972) suggested that the LPC score represents a two-level (primary and secondary) motivational system. That is, the primary orientation of the high-LPC leader is toward interpersonal relations. When that is achieved, the high-LPC leader focuses on task accomplishment (secondary motivation). On the other hand, the low-LPC leader focuses first on task accomplishment, and when that goal is reached or is about to be reached, the focus may shift to fostering warm interpersonal relations.

Situational favorableness

Situational favorableness reflects the degree to which the situation permits or facilitates the exercise of influence by the leader. According to Fiedler, three elements in the situation affect its favorableness: leader–member relations, task structure, and position power of the leader.

Leader–member relations refers to the degree to which the members like and respect the leader. Thus, the friendlier the members are, the easier it is for the leader to exert influence. Consider the case of the managers of the two fitness clubs in the previous example. Irrespective of whether the manager is task-oriented or employee-oriented, her attempts to influence subordinates will be more successful if they like her. If the subordinates are friendly with the manager, they may not mind her attempts to influence them, and they will be willing to express their friendship by following her directions and complying with her requests. Thus, the manager is in a favorable situation. If, on the other hand, the subordinates do not like or respect the manager, her attempts to influence the subordinates may fall on deaf ears. They are likely to see her actions as domineering if she is a task-oriented leader and manipulative if she is an employee-oriented leader. This would be an unfavorable situation for her. Fiedler viewed leader–member relations as the most important element contributing to the favorableness of the situation.

The second element in the situation affecting favorableness for the leader is the **task structure** itself. According to Fiedler, the more structured the task is, the more it contributes to situational favorableness. In the contingency model, the task of the group is considered to contribute to situational favorableness if (a) the goals are clearly defined; (b) the procedures to accomplish the task are limited; (c) the group's output can be easily measured; and (d) there is only one standard by which to evaluate performance. Take the case of the directors of two intercollegiate athletics departments. Let us assume that the two major goals of the first athletic department are winning more games and championships and generating more revenue. The goals of the second athletic department are to increase opportunities for students to pursue excellence in sport and to provide quality services in terms of coaching, facilities, and support services. Of the two athletic departments, the goals of the first department are more precise, the paths to attaining these goals are relatively limited, the outcomes of decisions can be more easily evaluated, and the number of correct solutions is limited. Hence, in Fiedler's model, the situation in the first athletic department is more favorable to the leader than it is in the second department. That is, the more structured the group task is, the easier it is for the leader to influence the group.

The **position power** of the leader, the final element of situational favorableness, reflects the authority invested in the leader's position and the degree of control he has over rewards and sanctions. For instance, the president and the athletic council of the university may curtail the power of the athletic director by requiring their approval for every decision. In addition, they may decide on salary raises for the coaches, as well as on punishing the coaches for violations. Under these conditions, the athletic director holds no power. According to Fiedler's model, this is an unfavorable situation for the leader because he has little potential to influence the members.

Contingency effects

Fiedler's research showed that task-oriented leaders (low-LPC) were more effective in situations very high or very low in favorableness. On the other hand, employee-oriented leaders (high-LPC) were more effective in moderately favorable situations. These contingent relationships between leader's style and situational favorableness are illustrated in Exhibit 11.5. The exhibit illustrates how situations can fall along a favorableness continuum. At one end, the most favorable situations are found: leader–member relations are good, task structure is high, and the leader power position is strong. At the other end are the most unfavorable situations—leader–member relations are poor, the task is unstructured, and the leader power position is weak.

Implications for sport managers

One implication of Fiedler's theory is that any leadership style can be effective provided it is matched with the situation and its favorableness. Sport seems to be an area where the situation might be most favorable to the leader (see Exhibit 11.6). Athletics is generally a voluntary activity. That is, individuals freely choose to participate. Quite often, athletes also have a choice of team (and, consequently, a choice of coach). Furthermore, both the coach and the athletes share the organizational goal of pursuit of excellence. And finally, the processes by which goals are to be achieved are also clearly understood and accepted by all members of the organization. As a result, the three elements—the leader, the members, and the situation—are in congruence with one another. Consequently, the situation is

exhibit 11.5 Fiedler's contingency model of leadership.

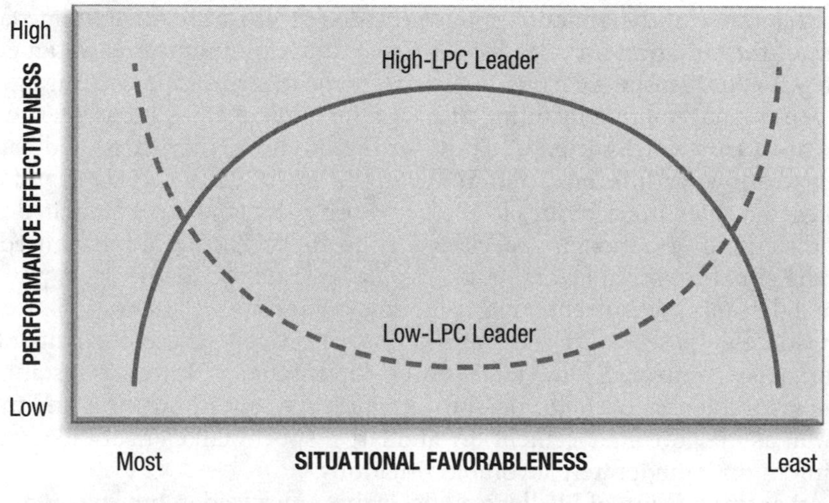

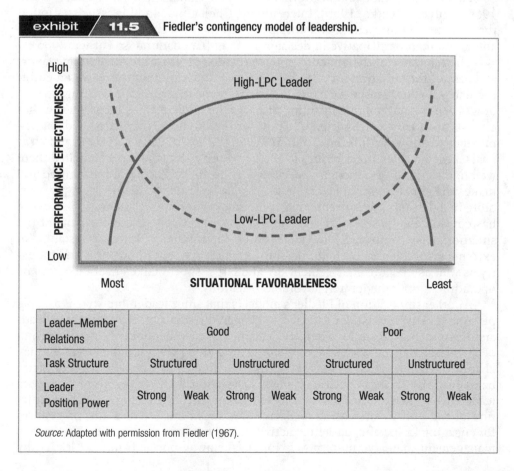

Leader–Member Relations	Good				Poor			
Task Structure	Structured		Unstructured		Structured		Unstructured	
Leader Position Power	Strong	Weak	Strong	Weak	Strong	Weak	Strong	Weak

Source: Adapted with permission from Fiedler (1967).

exhibit 11.6 Fiedler's model and sport (Chelladurai & Turner, 2006).

HIGH CONGRUENCE IN LEADER/MEMBERSHIP/SITUATION
■ Voluntary activity
■ Choice of team/coach
■ Common goal of pursuit of excellence in sport
■ Process of achieving goal understood and accepted by members
HIGH SITUATIONAL FAVORABLENESS
■ Autocratic task-oriented leadership style
■ Athletes' preference for autocratic rather than participative decision making

extremely favorable for the exercise of influence by the coach (an autocratic coach could be very effective). In short, Fiedler's proposal, that task-oriented and autocratic leaders are most effective in highly favorable situations, is reasonable in an athletic setting. In fact, a number of studies have found that coaches do tend to be generally autocratic and task-oriented in their leadership style (Hendry, 1968, 1969; Ogilvie & Tutko, 1966). Interestingly, Chelladurai and his associates found that athletes in Canadian universities preferred their coaches to be relatively more autocratic than participative in decision making (Chelladurai & Turner, 2006).

The reference to the athletic team is provided to illustrate the extreme favorableness of the situation for a leader. A similar situation might involve an entrepreneur who has just started a business such as a fitness club, a marketing agency, or an event management consulting firm. Assume that she has hired a few of her closest, most trustworthy friends. Thus, for the moment, there are good leader–member relations within the group. If the entrepreneur has set specific and clear goals, has identified the activities to achieve those goals, and has articulated them well to the employees, there is goal clarity. Thus, the task is highly structured and makes the situation more favorable for the leader. Finally, the position power is quite high because the entrepreneur is the sole owner of the business. Hence, she has considerable power over the employees. Collectively, these elements of the situation make it extremely favorable for the entrepreneur. However, instances of extreme favorableness of the leadership situation are rare in business and industry as well as in sport management. By and large, sport managers are likely to be operating in only moderately favorable situations.

Another implication of Fiedler's model is that since leadership style is a stable personality characteristic, it is easier to change the situation than to change leadership style. For example, when the leaders and members of a marketing group of a professional sport franchise are not getting along well, top management may change the composition of the marketing unit (that is, fire, hire, or transfer members) in order to improve leader–member relations. They may also change the leader if necessary. Alternatively, top management may change the task structure of the unit by increasing or decreasing the extent of rules and procedures for engaging in specific marketing activities and reporting the results. Finally, top management may give more power to, or take away power from, the leader. By altering these elements, top management can change the favorableness of the situation to be consistent with the leader's task or interpersonal orientation. In Fiedler's view, this approach is much more practical and productive than trying to change the orientation (personality) of the leader.

This perspective of the theory also provides a practical guideline for aspiring managers/leaders. That is, the theory provides a basis for individuals to assess their own leadership style, evaluate the various positions of leadership open to them, and then choose a position in which the situation's favorableness matches their personal leadership style.

Criticisms of Fiedler's theory

Fiedler's contingency model has been extensively tested in various organizational contexts. Not surprisingly, the research by Fiedler and his associates was supportive of the theory, because the theory itself was built on that research. However, subsequent research by others has highlighted some limitations of the theory. One issue pertains to the question of what the LPC scale actually measures. Initially, it was viewed as a measure of personality, but a subsequent interpretation advanced by Fiedler (1973) determined that the scale measures a hierarchy of goals (task accomplishment versus interpersonal relations). Larson and Rowland (1974) suggested that the LPC measures the cognitive complexity of the individual—that is, the extent to which an individual can process and assimilate numerous and complex bits of information.

Somewhat related to the aforementioned issue is the question of stability in a leader's orientation. Fiedler's model does not allow for the possibility of a shift in LPC scores owing to experience with different groups. Also, task orientation and interpersonal orientation are treated as extremes on a single continuum. The theory does not consider the possibility that a leader could be high on both orientations.

Another limitation is that the theory overlooks the possibility that the manager's leadership style could actually change the situational characteristics. For example, a leader might be operating under the condition of poor leader–member relations. If the leader is a high-LPC (relations-oriented) leader, then his activities will tend to improve leader–member relations, and over time, the situation will become more favorable.

Another comment on the theory relates to the issue of either task or relations orientation versus style of decision making. That is, according to the theory, a task-oriented leader is autocratic in arriving at a decision, and a relations-oriented leader is democratic. As noted in the earlier discussion of descriptions of leader behavior, the assumption that a task (or relations) orientation is associated with a particular style of decision making is unjustified.

It is also questionable whether situations representing the extreme ends of the favorableness continuum (refer back to Exhibit 11.5) are common in organizations. The least favorable situation on this continuum represents a chaotic situation that would not likely continue long-term. Similarly, the most favorable situation on this continuum represents an unlikely utopia.

In overview, despite the criticisms, Fiedler's contingency model was the first attempt to view leadership from a situational perspective. Fiedler emphasized the need to analyze leadership style as well as the situational characteristics. Although the meaning of the LPC score is questionable, the theory has highlighted the significance of (a) a leader's personality and orientations, and (b) the fit between the leader and the situation.

exhibit 11.7 McClelland's model of managerial motivation.

EFFECTS OF	SMALL ENTREPRENEURIAL ORGANIZATIONS	LARGE ORGANIZATIONS
Need for Affiliation	Irrelevant	Detrimental
Need for Achievement	Beneficial	Detrimental
Need for Power:		
■ Personal Power	Beneficial	Detrimental
■ Socialized Power	Irrelevant	Necessary and beneficial

McClelland's Model of Managerial Motivation

A second model that focuses on a leader's traits is that of McClelland and his associates (McClelland, 1961, 1975; McClelland & Burnham, 1976; McClelland & Winter, 1969). McClelland's well-known work deals with the human needs of affiliation, achievement, and power, and how they influence human behavior in general. His major contribution to research on **managerial motivation** was to show that the needs for affiliation, achievement, and power have specific relevance to organizational context. More specifically, McClelland and his associates demonstrated that the need for power is more critical to managerial effectiveness than the other two needs. Exhibit 11.7 summarizes this model.

Need for affiliation

The **need for affiliation** refers to the desire to be liked and accepted by the group. According to McClelland and Burnham (1976), the affiliation motive is least important to successful management. In fact, they suggest that it can even be detrimental to successful management. Managers with a high need for affiliation might tend to compromise on various rules in order to satisfy individual needs. For instance, an event manager, in his eagerness to be accepted by specific employees, may be a little lenient with them when they are late for work. Although the individual recipients may enjoy this preferential treatment, other members of the organization will consider these practices unfair, thus lowering the morale of the group.

Need for achievement

The **need for achievement** refers to "the desire to do something better or more efficiently than it has been done before" (McClelland & Burnham, 1976, p. 100). Individuals who have a high level of this need prefer a task that is moderately difficult rather than one that is too difficult or too easy. These same individuals also prefer rapid, specific feedback on how well they are doing. In addition, because achievement-motivated people try to improve their personal performance, they tend to do things themselves.

These characteristics would benefit the owner/manager of an individual business or a small firm. Thus, as Yukl (1981) pointed out, "the dominant motive for successful entrepreneurial managers appears to be need for achievement. Of course, success depends on the manager's ability as well as his motivation" (p. 79). When sport management graduates start their own businesses (for example, a pro shop, a fitness club, or a player agency), they are often in the position of having to do everything themselves, from sales to marketing to accounting. These new business owners will have a greater chance of being successful if they are highly achievement-oriented.

The perseverance, dedication, and work ethic that are characteristic of achievement-motivated people have led many theorists and practitioners to suggest that the need for achievement should be the dominant prerequisite for *all* successful managers. However, this is not necessarily the case in larger organizations where what the manager personally does is less important than what the subordinates do. As McClelland and Burnham (1976) suggested, "The manager's job seems to call more for someone who can influence people than for someone who does things better on his own. In motivational terms, then, we might expect the successful manager to have a greater 'need for power' than need to achieve" (p. 101).

Participation in decision making leads to (a) a greater understanding of the problem and its solutions by the members; (b) a belief that the problem is their own and the choice of a solution is their decision; and (c) the effective execution of the decision.

TO recap

Need for power

Need for power refers to "a desire to have impact, to be strong and influential" (McClelland & Burnham, 1976, p. 103). For example, the success of a departmental director of intercollegiate athletics or recreational sports is likely to be based on the degree to which he has influenced the members toward greater effort and achievement rather than on what he has personally accomplished. A director's willingness and ability to influence members is far more important than personal achievements. Similarly, the general manager of a professional sport franchise is responsible for many different activities. It stands to reason that he cannot carry out all those activities personally. Therefore, his success depends on how well his subordinates carry out their assignments. Thus, the general manager needs to be high on the need for power so that he will be oriented toward influencing subordinates to successfully perform tasks. On the other hand, the general manager should be relatively low on the need for achievement, which will inhibit his tendency to carry out the tasks by himself. In contrast, we noted earlier that in the case of the fitness entrepreneur, the need for achievement is most important.

McClelland and Burnham (1976) observed that the need for power must be moderated by a concern for the organization and the subordinates: "Above all, the good manager's power is not oriented toward personal aggrandizement but toward the institution which he or she serves. . . . This is the 'socialized' face of power as distinguished from the concern for personal power" (p. 103). Again, a comparison between a city recreation director and an entrepreneur helps clarify the distinction between "socialized power" and "personalized power." The director of a city recreation department should direct his attempts at influencing subordinates toward attaining organizational goals and promoting the welfare of the community rather than toward garnering personal glory and power. In the case of the entrepreneur, personal goals and organizational interests coincide, and few others, if any, are involved in the operation of the firm. Therefore, the personalized power motive may not be detrimental to the success of the firm. Consolidating the power, gaining control over the agenda of operation, and making more profit are all consistent with the notion of an entrepreneurial firm.

McClelland's emphasis on the power motive appears to be in opposition to a conventional "people orientation" and to the traditional reluctance to utilize an authoritarian form of management. McClelland and Burnham (1976), however, have argued that "the bogeyman of authoritarianism has in fact been wrongly used to downplay the importance of power in management. After all, management is an influence game. Some proponents of democratic management seem to have forgotten this fact, urging managers to be primarily concerned with people's human needs rather than with helping them to get things done" (pp. 104–105).

McClelland and Burnham (1976) noted that the presence of a power motive in management does not preclude the possibility that the manager can also adopt a democratic style. In fact, their research showed that successful managers were those who possessed a high need for power and a high concern for the organization, and who used a democratic managerial style. Subordinates under these types of managers possessed a high sense of responsibility and perceived a high degree of organizational clarity and team spirit (McClelland & Burnham, 1976). Chapter 6 described the advantages of member participation in decision making.

Given these advantages, the manager who wants to influence members to perform well in their jobs should include them in making decisions that affect them and their jobs. Note this conclusion pertains to managers of large organizations, such as a Division I athletic department or the NCAA. As we noted before, in the case of small firms and entrepreneurs, the achievement motive and personalized power motive might not adversely affect managerial effectiveness.

Comparing Fiedler's and McClelland's Views

In overview, the two approaches described above—Fiedler's contingency model of leadership effectiveness and McClelland's view of managerial motivation—emphasize the importance of the leader's specific personal traits. Although Fiedler's task orientation and McClelland's power motivation appear to be similar to the extent that both focus on task accomplishment, they differ in one significant aspect. While Fiedler's task-oriented leader is autocratic by definition, McClelland's power-motivated manager may also express the power motive in democratic ways. This difference notwithstanding, both Fiedler and McClelland have highlighted the significance of personal traits for effective leadership.

The Path–Goal Theory of Leader Effectiveness

Both Fiedler's contingency model of leadership and McClelland's model of managerial motivation emphasize leader traits. While the leader's traits and attributes are critical to the leadership phenomenon, the traits and attributes of the members are also critical. Members and their attributes are the focus of the **path–goal theory** of leader effectiveness. The theory was first proposed by Evans (1970) and later expanded upon by House and his associates (House, 1971; House & Dessler, 1974; House & Mitchell, 1974). House (1971) succinctly outlined the essence of the theory: "The motivational function of the leader consists of increasing personal pay-offs to subordinates for work-goal attainment, and making the path to these pay-offs easier to travel by clarifying it, reducing road blocks and pitfalls, and increasing the opportunities for personal satisfaction en route" (p. 323). Because the theory focuses on members' personal goals, their perceptions of the organizational goals, and the most effective paths to these goals, it is called the path–goal theory of leader effectiveness. That is, the theory attempts to specify how leadership should clarify the members' paths to the desired goals and rewards.

On the simplest level, every worker can be assumed to be seeking more monetary rewards from the organization. The leader can help the member by linking his personal goal to the incentive plans of the organization. In doing so, the leader will also identify the specific activities and performance levels necessary for receiving those incentives. In addition, the leader will also attempt to train the member in those tasks and remove any barriers that might hinder him from achieving the required performance level. In a similar manner, the director of the marketing department of an athletic enterprise can help her subordinates attain their personal objective of a promotion by suggesting the performance standards the employees need to achieve in order to be considered for promotion (such as securing a certain number of sponsorships or a certain dollar amount of sponsorships, and proposing and implementing innovative marketing strategies). In addition, the leader will also help the employees reach those standards by, for example, introducing them to prospective sponsors and training them in the art of making a presentation.

Leader behaviors related to the path–goal theory

As we noted in the discussion of the classification of leader behavior, four classes of leader behavior are taken into account in the path–goal theory: instrumental behavior, supportive behavior, participative behavior, and achievement-oriented behavior (House & Mitchell, 1974). **Instrumental behavior** is similar to the traditional initiating structure dimension discussed earlier. This leader behavior serves to clarify for members what is expected. It also involves leader behaviors associated with planning and coordinating. **Supportive behavior** reflects the leader's concern for the members' welfare and for a warm and friendly workplace environment. Thus, this dimension is very similar to the consideration dimension from the Ohio State studies. **Participative behavior** reflects the degree to which a leader shares information with members and allows them to participate in decision making. Finally, **achievement-oriented behavior** reflects the degree to which the manager sets challenging goals, expects good performance, and expresses confidence in the members. The path–goal theory, in essence, suggests that the extent to which the leader engages in these behaviors is a function of the situation that leader faces. These situational differences are described below.

Propositions of the path–goal theory

The path–goal theory is composed of two basic propositions: The first is that the leader's function is supplemental, and the second is that the motivational effect of leadership is a function of the situation.

Leadership function as supplemental. A leader's behavior will have an impact on member motivation and effort only to the extent that such behavior is seen as an immediate source of rewards and satisfaction, or as a path to future rewards and satisfaction. For example, when a supervisor of youth sports programs compliments a student volunteer on a job well done, this is an immediate reward and is likely to motivate the student to continue doing a good job. The supervisor may also teach and train the student in managing the programs and engage her in some managerial activities. These behaviors serve to enhance the student's experience and expertise, which in turn will serve the student well in her search for a job in the recreation field. Thus, the supervisor's behaviors are a source of future rewards. In addition, the leader's function supplements other factors that might contribute to member motivation and those that might be supportive of the individual. In our example of the student volunteer, other workers may provide the student with the same kind of support, positive feedback, and training. In addition, the programs' clients may also express their gratitude for the student's work. Under these circumstances, the supervisor's supportive and instrumental behaviors may become redundant. In other words, leadership is most necessary when there is a lack of motivation in the organizational context in which the members operate.

Motivation as a function of the situation. The second proposition of the path–goal theory is that the motivational effect of leadership is a function of the situation, which in turn is composed of the members and the environmental pressures and demands.

According to the theory, the personality and perceived ability of members (**member factors**) affect the degree to which they prefer or react to specific forms of leader behavior. For instance, subordinates with a high need for affiliation prefer supportive leadership behaviors, whereas subordinates with a high need for achievement would prefer achievement-oriented leadership behaviors (House & Dessler, 1974). Similarly, a member who has a high perception of personal ability would prefer less instrumental leadership behavior (and, in fact, would react negatively to such behavior).

Consider two different scenarios for the student volunteer in the youth sports program. If the student is highly achievement-oriented and has less need for affiliation, she is likely to be more motivated by the supervisor's help in enhancing her managerial competencies than by the supervisor's warm and friendly manner. In contrast, the competence-enhancing behaviors of the supervisor may not have much motivational impact if the student is not oriented toward achievement in that area.

Environmental factors are reflected in the nature of the task, the primary work group, and the organizational set. Tasks may vary in the degree to which they are routine or variable, the extent to which they are interdependent, and the degree to which they are inherently satisfying. Insofar as the leader's role is supplemental, the leader's behavior should vary according to the demands of the task. Thus, instrumental behavior is more appropriate when the task is variable than when it is routine. Similarly, interdependent tasks require a greater degree of coordination than independent tasks, and, therefore, a leader's efforts at coordination (one aspect of instrumental behavior) will be more appreciated in interdependent tasks than in independent tasks. In support of these propositions, Chelladurai and Carron (1982) found that athletes in interdependent sports (team sports) and athletes in variable sports (such as basketball) preferred more training and instruction (instrumental behavior) than athletes in independent sports and nonvariable sports (such as track and field). In short, the degree to which a leader's behavior will be acceptable to the members, and the degree to which that behavior will have a motivational impact, depends on the nature of the task.

The nature of the work group also influences the degree to which specific leader behaviors are necessary and relevant. For example, in a close-knit work group, senior members may provide guidance and coaching to junior members. In such a case, a leader's instrumental behavior is redundant. Similarly, supportive behaviors are unnecessary because the cohesive group fulfills that need. The final element in the situation is the **organizational set.** That is, the goals of the organization, the rules and procedures laid down, and other organizational practices serve to determine the need for and the effects of leader behavior. Thus, when an organization has extensive rules and procedures for each member concerning how to carry out assigned tasks, the leader's instrumental behavior becomes unnecessary.

Path–goal theory and individual motivation

The path–goal theory of leadership can be better understood if it is viewed from the perspective of individual motivation. In fact, the path–goal theory is largely based on the expectancy theory of individual motivation. Recall that the notion of expectancy is built into the Porter and Lawler model of motivation described in Chapter 10.

To facilitate an understanding of the relationship between the path–goal theory of leadership and individual motivation, Chelladurai (1981) presented a modified version of the Porter and Lawler (1968) model of motivation and discussed the relevance of the various dimensions of coaching/leader behavior (see Exhibit 11.8) to the motivational process.

As Exhibit 11.8 shows, motivation (effort in Porter and Lawler's terminology) will lead to performance, which in turn will lead to reward. The effort–performance relationship (Box 2 to Box 3) is moderated by the member's ability (Box 6) and the accuracy of the perception of her role (Box 7). Finally, the reward–satisfaction relationship (Box 4 to Box 5) is influenced by the member's perception of the equity of the rewards (Box 8).

Based on this framework of individual motivation, it is possible to identify the points along the motivation–performance–satisfaction sequence where the

exhibit 11.8 Leader behaviors and individual motivation.

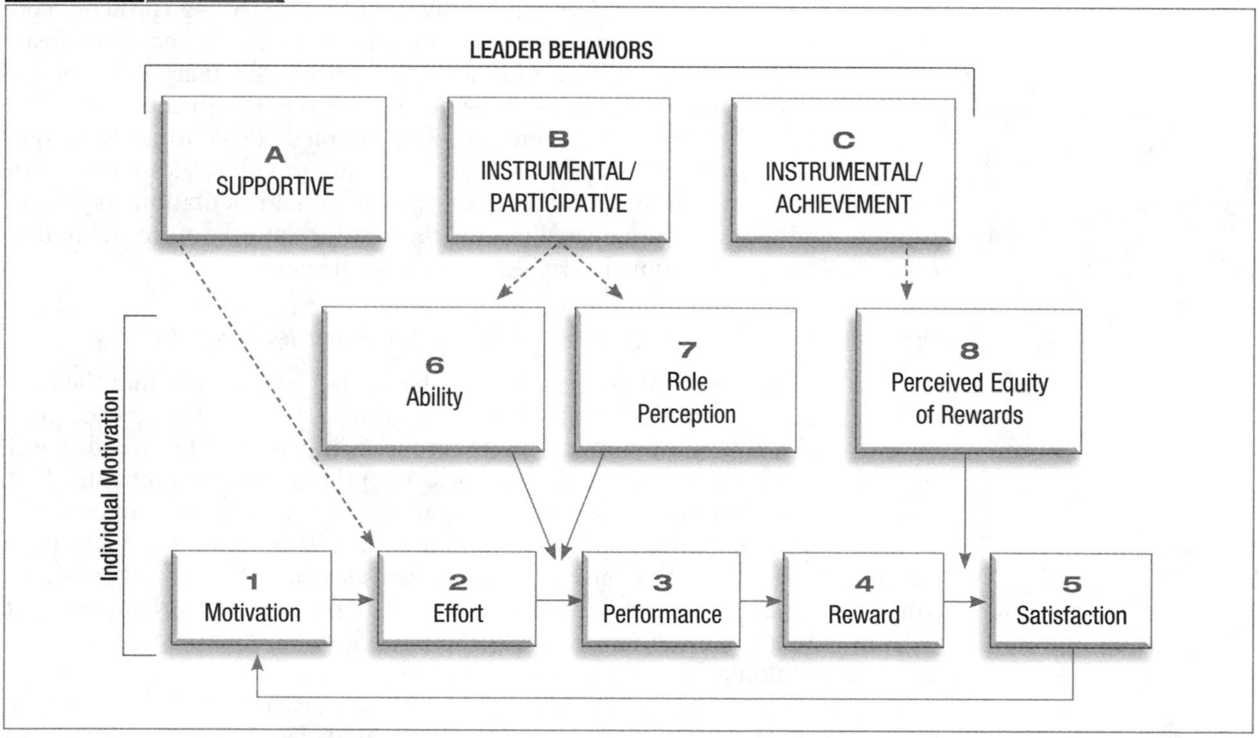

leader should intervene in an attempt to enhance the individual's motivational state. First, the value an individual attaches to intrinsic rewards is heightened when the leader sets challenging goals and expresses confidence in the member's capacity to attain those goals (achievement-oriented behavior, Box C). Supportive behavior (Box A) makes the effort phase enjoyable and frees it from any interpersonal frictions. Instrumental leader behavior (Box B) is beneficial when it leads to the development of the member's ability and when it serves to clarify role expectations. Thus, instrumental behavior strengthens the relationship between effort and performance. Participative behavior contributes to a member's role clarity as well as to feelings of involvement in decisions. Both of these effects of participative behavior enhance role performance. Finally, the equitable distribution of a leader's personal rewards (that is, equal rewards for equal performance) leads to a sense of equitability among the members.

The emphasis on personal rewards is deliberate. In small organizations, the manager may have considerable control over the rewards offered by the organization. In contrast, in larger organizations, the manager may not have a great deal of input into the determination of individual rewards. For example, pay raises and promotions in a bureaucracy are a function of some preset requirements or seniority. Under these circumstances, the manager must be content with providing personal rewards such as praise and encouragement.

In overview, although the path–goal theory of leadership includes a number of situational parameters, it places the greatest emphasis on the members, their ability, and their personal dispositions. Leadership is viewed as a process that helps members attain their personal goals (insofar as they are aligned with organizational goals). The path–goal theory contains the implicit assumption that a leader can change her leadership style according to situational exigencies. This notion that leader behavior is flexible contrasts with the inflexibility of leader behavior suggested by Fiedler's contingency model of leadership. In Fiedler's view, an individual's leadership style (task orientation versus interpersonal orientation) is a function of personality and, therefore, relatively more stable than situational variables, which can be altered.

Porter-Lawler model

The basic premise of the Porter and Lawler model of motivation is that an individual is motivated to work toward organizational goals only to the extent that (a) the individual values the rewards of attaining those goals, (b) the individual perceives that the efforts expended will lead to the level of performance expected by the organization, and (c) the rewards will be linked to such performance (refer back to Exhibit 10.6). The model also specifies that the relationship between one's effort and performance is dependent on the individual's having the necessary abilities and traits and on his or her correct perception of the job responsibilities. Finally, the linkages between performance, rewards, and satisfaction are a function of organizational practices in tying rewards to performance and distributing the rewards equitably based on relative performance.

TO recap

Implications of path–goal theory: Substitutes for leadership

As noted earlier, one of the propositions of the path–goal theory is that the leader's function is only supplemental. That is, the leader is expected to provide guidance and coaching, to structure activities for the members, and to provide social support only to the extent that these are lacking in the work environment. Clearly, whatever function the leader must perform may be partially accounted for by other factors in the environment. Kerr and Jermier (1978) have listed a number of such factors, which they refer to as *substitutes for leadership*. The most significant ones are the members' characteristics, their professional orientation and affiliation, the nature of their task and the work group, and the organizational structure (including the policies and procedures).

The significance of member characteristics and the nature of the task were discussed earlier in this chapter in connection with House's path–goal theory of leadership. The work group (or peer group) can also serve as a substitute for the leader. For example, fellow employees often provide the necessary guidance and coaching to help a new employee or volunteer carry out assignments. More importantly, the work group also provides the social support necessary when both personal and organizational problems arise.

If the organizational policies and procedures are elaborate and if they clearly specify what the employee should do, how to do it, and under what circumstances it should be done, then the leader's instrumental behavior becomes redundant. The employee simply has to follow the rules. However, since these service tasks are relatively routine and monotonous, the supervisor must attempt to create a warm climate and establish good interpersonal relationships within the group. Thus, the leader's supportive behavior is important.

In professional or human service organizations, the professional orientation of the members and their relationships with other professionals serve as substitutes for leadership. Professional orientation ensures that members are committed to providing a quality service. For instance, medical personnel and athletic trainers in university athletic departments (or exercise physiologists in fitness clubs) are expected to abide by their professional standards of providing quality service to their clients. Furthermore, their respective professional associations set standards of performance for their professions, and members internalize these standards. In addition, periodic peer meetings and professional publications provide some guidance and incentives for greater productivity. Given this orientation within professional services, it should not be necessary for the managers of these organizations to attempt to influence members.

IN brief

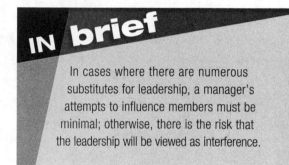

In cases where there are numerous substitutes for leadership, a manager's attempts to influence members must be minimal; otherwise, there is the risk that the leadership will be viewed as interference.

The Adaptive-Reactive Theory

Osborn and Hunt (1975) noted that the variables of the larger organizational system have an impact on both the leader and members and, therefore, must be treated as separate classes of contingency variables. One class of variables in the organizational system, called *macro variables,* includes unit size, level of technology, and formal structure of the organization. A second class of contingency variables, called *micro variables,* includes the task itself and differences among individual members. On the basis of these two classes of variables that influence a leader, Osborn and Hunt dichotomized leader behavior into *adaptive behavior* and *reactive behavior.* (See Exhibit 11.9.)

Adaptive behavior

Adaptive behavior refers to the degree to which the leader adapts to the requirements of the organizational system (macro variables). That is, the nature of the organization and its processes demand or constrain leader behavior in specific ways. Consider the differences in the constraints and demands faced by a director of NCAA Division I athletic programs, where performance expectations and attained excellence are high, versus a director in a Division III program, where both the excellence and the expectations for such excellence are relatively low. Thus, unit size and level of technology contribute to a need for different formal structures (the size of the coaching staff in football, and the hierarchy and differentiation among the coaching staff in Division I and III institutions). These, in turn, contribute to the emergence of different leader behaviors.

exhibit 11.9 Adaptive–reactive theory.

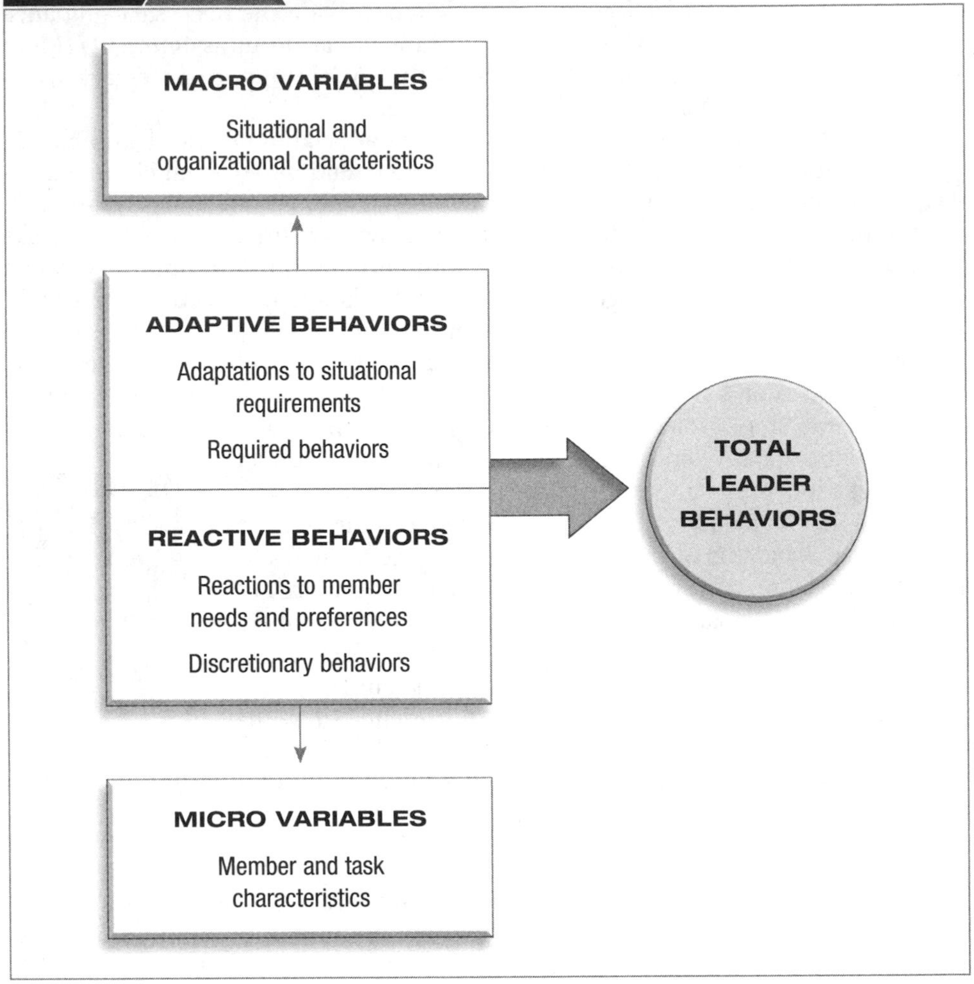

Reactive behavior

Reactive behavior refers to leader behaviors in reaction to member preferences and the differences among the tasks performed by the members. In Osborn and Hunt's theory, the nature of the task and individual differences are called the micro variables. Recall that House's path–goal theory also includes the nature of the task and individual differences as elements in the situation, which also included organizational characteristics. Osborn and Hunt separate the larger organizational variables (the macro variables) and the individual and task differences (the micro variables). The contrast between football and badminton illustrates the significance of the nature of the task. Whereas the individual tasks in football involve large muscle groups, badminton tasks involve finer movements. Also, though football is an interdependent sport, badminton is an independent sport. These differences, in turn, influence leader behavior.

For example, a football coach who shouts might positively affect the players and the team. But such behavior would likely be detrimental to the performance of the badminton players. It was already noted that individual differences relating to personality and ability also influence leader behavior. The leader behaviors influenced by the task and by individual differences are called the reactive behaviors—they reflect a leader's reactions to the needs and desires of the members.

Thus, according to the adaptive–reactive theory, the organizational variables (macro variables) control and constrain one set of leader behaviors (adaptive behaviors). Also, they do not permit the leader to deviate significantly from the organizational requirements. On the other hand, the micro variables elicit reactive behaviors that are largely under the control of the leader. The most important postulate of the adaptive–reactive theory is that the reactive behaviors reflect the *discretionary influence* exercised by the leader. Consequently, they will be motivational, to the extent that they match the needs and preferences of the members.

Consider the case of a supervisor in a large city recreation department overseeing eight other people. The supervisor and the subordinates may need to follow strict rules and procedures. The human resource management policies will be uniform across all units within the city government. Higher authorities may decide on monetary rewards for all employees. Under those circumstances, both the supervisor and the employees are aware that they are governed by the policy of the city government, a macro variable. In contrast, the supervisor may have the discretionary powers to assign the subordinates to different projects or to different facilities or playgrounds in the city. The supervisor can make such assignments with a view to accommodate the desires of as many subordinates as possible. These discretionary behaviors in reaction to member preferences are likely to be motivational.

Fiedler and House

The major focus of Fiedler's contingency theory is on the leader and his personality and leadership style. In contrast, House's path–goal theory of leadership emphasizes the members and their needs, preferences, and abilities. Although both Fiedler and House included organizational variables among the situational elements in their respective theories, their treatment of organizational requirements is superficial. In Fiedler's contingency model of leadership, the situation includes the variables of leader–member relations (whether members respect and like the leader or not), task structure (whether the task is simple and routine or complex), and the position power of the leader (the extent to which the leader has power to reward and punish members). The elements of task structure and power position can be seen as organizational variables. Similarly, House's path–goal theory of leadership includes as situational elements member characteristics (personality, preferences, and abilities), the nature of the task (routine or variable and independent or interdependent), the nature of the work group (friendly and cohesive or not), and the organizational set (goals, extent of rules and procedures, and so on).

TO recap

Implications for sport managers

The practical implication of the adaptive–reactive theory for sport managers is to adjust and abide to the demands and constraints of the macro variables that impinge on their respective organizations (e.g., government regulations that govern the operation of a fitness club, the NCAA rules governing collegiate sports, citizens' expectations for a city recreation department). By the same token, the managers also need to know the extent to which and the areas in which they have discretion in dealing with their employees. More importantly, they need to learn to make the best use of their limited discretionary behavior in motivating their subordinates.

LEADERSHIP AND POWER

In this chapter, leadership is defined as the interpersonal process of influencing members. The concept of *power* is often paired with leadership. Power refers to the capacity or ability to influence. That is, if managers have more power they have a better chance of influencing members.

But what are the bases or sources of power? The most commonly accepted framework of power was proposed by French and Raven (1959). They proposed that the social power one has may be classified into five categories based on the source of the power. These are labeled *legitimate power, reward power, coercive power, expert power,* and *referent power.*

Legitimate Power

Legitimate power is based on the position the person holds in the organization or group. As we noted in Chapter 7, a major tenet of bureaucracy is the hierarchy of authority. In other words, the higher-level position has the power over the lower-level position. This power differential is legitimized in a bureaucracy. This is evidenced in the power of the drill sergeant over the officer recruits. The managing director of a professional sport franchise has legitimate power over his subordinates. The athletic director of a university has legitimate power over the football coach even though the coach may get more than twice the salary of the athletic director. A coach has legitimate power over the multimillion-dollar athletes.

Reward Power

Another form of power closely linked to legitimate power is **reward power.** It simply refers to the fact that a person can bestow on another a desired reward. In many organizations, a manager at a particular level can decide on the merit pay for individuals or on the candidates to be promoted to higher positions. To the extent the subordinates desire these rewards, the manager has reward power over them. The coaches of team sports at any level have legitimate power as well as reward power. The reward power stems from the coach's authority over who the starters will be, who the substitutes will be, and who will play for how long. These opportunities are the rewards the athletes are seeking, and the coach is responsible for administering them. It must be noted here, however, that if no one wants the reward, then it has no power and the person holding the reward has no power, either. For example, individuals who do not want to be in charge of or responsible for others would not seek any higher-level positions in their organization. To them, a promotion is not a reward.

Coercive Power

An equally important source of power is the capacity to administer punishment to others. Just as a position in an organization may come with the power to reward others, it may also come with the power to punish others. For example, a drill sergeant does not have much reward power. However, he or she has considerable **coercive power** in dealing out punishments, such as making a cadet do extra push-ups or in submitting negative reports about the candidates to the higher-ups.

Punishment can take the form of withholding a reward, such as when the manager does not recommend a merit increase. Similarly, when a coach benches a player, the reward of playing is being withheld. From this perspective, the coercive power is as influential as the reward power.

Expert Power

Expert power refers to the expertise and specialized knowledge one possesses. In earlier times when most people were illiterate, the mere ability to read and write was a source of expert power. Now, expertise and specialized knowledge goes far beyond reading and writing. From a manager's perspective, expertise may reside in lawyers, accountants, financial experts, marketing specialists, and other specialized professionals. Another field in which expertise is sought after is technology use. Consider the case of a digital display used as a scoreboard and for action/fan close-ups in a football stadium; the manager of the stadium does not have much knowledge about the electronics or the computer software that controls the display. He or she relies on another person with expertise in software, and this other person is said to have expert power over the manager. Assume that the software person is the only expert available and that the digital display is the main attraction in the stadium; then the software specialist wields expert power. But as software experts for this technology become common, the manager can always hire someone else.

Referent Power

A person's **referent power** stems from the admiration other people have for him or her. Revolutionary leaders like Gandhi and Mandela wielded great referent power because the people of their respective countries and beyond had enormous admiration and liking for the sacrifices these individuals made for their country and their concern for the welfare of the common people. In our context, great coaches such as Vince Lombardi and John Wooden were bestowed with referent power, and, thus, they were able to influence their players to perform better.

Interrelationship of the Forms of Power

Note that in an organizational context, however, some power sources are likely to be interrelated. For instance, the notions of legitimate power, reward power, and coercive power are related because the organizational hierarchy assigns these powers differentially to various positions. Accordingly, these three forms of power are labeled *position powers* because they reside in the position and not the person. On the other hand, the expert power and referent power need not be related to the other three forms of power or to each other. Because these two forms of power reside in the person, they are **personal powers.** Moreover, the expert and referent power may reside anywhere in the organization and not necessarily in any hierarchical positions. A locker room attendant in the football practice facility may be an influential person. A senior employee in a recreation department may wield the greatest amount of referent power in the department.

Not all those who have power prefer to use it to influence others. The tendency to influence is derived from the need for power discussed earlier in the chapter. Persons who have a low need for power are not likely to use whatever power they may have. However, those individuals who have a high need for power and a great desire to impact the organization are likely to be more successful if they possess one or more of the forms of power described above.

SUMMARY

This chapter described various theories of leadership categorized under the trait, behavioral, and situational approaches to the study of leadership. It discussed the various dimensions of leader behavior developed by scholars at The Ohio State University (consideration and initiating structure) and the University of Michigan (employee orientation and production orientation).

Following this was a description of Fiedler's contingency model of leader effectiveness, with the emphasis on a match between leadership style as a personality characteristic (task orientation versus interpersonal orientation) and situational favorableness (defined by leader–member relations, task structure, and position power). We discussed the implications of Fiedler's model and the criticisms against it. Then we examined McClelland's view that the need for power in a manager is more critical than the needs for affiliation or achievement. House's path–goal theory states that the leader's role is to increase the members' personal payoffs for their efforts and to make the path to those payoffs easier. Leadership is seen as a supplemental role providing instrumental, supportive, and achievement-oriented behaviors. The effects of these behaviors are said to be dependent on environmental factors, including member characteristics and the nature of the task. We looked at the implications of the path–goal theory and the notion of substitutes for leadership. Next, we noted that the adaptive–reactive theory of leadership placed the emphasis on environmental demands and constraints. The chapter concluded with a discussion of leadership and power, focusing on the sources of power.

develop YOUR PERSPECTIVE

1. Are you relatively more task-oriented or relations-oriented? What is the basis of your self-perception?
2. In the case of an athletic team, what factors serve as "substitutes for leadership"?
3. Many believe that sport is generally an autocratic situation. Do you agree or disagree with this position? Why?

references

Bass, B. M. (1985). *Leadership and performance beyond expectations*. New York: The Free Press.

Bass, B. M. (1990). From transactional to transformational leadership: Learning to share the vision. *Organizational Dynamics, 18*(3), 19–31.

Bateman, T. S., & Snell, S. A. (2007). *Management: Leading and collaborating in a competitive world* (7th ed.). Boston: McGraw-Hill Irwin.

Bowers, D. G., & Seashore, S. E. (1966). Predicting organizational effectiveness with a four-factor theory of leadership. *Administrative Science Quarterly, 11*, 238–263.

Branch, D., Jr. (1990). Athletic director leader behavior as a predictor of intercollegiate athletic organizational effectiveness. *Journal of Sport Management, 4*, 161–173.

Chelladurai, P. (1978). *A contingency model of leadership in athletics*. Unpublished doctoral dissertation, University of Waterloo, Waterloo, Canada.

Chelladurai, P. (1981). The coach as motivator and chameleon of leadership styles. *Science Periodical on Research and Technology in Sport*. Ottawa: Coaching Association of Canada.

Chelladurai, P. (1993). Leadership. In R. N. Singer, M. Murphey, & L. K. Tennant (Eds.), *Handbook of research on sport psychology* (pp. 647–671). New York: Macmillan.

Chelladurai, P., & Carron, A. V. (1982). Task characteristics and individual differences and their relationship to preferred leadership in sports. *Psychology of motor behavior and sport—1982: Abstracts*. College Park, MD: North American Society for the Psychology of Sport and Physical Activity.

Chelladurai, P., & Turner, B. (2006). Styles of decision making in coaching. In J. M. Williams (Ed.), *Applied sport psychology: Personal growth to peak performance* (5th ed., pp. 140–154). Boston: McGraw-Hill.

De Neve, J-E., Mikhaylov, S., Dawes, C. T., Christakis, N. A., & Fowler, J. H. (2013). Born to lead? A twin design and genetic association study of leadership role occupancy. *Leadership Quarterly, 24,* 45–60.

Evans, M. G. (1970). The effects of supervisory behavior on the path–goal relationships. *Organizational Behavior and Human Performance, 5,* 277–298.

Fiedler, F. E. (1954). Assumed similarity measures as predictors of team effectiveness. *Journal of Abnormal and Social Psychology, 49,* 381–388.

Fiedler, F. E. (1967). *A theory of leadership effectiveness.* New York: McGraw-Hill.

Fiedler, F. E. (1972). How do you make leaders more effective? New answers to an old puzzle. *Organizational Dynamics, 1*(2), 3–18.

Fiedler, F. E. (1973). Personality and situational determinants of leader behavior. In E. A. Fleishman & J. G. Hunt (Eds.), *Current developments in the study of leadership.* Carbondale: Southern Illinois University Press.

Fineman, S., Gabriel, Y., & Sims, D. (2010). *Organizing and organizations* (4th ed.). Thousand Oaks, CA: Sage.

French, J. R. P., & Raven, B. (1959). The bases of social power. In D. Cartwright (Ed.), *Studies in social power* (pp. 150–167). Ann Arbor, MI: Institute for Social Research.

Halpin, A. W., & Winer, B. J. (1957). A factorial study of the leader behavior description. In R. M. Stogdill & A. E. Coons (Eds.), *Leader behavior: Its description and measurement.* Columbus: The Ohio State University.

Hemphill, J. K., & Coons, A. E. (1957). Development of the Leader Behavior Description Questionnaire. In R. M. Stogdill & A. E. Coons (Eds.), *Leader behavior: Its description and measurement.* Columbus: The Ohio State University.

Hendry, L. B. (1968). The assessment of personality traits in the coach–swimmer relationship and a preliminary examination of the "father-figure" stereotype. *Research Quarterly, 39,* 543–551.

Hendry, L. B. (1969). A personality study of highly successful and "ideal" swimming coaches. *Research Quarterly, 40,* 299–305.

Hill, A. (2013, May 21). Leadership that will mess with your head. *Financial Times,* p. 12.

Hitt, M. A., Black, J. S., & Porter, J. W. (2009). *Management* (2nd ed.). Upper Saddle River, NJ: Pearson Prentice Hall.

Hollander, E. P., & Julian, J. W. (1969). Contemporary trends in the analysis of leadership processes. *Psychological Bulletin, 71,* 387–397.

House, R. J. (1971). A path–goal theory of leader effectiveness. *Administrative Science Quarterly, 16,* 321–338.

House, R. J., & Dessler, G. (1974). The path–goal theory of leadership: Some post hoc and a priori tests. In J. G. Hunt & L. L. Larson (Eds.), *Contingency approaches to leadership.* Carbondale: Southern Illinois University Press.

House, R. J., & Mitchell, T. R. (1974). Path–goal theory of leadership. *Journal of Contemporary Business, 3,* 81–97.

Ivancevich, J. M., Konopaske, R., & Matteson, M. T. (2011). *Organizational behavior and management* (9th ed.). New York: McGraw-Hill Irwin.

Katz, D., Maccoby, N., Gurin, G., & Floor, L. (1951). *Productivity, supervision, and morale among railroad workers.* Ann Arbor: University of Michigan.

Katz, D., Maccoby, N., & Morse, N. (1950). *Productivity, supervision and morale in an office situation.* Ann Arbor: University of Michigan.

Kerr, S., & Jermier, J. M. (1978). Substitutes for leadership: Their meaning and measurement. *Organizational Behavior and Human Performance, 22,* 375–403.

Larson, L. L., & Rowland, K. (1974). Leadership style and cognitive complexity. *Academy of Management Journal, 17,* 36–45.

McClelland, D. C. (1961). *The achieving society.* New York: Van Nostrand.

McClelland, D. C. (1975). *Power: The inner experience.* New York: Irvington.

McClelland, D. C., & Burnham, D. H. (1976). Power is the great motivator. *Harvard Business Review, 54,* 100–110.

McClelland, D. C., & Winter, D. (1969). *Motivating economic achievement.* New York: The Free Press.

Morse, N. C., & Reimer, E. (1956). The experimental change of a major organizational variable. *Journal of Abnormal and Social Psychology, 51,* 120–129.

Northouse, P. G. (2010). *Leadership: Theory and practice* (5th ed.). Thousand Oaks, CA: Sage.

Ogilvie, B. C., & Tutko, T. A. (1966). *Problem athletes and how to handle them.* London: Pelham Books.

Osborn, R. N., & Hunt, J. G. (1975). An adaptive-reactive theory of leadership: The role of macro variables in leadership research. In J. G. Hunt & L. L. Larson (Eds.), *Leadership frontiers.* Kent, OH: Kent State University.

Porter, L. W., & Lawler, E. E. (1968). *Managerial attitudes and performance.* Homewood, IL: Richard D. Irwin.

Sheridan, J. E., Downey, H. K., & Slocum, J. W. (1975). Testing causal relationships of House's path–goal theory of leadership effectiveness. In J. G. Hunt & L. L. Larson (Eds.), *Leadership frontiers.* Kent, OH: Kent State University.

Stogdill, R. M. (1974). *Handbook of leadership.* New York: The Free Press.

Szilagyi, A. D., & Wallace, M. J. (1980). *Organizational behavior and performance.* Santa Monica, CA: Goodyear.

Taylor, J. C., & Bowers, D. G. (1972). *Survey of organizations: A machine-scored standardized questionnaire instrument.* Ann Arbor: Institute for Social Research, The University of Michigan.

Yukl, G. A. (1971). Toward a behavioral theory of leadership. *Organizational Behavior and Human Performance, 6,* 414–440.

Yukl, G. A. (1981). *Leadership in organizations*. Englewood Cliffs, NJ: Prentice Hall.

Yukl, G. (2006). *Leadership in organizations* (6th ed.). Upper Saddle River, NJ: Pearson-Prentice Hall.

Yukl, G., Gordon, A., & Taber, T. (2002). A hierarchical taxonomy of leadership behavior: Integrating a half century of behavior research. *Journal of Leadership and Organizational Studies, 9*, 15–32.

CHAPTER 12 CONTEMPORARY APPROACHES TO LEADERSHIP

manage YOUR LEARNING

After completing this chapter you should be able to:

- Explain the multidimensional model of leadership, its components, and the relationships among these components.
- Distinguish between transactional and transformational leadership, and their effects.
- Define charismatic leadership.

strategic CONCEPTS

actual leader behavior
charismatic leadership
congruent
performance
preferred leader behavior
punctuated equilibrium
required leader behavior
satisfaction
transactional leadership
transformational leadership

We see around us frantic efforts to change the structure and processes of all forms of organizations. Such efforts are variously called downsizing, right-sizing, re-engineering, restructuring, and refocusing. Any restructuring or repositioning of organizations requires strong leadership at the top. Those who guide their organizations to transform into innovative and profitable enterprises are called *transformational leaders*. Along with the pace of change, the study of these leaders and transformational leadership has also intensified in the past three decades.

EVOLUTION OF CONTEMPORARY THEORIES OF LEADERSHIP

The criticisms of existing theories of leadership are twofold. First, the leader is purported to act within the constraints imposed by the situation (see Exhibit 12.1). The dichotomy of adaptive and reactive leader behavior proposed by Osborn and Hunt (1975) suggests that the leader can only adapt to the situation and react to member preferences. This view reflects Stewart's (1982) demands–constraints–choices theory, which states that a leader's discretionary behavior is circumscribed by the demands and constraints in her environment. Stewart (1982) suggested that in any organizational context, the manager/leader will be faced with certain demands and constraints imposed on the position. Demands are those activities expected of a leader in a given situation that he must fulfill to be accepted by the group or organization. Constraints are the limits within which the leader can act. In other words, the leader is prohibited from acting in the domain beyond the boundaries set by the constraints. According to Stewart (1982), the area between demands and constraints of the situation represents the choices a leader has. Stewart's demands–constraints–choices the-

exhibit 12.1 Stewart's (1982) demands–constraints–choices theory.

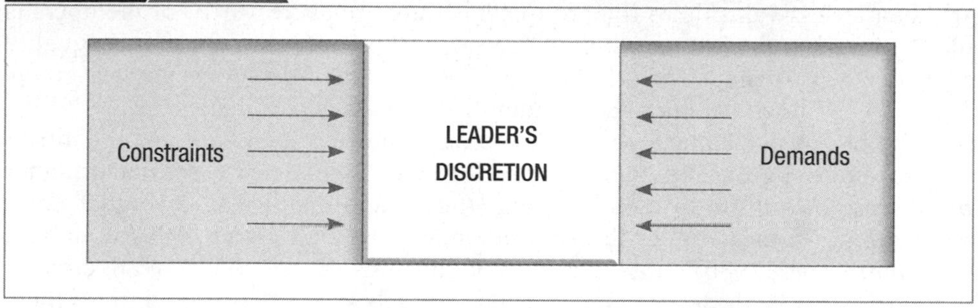

ory is illustrated in Exhibit 12.1. A significant portion of the demands and constraints stems from the members themselves. Thus, the leader needs to transact with members individually and collectively to have them perform their duties. Such transactions involve the leader providing some resources, including leader approval and support, in return for members' efforts toward the attainment of organizational goals.

The second focus of criticisms against the leadership theories described so far is the transactional nature of leadership as portrayed by the theories. For example, Osborn and Hunt's adaptive–reactive theory implicitly acknowledges this aspect when it states that the leader needs to react to members' needs and preferences. Chelladurai's (1978, 1993, 1999) model (to be discussed later in the chapter) also suggests that the leader's actual behaviors need to be consistent with the style of leadership preferred by members. The transactions with the members in general involve the leaders offering rewards to members, who in turn comply with leaders' directions and suggestions. The transaction may also take the form of punishment or threat of punishment in order to elicit the desired behavior or performance from the members.

TRANSACTIONAL THEORY

The theories mentioned earlier imply the transactional nature of leadership; therefore, they are rightfully called *transactional leadership* theories. Another prominent transactional theory is the leader–member exchange (LMX) theory.

Leader-Member Exchange Theory

When it was proposed in the 1970s, the leader–member exchange theory was known as the vertical dyadic linkage (VDL) model (see Dansereau, Cashman, & Graen, 1973; Dansereau, Graen, & Haga, 1975; Graen, 1976; Graen & Cashman, 1975). The essential thrust of the model is that effectiveness of leadership is a function of the extent to which the leader builds a unique relationship with each of the members. Instead of assuming that a leader will behave the same way with all members, this theory posits that the forms and quality of leader–member relationships will vary across the members of the group. The relationship between a member and the leader is based on the interpersonal exchanges between the two. The quality of such a relationship is characterized by mutual trust, respect, and support.

The implication of the theory is that a leader is likely to bestow trust and support upon those individuals the leader values as contributors to positive group functioning. The leader is not likely to be interacting as much with those who are seen as less valuable to the group. This differential treatment of members is likely to lead to the formation of an *in-group,* whose members have high-quality exchange relationships with the leader. The other members form the *out-group.* Exhibit 12.2 illustrates these differential leader–member exchanges.

The in-group members will tend to assume more responsibility and contribute more to the group. In turn, their performances will also be evaluated higher than those of out-group members, and these factors will lead to higher commitment and satisfaction of in-group members (Basu & Green, 1997; Duchon, Green, & Taber, 1986). Note that the relationships described above are circular in nature. That is, the leader identifies a few members as valuable and treats them with trust and respect. This will lead those members to reciprocate by taking on more responsibility to relieve the leader, perform better, and contribute more to the group. With such high performance and contributions, they are, in turn, likely to be evaluated higher than the others. More importantly, the leader is going to value them even more and further enhance his relationship with them. Note that the LMX theory is also transactional in nature—it involves the exchange of mutual feelings of trust, support, and performance.

Transactional Versus Transformational Leadership

Transactional leadership is not in itself a bad thing. In fact, it may even be a fruitful approach when the environment of the work group is somewhat stable and when both the leader and members are satisfied with the work group's purposes and processes. Moreover, it is assumed that members with a stable set of needs and desires will engage in transactions with the leader in order to benefit

exhibit 12.2 The quality of LMX and the formation of in-group and out-group.

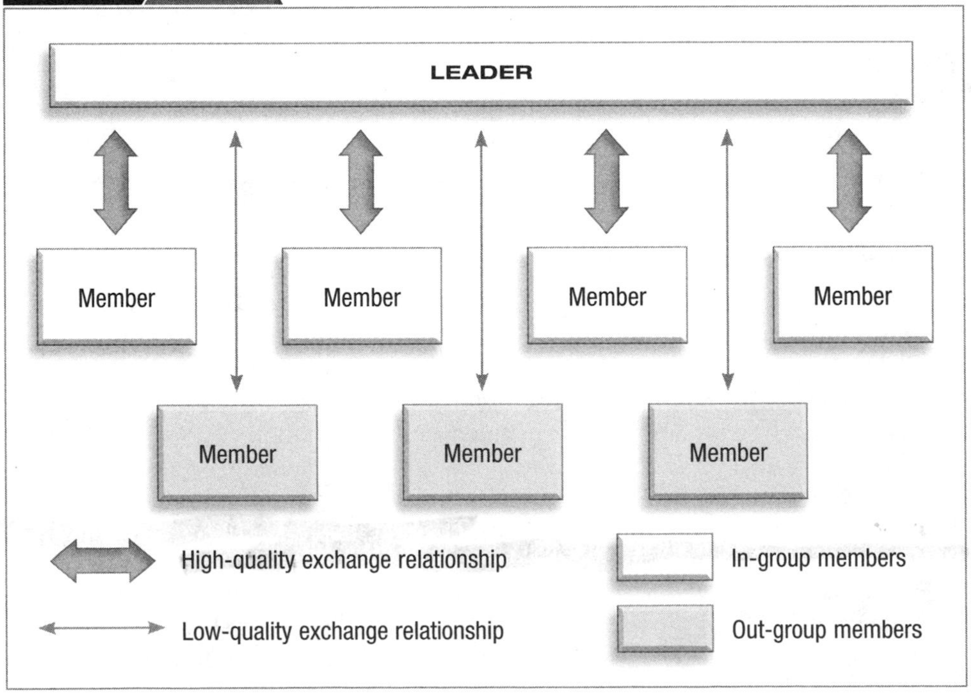

themselves, the leader, and the organization. Thus, transactional leadership can be effective in maintaining the status quo in terms of productivity and effectiveness. However, transactional leadership is not seen as very useful when an organization has to change in response to changes in the environment.

Transformational leadership, on the other hand, is defined as "the process of influencing major changes in the attitudes and assumptions of organization members (organizational culture) and building commitment for major changes in the organization's objectives and strategies" (Yukl & Van Fleet, 1992, p. 174). According to this definition, the transformation occurs at three levels: (1) changes in organizational objectives and strategies, (2) member commitment to the new set of goals and strategies, and (3) changes in the assumptions and attitudes of members. This shift in conceptualizing leadership has been spearheaded by different groups of scholars, each with their own unique perspectives. Bass and his associates (Bass, 1985, 1990, 1997; Bass & Avolio, 1993) used the terms *transformational* and *transactional* to label the two different aspects of leadership as defined above. They view these aspects as independent dimensions, meaning that a leader can be both transformational and transactional. Conger and Kanungo (1987, 1988, 1998) used the term *charismatic* to refer to leadership that is concerned with larger issues as opposed to that concerned with daily routines and maintenance. A third approach is that of House and his associates (House, 1977; House & Howell, 1992; House & Podsakoff, 1994; House & Shamir, 1993), who view charisma as a characteristic attributed to a transformational leader. Although there are differences among the theories, they do share a considerable overlap in their concepts and the relationships they espouse.

TRANSFORMATIONAL LEADERSHIP

The basis for transformational leadership is a general discontent with the status quo. Transformational leaders are concerned with creating a new vision and order for the organization. In the process of changing the total organization, a transformational leader (a) articulates the vision, (b) convinces the members of the viability of the vision, and (c) expresses confidence in their capacity to achieve that vision. Transformational leadership involves the arousal of members' higher-order needs, which in turn elevates the level of effort beyond expectations (Bass, 1985; Conger & Kanungo, 1987). Furthermore, it entails empowering the members to engage in innovative and creative ways to achieve the stated vision. More importantly, transformational leadership involves a new vision—an alternative to the status quo. In fact, the terms *transformational* and *visionary* are used interchangeably to describe this form of leadership. Exhibit 12.3 shows the contrasts between transformational and transactional leadership. Because the critical focus of transformational leadership is the vision, it is also appropriate to label it visionary leadership. Bennis (1984) uses the label *visionary leadership* and suggests that it calls for competency in four different areas: (1) *Management of attention* is garnering the attention of the followers to the vision that the leader has espoused. (2) *Management of meaning* is clarifying for the members what the vision means for

> **sidebar 12.1**
>
> **TRANSFORMATIONAL LEADERSHIP**
>
> In Bass's (1985) view, transformational leadership is composed of (a) charismatic leadership, meaning "the faith and respect in the leader and the inspiration and encouragement provided by his or her presence" (p. 209); (b) intellectual stimulation, defined as "the arousal and change in followers of problem awareness and problem solving, of thought and imagination, and of beliefs and values, rather than arousal and change in immediate action" (p. 99); and (c) individualized consideration, referring to treating each subordinate "differently according to each subordinate's needs and capabilities" (p. 82). Bass (1985) also developed the scale called the Multifactor Leadership Questionnaire (MLQ) to measure these three dimensions of transformational leadership.

exhibit 12.3 Transactional and transformational leadership.

LEADERSHIP	FACTORS AFFECTED	OUTCOMES
Transactional	Cognition Abilities Exchanges	Lower turnover/absence Satisfaction Expected performance
Transformational	Emotions Values/goals/needs Self-esteem	Higher aspirations Greater efforts Performance beyond expectations

them and for the organization, and how their activities contribute to attaining that vision. (3) *Management of trust* is creating a sense of trust among the followers that the leader is honest and trustworthy and deserves to be followed. (4) Finally, *management of self* is understanding and accepting one's own strengths and weaknesses and acknowledging that risk and failure are part of visionary leadership. In a later work, Bennis and Biederman (1997) observe that effective leaders of groups (a) provide the direction for the members and signify to them the importance of what they do, (b) generate trust among the group members including the leader, (c) make resolute but sometimes risky decisions, and (d) stimulate hope among the members that their efforts will be successful.

Readers will note that Bass (1985), Bennis (1984), and Bennis and Biederman (1997) refer to the same essential components even though they use different terms. Weese (1995) illustrates this perspective when he combines the works of Bass (1985), Bennis (1984), and Shaskin (1986) to propose a five-component model of leadership. He labels it the *Five "C" Model*. See the box on the facing page for his exposition of his model.

In contrast to Weese's five dimensions, Arnold, Arad, Rhoades, and Drasgow (2000), developed a measure named *Empowering Leadership Questionnaire* (ELQ) that measures five dimensions of leadership focused on empowering subordinates. As noted earlier, transformational leaders tend to empower their subordinates. These dimensions are described in Exhibit 12.4.

Many descriptions of transformational leadership imply that such leadership begins with the chief executive officer of an organization, and that it begins to filter down to lower levels through the empowerment of successive levels of subordinates. At the social and political

IN brief

Transactional leadership involves members' contributions in exchange for rewards from the leader in maintaining the status quo. In contrast, a transformational leader strives to change the goals and processes, to incite the higher-order needs of the followers, and to exhibit confidence in their capacity.

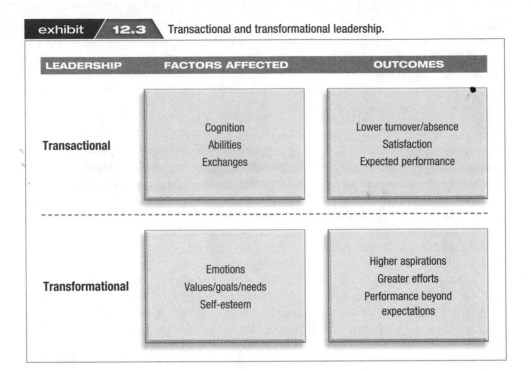

an expert's view / ON LEADERSHIP

Jim Weese is one of the founders and pillars of the North American Society for Sport Management and a recipient of its prestigious Earle Zeigler Award. He has also been its president. He is an ardent student of leadership, and he has proven his leadership mettle as an academic dean at two different universities.

WEESE'S FIVE C'S OF LEADERSHIP

Jim Weese

My lifelong study of leadership, informed and guided by the research of others, leads me to believe that there are some universal truths about effective leadership and they are captured in my "Five C's of Leadership." A discussion of each of the five areas is presented below.

Credibility (C1) is the foundation for leadership and leaders, and there are two components to this critical area. First, leaders need to be respected for having the relevant knowledge, insights, and experience to be seen as credible in the eyes of those they are leading. Secondly, they must be perceived as being honest, reliable, consistent, and trustworthy. People cannot impart effective, sustainable leadership without possessing and displaying both components. These are not static measures, however. Leaders and prospective leaders must stay current in leadership and in their respective fields, and they must always operate in an honest and trustworthy manner. If an individual fulfills these two components, he or she has the requisite foundation to lead. However, this is only the foundation.

Compelling vision (C2) refers to the leader's ability to focus the attention of followers on a desired and inspiring end. Effective leaders understand their industry, pay attention to internal and external cues, and they listen attentively to the needs, wants, and desires of stakeholders. They digest this information, blend in their own instincts and experience, and ensure that an inspiring vision is shaped and effectively communicated to members in a way that the overwhelming majority of (if not all) members see as important, uplifting, and their own.

Charismatic communicator (C3) refers to the leader's ability to formally and informally communicate with members. Effective leaders are exceptional communicators. They employ mechanisms to keep their members in the communication loop. They also share proof points that reinforce the vision's relevance and/or the unit or organization's progress towards its attainment. Effective leaders engage followers through their words and actions. The exciting developments in the emotional intelligence area (Goleman, Boyatzis, & McKee, 2002) support this key component of leadership. Effective leaders inspire both the hearts and minds of followers through their words and actions.

Contagious enthusiasm (C4) also draws on the emotional intelligence literature as it relates to leadership. Effective leaders have a passion for their role, their industry, and the people they lead. This is continually and consistently reflected in their words and actions. They go above and beyond the call of duty for their members who find their leader's enthusiasm and caring nature to be both exciting and uplifting. They challenge followers to perform beyond expectations. They regularly acknowledge and celebrate group and member achievements, and they are admired and respected by their followers.

Culture builder (C5) is the capstone feature of the model, and it is critical to long-term leadership success. Organizational culture refers to the dominant beliefs, values, and attitudes of members of a group or organization. Scholars like Schein (1990) suggest that developing and/or imbedding a desired culture for an organization is the most important responsibility for a leader. If leaders have the other four "C' components in place, they can, through their words, actions, human resource decisions, and reward systems, change and/or imbed a desired culture for their group or organization. This culture facilitates effective and sustainable leadership, brings forth higher commitment to the vision, and heightens member and organizational performance.

level, renowned transformational leaders such as Mohandas Gandhi of India and Nelson Mandela of South Africa could not have achieved what they did without the active cooperation of their immediate followers.

Within the context of sport organizations and sport management, several transformational leaders are recognized. Professors Earl F. Zeigler and James G. Mason were instrumental in transforming the field of administration of physical education and athletics into what is now the scholarly and professional field known as sport management. Donna Lopiano spearheaded the formation of the Women's Sports Foundation to promote women in sport and bring long-over-

exhibit 12.4 Dimensions of empowerment leadership.

DIMENSION	DESCRIPTION
1. Leading by example	Setting high standards for own behavior, working hard to maintain that standard, and setting an example of good behavior.
2. Participative decision making	Encouraging and listening to group's ideas and suggestions, and giving members a chance to voice their concerns.
3. Coaching	Providing help to members to improve performance, encouraging members to share ideas and to work together, and supporting group members.
4. Informing	Explaining organization's goals, policies, rules, decisions, and how group fits into the organization.
5. Showing concern/ interacting with the team	Caring about members' personal problems, their well-being, treating the members as equals, and getting along well with the members.

Source: Arnold & colleagues (2000).

due recognition and status to women's sport. The Women's Sports Foundation has become a model for similar organizations promoting the causes of women in sport around the world. On the commercial side, Phil Knight became a legendary figure because of the success of his Nike enterprise. His Excellency Juan Antonio Samaranch is credited with transforming the International Olympic Committee (IOC) and the Olympics itself into a multibillion-dollar enterprise.

Transformational leadership need not, however, be confined to large organizations with a hierarchical structure. Smaller organizations with fewer levels of management can practice transformational leadership as well. For instance, Doherty and Danylchuk (1996) found that coaches of intercollegiate athletics in Ontario, Canada, perceived their athletic directors to be more transformational than transactional in their behaviors. This perceived transformational leadership was associated with coaches' increased satisfaction and extra effort. Another typical example is that of a coach who transforms her team from a perennial doormat into a winning team. Such a coach uses a threefold approach: (1) sowing discontent with the current image of the team, (2) articulating a vision of the team performing in a winning fashion, and (3) convincing the members that they have the abilities to be a winning team. The only difference between the transformational leadership of a CEO of a large corporation and that of the coach is that the coach does not have to deal with several layers of managers. Instead, he interacts with the members directly.

Note, however, not all organizations need to be subjected to transformation, nor does an organization need to be transformed all the time. Transformation entails upheaval and turmoil, and that cannot be a permanent state. The organization must find its equilibrium promptly to achieve its designated

sidebar 12.2

CASCADING EFFECTS OF TRANSFORMATIONAL LEADERSHIP

A transformational leader encourages followers to develop their own leadership abilities. That is, the transformational leader serves as a role model for subordinates to follow and stimulates them to be effective leaders. This notion of the "cascading" effects of transformational leadership was tested by Kent and Chelladurai (2000) in the context of intercollegiate athletics. They assessed the perceptions of 75 third-tier employees of a large university athletic department regarding (a) the transformational leadership exhibited by the athletic director, (b) the quality of their relationship with their immediate supervisor (i.e., leader–member exchange), (c) their commitment to the organization (organizational commitment), and (d) their citizenship behaviors within the organization (organizational citizenship). Their results showed that perceived transformational leadership at the athletic director level was reflected in the quality of leader–member exchange between the second-level supervisors and their subordinates. In addition, both transformational leadership at the top and quality of leader–member exchange at the middle level contributed to employee commitment to the department and increased citizenship behavior. Thus, the study supported the notion of "cascading" effects of leadership.

In another study, Kent and Chelladurai (2001) investigated the effects of transformational leadership and leader–member exchange on organizational commitment of 283 third-tier employees of a state parks and recreation department. These employees' perceptions of transformational leadership of the executive chief of the department and the quality of leader–member exchange with their immediate supervisor were significantly correlated, which again supports the notion of the cascading effects of transformational leadership. The authors discovered that both transformational leadership and leader–member exchange had cumulative and unique effects on employee commitment to the organization. This latter result suggests that leadership provided by managers at different levels of an organization is critical in cultivating organizational commitment.

goals. Some authors have called the transition from transformation to equilibrium the **punctuated equilibrium** (e.g., Miller & Friesen, 1984). Transactional leadership is said to be more relevant to the steady-state or equilibrium stage. This does not mean that transactional leadership would be content with the current level of effectiveness or efficiency of the organization. Transactional leadership could indeed be focused on continuously improving the performance of the organization. In fact, Moore (2004) notes that three kinds of leader are needed—transformational leader, steady-state leader, and evolutionary leader. The *transformational leader* is one charging in from the outside with a great discontent with the status quo and little patience for those who support it, and who turns the place inside-out. The *steady-state leader* is usually an insider who knows how things are done in the organization and who is focused on regrouping and rebuilding the organization after the upheaval of the transformational process. Finally, the *evolutionary leader*, who may also be from within the organization, is not content with the steady state and focuses on steady improvement in organizational performance.

CHARISMATIC LEADERSHIP

A term that is often used in conjunction with transformational leadership is *charismatic leadership*. Although the two terms have been used synonymously in some contexts, it is useful to consider them as distinct concepts. Yukl and Van Fleet (1992) noted that **charismatic leadership** "refers to the follower perception that a leader possesses a divinely inspired gift and is somehow

sidebar 12.3

MANAGEMENT VERSUS LEADERSHIP

Some noted authors (e.g., Bennis & Nanus, 1985; Kotter, 1990) make a distinction between management and leadership. In such a view, management is concerned with stability, order, and efficiency, whereas the focus of leadership is on flexibility, innovation, and adaptation. Management is concerned with routine operations, whereas leadership is more attuned to creating a vision for the organization and setting its larger goals. This perspective is well illustrated by Bennis and Nanus's (1985) well-known quote: "Managers are people who do things right and leaders are those who do the right thing" (p. 21).

In Kotter's (1990) view, leadership deals with (a) developing and setting the future course for the organization involving organizational change, (b) explaining the new vision and convincing the members of the necessity and viability of such change, and (c) motivating them to attain the new vision. In contrast, management is concerned with (a) breaking down the grand vision into operational goals, (b) structuring and staffing the organization to suit the new operations, and (c) monitoring and controlling the activities to be consistent with established plans. In essence, the distinction rests on who sets the policy (i.e., vision and goals) and who executes the policy (i.e., achieving the new vision and goals). In addition, the distinction these authors make between leadership and management parallels the distinction made earlier between strategic planning and operational planning (see Chapter 5). Furthermore, the way they describe leadership is similar to transformational leadership at the top level. Note that other authors (e.g., Mintzberg, 1973; Yukl, 2006) have considered leadership as one of the functions of management. However, the nature and scope of leadership varies as a function of one's position in the organization. At the top levels of management in an organization, leadership must be transformational in nature—impacting the whole organization. In contrast, lower-level managers need to exhibit leadership that is narrowly focused on their specific units and their operational goals. Take the case of the NCAA and its compliance units at its headquarters. The association's governance structure at the top level—including its division-wide legislative bodies—sets the policies, rules, and regulations for the entire membership. Quite often those policies are transformational in nature. But the units subordinate to the top level have to be organized and structured in such a way as to be efficient in carrying out the mandate of the NCAA. Moreover, the members within these units need leaders to guide them in ensuring that member universities and colleges efficiently comply with the rules of the NCAA. The point is that there is leadership at both the top and lower levels of the NCAA, but the scope and focus differ at the two levels.

unique and larger than life. . . . They [followers] also idolize or worship the leader as a superhuman hero or spiritual figure. . . . Thus, with charismatic leadership, the focus is on an individual leader rather than on a leadership process that may be shared among multiple leaders" (p. 174).

In this view, charisma is something the leader is purported to have that enables her to transform the group or organization. Thus, charisma is a set of laudable attributes of the leader, as well as a set of beliefs the members have about the leader. From this perspective, charisma is a personal resource, which leaders exploit successfully in transforming their organizations and their members. Note that charisma is an attributional phenomenon—it involves attributions made by the followers regarding the abilities of the leader. As Yukl (2006) noted, followers are likely to attribute charisma to a leader if the leader

1. advances a mission that is radically different from the status quo but one that is achievable.
2. acts in unconventional ways (for instance, Gandhi went in his simple Indian clothing to meet the Prime Minister of England).
3. makes self-sacrifices (for instance, Nelson Mandela chose to go to prison rather than give up his mission).

4. exudes confidence about the vision and mission. Michael Krzyzewski, the famous Duke basketball coach, stated, "A basketball team is like the five fingers on your hand. If you can get them all together, you have a fist. That's how I want you to play."
5. inspires followers with emotional appeal. Knute Rockne, the famed Notre Dame coach, said, "Let's win one for the Gipper," when the star player was dying.
6. sees opportunities that others don't see. Saint Louis University football coach E. B. Coachems introduced the forward pass as an offensive strategy in 1906.

Such strong and positive attributions are the source of power that facilitates greater acceptance of the leader's pronouncements and the willingness to abide by his dictates and directions. The great followings enjoyed by leaders like Mohandas Gandhi, Nelson Mandela, Martin Luther King Jr., and John F. Kennedy were based partly on the significance of the causes they promoted, partly on the sacrifices they made, and partly on the beliefs their followers held about their superhuman qualities. For example, the success of Vince Lombardi, the legendary football coach, was said to be partly a function of his charisma. Similarly, the respect bestowed on Michael Jordan by his peers was largely based on his playing prowess, but it was also partly based on his charisma. On the commercial side, the charisma of Phil Knight, the former CEO of Nike Corporation and major shareholder, is said to have been a significant factor in the corporation's success.

IN brief

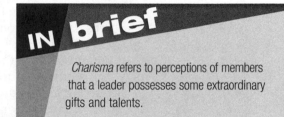

Charisma refers to perceptions of members that a leader possesses some extraordinary gifts and talents.

AN INTEGRATIVE FRAMEWORK: THE MULTIDIMENSIONAL MODEL OF LEADERSHIP

The multidimensional model of leadership (Chelladurai, 1978, 1993, 1999) is an attempt to synthesize and reconcile existing theories of leadership. A schematic illustration of the model is presented in Exhibit 12.5.

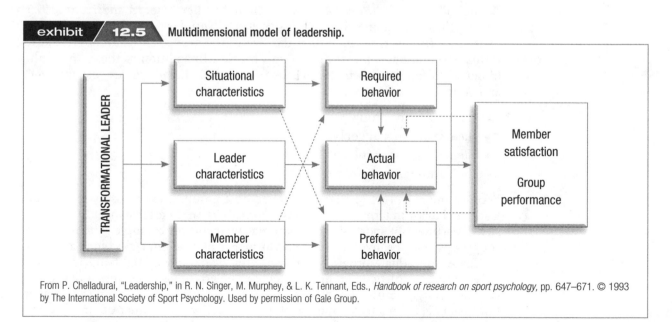

exhibit 12.5 Multidimensional model of leadership.

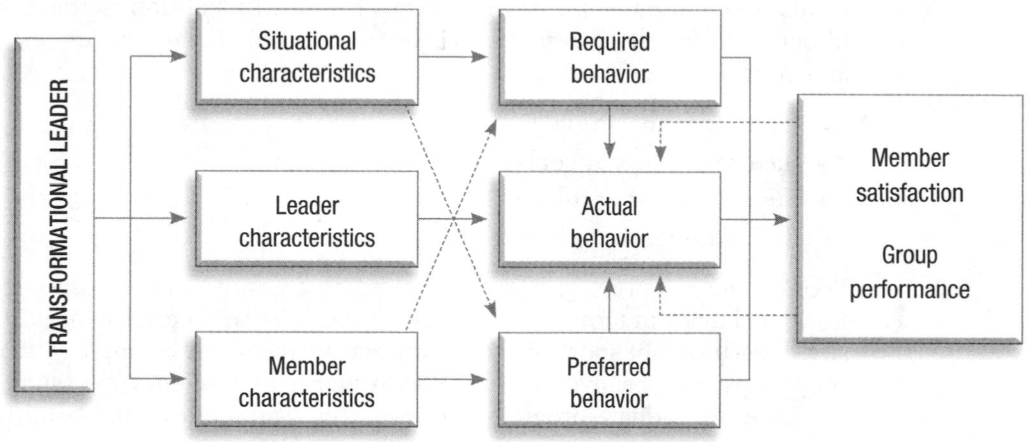

From P. Chelladurai, "Leadership," in R. N. Singer, M. Murphey, & L. K. Tennant, Eds., *Handbook of research on sport psychology*, pp. 647–671. © 1993 by The International Society of Sport Psychology. Used by permission of Gale Group.

Essentially, the model focuses on three states of leader behavior: required, preferred, and actual. The antecedent variables that determine these leader behaviors are classified as situational characteristics, member characteristics, and leader characteristics. In the model, required leader behavior is largely determined by situational characteristics, and the preferred leader behavior is a function of member characteristics. The actual leader behavior is influenced by leader characteristics, required leader behavior, and leader behavior preferred by the members. The consequences (outcome variables) in the model are group performance and member satisfaction.

Required Leader Behavior

Required leader behavior refers to what the leader needs to do as well as what the leader is not permitted to do. Note that the notion of required leader behavior as defined by the demands and constraints on leader behavior reflects Stewart's demands–constraints–choices theory and is the same as Osborn and Hunt's (1975) adaptive behavior (adaptations to the macro variables). For instance, a commissioner of a professional sport league is confronted with many demands and constraints from different groups. Beginning with the need to satisfy the contrasting and at times conflicting needs and preferences of the club owners and the players' union, the commissioner also must deal with the demands of the media, the sponsors, and other stakeholders. Although the commissioner may have some freedom in how she satisfies the interests of the different stakeholders, clearly they cannot be overlooked—hence the notion of required leader behavior. Add to these demands the constraints imposed on the commissioner, such as government rules and regulations, legal and accounting requirements, and the contracts entered into by the league as a whole and by its member clubs. Thus, a portion of the commissioner's behavior is required in terms of what has to be done (prescriptions) and what cannot be done (proscriptions).

Situational characteristics

What are those situational elements (demands and constraints) that have such strong influence on leader behavior? As noted earlier, Osborn and Hunt (1975) named these situational characteristics *macro variables*. As shown in Exhibit 12.6, Osborn and Hunt identified the size of the group, its technology, and its formal structure as some of the macro variables. In addition to these, the multidimensional model also includes other situational characteristics that influence and control leader behavior:

- the task of the group
- the organizational goals
- the norms of a particular social setting
- the nature of the group

Because the construct of leadership refers to a group, it is necessary to consider leader behavior in terms of group tasks, processes, and performance. In a university department of sport or recreation management, for example, different units (or groups) may be involved in the performance of different tasks (such as undergraduate or graduate programs in marketing or organizational behavior). Similarly, for each athletic team in a university, the group task becomes a part of the situation. Organizational goals also affect the total group, including the leader. For instance, the relative emphasis placed on quality versus quantity in a produc-

exhibit 12.6 Situational characteristics influencing required leader behavior.

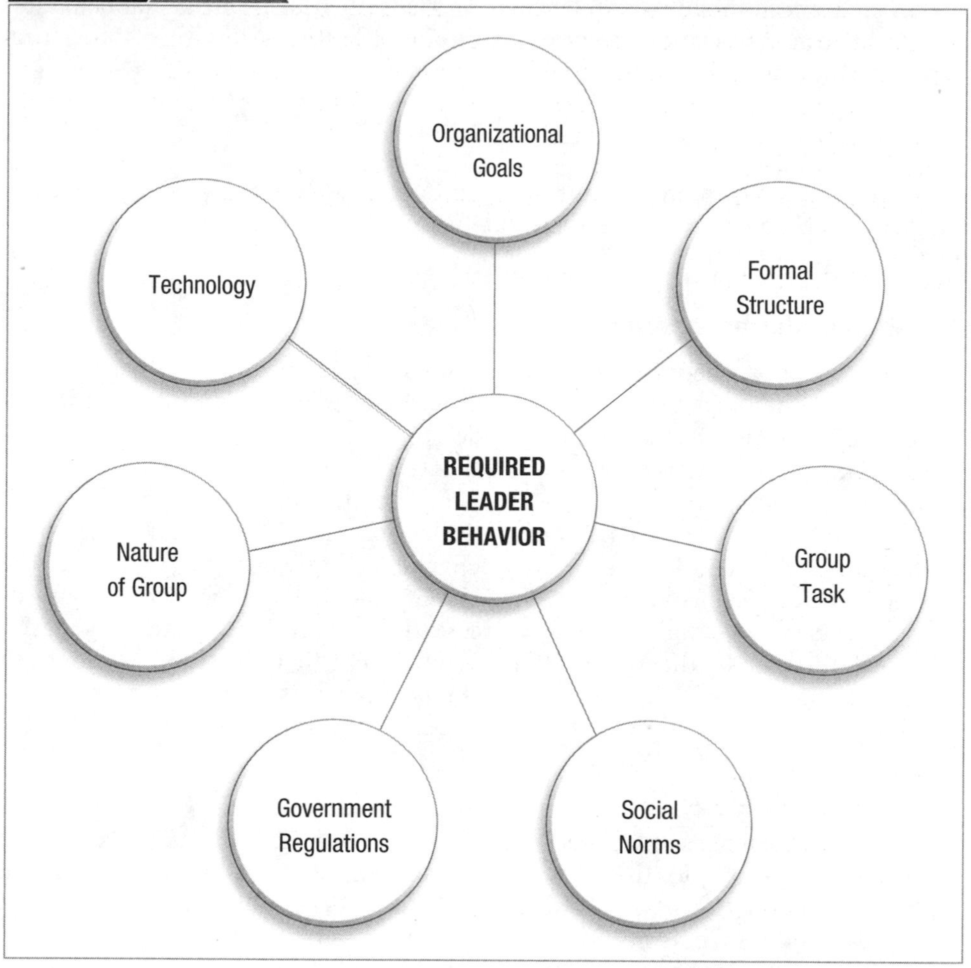

tion firm affects both the manager's and the employees' behavior. The norms and codes of conduct prevalent (or emerging) in a given social setting form a significant set of situational factors that impinge on leadership.

Chelladurai (1993, 1999) argued that the nature of the group as a whole also influences that segment of leader behavior required in a situation. For instance, the differences in orientations between volunteers and professionals will impose different demands on the leader. As another example, Hersey and Blanchard (1969, 1977) argued that leaders should vary their behaviors according to the maturity level of the subordinates. Thus, a leader would alter her behavior based on whether she is leading a youth, adult, or senior group. When viewed as an attribute of the group, ability or maturity influences how the leader should behave in a given context (i.e., required leader behavior). Note that we are concerned with the nature of the group as a whole and not with individual differences within the group. For instance, House (1971) refers to perceived ability as an individual difference variable. Whereas it is clear

IN brief

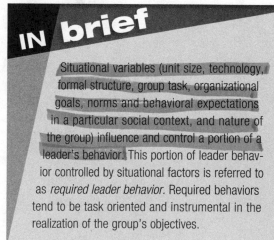

Situational variables (unit size, technology, formal structure, group task, organizational goals, norms and behavioral expectations in a particular social context, and nature of the group) influence and control a portion of a leader's behavior. This portion of leader behavior controlled by situational factors is referred to as *required leader behavior.* Required behaviors tend to be task oriented and instrumental in the realization of the group's objectives.

that individuals may vary in actual or perceived ability, we can also conceive of group differences in ability. Athletes at the Division I level of the National Collegiate Athletic Association are presumed to be of higher ability than those from Division III.

Preferred Leader Behavior

The preferences of members for specific leader behaviors (**preferred leader behavior**) stem from both the situational characteristics and the characteristics of the members themselves.

Situational characteristics

House's path–goal theory of leadership (House, 1971; House & Dessler, 1974) suggests that the impact of the task (particularly its characteristics of interdependence and variability) is an immediate determinant of member preferences. As noted earlier, the situational characteristics (see Exhibit 12.6) place some constraints and demands on the leader. The same situational characteristics influence member preferences for specific forms of leader behavior. Therefore, the members' preferences for certain forms of leader behavior will reflect the influences of the situation (Bass, 1985; House, 1971; Yukl, 1989; Yukl & Van Fleet, 1992). Consider a supervisor and employees of a city recreation department where the supervisor needs to abide by the organizational requirement that all salary decisions are made at a higher level. To the extent this requirement is known to the subordinates as well, they would not expect the supervisor to increase their salary.

Member characteristics

Individual differences influence members' preferences for particular leader behaviors. For example, the effect of task-relevant ability is highlighted in the path–goal theory (House, 1971; House & Dessler, 1974). Similarly, a number of personality traits such as need for affiliation and need for achievement influence members' preferences for different leader behaviors. Lorsch and Morse (1974) and Morse (1976) found that an individual's attitude toward authority affects his reactions to different types of supervision. For instance, people who have a high regard and respect for authority may not mind close supervision from a manager, whereas individuals who have a less positive attitude toward authority may resent close supervision. Cognitive complexity, which refers to the way individuals process information, also helps to determine the preference for structuring behavior from the leader (Wynne & Hunsaker, 1975). Employees who can manage in complex and ambiguous work situations may not need much guidance from the supervisor. On the other hand, individuals who have a lower capacity to handle complex situations may prefer the supervisor telling them what to do, when, and how. Authoritarianism and the need for independence affect the degree to which members prefer their leader to use participation in decision making (Vroom, 1959). Those persons high in achievement motivation prefer the leader to provide challenge, responsibility, and feedback (McClelland, 1961). The interpersonal needs (need for affiliation, succor, and so on) of members also affect their preferences for specific leader behaviors.

IN brief

Although all members operate under the influence of the same situational characteristics, their preferences for specific forms of leader behavior may vary. These variations are a function of member characteristics including ability, expertise, and personality.

Actual Leader Behavior

The third, and obviously the most central, state of leader behavior is **actual leader behavior**—that is, how a leader behaves in any given situation. Two of the determinants of actual leader behavior are the requirements of the situation (i.e., required leader behavior as discussed above) and the preferences of members (i.e., preferred leader behavior). As discussed previously, Stewart (1982) pointed out that the leader needs to abide by the demands and constraints of the situation in which he or she operates. Osborn and Hunt (1975) divided actual leader behavior into adaptive behaviors (adaptations to situational requirements) and reactive behaviors (reactions to member preferences). How a leader adapts to the demands and constraints of the situation and reacts to member preferences is also a function of the leader's personal characteristics—in particular, personality and ability. That is, two leaders facing the same situational contingencies and member preferences may not behave similarly because of differences in their personalities and abilities.

Leader characteristics

Significant leader characteristics include ability, knowledge, experience, and personality. We noted earlier that the leader's personality (task orientation versus people orientation) is the central focus of Fiedler's (1967) contingency model of leadership. Also, McClelland and Burnham (1976) isolated the needs for power, achievement, and affiliation as the most significant in the organizational context, particularly with reference to leaders or managers.

The leader's ability is made up of two components. The first is the leader's specific knowledge and expertise of the group's goal and the processes necessary for attaining it. This specific ability will vary with different leadership positions. In a university athletic department, a comprehension of the recruiting, eligibility, and league rules is likewise specific to the group task and processes.

IN brief

A leader's actual behavior is influenced by (a) the demands and constraints imposed by the situation, (b) the preferences of the members under the leader's charge, and (c) the leader's own personal characteristics.

The second component of the leader's ability is the capacity to conceptualize the organization as a whole, to analyze the complexities of a problem, and to persuade subordinates about the efficiency of a particular approach. This is a general ability that is transferable across situations. For instance, the director of the city recreation department is expected to comprehend how the department and its activities fit into the overall scheme of city governance, the politics within the department and in conjunction with other city departments, how other city recreation departments are run, the emerging trends in recreation and sport, and other major issues that will impact the department in both the short and long run. These general abilities of the recreation athletic director are relevant in many top managerial positions in other organizational contexts.

Performance and Satisfaction

The consequences included in the multidimensional model are **performance** and **satisfaction** (see Exhibit 12.5). The degree to which the three states of leader behavior are **congruent** (that is, that the actual behavior is consistent with both the preferred and required behaviors) is said to influence performance and satisfaction. Thus, any of the states of leader behavior could be a limiting factor.

For instance, the manager of a firm specializing in organizing and conducting sports events needs to abide by the rules and ordinances of the city where the event takes place. She also has to follow legal requirements in running the event and accept the demands and constraints of the parent body that sanctions the event (for example, the Special Olympics). If her behaviors deviate from the requirements (the required behavior), she may jeopardize the standing of the firm. By the same token, the employees of the firm should not prefer that their manager flout the situational requirements. In other words, member preferences should be consistent with situational requirements. From a different perspective, the manager must try to satisfy as much as possible the members' legitimate preferences (preferred behavior). Members will not be motivated to perform well and they will be dissatisfied with their manager if she continually disregards their needs and desires.

In the multidimensional model, the leaders are assumed to be flexible and capable of altering their behavior according to changing conditions. This perspective is consistent with the position taken by many scholars and researchers. If a leader finds that his behavior has not resulted in increased performance by the group, he is likely to alter his behavior with a view to enhance productivity (for example, the coach may spend more time and effort in training and instructing the players). By the same token, if the leader finds that the group is not cohesive and integrated, he could begin emphasizing those aspects of his own behavior that would foster warm interpersonal relations within the group.

Transformational Leadership Within the Multidimensional Model

The final component of the model (shown at the left of Exhibit 12.5) links transformational leadership to the elements of transactional leadership within the model. That is, a transformational leader attempts to alter the situational and member characteristics. Transformational leadership involves a new vision, meaning a new and higher set of goals, and innovative and creative ways of achieving those loftier goals. In creating this vision, the transformational leader may also change the value system guiding the organization. She also implies that perceived barriers to goal attainment are surmountable. Thus, the transformational leader alters the situational characteristics to some degree. As we noted, required behavior is a function of situational characteristics, including organizational goals, the values subscribed to by the organization, and the traditions of the organization.

IN brief

A critical proposition of the multidimensional model of leadership is that the performance of a group and the satisfaction of its members will be enhanced if there is congruence among three states of leader behavior: (1) the leader behavior required by the situational demands and constraints, (2) the leader behavior preferred by the members, and (3) the actual behavior of the leader.

Equally important to transformational leadership is its focus on members. Insofar as the members can only actualize the vision espoused by the leader, it is important to convince the members of the goodness and viability of the vision. Though the transformational leader tells the members that they have the ability to achieve those goals, he also expresses great confidence that the members and the organization will achieve the vision. In this sense, the transformational leader alters member characteristics in terms of their values, aspirations, and confidence in their abilities to reach the goal. In turn, these changes in member characteristics will affect their preferences for leadership and make them consistent with the new vision and order.

In the process of transforming all members, the transformational leader has to rely on immediate subordinates (that is, second-level managers). Thus, the

an expert's view / ON LEADERSHIP

Professor Kari Puronaho of HAAGA-HELIA University of Applied Sciences in Finland is well known for his capacity to translate theories and research findings into practical guidelines for managers. In this discussion, he has distilled the writings by various authors on leadership and management and offers what he sees as the essence of good leadership.

SMOOTH LEADERSHIP

Kari Puronaho

No resources are more important than human resources. The well-being of individuals leads to the well-being of organizations. This in turn leads to the well-being of cities and communities, then the well-being of countries and the world. People make your organization, your unique products, and services. How attractive your organization is, how you manage your people, and how you organize, coordinate, and manage will determine your level of success. The ways of leading and managing the organization are vital differentiators and the keys to competitive advantage and enhanced performance.

Goals are what we want; values are why we want them. A vision close to values is needed to inspire people. A leader must convince people to buy into the values behind the organization and the vision arising from those values. The closer the performed activity is to the espoused values, the more motivated the employees will be.

Creating a positive work climate, including positive relationships and communication, is vital to increasing performance as well as job satisfaction. Leaders must also realize that satisfaction is not confined just to the employees' jobs. It also includes external factors like family life; physical, psychological, and social health; leisure-time activities, and so forth. Leaders need to be flexible enough to recognize individual needs outside of work. Flexibility from the employer can lead to more flexibility on the part of employees in favor of the organization in terms of improved climate and performance.

Extending respect to colleagues, co-workers, and employees is a minimum requirement for effective leadership and management. It is also critical to clearly show why one is respected; explain the factors that engender such respect within the organization. If the employees are aware that their behaviors are respected, they are more likely to continue exhibiting them.

Positive relationships in the workplace enhance the emotional carrying capacity of individuals and result in stronger self-esteem, increased creativity, trust, and openness to new ideas. This creates a virtuous cycle of positive social interactions. It is not what people receive that makes a relationship productive but what they give. What they contribute to others accounts for these advantages. A positive climate in general is strongly associated with positive performance.

Finally, smooth leadership and management, with a view to enhanced performance, focuses on strengths rather than weaknesses, opportunities rather than threats, optimism rather than pessimism, good instead of bad. In the end, the leader must choose to know and respect the members, understand their values and sources of motivation, and create a positive atmosphere.

transformational leader must also influence her immediate subordinates to accept her vision and appeal to their aspirations and self-esteem by making them believe the vision is attainable.

SUMMARY

This chapter focused on contemporary theories of leadership. We first looked at the contemporary theories of transformational leadership, charismatic leadership, and leader–member exchanges. Whereas earlier theories were concerned with the transactions between a leader and the members, transformational leadership is focused on transforming both the organization (including its goals and vision) and its members. The leader–member exchange theory was described as focused on cultivating quality relationships between a leader and each of the members. We examined Osborn and Hunt's distinction between macro and micro variables and their impacts on leadership. Finally, we studied the multidimensional model of leadership, described as a framework integrating the earlier approaches of Fiedler, House, and Osborn and Hunt.

develop YOUR PERSPECTIVE

1. Recall one of your work experiences (either part-time or full-time). Describe your supervisor's leadership in terms of one of the leadership theories discussed in the chapter.
2. From your experiences in groups with formal leaders, recall a situation that had an in-group and an out-group. Contrast the specific relationships the leader had with members of the in-group versus members of the out-group. How did these relationships affect the total group and its effectiveness?
3. Based on your work experiences (either full-time or part-time), identify a leader who was transformational. Explain in detail the specific actions the leader took that transformed the situation. Were the members also transformed? Give details of the changes in members as well as in the total group as a result of the transformational leadership.

references

Arnold, J. A., Arad, S., Rhoades, J. A., & Drasgow, F. (2000). The Empowering Leadership Questionnaire: The construction and validation of a new scale for measuring leader behaviors. *Journal of Organizational Behavior, 21,* 249–269.

Bass, B. M. (1985). *Leadership and performance beyond expectations.* New York: The Free Press.

Bass, B. M. (1990). *Bass and Stogdill's handbook of leadership.* New York: The Free Press.

Bass, B. M. (1997). Does the transactional-transformational leadership paradigm transcend organizational and national boundaries? *American Psychologist, 52,* 130–139.

Bass, B. M., & Avolio, B. (1993). Transformational leadership: A response to critiques. In M. M. Chemers & R. Ayman (Eds.), *Leadership theory and research perspectives and directions* (pp. 49–80). New York: Academic Press.

Basu, R., & Green, S. G. (1997). Leader–member exchange and transformational leadership: An empirical examination of innovative behaviors in leader–member dyads. *Journal of Applied Social Psychology, 27*(6), 477–499.

Bennis, W. G. (1984). Good managers and good leaders. *Across the Board, 21*(10), 7–11.

Bennis, W. G., & Biederman, P. W. (1997). *Organizing genius: The secrets of creative collaboration.* Reading, MA: Addison-Wesley.

Bennis, W. G., & Nanus, B. (1985). *Leaders: The strategies for taking charge.* New York: Harper & Row.

Chelladurai, P. (1978). *A contingency model of leadership in athletics.* Unpublished doctoral dissertation, University of Waterloo, Waterloo, Canada.

Chelladurai, P. (1993). Leadership. In R. N. Singer, M. Murphey, & L. K. Tennant (Eds.), *Handbook of research on sport psychology* (pp. 647–671). New York: Macmillan.

Chelladurai, P. (1999) *Human resource management in sport and recreation.* Champaign, IL: Human Kinetics.

Conger, J. A., & Kanungo, R. N. (1987). Toward a behavioral theory of charismatic leadership in organizational settings. *Academy of Management Review, 12,* 637–647.

Conger, J. A., & Kanungo, R. N. (Eds.). (1988). *Charismatic leadership: The elusive factor in organizational effectiveness.* San Francisco: Jossey-Bass.

Conger, J. A., & Kanungo, R. N. (1998). *Charismatic leadership in organizations.* Thousand Oaks, CA: Sage Publications.

Dansereau, F., Cashman, J., & Graen, G. (1973). Instrumentality theory and equity theory as complementary approaches in predicting the relationship of leadership and turnover among managers. *Organizational Behavior and Human Performance, 10,* 184–200.

Dansereau, F., Graen, G., & Haga, B. A. (1975). A vertical-dyad linkage approach to leadership within formal organizations: A longitudinal investigation of the role making process. *Organizational Behavior and Human Performance, 13,* 46–78.

Doherty, A. J., & Danylchuk, K. E. (1996). Transformational and transactional leadership in interuniversity athletics management. *Journal of Sport Management, 10,* 292–309.

Duchon, D., Green, S. G., & Taber, T. D. (1986). Vertical dyad linkage: A longitudinal assessment of antecedents, measures, and consequences. *Journal of Applied Psychology, 71,* 56–60.

Fiedler, F. E. (1967). *A theory of leadership effectiveness.* New York: McGraw-Hill.

Goleman, D., Boyatzis, R., & McKee, A. (2002). *Primal leadership: Realizing the power of emotional intelligence.* Boston: Harvard Business School Press.

Graen, G. (1976). Role making processes within complex organizations. In M. D. Dunnette (Ed.), *Handbook of industrial and organizational psychology* (pp. 1201–1245). Chicago: Rand-McNally.

Graen, G., & Cashman, J. F. (1975). A role making model of leadership in formal organizations: A developmental approach. In J. G. Hunt & L. L. Larson (Eds.), *Leadership frontiers* (pp. 181–185). Kent, OH: Kent State University Press.

Hersey, P., & Blanchard, K. H. (1969). Life cycle theory of leadership. *Training and Development Journal,* May, 26–34.

Hersey, P., & Blanchard, K. H. (1977). *Management of organizational behavior.* Englewood Cliffs, NJ: Prentice Hall.

House, R. J. (1971). A path–goal theory of leader effectiveness. *Administrative Science Quarterly, 16,* 321–338.

House, R. J. (1977). A 1976 theory of charismatic leadership. In J. G. Hunt & L. L. Larson (Eds.), *Leadership: The cutting edge.* Carbondale: Southern Illinois University Press.

House, R. J., & Dessler, G. (1974). The path–goal theory of leadership: Some post hoc and a priori tests. In J. G. Hunt & L. L. Larson (Eds.), *Contingency approaches to leadership.* Carbondale: Southern Illinois University Press.

House, R. J., & Howell, J. M. (1992). Personality and charismatic leadership. *Leadership Quarterly, 3*(2), 81–108.

House, R. J., & Podsakoff, P. M. (1994). Leadership effectiveness: Past perspectives and future directions for research. In J. Greenberg (Ed.), *Organizational behavior: State of the science* (pp. 135–153). Hillsdale, NJ: Lawrence Erlbaum Associates.

House, R. J., & Shamir, B. (1993). Toward the integration of transformational, charismatic, and visionary theories. In M. Chemers & R. Ayman (Eds.), *Leadership theory and research perspectives and directions* (pp. 579–594). Orlando, FL: Academic Press.

Kent, A., & Chelladurai, P. (2000). *The differential effects of multiple sources of leadership on employee reactions in a state parks and recreation department.* Unpublished manuscript, The Florida State University, Tallahassee.

Kent, A., & Chelladurai, P. (2001). Cascading effects of transformational leadership on organizational commitment and citizenship behavior: A case study in intercollegiate athletics. *Journal of Sport Management, 15,* 135–159.

Kotter, J. P. (1990). *A force for change: How leadership differs from management.* New York: The Free Press.

Lorsch, J. W., & Morse, J. J. (1974). *Organizations and their members: A contingency approach.* New York: Harper & Row.

McClelland, D. C. (1961). *The achieving society.* New York: Van Nostrand.

McClelland, D. C., & Burnham, D. H. (1976). Power is the great motivator. *Harvard Business Review, 54,* 100–110.

Miller, D., & Friesen, P. (1984). *Organizations: A quantum view.* Englewood Cliffs, NJ: Prentice Hall.

Mintzberg, H. (1973). *The nature of managerial work.* New York: Harper & Row.

Moore, K. (2004, Feb. 6). An evolution in leaders. *Globe and Mail,* pp. C1 and C6.

Morse, J. J. (1976). Person–job congruence and individual adjustment and development. *Human Relations, 28,* 841–861.

Osborn, R. N., & Hunt, J. G. (1975). An adaptive-reactive theory of leadership: The role of macro variables in leadership research. In J. G. Hunt & L. L. Larson (Eds.), *Leadership frontiers.* Kent, OH: Kent State University.

Schein, E. H. (1990). *Organizational culture and leadership.* San Francisco: Jossey-Bass.

Shaskin, M. (1986). True vision in leadership. *Training and Development Journal, 40*(5), 58–61.

Stewart, R. (1982). The relevance of some studies of managerial work and behavior to leadership research. In J. G. Hunt, U. Sekaran, & C. Schriesheim (Eds.), *Leadership: Beyond establishment views* (pp. 11–30). Carbondale: Southern Illinois University Press.

Vroom, V. H. (1959). Some personality determinants of the effects of participation. *Journal of Abnormal and Social Psychology, 59,* 322–327.

Weese, W. J. (1995). A synthesis of leadership theory and a prelude to the Five "C" model. *European Journal of Sport Management,* 2(1), 59–71.

Wynne, B. E., & Hunsaker, P. L. (1975). A human information-processing approach to the study of leadership. In J. G. Hunt & L. L. Larson (Eds.), *Leadership frontiers.* Kent, OH: Kent State University.

Yukl, G. A. (1989). *Leadership in organizations* (2nd ed.). Englewood Cliffs, NJ: Prentice Hall.

Yukl, G. A. (2006). *Leadership in organizations* (6th ed.). Upper Saddle River, NJ: Pearson-Prentice Hall.

Yukl, G. A., & Van Fleet, D. D. (1992). Theory and research on leadership in organizations. In M. D. Dunnette & L. M. Hough (Eds.), *Handbook of industrial and organizational psychology* (2nd ed., pp. 147–197). Palo Alto, CA: Consulting Psychologist's Press.

MANAGING DIVERSITY

CHAPTER 13

manage YOUR LEARNING

After completing this chapter you should be able to:

- Define and describe diversity in the workplace and marketplace.
- Distinguish among forms of diversity.
- Differentiate among the concepts of affirmative action, valuing diversity, and managing diversity.
- Discuss the strategies of accommodation and activation in managing diversity.
- Identify the relationships between tasks and time factors in managing diversity.

strategic CONCEPTS

accommodation
activation
actualization
affirmative action
benefits of diversity
competence
cultural diversity
deep-level diversity
deficit
difference
diversity
managing diversity
strategies for managing diversity
surface-level diversity
task factor
time factor
valuing diversity

ORGANIZATIONS AND DIVERSITY

In the previous chapters, the descriptions of organizations and their management emphasized the variability associated with management. For instance, the cooperation among different people performing different roles is the essence of some definitions of an organization (see Chapter 2). Chapter 3 described organizations as open systems. We defined a system as a set of interrelated and interdependent parts that differ in their attributes but are arranged in an organized manner to produce a unified whole (Immegart & Pilecki, 1973; Robbins, Coulter, Leach, & Kilfoil, 2012; Waring, 1996). We also noted that one system might differ from another in terms of the parts and attributes of parts. An effective system is one in which different parts of the system and their attributes combine to make up a meaningful whole, and in which the activities of different parts are coordinated to facilitate the effective functioning of the system itself.

The notion of **diversity** also underlies the definition of sport management as "coordination of limited human and material resources, relevant technologies, and situational contingencies for the efficient production and exchange of sport services" (Chelladurai, 1994, p. 15). In this book we note that coordination is achieved through the functions of planning, organizing, staffing, leading, and evaluating (discussed in Chapters 5–12 and 14). These chapters highlight the concept of diversity (variability) of the elements that need to be coordinated. Thus, the concept of diversity underlies all managerial actions (Thomas, 1996). However, this chapter's emphasis is on diversity in human characteristics. The focus of this chapter is on the variability or diversity among people with whom an organization interacts, including its employees and customers.

Variability among people was emphasized in our discussion of planning. For instance, in setting goals and choosing the appropriate means to achieve those goals, managers need to be attuned to external as well as internal environmental conditions. The external conditions include individuals and groups (called constituents or stakeholders), who differ in their values and goal preferences (see Chapter 5). The internal conditions include the employees of the organization, who differ in their abilities, work experiences, goal preferences, and so on. Similarly, the organizing function entails breaking down the total work into distinct jobs and assigning those jobs to qualified individuals, and establishing a mechanism to coordinate these jobs and individuals (see Chapters 7 and 8). Implied in this description is the idea that the jobs as well as the people who perform them differ in terms of skills, abilities, and attitudes. Individual differences result in the varying preferences for leadership considered in the multidimensional model described in Chapter 14.

If we push the idea of differences among us far enough, we can conclude that each of us is distinct and different from anyone else in the world. This is certainly true in the biological sense, because our DNA compositions are unique in the universe (unless we have an identical twin). Even from a social-psychological perspective, we are characterized by differences in terms of abilities, attitudes, personality, values, and thinking styles. The factors that set us apart at the individual level are called *individual difference variables.* These variables help distinguish one individual from another of the same group, such as white Americans, African Americans, Asian Americans, males, and females. The individual difference variables have been the subject matter of study in fields such as human resource management, personnel psychology, and organizational behavior. In fact, individual differences are the subject of four entire chapters in Chelladurai's (2006) *Human Resource Management in Sport and Recreation.*

IN brief

The definition of management implies that an organization's diversity in resources, personnel, activities, and associated technologies needs to be coordinated. Thus, diversity underlies management.

Individual differences affect every managerial action and its effectiveness. Thus, a critical function of management is to take advantage of the differences among employees and coordinate them. Because diversity in the workforce presents unique opportunities as well as obstacles for organizational effectiveness, it is useful for us to understand the dynamics of diversity in the workplace and how to mobilize it for greater organizational effectiveness.

DIVERSITY DEFINED

The following is a sampling of definitions of diversity:

> Diversity is any mixture of items characterized by differences and similarities. (Thomas, 1996, p. 5)
>
> Diversity describes a wide spectrum of differences between people. (Gomez-Meija, Balkin, & Cardy, 2005, p. 458)
>
> Diversity is all the ways in which individuals differ, both on a personal basis and in terms of organization-related characteristics. (Hitt, Black, Porter, & Hanson, 2007, p. 534)

The personal characteristics they refer to may be (a) primary, such as ethnicity, gender, nationality, and ability; and (b) secondary, such as marital status, educational level, values, and beliefs. The organization-related characteristics would include position in the hierarchy, tenure, and full-time or part-time status.

> Today *diversity* refers to far more than skin color and gender. It is a broad term used to refer to all kinds of differences. . . . These differences include religious affiliation, age, disability status, military experience, sexual orientation, economic class, educational level, and lifestyle in addition to gender, race, ethnicity, and nationality. (Bateman & Snell, 2007, p. 359)

> Diversity is the presence of differences among members of a social unit that lead to perceptions of such differences and that impact work outcomes. (Cunningham, 2011a, p. 6)

> Diversity is a mix of people in one social system who have distinctly different, socially relevant group affiliations. (Cox & Beale, 1997, p. 1)

Note the subtle difference between Thomas's (1996) and the other definitions. Thomas's definition refers to a mixture of items including all organizational variables, material and human. In this broader view, diversity "applies not only to a company's people concerns but to many other critical areas" (Thomas, 1996, p. 5). For instance, Thomas would include acquisitions and mergers, cross-functional coordination, and managing change as issues of diversity. "The more lines of business you have, the more functions, the more races represented in your workforce, and the greater the differences among them, the greater the diversity" (Thomas, 1996, p. 9). As noted, Thomas's broader view is included in discussions of management in general. Many issues associated with diversity in products, structure and processes, and environments were discussed in previous chapters.

On the other hand, Gomez-Meija et al. (2005), Hitt et al. (2007), Bateman and Snell (2007), Cunningham (2011a), and Cox and Beale (1997) restrict their conception of diversity to human differences. Most scholars and practitioners take this perspective, restricting their discussion of diversity to human differences. Furthermore, differences among people can be at the group level or the individual level. Though the individual-level and group-level diversity is implied in all definitions, Cox and Beale (1997) are more direct in emphasizing group-level

sidebar 13.1

EVERYONE A MINORITY

One of the problems that plagues the management of diversity is that diversity issues are most often equated with minority issues and discrimination. Although minorities and their treatment is important, the two terms *diversity* and *minority* should not be lumped together, even though they are highly interrelated. In the United States, whites are in the majority and the other ethnic groups are in the minority. So the issues that arise in the management of diversity in the workforce could be cast against the backdrop of this majority–minority divide. But consider the report by the U.S. Census Bureau that by the year 2050, whites will be in the minority (Roberts, 2008). The rates for 2008 and future membership in different ethnic groups are shown in Exhibit 13.1. In other words, everybody in the United States will belong to a minority group. Thus, the majority–minority ethnic divide will diminish, but the issues of diversity and diversity management will remain. That is because the designation of a group as a minority is based on the numbers of people in different groups. But diversity refers to surface-level and deep-level differences among groups of people. Those differences will remain without reference to the various configurations of the composition of the members of an organization.

exhibit 13.1 Rates for 2008 and projected (2050) rates for ethnic group populations in the United States (Winslow, 2008).

ETHNIC GROUP	POPULATION IN MILLIONS AND PERCENTAGE (2008)	PROJECTED POPULATION IN MILLIONS AND PERCENTAGE (2050)
All U.S. Citizens	305	439
Hispanics	46.7 (15.4%)	132.8 (30.3%)
Black Population	41.1 (14%)	65.7 (15%)
Asian	15.5 (5.1%)	40.6 (9.2%)
Whites (non-Hispanic)	199.8 (66%)	203.3 (46%)

diversity. They note that group affiliations may relate to gender, nationality, age, physiological abilities or disabilities, ethnic identity, religion, and so on. Note also that a socially relevant group affiliation implies that some meaning is attached to interactions among members of the group. These authors note that wearing the same size shoes does not have the same effect or meaning as belonging to the same political party. Diversity at the individual level can be related to the abilities, talents, values, and beliefs an individual brings to the organizational context. The focus of this chapter will be on both group-level and individual-level diversity.

DIMENSIONS OF DIVERSITY

According to Schuler and Jackson (1996), the dimensions of diversity include gender, ethnicity, culture, age, functional areas of expertise, religion, and lifestyle. Similarly, Kossek and Lobel (1996) consider "diversity to be not only derived from differences in ethnicity and gender, but also based on differences in function, nationality, language, ability, religion, lifestyle, or tenure" (p. 2).

Milliken and Martins (1996) categorize these grouping characteristics as observable or readily detectable attributes, and less visible or underlying attributes. Observable attributes include race or ethnic background, age, and gender. Less visible attributes include education, technical abilities, and tenure in the organization. One reason they distinguish between observable and unobservable attributes is that "when differences between people are visible, they are particularly likely to evoke responses that are due directly to biases, prejudices, or stereotypes" (p. 404).

"Social philosophers are still debating the merits of encouraging members of a multicultural society to perpetuate their ethnic identities versus the merits of encouraging them to amalgamate into the 'American melting pot.' In recent years this national debate has been dominated by a single theme: ethnic, racial, and social diversity. However, as groups other than those identified by race or ethnicity (e.g., feminists, homosexuals, the aged, and disabled individuals) intensify their efforts to be recognized as legitimate entities in America's mosaic of humanity, social philosophers have begun to move beyond the rhetoric of ethnic, racial, and *cultural diversity* and toward the new rhetoric of 'diversity.'"

HOPKINS,
1997, pp. 3–4

In line with the above distinction between observable and unobservable group characteristics, Hopkins (1997, p. 3) categorizes group characteristics as:

- *ethnographic* descriptors, such as nationality, religion, and language.
- *demographic* descriptors, such as age, gender, and place of residence.
- *status* descriptors, such as social, economic, and educational background.
- *sexual orientation* descriptors, such as heterosexual, homosexual, or bisexual.
- a range of other descriptors relating to formal or informal membership affiliations, such as functional specializations and part-time or full-time employment status.

From a different perspective, Jehn, Northcraft, and Neale (1999) speak of three categories of diversity—informational diversity, social category diversity, and value diversity. *Informational diversity* refers to "differences in knowledge bases and perspectives that members bring to the group," which may arise from "differences in education, experience, and expertise" (p. 743). *Social category diversity* is born out of membership in specific social categories, such as race and gender. *Value diversity* "occurs when members of a workgroup differ in terms of what they think the group's real task, goal, target, or mission should be" (p. 745). The idea of differences in information and knowledge people possess suggests that people specializing in functional areas (e.g., marketing, accounting, coaching, fitness leadership) may also be diverse (Pelled, Eisenhart, & Xin, 1999). That is, the specialized training and education and experiences with specific task contingencies may lead to *functional diversity*—diverse orientations regarding what activities are important and how they should be carried out.

As you consider the factors that underlie diversity, note two caveats. First, each of us can be described as diverse under specific circumstances. For instance, a young student renting an apartment in a complex predominantly occupied by retirees would be diverse from the other occupants in terms of age. Similarly, a middle-aged person visiting a bar full of college students would be the odd one (that is, the old one). Second, because individuals belong to more than one group, judgments about individuals cannot be made on the basis of their membership in only one group. For example, the distinction between males and females implies that the males will be alike on certain characteristics in comparison to females. However, any two males may differ in their nationality, religion, or language. Similarly, contrasting white Americans from nonwhite Americans does not say anything about the sexual orientation, educational background, or religion of a white American or a nonwhite American. The issue of diversity and managing diversity is complex.

Another point of emphasis in Thomas's (1996) definition of diversity as "any mixture of items characterized by differences *and* similarities" (emphasis added) is that diversity includes both differences and similarities among groups. In his words, "One way of conceptualizing this is to think in terms of a macro/micro continuum. A micro perspective looks at the individual component and a macro perspective looks at the mixture. To get at the true nature of diversity (comprising differences *and* similarities) requires an ability to

sidebar 13.2

DIVERSITY AT HAND

I come from a family of nine children (five girls and four boys). Sibling rivalry often led us to arguments of who was better and who was better liked by our mother. When we took our arguments to mother, she would ask us to put up our right hand with fingers spread out. After pointing out that the five fingers are not alike, she would ask us which one of the five fingers we would not miss should it be cut off.

Extending this analogy, we can suggest that management of diversity consists of (a) recognizing the differences as well as similarities among people (the fingers); (b) realizing that each person, like a finger, has unique qualities that can contribute to the total effort; and (c) capitalizing on these unique features and coordinating them for productivity and effectiveness. Each finger is different, but it takes the coordination of all five to manipulate objects effectively.

assume both perspectives simultaneously; the micro facilitates identification of differences, and the macro enhances the ability to see similarities" (p. 6).

In a similar vein, Lawson and Shen (1998), noting that it takes longer to change a heart than a mind, suggested that "the critical challenge for each person and each organization around the world is to learn that diversity is a bridge to finding deeper similarities and interests among all human beings" (p. 69).

DIFFERENCES VERSUS DEFICITS

Any discussion of diversity or management of diversity must begin with the basic idea that **differences** are not **deficits.** The natural tendency to view anything different about an individual or a group of individuals as inferior to us must be resisted. As Weiner (1997) noted,

> For something to be "different," there must be a reference point, something for it to be different from. Typically "we" (whoever "we" are) see other cultures as different from "us," often unaware that we are different from them. . . . That is, we typically divide the world into an in-group (our group) and all other groups are out-groups; out-groups are seen as different. This would not be a problem except that in-group thinking typically defines those who are different as inferior, wrong or bad. (p. 2)

The same issue was illustrated by the cartoon character Hagar the Horrible. Hagar tells his stooge, Eddie, "Remember, Vikings are the chosen people." Eddie asks, "Who chose us?" The pat answer from Hagar is "We did." Such self-determined notions of the superiority of "our group" leads to stereotypes such as "members of certain groups lack leadership ability, have a propensity for certain kinds of work such as caring work or technical work, have good or poor work ethics and so on" (Weiner, 1997, p. 3). In this text, the term *different* carries no connotation of deficit. It simply means "not the same." "'Not the same' describes two or more things as being unlike or different; it does not mean that one is better than the other" (Weiner, 1997, p. 2).

It is crucial that managers and leaders understand what diversity is and learn how an organization may take advantage of the diversity of its workforce, its clients, and its customers.

In Chapter 1, after describing the various products of sport organizations, we noted that sport management is concerned with producing and marketing sport services. Implied in this statement is the need to tailor an organization's products to be consistent with the needs of its customers and to adopt marketing strategies that suit the characteristics of the customers. Marketers have long known that a market (i.e., the collection of customers) is not uniform. That is, a market can be subdivided into segments based on specific characteristics such as gender, age, and education; hence the terms *market segmentation* and *niche marketing*. Thus, any organization concerned with marketing its products must understand the nature of diversity in its market, and must learn appropriate marketing strategies, including market segmentation.

> **IN brief**
>
> Diversity can be described in terms of several dimensions such as gender, race, age, language, and religion. Note that differences in these dimensions are not deficits.

Weiner (1997) notes that globalization of industries and trade also directs a greater focus toward diversity. If the United States itself is characterized by diversity, the global economy is much more so. Any organization that deals at the international level has to be attuned to the diversity in the global market.

sidebar 13.3

NEGATIVE IMPACT OF DIVERSITY ON INDIVIDUAL OUTCOMES

The negative effects of diversity on employees of intercollegiate athletic departments have been demonstrated by Cunningham and his associates (Cunningham & Sagas, 2004a, 2004b, 2004c; Fink & Cunningham, 2005). Cunningham and Sagas (2004a) reported that greater diversity in terms of tenure and ethnicity was associated with lower occupational commitment and higher intention to leave the occupation among 235 Division IA football coaching staffs. However, diversity in age was not related to either of the outcomes. In another study of Division IA assistant football coaches, Cunningham and Sagas (2004b) found that coaches belonging to minority races perceived less career-related opportunity, were less satisfied with their careers, and had greater occupational turnover intentions than their white counterparts. The authors also found that perceived career opportunity affected career satisfaction, which, in turn, influenced the intention to leave the occupation.

Fink and Cunningham (2005) investigated the effects of differences in gender and race between subordinates (i.e., assistant/associate athletic directors, senior women's administrators, and coaches) and their athletic directors on an index of work experience. Their results showed that persons in mixed-gender dyads and those in mixed-race dyads had poorer work experiences than did persons in demographically similar dyads.

Cunningham and Sagas (2004c) studied the effects of being in a predominantly white or predominantly black staff on organizational commitment of Division I assistant basketball coaches. They found that black coaches in predominantly white or black staff expressed greater commitment than did black coaches in staffs with a relatively equal distribution of whites and racial minorities. In contrast, white coaches on predominantly black coaching staffs were less committed than whites in other settings. Cumulatively, these studies suggest that diversity in demographic characteristics could detrimentally affect the attitudes of minority members in work groups. Hence, it is important that managers recognize this and take steps to reduce the negative impact of diversity and enhance its potential benefits.

Moreover, as the global economy moves labor across national boundaries, organizations need to ensure smooth interactions among these diverse workers (Schneider & Northcraft, 1999).

Consider the National Basketball Association's program *Basketball Without Borders,* which uses the services of current and former NBA players to promote "friendship, healthy living, and education" (NBA, 2005) among nations on all continents. In the process, the NBA also promotes basketball and the NBA brand. The venture may also facilitate the recruitment of outstanding players from other continents. Another example is the Pittsburgh Pirates baseball organization, which signed two pitchers from India after they were discovered in a reality show competition called *Million Dollar Arm.* They had never played baseball, but their pitch speeds often exceeded 90 miles an hour. Neal Huntington, Pirates' General Manager, explained that they were broadening their horizons and trying to get into newer markets (Nightengale, 2008). For the NBA and MLB to be successful in penetrating foreign markets and to recruit players from many countries, they must understand and appreciate the diversity among nations in terms of language, culture, and political ideology. Currently, NBA, NHL, and MLB franchises have many players from European, Asian, and South American countries. The performance of these players and their teams is contingent on effective diversity management.

IN brief

Management needs to be concerned with diversity not only because of the increasing diversity in the American population and workforce, but also because of the increasing globalization of the economy, as well as of sport.

BENEFITS OF MANAGING DIVERSITY

As we noted, diversity implies that the market and the workforce comprise people of different demographic and ethnographic backgrounds, different socioeconomic groups, and different sexual orientations. It also implies that such diverse people bring to the organization various beliefs, values, and attitudes. What is more important in our context is that these diverse groups bring many talents and perspectives relevant to organizational processes. Effective management of diversity is based on capitalizing on these diverse talents and perspectives in order to solve organizational problems and enhance the effectiveness of organizational processes, thus reaping the **benefits of diversity**.

Cox and Beale (1997) argue that revenue enhancement is achieved through effective marketing strategies, problem solving, creativity, and innovation. *Effective marketing strategy* refers to selling to increasingly diverse consumers. This strategy is facilitated by a well-utilized, diverse workforce in two main ways: A diverse workforce provides public relations value for the organization, and a well-managed, diverse workforce enhances the reputation of the organization with its potential customers (Weiner, 1997). In addition, the organization will gain from the marketing insights available from diverse employees.

Problem solving is enhanced by diverse backgrounds and experiences, and by the insights from differing perspectives. These differing perspectives facilitate critical analysis and scrutiny of a given problem. By the same token, a diverse workforce is rich with creativity and innovation. Weiner (1997) echoes this view and underscores the many benefits to be derived from the contributions of talents of a multicultural workforce.

COSTS OF MANAGING DIVERSITY

Workforce diversity may increase the costs of running an organization if that diversity is not managed properly. Costs may arise from increased absenteeism and turnover because of employee dissatisfaction. Also, a diverse workforce may not result in positive contributions if communication is not efficient. Unresolved issues in intergroup dynamics may further increase the costs. In addition, harassment may increase, which in turn may lead to legal ramifications such as discrimination suits.

Effective management of diversity also involves some costs. As Weiner (1997) notes, the first obvious costs relate to monetary and material resources of the organization. In attempting to accommodate the needs of working mothers, for example, the organization may have to spend extra resources setting up a day care center. Similarly, it costs money to build a wheelchair ramp for workers who are disabled.

Less evident in the above examples is the amount of time needed to effectively manage a diverse workforce. We noted that a diverse workforce contributes greatly to problem solving and good decision making, but these processes take time. Group decision making is notorious for the time it takes. This process is more drawn out when diverse individuals are involved. It takes time for members to understand each other's perspectives and to arrive at a solution acceptable to the majority. Another cost alluded to by Weiner (1997) is the discomfort experienced by members of a diverse team and the resistance of members to understanding and appreciating different perspectives. Such discomfort may lead to the biggest potential cost of all: conflicts among members of a diverse workforce.

an expert's view / ON DIVERSITY IN SPORT

George B. Cunningham and his associates at Texas A&M University have carried out numerous research studies and published several articles in both sport management and general management journals. He established the Laboratory for Diversity in Sport at Texas A&M University and has secured grants from the NCAA for research on diversity issues in intercollegiate sport. Here he offers an overview of his research and perspectives on the topic.*

DIVERSITY OVERVIEW

George B. Cunningham

Of the many activities in which sport managers engage, ensuring that sport and sport organizations are diverse and inclusive is among the most important. The primacy of the topic stems from changing population and workplace demographics, societal expectations, legal mandates, team-based workplace structures, and the impact of employee differences and inclusive workplaces on important work processes and outcomes.

Researchers have devoted considerable attention to understanding how diversity and inclusion affect employees and the organizations in which they work. The collective results tell what might appear to be a contradictory story.

On the one hand, employees who differ from those who have historically held power frequently face prejudice and discrimination. For example:

- Women and racial minorities continue to be under-represented in coaching and top administrative positions (Acosta & Carpenter, 2012; DeHass, 2007).
- Lesbian, gay, bisexual, and transgender employees and athletes encounter hostility, abuse, and antiquated stereotypes (Cunningham, Sartore, & McCullough, 2010). Furthermore, most policies restrict the transgender athletes' participation opportunities (Buzuvis, 2012).
- Persons with physical and mental disabilities encounter treatment discrimination (Ren et al., 2008) and have fewer opportunities to engage in sport than do their able-bodied counterparts (DePauw & Gavron, 2005).
- Religious minorities are likely to be less satisfied with their work, especially when their religious beliefs are an important part of who they are as a person (Cunningham, 2010).
- The poor face various forms of classism—including that in the cognitive, interpersonal, and institutional domains—all of which restrict their opportunities for optimal health and well-being (Lott & Bullock, 2007).

On the other hand, other researchers have observed that differences within the workplace can add meaningfully to important work processes and outcomes. For instance, in a study of intercollegiate athletic departments, I observed that both gender and racial diversity of departmental employees was associated with a culture of workplace creativity (Cunningham, 2008). We have also theorized that employee diversity is associated with better decision making and improved marketplace understanding (Cunningham & Melton, 2011). These process improvements should translate into performance gains—a finding we have observed across various contexts, including the racial diversity of college football coaching staffs (Cunningham & Sagas, 2004a, b), the racial diversity of athletic department personnel (Cunningham, 2009), and the sexual orientation diversity of athletic department personnel (Cunningham, 2011b).

When a body of evidence provides what might seem to be equivocal patterns, it is useful to look for moderating factors; that is, something that influences the relationship between two variables. Examination of the diversity research points to such a variable: the inclusiveness of the workplace. We can consider inclusion to represent the organizational values, policies, procedures, and activities that provide access and opportunities to all persons, irrespective of their individual differences. For instance, sport organizations that offer partner benefits are more inclusive than those that do not.

A review of the diversity research suggests that the degree to which diversity is associated with subjugation or success largely depends on the inclusive culture of the team or organization. For instance, in my research with athletic departments (Cunningham, 2009, 2011b), the benefits of diversity were strongest when the organization was characterized by an inclusive culture. Anderson (2011) has also found this with sport teams, as gay athletes have very positive experiences when inclusive masculinity (i.e., an inclusive culture) pervades the team. Fink et al. (2012) have observed a similar pattern in their study of bisexual and lesbian athletes who disclosed their sexual orientation to others.

The message for sport managers is clear: diversity *and* inclusion matter. It is important to develop organizational policies and practices that ensure equity and access for all athletes, coaches, and administrators.

*See also *Diversity in Sport Organizations* (2nd ed.) by George Cunningham (Holcomb Hathaway, 2011) for more information on competencies in diversity management in sport.

PERSPECTIVES ON MANAGING DIVERSITY

Diversity in the workforce is not a matter of debate. It is a fact. But managing diversity may be a focus of debate. What are the effective ways of managing diversity? How do we capitalize on the advantages of a diverse workforce and minimize the disadvantages of diversity? These questions are of great concern among theorists and practitioners. Thomas (1991) noted that affirmative action, valuing diversity, and managing diversity are the three approaches to diversity in the workplace. Even though these processes are important in themselves, people at times are not clear about the distinctions among them. An effective manager needs to be clear about these terms and their implications for management. The following sections describe these approaches.

Affirmative action. **Affirmative action** is a government policy aimed at eliminating the discriminating effects of managerial policies and practices that preclude equal employment opportunities for all without reference to group membership. Affirmative action

> aims, through a variety of methods, to remedy discrimination and increase the representation of designated disadvantaged groups, namely women and ethnic minorities. The policy goes beyond advocating simple sex or color blindness in employment decision making by specifying that group membership be explicitly taken into account in such decisions. Thus, the assumption built into this policy is that nondiscrimination alone is not sufficient to counteract the consequences of prejudice and inequality—that something more is needed. (Heilman, 1994, pp. 126–127)

Valuing diversity. **Valuing diversity** refers to (a) genuinely accepting diversity as a given, (b) recognizing the advantages of a diverse workforce, and (c) clearly understanding that benefits of diversity can be derived only through appropriate managerial practices. "Valuing diversity is a philosophy about how diversity affects organizational outcomes that holds the presence of diversity represents a distinct organizational resource that, properly leveraged, can bring a competitive advantage against organizations that either are culturally homogeneous or fail to utilize their diversity" (Cox & Beale, 1997, p. 13).

Managing diversity. **Managing diversity** implies that "the organizational interventions that fall within the realm of this label focus on ensuring that the variety of talents and perspectives that already exist within an organization are

sidebar 13.4

CANADA'S MULTICULTURALISM ACT

"Dealing with differences in Canada is unique because Canada is the only country to have a legal commitment to multiculturalism. The federal *Multiculturalism Act* recognizes the diversity of Canadians with respect to race, national and ethnic origin, and religion as a fundamental characteristic of Canadian society. The Act commits the government to a policy of multiculturalism designed to preserve and enhance the multicultural heritage of Canadians while working to achieve equality for all Canadians in the economic, social, cultural and political life of Canada. The Act only affects the federal government and puts no requirements on work organizations. Still, it does provide a foundation and expectation for how work organizations will behave" (Weiner, 1997, p. 1).

sidebar 13.5

U.S. FEDERAL INITIATIVES TOWARD NONDISCRIMINATION

For decades, governments at all levels have been concerned with maximizing the benefits of diversity in the workforce. These governments have promulgated laws and regulations to curb discriminatory employment practices and promote equal employment opportunities for all members of society. Fernandez and Barr (1993) list the following as a sampling of federal government initiatives in this regard:

- *Equal Pay Act of 1963.* Prohibits gender-based pay differentials for equal work.
- *Title VII, 1964 Civil Rights Act* (as amended in 1972). Prohibits job discrimination based on race, religion, gender, or national origin.
- *Executive Order 11246* (1965). Requires contractors and subcontractors performing work on federal or federally assisted projects to prepare and implement affirmative action plans for minorities and women, persons with disabilities, and veterans.
- *Age Discrimination in Employment Act (ADEA)* (1967). Prohibits age discrimination in areas such as hiring, promotion, termination, leaves of absence, and compensation. Protects individuals age 40 and over.
- *Rehabilitation Act of 1973.* Prohibits contractors and subcontractors of federal projects from discriminating against applicants or employees who are physically or mentally disabled, if qualified to perform the job. Requires the contractor to take affirmative action in the employment and advancement of individuals with disabilities.
- *Vietnam Era Veterans Readjustment Assistance Act of 1972 and 1974.* Requires government contractors and subcontractors to take affirmative action with respect to certain classes of veterans of the Vietnam Era and Special Disabled Veterans.
- *Immigration Reform and Control Act of 1986 (IRCA).* Prohibits employers from discriminating against persons authorized to work in the United States with respect to hiring or termination from employment because of national origin or citizenship status.
- *The Americans with Disabilities Act of 1990, Title I.* Prohibits employers from discriminating against qualified applicants and employees with disabilities with regard to any employment practices or terms, conditions, or privileges of employment.
- *Civil Rights Act of 1991.* Grants to plaintiffs the right to a jury trial and makes available compensatory and punitive damages (capped at $300,000).

well utilized" (Schuler & Jackson, 1996, p. 4). According to Cox and Beale (1997), managing diversity is "creating a climate in which the potential advantages of diversity for organizational or group performance are maximized while the potential disadvantages are minimized" (p. 2). In Arredondo's (1996) view, managing diversity is a strategic organizational approach, and it "represents a shift away from activities and assumptions defined by affirmative action to management practices that are inclusive, reflecting the workforce diversity and its potential" (p. 17).

IN brief

Affirmative action is a *legal requirement* imposed by government. Valuing diversity is a philosophy in which diversity is accepted and the value and usefulness of all people is recognized. Managing diversity is a strategy for making the best use of the talents, abilities, and perspectives of diverse workers.

Henderson (1994) provides an elaborate description of affirmative action that incorporates valuing and managing diversity and the differences among such workers. Henderson notes that affirmative action is *legally* driven; valuing diversity is *ethically* driven; and managing diversity is *strategically* driven. This fundamental distinction among the three concepts provides for other differences that are outlined in Exhibit 13.2.

Valuing diversity and effectively managing it begin with a clear understanding of what diversity means and what implica-

exhibit 13.2 Distinctions among affirmative action, valuing differences, and managing diversity.

AFFIRMATIVE ACTION	VALUING DIFFERENCES	MANAGING DIVERSITY
Quantitative. The achievement of equality of opportunity is sought by changing organizational demographics. Progress is monitored by statistical reports and analyses.	*Qualitative.* The emphasis is on the appreciation of differences and the creation of an environment in which everyone feels valued and accepted. Progress is monitored by organizational surveys of attitudes and perceptions.	*Behavioral.* The emphasis is on building specific skills and creating policies that get the best from every employee. Efforts are monitored by progress toward achieving goals and objectives.
Legally driven. Written plans and statistical goals for specific groups are used.	*Ethically driven.* Moral and ethical imperatives are the impetus for cultural change.	*Strategically driven.* Behaviors and policies contribute to organizational goals, such as increased profits and productivity.
Remedial. Specific target groups benefit as prior wrongs are addressed. Previously excluded groups have an advantage.	*Idealistic.* Everyone benefits by feeling valued and accepted in an inclusive environment.	*Pragmatic.* The organization benefits: morale, profits, and productivity increase.
Assimilation model. Assumes that groups that are brought into the system will adapt to existing organizational norms.	*Diversity model.* Groups retain their own characteristics, shape the organization, and are shaped by it to create a common set of values.	*Synergy model.* Diverse groups create new ways of working together effectively in a pluralistic environment.
Opens doors. The focus is on hiring and promotion decisions.	*Opens attitudes, minds, and the culture.* The emphasis is on inclusion, not assimilation.	*Opens the system.* Managerial policies and practices are affected.
Resistance. Resistance arises from perceived limits to autonomy in decision making and fears of reverse discrimination.	*Resistance.* Resistance arises from the fear of change and discomfort with differences.	*Resistance.* Resistance arises from the denial of demographic realities, of the need for alternate approaches, and of the benefits of change.

From *Cultural diversity in the workplace: Issues and strategies,* by G. Henderson. Westport, CT: Quorum Books. ©1994 by G. Henderson. Reproduced with permission of Greenwood Publishing Group, Inc., Westport, CT.

tions it has for the organization and the people in it. In Weiner's (1997) view, *inclusivity* "requires recognizing differences while perceiving them as part of the whole. . . . The mind-set shift involves realizing that all groups are different and that all differences are equally valid, assuming they are relevant, and have something to contribute" (pp. 6–7). That is, the mind-set that is bound to the in-group versus out-group dichotomy should shift to valued differences among subgroups.

In a similar vein, Cox and Beale (1997) view *diversity competency* as "a process of learning that leads to an ability to effectively respond to the challenges and opportunities posed by the presence of social–cultural diversity in a defined social system" (p. 2). Learning to manage diversity consists of awareness, meaning recognizing and acknowledging diversity and its effects; understanding, which leads to a deeper grasp of the need for effective management of diversity; and action steps to change behavior. These stages (shown in Exhibit 13.3) relate to all managerial activities, including staffing and promotion decisions, training programs, performance evaluation and feedback, group formation and functioning, and conflict resolution.

exhibit 13.3 Learning process for diversity competency.

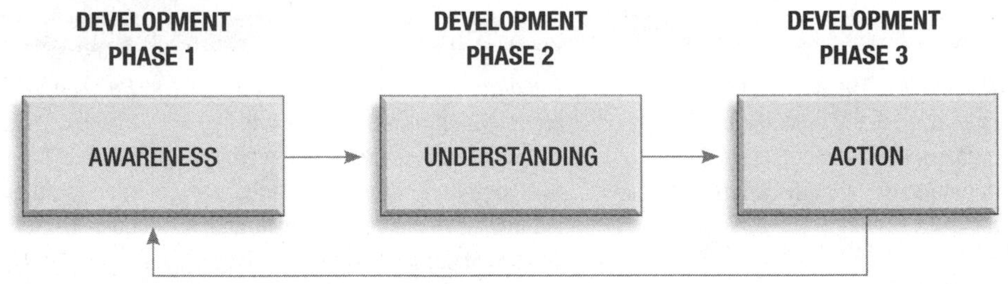

Source: Cox and Beale (1997, p. 5).

Robbins and Coulter (1996, p. 507) also note that coordination of heterogeneous groups requires understanding differences and the need to be fair and equitable; empathy (i.e., recognizing others' perspectives and preferences); tolerance for different perspectives, values, and behaviors; and communicating in nonthreatening ways.

OPTIONS FOR HANDLING DIVERSITY

Thomas (1996) identifies the following eight options for managers facing diversity issues. Note that diversity as defined by Thomas refers to a mixture of items characterized by differences and similarities. This view includes differences among organizational environments, structures, processes, and material as well as human resources. As noted, the focus in this book is on diversity in human terms, as seen in the workforce and the marketplace.

Option 1: Include/exclude. In this option, either the number and variability of elements in the mixture are increased, or diversity is excluded by minimizing the variability in the elements of the mixture. Thomas (1996) notes that the option of exclusion is prohibited for the most part by existing laws prohibiting discrimination and requiring equal employment opportunities. Despite such laws, however, some sport organizations still restrict their membership to certain categories of people.

Option 2: Deny. In this option, decision makers refuse to acknowledge differences among people; thus, there is less tolerance for gender or racial groupings. For instance, management may not encourage support groups for women or minorities. Again, as Thomas (1996) notes, this option is less prevalent as the workforce—both managers and employees—becomes more comfortable with ethnic and gender diversity.

Option 3: Assimilate. Managers operating under this option attempt to minimize diversity by insisting that the diverse elements conform to the dominant norms. Holding dominant norms and ways of operating as ideals, managers expect everyone to fit into a given mold. These managers also tend to emphasize organizational and task requirements as the basis for organizational behavior. Although we cannot ignore organizational or task requirements, we must also recognize that such requirements include preferences and traditions. "The corporate mold, comprising true requirements and also these preferences, traditions, and conveniences, was developed sometime in the past, by whatever race was dominant then" (Thomas, 1996, p. 92). The problem here is the confounding of *true* requirements of the task or organization and preferences and traditions that are unrelated to the task.

sidebar 13.6

DIVERSITY WITHIN DIVERSITY

Any discussion of diversity touches upon easily identifiable characteristics such as gender, skin color, and age as well as less discernible characteristics such as educational, economic, and social status. A more thorough analysis would show that the values, beliefs, and attitudes that individuals bring to the situation are also important sources of diversity in the workplace. Because people's beliefs, values, and attitudes stem partly from their cultures, the notion of **cultural diversity** has gained prominence in the discourse on diversity issues.

Culture is defined as a unique set of values, beliefs, attitudes, and expectations, as well as language, symbols, customs, and behaviors of individuals by virtue of some common characteristic(s) shared with others (e.g., DeSensi, 1994; Doherty & Chelladurai, 1999). When we speak of a "youth culture," a "gay culture," a "drug culture," an "African American culture," or a "Latino culture," we think of each consisting of a unique set of values, beliefs, attitudes, language, symbols, and behaviors shared by members belonging to the defined group.

Although cultural diversity among groups of people defined by race, gender, age, and other such characteristics is readily apparent, there are some dangers to generalizing this conception to all people of a group. First we need to understand that considerable differences exist among members of a group in the extent to which they accept and adhere to the values, beliefs, and attitudes of the group in general (Allison, 1988; Fine, 1995). In other words, the differences among groups (*intergroup* differences) should not be allowed to hide the differences among members of any one group (*intragroup* or *interindividual* differences).

The significance of the distinction between intergroup and intragroup differences is shown in Exhibit 13.4. The mean of Group A on a given cultural value such as authority relations is shown to be lower than that of Group B (intergroup difference). At the same time, there are considerable differences between members within each of the groups (intragroup differences). Whereas the scores for most members of Group A cluster around the mean for that group, the scores for A1 and A2 from Group A are far apart from each other. This is the same case with members B1 and B2 in Group B. Notice also that the scores for A1 and B1 (and those of A2 and B2) are almost the same, although they belong to two different groups.

A second confounding issue is that any one individual may belong to more than one distinguishing group. Consider these four individuals: an African American female, an African American male, a white female, and a white male. Each one of them belongs to different groups defined by race and gender. If we were to make any judgments about any one of them based on cultural indicators, we would be at a loss; any such judgment could be terribly wrong.

The point is that an individual may identify with more than one culture group based on a number of different personal characteristics (see Cox, 1993; Doherty & Chelladurai, 1999). For example, an individual may belong to several groups simultaneously, such as males or females, Christians or Buddhists or Muslims, and whites or nonwhites. The basic premise is that every group has its own culture, and therefore, a person may belong to several cultures at the same time (Doherty & Chelladurai, 1999). That is, an individual's personal culture is multifaceted. One view is that individuals will emphasize those facets of their personal culture that are associated with permanent characteristics such as gender, race, and age. Another view is that individuals may focus on different facets of their personal culture in different contexts (such as work and nonwork settings). The important thing for sport managers is to recognize the complexity and multifaceted nature of personal cultures that employees bring to the workplace. It would be inappropriate and counterproductive to pigeonhole an employee into any specific cultural box.

exhibit 13.4 Intergroup and intragroup differences.

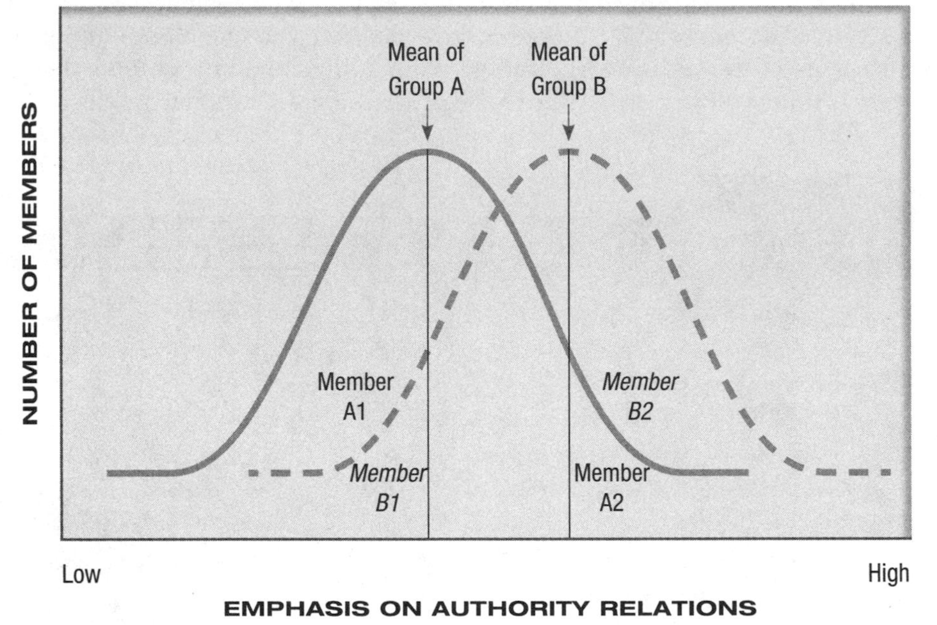

Option 4: Suppress. In seeking to minimize diversity in the workplace, managers may attempt to suppress manifestation of any racial differences. These managers may acknowledge and accept gender or racial differences outside the organization but not in the workplace. For example, a manager of a fitness club may insist that all aerobic instructors conform to standard attire and music, suppressing employees' preferences for specific styles of dress and music that reflect culture or heritage.

Option 5: Isolate. One way of reducing the complexity of managing diversity is to isolate groups defined by gender or race. Thomas (1996) gives the example of how a predominantly white church handled diversity in the congregation. When confronted with an influx of Hispanics, the church hired a Hispanic minister and arranged special services for the Hispanic members. One may argue that the move was based on good intentions because the Hispanic members are likely to be better served by a minister who speaks their language and understands their culture. Consider a fitness club that caters to young adults as well as senior citizens. Is it not reasonable for the management to schedule separate exercise sessions for the two groups? Similarly, it is not uncommon for a city recreation department to organize soccer competitions for different age groups and for males and females.

However, in an employment situation such segregation may be less defensible. For instance, relegating individuals to specific departments or tasks based on gender or race is discrimination in practice.

Option 6: Tolerate. Managers operating under this option acknowledge gender and racial differences, perhaps because of affirmative action equal employment regulations. Ostensibly, the attitude represented by this option is that there is room for everyone. However, although all are included in the workforce, they are not treated equally. They do not become full partners in organizational processes. As

Thomas (1996) noted, "To be tolerated is to be kept in limbo between full participation and exclusion" (p. 93).

Option 7: Build relationships. This option reflects management's efforts to manage diversity effectively. With acceptance and understanding of diversity, managers try to cultivate positive relationships and harmony among members of the diverse workforce with a view to enhancing productivity and effectiveness of the organization as a whole. Thomas (1996) notes that this is a significant and necessary—but not sufficient—step for effective management of diversity.

Option 8: Foster mutual adaptation. The most advanced option for effective management of diversity among Thomas's (1996) eight options is mutual adaptation, wherein every diverse element makes some changes in order to adapt to "true" organizational and task requirements and thereby achieve common objectives.

> By focusing on *true requirements* [italics added] and pushing individual and organizational preferences, conveniences, and traditions to the side, the parties identify the essentials for the relationship and free up room for negotiations around the *nonrequirements* [italics added]. This movement by both parties allows assimilation where it is necessary for organizational requirements and also some flexibility in other areas where the individual is comfortable with being different. (Thomas, 1996, pp. 94–95)

Thomas (1996) noted that only this last of the above eight options unequivocally endorses diversity, whereas the other seven options only attempt to eliminate or minimize diversity. He also noted that none of the options is inherently legitimate or illegitimate. The goodness/badness of an option depends on the situation. For example, the isolation of Hispanics in the church referred to by Thomas can be seen as a legitimate and good option if it was intended to set the stage for further reorganization of the church services. On the other hand, if the purpose were to minimize the interactions between Hispanics and whites, it would be a bad option. Despite the possible legitimacy of all options, the focus of this chapter is on fostering mutual adaptation in the pursuit of organizational goals.

In the above quote from Thomas (1996), I emphasized two significant terms—*true requirements* and *nonrequirements*. The requirements that Thomas (1996) refers to are those required for the effective functioning of the organization and successful performance of the job at hand. In managing diversity, we must be concerned that the diversity elements do not affect the true requirements of the job and we must also minimize the significance of non–task-related elements of diversity. There was a time in American sport when players of a team were all required to have a crew cut. In fact, when I was coaching a high school basketball team in Canada, the principal of the school asked me to have one of my players cut his hair short before we went to another town for a friendly game. The principal suggested that players, as ambassadors of the school, should project a clean-cut image. Bill Walton, who played for the famous coach John Wooden, had to cut his hair short. However, coaches have recognized that the length of the hair does not have anything to do with the performance of the athlete in most sports (except perhaps in swimming). With this perspective, today's coaches and organizations permit players to wear long hair and have facial hair and tattoos. But coaches still insist on strict adherence to team rules and rules of the game such as wearing team uniforms during the game. In essence, management and coaches make the best use of the skills and abilities of the athletes while accommodating their idiosyncratic preferences and behaviors that are unrelated to task performance. This example highlights two distinct strategies in managing diversity—*accommodation* and *activation*. We will discuss these two strategies in detail in a later section of the chapter.

CONCEPTUAL FRAMEWORKS OF DIVERSITY IN SPORT

The study of diversity in sport organizations has been rather limited. Notable exceptions are the works of DeSensi (1994, 1995), Doherty and Chelladurai (1999), Fink and Pastore (1999), and Fink, Pastore, and Riemer (2001, 2003). Patterned after Chesler and Crowfoot (1992) and Cox (1991), DeSensi (1995) identified three forms of organizations in which diversity is differentially managed—monocultural, transitional, and multicultural organizations. *Monocultural organizations* tend to emphasize one culture and expect the employees of different cultural backgrounds to adapt to the dominant culture. At the other extreme are *multicultural organizations,* where all cultural backgrounds are valued and accommodated. In between are the *transitional organizations,* which are changing in order to accommodate the increasing diversity in the workforce and customer base. These three forms of organizations are said to vary along the five dimensions of mission, culture, power, informal relations, and major change strategies, as shown in Exhibit 13.5.

Doherty and Chelladurai (1999) maintain that individuals bring to the organization their own "personal culture," composed of a unique set of values and beliefs about the world around them. Individuals derive these values and beliefs from their association with different cultural groups, and they are not necessarily confined to one cultural group. This perspective differs from viewing employees as belonging to one specific cultural group that assumes one set of values and beliefs for all members in that group. In these authors' view, the benefits and problems associated with personal cultures are accentuated by how diversity is managed, which in turn is a function of the culture of the organization.

The organizational *culture of similarity* is characterized by the values and assumptions of parochialism, ethnocentrism, rigidity, task orientation, and intolerance of ambiguity. This type of organizational culture is manifested in closed group membership, one-way or closed communication, and unilateral decision making. In contrast, the organizational *culture of diversity* is characterized by flexibility, people orientation, a high degree of respect for differences, and tolerance for ambiguity. Such an organizational culture encourages two-way, open communication; multilevel decision making; and open group membership.

Fink and Pastore (1999) proposed a framework that outlines four different levels of managing diversity in the context of intercollegiate athletics. At the lowest end is the strategy of noncompliance to regulations relating to diversity, a characteristic of monocultural organizations. The next level of strategy is simply compliance to all existing regulations with a view to avoid litigation and other conflicts. The organization itself is still largely monocultural in its orientation. At the third level is the reactive strategy, where any problem arising out of diversity in the workplace is immediately addressed and solved. At the top is the proactive strategy, where diversity is defined more broadly than race and gender, and is valued to a great extent. Accordingly, this strategy would involve changing policies to attract and retain diverse people and to benefit from diversity.

Based on Fink and Pastore (1999), Fink and colleagues (2001) investigated the beliefs of top management people (athletic directors, senior women's administrators, assistant or associate athletic directors) and softball and baseball coach-

exhibit 13.5 Organizational stages of multiculturalism.

DIMENSION	MONOCULTURAL	TRANSITIONAL	MULTICULTURAL
Mission	Deliberately exclude or ignore diversity.	Announce desire/need for diversity.	Positively value diversity. Link diversity to "bottom line" and social justice values. Global perspective.
Culture	White, male, and Eurocentric norms prevail. Prejudice and discrimination evident. Encourage assimilation into dominant community. Emphasize individualism.	White and male norms are questioned but prevail. Prejudice and discrimination are lessened, but still exist. Seek accommodation to and comfort/tolerance for minorities. Reify particular group identities.	Prejudice and discrimination constantly confronted publicly and negatively sanctioned. Alternative norms are publicized and embraced. White, male, and Eurocentric symbols are changed. Synthesis of individual characteristics, group identities, and a transcendent community.
Power	White and male throughout. Others excluded or at bottom. Access limited to the "club." Strong hierarchy.	A few minority members who can adapt reach higher status. White and male sponsors of minorities and women. Narrow access.	Multicultural team of leaders. Relatively flat and multilevel decision making. Wide access. Value different decision-making styles.
Informal relations	Exclusionary with segregated social events. Communications within racial/gender groups. No external intergroup contact.	Distant but cordial relations. Open to assimilated minorities. Communication on deeply held issues mostly within social identity groups. Some external intergroup social contact.	Proactive inclusiveness. Homogeneous and heterogeneous groupings coexist. Much communication across race/gender lines. Sense of community (yet differentiated).
Major change strategies	Litigation and countersuit. External demand/protest and coercion. Some listening by elite.	"Awareness" and training programs evident. Administrative mandate. Affirmative action programs. Assessments and audits.	Continuous (re)education and growth of individuals and organization. Reward multicultural work. Multicultural norms and leadership. Coalition formation. Combat external social oppression.

Reprinted, by permission, from J. T. DeSensi, 1995. Understanding multiculturalism and valuing diversity: A theoretical perspective, *Quest, 47* (1), 37–38. Originally from *Visioning change: Stages in the movement from monocultural to multicultural organizations,* by M. Chesler and J. Crowfoot, 1992, University of Michigan, Ann Arbor. Used with permission.

es at Division IA athletic departments about managing diversity. In general, top administrators believed in the benefits of diversity. Furthermore, these beliefs were reflected in the extent of diversity management practices. That is, strong beliefs in the benefits of diversity were associated with proactive management practices. In contrast, the other respondents (baseball and softball coaches) perceived that their institutions were characterized by compliance strategies to a fair

Annelies Knoppers, one of the most renowned critical theorists in sport, contributes the following perspective on managing diversity.

QUESTIONING THE IDEA OF MANAGEMENT OF DIVERSITY

Annelies Knoppers

An organizational emphasis on management of diversity has become popular. Many organizations indicate on their websites and in formal documents that they consider diversity to be an important organizational value. Critical theorists, however, pose questions such as: Is it appropriate to associate diversity with organizational performance and efficiency? Is diversity an organizational dynamic that *should* be managed and if so, by whom? In the following, I summarize these and other critical perspectives on the idea of managing diversity.

One of the claims for developing and implementing policies to increase the demographic diversity of an organization is that a socially diverse workforce enhances (or will enhance) efficiency and productivity. This claim assumes that organizational acceptance of cultural, religion, (dis)ability, sexual, and gender diversity results in satisfied and productive workers because it allows them to make choices that fit their needs and preferences. Satisfied and productive workers are assumed to influence organizational productivity in a positive manner. Thus, diversity is assumed to be good for both the individual and organization. Critical theorists point out there is relatively little consistent evidence that this occurs. For every study that shows positive results, another shows a decrease in organizational performance associated with an increase in social diversity. Critical theorists argue that organizational performance and diversity are dynamic concepts that cannot be captured in quantifiable ways that enable them to be linked in a valid manner and be used to show causality. Even if organizational performance and social diversity could be quantified in a valid manner and shown to be related, then how do we know that changes in performance and efficiency are influenced by increases in social diversity? If two variables are related, the relationship is not necessarily causal or unidirectional. How do we know that changes in the diversity of the workforce actually cause the output to change for the better (or, worse)? We can only state that an increase in productivity possibly resulted in social diversity. Claims that are made for diversity with respect to efficiency and productivity should therefore be viewed with caution.

Critical theorists see management of diversity as a practice of power in which managers decide what the definition of diversity is, what its boundaries are, how differences may be practiced, which differences will be honored, and which ones will be ignored. For example, Knoppers, Claringbould, and Dortants (in press) found that managers in nonprofit organizations thought that gender and ethnic diversity at the employee level contributed in a positive manner to organizational image and productivity and were willing to do what they thought needed to be done to enhance it. They saw no added value in fostering diversity with regard to sexual orientation in their organization, however, and therefore did not take steps to address this. In contrast, Cunningham (2011b) and Cunningham and Melton (2011) found that athletic directors were willing to address issues of sexual orientation because doing so might enable the university to tap into the gay alumni and gay community base.

Management of diversity is assumed to enable the individual to make choices that fit her or his social demographic especially with respect to needs such as specific foods, accessibility of buildings, holidays, religious practices, and communicative styles. In addition, employees may be trained in cultural sensitivity and communication skills to develop their intercultural competencies so that every individual will feel welcome in their workplace. Managers decide on how these practices play out. In other words, managers have a great deal of power in deciding how diversity or difference can be practiced in an organization. Employees may have little say in which issues are important to them. Fundamental issues such as the effects of part time work, work family life balance, gendered division of labor, misogynist, homophobic or colorblind workplace cultures often resulting in marginalization, exclusion, and trivialization may be of more importance to employees than sensitivity workshops. These issues tend to be ignored in management of diversity discourses. Such results have led critical scholars to conclude that management of diversity is a practice that primarily benefits managers and pays little attention to the lack of diversity at the director or managerial level. There are those who manage (the managers) and those who are diverse (the employees). Management of diversity as an organizational value has thus far produced little change in the status quo, especially at the managerial level where women and minorities continue to be significantly underrepresented and the culture is often shaped by white masculinist practices.

A critical perspective on diversity stimulates and encourages diversity in people, in ways of thinking and in practice. It begins at the managerial level and addresses diversity among managers. A critical perspective on diversity requires managers to reflect on how they and the rest of the organization create differences and identities and what and who is marginalized and privileged. This includes paying special attention to the practices and assumptions of historically advantaged groups and how their ways of doing are preferred or seen as normal in most levels of the organization. A critical perspective requires critical examination of practices asking questions such as how masculinity is done or performed in an organization, what is associated with being white, how disability is defined and created, etc. In addition, how do these definitions shape organizational practices of exclusion and inclusion and identities?

A critical perspective requires managers to foster a climate where differences among people and ways of thinking and acting are valued, encouraged, and accompanied by questions about how differences are created. The purpose of stimulating organizational diversity is not necessarily to increase organizational efficiency in the traditional sense. Reflecting on and stimulating diversity is encouraged because it is the morally right thing to do. A critical perspective of diversity, therefore, is not based on arguments about productivity and efficiency but on those about social justice. This is accompanied by an exploration of how differences are created and made to matter and by the development of creative ways of looking at organizations and their values.

extent and by proactive strategies to a lesser extent. Based on these and other findings, Fink and colleagues (2001) came to a general conclusion that Division IA athletic departments operate in a culture that values similarity as defined by Doherty and Chelladurai (1999).

In a subsequent study, Fink, Pastore, and Riemer (2003) examined the dynamics of diversity management and individual and organizational outcomes at the level of NCAA Division III intercollegiate athletics. The authors found that perceptions of proactive diversity management were significantly associated with enhancement of all outcomes, which included organizational outcomes of

1. attraction of talented employees
2. retention of talented employees
3. attraction of a diverse customer (fan) base
4. avoidance of discrimination lawsuits
5. a diverse workforce

and individual outcomes of

1. a creative organization
2. an organization in which all employees are involved in decision making
3. an organization in which employees are satisfied
4. a productive organization

Interestingly, the researchers also found that perceptions of enhanced diversity management contributed more to individual-level outcomes than to organizational-level outcomes. Furthermore, the strategy of compliance was also related to these outcomes, whereas the reactive strategy was unrelated to any of the outcomes.

AN INTEGRATIVE FRAMEWORK

In the following sections, we will use a framework that integrates various approaches to managing diversity. We propose that managers can better manage diversity if they take a contingency perspective and consider the forms of diversity they must deal with, diversity management strategies, and the task and time factors that will impact diversity management. Exhibit 13.6 illustrates the integrative framework. Before discussing these elements of the framework and

exhibit 13.6 An integrative framework for managing diversity.

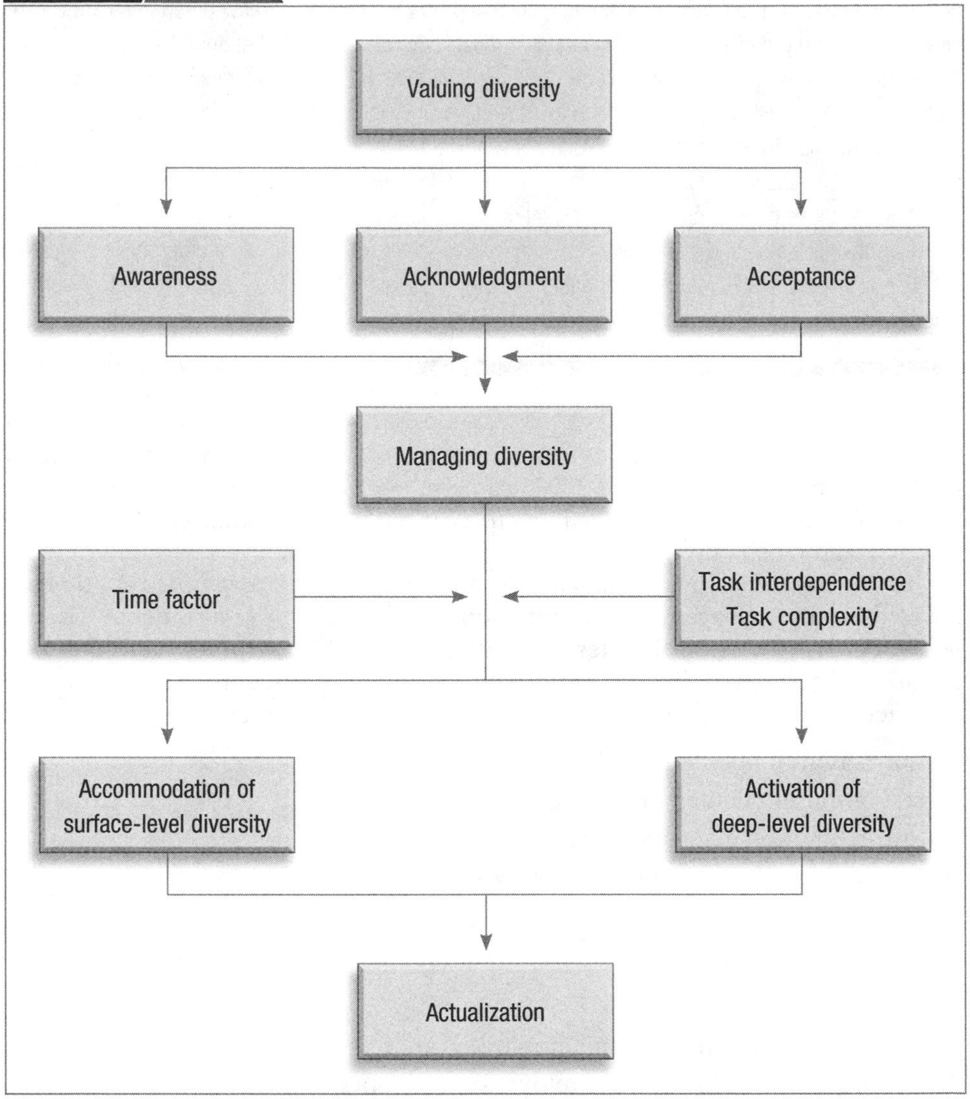

their interrelationships, we must emphasize a fundamental principle of management, including management of diversity: competence is the basis for involving members in specific jobs. Also before presenting the integrated framework, we will discuss the forms of diversity significant to the framework.

Competence as the Cornerstone

Recall that **competence** is one of the tenets of bureaucracy discussed in Chapter 7. Theorists have also emphasized the significance of competence in diversity management. For instance, Thomas (1996) noted that competency must be a primary consideration in managing diversity. Similarly, Lawson and Shen (1998) believe that a focus on job performance–related skills and abilities in hiring and promotion processes would prove beneficial to both the individuals and the organization. On the other hand, a preferential focus on job-irrelevant attributes would prove detrimental for the organization and the individuals themselves. In Lawson and Shen's view, competence, commitment, and compassion should be the cornerstones for harnessing diversity. From this perspective, these authors state the rule as follows: "Seek competence first, keep an open mind, pursue a mix of members, and rely on job performance-related data. No one group of members has a monopoly on competence: rather, different persons have different competencies. You will not do your organization, yourself, or others any favor if you hire and promote individuals who lack competence unless they agree to participate in competence-enhancement education provided by the organization" (Lawson & Shen, 1998, p. 80).

The emphasis here is on current competence to carry out a specific job. Assume that there are 10 applicants for a specific job (e.g., marketing director); one perspective would hold that you as a manager should choose the *most competent* candidate in terms of the current qualifications such as education, specialized training, experience, and past performance. Another perspective could be that anyone who has the *necessary competence* to carry out the job to perform *well enough* can be hired. In this perspective, the manager can create a diverse workforce when hiring for several jobs over a period of time. Because most jobs in most organizations would fall under this category, the organizations can and should enlist people of diverse backgrounds who have the necessary competence to carry out these jobs.

Neither of the above two perspectives addresses a serious issue raised by Cunningham (2011a) of what to do with those people who do not have the necessary competence at the moment because of historical reasons. He notes that "in some situations, however, this practice [of focusing on competence] can have an adverse impact on members of particular social groups" (p. 297). He gives us the example of admission to universities where academic competence is the sole requirement for admission. Those students who can afford to attend prestigious schools, take college preparatory courses, or have a private tutor would have a better chance of admission to such universities. Students who cannot afford these preparatory ventures (particularly those individuals belonging to racial minorities and lower socioeconomic groups) would lose out in the admission process. Cunningham concludes by saying, "Although competence should be the cornerstone, other factors must be considered, such as one's ability to learn or be trained, motivation, personality, and overall fit with the organization" (p. 297).

Cunningham is absolutely right about the potential for competence being spread around in every group. But unfortunately such potential has not been tapped in the past. People belonging to specific groups have been denied the opportunities to maximize their potential. The bright side of this problem is that society and organizations including sport organizations have begun to realize this predicament and are making attempts to redress the situation. For instance, the NCAA has specific programs to offer minorities and women opportunities to be trained and mentored for jobs in intercollegiate sport. Educational institutions also have instituted policies that would give minorities the opportunity to obtain a higher education. In developing and offering such developmental programs, the organizations underscore the importance of competence in a given job. By the same token, such efforts also highlight the fact that the two processes of developing the potential competence and hiring the competence are distinct. As was discussed in Chapter 9, it is also a common practice in organizations to hire people with potential competence and then train and develop them for specific jobs before placing them in those jobs, as shown in Exhibit 13.7.

exhibit 13.7 Hiring the competence (a) versus developing the competence (b).

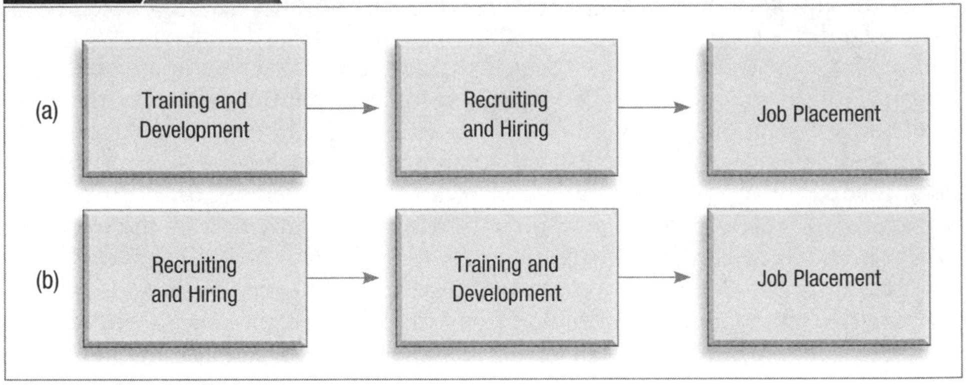

Forms of Diversity

Earlier in the chapter, we discussed the different forms of diversity. We noted that some forms of diversity are observable (color, gender, age, height, and so on) and some are nonobservable (values, beliefs, education). Some authors have used the term **surface-level diversity** to refer to observable differences and the term **deep-level diversity** to refer to non-observable differences. For the purposes of managing diversity, it is useful to consider diversity in the forms of:

1. Appearance or visible features of individuals, such as gender, age, color, and race. These are some of the surface-level differences noted earlier.
2. Behavioral preferences (such as dress and food preferences). These also belong to the category of surface-level differences.
3. Value and attitudinal differences (individualism versus collectivism, attitudes toward athletics, and so on). These belong to the deep-level differences alluded to earlier. These differences can be identified only through observation of decisions people make or the positions they take on specific issues.
4. Cognitive orientations and skills of individuals. These are also deep-level differences that can be discerned only through observing the individuals in task performance. Recall the three forms of managerial skills discussed in Chapter 4. We noted that people differ in the extent to which they possess technical, human, and conceptual skills.

These forms of diversity are expressed in two significant ways. We may call the first type of expression *symbolic,* because it is identified through symbols. For example, the clothing worn by many Arabs, Indians, or Chinese are symbolic expressions of their background. Similarly, the foods people eat are often expressions of their preferences based on tradition and practice.

The second set of expressions of diversity is substantive in nature. I label it *substantive* because these expressions reflect the values, beliefs, and attitudes people hold on vital issues affecting the organization, including the goals and processes of the organization. For instance, Trail and Chelladurai (2000) noted that calls for reform in intercollegiate athletics are based on the divergent values both within and among stakeholders of intercollegiate athletics. The authors have shown that values are related to the choice of goals for athletics and approval of the processes to achieve those goals. In their study, those faculty and students who held power-related values endorsed athletic performance–related goals, and those high on universalism values chose the student development–related goals. Thus, differences between value orientations lead to differences in choices of goals and processes.

Diversity Management Strategies

Several authors have proposed **strategies for managing diversity** in the context of sports (Cunningham, 2011a; DeSensi, 1995; Doherty & Chelladurai, 1999; Fink & Pastore, 1999; Taylor, Doherty, & McGraw, 2008) and in other contexts (Bateman & Snell, 2007; Cox, 1993; Cox & Beale, 1997; Thomas, 1996). A distillation of these perspectives and strategies suggests that valuing diversity is the first necessary condition for managing diversity. Second, managing diversity includes two distinct strategies—accommodation and activation—that can be variously implemented based on the task type. These are explicated below.

Valuing diversity

We noted earlier that valuing diversity means accepting diversity and viewing it as an asset to the organization. This basic requirement for effective diversity management is composed of awareness, acknowledgment, and acceptance of diversity. A sport manager must first be aware of the existence of diversity, acknowledge it openly, and accept it with all its opportunities and obstacles. For example, a manager may see two men or two women of the same color. The most obvious diversity factor is color, and the color itself sets each pair apart from those of another color. However, as stated earlier, the individuals within each pair may be quite different from each other on several other diversity factors, such as country of origin, religion, political leanings, and language. As Lewis (2002) noted, "A healthier sense of belonging in contemporary organizations requires a deep, social acceptance of differences, aided by critical examination of artificial distinctions" (p. 770). Thus, effective diversity management would require that management be aware of these differences, acknowledge them, and accept them as legitimate and beneficial to the organization.

Recall that Thomas (1996) outlined several options an organization can undertake in dealing with diversity. He also noted that only one of those options—mutual adaptation—was focused on truly understanding diversity and maximizing its benefits. Extending this line of reasoning, we find that there are two broad classes of strategies for managing diversity: accommodation and activation.

Accommodation

Accommodation simply refers to permitting and facilitating the symbolic expression of behavioral preferences of diverse individuals. For instance, if women of Indian origin wish to wear saris to work and if task performance is not affected by wearing them, then management should permit it. Similarly, if workers of Islamic faith prefer to pray during lunch break, management can set aside a room for such purposes. If some workers are vegetarians, management should make such food available in the cafeteria. In essence, the strategy of accommodation is aimed at satisfying preferences for symbolic expressions of diversity. Because a strategy such as this reflects the reactions of management to preferences of diverse individuals, it is to some extent similar to the reactive strategy of Fink and Pastore (1999). This strategy would also be part of the organizational culture of diversity proposed by Doherty and Chelladurai (1999).

sidebar 13.7

INTERSECTION OF RELIGION AND SPORTS

The following is an example of the principle of accommodation. Consider the case of Bilqis Abdul-Qaadir, who in January 2009 set the scoring record in Massachusetts high school basketball with 3,000 points. Wearing long sleeves and full-length leggings under her school uniform and a *hijab* on her head, this 5-foot 3-inch player had no difficulty performing the tasks of a basketball player. She was heavily recruited and signed by Melissa McFerrin, the first-year coach at the University of Memphis, and will be the first player at the top tier of Division I to play in Muslim dress. Her success and recruitment show that fans, players, and coaches believe it is the performance that matters and will accommodate diversity when called upon to do so.

This has not always been the case in international soccer. Only in 2012 did the Fédération Internationale de Football Association (FIFA), the international federation that governs the sport of soccer worldwide, allow Muslim women to wear their *hijabs* during competitions. However, in early 2013, the soccer association of Quebec disallowed Sikh male children to wear their *dastar*, the turban that is used to cover their long, uncut hair. The reason behind the ban was that the *dastar* was not allowed by the rules, and that it was dangerous even though there were no reported incidents of harm to anyone. In this case, the Quebec association did not accommodate the preferences of one set of members of the association. However, the Canadian Soccer Association insisted that the ban be lifted under the threat of suspension. The International Football Association Board (IFAB), the rule-making body of FIFA, affirmed the Canadian Soccer Association's position and said that males could wear head covers under the conditions that the head cover must (a) be of the same color as the jersey, (b) be in keeping with the professional appearance of the player's equipment, (c) not be attached to the jersey, and (d) not pose any danger to the player wearing it or any other player (e.g., opening/closing mechanism around the neck).

Interestingly, highly acclaimed international soccer stars such as Ronaldinho, Didier Drogba, Sergi Ramos, Fernando Toress, and several others have used some kind of bandana to keep their hair in place. There has been no concern with that practice. Yet, when some belonging to a religion (Islam or Sikhism) uses similar head covers in adhering to the code of their religion, it becomes an issue with some people and some organizations. It is, however, encouraging that the powers that be (i.e., the Canadian Soccer Association and FIFA) are increasingly accommodating to the dress preferences of minority groups.

Activation

Activation is the process of deliberately bringing divergent perspectives to bear on a task or project. In other words, management consciously encourages members to express their preferences for specific goals or courses of action, or their perspectives on a problem and solutions for it. In fact, management facilitates substantive expressions of diversity (the effects of less observable elements such as values, beliefs, and attitudes) with a view to capitalizing on the strengths of diversity.

Of course, managing these substantive expressions is relatively more difficult. At the same time, this task is more important because these substantive expressions represent unique and innovative ways of perceiving and thinking about organizational affairs. The varying substantive expressions can lead to debates and discussions necessary for optimal decisions and creative problem solving. Thus, it is necessary to activate the richness of the resources offered by diversity toward actualizing the full potential of the members and the organization.

It was noted that producing and marketing of any sport service need to be geared to the increasing diversity in the marketplace. Suppose a fitness club is operating in an area where several immigrant groups reside. Suppose also that the club has hired a few employees from these immigrant groups. If the club wants to make its operations culturally sensitive, it would make sense to engage these immigrant employees in group discussions because they bring to the situation perspectives that are culturally derived. If management activates this special expertise and these unique insights, it is likely to make more informed and practically useful decisions. In the context of marketing spectator sports to African Americans, Armstrong (1998) alludes to the notion of activation. She suggests that African American experts in consumer behavior, media, and African American culture should be involved in designing and implementing these marketing strategies because they bring unique perspectives that are relevant to the African American segment of the market.

Task Factors

Although the management strategies of accommodation and activation are somewhat straightforward, the issue of *what* to accommodate and *when* to activate is more complex. A useful way to address this issue is to look at the nature of the task in which culturally diverse people are involved. The following sections discuss two significant **task factors** that moderate the effects of diversity on performance. Doherty and Chelladurai (1999) include *task complexity* and *task interdependence* as moderators of the effects of diversity on organizational and group outcomes.

Simplicity and complexity of tasks

A task is said to be simple when the purposes and processes of executing it are relatively straightforward. Examples of simple tasks are those of the locker room attendants and ticket takers at a sports venue. In these cases, the persons deal with a narrow set of activities that can be made routine and standard. As Jehn

sidebar 13.8

BUT IS IT DISCRIMINATION?

After analyzing a report by Lapchick (1991), DeSensi (1995) noted that racial discrimination was evident in the stacking of African American players in professional football. The term *stacking* was first introduced by Loy and McElvogue (1970) to refer to the finding that playing positions are staffed differentially by race. That is, black players were disproportionately represented in the so-called noncentral positions—cornerbacks, running backs, and wide receivers. In contrast, white players tended to occupy the so-called central positions—quarterback, center, linemen, and linebackers. Stacking was said to be the process of excluding African American players from central positions and placing them in the noncentral positions. Note that central positions are those at the center of the configuration of all players at the time of the snap.

Regardless of whether or not this practice continues today, the argument that stacking is a manifestation of discrimination is suspect. The fundamental basis for this argument is that the so-called central positions are more important than the noncentral positions. Chelladurai and Carron (1977) argued that geographical centrality in football does not parallel the functional centrality of the game itself. In football, it is the running backs and wide receivers who are engaged in advancing the ball for a touchdown. Thus, these positions are central to the functions of the offensive unit. Although the quarterback is the most central position both geographically and functionally, all actions initiated by the quarterback have to be completed by one of the geographically noncentral but functionally central positions. The other positions jointly play only a supporting role. Thus, the assertion that there is discrimination against black players in football cannot be sustained by these data. In fact, it can be argued that it is whites who are precluded from the functionally central positions.

On the other hand, any data showing that African American players are paid less than white players in comparative playing positions, or that disproportionately fewer blacks are found in coaching and administrative positions, would indicate discrimination.

and colleagues (1999) noted, "When a task is simple and well understood group members can rely on standard operating procedures" (p. 746). Thus, the effects of diversity (both positive and negative) are minimal in simple and routine tasks. Insofar as there is no room for substantive expressions while performing simple tasks, effective management of diversity is restricted to accommodating the symbolic expressions of individuals.

Task complexity refers to difficult and multifaceted tasks (such as policy development, project management, and so on), where the environment is not stable and information is lacking. Such complex tasks are not well understood and do not have prior procedures to handle them. More importantly, they require problem-solving skills (Jehn et al., 1999). In Doherty and Chelladurai's (1999) view, the beneficial effects of diversity are enhanced in complex tasks because members bring different perspectives to addressing the issues posed by the task and to proposing and revising solutions. Jehn and his colleagues (1999) refer to *informational diversity,* meaning "differences in knowledge bases and perspectives that members bring to the group" (p. 743). These authors maintain that education, experience, and expertise are the bases of informational diversity. We can extend that argument and suggest that the personal values and beliefs of members of a group also bring different perspectives to bear on the task at hand. That is, substantive expressions of diversity are critical in complex tasks. Harnessing these differing perspectives and their expressions toward accomplishment of group and organizational tasks is management's task. By the same token, properly managing the negative effects of diversity can prevent them from becoming a problem.

Task interdependence

Doherty and Chelladurai (1999) state that insofar as people of diversity are engaged in relatively independent tasks involving little or no interaction with others, the effects of diversity (both positive and negative) will be neutralized except in the case of symbolic expressions. Accommodating these symbolic expressions need not be a major concern in independent tasks.

In contrast, the effects of diversity can be enhanced in interdependent tasks, where members need to rely on one another to complete their tasks. Interdependent tasks require smooth interaction among group members, who need to communicate, cooperate, and coordinate their efforts (Jehn et al., 1999). Management needs to promote the use of the strengths of such diversity and garner its potential benefits. That is, management needs to facilitate the substantive expressions (creativity, innovative solutions, and so on). If management does not value diversity but rather attempts to stifle it, the potential benefits of diversity are minimized, and the negative effects of diversity (miscommunication, mistrust, confusion, and stress) will increase.

Time Factor

In attempting to harness the benefits of diversity, managers must also consider the **time factor** and its impact on the effects of diversity. In general, members of a newly formed group tend to categorize others based on surface-level differences (such as gender, race, or age), and to make judgments about them based on stereotypes (see Harrison, Price, & Bell, 1998). Given some time, members develop a better understanding of the others' psychological features or deep-level differences and similarities. Any perceived similarity in values, beliefs, and attitudes between the focal person and the others would strengthen the bond

sidebar 13.9

EQUILIBRIUM IN DIVERSITY MANAGEMENT

Chelladurai (2001) employed the metaphor of the solar system to illustrate and highlight the diversity management strategies of accommodation and activation. Two forces are operating in the solar system: the centripetal force created by gravity that pulls the planets toward the sun, and the centrifugal force created by the velocity of the planets that causes them to pull away from the sun. If the centripetal force exceeded the centrifugal force, the planets would be sucked into the inferno of the sun. If, on the other hand, the centrifugal force were greater than the centripetal force, the planets would break loose and hurtle away from the sun. The point is that the dynamic equilibrium among the planets and the sun is maintained by the equality of these two forces.

In our context, the planets correspond to the individuals and groups, and to the organization with its purposes. The "centrifugal forces"—the different sets of values and beliefs of the groups—can impel the individuals and groups outward, away from the purposes of the organization. In contrast, "centripetal forces" from organizational structures and processes can integrate the groups into collective action and pull them toward organizational purposes. Valuing diversity means recognizing, accepting, and allowing the centrifugal forces to operate. Managing diversity requires the creation of the centripetal forces to draw the groups toward the organization and create the dynamic equilibrium and integration of diversity. It is the balance between the two forces that makes for effective diversity management.

between them. Then, even if members perceive differences in values and beliefs, judgments about the others and interactions with them will be based more on observed behavior than on stereotypes (Harrison et al., 1998).

As group members become familiar with each other, they may also become more disposed to developing and understanding an appreciation for different perspectives (Pelled et al., 1999). By the same token, individuals may cultivate the ability to frame and state their views in juxtaposition with others' perspectives. Thus, members may develop a shared understanding of the task and its requirements, as well as of the processes involved in solving problems. The development of such understandings leads to the blurring of the in-group and out-group boundaries. In fact, over time, all members may come to think that they belong to the in-group (that is, the entire group) and to perceive members of the other groups as the out-group (Pelled et al., 1999). But this positive transformation takes time, however. Research has shown that homogeneous groups perform well in the short run, while diverse groups perform well in the long run (see Harrison et al., 1998; Pelled et al., 1999; Schneider & Northcraft, 1999). Note that the negative effects of diversity may take hold in the short run, causing the group to experience conflict and discomfort. Thus, the interactions early on among members of a diverse group may be contrived and artificial. Members may also be restrained from freely expressing their views for fear of rejection.

A CONTINGENCY PERSPECTIVE

We have looked at two distinct forms of expressions of diversity—symbolic and substantive. After discussing two strategies for managing diversity (accommodation and activation), we identified task and time factors as moderators of the effects of diversity on task performance. Given performance imperatives, sport managers need to take a contingency view in deciding on the extent to which the strategy of activation will be practical or beneficial. Readers will recall that those task situations characterized by low interdependence and low complexity may not require activation of substantive differences. That is, when tasks are well defined and the processes of completing the tasks are clear cut, there is little need to exchange opinions and discuss options (Pelled et al., 1999). Thus, the utility of the strategy of activation may be minimal. In contrast, creative problem solving in a complex task may call for activation of the substantive expressions of divergent perspectives. Such a process would yield the benefits of divergent perceptions, orientations, and problem-solving skills.

Note that task factors have more effect on the extent and utility of the strategy of activation of substantive expressions of diversity. The strategy of accommodation is not affected to the same extent by task factors because accommodation deals with symbolic expressions of cultural diversity that do not normally affect task performance. For this reason, accommodating symbolic expressions of diversity can be more easily implemented. Thus, the strategy of accommodation can be thought of as a universal process. That is, the strategy of accommodation should be adopted as a general policy, whereas the strategy of activation should be linked to task factors. Exhibit 13.8 shows these differential approaches to the two strategies.

Though the universal application of the strategy of accommodation generally works, there may be circumstances where accommodation may be circumscribed by organizational or task factors. For instance, a soldier wearing a sari in combat is not conducive to performing effectively in that situation. Similarly, volunteers at The Ohio State University football games are required to wear red coats so as to be identifiable by supervisors, coworkers, and spectators. Under these circumstances, the organization may not be able to accommodate the behavioral preferences of its members.

The time available for making decisions or solving problems also influences the extent to which management may activate substantive expressions of diversity. As we noted, diverse groups take more time to understand their differing orientations and come to some common understanding of the problem at hand and

exhibit 13.8 Strategy of activation in relation to task factors.

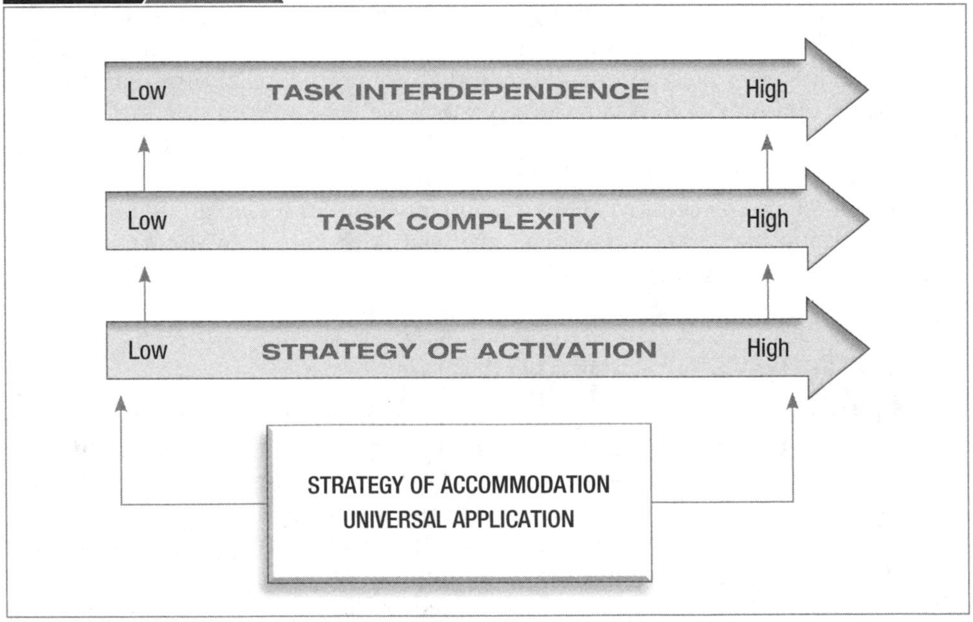

sidebar 13.10

COMMON IN-GROUP IDENTITY: A STRATEGY FOR MANAGING DIVERSITY

Cunningham (2004) and Cunningham and Chelladurai (2004) suggested that one method to reduce the possible negative effects of group diversity is by forming a common in-group identity, such that group members come to consider the aggregate (i.e., the total group) as representing a single, superordinate group. Indeed, within the context of cross-functional teams, Cunningham and Chelladurai (2004) found that the presence of a common in-group identity resulted in greater coworker satisfaction and a stronger preference to work with the team. Therefore, managers seeking to mitigate diversity's negative effects should seek to reinforce the common identity of all members of the group.

Readers will note that this strategy of creating a common in-group identity is employed by coaches. As Cunningham (2004) noted, quite often they achieve this by identifying a common goal of athletic excellence, a common enemy (e.g., the rival basketball team), or a common fate (i.e., everybody loses if the team loses, or everybody gains when the team wins). Note that politicians also whip up support by extolling the virtues of the in-group, and the need to unite to defeat the other group.

possible solutions. Therefore, managers may assign decision making and problem solving to homogeneous groups. If a diverse group has to deal with them at all, a useful strategy for managers is to be more directive in structuring the problem and channeling discussions. That is, the substantive expressions of diversity are minimized with a view to saving time. If there is more time, managers are advised to employ the strategy of activation in order to generate creative and more productive ways of tackling the problem.

ACTUALIZATION

Borrowing from Maslow (1943), I use the term **actualization** to refer to the organization as a whole, including its members and groups, attaining its full potential. Managing diversity is about improving organizational performance by optimally utilizing every member's abilities and by leveraging diversity as an organizational resource (Cox & Beale, 1997). Thus, the most important rationale for management of diversity is the optimization of individual potential and the quality of life for all. A critical caveat here is that the concern with diversity should not be mistaken for concern with minority issues. On the contrary, our earlier discussion shows that diversity in certain dimensions (such as values, beliefs, attitudes, education, and age) can be found even within the majority group. Thus, the central purpose of managing diversity should be the promotion of the potential and quality of life of all members. In sum, the concept of actualization refers to management's relative success in optimizing individual potential, enhancing quality of life for all, and thus increasing organizational productivity.

SUMMARY

This chapter highlighted the need for sport managers to be aware of the significance of diversity in the workforce and marketplace. The dimensions of diversity include observable or surface-level factors such as gender, race, and color, and less observable or unobservable differences in behavioral preferences, values and attitudes, and cognitive orientations. In discussing these dimensions of diversity, we emphasized that differences are not deficits. Affirmative action can be compared to a genuine sense of valuing diversity and managing that diversity. Strategies for managing diversity include the negative options of denying the existence of diversity and suppressing or isolating diversity. Positive strategies include building relationships and fostering mutual adaptations among diverse members.

The final sections of the chapter present an integrative framework for managing diversity. The two cornerstones of managing diversity are a genuine valuing of diversity and a focus on competence. All dimensions of diversity are expressed in two significant ways—symbolic expressions, such as preferences for specific dress and food, and substantive expressions, such as expressions of one's values, attitudes, and preferences for certain courses of action.

The two major strategies for managing diversity are (1) accommodating symbolic expressions of diversity, such as specific attire, food, language, and so forth; and (2) activating substantive expressions of diversity in values, needs, and preferences as well as diversity in information and expertise. We noted that the employment of these two strategies is contingent on the nature of the task. In independent or simple tasks, the accommodation of symbolic expressions is necessary and sufficient. In the case of interdependent and complex tasks, in addition to accommodating symbolic expressions, management must also activate substantive expressions of diversity. This leads to better decisions acceptable to most participants.

develop YOUR PERSPECTIVE

1. Consider your closest friends. In what ways are they similar to you? In what ways do they differ? What specific similarities and differences affect your relationships, and in what ways? How do you and your friends manage the diversity among you?
2. Identify a sport organization you are familiar with. Describe the diversity among members of that organization. Explain the effects of this diversity on the functioning of the organization. What conscious efforts is that organization making to capitalize on the strengths of its diversity?
3. Can you identify situations in sport management in which the strategy of accommodation of symbolic expressions can easily be followed without disrupting the work processes? Similarly, can you identify circumstances in sport management where accommodation would be detrimental to work performance?
4. The strategy of activation is fruitful only in some circumstances. Identify and describe some circumstances in sport management that require activation and some that prohibit it.

references

Acosta, R. V., & Carpenter, L. J. (2012). *Women in intercollegiate sport: A longitudinal study—thirty-five year update—1977–2012.* Unpublished manuscript, Brooklyn College, Brooklyn, NY.

Allison, M. T. (1988). Breaking boundaries and barriers: Future directions in cross-cultural research. *Leisure Sciences, 10,* 247–259.

Anderson, E. (2011). Updating the outcome: Gay athletes, straight teams, and coming out in educationally based team sports. *Gender & Society, 25,* 250–268.

Armstrong, K. L. (1998). Ten strategies to employ when marketing sport to black consumers. *Sport Marketing Quarterly, 7*(3), 11–18.

Arredondo, P. (1996). *Successful diversity management initiatives: A blueprint for planning and implementation*. Thousand Oaks, CA: Sage Publications.

Bateman, T. S., & Snell, S. A. (2007). *Management: Leading & collaborating in a competitive world* (7th ed.). Boston: McGraw-Hill Irwin.

Buzuvis, E. (2012). Including transgender athletes in sex-segregated sport. In G. B. Cunningham (Ed.), *Sexual orientation and gender identity in sport: Essays from activists, coaches, and scholars* (pp. 23–34). College Station, TX: Center for Sport Management Research and Education.

Chelladurai, P. (1994). Sport management: Defining the field. *European Journal of Sport Management, 1,* 7–21.

Chelladurai, P. (2001). *Athletic teams as models for managing diversity*. Opening keynote presentation at the 9th Congress of the European Association for Sport Management. Vittoria-Gasteiz, Spain. September 19–23.

Chelladurai, P. (2006). *Human resource management in sport and recreation* (2nd ed.). Champaign, IL: Human Kinetics.

Chelladurai, P., & Carron, A.V. (1977). A reanalysis of formal structure in sport. *Canadian Journal of Applied Sport Sciences, 2,* 9–14.

Chesler, M., & Crowfoot, J. (1992). *Visioning change: Stages in the movement from monocultural organizations*. Ann Arbor: University of Michigan.

Cox, T. (1991). The multicultural organization. *Academy of Management Executive, 5,* 34–46.

Cox, T. (1993). *Cultural diversity in organizations: Theory, research, and practice*. San Francisco: Berrett-Koehler.

Cox, T., Jr., & Beale, R. L. (1997). *Developing competency to manage diversity: Readings, cases, & activities*. San Francisco: Berrett-Koehler.

Cunningham, G. B. (2004). Strategies for transforming the possible negative effects of group diversity. *Quest, 56,* 421–438.

Cunningham, G. B. (2008). Commitment to diversity and its influence on athletic department outcomes. *Journal of Intercollegiate Sport, 1,* 176–201.

Cunningham, G. B. (2009). The moderating effect of diversity strategy on the relationship between racial diversity and organizational performance. *Journal of Applied Social Psychology, 36,* 1445–1460.

Cunningham, G. B. (2010). How closely do you identify? The interactive effects of perceived religious dissimilarity and religious personal identity on perceived value dissimilarity and job satisfaction. *Social Justice Research, 23,* 60–76.

Cunningham, G. B. (2011a). *Diversity in sport organizations* (2nd ed.). Scottsdale, AZ: Holcomb Hathaway.

Cunningham, G. B. (2011b). The LGBT advantage: Examining the relationship among sexual orientation diversity, diversity strategy, and performance. *Sport Management Review, 14,* 453–461.

Cunningham, G. B., & Chelladurai, P. (2004). Affective reactions to cross-functional teams: The impact of size, relative performance, and common in-group identity. *Group Dynamics: Theory, Research, and Practice, 8*(2), 83–97.

Cunningham, G. B., & Melton, E. N. (2011). The benefits of sexual orientation diversity in sport organizations. *Journal of Homosexuality, 58,* 647–663.

Cunningham, G. B., & Sagas, M. (2004a). Group diversity, occupational commitment, and occupational turnover intentions among NCAA Division IA football coaching staffs. *Journal of Sport Management, 18,* 236–254.

Cunningham, G. B., & Sagas, M. (2004b). Racial differences in occupational turnover intent among NCAA Division IA assistant football coaches. *Sociology of Sport Journal, 21,* 84–92.

Cunningham, G. B., & Sagas, M. (2004c). The effect of group diversity on organizational commitment. *International Sports Journal, 8*(1), 124–131.

Cunningham, G. B., Sartore, M. L., & McCullough, B. P. (2010). The influence of applicant sexual orientation and rater sex on ascribed attributions and hiring recommendations of personal trainers. *Journal of Sport Management, 24,* 400–415.

DeHass, D. (2007). *2005–06 ethnicity and gender demographics of NCAA member institutions' athletics personnel*. Indianapolis, IN: National Collegiate Athletic Association.

DePauw, K. P., & Gavron, S. J. (2005). *Disability sport* (2nd ed.). Champaign, IL: Human Kinetics.

DeSensi, J. T. (1994). Multiculturalism as an issue in sport management. *Journal of Sport Management, 8,* 63–74.

DeSensi, J. T. (1995). Understanding multiculturalism and valuing diversity: A theoretical perspective. *Quest, 47,* 34–43.

Doherty, A. J., & Chelladurai, P. (1999). Managing cultural diversity in sport organizations: A theoretical perspective. *Journal of Sport Management, 13,* 280–297.

Fernandez, J. P., & Barr, M. (1993). *The diversity advantage: How American business can outperform Japanese and European companies in the global marketplace*. San Francisco: Jossey-Bass. First published by Lexington Books.

Fine, M. G. (1995). *Building successful multicultural organizations*. Westport, CT: Quorum Books.

Fink, J. S., Burton, L. J., Farrell, A. O., & Parker, H. M. (2012). Playing it out: Female intercollegiate athletes' experiences in revealing their sexual identities. *Journal for the Study of Sports and Athletes in Education, 6,* 83–106.

Fink, J. S., & Cunningham, G. B. (2005). The effects of racial and gender dyad diversity on work experiences of university athletics personnel. *International Journal of Sport Management, 6,* 199–213.

Fink, J. S., & Pastore, D. L. (1999). Diversity in sport? Utilizing the business literature to devise a comprehensive framework of diversity initiatives. *Quest, 51,* 310–327.

Fink, J. S., Pastore, D. L., & Riemer, H. A. (2001). Do differences make a difference? Managing diversity in Division 1A intercollegiate athletics. *Journal of Sport Management, 15,* 10–50.

Fink, J. S., Pastore, D. L., & Riemer, H. A. (2003). Managing employee diversity: Perceived practices and organizational outcomes in NCAA Division III athletic departments. *Sport Management Review, 6*(2), 147–168.

Gomez-Meija, L. R., Balkin, D. B., & Cardy, R. L. (2005). *Management: People, performance, change.* Boston: McGraw-Hill Irwin.

Harrison, D. A., Price, K. H., & Bell, M. P. (1998). Beyond relational demography: Time and the effects of surface- and deep-level diversity on work group cohesion. *Academy of Management Journal, 41*(1), 96–107.

Heilman, M. E. (1994). Affirmative action: Some unintended consequences for working women. *Research in Organizational Behavior, 16,* 125–169.

Henderson, G. (1994). *Cultural diversity in the workplace: Issues and strategies.* Westport, CT: Quorum Books.

Hitt, M. A., Black, J. S., Porter, L. W., & Hanson, D. (2007). *Management.* Frenchs Forest, NSW: Pearson Education Australia.

Hopkins, W. E. (1997). *Ethical dimensions of diversity.* Thousand Oaks, CA: Sage Publications.

Immegart, G. L., & Pilecki, F. J. (1973). *An introduction to systems for educational administrators.* Reading, MA: Addison-Wesley.

Jehn, K. A., Northcraft, G. B., & Neale, M. A. (1999). Why differences make a difference: A field study of diversity, conflict, and performance in workgroups. *Administrative Science Quarterly, 44,* 741–763.

Knoppers, A., Claringbould, I. & Dortants, M. (in press). Discursive managerial practices of diversity and homogeneity. *Journal of Gender Studies.*

Kossek, E. E., & Lobel, S. A. (1996). Transforming human resource systems to manage diversity: An introduction and orienting framework. In E. E. Kossek & S. A. Lobel (Eds.), *Managing diversity: Human resource strategies for transforming the workplace* (pp. 1–19). Cambridge, MA: Blackwell Business.

Lapchick, R. E. (1991). Professional sports: The racial report card. *Center for the Study of Sport and Society Digest, 2*(1), 4–8.

Lawson, R. B., & Shen, Z. (1998). *Organizational psychology: Foundations and applications.* New York: Oxford University Press.

Lewis, M. (2002). Exploring paradox: Toward a more comprehensive guide. *Academy of Management Review, 25,* 760–776.

Lott, B., & Bullock, H. E. (2007). *Psychology and economic injustice: Personal, professional, and political intersections.* Washington, DC: American Psychological Association.

Loy, J. H., & McElvogue, J. F. (1970). Racial segregation in American sport. *International Review of Sport Sociology, 5,* 5–24.

Maslow, A. H. (1943). A theory of human motivation. *Psychological Review, 50,* 370–396.

Milliken, F. J., & Martins, L. L. (1996). Searching for common threads: Understanding the multiple effects of diversity in organizational groups. *Academy of Management Review, 21,* 402–433.

NBA (2005). Basketball Without Borders expands to four continents. Retrieved from www.nba.com/bwb/four continents2005.html.

Nightengale, B. (2008). Novice pitchers from India sign with Pirates. *USA Today.* Retrieved from www.usatoday.com/sports/baseball/nl/pirates/2008-11-24-indian-pitchers-sign_N.htm.

Pelled, L. H., Eisenhart, K. M., & Xin, K. R. (1999). Exploring the black box: An analysis of work group diversity, conflict, and performance. *Administrative Science Quarterly, 44,* 1–28.

Ren, L. R., Paetzold, R. L., & Colella, A. (2008). A meta-analysis of experimental studies on the effects of disability on human resource judgments. *Human Resource Management Review, 18,* 191–203.

Robbins, S. P., & Coulter, M. (1996). *Management* (5th ed.). Upper Saddle River, NJ: Prentice Hall.

Robbins, S. P., Coulter, M., Leach, E., & Kilfoil, M. (2012). *Management* (10th ed.). Don Mills, Ontario: Pearson Canada.

Roberts, S. (2008, August 14). Minorities in U.S. set to become majority by 2042. *New York Times.* Retrieved from http://www.nytimes.com/2008/08/14/world/americas/14iht-census.1.15284537.html?_r=0.

Schneider, S. K., & Northcraft, G. B. (1999). The social dilemmas of workforce diversity in organizations: A social identity perspective. *Human Relations, 52,* 1445–1467.

Schuler, R. S., & Jackson, S. E. (1996). *Human resource management: Positioning for the 21st century* (6th ed.). Minneapolis, MN: West.

Taylor, T., Doherty, A., & McGraw, P. (2008). *Managing people in sport organizations: A strategic human resource perspective.* Burlington, MA: Butterworth-Heineman.

Thomas, R. R. (1991). *Beyond race and gender: Unleashing the power of your total workforce by managing diversity.* New York: AMACOM.

Thomas, R. R. (1996). *Redefining diversity.* New York: AMACOM.

Trail, G., & Chelladurai, P. (2000). Perceptions of goals and processes of intercollegiate athletics: A case study. *Journal of Sport Management, 14,* 154–178.

Waring, A. (1996). *Practical systems thinking.* London: International Thomson Business Press.

Weiner, N. (1997). *Making cultural diversity work.* Scarborough, ON, Canada: Carswell (Thompson Professional Publishing).

Winslow, O. (2008). Census report sees minorities becoming majority by 2042. Retrieved from www.newsday.com/news/printedition/longisland/nylicens145800578aug14,0,2712431.story.

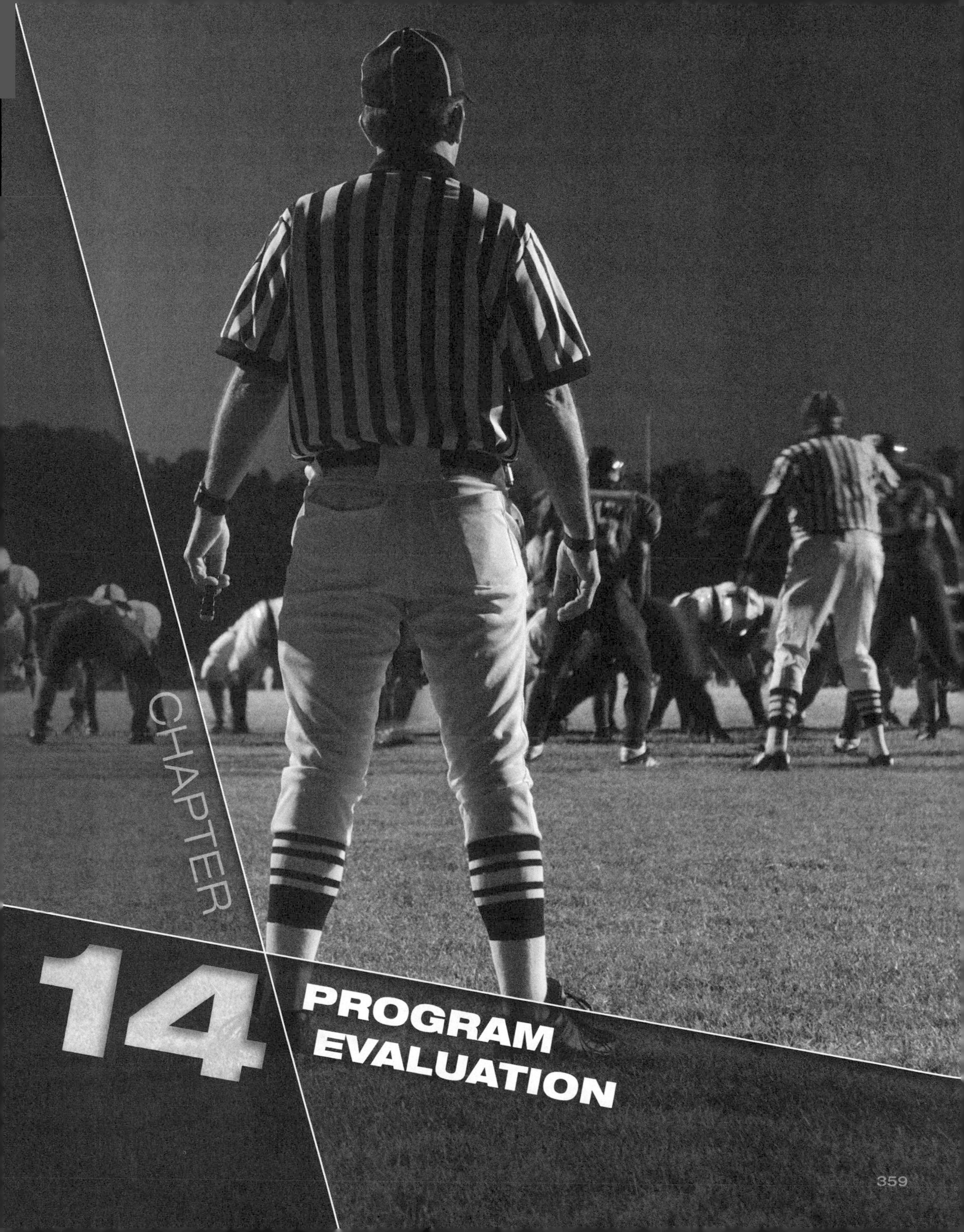

CHAPTER 14 PROGRAM EVALUATION

manage YOUR LEARNING

After completing this chapter you should be able to:

- Distinguish the performances at individual, unit, and organizational levels.
- Understand the relationships between planning and programming.
- Define and describe a program and its components from a systems perspective.
- Distinguish between the outputs and impacts of a program.
- Describe the various types of programs.
- Define program evaluation, its purposes, and its processes.
- Understand the differences among various standards applied to programs.

strategic CONCEPTS

client satisfaction
cost–benefit analysis
cost-effective
impact
meeting objectives
output
performance appraisal
planning
professional judgment
program
program evaluation
program logic
program profile
public and nonprofit programs
social intervention
socioeconomic evaluation
standards of evaluation

EVALUATION DEFINED

The previous chapters have been devoted to describing the managerial processes of planning, organizing, and leading. The identification of desired goals and the selection of activities and programs to achieve those goals are the essence of the planning process as outlined in Chapters 5 and 6. Grouping the activities into meaningful units, establishing appropriate rules and regulations to govern and coordinate these units, and hiring and assigning the right people to the right jobs are part of the organizing process, which we discussed in Chapters 7, 8, and 9. The leading function aims at motivating and influencing the members toward organizational goals (see Chapters 10, 11, and 12). All of the time and effort that the managers spend on these processes are expected to lead to some specified results. Now comes the equally critical function of evaluating, whereby the organization and its units are judged on the basis of their achievements.

Individual-, Unit-, and Organizational-Level Performances

As shown in Exhibit 14.1, there are three major categories to be considered in the evaluation stage: performances at the individual, unit, and organizational levels. Consider the case of a sport team. The coach as an individual can be evaluated based on how well he motivates the players and makes them perform their

exhibit 14.1 Evaluation of performance at different levels.

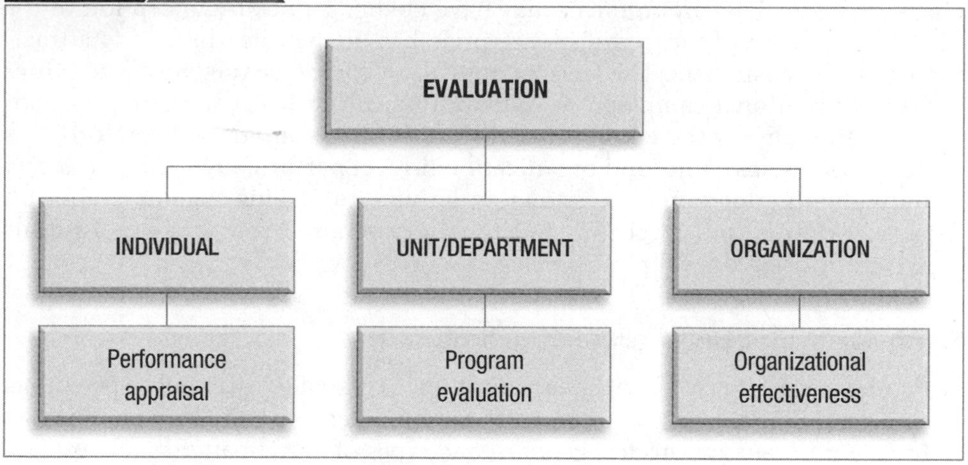

best. The team as a unit can also be evaluated based on its performance both on and off the field. Finally, the organization to which the team belongs (the school, university, or the professional league) can be evaluated on the basis of attaining its goals. The first concern pertains to performances of individual employees. The analysis focuses on finding out whether every employee has completed effectively the tasks assigned to that individual. This issue is fundamental to all of management because the whole enterprise is ultimately dependent for its success on the members and their performances.

The assessment or evaluation of the work of individual employees is called **performance appraisal** and is an integral part of human resource management. Performance appraisal is so important that many organizations have separate departments to address it. Chelladurai (2006) deals extensively with the topic. Briefly, performance appraisal has two purposes. The first is the developmental purpose, whereby managers (a) appraise individual performances; (b) identify strengths and weaknesses; (c) discuss with the individual any areas where improvements can be made; and (d) determine how to overcome the barriers, if any, to enhancing performance. The second is the evaluative purpose, by which the performances of all employees are appraised on some common and standard criteria and then compared with each other, and the resulting comparisons are used to distribute organizational rewards (promotions, merit pay, bonuses, and so on).

IN brief

Evaluating is one of the four major functions of management. It involves evaluating the performance of (a) individuals (performance appraisal), (b) individual programs (program evaluation), and (c) the total organization (organizational effectiveness).

From a macro perspective, managers must also be concerned with how well the different units are doing and how effective the total organization is. Even when individuals in an organization carry out their assigned tasks effectively, the units within an organization and the total organization may not be achieving the goals specified for them. We can identify several reasons for the lack of correspondence between employee-level performance and unit- or organizational-level performance. The unit- or organizational-level goals may have been too high or inappropriate in the first place. For example, a promotional program aimed at recruiting 200 new customers for a fitness/health club may not achieve that goal despite the best efforts of the employees, simply because the goal is too high. Or it could be because severe constraints have been overlooked in the planning stage, such as the inaccessibility of the club's location. The environment may have changed since the inception of the plan in that a new fitness/health enterprise has opened nearby and is attracting would-be customers. The failure could also be because the chosen activities for the promotional campaign were inappropriate or because there was poor coordination among the employees involved in the promotion. Therefore, it is important to assess unit- and organizational-level performance independently of individual performances, as shown in Exhibit 14.1. This chapter deals with the evaluation of unit-level performance (or programs), and Chapter 16 deals with organizational-level performance.

Organizational Units and Programs

Very often each of the units in an organization is created to carry out a specific set of activities. For instance, a city recreation department may create separate units to handle different age groups, genders, and types of participation, such as competitive, recreational, and instructional programs. Each of these units is assigned specific tasks or activities. Therefore, whenever we speak of the effectiveness of a unit, we really mean whether that unit's assigned activities are carried out according to specifications, and whether those activities achieve the objectives they were designed to achieve. The terms *program management, program planning,* and *program evaluation* indicate the respective functions pertaining to a program. The following sections outline the evaluative function with respect to a program.

PROGRAMS DEFINED

According to Marinaccio and Trojanowski (2012), "Programs comprise a group of related projects coordinated and managed to obtain benefits that would not be realized if managed individually. Typically, programs focus on outcomes—usually a change or improvement—and use project outputs to deliver the benefits the program was designed to achieve" (p. 47). According to this definition, those activities attempting to achieve a specific goal or a set of goals are grouped together as a program. For instance, a youth sports program aimed at fostering sports participation among teenagers may consist of several activities, such as scheduled daily or weekly instructional, competitive, or recreational sessions.

In addition, it is also conventional for the group of activities associated with a program to be assigned to one unit or department rather than being spread across different units. Locating an entire program and its activities in one unit makes for better coordination and control. This does not mean that each unit will be restricted to only one program. For instance, the city recreation department may offer programs such as adult sports, youth sports, adapted recreation, hobby and art workshops, and park maintenance. It is also essential to conceive of a program as a distinct entity from the unit that runs the program.

Another element common to all programs is that some resources (human, material, and monetary) are allocated to a given program. It is conventional for a university athletic department to speak of its sports teams as programs (football program, men's and women's basketball programs, and so on). It is also conventional to allocate certain resources to each of these programs. In addition to the facilities and support services assigned to each one, a certain dollar amount is also allocated. Recall that such allocation of resources is referred to as program budgeting (see Chapter 5).

Planning and Programming

Owen (1993) states that a program is "a manifestation of the planning process . . . [and that] program development means converting value choices into concrete directions for action by choosing from among alternatives and allocating resources to achieve defined goals" (p. 5). The foregoing description of a program parallels that of **planning** and goals discussed in Chapter 5. The notable difference is that the objectives of a program are narrow, with a limited number of activities, and that a program is usually targeted toward a specific client group (as in a youth sport program).

TO recap

planning and budgeting

In Chapter 5, we noted that planning includes budgeting—the allocation of resources to various activities chosen to achieve the desired ends. We also noted that organizations need to take a rational, comprehensive approach to planning. Such an approach would entail assessing the importance of the various programs (or activities) and their effectiveness in contributing to organizational goals. We noted that this is the essence of the budgeting technique known as the Planning–Programming–Budgeting System (PPBS). Thus, the process of program evaluation discussed in this chapter feeds back into the planning and budgeting processes described earlier.

Programs Versus Projects

We must distinguish between a program and a project. A **program** is a set of activities carried out on a continuing basis. For example, the coaching and associated activities provided for an athletic team in an educational setting are a program because these activities are carried out every year on a continuous basis. Similarly, the organization and conduct of competitions in one or more sports by a university recreation department is a program, because it is done on a continuous basis. In contrast, projects are "temporary undertakings aimed at creating a product, service, or result according to predefined schedule, cost, and quality constraints. Typically, the process involves assembling a temporary project team that works to create a defined output" (Marinaccio & Trojanowski, 2012, p. 47). For example, a city recreation department may begin a project of sports competitions for wheelchair athletes. Just as in a program, a set of resources will be expended on specified activities for the benefit of the target group.

What distinguishes a project from a program is that the project is carried out for the first time without any prior intention to continue it in the coming years. However, after the project's initial run, administrators may find that it was successful and of great benefit to everyone concerned. At this point the managers may decide to continue with the project every year. When that happens, the project becomes a program. Apart from this difference, a program and a project are planned and executed in similar ways. Therefore, the following sections are applicable to both.

IN brief

A program and a project, while similar in most respects, exhibit one significant difference. A program is repeated on a continuing basis, whereas a project is a one-shot affair. However, a project may be later converted into a regular program.

Public and Nonprofit Programs

The terms *program* and *program evaluation* are more often used in the context of public and nonprofit organizations than in the business context. We are all familiar with the welfare programs, drug education programs, and highway maintenance programs of the federal, state, and city governments. These types of **public and nonprofit programs** are often aimed at improving the conditions of targeted groups and thereby benefiting the society at large. A recent phenomenon is for a profit-oriented organization to form a nonprofit subunit to carry out programs to help specific groups. For example, the NFL's "Play 60" campaign is aimed at encouraging youth physical activity, and the Cincinnati Reds Rookie Success League is aimed at providing sport opportunities for underprivileged youth.

In a similar manner, the International Olympic Committee and its administrators may embark on a specific program to improve sport performance around the world. The IOC then selects certain developing countries and embarks on a program of activities (training coaches and athletes, educating administrators, and so on). Along similar lines, sport-governing bodies offer coaching programs to teach the skills of the sport; the knowledge associated with that sport, such as its history, psychophysical requirements, and rules; sportsmanship; and respect for rules, officials, and opponents.

The NCAA institutes programs to educate prospective university athletes about various regulations, the rights and responsibilities of athletes, and the dangers of drug use and gambling. For instance, the NCAA's Leadership Advisory Board "provides an important leadership perspective from outside the NCAA governance structure; plays an active and meaningful role in advancing the mission of the student-athlete and the NCAA" (NCAA, 2007a). With this mission in mind, the board offers the following programs in support of student-athletes:

- Student-Athlete Advisory Committees
- Leadership Advisory Board
- Leadership Conferences for Student-Athletes
- National Student-Athlete Day
- Fellows Leadership Development Program
- Leadership Institute for Ethnic Minority Males and Females
- CHAMPS/Life Skills Program
- Conference Intern Seminar (NCAA, 2007b)

In addition, the goals of the NCAA's Ethnic Minority and Women's Enhancement Program are to increase the pool of and opportunities for qualified minority and female candidates in intercollegiate athletics through postgraduate scholarships. With this in mind, the NCAA awards 13 scholarships to ethnic minorities and 13 scholarships to female college graduates who will be entering their initial year of postgraduate studies (NCAA, 2007c).

One of the most popular programs of the Government of Canada is called ParticipACTION, which advocates an active lifestyle through its innovative slogans and advertisements. In the United States, the President's Council on Physical Fitness and Sports advises the President through the Secretary of Health and Human Services about physical activity, fitness, and sports. Partnering with the public, private, and nonprofit sectors, the council promotes health, physical activity, fitness, and enjoyment among all Americans through participation in physical activity and sports (President's Council on Physical Fitness and Sports, 2008a). The most significant of its programs is the President's Challenge, which encourages all Americans to be active in their everyday lives. Individuals can earn points for their daily activities, and when they earn a certain number of points, they will receive a Presidential Award (President's Council on Physical Fitness and Sports, 2008b).

Programs in the Commercial/Profit Sector

Programs and program evaluation are equally relevant to every kind of organization, including commercial, profit-oriented organizations. A public or media relations program in, for example, a professional sport franchise may consist of several activities (e.g., media relations, advertising, lobbying), all of which are expected to achieve a positive public image for the franchise. Consider the NBA's "I love this game" campaign to promote the game of basketball and the NBA itself.

Sponsorship, defined as "the acquisition of rights to affiliate or directly associate with a product or event for the purpose of deriving benefits related to that affiliation or association" (Mullin, Hardy, & Sutton, 2007, p. 315), is a program in itself. Coca-Cola, for example, sponsors various sporting enterprises and/or events with a view to publicize the company and its products among specific market segments. Coca-Cola's sponsorship activities are unique from other forms of advertising and marketing of its products, and as each sponsorship is affiliated with a distinct sporting enterprise and the associated market segment, we designate sponsorship activities as a program unto itself.

Programs in Small Organizations

Many of the foregoing examples of programs are drawn from large and rich organizations (both profit and nonprofit) and may involve significant sums of money, impact a vast number of people, and cover a large territory. Because of their size and scope, such programs are often in the news, and the public, politicians, and commentators debate over their purposes and outcomes.

Programs and program evaluation are just as relevant to smaller organizations. For instance, the intramural department in a small university may enact a program designed to encourage greater participation by the students, staff, and faculty of the university. This example is a program by itself, and evaluation would shed some light on where improvements could be made, how the program could be made more cost-effective, and how it could be made attractive to prospective customers.

The efforts and funding that go into such a program may be much smaller than in the programs of larger organizations. However, those funds may be comparatively large when considered as a percentage of the overall budgets of these units. The point here is that if substantial effort and money go into a program, then it is incumbent upon the managers to verify whether the program achieves what it is supposed to achieve.

PROGRAMS FROM A SYSTEMS PERSPECTIVE

It is important to note that the definitions of a program cited so far highlight (a) resources, (b) activities, and (c) outputs. As shown in Exhibit 14.2, these elements resemble the input, throughput, and output of a system as described in Chapter 3. In the case of the USA Football Player Academy (a program of the USA Football organization), the personnel, money, and sponsorships are the inputs; the activity is the three-day camp teaching football fundamentals through both classroom and on-field teaching and coaching; and the outputs are what the youth learn about football fundamentals and the additional revenue that USA Football raises. Additional program impacts could be increased interest in football, improvement of a football team, or increased community involvement in football.

In essence, resources refer to the dollars, the labor (number of employees, number of hours they spend on the program), and other inputs allocated to the program. For instance, the resources of the football, volleyball, and cross-country programs of a university athletic department can be compared on the basis of the budgets allotted to each, the number of full- and part-time coaches, and the effort and expenditure of maintaining the practice and competition facilities.

exhibit 14.2 A systems view of a program.

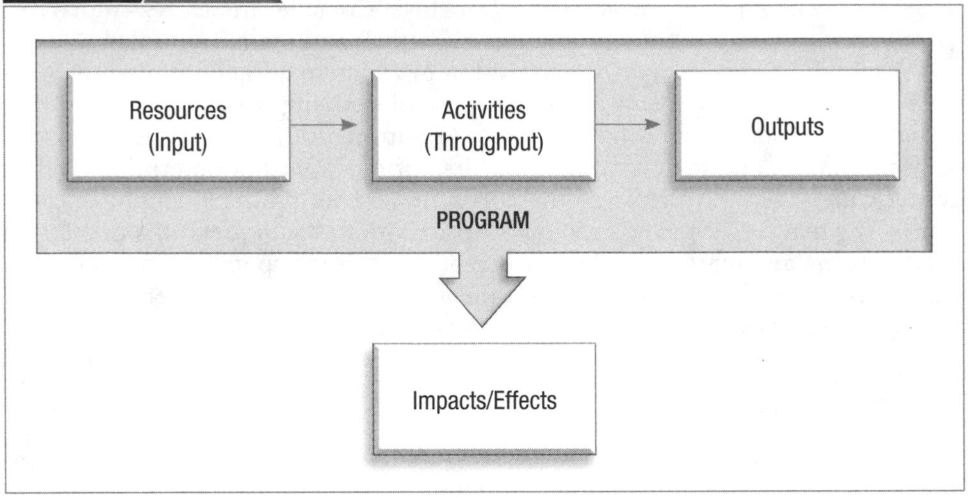

The activities are the major tasks undertaken to achieve the goals of the program. These activities also include the arrangement of positions and powers among the program's personnel. As noted in Chapters 7 and 8, this refers to the distribution of responsibilities and authority, and to the methods of coordination of the activities of the members assigned to the program. For example, the American Sport Education Program is involved in developing multilevel curricular programs and offering courses for coaches (called SportCoach), for sport administrators (SportDirector), and for parents (SportParent). Similarly, the coach education program undertaken by the Coaching Association of Canada includes the preparation and production of instructional material, different levels of coaching classes, and various methods of assessment of trainees. These activities are often carried out with the collaboration of national and provincial sport-governing bodies, educational institutions, and local recreation departments. They are also governed by a hierarchically arranged system composed of a director, several assistant directors, regional coordinators, and many more instructors throughout Canada. From a systems perspective, these are the throughput processes.

The **outputs** are the intended (and sometimes unintended) results of the program. The Coaching Association of Canada may count among its outputs the number of classes offered at various levels and in different regions, the sales of its publications, and the quality of the instructional materials. Thus, outputs as described here are direct effects and outcomes of the program.

Outputs and Impacts

In addition to the direct outputs, programs may have **impacts** and effects beyond the intended outputs. Consider a university athletic department program for generating revenue through licensing concessions. The immediate and readily apparent outputs are the dollar amounts generated and the number of spectators served. However, the holders of these concessions may invest money and labor in their respective enterprises (to buy and sell their products) and thereby generate a distinct sphere of economic activity. These activities reflect the significant impact a program may have on the economic front.

If the athletic department allows nonprofit organizations to sell their products during a game, the impact is partly on the economic side and, more important, on the public relations side as well. The political and social impact of the program may be even greater. If a university has a winning football team, its public image may be greatly improved; recruitment of quality students becomes easier; influence with the lawmakers increases; and solidarity with the local and regional community, the media, and alumni across the nation is vastly enhanced. In the case of the Coaching Association of Canada, the impact is evidenced by the quality of coaching offered by its trainees and by the quality of the experience of participants in youth sport across the country.

Programs as Social Interventions

From a different perspective, almost all the programs of public (government) and nonprofit organizations may be considered as **social interventions** (Owen, 1993). This means that these organizations may initiate and execute programs for the benefit of society in general and a specific client group in particular (such as the programs of the Red Cross, Salvation Army, and educational institutions, and the welfare programs of the federal, state, and city governments). The concept of intervention implies that a need exists that must be addressed or satisfied—that is, a need exists to improve some neglected or deficient aspect in the society.

Note that the idea of social intervention need not be restricted to public and nonprofit organizations. Some commercial enterprises may devise and undertake specific programs to solve a problem for the society or a segment of the society. As mentioned previously, profit-oriented enterprises may initiate programs to encourage greater participation in sport and physical activity. For example, programs such as street basketball, three-player basketball, charity runs, walkathons, and the NFL's "Play 60" may be organized by profit-oriented firms to promote participation in these activities. To the extent these programs are aimed at changing the community's health and fitness habits, they may be considered social interventions. However, this does not negate the fact that when commercial enterprises create programs for the good of society, they usually do so as a public relations strategy to promote themselves and their products. In fact, the promotion and sponsorship of many sport events are primarily business propositions from the companies' perspective. For our purposes here, however, they are still programs of social intervention.

PROGRAM EVALUATION

Now that we have defined and described programs and their types, let us look at **program evaluation** itself. According to Newcomer and colleagues (1994), "*program evaluation* is the systematic assessment of program results and, to the extent feasible, systematic assessment of the extent to which the program caused those results. . . . [It also] includes process evaluations which assess the extent to which a program has been implemented as intended, even when such evaluation does not assess the longer-term results of the program implementation" (p. 3).

Program evaluation is also a "review and assessment of . . . the adequacy of its objectives, its design and its results both intended and unintended" (Treasury Board of Canada, 1981, p. 19). Three significant questions are addressed in this description of program evaluation. First, has the program achieved its goals or reached the intended outcomes? The second question is, have the activities been carried out in accordance with specifications? If the activities deviated from what was planned, one cannot necessarily expect the program to achieve its objective. Even when the processes are in order, and even when the objectives are achieved, a third question remains: Were the objectives achieved because of the program and its activities or because of something else? For instance, a government organization that promotes physical activity may experience increased participation in the three months following its marketing program, but that increase could be a function of changing weather conditions. That is, if the marketing campaign was launched in February and March and if the increase in participation came about in June and July, was it an effect of the marketing efforts, or was it an effect of the better weather?

Finally, an underlying theme in any program evaluation is to verify whether the program should exist at all given its cost relative to its impact on the public. In many cases the costs associated with a program may exceed the value of its outcomes and benefits. The issue of estimating benefits is a difficult one and will be discussed later in the chapter. In addition to the **cost–benefit analysis**, there is the question of whether alternate programs could achieve the same results with less cost. For example, a national government may decide on improving the performance level of its athletes. It may institute several programs to achieve this end such as

- financial aid to cover the training and competition expenses of top athletes
- scholarships so that the athletes can enroll in institutions with strong athletic traditions
- grants to educational institutions, enabling them to nurture and foster athletic talent
- government-financed sport schools/colleges to recruit top talents and train them in both academics and athletics

Evaluation of these programs would show which ones are more effective in achieving the goal (producing international-caliber athletes) and which ones are **cost-effective** (i.e., low cost in relation to what they achieve).

sidebar 14.1

PROGRAM EVALUATION FOR EXERCISE LEADERS

In outlining the importance of program evaluation for exercise leaders, Myers (1999) noted that it is critical "whether you work or intend to work in the fitness or health club sector, the corporate sector, the clinical sector, the community sector, the public health sector, or as an independent entrepreneur. In today's competitive fitness market, commercial facilities and personal trainers must position themselves or find their niche in their marketplace. Nonprofit exercise programs similarly want to attract and keep clients, deliver high-quality services that meet client expectations, maximize client benefits, and minimize adverse effects such as injuries. Evaluation shows how well you are doing in each area and provides direction for improving your services" (p. xiii).

The essential points here are that (a) program and program evaluation are meaningful in every type of organization, including individually owned enterprises; (b) a program may involve recruiting and retaining clients and/or providing quality services and other benefits to clients; and (c) every one of these programs can be evaluated.

Purposes of Program Evaluation

The many reasons given by scholars for why organizations and their management engage in periodic program evaluations (e.g., Affholter, 1994; Farley, 1984; Kestner, 1996; Royse & Thyer, 1996; Scheirer, 1994; Wholey, 1981) can be summarized as

- accountability/credibility
- improved performance
- cost-effectiveness
- safety of participants
- breadth of programs
- accessibility of programs

Because many sport organizations are third-sector organizations (see Chapter 2) funded by government agencies or by donations and membership fees, they are accountable to those who provide the resources. Therefore, it is imperative that they justify their operations by demonstrating that their programs are effective and are achieving the ends sought. Program evaluations will provide data and results to support the claims and lend credibility to an organization and its programs.

Program evaluations also show which aspects of a program are weak and how even a successful program can be improved. A concomitant benefit is the identification of measures that could make a program more cost-effective. That is, the evaluation will show how the available resources can best be used to improve the performance of the program.

IN brief

Program evaluation will show if (a) the goals of the program are achieved, (b) the activities are carried out as planned, and (c) the program can be justified.

The next three benefits are quite relevant to sport and recreation programs. Kestner (1996) points out that evaluation of a sport program can identify the factors that may jeopardize the safety of the program participants. An equally important consideration is to verify if the programs are sufficiently broad to include many segments of the community, and if those programs are easily accessible to all members. The NCAA Women's Enhancement Program and the Ethnic Minority Enhancement Program, described earlier, were initiated to increase opportunities for women and minorities in intercollegiate athletics.

In sum, proper evaluation of a program can (a) provide information to the administrators for more informed decision making; (b) clarify the program and its logic for its users, service providers, and administrators; and (c) offer advance information for any proposed new program (Owen, 1993). Through such an evaluation, the manager will also gain confidence not only in organizational performance but also in his own abilities, including the ability to conduct successful evaluations.

Program Profile

A useful way to begin the evaluation of a program is to draw up a **program profile** (Owen, 1993). This is a description of the program that includes background information, the structure and processes of the program, and expected outcomes and impacts. The background information should outline the genesis of and reasons for creating the program, its scope and objectives, the population it serves or the market it targets, and the amount of resources assigned to the program.

The profile should also describe

- the activities chosen for the delivery of the program and the interrelationships among them
- the personnel involved in the program
- the distribution of responsibilities and authority among the personnel (who does what, who is responsible for what, and who reports to whom)

IN brief

A program profile outlines the genesis of the program and its goals, the resources assigned to it, the activities to be carried out, and the expected outcomes. It also highlights the relationships among the goals, resources, processes, and outcomes.

The final section of a program profile should describe the expected outcomes and the impact of those outcomes.

The advantages of drawing up a program profile are twofold. First, the evaluator gains some insight into the logic of the program. **Program logic** refers to the interrelatedness among the objectives, activities, personnel, structure, and expected outcomes of the program. The connections among these factors must be based on correct reasoning. Any inconsistencies in the logic of the program would suggest redesigning the program to eliminate the flaws in the logic.

The second benefit of a program profile is that it distinguishes the structural and process attributes of the program from the expected outcomes. That is, the focus of evaluation could be on (a) whether the program was implemented as it was designed or (b) whether the program achieved what it was supposed to achieve. A program profile makes it easier to focus on evaluating the processes, the outcomes, or both. In essence, a program profile shows if (a) the goals and objectives of the program are meaningful and attainable, (b) the links between ends and means are strong, and (c) the cause–effect relationships within the program are sound (Wholey, 1981).

Standards of Evaluation

Earlier, in discussing the purposes of program evaluation, we identified its benefits. Although that discussion established the reasons for evaluating programs, it is also critical to decide on the standards by which a program will be judged to be effective (**standards of evaluation**). For instance, if a person clears 6 feet in the high jump, how do we judge that performance? What standards should we apply? The standards could be others' performances, the individual's own resources (height), the training time and expenses, or the goals that were set earlier (for example, the goal of clearing 5'9" versus 6'3"). Thus, the final determination about the high jumper's performance depends on the standards we choose to apply. The same issue often comes up in program evaluation. Theobald (1987) provided a historical account of the various standards that have been used in evaluating recreation programs and services. These are described in the following sections.

Meeting objectives

A program by definition is intended to achieve certain objectives; therefore, its effectiveness can best be judged by the extent to which it **meets the objectives.** This is obviously a straightforward and logical approach. For instance, a sponsorship program can be evaluated on the basis of whether the program has met the commercial objectives of increased awareness of and positive attitudes toward the sponsor or its products; increased sales of the products; and media exposure due to sponsorship relative to the cost of equivalent advertising space or time.

However, the attainment of objectives cannot be adequately measured in all cases. Take, for example, a program of instruction to cultivate sportsmanship, citizenship, or awareness about drug abuse. It will be extremely hard to judge whether the athletes have in fact changed their attitudes and behavior because of the program. In such cases, the standard of achieving the objectives may not be so meaningful.

sidebar 14.2

MEASURING SPONSORSHIP IMPACT

To measure the impact of sponsorship, Horn and Baker (1999) suggest asking the following questions:

1. What was the business objective? Was it increased sales, volumes, shares, or prices?
2. What was the target audience? Was it customers, key accounts, vendors, financial institutions, investors, community and civic organizations, or employees?
3. What was the desired action on the part of the audience? Was it trial of a new brand, in-home consumption of a brand, or change in beliefs about or perceptions of a brand?
4. What did happen? How far did the desired actions go?
5. What were the reasons for the results, either good or bad?
6. What have we learned from the experience, and what will we do better next time?

Standards set by experts

In many instances, experts from among scholars and practitioners may decide that if a program is to be effective in achieving its stated purposes, it must include certain processes and be structured in specific ways. For example, the Commission on Sport Management Accreditation (COSMA) provides accreditation and related services for sport management programs in colleges and universities. Its major purpose is to ensure excellence in sport management education programs through its accreditation processes. COSMA has established principles on which it evaluates a given degree program. The eight main principles include subprinciples: 1, 2, 3.1–3.7, 4.1–4.6, 5, 6.1–6.5, 7.1–7.8, 8 (see Exhibit 14.3 for examples). Note that COSMA uses the term *principles* instead of *standards.*

Any college or university with degree programs in sport management may apply to COSMA for accreditation. After careful scrutiny of the course offerings, their content, the number of professors involved, and purposeful visitations and interviews, COSMA may accredit the degree program. It must also be noted that the colleges or universities themselves also have their own structures and procedures for sanctioning a degree program or a course.

Professional judgment

Another standard of evaluation is **professional judgment.** That is, one or more professionals may be asked to determine whether a program is effective. In making their judgments, they will focus more on the outcomes than on the structure and processes of the program. This is in contrast to the "standard of norms" cited above, in which the focus is on the processes and not on the outcomes.

One of the objectives of the Kamloops Women's Action Project in the Canadian province of British Columbia is to enhance recreation opportunities for those living in poverty (Frisby, 1998). Accordingly, the organization offers three different programs at no cost: Self-Defense, Fun and Games for Moms & Preschoolers, and Fun & Friendly Fitness. The project has laid out several ways of evaluating the success of these programs. One of these ways is for leaders and experts to visit the centers where these programs are offered. These individuals observe the interactions (including facial expressions and body gestures) among the participants, instructors, and volunteers; listen to their casual comments; and note any conflicts or issues that may arise. Opinions about the program based on these observations would be labeled professional judgments.

exhibit 14.3 Examples of COSMA principles for accreditation of sport management programs.

7.4	Business and Industry Linkages	Excellence in sport management education requires that the academic unit/sport management program have current and meaningful linkages to sport management practitioners and organizations.
7.6	International Cooperation	Excellence in sport management education supports that sport management students be prepared to function effectively in a changing global environment. Therefore, the academic unit/sport management program, through its curricula and co-curricular programs, should ensure that students possess the knowledge, skills, and experiences to understand and deal effectively with critical issues in a dynamic global environment.
7.7	Diversity in Sport	Excellence in sport management education includes diversity. Sport management students should be prepared to function effectively in an increasingly diverse sport industry. Therefore, the academic unit/sport management program, through its curricula and co-curricular activities, should ensure that students possess the knowledge, skills, and experiences to understand and deal effectively with diversity in a diverse sport environment.
8	Educational Innovation	Excellence in sport management education requires adapting to changes in sport management and society. Therefore, the academic unit/sport management programs should provide an environment that encourages and recognizes innovation and creativity in the education of sport management students.

Socioeconomic evaluation

Some programs are instituted to serve the public at large equitably. Any judgment of the program's effectiveness should consider whether the extensions of the facilities and services were related to the needs of all the different communities. For example, the population density and the social and economic status of the communities within the city reflect the needs of those communities. Thus, if the recreation department has distributed its facilities and services in relation to these needs, the program may be judged to be effective. This is called **socioeconomic evaluation.**

Accessibility and safety

When a program is established for the benefit of the public or a segment of it, it is important that the program be accessible to all those who are entitled to its services. An obvious example is that it is now law that the facilities of a university be accessible to persons with disabilities. In the university where I teach, professors are required to state at the beginning of their course outlines that alternate formats of the course outline are available on request for those whose vision is impaired. In addition, the safety standards for the equipment and facilities in a fitness club or a weight training room in an athletic department, for example, are important in evaluating the respective programs.

Cost–benefit

A standard often applied to programs is the cost–benefit analysis. The essence of this standard is that the benefits accruing from a program should exceed the costs of the program. A program of licensing concessions as a means of generating revenue for an intercollegiate athletic program certainly will cost some money in terms

> "A cost-effectiveness analysis does not produce a 'bottom line' number, with benefits exceeding costs or costs exceeding benefits. If a program costs $1 million and produces 10 units of outcome X, 12 units of outcome Y, and 20 units of outcome Z, how is the evaluator to make a judgment concerning the cost-effectiveness of the program? The question for the decision maker is whether the outcomes produced are worth the $1 million expenditure."
>
> **KEE, 1994,** *p. 459*

of building the concessions and maintaining them, administration and staffing, and legal fees in monitoring and enforcing the licensing agreements. If the revenues do not exceed the costs, then the program is judged to be ineffective. This is a straightforward business proposition. However, a monetary value cannot be assigned to the outcomes of many programs. Take the case of the drug education program of the NCAA. Assuming that the program costs $500,000, what value do we place on the redemption of a person from drug abuse? What value do we place on a life saved? When strict monetary values cannot be assigned to a benefit or outcome, a cost–benefit analysis would be inappropriate.

Cost-effectiveness

While it is true that there is no dollar value on recovery from drug abuse (or a life saved), it cannot be denied that if the incidence of drug abuse falls to 50 players from 100, we can confidently say that the program was successful even though its costs were high, say $500,000. Here our concern lies with the number of athletes who have given up drugs, and not with the dollar value of "not using drugs." That is, the program was effective in the sense it helped 50 athletes give up drug use. If another program can be shown to save the same number of athletes from drug use at a cost of only $250,000, then the second program would be more cost-effective.

Client satisfaction

A final, and perhaps the most important, standard that can be applied to a program is **client satisfaction.** If a program is carried out for the benefit of a specific group, then it stands to reason that those clients should be the ultimate arbiters of the program. This is the central argument offered by proponents of total quality management and service quality management (see Goetsch, 1994; Schneider & Bowen, 1995; Zeithaml, Parasuraman, & Berry, 1990).

In the context of sport, Chelladurai and Riemer (1997) and Riemer and Chelladurai (1998) have argued that the success of intercollegiate athletics should be based on the satisfaction of athletes in various facets of their experience in athletics, mainly because the athletes are the prime beneficiaries or clients of intercollegiate athletics. The evaluators of a program could develop a survey to gauge clients' reactions to specific attributes of a program. This was the approach taken by Riemer and Chelladurai in developing the Athlete Satisfaction Questionnaire (ASQ). The ASQ has 56 items to measure 15 facets of athlete satisfaction. Examples of the items and their facets include how the team works to be the best (team's task contribution), competencies of the medical personnel (medical personnel), the extent to which all team members

sidebar 14.3

ECONOMIC EQUIVALENCY INDEX

Can we calculate the monetary benefits of a parks and playground program of a city recreation department? Theobald (1987) refers to the economic equivalency index (EEI), which is calculated as follows:

EEI = number of participants
x hours of participation
x minimum wage

From a different perspective, we could argue that the value derived through the above formula could be treated as a cost incurred by the participants rather than a benefit to them.

are ethical (team ethics), the funding provided to a team (budget), the training received from the coach (training and instruction), and the academic support services provided (academic support services).

Such information can also be gathered through well-designed interviews with selected clients. We might assemble a group of clients together and let them discuss the various attributes of a program. This latter technique, known as the focus group, would identify the benefits from the clients' viewpoint. It would also reveal which of the processes or activities of the program are considered efficient and useful, and which are not. For instance, the city recreation department, in evaluating its sports program for wheelchair athletes, may assemble some of the participants in a focus group. In such a session, participants will describe what they enjoyed about the program and what they disliked about it. They may also be encouraged to suggest new elements that might be added to the program and what elements might be eliminated. Such free discussions among clients would yield valuable insights into the program and its effectiveness. Of course, such discussions need to be moderated by someone well versed in focus group techniques.

Thus, evaluators have a choice of means of assessing clients' reactions to a program and its attributes.

SUMMARY

This chapter emphasized the significance of evaluating an organization's programs of activities. After defining a program as a set of resources and activities designed to achieve a narrow set of goals, we contrasted performance appraisal (evaluation of individual performance) with organizational effectiveness (evaluation of organizational performance). We noted that the concepts of program and program evaluation are applicable to all organizations—public and private, profit and nonprofit, large and small. A program was also described as a system in itself, consisting of inputs, throughputs, and outputs. After this, the chapter outlined the purposes of program evaluation and described the standards that can be employed to evaluate programs. These included meeting objectives, standards set by experts, professional judgment, socioeconomic evaluation, accessibility and safety, cost–benefit evaluation, and cost-effectiveness.

develop YOUR PERSPECTIVE

1. Identify a sport-related program you are familiar with, and describe its profile in terms of its objectives, activities, finances, and outcomes.
2. Referring to the program you have described, discuss the logic of the program (cause–effect and means/ends relationships).
3. Can you place a monetary value on the benefits of the program? Explain.
4. Bearing in mind the distinction between cost–benefit evaluation and cost-effectiveness evaluation, identify sport-related programs that could be subjected to either of these evaluations.
5. Consider the economic equivalency index suggested by Theobald (1987). Discuss its merits from the perspective of program evaluation.

6. Visit http://cosmaweb.org/accredmanuals and download the COSMA Sport Management Accreditation Manual. What are your reactions to the guidelines for sport management degree programs as presented in the manual? Do you agree with the standards? Why? What other standards would you suggest? Why? Do we need a certification program?

references

Affholter, D. P. (1994). Outcome monitoring. In J. S. Wholey, H. P. Hatry, & K. E. Newcomer (Eds.), *Handbook of practical program evaluation* (pp. 96–118). San Francisco: Jossey-Bass.

Chelladurai, P. (2006). *Human resource management in sport and recreation* (2nd ed.). Champaign, IL: Human Kinetics.

Chelladurai, P., & Riemer, H. A. (1997). A classification of facets of athlete satisfaction. *Journal of Sport Management, 11*, 133–159.

Farley, M. (1984). Program evaluation as political tool. *Journal of Physical Education, Recreation, and Dance, 55*(4), 64–67.

Frisby, W. (1998). *Leisure access: Enhancing recreation opportunities for those living in poverty*. Vancouver, BC: British Columbia Health Research Foundation.

Goetsch, D. L. (1994). *Introduction to total quality: Quality, productivity, competitiveness*. New York: Macmillan.

Horn, M., & Baker, K. (1999). Measuring the impact of sponsorship. *International Journal of Sport Marketing and Sponsorship, 3*(1), 296–301.

Kee, J. E. (1994). Benefit–cost analysis in program evaluation. In J. S. Wholey, H. P. Hatry, & K. E. Newcomer (Eds.), *Handbook of practical program evaluation* (pp. 456–491). San Francisco. Jossey-Bass.

Kestner, J. L. (1996). *Program evaluation for sport directors*. Champaign, IL: Human Kinetics.

Marinaccio, M. D., & Trojanowski, M. R. (2012). Projects programs defined. *Internal Auditor, 69*(2), 46–50.

Mullin, B. J., Hardy, S., & Sutton, W. A. (2007). *Sport marketing* (3rd ed.). Champaign, IL: Human Kinetics.

Myers, A. M. (1999). *Program evaluation for exercise leaders*. Champaign, IL: Human Kinetics.

NCAA (2007a). NCAA Leadership Advisory Board. Retrieved from http://www.ncaa.org/leadership_advisory_board/index.html.

NCAA (2007b). Retrieved from http://www2.ncaa.org/portal/academics_and_athletes/leadership/.

NCAA (2007c). Ethnic minority and women's enhancement postgraduate scholarship for careers in athletics. Retrieved from http://www1.ncaa.org/membership/ed_outreach/prof_development/minority-womens_scholarships.html.

Newcomer, K. E., Hatry, H. P., & Wholey, J. S. (1994). Meeting the need for practical evaluation approaches: An introduction. In J. S. Wholey, H. P. Hatry, & K. E. Newcomer (Eds.), *Handbook of practical program evaluation* (pp. 1–10). San Francisco: Jossey-Bass.

Owen, J. M. (1993). *Program evaluation: Forms and approaches*. St. Leonards, NSW, Australia: Allen & Unwin.

President's Council on Physical Fitness and Sports (2008a). Retrieved from http:// www.fitness.gov/about/index.html.

President's Council on Physical Fitness and Sports (2008b). Retrieved from http://www.fitness.gov/home_pres_chall.htm.

Riemer, H. A., & Chelladurai, P. (1998). Development of athlete satisfaction questionnaire (ASQ). *Journal of Sport and Exercise Psychology, 20*, 127–156.

Royse, D., & Thyer, B. A. (1996). *Program evaluation: An introduction*. Chicago: Nelson-Hall.

Scheirer, M. A. (1994). Designing and using process evaluation. In J. S. Wholey, H. P. Hatry, & K. E. Newcomer (Eds.), *Handbook of practical program evaluation* (pp. 40–68). San Francisco: Jossey-Bass.

Schneider, B., & Bowen, D. E. (1995). *Winning the service game*. Boston: Harvard Business School Press.

Theobald, W. (1987). Historical antecedents of evaluation in leisure programs and services. *Journal of Park and Recreation Administration, V*, 1–8.

Treasury Board of Canada–Comptroller General (1981, May). *Guide on the program evaluation function*. Ottawa, ON: Minister of Supply and Services Canada.

Wholey, J. S. (1981). Using evaluations to improve program performance. *The Bureaucrat, 20*(2), 55–59.

Zeithaml, V. A., Parasuraman, A., & Berry, L. L. (1990). *Delivering service quality: Balancing customer perceptions and expectations*. New York: Free Press.

SERVICE QUALITY

15

CHAPTER

manage YOUR LEARNING

After completing this chapter you should be able to:

- Define and describe the notion of quality in sport services.
- Understand the dimensions of a service.
- Describe the various dimensions of quality.
- Explain the standards that could be applied in evaluating a service.
- Understand the relevance of the varying standards to different types of services.
- Explain the gaps in translating customer expectations into the desired service.

strategic CONCEPTS

consumer services
customer expectation
dimensions of services
human services
professional services
service quality
service quality dimensions
standards of quality

INTRODUCTION

In Chapter 1, sport management is defined as "a field concerned with the coordination of limited human and material resources, relevant technologies, and situational contingencies for the efficient production and exchange of sport services" (Chelladurai, 1994, p. 15). Because sport management is a service industry, Chapter 1 focused on the concept of services and their attributes. In doing so, I also compared various forms of services such as consumer, professional, and human services. More specifically, the discussion focused on participant sport services, spectator sport services, sponsorship services, and so on.

Chapter 1 defined a service as a "time-perishable, intangible experience performed for a customer acting in the role of co-producer" (Fitzsimmons & Fitzsimmons, 2011, p. 4). We also noted that an organization would be considered effective if its outputs are acceptable to the environment, including the clients, and if the throughput processes of the organization (i.e., the processes of production) are also deemed appropriate (see Chapter 14). The underlying theme in all these arguments is that the client/customer who receives the services should accept the "quality" of the service itself and the "quality" of the experiences they undergo in receiving that service. Hence, organizations must focus on **service quality.** Sport management scholars have dealt with the issue of quality in various types of sport services. Before we discuss such efforts, let us look at some of the definitions of service quality.

DEFINITION OF SERVICE QUALITY

Quality has been variously defined as

- conformance to clearly specified requirements (Crosby, 1985; Deming, 1986);
- fitness for use, meaning that the product meets customer needs, and is free of deficiencies (Juran, 1989);
- the features of a product or service that satisfy stated or implied needs (British Standards Institute, 1991); and
- a source of satisfaction or delight for the customer, satisfying or exceeding customer expectations (e.g., Goetsch, 1994; Zeithaml, Parasuraman, & Berry, 1990).

Focus on the Product

The first two definitions seem to focus on products and the processes of producing them. In the perspective of quality as conformance to specifications (Crosby, 1985, 1989; Deming, 1986; Feigenbaum, 1991; Juran, 1989), consumer needs and desires are translated into clear specifications for the product. Such specifications stem from the efforts of marketing experts who identify the needs of the customers and the design specialists who devise the product's features to satisfy client needs and specify the production processes. Thus, following the design and production specifications results in quality tangible goods, such as automobiles, television sets, home appliances, exercise cycles, tennis rackets, basketball shoes, and hockey sticks. It would appear that such specifications are not appropriate to services because the nature and quality of the service is largely determined by individual differences that characterize each employee and client. However, specifications are employed in service operations. For example, front desk personnel in fitness clubs may be required to wear specific attire on the job, greet the customers in specific ways, and schedule their activities according to specific guidelines. While it is true that such specifications are easier to make and follow in providing consumer goods, we also see such specifications in human services. For example, the physical education curricula drawn up for various grade levels by the U.S. Department of Education is in fact a set of specifications. When we teach the skills of a particular sport (e.g., a layup in basketball), we specify the "one best way" it should be executed.

Focus on the Client

The next two definitions of quality in the above list, which apply to both products and services, emphasize the customers' needs and expectations. A product has value for a client only if it satisfies his or her needs. For a tennis novice, the quality of a tennis racket lies in its ability to absorb the velocity of a shot and reduce its impact on the player's elbow. Similarly, quality tennis instruction would be judged by a player's improved strokes. In both of these cases, satisfying the novice's expectations is the focus in judging quality.

The last definition underscores **customer expectations** as the basis for judgments of quality. When people join a fitness club, they have some expectation of the services they will receive. They may expect that the parking facilities will be adequate and easily accessible, the locker rooms and showers will be clean, and the equipment will be well-maintained and safe. If the new customers' expectations in these matters are not met, they will be disappointed and judge the service to be of poor quality. Similarly, when fans attend an NCAA Division I football or basketball game, or a soccer game in the English Premier League, they are of course focused on the quality of the product (i.e., the game itself and the skills exhibited by players of both teams). In addition, they will judge the quality of the traffic and parking, the quality of the seating arrangements, access to the concessions, the food in the concessions, and so on.

SERVICE QUALITY DIMENSIONS

As noted above, customers and clients may evaluate a service based on several factors. What are these factors and how do they enhance or detract from the service experience?

SERVQUAL Model

Parasuraman, Zeithaml, and Berry (1985, 1988) offered a model of **service quality dimensions** that comprises the following five factors, which they dubbed SERVQUAL:

- *Reliability:* Whether the promised service is performed dependably and accurately.
- *Assurance:* Whether the employees cultivate trust and confidence through their knowledge and courtesy.
- *Tangibles:* Whether the physical facilities and equipment are clean and adequate.
- *Empathy:* Whether caring and individualized attention is paid to customers.
- *Responsiveness:* Whether the employees are willing to help customers and provide prompt service.

People experience the dimension of tangibles in various ways. For instance, at the auto repair shop, the waiting room may be outfitted with conveniences such as television, magazines, newspapers, and even coffee to help pass the time. Such facilities and amenities are labeled the *servicescape* (Bitner, 1992). Wakefield, Blodgett, and Sloan (1996) extended this emphasis on physical surroundings to sport stadiums and arenas and labeled them the *sportscape* (discussed below). Servicescape includes the facilities (e.g., clubhouses in golf courses), the surrounding scenery, the quality of playing surfaces (e.g., tennis courts), and the equipment (e.g., treadmills in a fitness club).

Parsuraman and associates' scheme is applicable to all forms of services and every component of a service. For example, spectators may evaluate the parking services, ticketing operations, or seating arrangements using the SERVQUAL dimensions. Of course, some of the dimensions are more relevant to some of the services than to others.

Specialized services have unique attributes that may involve sequential steps or stages of service delivery. As shown in Exhibit 15.1, those attending a professional basketball game will be concerned with access to the arena and parking, the signage guiding them to parking and the stadium entrances, the seating, the actual game, the food and beverage services, and the ease of exit from the arena. Similarly, a customer in a fitness club may first encounter the front desk personnel, followed by individuals at different stations taking the person's weight, testing his or her fitness, and prescribing a fitness program to be supervised by a personal trainer. Customers in health-care services may encounter the receptionist first, followed by a qualified individual taking down the history of an ailment or injury, after which the physician diagnoses the problem, prescribes medication and other remedial measures, and recommends a follow-up visit. These components are known as service dimensions (as opposed to service quality dimensions).

exhibit 15.1 Sequential steps (service dimensions) in delivery of various services.

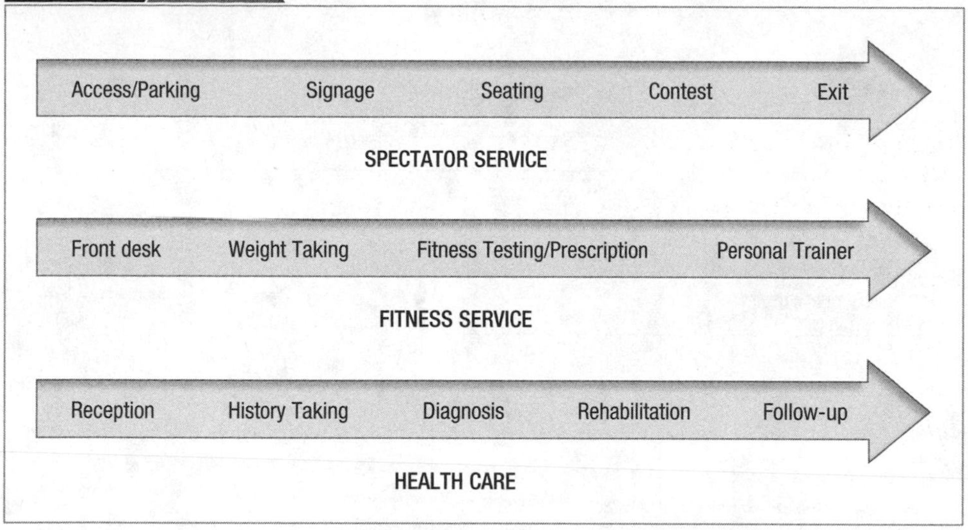

Quality Dimensions in Sport Management Services

Based on this idea of differentiation among services, sport management scholars have articulated sets of dimensions of various types of services within the industry. Some of the schemes pertaining to various sport services are outlined below.

Quality in fitness services

In perhaps the first such effort in sport management, Chelladurai, Scott, and Haywood-Farmer (1987) described a model of the dimensions of fitness services shown in Exhibit 15.2. They distinguished between primary and secondary services offered by fitness clubs. Their distinction was based on the fact that the clubs may include some services that may not relate to fitness per se. For instance, when a fitness club sells T-shirts, sport drinks, and nutrition bars, such services are not related to fitness itself. Therefore, these services are secondary to the primary concern of fitness. In their words, "The primary segment includes all aspects of the service that relate to fitness, such as instructors, equipment, reservation system, and courts. The secondary segment includes all those goods and services within the fitness club that do not relate to fitness per se. Food and beverage services are examples of the secondary segment" (p. 161).

The authors also distinguish between core services and peripheral services. Core services define the essential nature of a business, just as the preparation and serving of food defines the essential features of a restaurant. In the case of fitness clubs, fitness testing, prescribing an exercise program, maintaining the equipment and facilities, providing personal training, and leading fitness classes are core elements that define the nature of the business. On the other hand, peripheral services facilitate and support the provision of primary services. Laundry, parking, day care, and such other services are peripheral to the core business but they are essential in the sense they facilitate the production and consumption of the core services. Chelladurai and associates also employed the distinction between professional and consumer services as discussed in Chapter 1. **Professional services** include exercise testing and prescription, personal training, and exercise leadership, whereas **consumer services** include reception, reservation, and towel services. All of these

exhibit 15.2 Dimensions of fitness services (from Chelladurai, Scott, Haywood-Farmer, 1987).

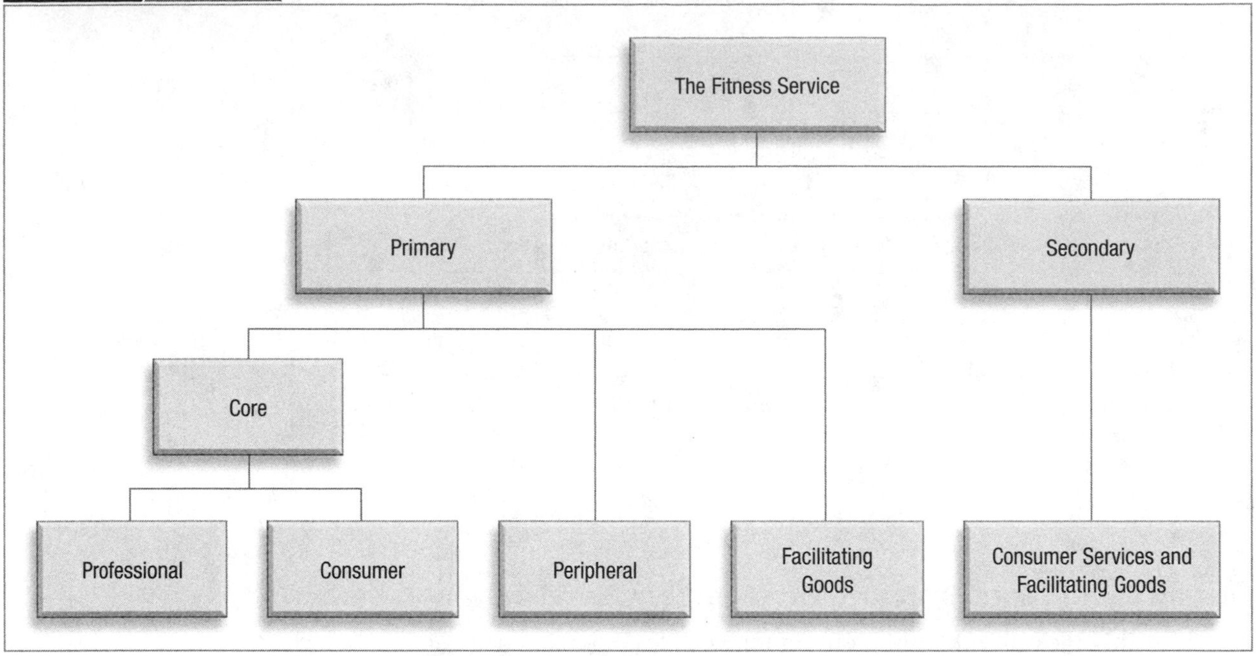

services are offered within the confines of a building and with the use of suitable equipment. Chelladurai and associates labeled these the facilitating goods.

In a later study, Chang and Chelladurai (2003) employed the input–throughput–output view of a system to define the quality dimensions as shown in Exhibit 15.3. Their input stage included management actions in terms of (a) cultivating a climate for service, (b) management commitment to service quality, and (c) designing the programs of services to be offered. The throughput stage was composed of employee–client interactions of a personal nature as well as the interactions related to the task at hand. In addition, other clients and their behavior are considered important factors in determining the quality of experiences. Clients who do not respect fellow clients or employees, are noisy and unruly, and do not follow the rules of conduct or common courtesy detract from the quality of experiences of other customers. Another significant dimension in the throughput stage is the extent to which there are service failures and how quickly they are addressed and fixed. The only dimension at the output stage is client perception of service quality. This is obviously the most important dimension because it influences clients' intentions to continue the membership or cancel it. Chang and Chelladurai's use of the input–throughput–output scheme to describe fitness services parallels Golder, Mitra, and Moorman's (2012) conceptualization that distinguishes among *quality production process, quality experience process,* and *quality evaluation process.*

Quality in sport tourism

Shonk and Chelladurai (2008) studied quality in sport tourism and identified the following dimensions:

- *Access quality* relates to the ease and speed of reaching (a) the destination (e.g., city) where the event is held, (b) the sport venue, and (c) lodging/place of accommodation.

exhibit 15.3 Systems view of dimensions of fitness services.

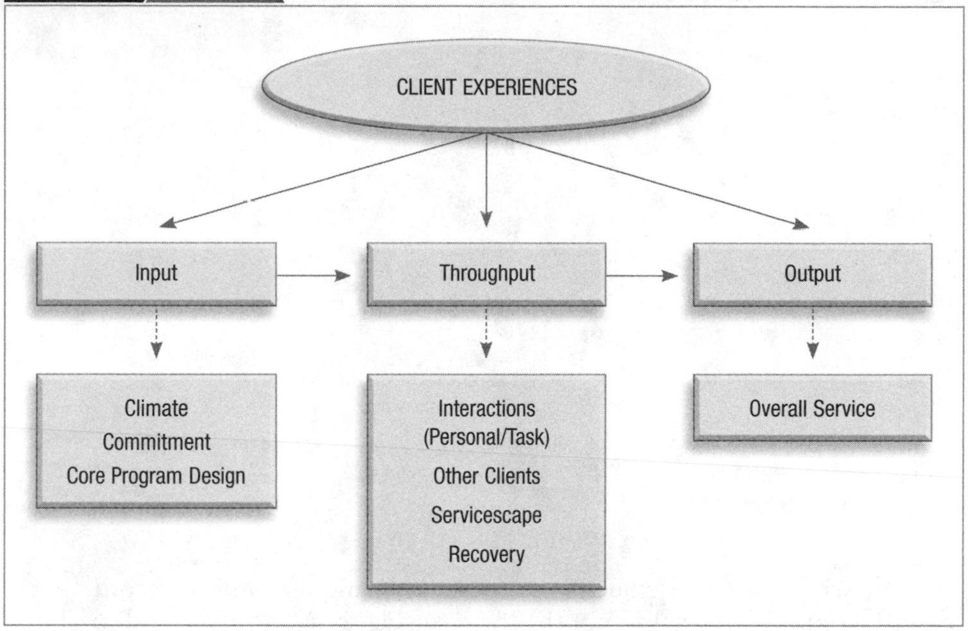

- *Accommodation quality* refers to the place of stay (hotels, motels, etc.) including (a) interactions with hotel personnel and other guests, (b) the environment (noise level, odors, temperature, etc.), and (c) the value as a function of costs and benefits.
- *Venue quality* relates to the facility where the event is held including (a) the interactions with stadium employees and other spectators; (b) its cleanliness, seating, sound system, parking, restrooms, food and beverage areas, signage, and facility layout design; and (c) its value as a function of cost–benefit analysis.
- *Contest quality* includes process quality, which refers to officiating, announcements, display of scores, replays, and crowd control, and product quality, which refers to the quality of play exhibited by both teams.

Quality in spectator sport

Spectator sports also have been subjected to some quality analysis. For instance, Wakefield and his associates (Wakefield et al., 1996; Wakefield & Sloan, 1995) have isolated the context (e.g., the stadium in which a contest takes place) and labeled it *sportscape* after Bitner's (1992) notion of *servicescape*. The dimensions of the sportscape shown in Exhibit 15.4 are (1) *stadium access and parking layout and accessibility,* (2) *facility aesthetics and cleanliness,* (3) *scoreboard quality,* (4) *seating comfort,* (5) *layout accessibility,* (6) *space allocation,* (7) *crowding,* (8) *signage,* (9) *food service,* and (10) *fan control*. In their view, these contextual elements of a service constitute added value. McDonald, Sutton, and Milne (1995) developed the TEAMQUAL scale, consisting of 39 items that measure five **dimensions of service** quality in professional team sports, which is patterned after the dimensions identified in SERVQUAL (Parasuraman et al., 1988).

In a more recent study of the effects of service quality on spectator intention to attend a professional sport game, Byon, Zhang, and Baker (2013) distinguished between core service and peripheral service factors.

exhibit 15.4 Dimensions of the sportsscape.

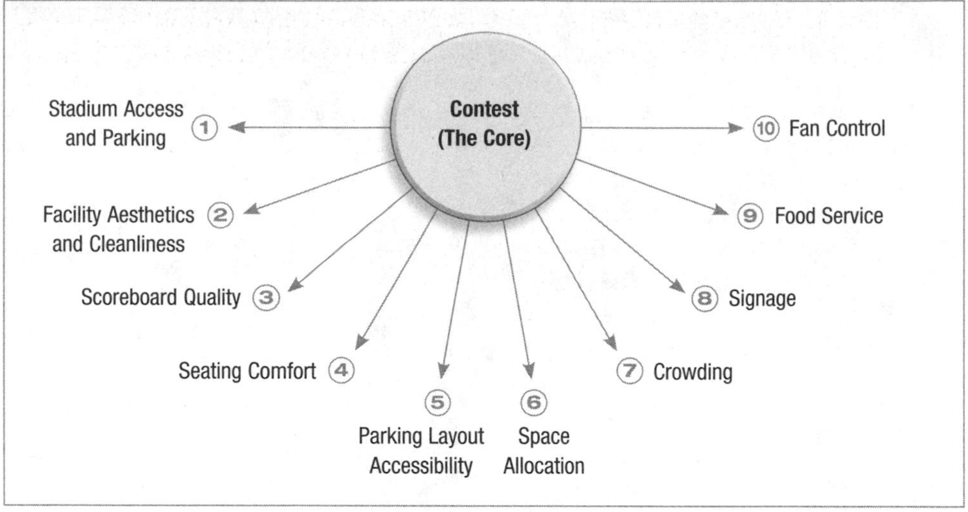

- *Core service factors* include (a) the *home team* and its win/loss record, reputation, and league standing; (b) the *opposing team* and its overall performance, reputation, quality of players/team, and exciting play; (c) *economic considerations* such as ticket price, affordability, and discounts; (d) *game promotion,* including advertising, direct mail, and sales promotions; and (e) *schedule convenience,* including game time of the day and day of the week.
- *Peripheral service factors* include (a) *game amenities* such as pregame, halftime, and postgame entertainment, cheerleading activities, and concourse activities; (b) *ticket services,* including phone and Internet ordering, will-call service, and ticket exchange program; and (c) venue quality, including staff courtesy, restroom availability, arena/stadium cleanliness, ease of entrance, security, and parking.

Their results showed that home team, opposing team, game promotion, game amenities, venue quality, and perceived value were all predictive of behavioral intentions.

Quality in campus recreation

In assessing customer perceptions of service quality in campus recreation programs, Ko and Pastore (2007) identified four dimensions. They are (a) *program quality,* referring to the range and timing of programs and access to information; (b) *interaction quality,* referring to employee-client and inter-client interactions; (c) *outcome quality,* referring to changes in one's physical self, positive social experiences, and evaluation of the service as good or bad; and (d) *physical environment quality,* referring to the ambience and design of the building and the quality of the equipment.

See Sidebar 15.1 for service quality dimensions in the leisure services area.

ROLE OF CLIENTS IN SERVICE QUALITY

As discussed in Chapter 1 and in this chapter, the client is integral to the production of a service. In the input–throughput–output view of a system, clients are the major input; they are involved in the throughput process of producing the service; and finally, they are the output in the form of some altered

sidebar 15.1

SPORT ENGLAND'S NATIONAL BENCHMARKING SERVICE FOR SPORT AND LEISURE SERVICES

"Sport England is focused on helping people and communities across the country to create a sporting habit for life. . . . We also have a role protecting sports provision and must be formally consulted on any English planning applications that affect playing fields" (Sport England, 2013, p. 1). With this mission in mind, Sport England has set up the National Benchmarking Service (NBS) for sports halls and swimming pools to evaluate the performance of sports and leisure centers and provide feedback to the local authorities who own and run them. According to NBS (2013), the major performance indicators they evaluate are access, utilization, financial, and service quality. Service quality is evaluated based on

- *accessibility* in terms of convenient timing of activities, ease of booking for those activities, and the fees for those activities;
- the *availability* of car parking, crèche facilities (e.g., day care or nursery), food and drink, range of activities, and equipment;
- the *quality of facility,* referring to flooring, lighting, water quality in pool, number of people in pool, and quality of food and drink;
- the *cleanliness* of the reception area, locker rooms, and café/bar;
- the *staff,* referring to the helpfulness and friendliness of reception and other staff, availability, and standard of coaching; and
- the *value for money* for activities, food and drink, and overall.

and improved condition. Therefore, we can expect that the client has much to do with the quality of the service. Accordingly, the client's role in enhancing the quality of the service is outlined below.

Client–Employee Interactions

As a service is simultaneously produced and consumed, the interactions between the service provider and the client become significant. Such interactions include the helping behavior of the employee, the courtesy and care toward clients, and the prompt delivery of individualized attention (Bitner, Booms, & Mohr, 1994, Price, Arnold, & Terney, 1995). Others labels attached to this dimension are *quality in contact* (Church, Javitch, & Burke, 1995); *interactive quality* (Lehtinen & Lehtinen, 1991); *assurance* and *emotion* (Schvaneveldt, Enkawa, & Miyakawa, 1991); and *responsiveness, assurance,* and *empathy* (Zeithaml et al., 1990).

Inter-Client Interactions

While the interactions between the client and service providers as outlined above are critical to all service operations, many sport settings present other targets for evaluation. Many of our services are offered to a group of clients simultaneously, as in teaching and coaching in schools, Zumba or spin classes in fitness clubs, and youth sport programs offered by city recreation departments. As Chang and Chelladurai (2003) noted, the interactions among a group of clients who are served at the same time become significant. The nature and intensity of task and nontask interactions among the members of the group impact the quality of the service they experience. Such interactions can be positive and supportive or they may disrupt the service provider's efforts or the other clients. Thus, such interclient interactions constitute a target for judging quality. Take the case of spectators at a sporting event. The miscreant behaviors of some spectators may disrupt the event and thus reduce the quality of the experience for other spectators. Thus, when crowd control is viewed as a target for judging quality (Wakefield et al., 1996), the focus is largely on the interactions among the spectators.

Client Participation

Many sport services involve the energetic and vigorous participation of the client. As noted, clients' contributions to service production could be in the roles of (a) a resource, (b) a co-producer, (c) a buyer, (d) a user, and (e) a product. In **human services**, each client is simultaneously a resource and the product of the service enterprise as well as a co-producer of the service (Lengnick-Hall, 1996). Clients' perceptions of the quality of their own involvement are critical for their continued participation in that activity. The literature on youth sport clearly shows that a lack of quality in their participation is the main reason that many drop out of sport. Lehtinen and Lehtinen (1991) labeled this target of quality (i.e., client participation) as *process quality*.

MEASUREMENT OF SERVICE QUALITY

One approach to measuring quality of services, first proposed by Parasuraman and his colleagues, is to assess both the consumer's expectation for a service or an attribute of that service and his or her perception of the experience. The difference between the two estimates (i.e., expectation and perception) is a measure of service quality. A service would be considered low quality if the consumer's expectation was higher than his or her perception of the experience. On the other hand, the quality would be considered high if the consumer's experience was rated higher than his or her expectation. However, this method has fallen into disfavor because of the statistical issues associated with difference scores and because respondents have to respond twice to the same items (once for expectation and once for perception). Furthermore, some research shows that measuring only the perception of the performance of a service is as good in predicting customer satisfaction as using different scores for expectation and perception (e.g., Cronin & Taylor, 1992, 1994). Given these considerations, much of the research on the quality of sport services has adopted the approach of measuring perceptions only.

Service quality measurement plans related to various sport services (e.g., sport tourism, spectator sport, campus recreation) identify several dimensions. While it is important to identify these relevant dimensions and assess their quality, be aware that not all attributes will be important to every consumer. For example, parking at a football game will be of no importance to fans who live near the stadium. Similarly, value is less important to wealthy individuals than it is to those of modest means. Thus, sport managers striving to improve the quality of their services should focus on the dimensions that are most important to a majority of their consumers before attending to dimensions that are important to only a few.

ISSUES IN EVALUATING SERVICE QUALITY

Apart from using the attributes of various sport services in evaluating service quality, Chelladurai and Chang (2000) highlighted two other issues: (a) standards by which a service is evaluated, and (b) who should be the judge of the quality of the service.

Standards of Quality

Based on Reeves and Bednar (1994), Chelladurai and Chang (2000) identified four **standards of quality:** (a) *quality as excellence,* (b) *quality as value,* (c) *quality as conformance to specifications,* and (d) *quality as meeting or exceeding customers' expectations.*

Quality as excellence

Excellence refers to the best attainable standard, which requires large investments and hiring those with the best talent and skills for delivering the service. Services like brain surgery or coaching of a national team require excellence and need to be evaluated on that basis.

Quality as value

In some cases, quality may be judged by the relative price one pays for a certain level of performance. It does not imply the best product or the cheapest price, but the "best bargain," meaning the optimal combination of product and price. Value "is a question of the consumers' own personal assessment of what they get in relation to the price they are able to and willing to pay" (Gummesson, 1992, p. 184).

Quality as conformance to specifications

As noted, the features of a product and the steps in the production process are clearly specified before the production. If these specifications are followed, then the product should meet the quality requirements. Therefore, quality is a function of the extent to which the specifications are met. In other words, quality is conformance to specifications. As an example, a golf club may specify that all golf carts be inspected and washed daily, or a ticketing operation may prescribe certain specifications to be followed by its service employees.

Quality as meeting or exceeding customers' expectations

Zeithaml et al. (1990) noted that "the only criteria that count in evaluating service quality are defined by customers. Only customers judge quality; all other judgements are essentially irrelevant" (p. 16). That is, consumers know the quality of a service as they experience it, and their expectations become the standard for evaluating quality. As long as a service meets or exceeds customers' expectations, the service is deemed to be of quality. This concept was labeled *user-based quality* by Garvin (1988).

Service types and standards of quality

Now comes the issue of which standard is appropriate to which type of service. The classification of sport services based on the distinctions between consumer and human services provides a partial answer. The definition of consumer services implies that (a) the client knows what he or she wants, and (b) the client has specific expectations for that service (Mills & Margulies, 1980). Accordingly, the quality of consumer services can be evaluated based on meeting customer expectations. By the same token, the standard of quality as value is also an appropriate standard in the case of consumer services. When a golfer goes to a golf course, he or she has some expectations about the layout of the holes, the greens, and the crowding at the greens. If those expectations are met, the golfer will be satisfied with the quality. Another standard the golfer may use is the price paid for the privilege of using the course. If the price is lower than that of other courses, the customer might be satisfied with a lower-quality experience.

In the case of professional and/or human services, however, the client may not be aware of all aspects of the service (Mills & Margulies, 1980). For instance, in cardiac rehabilitation through exercise, the core service may not be fully understood by the client; thus, the client may lack the knowledge and expertise to evaluate the service and may require professional judgments by the service providers. Therefore, the appropriate standards of quality in this context are quality as excellence, and quality as conformance to professional standards. The above contingent view of differential application of standards to different types of services is illustrated in Exhibit 15.5.

This line of thinking also help us resolve another issue regarding the bases for judgments of quality. The gap theory suggests that consumers judge quality based on the discrepancy between what they expected to get and what they think they got (e.g., McDonald et al., 1995; Parasuraman et al., 1985; Wright, Duray, & Goodale, 1992). In contrast, the performance theory holds that overall service quality is primarily determined by the service provider's performance (e.g., Cronin & Taylor, 1992, 1994; Patterson & Johnson, 1993). In this context, we can adopt a contingent view, meaning that both perspectives are valid provided they are linked to the type of service—consumer and human services. Because clients know what they want in a consumer service, their expectations are definite and correct. Therefore, the gap model would be relevant in the case of consumer services. In the case of human services, a customer may be unaware of the critical elements of the service, and may not be able to form any clear expectations for it. Thus, the performance of the service provider becomes the proper base for judging quality. That is, the performance theory is more relevant.

exhibit 15.5 Contingent view of standards of evaluation and types of services.

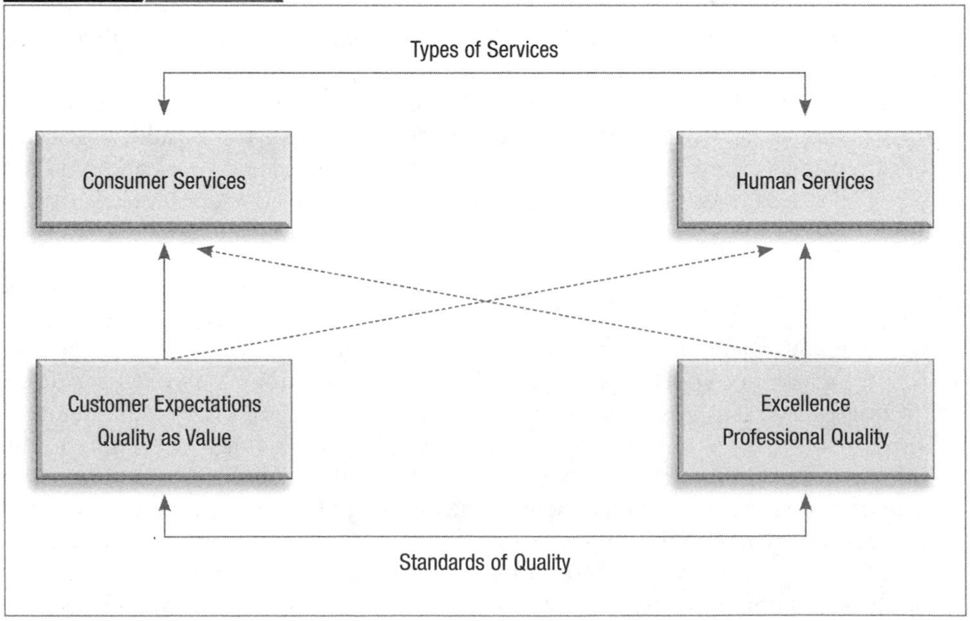

Sequential steps in service delivery

As noted earlier, many services involve a series of sequential steps or elements. And each of these may be characterized by varying degrees of simplicity, routine, and predictability (Vuori, 1982). For instance, a client entering a fitness club may interact with different employees involved in different processes, such as the front desk personnel; a fitness specialist who records the client's body composition, blood pressure, and so on; the personal trainer who assesses the client's fitness level and designs a customized exercise program; and an instructor who leads the client in the club's fitness classes. These client–employee interfaces may be seen as an assembly line involving operations of varying degrees of complexity. The operations at the front desk are routine and standardized, which permit the client to form certain expectations, and satisfying those expectations is a primary criterion of quality. On the other hand, the process associated with the personal trainer is more complex, and the quality of that process is primarily judged by professional and human service standards rather than consumer expectation.

Evaluators of Service Quality

We have discussed up to this point what is to be evaluated from a quality perspective (i.e., targets), and how it is to be evaluated (i.e., standards). A related issue is who among the clients, service providers, and managers should evaluate quality in a service. The standards themselves discussed above suggest who will be the evaluators. For instance, the client is expected to be the judge when quality as meeting customer expectations and/or quality as value are the standards. In the case of quality as excellence and/or quality as conformance to specifications, the professionals and the organizations are likely to be the judges of quality.

GAPS IN SERVICE DELIVERY

All sport organizations and their managers intend to provide high-quality services. They carefully plan their offerings based on their understanding of what the clients or customers want and what will please them. However, despite all the good intentions and thoughtful planning, the organization may not be delivering services to the clients' satisfaction. According to Parasuraman et al. (1985), failure to satisfy customers happens because of five gaps in the process of assessing what the customer desires and what is delivered. These gaps are illustrated in Exhibit 15.6.

Gap 1

The first gap is between what the customer expects and what the management thinks the customer expects. For example, the person who takes ticket orders for a college football game may specify that the tickets will be mailed to the customer when the customer would prefer to pick them up at the will call window.

Gap 2

The second gap is between what the management thinks the customers expect and how management specifies for the service to be delivered to satisfy those expectations. For example, in the above case, the customer may expect the tickets to be mailed to him, but the ticket salesperson may make a mistake in taking down his address.

exhibit 15.6 Gaps in the process of delivering expected service.

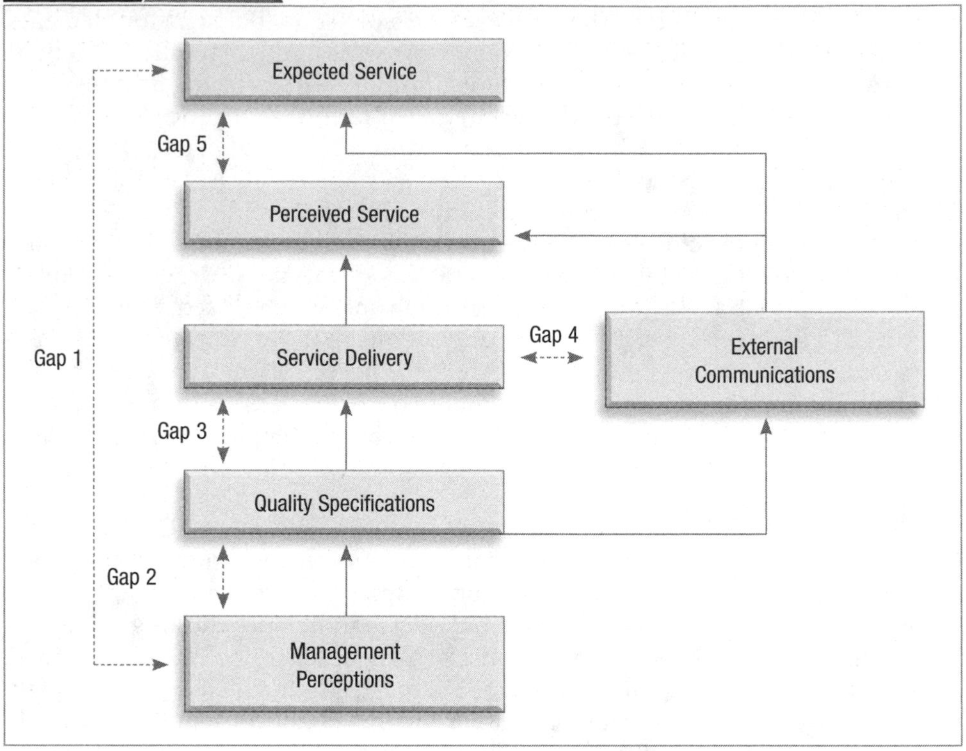

Source: Parasuraman, A., Berry, L.L., & Zeithaml, V.A. (1985). A conceptual model of service quality and its implications for future research. *Journal of Marketing, 49(4),* 41–50. (Figure 1; p. 44) Reprinted with permission via Copyright Clearance Center.

Gap 3

The third gap occurs when the employee or the service provider fails to abide by the process the management has specified. In the above case, the employee in charge of mailing out the tickets may inadvertently skip the name of the customer in question and fail to mail the tickets.

Gap 4

The fourth gap refers to what was communicated to the customer and what was delivered. The person who took the ticket order may have promised seats in a good location but sent tickets for obstructed view seats.

Gap 5

The final and fifth gap is between what the customer expected and what he or she perceived the service to be. This is, in fact, a cumulative effect of the previous four gaps. Obviously, this final gap is of utmost importance, as the customer's satisfaction and intent to continue with the service are based on how wide this gap is.

Service Failure and Recovery

Despite all the planning and practice, some elements of the service may not live up to expectations. For instance, tennis nets might not have been put up by the time the clients arrive, a minor issue that can be rectified quickly. On the other hand, the problem is more serious if the tennis pro does not show up when 15 clients are waiting for instruction. Such failures influence consumer satisfaction with the service (Howat, Murray, & Crilley, 1999; Zeithaml, Parasuraman, & Berry, 1996). Hence, the extent and severity of service failures do constitute a target of evaluation.

The negative impact of a service failure can be alleviated if the firm is prepared for such failures and is willing to remedy the situation. Such preparedness and willingness constitute a target of quality evaluations, but neglecting to recover from the failures may cause even higher levels of customer dissatisfaction (Hart, Heskett, & Sasser, 1990). Lilienthal (1997) found that a superior recovery effort following service failures in golf courses resulted in higher levels of post-recovery satisfaction than poor recovery efforts. Similarly, Howat et al. (1999) found that those who experienced a problem but had the problem resolved successfully expressed higher levels of satisfaction than those whose problems were not resolved successfully. So, managers of sport organizations should be vigilant in detecting service failures and rectifying them. An equally important step is to compensate those customers who experience such failures. Compensation could include simple formal apologies to the customers, waiver of dues associated with the failure, and additional benefits that the club may be able to afford, such as a free lunch in its café or an extension of membership by a month.

SUMMARY

We have distinguished between the targets of quality and the standards to be applied in evaluating quality of a given sport service. The process begins by identifying the targets of quality evaluations (i.e., breaking down a service into distinct elements) and verifying the extent to which they are consumer services or human services. We have discussed a contingent perspective to facilitate the choice of the standards to be applied to a given service. That is, the standards of meeting customer expectations and quality as value are more appropriate to consumer services, and standards of quality as excellence and quality as conformance to professional standards are more appropriate to human services.

develop YOUR PERSPECTIVE

1. Explain the concept *service quality.*
2. Describe the dimensions of service quality.
3. What standards can be applied to judge the quality of a service?
4. A critical issue in relation to service quality relates to who should be the judge of service quality. Explain who should judge quality in various types of services.
5. Although service organizations and their managers aim to provide quality services, they may fail to do so because of the gaps in what they perceive to be customer preferences and what the customer receives. Describe possible gaps in service delivery processes.

Bitner, M. J. (1992). Servicescapes: The impact of physical surroundings on customers and employees. *Journal of Marketing, 56*(2), 57–71.

Bitner, M. J., Booms, B. H., & Mohr, L. A. (1994). Critical service encounters: The employee's viewpoint. *Journal of Marketing, 58,* 95–106.

British Standards Institute (1991). *BS5750 part 8: Guide to quality management and system elements for services.* Milton Keynes, UK: British Standards Institute.

Byon, K. K., Zhang, J. J., & Baker, T. A. (2013). Impact of core and peripheral service quality on consumption behavior of professional team sport spectators as mediated by perceived value. *European Sport Management Quarterly, 13*(2), 232–263.

Chang, K., & Chelladurai, P. (2003). System based quality dimensions in fitness services: Development of the Scale of Quality (SQF). *Service Industries Journal, 23*(5), 65–83.

Chelladurai, P. (1994). Sport management: Defining the field. *European Journal for Sport Management, 1*(1), 7–21.

Chelladurai, P., & Chang, K. (2000). Targets and standards of quality in sport services. *Sport Management Review, 3,* 1–22.

Chelladurai, P., Scott, F. L., & Haywood-Farmer, J. (1987). Dimensions of fitness services: Development of a model. *Journal of Sport Management, 1,* 159–172.

Church, A. H., Javitch, M., & Burke, W. W. (1995). Enhancing professional service quality. *Managing Service Quality, 5,* 29–33.

Cronin, J. J., & Taylor, S. A. (1992). Measuring service quality: A reexamination of extension. *Journal of Marketing, 56,* 55–68.

Cronin, J. J., & Taylor, S. A. (1994). SERVPERF versus SERVQUAL: Reconciling performance-based and perceptions-minus-expectations measurement of service quality. *Journal of Marketing, 58,* 125–131.

Crosby, P. B. (1989). *Let's talk about quality.* New York: McGraw-Hill.

Crosby, P. B. (1985). *Quality without tears.* New York: Signet.

Deming, W. E. (1986). *Out of the crisis.* Cambridge, MA: MIT Press.

Feigenbaum, A. V. (1991). *Total quality control* (4th ed.). New York: McGraw-Hill.

Fitzsimmons, J. A., & Fitzsimmons, M. J. (2011). *Service management* (7th ed.). New York: McGraw-Hill.

Garvin, D. A. (1988). *Managing quality: The strategic and competitive edge.* New York: Free Press.

Goetsch, D. L. (1994). *Introduction to total quality: Quality, productivity, competitiveness.* New York: Macmillan.

Golder, P. N., Mitra, D., & Moorman, C. (2012). What is quality? An integrative framework of processes and states. *Journal of Marketing, 76,* 1–23.

Gummesson, E. (1992). Quality dimensions: What to measure in service organizations. *Advances in Services Marketing and Management, 1,* 177–205.

Hart, C. W. L., Heskett, J. L., & Sasser, W. E., Jr. (1990). The profitable art of service recovery. *Harvard Business Review, 68,* 148–156.

Howat, G., Murray, D., & Crilley, G. (1999). The relationship between service problems and perceptions of service quality, satisfaction, and behavioural intentions of Australian public sports and leisure center customers. *Journal of Parks and Recreation Administration, 17*(2), 42–64.

Juran, J. M. (1989). *Juran on leadership for quality.* New York: Free Press.

Ko, Y. J., & Pastore, D. L. (2007). An instrument to assess customer perceptions of service quality and satisfaction in campus recreation programs. *Recreational Sports Journal, 31*(1), 34–42.

Lehtinen, U., & Lehtinen, J. R. (1991). Two approaches and service quality dimensions. *Service Industry Journal, 11,* 287–303.

Lengnick-Hall, C. A. (1996). Customer contributions to quality: A different view of the customer-oriented firm. *Academy of Management Review, 21,* 791–824.

Lilienthal, S. K. (1997). Service recovery in sport service contexts: An investigation of the veracity of the recovery paradox. Unpublished doctoral dissertation. The Ohio State University.

McDonald, M. A., Sutton, W. A., & Milne, G. R. (1995). TeamqualTM: Measuring service quality in professional team sports. *Sport Marketing Quarterly, 4*(2), 9–15.

Mills, P. K., & Margulies, N. (1980). Toward a core typology of service organizations. *Academy of Management Review, 5,* 255–265.

NBS (2013). Data analysis—What is involved? Retrieved from http://www.questnbs.org/nbs-options-what-is-involved.

Parasuraman, A., Zeithaml, V. A., & Berry, L. (1985). A conceptual model of service quality and its implications for future research. *Journal of Marketing, 49*(4), 41–50.

Parasuraman, A., Zeithaml, V. A., & Berry, L. (1988). SERVQUAL: A multiple-item scale for measuring consumer perceptions of service quality. *Journal of Retailing, 64,* 12–40.

Patterson, P. G., & Johnson, L. W. (1993). Disconfirmation of expectations and the gap model of service quality: An integrated paradigm. *Journal of Consumer Satisfaction, Dissatisfaction & Complaining Behavior, 6,* 90–99.

Price, L. L., Arnold, E. J., & Terney, P. (1995). Going to extremes: Managing service encounters and assessing provider performance. *Journal of Marketing, 59,* 83–97.

Schvaneveldt, S. J., Enkawa, T., & Miyakawa, M. (1991). Consumer evaluation perspectives of service quality:

Evaluation factors and two-way model of quality. *Total Quality Management, 2,* 149–161.

Shonk, D., & Chelladurai, P. (2008). Service quality, satisfaction, and intent to return in event sport tourism. *Journal of Sport Management, 22*(5), 587–602.

Sport England (2013). What we do. Retrieved from http://www.sportengland.org/.

Vuori, H. V. (1982). *Quality assurance of health services: Concepts and methodologies* (16th ed.). Geneva, Switzerland: World Health Organization.

Wakefield, K. L., Blodgett, J. G., & Sloan, H. J. (1996). Measurement and management of the sportscape. *Journal of Sport Management, 10,* 15–31.

Wakefield, K. L., & Sloan, H. J. (1995). The effects of team loyalty and selected stadium factors on spectator attendance. *Journal of Sport Management, 9,* 153–172.

Wright, B. A., Duray, N., & Goodale, T. L. (1992). Assessing perceptions of recreation center service quality: An application of recent advancements in service quality research. *Journal of Park and Recreation Administration, 10,* 33–47.

Zeithaml, V. A., Parasuraman, A., & Berry, L. L. (1990). *Delivering quality service: Balancing customer perceptions and expectations.* New York: Free Press.

Zeithaml, V. A., Parasuraman, A., & Berry, L. L. (1996). The behavioral consequences of service quality. *Journal of Marketing, 60,* 31–46.

CHAPTER

16 ORGANIZATIONAL EFFECTIVENESS

manage YOUR LEARNING

After completing this chapter you should be able to:

- Explain the concept of organizational effectiveness and its complexities.
- Distinguish between the multidimensional aspects and multiple perspectives of organizational effectiveness.
- Explain the differences and the relationships among the goals, system resource, and process models of organizational effectiveness.
- Understand the relationships between values and organizational effectiveness.
- Discuss the primacy of multiple perspectives of organizational effectiveness.
- Debate the utility of the "prime beneficiary" approach to organizational effectiveness.

strategic CONCEPTS

competing values approach (CVA)
evolutionary perspective
goals model
human relations model
internal process model
multidimensional perspective
multiple constituencies
multiple perspectives
open system model
organizational effectiveness
organizational paradox
power perspective
prime beneficiary
process model
rational goal model
relativistic perspective
social justice perspective
system resource model

INTRODUCTION

As discussed in Chapter 4, *evaluating* is defined as the process of assessing the degree to which the organization as a whole and various units and individuals have accomplished what they set out to do. It was also pointed out that the four managerial functions—planning, organizing, leading, and evaluating—must be considered ongoing processes that are intricately intertwined. Thus, the planning process sets the stage for organizational initiatives, while the evaluating function provides the rationale for the revision or reorganization of organizational activities. From this perspective, evaluating is critical to the management of any organization.

Evaluating, as defined above, is a broad concept encompassing the organization as a whole, the units within it, and its members. Theorists and practitioners have traditionally distinguished between evaluating the organization and its units—organizational effectiveness and program evaluation—and evaluating individuals' performances. Because this text is concerned with macro issues relating to sport and recreation organizations, we examine only the concepts of program evaluation and organizational effectiveness. We studied program evaluation in Chapter

14, and now we will look at organizational effectiveness, which is "a measure of how appropriate organizational goals are and how well an organization is achieving those goals" (Robbins, Coulter, Leach, & Kilfoil, 2012, p. 478).

Note that although the successes of various programs may contribute to the effectiveness of the organization as a whole, organizational effectiveness is a larger concept. As Herman and Renz (1999) noted, "An organization is not the sum of its parts or functions. It is possible to assess the effectiveness of a program or the use of service volunteers in an organization; however, such assessments do not necessarily reveal much about overall organizational effectiveness" (p. 108).

program evaluation

As noted in Chapter 14, activities intended to achieve a specific goal or set of goals are grouped together as a program. Evaluating a program consists of determining whether (a) the program has achieved its goals, (b) the activities were carried out in accordance with specifications, and (c) the objectives were achieved because of the program and its activities or because of something else.

TO recap

EFFECTIVENESS AND EFFICIENCY

The terms *effectiveness* and *efficiency* are often used interchangeably. However, from an organizational perspective, they are quite different (see Etzioni, 1964; Ostroff & Schmitt, 1993; Steers & Black, 1994). As Steers and Black (1994) noted, "*Effectiveness* is the extent to which operative goals can be attained; *efficiency* is the cost/benefit ratio incurred in the pursuit of those goals" (p. 330). Consider two comparable sport marketing firms, A and B. Both set the goal of making a $200,000 profit in a year. If Firm A makes the $200,000 and Firm B makes only $175,000, Firm A would be considered more effective because it reached its goal. However, consider that Firm A invested $2 million in its operations and Firm B invested only $1.5 million, and we can make a different judgment. Because Firm B had a better rate of return on its capital than Firm A, Firm B would be considered more efficient than Firm A. These two evaluations are illustrated in Exhibit 16.1. Thus, *effectiveness* and *efficiency* are distinct concepts, and we should avoid the tendency to use them synonymously.

sidebar 16.1

ORGANIZATIONAL EFFECTIVENESS AND PERFORMANCE MANAGEMENT

A concept that parallels the notion of organizational effectiveness is organizational performance. Performance measurement and performance management have become part of management discourse, and several books and articles have been written on the topic. Performance measurement is "a process of monitoring and reporting on how well someone or something is doing. In theory, it is a broad concept applicable to people, things, situations, activities, and organizations. Strategic performance measurement is defined as the measurement and reporting system that quantifies the degree to which managers achieve their objectives" (Verweire & Van Den Berghe, 2004, p. 6). Recall that we have labeled the measurement of an individual's performance as performance appraisal. If the measurement is concerned with a program, it is considered program evaluation. When the measurement targets the organization, it is considered organizational effectiveness, which is the focus of this chapter. Much of what is written on performance management underscores the significance of goals and the strategies to achieve them. This was highlighted by Verweire and Van Den Berghe (2004) when they stated that "the purpose of performance management is to achieve organizational effectiveness" (p. 7). Similarly, Bayle and Madella (2002) consider that organizational performance consists of effectiveness and efficiency. In their words, "*Effectiveness* is traditionally defined as the capacity to achieve the institutional goals. *Efficiency* compares the means used and the real production without examining the satisfaction of the user" (p. 2).

exhibit 16.1 Effectiveness and efficiency in organizations.

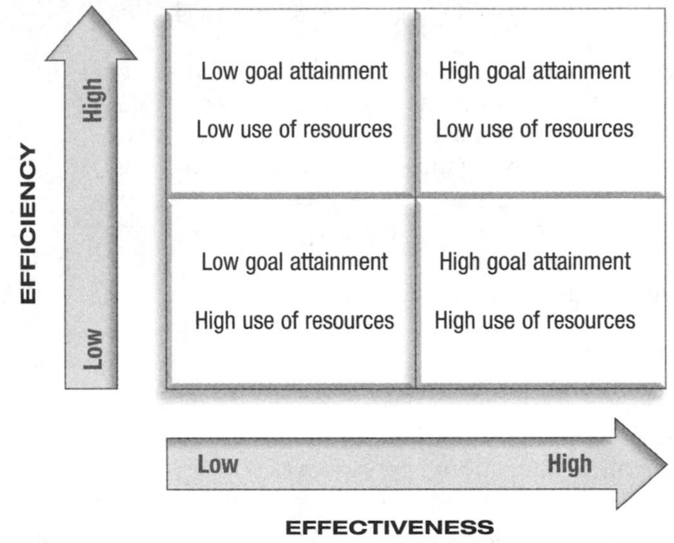

It is, however, conceivable that an organization may set efficiency itself as a goal. For example, a university athletic department, concerned with revenue generation, may embark on a fundraising campaign. At the same time, it may also set a second goal of reducing its expenses while maintaining the same levels of service and performance. The latter effort is aimed at making operations more efficient. If the department becomes more efficient, then it will have reached that objective. Many profit-oriented organizations are geared toward efficiency in order to maximize their profits. For our purposes here, it is useful to consider the two concepts—effectiveness and efficiency—as separate entities while treating the attainment of efficiency as a measure of effectiveness (if indeed that was the goal of the organization).

> **IN brief**
>
> *Effectiveness* refers to the attainment of a goal, whereas *efficiency* refers to the ratio of cost to benefits of achieving the goal. Organizations may set efficiency as a goal in itself.

ORGANIZATIONAL EFFECTIVENESS: THE ULTIMATE CONCERN

Organizational effectiveness is the ultimate dependent variable in any organizational analysis. Organizations, as noted earlier, are social entities that set out to achieve certain purposes. All of the managerial functions and processes discussed in the preceding chapters are aimed at reaching the specified ends. Thus, whether those purposes are achieved or not is critical to the analysis of an organization and its management. That is why both scholars and practitioners consider organizational effectiveness the bottom-line concern of all managerial activities.

Despite its importance, organizational effectiveness is, perhaps, the most controversial and complex concept in management. A number of authors have studied organizational effectiveness from different perspectives and with different criteria (see Campbell, 1977; Steers, 1975; Steers & Black, 1994). Some authors have used

sidebar 16.2

MANAGEMENT EFFICIENCY VERSUS EFFECTIVENESS

Robbins, Coulter, Leach, & Kilfoil (2012) define management as "the process of coordinating work activities so that they are completed efficiently and effectively with and through other people" (p. 6). They expand on this definition by saying that "efficiency refers to getting the most output from the least amount of inputs. . . . Because managers deal with scarce resources—including resources such as people, money, and equipment—they're concerned with the efficient use of those resources by getting things done at the least cost. . . . It is not enough just to be efficient, however. Management is also concerned with being effective, completing activities so that organizational goals are achieved. . . . Whereas efficiency is concerned with the means of getting things done, effectiveness is concerned with the ends, or attainment of organizational goals" (p. 9).

a single criterion of effectiveness while others have used multiple criteria. Some have approached the problem from a normative perspective (what *ought to be*). This perspective simply reflects the theoretical expectations for an organization. Other authors have taken a descriptive approach (what *is*).

Thus, as summaries of the literature suggest, the effectiveness concept has proved to be imprecise—there is no consensus on its definition or, therefore, on its measurement (e.g., Campbell, 1977; Molnar & Rogers, 1976; Steers, 1975; Steers & Black, 1994). It is possible, however, to reconcile the various theoretical orientations toward organizational effectiveness and produce a gestalt view of the construct. This is the approach adopted in this book.

Specifically, the five significant models of organizational effectiveness—the *goals model,* the *system resource model,* the *process model,* the *multiple-constituency model,* and the *competing values approach*—are examined within the general framework of a systems perspective. (Chapter 3 contains a lengthy discussion of the systems view of organizations.) To facilitate the discussion of the first four models, the input–throughput–output model of a system is reproduced in Exhibit 16.2. The figure also shows how the various models of effectiveness relate to the specific elements of the input–throughput–output cycle of an open system.

THE GOALS MODEL

The most fundamental approach to the study of organizational effectiveness is suggested in the description provided above. In the **goals model**, effectiveness is the degree to which an organization has achieved its goals (Etzioni, 1964; Price, 1972). Implicit in this definition is the assumption that because organizations exist to achieve some specific purpose, an organization's effectiveness is a function of the degree to which it has achieved that purpose. Thus, a national sport-governing body might set a goal that its national team will be ranked in the top 10 in the world within a two-year period. If the team is only ranked 15th at the end of that period, the organization can be considered ineffective. Many university athletic departments set the goal for their teams to finish the season in the top half of their respective leagues. A team (and the entire department) will be considered effective if it reaches that plateau and ineffective if it does not.

Two underlying conditions for the goals model of effectiveness become evident from the examples given above. The first is that a goal must be identifiable.

exhibit 16.2 Models of organizational effectiveness.

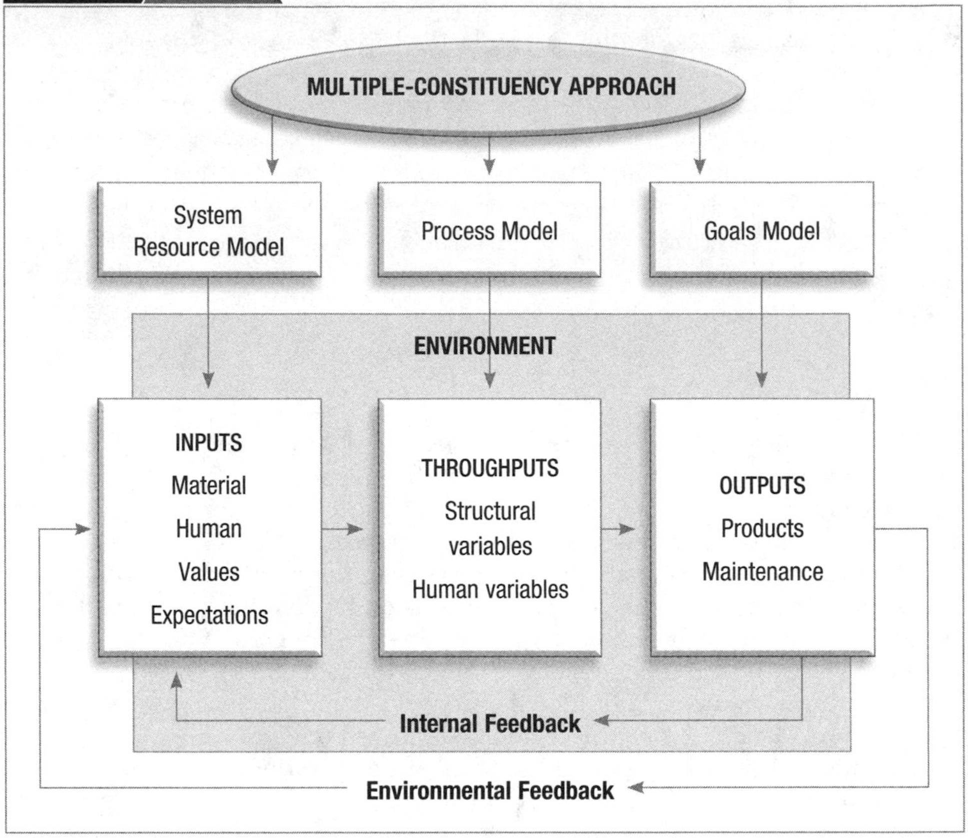

In the first example, the goal is a world ranking for the sport-governing body. The second condition is that organizational performance must be clearly measurable. It is easy to measure the world ranking attained by a sport-governing body. In our examples, the criteria of effectiveness are crystallized (the goals are clear and precise), and they are also observable and measurable (Hasenfeld, 1983). Though the goals model is intuitively appealing, the two conditions behind the model—clarity of goals and measurement of goal attainment—may not be valid for all types of organizations.

The Need for Clear Goals

As noted in Chapter 5, many organizations tend to proclaim their goals in broad, global terms. That is, their goals are designed to delineate a domain of activity, and their charters and official notifications are formulated to rationalize their existence and to justify support from the larger community (Perrow, 1961). However, global statements (*official goals* in Perrow's terminology) do not provide a focus for organizational analysis. In other words, if you did not specify where you wanted to go in the first place, how can you know whether you have arrived?

Price (1972), while acknowledging the difficulty of identifying organizational goals, suggested that there are ways to overcome this limitation. For example, he felt that it is possible to identify the real, or operative, goals of the organization by focusing on the major decision makers. Their statements and their decisions regarding major organizational processes (such as budgeting and staffing) should reveal the organization's priorities. Price also argued that the actual activities of the organization and its members will clearly reveal what the organization's goals are. We noted in Chapter 5 that operative goals can be identified through an analysis of organizational processes and decisions. For example, when a university athletic department fires a coach after a losing season without considering his accomplishments in other aspects of coaching, it can be inferred that winning is important to that department, despite all protestations to the contrary.

Although Price's proposals have some merit, there are problems in their implementation. For example, his assumption that there will be consensus among the major decision makers on the goals for an organization may not be true in all cases (see Lawrence & Lorsch, 1967; Steers & Black, 1994). Also, as noted in Chapter 5, an organization's operative goals may not remain stable over time. Insofar as the major decision makers may have fluctuating preferences, and insofar as their power to influence decisions is subject to change (this reflects the notion of dominance of coalitions referred to in Chapter 6), the operative goals of an organization also might shift. Thus, it might not be possible to obtain the clarity and focus necessary to apply the goals model.

Many organizations pursue multiple goals, and this limits the utility of a goals model approach for analyzing organizational effectiveness. For instance, the sport-governing body in the above example might have two goals—to increase the number of its registered clubs and to improve its world ranking. These two goals are reflected in its two programs, usually referred to as mass sport and elite sport. Before assessing the relative goal attainment of the organization, it is necessary to know the relative weight attached to each goal (that is, the relative importance of the two programs).

The problem of multiple goals is further complicated by the fact that some organizational goals can be in conflict with each other (see Chapter 5). When this is the case, the attainment of one goal may contribute to the failure of the second. That is, the organization would be effective in terms of one goal but would be ineffective in terms of the conflicting goal. In the case of an intercollegiate athletic program, for example, the goal of promoting a large number of sports and the goal of winning national championships in many sports might not be attainable simultaneously within the context of budget constraints. This issue of multiple and conflicting goals is not addressed by the goals model.

The Need for Measurable Goals

The second assumption of the goals model is that the outcomes of the organization can be measured and compared against the priority established for the goals. However, objectively measuring outputs (i.e., goal attainment) is a problem in service organizations. For example, many university athletic departments state that one of their goals is to develop their athletes to be responsible citizens. It should be obvious that it is not possible to determine with any validity the degree to which this goal is attained or approached. Similarly, the university as a whole may have as its goal "the education of youth." Again, this goal is not easily quantifiable.

To the extent goals are intangible and their attainment is not easily measured, the goals model appears to have little utility. This issue extends to services in general because they are intangible, and, therefore, the quality of services cannot be easily ascertained. Thus, the problem of measuring outputs is acute in all service organizations, particularly in professional service organizations.

Substitution of Surrogate Measures

Given the difficulty of measuring intangible goals, it is not uncommon for organizations to use some quantitative measures as indicators of qualitative outcomes. For example, quantitative measures such as the number of graduating students or students' scores on standardized tests are often used by educational institutions as indicators of their effectiveness. In our own context, the percentage of graduating athletes is often used as a measure of the effectiveness of university athletic departments.

IN brief

In the goals model of effectiveness, goal attainment is the criterion of effectiveness. The model is useful only to the extent that goals are specific and unambiguous and goal attainment can be easily measured.

As Hoy and Miskel (2008) point out, assessing school (or athletic department) effectiveness through such measures is based more on expediency than on theory. That is, such quantitative measures are readily available and easily understood by those who demand that the schools or departments remain accountable. Although such measures are significant by themselves, they may not indicate effectiveness in terms of educating the youth. For example, a high number of graduating students might simply reflect low standards. Standardized tests measuring cognitive skills are just tests. They do not measure criteria in the affective domain, such as motivation, creativity, self-confidence, and aspirations.

THE SYSTEM RESOURCE MODEL

An alternate model of effectiveness, the **system resource model**, focuses on the inputs of the organization (refer back to Exhibit 16.2). Yuchtman and Seashore (1967), who proposed this model, defined effectiveness as "the ability of the organization, in either absolute or relative terms, to exploit its environment in the acquisition of scarce and valued resources" (p. 898). Every organization must compete with other organizations for resources from the larger society. Thus, an effective organization is one that gains an advantageous bargaining position relative to other organizations that share the same environment. The significance of the organization's bargaining position in the context of its environment was highlighted in Chapter 8. It was suggested that the members of the institutional and managerial subsystems must be able to influence the elements in the distal and task environments respectively.

Consider the case of a university seeking large donations and government subsidies to finance a new athletics arena. It has to compete with other universities and other nonprofit organizations in the region for donations and subsidies. According to the system resource model of effectiveness, the university will be considered effective if it secures the funds necessary to construct the arena. That, of course, is a function of the relative influence and bargaining power of the competing organizations. The case would be the same with professional sport franchises seeking financial support from municipal governments. They are competing with other organizations for municipal dollars.

When coaches use the number and quality of athletes who tried out for the various teams, or athletic administrators cite the season tickets sold as a measure of effectiveness, they are also using a system resource approach. By the same token, the athletic department itself may use the donations, endorsements, and sponsorships it receives as indicators of effectiveness.

sidebar 16.3

A THEORY OF SYSTEM RESOURCES

The significance of securing necessary resources is highlighted by the popular resource based view (RBV) of organizations. The RBV holds that an organization can gain and sustain a competitive advantage if it can garner critical resources and exploit those resources profitably (Barney, 1991, 1995). Resources are "all assets, capabilities, organizational processes, firm attributes, information, knowledge, etc., controlled by a firm that enable the firm to conceive of and implement strategies that improve its efficiency and effectiveness" (Barney, 1991, p. 101). According to Barney (1991, 1995), these resources can be *physical capital* (e.g., facilities, equipment, geographic location), *human capital* (e.g., the expertise and experience of managers and coaches, the talents of athletes), *organizational capital* (e.g., history, tradition, and culture of the university and its athletic department), or *financial capital* (e.g., reserves, debt, surplus revenue).

Resources are either *tangible* (e.g., facilities, raw materials, and other equipment), or *intangible* (e.g., organizational culture, reputation, and motivation of employees or players). As Carmeli (2004) noted, an organization can easily acquire tangible resources (or imitate them) and put them to various uses. In contrast, intangible resources take time to develop and cannot be easily imitated. Hence, "intangible, more than tangible, resources have potential for competitive advantage creation" (p. 112). For example, the sale of licensed merchandise is a source of income for many universities. Universities like the University of Notre Dame and The Ohio State University make more money through the sale of such merchandise than some other universities. This advantage is based not on the quality of the products, but on intangible resources such as university tradition and the loyalty of alumni and fans.

The criticalness of a given resource for competitive advantage is based on how *valuable, rare, imperfectly imitable,* and *hardly substitutable* it is (Barney, 1991). A resource is valuable only if it can contribute to organizational performance and goals. For instance, an individual's height may be a very valuable resource in the context of basketball and volleyball, but it does not have any relevance to conducting research if the individual chooses to become a scientist. Similarly, a large stadium is valuable only in the context of a football, baseball, or soccer competition; its value is less certain in the context of a hockey game.

The second attribute of resources that create competitive advantage is their rarity. If all organizations can have a resource (i.e., the resource is not rare), then a particular organization cannot gain a competitive advantage through that resource. For example, coaches were able to understand the significance of the 7-foot, 3-inch Hasheem Thabeet from Tanzania and draft him to the Oklahoma City Thunder basketball team. If there were hundreds of players as tall and talented as Hasheem, then his height and skill would not be a rare resource—other teams could recruit such players and nullify Thabeet's advantage for the Thunder. This explains the intense and expensive efforts to recruit or draft talented athletes. *Imperfect imitability* refers to the inability of other organizations to imitate a given resource. The fourth attribute of a resource contributing to competitive advantage is low substitutability. That is, a basketball coach may exploit other resources (e.g., speed, agility, skills, or strategies) to make up for lack of height and to nullify the height advantages of another team. Take the case of the NBA Finals of 2004, which the Detroit Pistons won against the Los Angeles Lakers. The then-Pistons' coach, Larry Brown, employed strategies of "hustle and bustle" and of double-teaming or triple-teaming Shaq O'Neal and Kobe Bryant, the stars of the Lakers. In other words, the coach substituted the speed and agility of his players for Shaq's height and Kobe's shooting ability. According to Bacon (2004), "The Pistons transformed the game itself from a star-centered run-a-thon to a selfless, disciplined game of Brown ball" (p. 40).

Simon, Gove, and Hitt (2008) argue that while having critical scarce resources offers a competitive advantage, they are not sufficient for winning competitions. In their view, "such resources must be effectively bundled and deployed to exploit opportunities and/or mitigate threats in specific competitive engagements for a firm to *realize* a competitive advantage" (p. 919). Effective bundling and deploying of resources is, in essence, *resource management,* which Simon and colleagues define "as the comprehensive process of structuring a firm's resource portfolio, bundling the resources to build capabilities, and leveraging those capabilities to *realize* a competitive advantage" (p. 922). *Structuring* is the process of securing the resources, *bundling* is the process of creating capabilities by integrating the available resources, and *leveraging* is configuring and deploying the capabilities to a particular market context. Furthermore, they argue that this process of resource management (i.e., bundling and deploying) is more critical in

(continued)

the case of human resources because the process is possible only through individuals whose skills may vary across different tasks. These authors used data from professional baseball competitions to illustrate their contention. Baseball managers (a) select a starting line up and the batting order (i.e., the bundling and deploying of batting, fielding, and pitching skill sets), (b) rebundle the skill sets through substitutions, and (c) make decisions on specific plays (hit and run, steals, intentional walks, etc.). The manager's effectiveness in these processes results in the team's victories. In the final analysis, according to these authors, when competing organizations are equal in resources, resource management (i.e., bundling and deploying) is more critical than the resources themselves.

Similar thoughts were advanced by Holcomb, Holmes, and Connelly (2009) with reference to football. In their view, football coaches understand the proficiencies each player brings to the team and bundle them into specialized units with every player performing a role appropriate to the task at hand. Then the coaches deploy these bundles in a given competitive context, such as offensive bundles for running and passing and defensive bundles to protect against the run and the pass. Thus, "success is more likely when managers create superior bundles and deploy them effectively" (p. 462).

Not surprisingly, considering the above football and basketball examples, the RBV framework has been the basis of studies in sport management. Cunningham (2003) used the average of the coaches' salaries and the recruiting budget as indicators of human resources and found that this measure was related to the success of athletic programs as indicated by the Sears Directors' Cup scores. In another study, Cunningham and Sagas (2004) found that the coaching experience and racial diversity of coaching staff (strength of human resources) were related to football program success.

In a more comprehensive study, Won and Chelladurai (2005) investigated the influence of several types of resources contributing to competitive advantage in intercollegiate athletics with reference to two sets of outcomes—*athletic performance* and *academic performance.* The authors found that the intangible resources of an athletic department (e.g., the athletic and academic reputations of the university) were the *contributing resources* that facilitated the generation of other more tangible resources (i.e., human and financial resources). The tangible resources were found to influence the attainment of athletic performance goals (i.e., a winning record) and athlete development goals (i.e., graduation rates and gender equity).

System Resource Versus Goals Model

It might appear at first glance that the goals model and the system resource model are significantly different—the former emphasizes the outputs of the organization, whereas the latter emphasizes the inputs. This is not the case, however. They are integrally linked if the organization is viewed as an open system. This idea of a link between the outputs of a system and its inputs is illustrated as the feedback loop from outputs to inputs (see Exhibits 3.2 and 16.2). That is, the feedback loop indicates the acceptability of organizational outputs and the availability of needed resources.

As an open system, any organization must be in a profitable exchange position with its environment. That is, it must be able to obtain essential inputs from the environment. However, this is possible on a continuing basis only when its outputs are acceptable to the environment. Thus, a measure of the degree to which the system is able to obtain its resources is, in fact, a measure of the acceptability and utility of its outputs. In short, the quality of the services provided by organizations may be inferred from the quantity of demand for their services. These demands, in turn, translate into inputs for the organization. For example, if a university athletic department is able to secure a large number of donations from the public, it is probably because the public appreciates the department's achievements. Thus, the system resource model quantifies one element (inputs) and uses it as a surrogate or substitute measure for another element (outputs), which is not as easily quantifiable (see Exhibit 16.3).

exhibit 16.3 Resource acquisition as a surrogate measure of goal attainment.

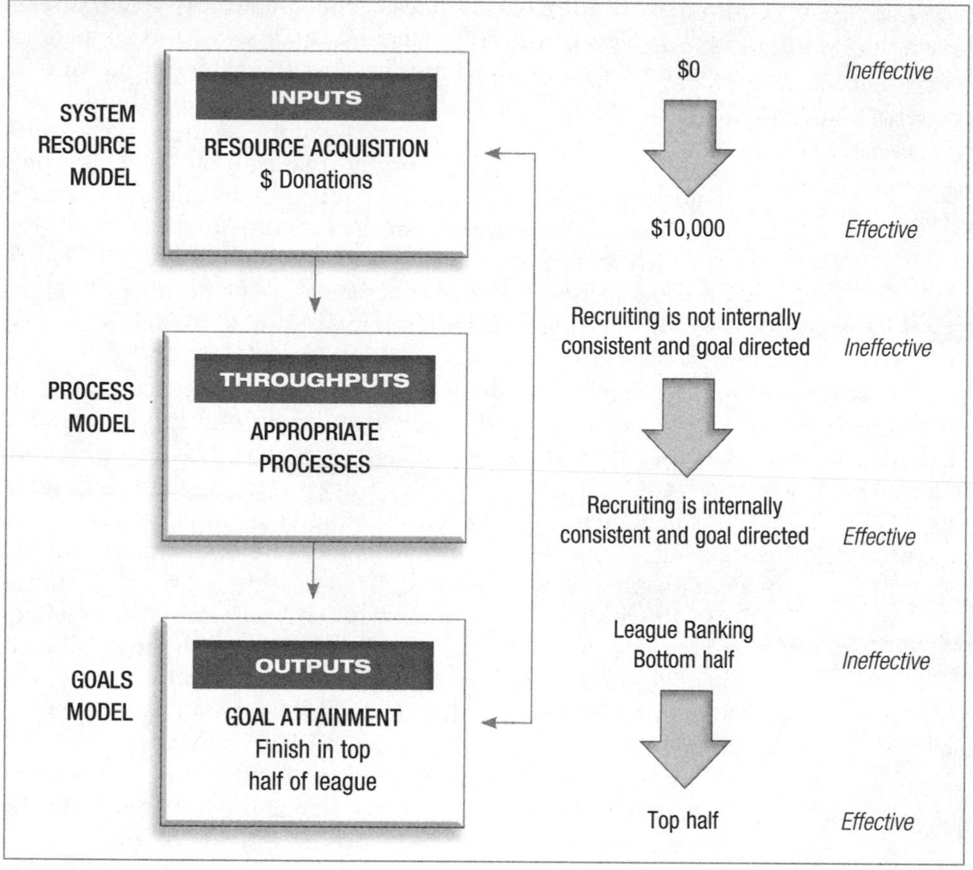

Obtaining System Resources as an Operative Goal

Viewed from a different perspective, an operative goal of an organization might be to obtain resources from the environment. Thus, measuring the extent of resource acquisition is the equivalent of measuring goal attainment. Yuchtman and Seashore (1967) made reference to this when they noted that

> The better the bargaining position of an organization, the more capable it is of attaining its varied and often transient goals [operative goals], and the more capable it is of allowing the attainment of personal goals of members. Processes of "goal formation" and "goal displacement" in organizations are thus seen not as defining ultimate criteria of effectiveness, but as strategies adopted by members for enhancing the bargaining position of their organization. (p. 898)

Note the authors' emphasis on "goal formation" and "goal displacement." Earlier we noted that the operative goals are set by the dominant coalition. The dominant coalition would, of course, include the resource providers, who would influence the formation or displacement of organizational goals.

Applicability of the System Resource Model

When Yuchtman and Seashore (1967) outlined the system resource model of organizational effectiveness, they felt that it was valid and applicable to

public, private, third sector

Chapter 2 described the distinctions among public, private, and third sector organizations. Basically, public organizations are government agencies at the federal, state, and municipal levels. Their finances come from taxes. Private organizations are those funded by private investors or donations. Third-sector organizations are private organizations that are heavily funded by government agencies.

TO recap

all organizations, and, indeed, the model provides a useful framework in many instances. The system resource model is highly relevant for professional/human service organizations because their output cannot be objectively measured. Consequently, their effectiveness is best measured by the demand for their services. The system resource model is also relevant for volunteer and nonprofit organizations (NPOs). Their major source of funding is the contributions and donations of members of the larger community. Consequently, the degree to which these organizations are able to attract financial support is a measure of their effectiveness. The number of volunteers in the organization (input of human resources) is also an indicator of organizational effectiveness.

There is some question, however, whether public sector and third sector organizations (see Chapter 2 again) can legitimately use the system resource model. A distinguishing characteristic of these organizations is that their resources are guaranteed (to some extent, at least) by a superior organization (such as government). The total funds generated by a sport-governing body could ordinarily be a legitimate measure of effectiveness. However, this measure is meaningless if the government provides subsidies. Also, an intercollegiate athletic program cannot use the athletic fees paid by students as a measure of effectiveness if those fees are levied and collected by the university. The student fees are a requirement of enrollment, and the total amount generated through the fees is a function of the total number of students in the university.

IN brief

In the system resource model, the input of resources is the measure of organizational effectiveness because these inputs are indicative of the acceptability of the outputs. However, the model's applicability is limited when an organization's inputs are underwritten by a superior authority.

It would be legitimate, however, for the third sector organizations in the above examples to claim effectiveness on the basis of the acquisition of resources outside of government support. A sport-governing body might generate a considerable amount of money through corporate sponsorships and private donations. It might also secure superior human resources in terms of athletes, volunteer coaches, and other officials.

PROCESS MODEL

If an organization cannot use the goals model because it cannot objectively measure its outputs, and if it cannot use the system resource model because its resources are underwritten by a superior organization (such as a government), how can it evaluate its effectiveness? A number of authors (e.g., Pfeffer, 1977; Steers, 1977) have suggested, as a partial solution, that the organization focus on its internal processes rather than on its proposed end results. From a systems perspective, this involves an emphasis on the throughputs, which link the inputs to outputs (see Exhibits 3.2 and 16.3).

The underlying rationale for the **process model** of effectiveness is that the conversion of inputs into acceptable outputs is based on the throughput processes adopted by the organization. If those throughput processes are internally logical, consistent, and without friction, then it can be assumed that the organization is effective. Furthermore, as Mott (1972) pointed out, organizational processes are expected to be adaptable to changes in the environment and flexible to accommodate fluctuating workloads. That is, the organization is doing what is rational in the context of its goals and its environment.

The process model can be illustrated by an athletic program. The program can be judged on the basis of such processes as recruiting, training, and scheduling competitions. An evaluation of these processes would be one measure of the relative effectiveness of the respective systems. Another measure would be the general policies and procedures, the satisfaction expressed by both coaches and athletes, and the lack (or presence) of conflict within the athletic department.

The arguments for the process model of effectiveness are equally applicable to private, profit-oriented organizations. In fact, the identification and specification of appropriate processes are the foundation of the movement labeled total quality management (TQM). In this approach, the quality of a product is best judged by the extent to which the processes specified by experts are strictly followed (Crosby, 1985; Deming, 1986). Any deviations from the specifications will detract from the quality of the product. Assembly lines require that certain processes are followed strictly. Traffic and crowd control before, during, and after a professional football game also require strict protocol, which is determined by experts who have carefully analyzed the situation. Strict adherence to this protocol is necessary to ensure the safety of spectators and the public. Of course, the success of the event management is judged on the basis of the smooth flow of traffic without any bottlenecks, as well as on the orderly behavior of the spectators. Such successes are attributed to the processes adopted by the sport franchise.

IN brief

The process model emphasizes the logic of the internal processes linking inputs to desired outcomes. However, the danger lies in treating a process as the one best way, thereby making it an end in itself.

Pros and Cons of the Process Model

As is the case with the goals and system resource models, the process model of effectiveness has some advantages. However, the evaluation of internal processes also poses problems. The process model presupposes that a body of experts can judge the appropriateness of specific processes. And, because experts' judgments are accepted as correct, there is a tendency to specify the "appropriate" processes and procedures in advance for all similar organizations to follow. When this happens, every organization must be judged as effective if it followed the specified processes.

This trend is evident in third sector organizations that depend heavily on the government for financial support. For example, many governments offer financial assistance to sport-governing bodies for specific programs. These programs are assumed to lead to better management of the sport-governing bodies, better recruitment and training of the national team, and so on. The sport-governing bodies in turn must follow these guidelines and institute the suggested programs in order to receive government grants. Thus, all sport-governing bodies tend to become identical in terms of their internal processes. In a similar manner, the traffic and crowd control processes adopted by various athletic departments and professional sport franchises tend to become similar across the country because these organizations "benchmark" and adopt the best practices of other organizations.

equifinality and multifinality

As we noted in Chapter 3, *equifinality* refers to the idea that two systems starting from different positions can end up at the same final position. Any two systems (organizations) can differ in the number and nature of their subsystems and the environments they face. Therefore, the particular internal processes within each system may also differ. The concept of equifinality suggests that the systems can be equally effective, because in each system the subsystems and their processes might be consistent with each other and with the task environment. On the other hand, the concept *multifinality* suggests that any two organizations following the same processes may still vary in the degree to which they achieve their goals.

TO recap

Max Weber's concept of a bureaucracy is another instance in which the problems associated with the use of internal processes are highlighted. Weber's bureaucratic prescriptions are normative in the sense that they suggest that all organizations must be bureaucratized in order to be efficient (see Chapter 7). However, the best judgment that can be made about an organization using the process model is whether the organization is more or less bureaucratized. To relate the degree of bureaucratization to effectiveness would be inappropriate.

Thus, the danger in the use of the process model of effectiveness is that organizations tend to deify the processes irrespective of their relationship to effectiveness. An emphasis on processes could be counterproductive from a systems perspective.

MULTIDIMENSIONALITY OF ORGANIZATIONAL EFFECTIVENESS

Given the difficulty in exclusively applying the goals, system resource, or process model, it may be necessary to assess the effectiveness of an organization from a **multidimensional perspective.** Evan (1976) suggested that "to appraise the effectiveness of an organization with the aid of systems theory . . . one must measure its performance with respect to all four systemic processes as well as their interrelationships" (p. 19). The four systemic processes that Evan referred to are the inputs, throughputs, outputs, and feedback of a system (see again Exhibits 3.2 and 16.2). Also, it may be necessary for some organizations to measure effectiveness at different points in the input–throughput–output cycle since no (or only a few) output measures may be available or feasible.

To illustrate how different dimensions of effectiveness can be superimposed on the input–throughput–output cycle (i.e., system resources model, process model, and goals model), consider Karteroliotis and Papadimitriou's (2004) five dimensions of the effectiveness of sport-governing bodies in Greece. These dimensions are (1) caliber of the board and external liaisons, (2) interest in athletes, (3) internal procedures, (4) long-term planning, and (5) sport-science support. Recall that in Parsons' hierarchical differentiation of subsystems described in Chapter 8, the major function of the institutional system was to interact effectively with elements in the distal environment. That point is highlighted by the first of the dimensions listed above. The caliber of the board can be seen as the input of human resources. The second dimension, interest in athletes, is the goal of the organization and thus can be mapped to the output stage in Exhibit 16.2. The other three dimensions are the processes in the throughput stage.

Bayle and Madella (2002) identified six dimensions of performance of national sport organizations (NSOs):

1. *Institutional:* This dimension is concerned with the sport organization strong national teams and gaining new members.
2. *Social–internal:* The focus in this dimension is the positive and friendly atmosphere among the employees of the organization and between supervisors and employees.
3. *Social–external:* This dimension is concerned with cultivating good relationships with external stakeholders by achieving organizational goals.
4. *Economic–financial:* This dimension refers to securing resources and managing financial ties with public institutions.
5 *Promotional:* This dimension focuses on increasing media coverage and creating public awareness of the organization.

6. *Organizational:* This dimension refers to the managing of the organization to be consistent with environmental demands.

Each of these six dimensions can easily be placed under the input, throughput, or output components of the model shown in Exhibit 16.2.

Kushner and Poole (1996) suggested that the performance of a nonprofit organization can be evaluated on four components—resource acquisition, efficiency, goal attainment, and client satisfaction. Resource acquisition relates to the input stage, reflecting the system resource model; efficiency to the throughput stage or the process model; and goal attainment and client satisfaction to the output stage or the goals model.

The need to measure organizational effectiveness at various stages in the input-throughput-output cycle may be greater in organizations with more than one domain of activities, in which each domain has its own distinctive goals. In those cases, the three models of effectiveness may be differentially relevant to the domains of organizational activity. For example, Chelladurai, Szyszlo, and Haggerty (1987) identified the relative importance of six dimensions of effectiveness according to the administrators of Canadian national sport organizations. These dimensions were derived by superimposing the three phases of the input–throughput–output cycle on the two domains of NSO activities—mass sport (promotion of public participation in the sport) and elite sport (promotion of excellence in the sport and winning in international competitions). Thus, the six dimensions were input-human resources, input-monetary resources, throughput-mass, throughput-elite, output-mass, and output-elite. These administrators rated input-human resources, throughput-mass, throughput-elite, and output-elite as the more important effectiveness dimensions than input-monetary resources and output-mass. (See Exhibit 16.4.)

IN brief

Given that each of the three models (goals, system resource, and process) has limitations, organizations tend to use all three models to assess and portray their effectiveness. Different models may also be applied to evaluate various programs of an organization.

exhibit 16.4 Differential evaluation of elite and mass sport.

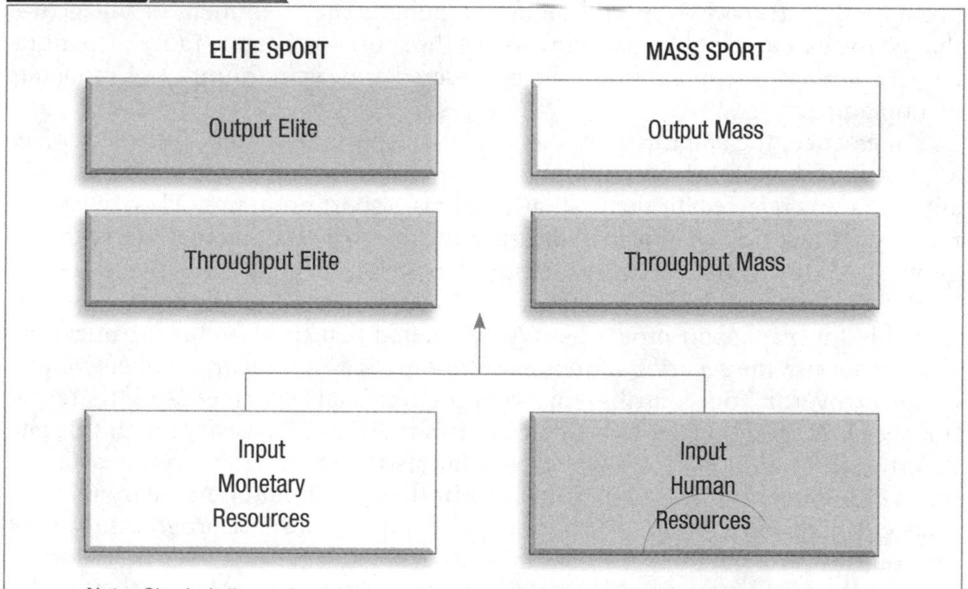

Note: Shaded dimensions were rated as more important than unshaded dimensions.

sidebar 16.4

EFFECTIVENESS OF THE NCAA

In Chapter 8 we discussed the nature and functions of interorganizational networks. O'Rourke and Chelladurai (2006) assessed the effectiveness of the NCAA from that perspective. Noting that the NCAA has 16 guiding principles (NCAA, 2004a, 2004b), which influence the development of policies and practices of the NCAA, they argued that the extent to which the NCAA enforces these principles would be an indication of its effectiveness. Their results showed that these varied activities could be grouped into six dimensions: *general equity concerns, institutional autonomy, competitive equity, rule enforcement, student-athlete welfare,* and *student-athlete status.* These are described in Exhibit 16.5.

In addition, they included the critical functions of a network organization noted in Chapter 8. These were (1) creating greater access to resources for member organizations, (2) helping to increase the financial performance of members, (3) facilitating innovation and sharing of knowledge and learning among member institutions, (4) reducing variety and uncertainty in transactions and economic uncertainty, and (5) reducing the costs associated with gathering and disseminating information. In O'Rourke and Chelladurai's (2006) study, these varied network functions were collapsed into *marketing and development, management enhancement,* and *image projection.* These are also described in Exhibit 16.5.

O'Rourke and Chelladurai (2006) found that the senior administrators in their study perceived all these factors to be very important, and that they were satisfied with the extent to which the NCAA carried out these functions. But the ratings on effectiveness of achieving them were lower than the importance attached to the functions. Furthermore, the factors of image projection, student-athlete status, and marketing and development were the more dominant influences in administrators' perceptions of NCAA effectiveness.

It is not surprising that the input of monetary resources was not considered as important as the other dimensions. At the time of this study, the Canadian government contributed an average of 75 percent of the budget of the national sport-governing bodies. Hence, the administrators did not place much importance on that dimension. These administrators also did not place much emphasis on the output dimension of mass sport. The goal of sport-governing bodies is to promote their respective sports among the public. The attainment of this goal—that is, the extent of public participation in the sport—is hard to judge. The number of fee-paying members could be considered a measure of input of monetary or human resources.

In essence, the administrators of Canadian sport-governing bodies endorsed a goals model approach for evaluating their elite sport programs. However, this approach was rejected for the evaluation of mass sport programs. This, of course, reflects the fact that an objective measure for the goal attainment of an elite program is readily available (for example, the performance record of the national team in international competitions). However, an objective measure is not available for mass sport programs. We also noted that third sector organizations should not use the securing of monetary resources as a measure of effectiveness, because governments contribute most of the financial resources, and, therefore, finances lose their potency as an effectiveness indicator. Consistent with this perspective, these authors found that sport administrators did, in fact, emphasize the input of human resources to a greater extent than the input of monetary resources as effectiveness indicators of both the elite and mass sport programs. Finally, the administrators in this study rated the process model of effectiveness as important for the evaluation of both elite and mass programs. In essence, they took a multidimensional approach to evaluating sport-governing bodies.

exhibit 16.5 Dimensions of effectiveness of NCAA based on its principles and functions.

DIMENSION	DESCRIPTION
Based on NCAA Principles	
General equity concerns	Promoting gender equity, commitment to gender and ethnic diversity, and activities free of biases
Institutional autonomy	Encouraging member institutions to conform to their own constitutional bylaws, allowing members to control their own programs, and promoting the financial stability of member institutions
Competitive equity	Creating competitive equity by ensuring that athletes are bona fide students, stating clear recruiting rules, encouraging reporting of violations, and deterring athlete–agent contacts
Rule enforcement	Consistently enforcing its rules, hiring qualified administrative personnel, and specifying clear academic requirements and eligibility
Student-athlete welfare	Ensuring harassment-free interactions of athletes with their coaches, their academic eligibility, the quality of their experiences, accountability of member institutions, and appropriate recruiting rules
Student-athlete status	Emphasizing the athletes as an integral part of the student body, their dignity, and their rights
Based on Network Functions	
Marketing and development	Helping members develop and market new products and services, and securing funds through donations, sponsorships, and grants
Management enhancement	Assisting member institutions to enhance their managerial skills and techniques, and improve their day-to-day operations
Image projection	Protecting the integrity of and projecting a positive image for intercollegiate athletics and member institutions

THE MULTIPLE-CONSTITUENCY MODEL

Connolly, Conlon, and Deutsch (1980) criticized both the goals and system resource models of effectiveness for their assumption that "it is possible, and desirable, to arrive at a *single* set of evaluative criteria, and thus at a *single* statement of organizational effectiveness" (p. 212). Thus, they proposed "a view of organizational effectiveness in which several (potentially, many) different effectiveness statements can be made about the focal organization, reflecting the criterion sets of different individuals and groups we shall refer to as 'constituencies'" (p. 212).

The constituencies they refer to are the owners, managers, employees, clients, suppliers, and other stakeholders. The constituent groups may be within the organization (senior administrators, employee groups), or they may belong to the environment (consumer groups, suppliers). In the case of a department of sport management, the students, the faculty, the

IN brief

Because different constituents of an organization may hold different goals for the organization, their perspectives on organizational effectiveness will also differ.

sidebar 16.5

STAKEHOLDERS BEHIND THE PLATE

That multiple stakeholders (or constituents) hold differing judgments of an organization's effectiveness was humorously illustrated by Herman and Renz (1999) in the story of the three baseball umpires:

> The first says he calls balls and strikes "as they are," and the second says, "I call 'em as I see 'em." The third says, "They ain't nothing 'til I call 'em." (p. 110)
>
> There are pitches, but a pitch is neither a ball nor a strike until the umpire calls it. . . . Of course, unlike the baseball analogy, in NPOs there is no single umpire (all stakeholders are permitted to determine effectiveness, although some stakeholders may be considered more credible than others) and no regular procedure for determining effectiveness (all stakeholders are free to send messages, with varying degrees of justification, about effectiveness and to focus on different activities as more relevant for determining effectiveness). Effectiveness is stakeholder judgment, formed and changed in an ongoing process of sense making and negotiation. (p. 118)

staff, and the dean and other administrative heads form the internal constituencies. External constituencies include university administrators, the senate, alumni, and other faculties. Beyond the university, the external constituencies are professional and semiprofessional sport franchises, city recreation departments, fitness clubs, and other organizations that have a stake in how the sport management department operates and in its graduates. These constituencies will have varying perspectives on what the sport management program should achieve.

Connolly and colleagues (1980) pointed out that the **multiple-constituency** approach to effectiveness incorporates the notion that different goals will be held by different groups in an organization. Insofar as differences in the perception of goals exist, there will also be differences in the perception of organizational effectiveness. Connolly and his colleagues noted that it was "somewhat arbitrary to label one of these perspectives a priori as the 'correct' one" (p. 212) and suggested that effectiveness must be considered as a plural concept—it is *effectivenesses* that should be considered, not *effectiveness.*

Note that the Connolly et al. (1980) approach hinges on the idea that different constituents hold different goals. This approach implies that different constituents will use different criteria in evaluating the effectiveness of a given organization. For instance, the faculty and alumni of a university may hold different goals for their intercollegiate department. Therefore, they may be expected to apply different criteria in judging the athletic department's effectiveness. Hypothetically, the alumni may hold the view that intercollegiate athletics should be concerned with only the major sports such as football and basketball. Accordingly, their effectiveness criteria would be focused on football and basketball operations. The faculty, in contrast, may emphasize the breadth of the athletic program and greater opportunities for more students to pursue excellence in sports. Thus, their effectiveness criteria are likely to be broad-based. This multiplicity of criteria is born out of the different goals held by different constituents (see Exhibit 16.6).

multiple stakeholders/ constituencies

The *multiple constituencies* referred to by Connolly et al. (1980) are the same as the stakeholders discussed in Chapter 3. Stakeholders were defined as "persons or groups that have or claim ownership, rights, or interests in a corporation and its activities, past, present, or future" (Clarkson, 1995, p. 106). In Chapter 5, on planning, we also noted that the stated goals of an organization tend to be global and vague. This vagueness allowed for the accommodation of varied expectations of multiple stakeholders or constituencies. Thus it is not surprising that the problems associated with specifying organizational goals also arise in the case of evaluating organizational effectiveness.

TO recap

exhibit 16.6 Multiple-constituency model.

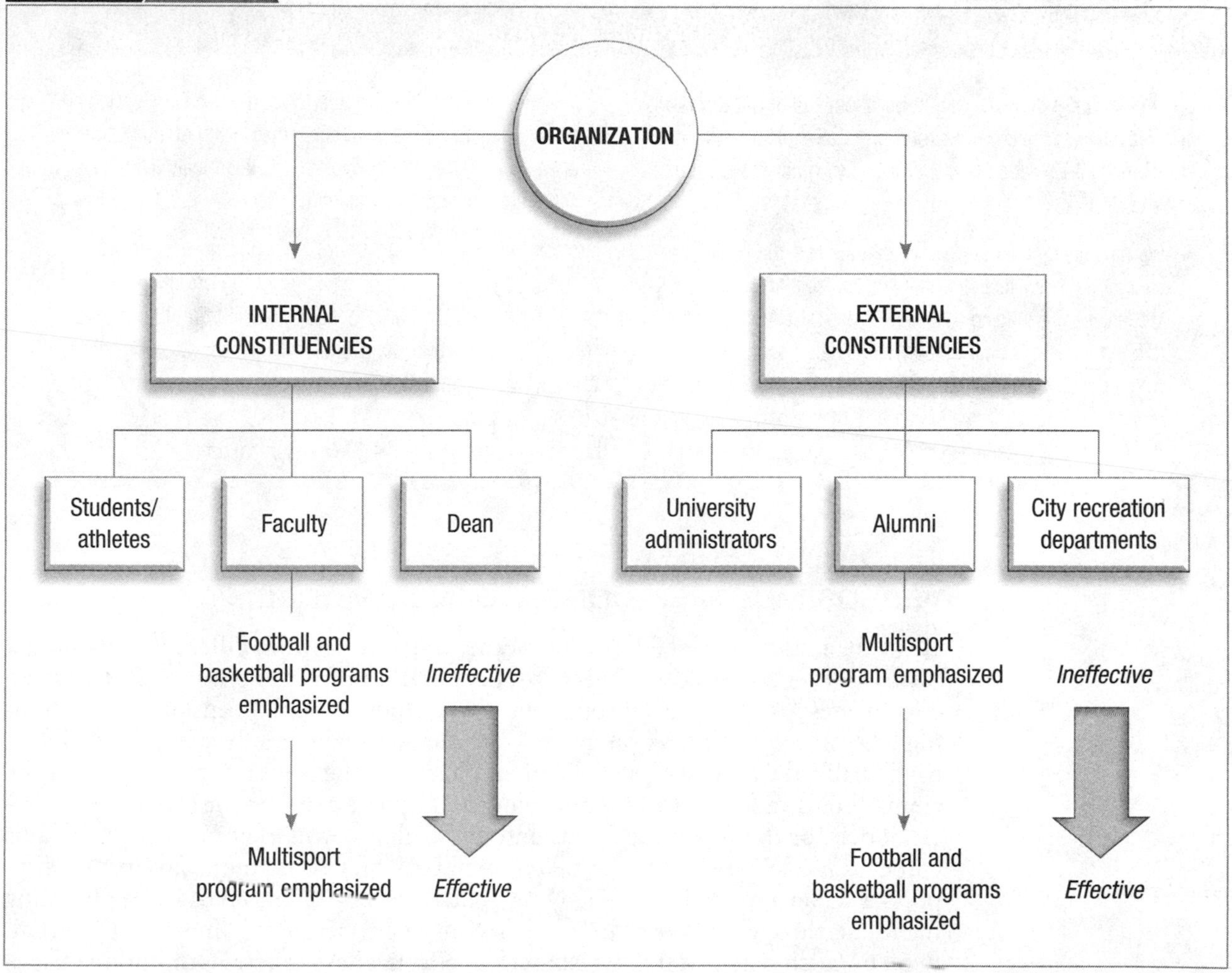

The problem of multiple goals and thus the multiple conceptions of organizational effectiveness is much more pronounced in nonprofit organizations than in commercial enterprises. Commercial enterprises have at least one objective and quantitative bottom-line criterion of effectiveness—making profits for the owners or shareholders. Herman and Renz (1999) highlighted this when they advanced the following six theses about the effectiveness of NPOs:

1. Nonprofit organizational effectiveness is always a matter of comparison.
2. Nonprofit organizational effectiveness is multidimensional and will never be reducible to a single measure.
3. Boards of directors make a difference in the effectiveness of NPOs, but how they do this is not clear.
4. More effective NPOs are more likely to use correct management practices.
5. Nonprofit organizational effectiveness is a social construction.
6. Program outcome indicators as measures of NPO effectiveness are limited and can be dangerous. (p. 107)

sidebar 16.6

RECOMMENDATIONS FOR NPOS

Based on the notion of multiple perspectives of organizational effectiveness held by the multiple stakeholders, Herman and Renz (1997) recommend the following for the managers of NPOs:

> We have suggested to these managers that the basic implication of our results is that they recognize that different constituencies are judging their organizations' effectiveness in different ways and that they (the managers) should find out what criteria are important to the different constituencies and provide favorable information on how their organizations are doing on those criteria. In effect, we are recommending tailoring the effectiveness message to each audience. Some managers tell us this is not something they have not thought of or already done. The more cynical have stated that all good managers are "spin doctors." (p. 202)

Herman and Renz also advocate "recognizing that how and on what bases different constituencies reach effectiveness judgments varies and that differentially emphasizing information of interest to differing constituencies is not tantamount to advocating lying. Managers can (and many do) present information that is as accurate as possible while still presenting it in ways that make a good case for their organization" (p. 202).

MULTIDIMENSIONALITY PERSPECTIVE VERSUS MULTIPLE-CONSTITUENCY MODEL

The multiplicity of effectiveness criteria stemming from different goals should not be confused with the criteria stemming from the issue of measuring effectiveness at the input, throughput, and output stages. For instance, the alumni group in the previous example may be unanimous in emphasizing football and basketball, but they may be split in emphasizing the winning percentage of the teams (goals model), the revenue generated by the department (system resources model), or the recruiting and training of athletes or marketing of the programs (process model). By the same token, members of a constituent group that supports a wider range of sports may be divided among themselves in emphasizing the input, throughput, or output dimensions of effectiveness. Thus, it is important to distinguish between the two sources of effectiveness criteria—multidimensionality of effectiveness versus **multiple perspectives** on effectiveness.

sidebar 16.7

ASSESSMENTS OF EFFECTIVENESS

According to Forbes (1998), "Assessments of effectiveness are not regarded as objective facts but neither are they regarded as arbitrary or irrelevant. Rather, the emergent approach holds that definitions and assessments of effectiveness have meaning but the meaning is (a) created by the individual or organizational actors, (b) specific to the context in which it was created, and (c) capable of evolving as the actors continue to interact" (p. 195).

Along the same lines, Hall (1996) noted that "while there is agreement that effectiveness as an overall concept has little or no utility, it would be a major mistake to simply ignore issues and findings that have been developed in regard to effectiveness. This seeming paradox can be resolved if a contradiction model of effectiveness is used. Put very simply, a contradiction model considers organizations to be more or less effective in regard to the variety of goals which they pursue, the variety of resources which they attempt to acquire, the variety of constituents inside and outside of the organization, and the variety of time frames by which effectiveness is judged. The idea of variety in goals, resources, and so on is key here, since it suggests that an organization can be effective in some aspects of its operations and less so in others" (p. 257).

An example from the commercial sector is the Nike Corporation, which is quite well known for its creativity and entrepreneurial efforts in offering quality footwear and apparel for public consumption. However, a constituent group criticized Nike for producing its goods in sweatshops in developing countries. While other groups (athletes, general consumers, business analysts, shareholders, sport organizations) may consider Nike an effective manufacturer and merchandiser, this particular constituency evaluated it very negatively. Similarly, it is not uncommon for the owners and shareholders of a professional sport franchise to consider their franchise effective because it generates large revenues and profits, while the fans evaluate the franchise as a failure based on its poor win–loss record.

Although Connolly and his colleagues emphasized the flexibility of the multiple-constituency model in terms of its accommodating various perspectives among the constituencies over time, they did not clarify how an organization could use the differing evaluations (by the constituencies) to improve its performance. The fact that managers have to make choices from among these perspectives is not addressed in their model. We will address this issue later in this chapter.

COMPETING VALUES MODEL

The foregoing discussion shows that the issue of effectiveness becomes more complex when the various interest groups (the multiple constituencies) hold a number of incompatible goals for the organization. Because multiple constituencies could have different preferences for organizational performance, and therefore would select different criteria for assessing organizational effectiveness, the values underlying these differing sets of criteria are important (Quinn & Rohrbaugh, 1983; Zammuto, 1984). As Zammuto (1984) suggested, "Organizational effectiveness fundamentally is a value-based concept in that the whole of the evaluation process requires the application of value judgments, from the selection of constituencies and the weighting of their judgments to the development of recommendations for future organizational performance" (p. 614). Values held by key decision makers and their judgments about effectiveness are related to operative goals that are, in the first place, subjective. This is reality, and we must realize that all the objective computations and calculations cannot mask this fact.

Connolly and colleagues (1980) and Zammuto (1984) highlight the significance of values underlying multiple perspectives on organizational effectiveness. Their findings suggest that the issues surrounding the concept of organizational effectiveness can be framed as a set of competing values. Quinn and Rohrbaugh (1983) used this basis in proposing their **competing values approach (CVA)** to organizational effectiveness. The authors selected 17 of 30 effectiveness criteria collated earlier by Campbell (1977). Then they asked a group of experts to judge the similarity between pairs of criteria. These similarity judgments were subjected to multidimensional scaling (a statistical procedure appropriate for such data). The results showed that the criteria could be grouped in the space defined by three dimensions: (1) internal versus external, (2) flexibility versus stability, and (3) means versus ends.

Internal Versus External

The first dimension reflects the organizational focus "from an internal, micro emphasis on the well-being and development of people in the organization to an external, macro emphasis on the well-being and development of the organization itself" (Quinn & Rohrbaugh, 1983, p. 369). Thus, this dimension has the people and the organization as its polar ends.

For example, a university athletic department may be concerned with generating more revenue. Therefore, its processes may reflect cost reduction in all its operations. This, in turn, may negatively affect the athletes, coaches, and other staff. Another university athletic department, with a greater focus on the welfare of its athletes and coaches, may spend more money on positively enhancing the experiences of its people. In the process, the department's surpluses may be reduced. Much of the debate on intercollegiate athletics is focused on this pair of competing values. Different constituencies of the athletic department may employ either of the focuses in evaluating an athletic department. The divergent focuses on people versus the organization are also relevant to other sport organizations, including commercial organizations such as a professional sport franchise, a commercial fitness club, or a sport-marketing consulting firm.

Flexibility Versus Stability

The second dimension derived by Quinn and Rohrbaugh (1983) reflects the competing views on organizational structure, "from an emphasis on stability to an emphasis on flexibility" (p. 369). The decision makers in a city recreation department may be more concerned with the stability and consistency of their operations. Therefore, they may structure their department to ensure greater control of their operations. Such a structure would emphasize centralized decision making. In contrast, the decision makers in another city recreation department may be concerned with being open to client demands and satisfying their needs. The decision makers may also be interested in identifying and implementing new trends in recreation. Accordingly, they are likely to make the structure more flexible to permit decentralized decision making. It follows that different constituents (including the decision makers) may apply either of the competing orientations toward structure in evaluating the effectiveness of the departments.

Means Versus Ends

The third dimension of Quinn and Rohrbaugh (1983) pertains to organizational means and ends, "from an emphasis on important processes (e.g., planning and goal-setting) to an emphasis on final outcomes (e.g., productivity)" (p. 369). The ends sought by a commercial fitness club may be profit or market share. The means employed by the club may be extensive planning to streamline its operations, offer new programs, and install new equipment. The dichotomy represented by this dimension reflects the distinction between the goals and process models of organizational effectiveness discussed earlier in the chapter.

In overview, these three dimensions of competing values highlight (a) attention orientation (internal/external focus), (b) structural preferences (flexibility/control or centralization/decentralization), and (c) the means–ends dichotomy. When these three dimensions are crossed with each other, they yield eight cells as shown in Exhibit 16.7. Note that each cell combines one extreme of each of the three value dimensions.

Quinn and Rohrbaugh (1983) went a step further to propose four models of effectiveness, each consisting of two of the eight cells shown in Exhibit 16.7. The **human relations model** focuses on flexibility and internal focus with a view to enhancing human resource development (ends) through such means as cohesion and morale (cells 1 and 2). The **internal process model** reflects an emphasis on

exhibit 16.7 Competing values model of organizational effectiveness.

People				Organization			
Flexibility		Stability		Flexibility		Stability	
Means (1)	Ends (2)	Means (3)	Ends (4)	Means (5)	Ends (6)	Means (7)	Ends (8)

	CELL	EMPHASIS
Human Relations Model	Cell 1 (PFM):	Group cohesion, morale, member commitment
	Cell 2 (PFE):	Human resource management processes
Internal Process Model	Cell 3 (PSM):	Information management, communication
	Cell 4 (PSE):	Stability, control, continuity, equilibrium
Open System Model	Cell 5 (OFM):	Flexibility, readiness, adaptability
	Cell 6 (OFE):	Resource acquisition, external support
Rational Goal Model	Cell 7 (OSM):	Planning, goal-setting
	Cell 8 (OSE):	Productivity, efficiency

control and internal focus to bring about control and stability (ends) through the means of information management and communication (cells 3 and 4). The **open system model** emphasizes flexibility and external focus in order to secure resources and external support (ends) through such means as being ready for and adaptable to environmental changes (cells 5 and 6). Finally, the **rational goal model** features a heavy emphasis on control and external focus to ensure productivity and efficiency (ends) through such means as planning and goal-setting (cells 7 and 8).

As Robbins (1990) noted, the competing values approach

> goes significantly beyond merely acknowledging diverse preferences. It assumes [demonstrates] that these diverse preferences can be consolidated and organized. The competing-values approach argues that there are common elements underlying any comprehensive list of OE [organizational effectiveness] criteria and that these elements can be combined in such a way as to create basic sets of competing values. Each one of these sets then defines a unique effectiveness model. (p. 69)

In addition, the competing values model identifies three dimensions that reflect the perennial dilemmas faced by managers. That is, the dimensions have an impact on all managerial functions. For instance, in the planning function of selecting goals for the organization, what priority would be given to the welfare of the personnel relative to corporate welfare (that is, the polar ends of Quinn and Rohrbaugh's first dimension)? Similarly, their means–ends dimension affects the setting of goals and the choice of activities (or programs) to achieve those goals. Their second dimension relates to the organizing function, where the rigidity or flexibility of the organizational structure and coordinating mechanisms is determined. From this perspective, Quinn and Rohrbaugh's competing values model provides a global perspective on all of management—not just on the concept of organizational effectiveness.

Shilbury and Moore (2006) employed Quinn and Rohrbaugh's (1983) competing values approach in studying the effectiveness of Australian sport-governing bodies. Based on the model, Shilbury and Moore proposed eight dimensions of organizational effectiveness that parallel the dimensions listed in Exhibit 16.7. They developed a scale to measure the performance of the sport-governing bodies. However, the analysis of their questionnaire data showed that there were two subdimensions in each of cells 1 and 2. Cell 1, which they called Skilled Workforce, was composed of two subdimensions relating to Professional and Volunteers respectively. Cell 2, labeled Cohesiveness of the Workforce, was broken into Motivation/Recognition and Work Harmony.

A differing perspective on Quinn and Rohrbaugh's model is that "it is not so much a theory of organizational effectiveness but more an account of where managers put their major emphasis in conducting the affairs of an organization, which by implication tells us something about how they evaluate its effectiveness" (Rollinson, 2002, p. 474). That is, the model can be seen as a scheme contrasting approaches managers can take in carrying out the different functions of management, such as planning, organizing, and leading. For instance, one fitness club manager, in contrast to another, may focus on the means (e.g., offering different programs and ensuring the quality of services offered) of achieving a given set of goals (e.g., making a 20 percent return on investment) rather than on the goals themselves. This approach illustrates Quinn and Rohrbaugh's means–ends distinction (see Chapter 5 on planning, which discusses setting goals and generating alternative courses of action to achieve those goals).

Similarly, one manager of a professional sport franchise may set up a bureaucratic structure to ensure stability and consistency of operations, whereas another may adopt the systems approach in making the structure more flexible to adapt to environmental conditions (see Chapters 7 and 8, which explain classical forms of organizing and systems-based organizing). These differing approaches are what Quinn and Rohrbaugh label the flexibility–stability dimension.

Finally, one athletic director may be more people-oriented in leading the members of the organization, whereas another may be more task- or organization-oriented (see Chapters 11 and 12 for a discussion of the different approaches to leadership). This trend illustrates what Quinn and Rohrbaugh call the people-versus-organization focus or the internal-versus-external focus.

From the above perspective, one can see the competing values model as a depiction and classification of the structures and processes adopted by organizations and their managers. However, the thrust of the model is that the adoption of different configurations of structures and processes also leads to the selection of criteria for evaluating the effectiveness of the organization. In one sense, the structures and processes adopted by the organization reflect the goals the organization has set for itself, and thus an effectiveness evaluation could legitimately focus on how well those structures and processes are implemented.

PARADOXICAL NATURE OF ORGANIZATIONAL EFFECTIVENESS

When the focal organization has to satisfy contradictory sets of criteria, it is forced to engage in activities that may mutually undermine each other's effects. This action exemplifies what Cameron (1986) calls **organizational paradox.** According to him, "Organizational effectiveness is inherently paradoxical. To be effective, an organization must possess attributes that are simultaneously contradictory, even mutually exclusive" (p. 545). Although Cameron uses the notion of paradox mainly to refer to conflicting organizational processes, the concept is relevant to the contradictions inherent in the viewpoints of the mul-

> In a sense, the paradoxical model [and the competing values model as well] can be viewed as a more complex form of its predecessors—it allows for the likelihood of organizations operating simultaneously in different environmental domains, with each domain conveying different expectations. Whereas contingency theory assumed a single domain, for the sake of matching organizational and environmental characteristics, the paradoxical extension allows for multiple domains requiring multiple, simultaneous, and inherently contradictory matches.
>
> **WHETTEN & CAMERON,** *1994, p. 141*

tiple constituents. The organization faces paradox, and its activities are paradoxical when it attempts to satisfy those "contradictory, even mutually exclusive" viewpoints. In fact, Cameron (1986) found that "the organizations that achieved the highest levels of effectiveness were also those that satisfied the most separate constituency group expectations, even when different constituencies held contradictory expectations. Highly effective organizations were paradoxical in that they performed in contradictory ways to satisfy contradictory expectations" (p. 550).

Consider university athletics. The expectations of the alumni, the student body, and the athletes could diverge and even conflict with each other. Many universities have succeeded in bringing about a balance between these opposing and "paradoxical" expectations. On the other hand, some universities have allowed one of the constituencies—for example, the alumni—to assume a dominant position that has resulted in great repercussions for athletics as well as the universities concerned. This situation is akin to what Cameron calls *schismogenesis,* "a process of self-reinforcement where one action or attribute in the organization perpetuates itself until it becomes extreme and therefore dysfunctional" (p. 546). The problem with the emphasis on dominant coalitions in the assessment of organizational effectiveness is that it sets the process of schismogenesis in motion. Choosing the criteria of the most powerful groups makes them more and more dominant, until they are able virtually to dictate what the organization should do. Organizations and their administrators need to be concerned about such negative processes.

PRIMACY AMONG MULTIPLE PERSPECTIVES

The foregoing discussion shows that there are multiple perspectives on organizational effectiveness, and that these differing perspectives are rooted in the values held by different stakeholder groups. While this is doubtless the case, these discussions do not provide any guidelines for the practicing manager. Given a multitude of claims and counterclaims, the manager must emphasize one of these perspectives over the others. Zammuto (1984) suggested that the writings on multiple constituencies and their perspectives can be synthesized into four classes, each one giving a particular constituency primacy in the evaluation of organizational effectiveness. These classes are described below.

Relativistic Perspective

The **relativistic perspective** holds that the evaluations by all of the various constituencies are legitimate, and therefore the primacy of one view over the others cannot be established. As explained earlier, Connolly et al. (1980) strongly supported this perspective. In suggesting that the evaluator's task is only to collect effectiveness ratings from multiple constituencies for the use of the superiors, the relativistic approaches do not really address the distributive issue. That is, the suggestion that the various constituencies may emphasize different values, which lead to differential emphases on organizational goals, does not provide any guidelines for the top administrators or the researchers who have to select a specific perspective to guide their actions.

Power Perspective

The **power perspective** (see Miles, 1980; Pennings & Goodman, 1977; Pfeffer & Salancik, 1978) is categorical in asserting that the preferences of the most powerful constituents, or of the coalition of powerful constituents, need to be satisfied. The models that subscribe to the power perspective emphasize the identification of the critical goals held by different constituents. For instance, Miles (1980) would require the preferential ordering of the various goals held by different constituencies, based on the relative power of the constituencies.

The relative power of a constituency depends on its ability to influence or control the activities of the focal organization. Power is often, but not always, a function of the resource contributions made by that constituency. For example, in many American universities, the alumni association has considerable influence in the affairs of the athletic programs because of its significant contribution of resources. In contrast, the athletic programs in many Canadian universities are financed through the activity fees paid by the students. The students, however, do not possess the degree of influence and power commensurate with their resource contribution. This is analogous to the citizens who pay taxes not having a say in the distribution of those taxes. These and similar situations could be an artifact of the diffusion of power among a large number of benefactors, or of benefactors' disinterestedness.

IN brief

In addressing the varying perspectives of its constituents, an effective organization engages in contradictory activities, which contributes to the paradox of organizational effectiveness.

According to Miles (1980), once the priorities of the powerful constituents are identified, effectiveness is evaluated on the basis of attainment of these prioritized goals. However, despite the model's sophistication in the assessment of relative power of the constituent groups and the establishment of priorities among the goals they hold, it still does not solve the problem that arises when two equally strategic interest groups hold conflicting values or goals for the organization.

Social Justice Perspective

The focus of the **social justice perspective** (Keeley, 1978) is on satisfying the needs of the less powerful or the less advantaged constituents. The social welfare programs of many countries, aimed at assisting disadvantaged citizens, rise out of this perspective. Many critics of intercollegiate athletic programs in the United States take this stance when they point to the inequity in the distribution of resources to various sports. For example, the social justice perspective would suggest that the use of the gymnasiums be equally distributed among basketball, volleyball, and badminton teams.

Evolutionary Perspective

Finally, the emphasis in Zammuto's (1984) **evolutionary perspective** is on "the continual process of becoming effective rather than on being effective" (p. 608). That is, organizational effectiveness is viewed in terms of how the organization attempts to satisfy the divergent needs over the long term as the constituents and their needs change over time. For example, an athletic department in a smaller institution may buy new equipment and uniforms for its teams in successive years. In any one year, only a few teams may get the new equipment, but in the long run every team gets its turn.

PRIME BENEFICIARY APPROACH

As noted earlier, the multiple-constituency approach addresses the question: which of the multiple perspectives should prevail? The various approaches discussed above tend to be mutually exclusive, and at times seem to ignore organizational purposes. Chelladurai (1987) proposed an alternate approach based on Blau and Scott's (1962) criterion of **prime beneficiary** (see Chapter 2 for a discussion of Blau and Scott's work).

With the relatively clear specifications developed by Blau and Scott, it is easier and more justifiable to uphold the perspective of the prime beneficiary in the evaluation of organizational effectiveness.

The players' unions in various sports are examples of mutual benefit associations, and the players are the prime beneficiaries. Accordingly, the players' views on the union's effectiveness should reign supreme as the measure of effectiveness. Similarly, evaluations of the organizational effectiveness of a private golf club should be based on members' views, because they are the prime beneficiaries.

In the case of a professional sports club (a business concern), the prime beneficiaries are the owners. The notion that their view should reign supreme is generally accepted in North American society. For instance, when the former Cleveland Browns football team was moved to another city, the city administrators, the fans, and the media expressed concerns. In the end, however, the primacy of the owners' views was upheld. By the same token, the owners also are the supreme judges of the effectiveness of their own respective organizations.

An example of a service organization (in Blau and Scott's terminology) would be a city or university recreation department. The department provides facilities and programs for the benefit of local residents or students. Thus, as the prime beneficiaries of the department, their judgments about the effectiveness of the department should be of paramount influence in managerial decisions. In a similar manner, many organizations offer sport and recreation programs to the disabled and disadvantaged. All of these organizations exist to serve the people who come into contact with them. There are no good examples of a commonweal organization in sport and recreation; however, many sport and recreation programs for youth may be considered to benefit the larger community if they are designed to "keep kids off the street."

The foregoing examples show that the prime beneficiary approach includes two of the various approaches suggested by Zammuto (1984). Because the owners of a professional sport franchise are the prime beneficiaries of the organization, they hold the power to make decisions. Therefore, the notion of prime beneficiary encompasses the power perspective suggested by Zammuto. In mutual benefit associations (such as labor unions or recreational clubs) where members are the prime beneficiaries, fairness among all members is paramount. Therefore, Zammuto's social justice perspective is applicable. In a similar manner, the social justice perspective on the primacy of constituents would hold in service organizations whose prime beneficiaries are the clients in contact. It must be noted that Zammuto's (1984) other two approaches do not really establish the primacy of

sidebar 16.8

PRIMARY STAKEHOLDERS VERSUS PRIME BENEFICIARIES

It is important to distinguish between the concept of primary stakeholder (discussed in Chapter 3) and prime beneficiary (discussed in Chapter 2).

Primary stakeholder refers to any group without whose cooperation and participation the organization cannot survive. Thus, the coaches and athletes of a professional sport franchise are primary stakeholders because without them the franchise cannot play games and provide entertainment. Similarly, the coaches and athletes of a university athletic department are primary stakeholders. In both examples, the coaches and athletes are treated equally as primary stakeholders.

However, the *prime beneficiaries* of professional sport franchises are the owners, while the players and coaches are "costs" of running the business. That is, the coaches and athletes are paid their salaries with a view that their performances will result in profits for the owners. In the case of intercollegiate athletics, the athletes are the prime beneficiaries, while the coaches are "cost" items. The coaches are paid their salaries so that they will serve the athletes—the prime beneficiaries—by coaching, instructing, and training them to be better athletes.

Although sport managers must satisfy the needs and preferences of primary stakeholders in order to make an organization more effective, they should base their judgment of organizational effectiveness on how well the prime beneficiaries are served.

any one constituent. The relativistic perspective simply says that all perspectives of the multiple constituents are legitimate, and, therefore, primacy of any one cannot be established. In a similar vein, the evolutionary approach implies that all perspectives are legitimate, and that the organization should attempt to satisfy as many constituents as possible in a sequential manner.

To acknowledge the perspective of the prime beneficiary is not to minimize the need for any organization to secure resources by catering to the wishes of other constituent groups. From Cameron's (1986) perspective of organizational effectiveness as a paradox, it is necessary for an organization to accommodate some of the expectations of other groups even though they may be inconsistent with the needs of the prime beneficiaries. The essential point is that an effective organization attempts to satisfy these contradictory expectations only with a view to increasing the payoffs to its prime beneficiaries. In one sense, satisfying the other constituents may be viewed as a cost incurred by the organization in order to better serve the prime beneficiaries. For instance, if an athletic department raises the salaries of its coaches, it satisfies that constituency. But the additional cost is incurred only to make sure that the coaches serve the athletes, the prime beneficiaries. "To keep the prime beneficiary in perspective is to keep the ultimate purpose of the organization in perspective" (Chelladurai, 1987, p. 45).

IN brief

One way to decide on the primacy of different perspectives on organizational effectiveness is to focus on the prime beneficiary of that organization (i.e., the constituent for whose benefit the organization exists).

A final comment on the need to distinguish between a multidimensional approach and the multiple-constituency approach to effectiveness: The multidimensional approach simply suggests that an organization should be evaluated on different dimensions—resource acquisition, productivity, smooth functioning of internal processes, and so on (Evan, 1976; Steers, 1975). The problems associated with it are *scientific* to the extent they are concerned with *what* is to be measured and *how* it should be measured. In the multiple-constituency model, however, various groups evaluate a focal organization on the same dimensions. For example, a youth recreational sports program would be evaluated by participants, parents, coaches, volunteers, community members, and local government officials. Thus, the multiple-constituency approach focuses on *whose perspective or preferences* should be the basis for evaluation rather than on what should be evaluated. The critical issue addressed here is *political* in nature to the extent that it focuses on appeasing various claimants and their perspectives.

SUMMARY

As noted at the beginning of the chapter, various models of effectiveness—the goals, system resource, process, multiple-constituency, and competing values models—can be synthesized into a gestalt view of effectiveness. As Yuchtman and Seashore (1967) pointed out, since the three processes of an open system—acquisition of resources, transformation of the inputs (throughputs), and disposal of the outputs—are integrally linked to each other, the effectiveness of the system can be measured at any point in the input–throughput–output cycle. This finding is highlighted by the fact that each model of effectiveness focuses on one of the elements in the cycle (see Exhibit 16.2). In addition, the chapter discussed the issue of multiple constituencies and their differential evaluations of organizational effectiveness. We also noted that the values individuals have underlie their perspectives on organizational effectiveness. The critical issue of the primacy of these different views was discussed from the perspective of prime beneficiaries of organizations.

A careful examination of the five models discussed in the chapter shows that all of them have goal attainment as the primary concern in assessing effectiveness. For example, the underlying assumption of the system resource model is that the ability of the organization to secure resources reflects the environment's acceptance of the organization's outputs. Thus, the degree to which the organization secures its resources reflects its goal attainment. Similarly, the process model of effectiveness links organizational processes to the outputs. Finally, the multiple-constituency and the competing values models also emphasize the operative goals held by different groups. The degree to which the organization achieves the goals of the various constituencies is a measure of its effectiveness.

In short, in choosing the criteria of effectiveness for their organizations, managers should focus on what Campbell (1976) calls *closeness to the final payoff*. That is, a criterion that is more closely related to the goal should be selected over those more remotely connected. For instance, if the academic achievement of the athletes is set as a significant goal, then the actual graduation rate is a more suitable effectiveness criterion than is the existence (or not) of a study table for the athletes. The former reflects goals attainment (it is actually the payoff), whereas the study table reflects only the process to attain that payoff.

develop YOUR PERSPECTIVE

1. Select a sport organization. What criteria would you use to evaluate its effectiveness? Why?
2. Give examples of sport organizations where each of the four models of effectiveness—goals, system resource, process, and multiple-constituency models—would be appropriate.

3. List as many criteria of effectiveness as possible for a sport organization. Place them on Campbell's (1976) continuum of closeness to the final payoff.
4. According to your perceptions, what are the effectiveness criteria used in evaluating your faculty or department? Who decides on these criteria? Can you infer their operative goals from these criteria?
5. Select a variety of sport organizations and identify the prime beneficiaries of each organization. Explain the extent to which their views are upheld in the evaluation of organizational effectiveness, and the manner in which this occurs.

references

Bacon, J. U. (2004). New balance. *NWA World Traveler, 36*(12), 36–40.

Barney, J. (1991). Firm resources and sustained competitive advantage. *Journal of Management, 17*(1), 99–120.

Barney, J. (1995). Looking inside for competitive advantage. *Academy of Management Executive, 9*(4), 49–61.

Bayle, E., & Madella, A. (2002). Development of a taxonomy of performance for national sport organizations. *European Journal of Sport Science, 2*(2), 1–21.

Blau, P. M., & Scott, W. R. (1962). *Formal organizations.* San Francisco: Chandler.

Cameron, K. S. (1986). Effectiveness as a paradox: Consensus and conflict in conceptions of organizational effectiveness. *Management Science, 32*(5), 539–553.

Campbell, J. P. (1976). Contributions research can make in understanding organizational effectiveness. In L. S. Spray (Ed.), *Organizational effectiveness: Theory–research–utilization.* Kent, OH: Graduate School of Business Administration, Kent State University.

Campbell, J. P. (1977). On the nature of organizational effectiveness. In P. S. Goodman & J. M. Pennings (Eds.), *New perspectives on organizational effectiveness.* San Francisco: Jossey-Bass.

Carmeli, A. (2004). Assessing core intangible resources. *European Management Journal, 22*(1), 110–122.

Chelladurai, P. (1987). Multidimensionality and multiple perspectives of organizational effectiveness. *Journal of Sport Management, 1,* 37–47.

Chelladurai, P., Szyszlo, M., & Haggerty, T. R. (1987). Systems based dimensions of effectiveness: The case of the national sport organizations. *Canadian Journal of Sport Sciences, 12,* 111–119.

Clarkson, M. B. E. (1995). A stakeholder framework for analyzing and evaluating corporate social performance. *Academy of Management Review, 20,* 92–117.

Connolly, T., Conlon, E. J., & Deutsch, S. J. (1980). Organizational effectiveness: A multiple-constituency approach. *Academy of Management Review, 5,* 211–217.

Crosby, P. B. (1985). *Quality without tears.* New York: Signet.

Cunningham, G. B. (2003). Human resources as sources of competitive advantage: A resource-based view of the athletic department. *Applied Research in Coaching and Athletics Annual, 203,* 37–58.

Cunningham, G. B., & Sagas, M. (2004). People make the differences: The influence of the coaching staff's human capital and diversity on team performance. *European Sport Management Quarterly, 4,* 3–21.

Deming, W. E. (1986). *Out of the crisis.* Cambridge, MA: MIT Press.

Etzioni, A. (1964). *Modern organizations.* Englewood Cliffs, NJ: Prentice Hall.

Evan, W. M. (1976). Organization theory and organizational effectiveness: An exploratory analysis. In L. S. Spray (Ed.), *Organizational effectiveness: Theory–research–utilization.* Kent, OH: Graduate School of Business Administration, Kent State University.

Forbes, D. P. (1998). Measuring the unmeasurable: Empirical studies of nonprofit organization effectiveness from 1977 to 1997. *Voluntary and Nonprofit Sector Quarterly, 27*(2), 183–202.

Hall, R. H. (1996). *Organizations: Structures, processes, and outcomes* (6th ed.). Englewood Cliffs, NJ: Prentice Hall.

Hasenfeld, Y. (1983). *Human service organizations.* Englewood Cliffs, NJ: Prentice Hall.

Herman, R. D., & Renz, D. O. (1997). Multiple constituencies and the social construction of nonprofit organization effectiveness. *Nonprofit and Voluntary Sector Quarterly, 26*(2), 185–206.

Herman, R. D., & Renz, D. O. (1999). Theses on nonprofit organizational effectiveness. *Nonprofit and Voluntary Sector Quarterly, 28*(2), 107–126.

Holcomb, T. R., Holmes, Jr., R. M., & Connelly, B. L. (2009). Making the most of what you have: Managerial ability as a source of resource value creation. *Strategic Management Journal, 30,* 457–485.

Hoy, W. K., & Miskel, C. G. (2008). *Educational administration: Theory, research, and practice.* Boston: McGraw-Hill.

Karteroliotis, K., & Papadimitriou, D. (2004). Confirmatory factor analysis of the sport organizational effectiveness scale. *Psychological Reports, 95,* 366–370.

Keeley, M. (1978). Social justice approach to organizational evaluation. *Administrative Science Quarterly, 22,* 272–292.

Kushner, R. J., & Poole, P. P. (1996). Exploring structure–effectiveness relationships in nonprofit arts organizations. *Nonprofit Management and Leadership, 6*(2), 171–180.

Lawrence, P. R., & Lorsch, J. W. (1967). *Organization and environment: Managing differentiation and integration.* Cambridge, MA: Harvard Graduate School of Business Administration.

Miles, R. H. (1980). *Macro organizational behavior.* Santa Monica, CA: Goodyear.

Molnar, J. J., & Rogers, D. L. (1976). Organizational effectiveness: An empirical comparison of the goal and system resource approaches. *Sociological Quarterly, 17,* 401–413.

Mott, P. E. (1972). *The characteristics of effective organizations.* New York: Harper & Row.

NCAA (2004a). The National Collegiate Athletic Association's purposes. Retrieved from www.ncaa.org/about/purposes.html.

NCAA (2004b). Principles for conduct of intercollegiate athletics. Retrieved from www.ncaa.org/library/membership/division_i_manual/2000-01/article_2.pdf.

O'Rourke, S. M., & Chelladurai, P. (2006). Effectiveness of the National Collegiate Athletic Association: Perceptions of intercollegiate athletic administrators. *International Journal of Sport Management, 7,* 82–101.

Ostroff, C., & Schmitt, N. (1993). Configurations of organizational effectiveness and efficiency. *Academy of Management Journal, 36,* 1345–1361.

Pennings, J. M., & Goodman, P. S. (1977). Toward a workable framework. In P. S. Goodman & J. M. Pennings (Eds.), *New perspectives on organizational effectiveness.* San Francisco: Jossey-Bass.

Perrow, C. (1961). The analysis of goals in complex organizations. *American Sociological Review, 26,* 854–866.

Pfeffer, J. (1977). Usefulness of the concept. In P. S. Goodman & J. M. Pennings (Eds.), *New perspectives on organizational effectiveness.* San Francisco: Jossey-Bass.

Pfeffer, J., & Salancik, G. R. (1978). *The external control of organizations.* New York: Harper & Row.

Price, J. L. (1972). The study of organizational effectiveness. *Sociological Quarterly, 13,* 3–15.

Quinn, R. E., & Rohrbaugh, J. (1983). A spatial model of effectiveness criteria: Towards a competing values approach to organizational analysis. *Management Science, 29*(3), 363–377.

Robbins, S. P. (1990). *Organization theory: Structure, design, and applications* (3rd ed.). Englewood Cliffs, NJ: Prentice Hall.

Robbins, S. P., Coulter, M., Leach, E., & Kilfoil, M. (2012). *Management* (10th ed.) Don Mills, Ontario: Pearson Canada.

Rollinson, D. (2002). *Organisational behaviour and analysis: An integrated approach* (2nd ed.). Harlow, UK: Financial Times Prentice Hall.

Shilbury, D., & Moore, K. A. (2006). A study of organizational effectiveness for national Olympic sporting organizations. *Nonprofit and Voluntary Sector Quarterly, 35*(1), 5–38.

Simon, D. G., Gove, S., & Hitt, M. A. (2008). Resource management in dyadic competitive rivalry: The effects of resource bundling and deployment. *Academy of Management Journal, 5*(5), 919–935.

Steers, R. M. (1975). Problems in the measurement of organizational effectiveness. *Administrative Science Quarterly, 20,* 546–558.

Steers, R. M. (1977). *Organizational effectiveness: A behavioral view.* Pacific Palisades, CA: Goodyear.

Steers, R. M., & Black, J. S. (1994). *Organizational behavior* (5th ed.). New York: HarperCollins.

Verweire, K., & Van Den Berghe, L. (2004). Integrated performance management: New hype or new paradigm? In K. Verweire & L. Van Den Berghe (Eds.), *Integrated performance management: A guide to strategy implementation* (pp. 1–14). London: Sage Publications.

Whetten, D. A., & Cameron, K. S. (1994). Organizational effectiveness: Old models and new constructs. In J. Greenberg (Ed.), *Organizational behavior: State of the science* (pp. 135–153). Hillsdale, NJ: Lawrence Erlbaum Associates.

Won, D., & Chelladurai, P. (2005, June). *Competitive advantage in intercollegiate athletics: Roles of intangible resources.* Paper presented at the 20th Annual Conference of the North American Society for Sport Management, Regina, Saskatchewan, Canada.

Yuchtman, E., & Seashore, S. E. (1967). A system resource approach to organizational effectiveness. *American Sociological Review, 32,* 891–903.

Zammuto, R. E. (1984). A comparison of multiple constituency models of organizational effectiveness. *Academy of Management Review, 9*(4), 606–616.

author index

subject index